Major U.S. Interstates, West-East

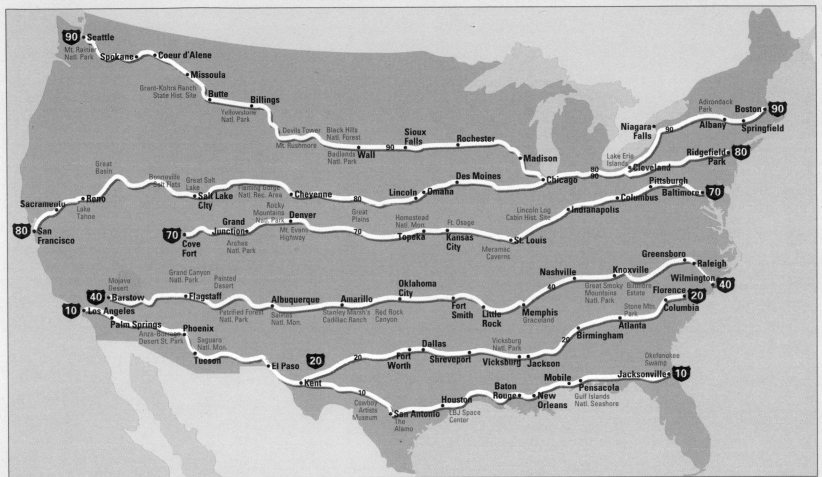

	Beginning to End	Length	Driving Time (no stops)	Don't Miss
90	Seattle, Washington to Boston, Massachusetts	3,163 miles	53 hours, 47 min.	Yellowstone
80	San Francisco, California to Ridgefield Park, New Jersey	2,907 miles	51 hours, 35 min.	Great Salt Lake
70	Cove Fort, Utah to Baltimore, Maryland	2,175 miles	36 hours, 34 min.	Mt. Evans Highway
40	Barstow, California to Wilmington, North Carolina	2,463 miles	45 hours, 20 min.	Great Smokies
20	Kent, Texas to Florence, South Carolina	1,536 miles	26 hours, 39 min.	Vicksburg Natl. Park
10	Los Angeles, California to Jacksonville, Florida	2,460 miles	41 hours, 34 min.	Okefenokee Swamp

2

Table of Contents

4, 5 Alaska (1750x1750 miles)
6, 7 Puerto Rico, U.S. Virgin Islands and Hawaii (250x250 miles)

250x250 miles

6-81 The United States, organized the way you drive it. Each page represents 250x250 miles, with all 48 mainland states mapped at the same scale. Interesting local notes appear on every page.

Special Pages
57 Food
68 Museums & Amusement Parks
75 Architecture

77 National Calendar of Events
79 Geographic & Weather Extremes
81 Cities & Town Names

25x25 miles

40 major metropolitan centers are marked in yellow on the 250x250 maps. Each shows the area covered by a 25x25 mile detail. We give you a sense of the city—whether you drive into it or around it.

82 Seattle
83 Portland
84 San Francisco
   Bay Area
86 Los Angeles
88 Orange County
89 San Diego
90 Salt Lake City
91 Phoenix
92 Kansas City
93 Denver

94 Fort Worth
95 Dallas
96 San Antonio
97 Houston
98 New Orleans
99 Nashville
100 Minneapolis/
    Saint Paul
101 Milwaukee
102 Chicago
103 Detroit

104 St. Louis
105 Indianapolis
106 Cleveland
107 Pittsburgh
108 Cincinnati
109 Columbus
110 Boston
111 New York
112 Stamford
113 Bridgeport/
    New Haven

114 Philadelphia
115 Baltimore
116 Washington DC
117 Charlotte
118 Durham
119 Raleigh
120 Orlando
121 Atlanta
122 Tampa/
    St. Petersburg
123 Miami

5x5 miles

11 downtown centers are marked in orange on the 25x25 maps. Each area shows the area covered by a 5x5 mile section of the city.

124 San Francisco
125 Santa Monica
126 Los Angeles

128 Las Vegas
129 Atlantic City
130 Chicago

131 Philadelphia
132 New York
134 Boston

135 Washington DC
136 Atlanta

137 Index
155 Acknowledgements
156 Answers to Questions

Inside Front Cover: **Interstate Maps**
Inside Back Cover: **Mileage Chart**

Key to the Maps

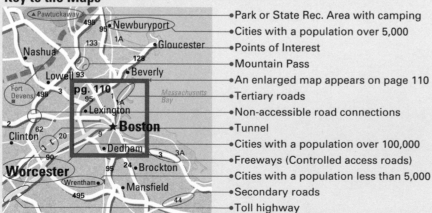

- Park or State Rec. Area with camping
- Cities with a population over 5,000
- Points of Interest
- Mountain Pass
- An enlarged map appears on page 110
- Tertiary roads
- Non-accessible road connections
- Tunnel
- Cities with a population over 100,000
- Freeways (Controlled access roads)
- Cities with a population less than 5,000
- Secondary roads
- Toll highway

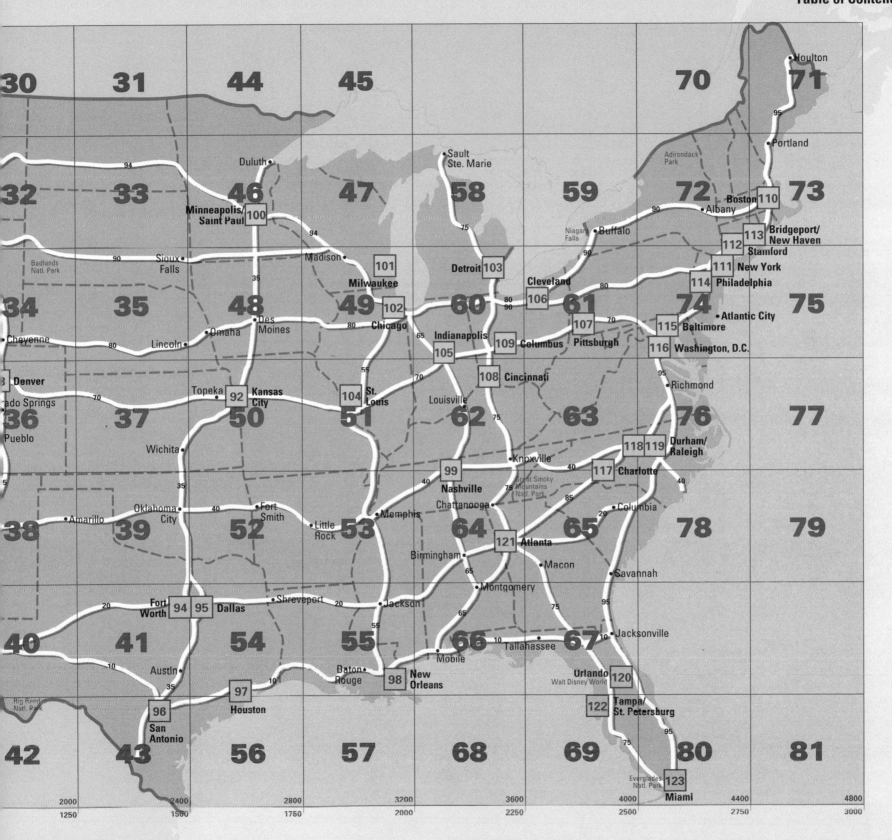

30   31   44   45   70   71
• Houlton
95
• Portland

32   33   46   58   59   72   73
Duluth •   Minneapolis/   Sault   Adirondack   Boston 110
Saint Paul 100   Ste. Marie   Park   • Albany   Bridgeport/
94   94   75   Niagara • Buffalo   90   112 113   New Haven
Falls   90   111 Stamford
90   New York

34   35   48   49   60   61   74   75
Sioux   Madison •   Detroit 103   Cleveland   80   114 Philadelphia
Falls   Milwaukee   80   106   107   115 • Atlantic City
35   102   90   61   116 Baltimore
Des   Chicago   Indianapolis   109 Columbus Pittsburgh   Washington, D.C.
• Omaha   Moines   65   105   70   95
Lincoln •   80   108 • Cincinnati   • Richmond

Denver   36   37   50   51   62   63   76   77
Topeka 92 Kansas   St.   Louisville   118 119 Durham/
ado Springs   City   104 Louis   75   117 Raleigh
Pueblo   70   55   70   Knoxville   40   Charlotte
Wichita   Great Smoky   85
99   Mountains   20 • Columbia
Nashville   Natl. Park   75
38   39   52   53   64   65   78   79
Amarillo   Oklahoma   40   Fort   40   121 Atlanta
City   Smith   Memphis   Chattanooga
Little   Birmingham •   • Macon
Rock   65   • Savannah

40   41   54   55   66   67
20 Fort   Shreveport   20   Montgomery   75   95
Worth 94 95 Dallas   Jackson   65   • Jacksonville
Austin •   55   66   10   Tallahassee   10
35   Baton   Mobile   Urlando   120
97   Rouge 98 New   Walt Disney World
42   43   56   57   68   69   80   81
96   Houston   122 Tampa/
San   St. Petersburg
Antonio   75   95
Everglades   123
Natl. Park   Miami

2000   2400   2800   3200   3600   4000   4400   4800
1250   1500   1750   2000   2250   2500   2750   3000

Is Alaska the westernmost or easternmost of the 50 states? *See page 156.*

Anchorage Bests, according to Mayor Tom Fink:
Sighting moose on the Coastal Trail.
The ride and the view at the Alyeska Ski Resort Chair Lift in Girdwood.
The friendliness and helpfulness of Anchorage residents.
The Anchorage Museum of History and Art.

There is more land dedicated to national parks in Alaska than in the other 49 states combined.

Of Alaska's 5000 glaciers, at least one is bigger than the state of Rhode Island.

1989's most infamous oil spill: What's the estimate on the *Valdez* damage? Prince William Sound *(pg. 5, C4)* might look cleaner, but the wildlife may not recover for 70 years.

The summer sun in Barrow *(pg. 5, C1)* "rises" on May 10 and doesn't set until August 2.

Alaska's official state sport is dog mushing. Catch the world's most comprehensive exhibit on the sport, and a live show, at the Dog Musher's Museum in Fairbanks *(pg. 5, C3)*.

North America's strongest recorded earthquake—8.5 on the Richter scale—rocked Alaska on Good Friday, 27 March 1964.

Let it Snow—at Thompson Pass *(pg. 5, D4)* it does, by the bucketful.
Most snow in a season:
974.5 inches (1952-53)
Most snow in a month:
297.9 inches (February 1953)
Most snow in 24 hours:
62 inches (December 1955)

Fire with ice—Mt. Redoubt *(pg. 5, C4)* has started up again, periodically spewing ash and steam, and sometimes dusting the streets of Anchorage.

Alaska-
It's the northwesternmost point in North America; 2 1/2 times the size of Texas; 1/5 the size of the continental US. Traveling from Ketchikan to Point Barrow is like going from Florida to Minnesota. If Alaska was mapped at the same scale as the other states in this book, you'd be looking at 16 pages of Alaska instead of 2.

A B C D E F G

U S S R

Sea of Okhotsk

• Tigil

KAMCHATKA PENINSULA

Karaginski Island

• Anadyr

KURIL ISLANDS

• Ust' Kamchatsk

• Olyutorskiy

Gulf of Anad

• Petropavlovsk Kamchatskiy

International Date Line (Monday) (Sunday)

Bering Sea

Attu Island • Attu
Near Islands

Agattu Island

Buldir Island

Cape St. Stephen

Kiska Island

Rat Islands

ALEUTIAN ISLANDS

Semisopochnoi Island

Amchitka Island

Gareloi Island

Delarof Islands

Tanaga Island

Kanaga Island

• Adak

Atka Island • Atka

Amlia Island

Seguam Island

Aleutian Time Alaska Time

Andreanof Islands

Islands of the Four Mountains

Fort Glenn •

Dutch Harbo

Nikolski •
Umnak Island

• Kashe
Una Islar

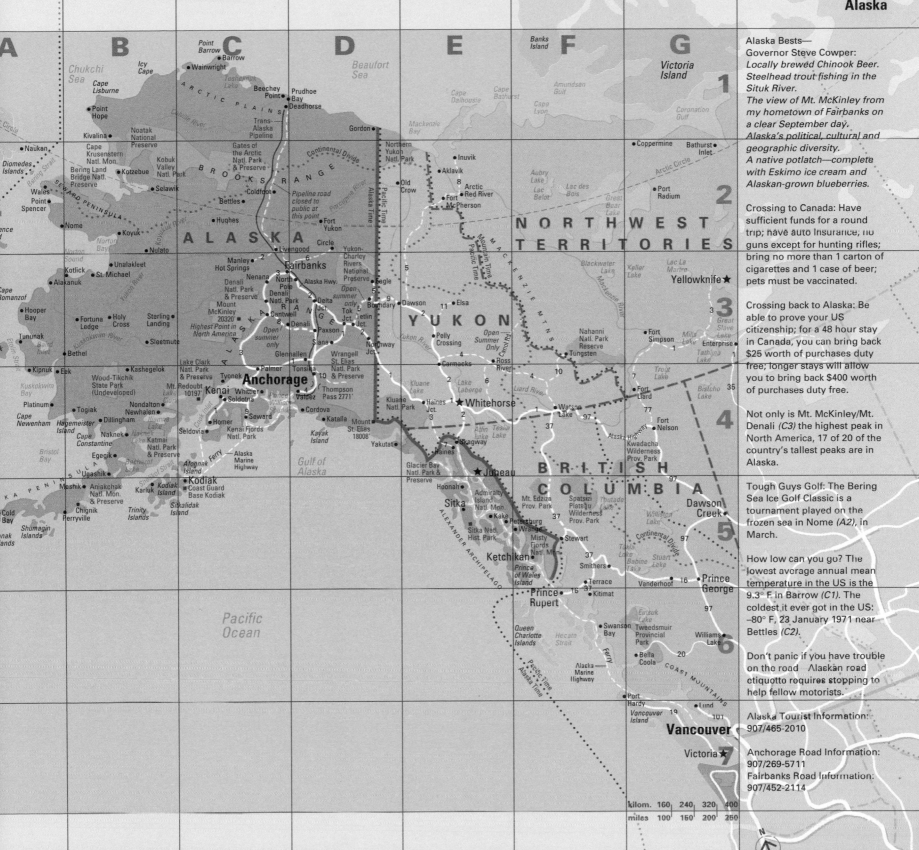

A   B   C   D   E   F   G

Alaska Bests—
Governor Steve Cowper:
Locally brewed Chinook Beer.
Steelhead trout fishing in the
Situk River.
The view of Mt. McKinley from
my hometown of Fairbanks on
a clear September day.
Alaska's political, cultural and
geographic diversity.
A native potlatch—complete
with Eskimo ice cream and
Alaskan-grown blueberries.

Crossing to Canada: Have
sufficient funds for a round
trip; have auto insurance; no
guns except for hunting rifles;
bring no more than 1 carton of
cigarettes and 1 case of beer;
pets must be vaccinated.

Crossing back to Alaska: Be
able to prove your US
citizenship; for a 48 hour stay
in Canada, you can bring back
$25 worth of purchases duty
free; longer stays will allow
you to bring back $400 worth
of purchases duty free.

Not only is Mt. McKinley/Mt.
Denali (C3) the highest peak in
North America, 17 of 20 of the
country's tallest peaks are in
Alaska.

Tough Guys Golf: The Bering
Sea Ice Golf Classic is a
tournament played on the
frozen sea in Nome (A2), in
March.

How low can you go? The
lowest average annual mean
temperature in the US is the
9.3° F in Barrow (C1). The
coldest it ever got in the US:
–80° F, 23 January 1971 near
Bettles (C2).

Don't panic if you have trouble
on the road. Alaskan road
etiquette requires stopping to
help fellow motorists.

Alaska Tourist Information:
907/465-2010

Anchorage Road Information:
907/269-5711
Fairbanks Road Information:
907/452-2114

The Virgin Islands are 1100 miles south of Miami—and are the easternmost of any US Atlantic landholdings.

Paradise found—the winter temperature for both Puerto Rico and the USVI averages 77°; in the summer it's only five degrees warmer.

The Virgin Islands were once the Danish West Indies. One lasting legacy—driving on the *left* side of the road.

You can bring back $800 worth of goods duty free—and the shopping here is phenomenal! St. Thomas is best known for high-end goods at low-end cost.

There was a pirate famed for being fatally disciplinary with his brides. Nowadays, if you really trust your groom, you can spend your honeymoon on St. Thomas in the tower once occupied by him. Remember his name? See page 156.

Sailing: St. Thomas has the largest charter yacht fleet in the Caribbean, and the island's port, Charlotte Amalie *(D3)*, is the area's busiest cruise port.

If you don't want to get wet, the underwater Coral World tower offers a spectacular view of the St. Thomas reef.

Travel to Puerto Rico and the USVI—since they're US Territories, you don't need a passport, but you do need to prove your US citizenship. A birth certificate will suffice.

Puerto Rico Tourist Information:
809/725-2110
Virgin Islands Tourist Information:
809/774-8784

A	B	C	D	E

1

Niihau
(Private Island)
• Puuwai

Haena St. Park
Na Pali Coast State Park
Waimea Canyon St. Park
Russian Fort Elizabeth
Kokee St. Park
Hanapepe

Lumahai Beach
Haena • Hanalei
56
Mt. Waialeale 5170'
550
50

• Kapaa
Wailua River State Park
Lihue
Lihue Airport

Kauai

Kaulakahi Channel

Kauai Channel

2

Atlantic Ocean

3

Puerto Rico

Aguadilla
• Arecibo
Parque Las Cavernas
San Sebastián
115   109   129   Utuado
2
Mayagüez •   105

2   130   22
10
111
518
143   723
155

2
160   22
155
• Morovis
Cerro de Punta 4390'
52
181
14
1   52   15

Castillo Del Morro ★ **San Juan**

Caguas •

3
El Yunque 3494'

30
• Humacao
3   *Pasaje de Vieques*
182
• Yabucoa

Cabezas de San Juan

Culebra Island

• Fajardo
• Culebra (Dewey)
Ferry
• Vieques
Vieques Island
Vieques (Isabel Segunda)

St. Thomas •
Charlotte Amalie

Cruz Bay •
St. John

Tortola (Britain)
Virgin Islands Natl. Park

Virgin Islands

San Germán •
100
■ Museo Porta Coeli
2
116
Cabo Rojo
■ Bahia Fosforecente

CORDILLERA CENTRAL
10
Ponce
1
Museo de Ponce
3

4

Buck Island Reef Natl. Monument

Christiansted
Frederiksted •   70 •

St. Croix

5

Caribbean Sea

kilom. 20   40   60   80
miles 10   20   30   40   50

The map on this page is 250x250 miles.

A B C D E

1

The Royal Hawaiian: Honolulu's Iolani Palace is America's only royal palace.

South Pacific fans: Bali Hai is Haena State Park *(pg. 6, D1)* on Kauai. That island is also where the nurses washed those men right out of their hair—on Lumahai Beach *(pg. 6, D1)*.

2

What are the 12 letters of the Hawaiian alphabet? *See page 156.*

The only snakes you'll find in Hawaii are in Honolulu Zoo. The residents will tell you there is no rabies here either. Strict quarantine helps.

The first high school west of the Rockies was built in Lahaina *(C3)*, in 1831.

3

Best drive—Hana Hwy. *(D3)*, Maui—it's hair-raising, spectacular and worth every skipped heartbeat.

The Big Island is also the biggest island in the US.

At the end of Hwy. 550 on Kauai *(pg. 6, D1)* is a breathtaking viewpoint, Kalalau Valley Lookout, with waterfalls tumbling into a lush valley and a distant glimpse of the sea.

4

Even with all the recent eruption activity, Kilauea *(E5)* is still very approachable.

You've been warned—Pele the fire goddess makes trouble for those who steal lava rocks from her volcanoes for souvenirs.

5

It does snow (you can even ski) in Hawaii—on the summits of Mauna Loa *(D5)* and Mauna Kea *(D4)*, the Big Island.

Hawaii Tourist Information: 808/923-1811

HAWAIIAN ISLANDS

Pacific Ocean

Oahu
Kahuku Point
Sunset Beach
Laie
Kaena Point State Park
Sacred Falls State Park
Haleiwa
Kahana Valley State Park
Wahiawa
Vaianae
Kaneohe
Kailua
Hanauma Bay State Underwater Park
Pearl Harbor
Honolulu
Honolulu International Airport
930, 93, 99, 803, 83, 750, H2, 99, 63, 61, 72, 93, H1, H1

Molokai
Ilio Point
Molokai Airport
Hoolehua
Kalaupapa National Historic Park
Halawa
Maunaloa
Kaunakakai
460, 470, 450, 460
Kaiwi Channel
Kalohi Channel

Maui
Honokohau
Kapalua
Kahului
The Needle
Kahului Airport
340, 360
Shipwreck Beach
Lanai City
Lahaina
Wailuku
Kaumahina State Wayside
Hana Hwy.
Maalaea
Kihei
360, Ilana Airport
Hana
Wailea
377, 378, 31, 37
Keokea
Haleakala Natl. Park
Kipahulu
30, 440

Lanai
Auau Channel
Kealaikahiki Channel
Alalakeiki Channel

Kahoolawe
Military Reserve
Alenuihaha Channel

Hawaii
Upolu Point
Upolu Airport
Hawi
270
Kukuihaele
Honokaa
240
Kawaihao
Waimea (Kamuela P.O.)
250, 19, 270
Puukohola Heiau Natl. Historic Park
Launahnehoe Park
Akaka Falls State Park
Honomu
220
Waimea-Kohala Airport
Mauna Kea 13796'
Mauna Kea St. Rec. Area
19, 200, 190
Ke-ahole Airport
Hilo
Gen. Lyman Field (Hilo Airport)
Hulihee Palace State Monument
Kailua-Kona
Keaau
11, 200
Weather Observatory
Cape Kumukahi
Kealakekua Bay State Underwater Park
Captain Cook
Mauna Loa 13680'
Namakani Paio
Kilauea Visitor Center
Pahoa
Lava Tree State Mon.
Kealakekua Bay State Historic Park
Hawaii Volcanoes National Park
130
Opihikao
Pu'uhonua o Honaunau Natl. Historic Park
Keokea
Kilauea Caldera
Kupaahu
Kipuka Nene
Kamoamoa
11
Manuka Wayside
Naalehu
Pahala
Apua Point
Ka Lae (South Cape)
KONA COAST

Note: You are not permitted to drive rental cars on certain roads, or may do so only "at your own risk". Read your car rental contract carefully.

The map on this page is 250x250 miles.

N

The country's most extensive and most used ferry system is found in Washington state.

Bring an umbrella to Lake Quinault *(D3)* on the Olympic Peninsula—an average of 200 inches of rain falls here a year.

The plentitude of precipitation trapped by the Olympic Mountains creates the only non-tropical rainforest in the country—and one of the few in the world.

Olympic National Park *(D3)* is a wilderness area—don't expect lots of paved roads and deluxe lodgings. Settle for the tremendous views and the backwoods hiking.

Another beautiful sight, in Long Beach *(D5)*—thousands of kites airborne at the Washington State International Kite Festival in August. Records are set here.

Cape Disappointment, WA *(D5)*, at the mouth of the Columbia River, tops the short list of foggiest spots in the US. So many ships foundered and sank here that it became known as "the graveyard of the Pacific"—not coincidentally, the first lighthouse in the Northwest was built near here.

Washington bests according to Governor Booth Gardner:
The North Cascades Highway.
The Washington State Ferry rides through the Puget Sound.
Mt. Rainier.
Seattle's Pike Place Market.
The Museum of Flight.

Astoria, OR *(D5)* is the oldest city in the Pacific Northwest—who's it named after? *See page 156.* Climb the 123-foot Astoria Column for the best view in town.

A **B** **C** **D** **E**

1 **2** **3** **4** **5**

kilom. 20 40 60 80
miles 10 20 30 40 50

The map on this page is 250x250 miles.

Pacific Ocean

Pacific Rim National Park
Ucluelet
Kildonan
Barkley Sound
Bamfield
Nitinat Lake
Clo-oose
Pacific Rim National Park
Cape Flattery
Neah Bay
Sekiu
Ozette
Ozette Lake
Clallam Bay
Slip Point Lighthouse
Butler Cove
Olympic National Park
Forks
La Push
Bogachiel
Soleduck
Boulder Creek
Altaire
Hoh
Mt. Carrie 6995'
Mt. Olympus 7965'
Olympic National Park
OLYMPIC MTNS
Kalaloch
Kalaloch
Queets
Queets
Graves Creek
Lake Quinault
Staircase
Taholah
109
Neilton
Lake Cushman
Lake Cushman
Sunset Beach
Hoodsport
Potlatch
Belfair
Pacific Beach
Ocean City
101
Ocean City
Ocean Shores
Grays Harbor
Hoquiam
Aberdeen
Schafer
101
Elma
Westport
Twin Harbors
105
12
107
Montesano
8
12
Grayland
Grayland
105
101
Tokeland
Bruceport Park
Raymond
Oakville
5
South Bend
Willapa Bay
Ocean Park
Nemah
6
Lebam
Long Beach
103
101
Cape Disappointment
Fort Canby
4
Rainbow Falls
6
Cape Disappointment Lighthouse
Toll Bridge
101
401
Megler
Grays River
Fort Stevens
Astoria
Fort Clatsop Natl. Memorial
30
Cathlamet
409
Castle Rock
504
Seaside
202
Westport
4
Longview
Kelso
432
Saddle Mtn.
47
Rainier
433
101
OREGON
26
Necanicum
47
30
5
Kalama
Cougar

Port Alberni
4
Parksville
101
Gibson
Departure Bay
Ferry
Nanaimo
Gabriola Gabriola Is.
Valdes Is.
Strait of Georgia
Ladysmith
Youbou
Chemainus
Galiano Is.
Cowichan Lake
Honeymoon Bay
18
Lake Cowichan
Salt Spring Island
Duncan
Port Renfrew
Sidney
17
14
San Juan Islands Hist. Pa.
Jordan River
Sooke
14
1
San Juan Island
112
E. Sooke
1A
Sappho
112
Victoria
Lake Crescent
101
Port Angeles
Sequim
Altaire
Heart O The Hills
Towns
Sequim Bay
Discovery Bay
101
Dosewallips
Quilcene
Elkhorn
Falls View
Seal Rock
Dosewallips
Hamma Hamma
COAST RANGE
Shelton
Jarrell Cove (Marine)
Purdy
106
302
3
Bremerton
300
Belfair
Olympia
Fort Lewis
Millersylvania
510
Yelm
507
Tenino
Centralia
Chehalis
508
Mayfield Lake
Marys Corner
12
505
Riffe Lake
Seaquest
Mt. St. Helens Natl. Volc. Monument
Mount St. Helens

↓ pg. 10

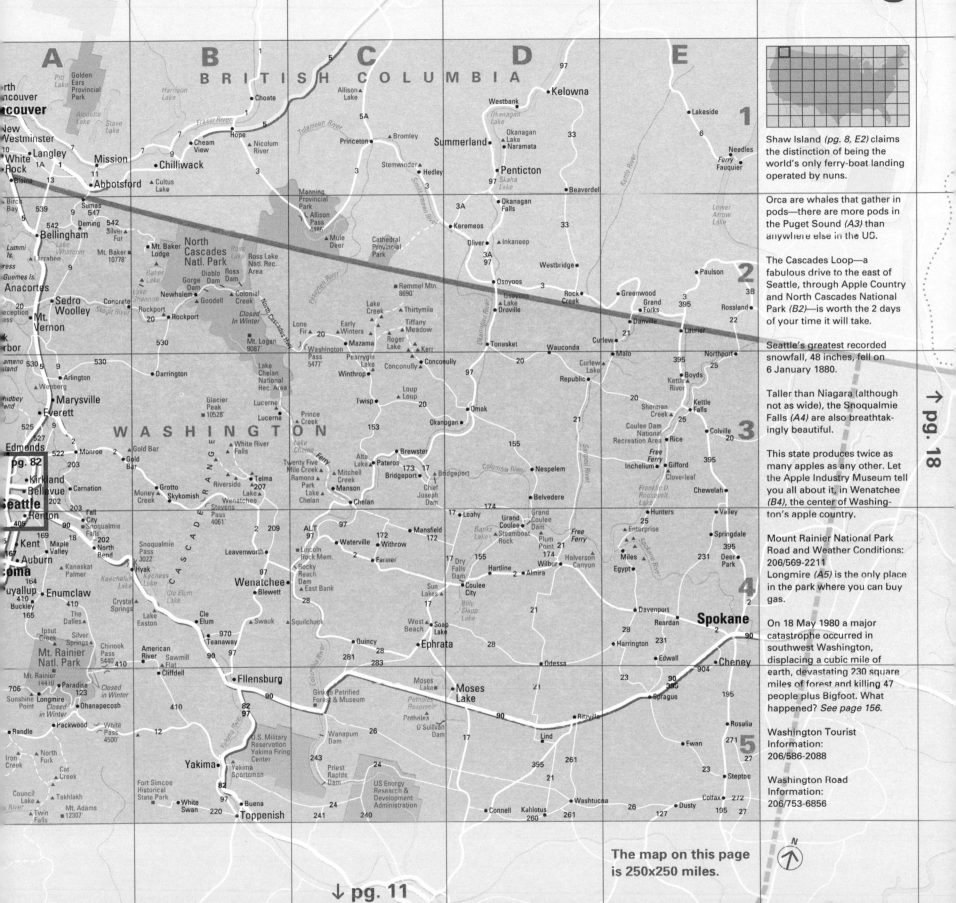

British Columbia / Washington Map

A B C D E

BRITISH COLUMBIA

North Vancouver, Vancouver, New Westminster, White Rock, Blaine, Langley, Mission, Abbotsford, Sumas, Deming, Silver Fir, Bellingham, Larrabee, Anacortes, Sedro Woolley, Mt. Vernon, Concrete, Rockport, Darrington, Arlington, Wenberg, Marysville, Everett, Edmonds, Monroe, Gold Bar, Gold Bar, Kirkland, Bellevue, Carnation, Seattle, Renton, Kent, Maple Valley, Auburn, Tacoma, Enumclaw, Buckley, Puyallup, Mt. Rainier Natl. Park, Paradise, Longmire, Ohanapecosh, Packwood, Randle, Yakima, Toppenish

Pitt Lake, Golden Ears Provincial Park, Harrison Lake, Choate, Cheam View, Hope, Nicolum River, Chilliwack, Cultus Lake, Manning Provincial Park, Allison Pass, Mule Deer, Cathedral Provincial Park

Fraser River, Tulameen River, Allison Lake, Princeton, Bromley, Stemwinder, Hedley, Keremeos

Westbank, Summerland, Penticton, Kelowna, Okanagan Lake, Naramata, Skaha Lake, Beaverdel, Okanagan Falls, Oliver, Inkaneep, Osoyoos, Osoyoos Lake, Westbridge, Rock Creek, Greenwood, Grand Forks, Danville, Laurier

Lakeside, Needles, Ferry, Fauquier, Lower Arrow Lake, Paulson, Rossland

North Cascades Natl. Park, Mt. Baker Lodge, Mt. Baker 10778', Diablo Dam, Gorge Dam, Ross Dam, Ross Lake Natl. Rec. Area, Newhalem, Goodell, Colonial Creek, Closed In Winter, Mt. Logan 9087', Washington Pass 5477', Lone Fir, Early Winters, Mazama, Roger Lake, Kerr, Remmel Mtn. 8690', Thirtymile, Tiffany Meadow

Lake Chelan National Rec. Area, Glacier Peak 10528', Lucerne, Lucerne, Prince Creek, Pearrygin Lake, Winthrop, Conconully, Conconully, Loup Loup, Twisp, Omak, Okanogan

Tonasket, Wauconda, Curlew, Curlew Lake, Republic, Sherman Creek, Kettle Falls, Colville, Rice, Free Ferry, Inchelium, Gifford, Cloverleaf, Chewelah, Valley, Springdale, Deer Park

Kettle River, Malo, Boyds, Northport

White River Falls, Telma, Riverside, Grotto, Money Creek, Skykomish, Ramona Park, Manson, Chelan, Lake Chelan, Twenty Five Mile Creek, Mitchell Creek, Alta Lake, Pateros, Bridgeport, Brewster, Chief Joseph Dam, Belvedere, Nespelem, Leahy, Grand Coulee, Grand Coulee Dam, Steamboat Rock, Plum Point, Halverson Canyon, Hunters, Enterprise, Miles, Egypt, Davenport, Reardan, Spokane, Harrington, Edwall, Cheney

Stevens Pass 4061', Snoqualmie Pass 3022', North Bend, Fall City, Snoqualmie Falls, Hyak, Kachess Lake, Cle Elum Lake, Leavenworth, Wenatchee, Blewett, East Bank, Rocky Reach Dam, Waterville, Withrow, Farmer, Mansfield, Dry Falls Dam, Hartline, Almira, Wilbur, Odessa, Sprague

Keechelus Lake, Crystal Springs, Lake Easton, Cle Elum, Swauk, Teanaway, American River, Sawmill Flat, Cliffdell, Ellensburg, Squilchuck, Quincy, Soap Lake, West Beach, Coulee City, Sun Lakes, Ephrata, Moses Lake, Ritzville, Lind, Washtucna, Connell, Kahlotus

Chinook Pass 5440', Paradise, Sunshine Point, Closed in Winter, White Pass 4500', North Fork, Cat Creek, Council Lake, Takhlakh, Mt. Adams 12307', Twin Falls, Iron Creek

Ginkgo Petrified Forest & Museum, Wanapum Dam, U.S. Military Reservation Yakima Firing Center, Yakima Sportsman, Fort Simcoe Historical State Park, Priest Rapids Dam, Potholes Reservoir, O'Sullivan Dam, US Energy Research & Development Administration, Buena, White Swan, Steptoe, Colfax, Dusty, Rosalia, Ewan

CASCADE RANGE, WASHINGTON

Skagit River, Baker Lake, Lake Shannon, Pasayten River, Columbia River, Okanogan River, Sanpoil River, Franklin D. Roosevelt Lake, Spokane River, Banks Lake, Billy Clapp Lake, Potholes, Yakima River

↑ pg. 18

pg. 82

↓ pg. 11

Shaw Island (pg. 8, E2) claims the distinction of being the world's only ferry-boat landing operated by nuns.

Orca are whales that gather in pods—there are more pods in the Puget Sound (A3) than anywhere else in the US.

The Cascades Loop—a fabulous drive to the east of Seattle, through Apple Country and North Cascades National Park (B2)—is worth the 2 days of your time it will take.

Seattle's greatest recorded snowfall, 48 inches, fell on 6 January 1880.

Taller than Niagara (although not as wide), the Snoqualmie Falls (A4) are also breathtakingly beautiful.

This state produces twice as many apples as any other. Let the Apple Industry Museum tell you all about it, in Wenatchee (B4), the center of Washington's apple country.

Mount Rainier National Park Road and Weather Conditions: 206/569-2211
Longmire (A5) is the only place in the park where you can buy gas.

On 18 May 1980 a major catastrophe occurred in southwest Washington, displacing a cubic mile of earth, devastating 230 square miles of forest and killing 47 people plus Bigfoot. What happened? See page 156.

Washington Tourist Information: 206/586-2088

Washington Road Information: 206/753-6856

The map on this page is 250x250 miles.

N

The West's largest cheese factory is in Tillamook *(D1)*. Stop by for a tour and a taste.

At the end of the Oregon Trail you'll find Oregon City *(E1)*, the first incorporated town west of the Rockies.

Surely one of the few places in the nation where you can fuel-up under the protection of a B-17 bomber: Look for the gas station on Rte. 99E in Milwaukie, OR *(E1)*.

The Willamette is one of only three rivers in the world that flows north *(D3)*.

A must-visit place: The Willamette Valley *(D2)*, with its preserved buildings, wineries and most of Oregon's 50-plus covered bridges.

Rent a dune buggy and explore the largest ocean dunes in North America at the Oregon Dunes National Recreation Area *(C3)*.

Eugene has made a name for itself as "The Track Capital of the World." World-class athletes and Olympic hopefuls can be found beside the amateur enthusiasts here.

Oregon's only national park is a beauty—Crater Lake *(D5)*, with the bluest water imaginable. What other record does it hold? *See page 156.*

Get a grip, or try to, at the Oregon Vortex in Gold Hill *(C5)*, where weird things happen to gravity.

Oregon Tourist Information: 1-800-547-7842

Oregon Road Information: 503/889-3999

A **B** **C** **D** **E**

1 **2** **3** **4** **5**

Pacific Ocean

kilom. 20 40 60 80
miles 10 20 30 40 50

The map on this page is 250x250 miles.

pg. 83

Portland · Vancouver
Camas

Vernonia · St. Helens · Yale
Yale Lake
26 47 30 503
Buxton 502
Manning 5
Nehalem 8 26 30 5 205
Mohler Forest Grove 205 84
Nehalem Bay Beaverton 217 5 26 30
101 Garibaldi 47 Newberg 99W Milwaukie
Tillamook Bay McMinnville Oregon City 205 212
Cape Meares Lighthouse 6 22 18 18 Spring · Sandy
Beaver Creek 211 21
Cape Lookout Hemlock 99E McLoughlin 224
Sand Beach House Natl. Milo · Estacada
Hebo Hist. Site McIver 224
Castle Rock 211
Lincoln City Devil's Lake 99W Crown State Park
Kernville North Creek Valley Jct. Dallas 22 Silverton
Cape Foulweather 229 Mill Creek Rec. Area Rickreall 214
Depoe Bay 223 Salem Silver Falls
Yaquina Head Lighthouse Beverly Beach Monmouth 22 Riversi
Newport Chitwood N. Santiam River Mill City Bagby Hot Springs
South Beach Toledo · Eddyville Corvallis 34 Humbug
101 20 34 20 Albany Detroit Lake · Detroit
Waldport Tidewater Lebanon 99W Bre
Beachside Slide Detroit Lake
Yachats Missouri Bend · Alsea Monroe · Halsey Mt. Jef
Cape Perpetua Rock Creek 99E 228 Sweet Home Green Peter Lake
Keller Creek Junction City Cascadia 22
Heceta Head Lighthouse Carl G. Washburne 36 99 5 20 Santiam Jct.
Florence 126 Greenleaf Fernview House Rock
Honeyman Mapleton Fern Ridge Lake Vida 126 McKenzie Lava Be
Siltcoos Dunes City Richardson 126 105 126 St. Park Belknap Springs
Driftwood Lagoon Oregon Dunes Natl. Smith River Falls Veneta Eugene · Springfield McKenzie Pass 5325'
Winchester Bay Rec. Area Vincent Creek Goshen 99 58 242 French Pete Satan Creek
Eel Creek Reedsport 38 Cottage Grove Dexter Cougar Lake Te
Umpqua Lighthouse Elkton Lookout Point Lake Twin Springs Beach
Horsfall Beach 38 99 Black Canyon Mt. B. Ski Area
Cape Arago Lighthouse North Bend Drain Pine Meadows Dorena Lake Oakridge Deschutes Bridge
Sunset Bay Coos Bay Tyee Ferrin Hills Creek Lake La Pine
Coquille River Lighthouse 101 42 138 5 McCredie Springs Waldo Lake
Bullards Beach 42S Coquille Roseburg Bogus Creek 58 Sand Prairie Davis Lake
Bandon Myrtle Point Idleyld Park Steamboat Willamette Pass 5128' Wickiup Reservoir
Cape Blanco Lighthouse Denmark Winston Lone Rock Rec. Area Susan Creek Boulder Flat Crescent Lake Crescent
Cape Blanco Coquille Myrtle Grove St. Park 42 Camas Valley Boulder Creek Horseshoe Bend 138 Poole Creek 58
Port Orford Powers Bear Creek Dumont Creek S. Umpqua Falls Clearwater Falls Chemult
Myrtle Creek Canyonville Diamond Lake Diamond Lake
Humbug Mtn. Prehistoric Gardens Tiller Crater Lake Natl. Park Beaver Marsh
Ophir Rogue River 5 Drew Closed in Winter 138
Agness Union Creek 230 Crater Lake Mt. Scott 8926'
Wolf Creek River Bridge 62 Wizard Island Kirk
Gold Beach Wolf Creek Whiskey Creek Spring Creek
Cape Sebastian Stewart · Prospect Williamson Collier Mem.
Pistol River Grants Pass Gold Hill Trail 234 62 97
101 238 Murphy Valley of the Rogue 99 5 Butte Falls Upper Klamath Lake
Harris Beach Brookings 199 Cave Jct. 238 Ruch Medford Lakecreek Chiloquin
46 99 140

Illinois River

COAST RANGE

CASCADE RANGE

Umpqua River

McKenzie River

Willamette River

Alsea River

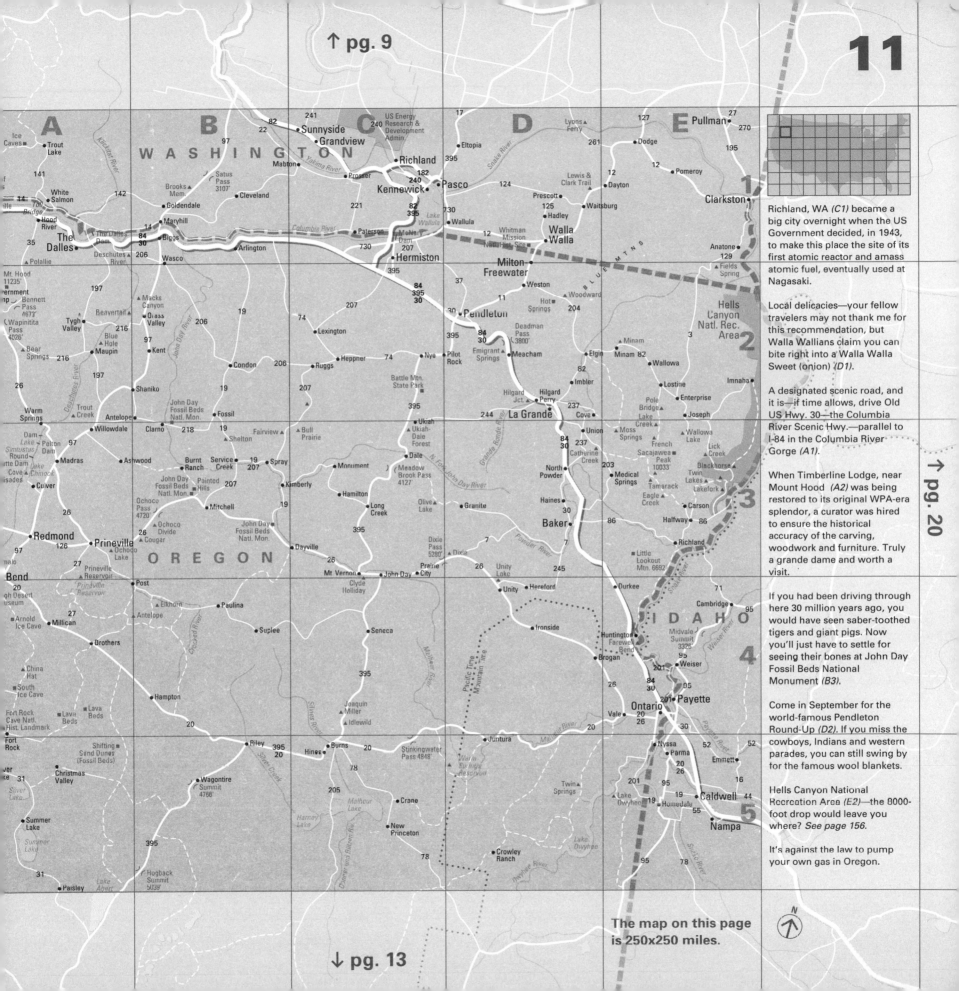

→ pg. 20

Richland, WA *(C1)* became a big city overnight when the US Government decided, in 1943, to make this place the site of its first atomic reactor and amass atomic fuel, eventually used at Nagasaki.

Local delicacies—your fellow travelers may not thank me for this recommendation, but Walla Wallians claim you can bite right into a Walla Walla Sweet (onion) *(D1)*.

A designated scenic road, and it is—if time allows, drive Old US Hwy. 30—the Columbia River Scenic Hwy.—parallel to I-84 in the Columbia River Gorge *(A1)*.

When Timberline Lodge, near Mount Hood *(A2)* was being restored to its original WPA-era splendor, a curator was hired to ensure the historical accuracy of the carving, woodwork and furniture. Truly a grande dame and worth a visit.

If you had been driving through here 30 million years ago, you would have seen saber-toothed tigers and giant pigs. Now you'll just have to settle for seeing their bones at John Day Fossil Beds National Monument *(B3)*.

Come in September for the world-famous Pendleton Round-Up *(D2)*. If you miss the cowboys, Indians and western parades, you can still swing by for the famous wool blankets.

Hells Canyon National Recreation Area *(E2)*—the 8000-foot drop would leave you where? *See page 156.*

It's against the law to pump your own gas in Oregon.

The map on this page is 250x250 miles.

12

Crowded but great—the Oregon Shakespeare Festival which happens each summer in Ashland (D1).

No wonder it's so pretty—Smith River, CA (B1) is the Easter Lily Capital of the World. If you grow lilies, chances are the bulbs came from here.

You can walk (at low tide) to Battery Point Lighthouse near Crescent City (B1). It's the oldest (1856) working lighthouse on the Pacific Coast.

The world's tallest tree (367.8 feet) in the Redwood National Park (B1) was even taller before lightning struck it several years ago. Leggett (B3) is where you can drive through a redwood.

The smallest and strangest trees, by the way, are in the Pygmy Forest of Van Damme State Park (B4).

Gold Country—drive Hwy. 49 for 49er history. How much gold was really here? The Grass Valley area alone produced $960 million worth, earning Nevada City the title of Queen City of the Northern Mines (D5).

Donner Memorial State Park (E5) in Truckee, CA explains the hardships and extremes that beset the snowbound Donner Party in 1847. What's the worst that happened? See page 156.

Lake Tahoe (E5) certainly is among the nation's most beautiful lakes—and among the largest and deepest. At one point it's 1600 feet to the bottom. There's enough water here to cover the entire state of California to a depth of 1 foot.

No. California Road Information: 415/557-3755

The map on this page is 250x250 miles.

A B C D E

1 2 3 4 5

Pacific Ocean

CALIFORNIA

Ashland, Klamath Falls, Yreka, Redding, Anderson, Red Bluff, Corning, Chico, Paradise, Oroville, Willows, Colusa, Marysville, Yuba City, Grass Valley, Nevada City, Susanville, Greenville, Quincy, Eureka, Arcata, Fortuna, Ferndale, Ukiah, Fort Bragg, Mendocino, Willits, Clearlake, Lakeport, Healdsburg, Geyserville, Cloverdale, Auburn, Crescent City, Smith River, Klamath, Weaverville, Mt. Shasta, Weed, McCloud, Dunsmuir, Burney

kilom. 20 40 60 80
miles 10 20 30 40 50

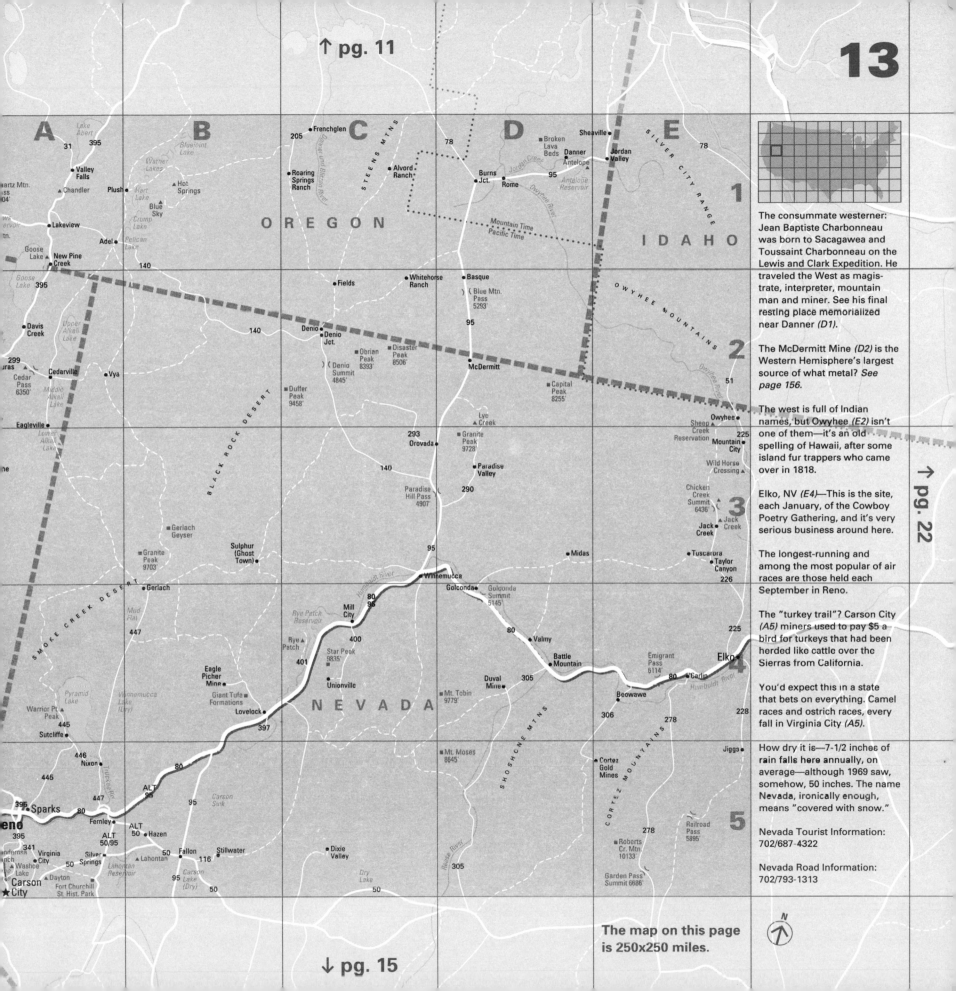

A B C D E

205 Frenchglen
Sheaville
78
Broken Lava Beds
Danner
Antelope
Jordan Valley

Valley Falls
Chandler Plush
Hot Springs
Roaring Springs Ranch
Alvord Ranch
Burns Jct.
Rome
95
Antelope Reservoir

31 395
Lake Abert
Bluejoint Lake
Warner Lakes
Hart Lake
Blue Sky
Crump Lake
Pelican Lake

O R E G O N

STEENS MTNS

S I L V E R   C I T Y   R A N G E

1

I D A H O

Lakeview
Adel
New Pine Creek
Goose Lake
140

Fields
Whitehorse Ranch
Basque
Blue Mtn. Pass 5293'
95

O W Y H E E   M O U N T A I N S

Mountain Time
Pacific Time

Davis Creek
Upper Alkali Lake
Cedar Pass 6350'
Cedarville
Vya
Denio
Denio Jct.
Obrian Peak 8393'
Disaster Peak 8506'
McDermitt
Capital Peak 8255'
140
51

2

Eagleville
Middle Alkali Lake
Lower Alkali Lake
Duffer Peak 9458'
Denio Summit 4845'

B L A C K   R O C K   D E S E R T

Lye Creek
Owyhee
Sheep Creek Reservation
Mountain City
225

299

293
Orovada
Granite Peak 9728'
Wild Horse Crossing
Chicken Creek Summit 6436'

3

Gerlach Geyser
Sulphur (Ghost Town)
Granite Peak 9703'
140
Paradise Valley
Paradise Hill Pass 4907'
290
Jack Creek
Jack Creek
Tuscarora
Taylor Canyon
226

Gerlach
95
Midas

Winnemucca
Golconda
Golconda Summit 5145'

S M O K E   C R E E K   D E S E R T

Mud Flat
Rye Patch Reservoir
Mill City
Humboldt River
80 95
Valmy
Battle Mountain
Emigrant Pass 5114'
Elko
225

4

447
Rye Patch
Star Peak 9835'
400
401
Eagle Picher Mine
Giant Tufa Formations
Unionville
Lovelock
Duval Mine
305
Mt. Tobin 9779'
Beowawe
Carlin
Humboldt River
80
228

Warrior Pt. Peak
Pyramid Lake
Winnemucca Lake (Dry)
445
Sutcliffe
397
306
278

N E V A D A

S H O S H O N E   M T N S

C O R T E Z   M O U N T A I N S

Nixon
Mt. Moses 8645'
Cortez Gold Mines
Jiggs
445
446
80
278
Railroad Pass 5895'

5

Sparks
Fernley
Hazen
50
Fallon
116
Stillwater
Dixie Valley
Roberts Cr. Mtn. 10133'
Garden Pass Summit 6686'
305

Reno
395
341
Virginia City
Silver Springs
Lahontan
Carson Sink
Carson Lake (Dry)
Dry Lake
50

Carson City
Dayton
Fort Churchill St. Hist. Park
Washoe Lake
Lahontan Reservoir

The consummate westerner: Jean Baptiste Charbonneau was born to Sacagawea and Toussaint Charbonneau on the Lewis and Clark Expedition. He traveled the West as magistrate, interpreter, mountain man and miner. See his final resting place memorialized near Danner (D1).

The McDermitt Mine (D2) is the Western Hemisphere's largest source of what metal? *See page 156.*

The west is full of Indian names, but Owyhee (E2) isn't one of them—it's an old spelling of Hawaii, after some island fur trappers who came over in 1818.

Elko, NV (E4)—This is the site, each January, of the Cowboy Poetry Gathering, and it's very serious business around here.

The longest-running and among the most popular of air races are those held each September in Reno.

The "turkey trail"? Carson City (A5) miners used to pay $5 a bird for turkeys that had been herded like cattle over the Sierras from California.

You'd expect this in a state that bets on everything. Camel races and ostrich races, every fall in Virginia City (A5).

How dry it is—7-1/2 inches of rain falls here annually, on average—although 1969 saw, somehow, 50 inches. The name Nevada, ironically enough, means "covered with snow."

Nevada Tourist Information: 702/687-4322

Nevada Road Information: 702/793-1313

→ pg. 22

The map on this page is 250x250 miles.

N

14

Pacific Rim, Melting Pot—you name it—the highest concentration of Hispanics, Asians, Native Americans and even Danes live in California.

The Russians came, and went, at Fort Ross near Jenner *(B1)*. The fort and a Russian Orthodox church still stand.

There's a museum in Santa Rosa built, believe it or not, with planks from a single redwood tree. Can you guess what museum? *See page 156.*

California accounts for more than 90% of US wine production. Take Hwy. 29 *(C1)* to see Napa Valley in action. Try to avoid summer weekends—it's more interesting (and less crowded) during fall harvest.

1 million people visit Yosemite National Park each summer *(E2)*. You might want to visit at another time.
Information: 209/372-0264

Santa Cruz *(C3)* is home to the Surfing Museum as well as the West Coast's only genuine boardwalk. Incidentally, what's thought of as the San Francisco quake of '89 actually was much closer to, and did more damage to, this town.

Great American Drives: Hwy. 1 *(C4)* from Carmel to Big Sur. If this drive doesn't take your breath away, you're not breathing.

Since 1947, California has led the nation in agricultural production, and is the leading producer of over 50 crops, from avocadoes to tomatoes.

If your home movies don't feature Hollywood stars, stop by Hearst Castle *(C5)*. William Randolph Hearst's do.

kilom. 20 40 60 80
miles 10 20 30 40 50

The map on this page is 250x250 miles.

A B C D E

1 2 3 4 5

Jenner
Guerneville
Calistoga
Sonoma Coast
116
Sebastopol
Santa Rosa
St. Helena
Lake Berryessa
Woodland
16
5
70
99
Auburn
McClellan A.F.B.
Roseville
80
Coloma
49
Vikingsholm
Bodega Bay
116
Cotati
12
Glen Ellen
29
Yountville
505
113
Davis
80
Folsom Dam
Folsom Lake
50
Placerville
S. Lak
Petaluma
Sonoma
121
121
12
Napa
Vacaville
80
Sacramento
49
Fair Play
Fiddletown
50
Kirkwood Ski Are
Point Reyes National Seashore
1
12
Fairfield
Travis A.F.B.
16
Plymouth
Sutter Creek
Jackson
West Point
88
Olema
Novato
37
80 680
Benicia Capital St. Hist Park
12
Rio Vista
Brannan Island
88
Mokelumne River
Golden Gate Natl. Rec. Area
San Rafael
101
580
Vallejo
pg. 85
Antioch
Lodi
49
Silvertip
Richmond
4
San Andreas
Big Trees
Calaveras Big Trees
Farallon Islands
Sausalito
Berkeley
Concord
Murphys
San Francisco
80
24
Walnut Creek
Stockton
Angels Camp
Fraser Flats
108
Daly City
Oakland
880 580
Dublin
J4
4
Sonora
Pacifica
101
580
Livermore
205
Manteca
49
108
Hayward
92
Tracy
580
120
Modesto
Groveland
San Mateo
Union City
84
99
132
Coulterville
Buck Meadows
Half Moon Bay
Palo Alto
84
880
Fremont
Hodgdon Meadows
San Gregorio
84
Mountain View
Milpitas
680
132
Indian Flat
Sunnyvale
130
Patterson
33
Turlock
Pomponio St. Beach
Bean Hollow St. Beach
35
Santa Clara
Los Gatos
pg. 84
San Jose
Mt. Hamilton
4208'
Lick Observatory
101
McConnell
140
Año Nuevo State Reserve
BUS 101
Epicenter of the 1989 earthquake
Morgan Hill
Gustine
Atwater
Castle A.F.B.
140
Mariposa
Wav
Pacific Ocean
9
17
101
San Joaquin River
165
140
Merced
140
Santa Cruz
Aptos
152
Gilroy
152
Pacheco Pass
1368'
Los Banos
59
49
Oakhurst
Capitola
Seacliff
Watsonville
San Juan Bautista Mission
233
Chowchilla
Raymond
Monterey Bay
Sunset
101
156
Hollister
Dos Palos
41
Castroville
156
25
145
Mill
Seaside
183
Salinas
Paicines
Firebaugh
Madera
Dam
Pacific Grove
Ft. Ord
Paicines
J1
33
145
Monterey
68
G20
Mendota
180
Clovi
17 Mile Drive
Carmel
Carmel Mission
101
25
Kerman
Fresno
180
Pt. Lobos State Reserve
Carmel Valley
Pinnacles Natl. Mon.
33
Andrew Molera
G16
Soledad
146
San Benito Mtn. 5,241'
COAST RANGE
Selm
China
G16
Greenfield
CALIFORNIA
Big Sur
Pfeiffer Big Sur
Arroyo Seco
25
145
Coalinga
41
99
Julia Pfeiffer Burns
Junipero Serra Pk. 5862'
King City
198
Priest Valley
198
Lemoore Naval Air Station
198
Hanford
Lucia
Kirk Cr. Vista
G14
Mission San Antonio De Padua
101
Stratford
Plaskett Cr.
Jolon
San Antonio Reservoir
G18
269
Avena
Parkfield
Tulare
Camp Roberts
San Miguel
San Miguel Mission
Corcoran
San Simeon
Hearst San Simeon St. Hist. Mon.
G14
Cholame
Kettleman City
Tipto
San Simeon Beach
Cambria
Nacimiento Reservoir
Paso Robles
46
41
43
Harmony
46
46
Devils Den
Colonel Allensworth St. Hist. Park
Earlimart
1
San Joaquin Valley
Lost Hills
46
Delan
Cayucos
41
Atascadero
58
33
Was
Morro Bay
Morro Bay
Santa Margarita
101
5

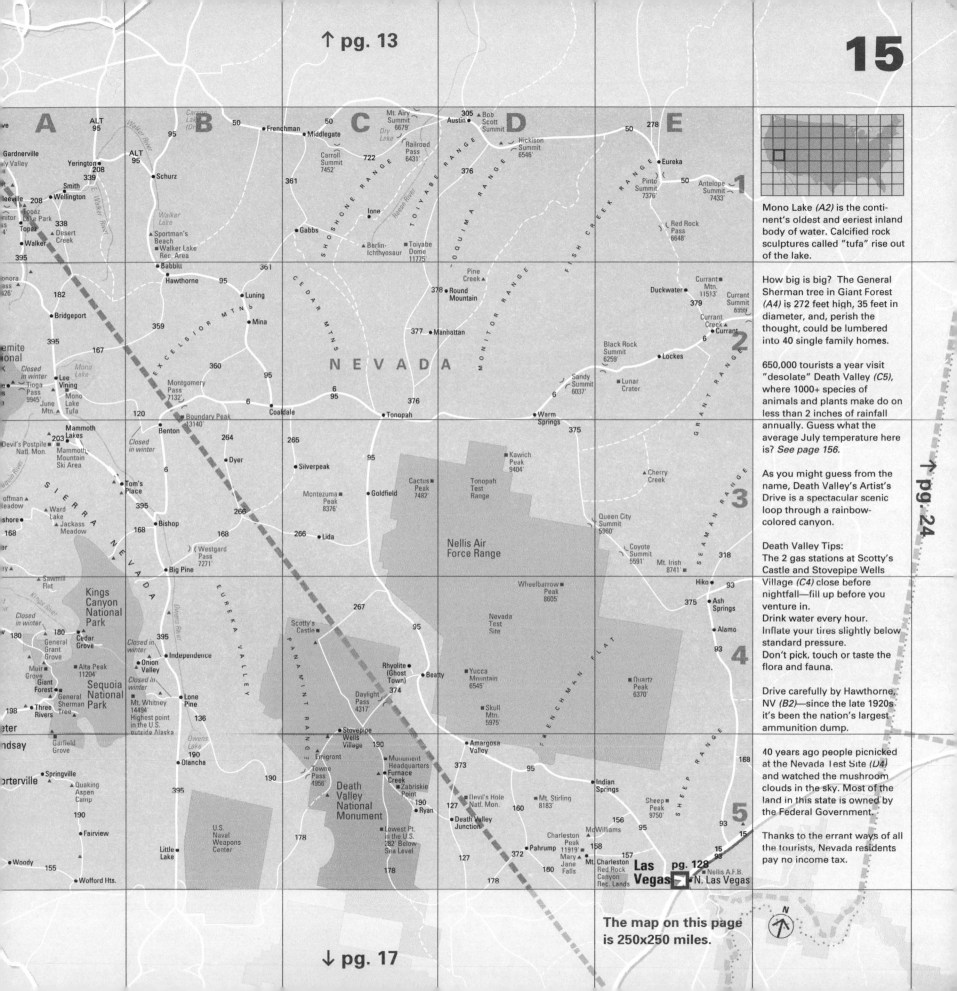

Mono Lake (A2) is the continent's oldest and eeriest inland body of water. Calcified rock sculptures called "tufa" rise out of the lake.

How big is big? The General Sherman tree in Giant Forest (A4) is 272 feet high, 35 feet in diameter, and, perish the thought, could be lumbered into 40 single family homes.

650,000 tourists a year visit "desolate" Death Valley (C5), where 1000+ species of animals and plants make do on less than 2 inches of rainfall annually. Guess what the average July temperature here is? See page 156.

As you might guess from the name, Death Valley's Artist's Drive is a spectacular scenic loop through a rainbow-colored canyon.

Death Valley Tips:
The 2 gas stations at Scotty's Castle and Stovepipe Wells Village (C4) close before nightfall—fill up before you venture in.
Drink water every hour.
Inflate your tires slightly below standard pressure.
Don't pick, touch or taste the flora and fauna.

Drive carefully by Hawthorne, NV (B2)—since the late 1920s it's been the nation's largest ammunition dump.

40 years ago people picnicked at the Nevada Test Site (D4) and watched the mushroom clouds in the sky. Most of the land in this state is owned by the Federal Government.

Thanks to the errant ways of all the tourists, Nevada residents pay no income tax.

The map on this page is 250x250 miles.

San Luis Obispo *(D1)* is the holder of the title of Best Micropolitan Area in the US (that's a small city not part of a metropolitan area). Best sights:

Madonna Inn—a pink palace of 109 fantasy rooms, each decorated in a different theme (Caveman, Race Cars …).

Bubblegum Alley—where hundreds of chewers have left their wads stuck to the wall.

Cal Poly San Luis Obispo—a top agricultural, architectural and engineering university. Tour the campus and research facilities.

The Danish Capital of America is Solvang *(D2)*. Enchanting architecture, crafts and food are just like you'd find in the Old World.

Santa Barbara *(D2)* is a kind of West Coast Camelot—things are beautiful here by decree, or at least strict building codes which have been in effect for over 50 years.

So naturally it's Mission Santa Barbara (D2) that's called "Queen of the California Missions." If you only visit one, make it this one.

Who lives at Rancho del Cielo? *See page 156.*

Floating off the coast of Ventura are the Channel Islands *(D2)*—the wildlife preservation is total and the beauty unspoiled by modern day amenities.

California Tourist Information: 916/322-2881

S. California Road Information: 213/626-7231

A

B

C

D

E

1

2

3

4

5

kilom. 20   40   60   80
miles 10   20   30   40   50

The map on this page is 250x250 miles.

Montana de Oro ▲
Pismo Beach
San Luis Obispo
101
227
Arroyo Grande
58
33
San Luis Obispo Bay
Pismo Beach ▲
McKittrick
Bakersfi
43
Twitchell Reservoir
166
Buena Vista ▲ Aquatic Rec. Area
Guadalupe
1
166
Santa Maria
166
Taft
Maricopa
166
Vandenberg Air Force Base
New Cuyama
Cuyama
Surf
246
135
Los Alamos
33
Lompoc
1
Point Arguello
246
33
G
Fort St. Hi
Jalama
Jalama County Beach Park
1
Las Cruces
101
Soivang
154
Santa Ines Mission
Cachuma Reservoir
Ozena ▲
Fra
Reyes Creek
Point Conception
Gaviota Tunnel
Gaviota
154
Santa Barbara
33
Wheeler Gorge
Refugio Beach
El Capitan Beach
101
Mission Santa Barbara
Carpinteria
Carpinteria Beach
Ojai
150
Sant
Paul
Santa Barbara Channel
Rincon Point
Lake Casitas
Ventura
33
126
San Miguel Island
Channel Islands
Oxnard
101
118
Santa Rosa Island
Santa Cruz Island
Port Hueneme
Thousan Oak
Pt. Mugu ▲
Santa Rosa and Santa Cruz Islands are currently under private ownership
Anacapa Island
Leo Carrillo Beach
San Natl.
Channel Islands National Park
U.S. Naval Reservation
Santa Barbara Island
San Nicolas Island
Pacific Ocean
San Cle
U.S. Rese

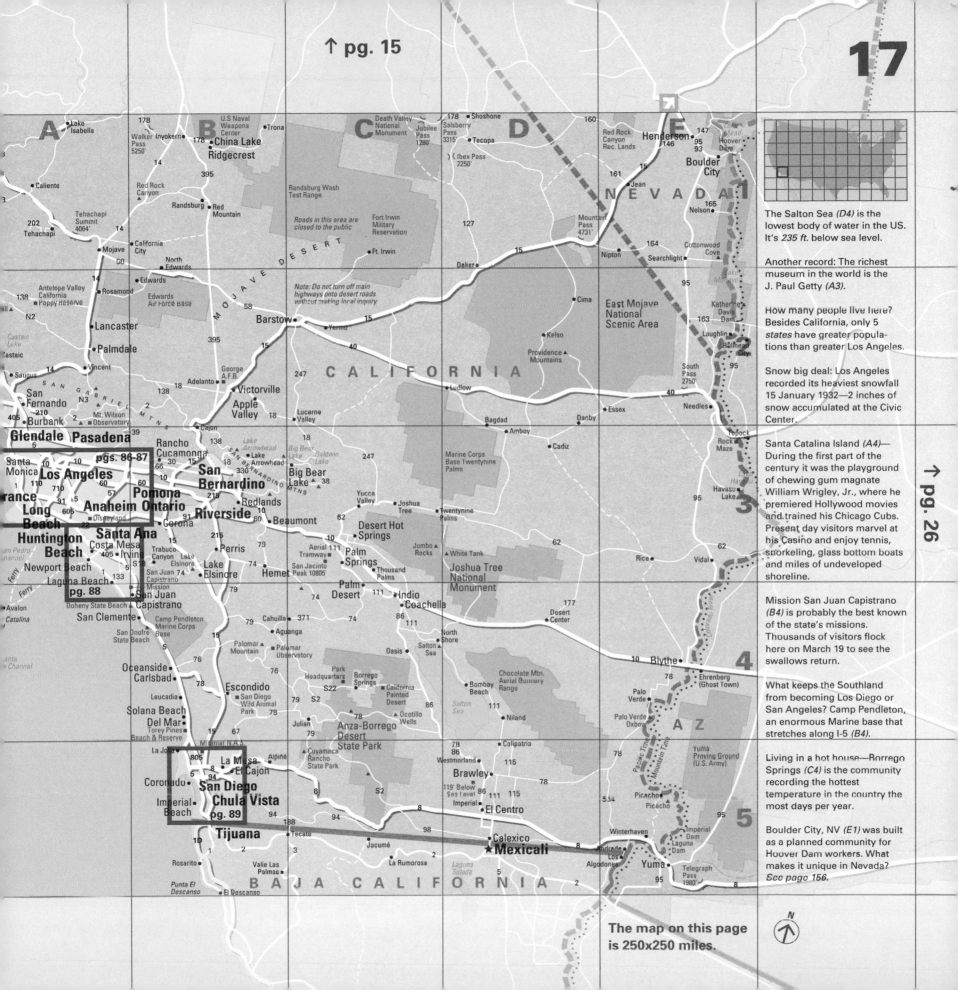

↑ pg. 15

17

→ pg. 26

The Salton Sea (D4) is the lowest body of water in the US. It's *235 ft.* below sea level.

Another record: The richest museum in the world is the J. Paul Getty (A3).

How many people live here? Besides California, only 5 *states* have greater populations than greater Los Angeles.

Snow big deal: Los Angeles recorded its heaviest snowfall 15 January 1932—2 inches of snow accumulated at the Civic Center.

Santa Catalina Island (A4)— During the first part of the century it was the playground of chewing gum magnate William Wrigley, Jr., where he premiered Hollywood movies and trained his Chicago Cubs. Present day visitors marvel at his Casino and enjoy tennis, snorkeling, glass bottom boats and miles of undeveloped shoreline.

Mission San Juan Capistrano (B4) is probably the best known of the state's missions. Thousands of visitors flock here on March 19 to see the swallows return.

What keeps the Southland from becoming Los Diego or San Angeles? Camp Pendleton, an enormous Marine base that stretches along I-5 (B4).

Living in a hot house—Borrego Springs (C4) is the community recording the hottest temperature in the country the most days per year.

Boulder City, NV (E1) was built as a planned community for Hoover Dam workers. What makes it unique in Nevada? *See page 156.*

The map on this page is 250x250 miles.

Would you believe that the hottest it ever got in Canada was in Gleichen *(E1)*—115° F on 28 July 1903.

No argument—Idaho has the least percentage of population living in metropolitan areas.

You thought Kentucky was the bluegrass state? Post Falls, ID *(A4)* is the center of the largest bluegrass seed producing region in the US.

A popular pasttime—summer cruises on beautiful Coeur d'Alene Lake *(A5)*.

Shoshone County has yielded more silver than any other region in the world. I-90 through Wallace *(B5)* brings you there.

Who were the first US citizens to see the Rocky Mountains and the Continental Divide *(D3)? See page 156.*

There are at least 50 glaciers in Glacier National Park *(D3)*—remnants of the last Ice Age. Canada's Waterton Lakes National Park forms with Glacier National Park a "peace park" of international friendship. (Each has separate admissions though!) Information: 406/888-5441

A great Montana drive (and a great name)—the Going-to-the-Sun Road *(D3)* in Glacier National Park.

Celebrate Montana's deep Indian heritage at Indian Days—a huge gathering of US and Canadian tribes in Browning *(E4)* in July.

The St. Ignatius Mission in St. Ignatius, MT *(D5)* dates from 1893 and boasts 58 magnificent frescoes by the mission cook.

← pg. 9

The map on this page is 250x250 miles.

A | B | C | D | E

Bassano
36
1
Dinosaur
544
Brooks
▲ Tillebrook
539
Lake Newell
535 Kinbrook Island
875

Jenner
886
Buffalo
555
884

THE MIDDLE SAND HILLS

Canadian Forces Base Suffield
Tide Lake

41
41

Red Deer River

Cabri Lake
21
649
Eston
44
Ferry
30
Ferry
Leader
S. Saskatchewan River
32
Abbey
Cabri
Pennant

Elrose
42
4
42
342
Kyle
COTEAU HILLS

Diefenbaker Lake
Ferry

1

36
524
524
Ralston
Redcliff
Medicine Hat
S. Saskatchewan River
Vauxhall
Taber ● Purple Springs
3
Bow Island
Seven Persons
Irvine
Walsh
1
41
887
Bitter Lake
Maple Creek
371
Fox Valley
321
GREAT SAND HILLS
Hazlet
37
332
Crane Lake
Bigstick Lake
Tompkins
Gull Lake
Antelope Lake
32
4
Herbert
Morse
1
Swift Current
Beverley
363
Neville
43 Vanguard

S A S K A T C H E W A N

2

Wrentham
61 Skiff
Foremost
Etzikom
61 Orion
879
Manyberries
Pakowki Lake
887
501
Warner
4
Milk River
501
Writing-on-Stone
Milk River

Elkwater
Cypress Hills Prov. Park
C Y P R E S S   H I L L S
Cypress Hills
21
Cypress Lake
Robsart
Consul
Govenlock
41
502
21
Willow Creek
Wild Horse

Instow
Shaunavon
13
13
Eastend
Notukeu Cr.
Frenchman River
Climax
18
37
Masefield
Val-Marie
Cadillac
Aneroid
13
4
19
18
Pinto Butte 3350'
Mankota
Wood Mountain

3

Coutts
Sweetgrass
15
M O N T A N A

Shelby
Dunkirk
2
Lothair ● Chester
Joplin
Hingham
Lake Elwell ▲
Sanford Park
Tiber Dam
Lake Elwell
Conrad
232
Fresno Reservoir
Fresno Rookery
Fresno
Dam
2
Havre
87
233
Chinook
Harlem
241
Turner
242
Treelon
Monchy
Loring ● Whitewater
242 Nelson Reservoir ● Nelson
Saco

Grasslands National Park (undeveloped)

4

365
1 ● Dutton
15
Benton Lake
Great Falls
▲ Malmstrom A.F.B.
Vaughn
Teton River
87
Fort Benton
80
Great Falls
Marias River
223
Big Sandy
Loma
236
B E A R S   P A W   M O U N T A I N S
Beaver Creek
Cow Creek
Geraldine
191
Missouri River
66
191
Dodson
2
Malta
Malta Trafton Park
Lake Bowdoin
Hinsdale
2

5

→ pg. 30

↓ pg. 21

The map on this page is 250x250 miles.

N

The border crossing at Sweetgrass, MT *(A3)*, is the busiest between Washington and Minnesota. Maybe they're all driving to Edmonton *(off map)* to see gigantic West Edmonton Mall (110 acres!).

Lewis and Clark thought highly of the Nez Percé tribe; 70 years later the cavalry evidently did not agree—the tribe was driven from its homeland and after weary months on the march, their chief, Chief Joseph, gave the following remarkable speech:

"I am tired of fighting ... it is cold and we have no blankets. The little children are freezing to death. My people, some of them, have run away to the hills, and have no blankets, no food; no one knows where they are—perhaps freezing to death. I want to have time to look for my children and see how many I can find. Maybe I shall find them among the dead. Hear me, my chiefs. I am tired; my heart is sick and sad. From where the sun now stands, I will fight no more forever."

And you thought Route 66 was it—Hwy. 2 is the last of the trans-continental highways. No wide interstate this, scenery and small towns make getting there half the fun.

Great Falls, MT *(A5)* hit the record low (48 states) temperature of -70°F on 20 December 1954. What other weatherwise distinction does this city—and not Chicago—claim? *See page 156.*

The "Great Falls" are only a reminder of their own splendid past. A dam reduced the roar to a more "civilized" flow.

↑ pg. 18

Lewiston, ID *(A1)* is a seaport, via the Columbia and Snake Rivers.

No wonder he was so convincing in High Noon— Gary Cooper hailed from Helena, MT *(E2)*.

A scenic route in already stunning country: the trip from Sun Valley *(C5)* to Stanley *(B4)*, Challis *(C4)*, Mackay *(C5)*, Arco *(pg. 22, C1)*, Hailey *(pg. 22, B1)* and back.

Most state capitols are full of hot air; Idaho's, in Boise, is full of hot water (natural geothermal heating).

An unforgettable sight—rare peregrine falcons and eagles up close at the World Center for Birds of Prey in Boise.

Missoula's Smokejumpers Center trains forest fire fighters from all over the country *(D1)*.

Montana's state motto is "Oro y Plata" (gold and silver) but it's claim to fame is another mineral—what? *See page 156.* (20 billion pounds have been mined from the soil here.)

The aforementioned gold gave Helena more millionaires per capita than any other city in America during the boom of 1864-94. One of them used his riches to build the Cathedral of St. Helena, modeled after the cathedral of Cologne.

Woodburning stoves are so numerous in Montana, that parts of the state are now Big (Smoky) Sky Country.

Idaho Tourist Information: 1-800-635-7820

Idaho Road Information: 208/334-8000

← pg. 11

The map on this page is 250x250 miles.

↓ pg. 22

A B C D E

Map labels (grid A–E, rows 1–5):

Moscow, Bovill, Deary, 3, 8, 3, Kendrick, Freeman Creek, Nez Perce Natl. Hist. Park (Spalding Area), Dworshak Dam, Dworshak Reservoir, Orofino, Pot Mtn. 7139', Kelly Forks, N. Fork Clearwater River, 257, 90, 93, 200, Rattlesnake Natl. Rec. Area, Clark Fork, Huson, Big Larch, Placid Lake, Clearwater, Seeley Lake, 83, Ovando, 200, 200

Lewiston, 95, 12, E.C. Rettig, Hollywood, Rhodes Pk. 7940', Lolo Pass 5233', Lolo Hot Springs, Lolo, 93, 12, 12, Pattee Canyon Rec. Area, Missoula, Potomac, Lincoln, Hooper, Aspen Grove, Wilborn, 279

Winchester, Craigmont, Greer, Fraser Park, 11, Pierce, 12, Whitehouse, White Sand, Wendover, Powell, Lochsa River, Jerry Johnson, Chief Looking Glass, Florence, Sapphire Mtns, Clark Fork, Drummond, 90, 12, Garnet Range, Upper

Kamiah, Nez Perce Natl. Hist. Park (Cottonwood Skirmish), Kooskia, Lowell, Major Penn, Round Top Mtn. 7100', Grave Peak 7878', 93, Hamilton, Grantsdale, 38, Closed in Winter, Philipsburg, Garrison, Elliston, 12, Helena, MacDonald Pass 6320', Grant-Kohrs Ranch Natl. Hist. Site, Deer Lodge, Elkhorn, Continental Divide, 15, Bou, 69

2 Hells Canyon Natl. Rec. Area, Pine Bar, Cottonwood, Grangeville, Hammer Creek, 13, Harpster, White Bird, 14, South Fork Clearwater, Golden, Elk City, South Fork Clearwater River, Squaw Pk. 7677', Durland Park Rec. Area, Darby, Black Bear, Skalkaho Pass 7260', Georgetown Lake, Porters Corners, Anaconda, Butte, Elk Park, Pass 6368', Deer Lodge Pass 5902', 90, Whitehall, 2, 41, 55

3 Grand Canyon of the Snake River, Hells Canyon, 95, Salmon River, Salmon River Canyon, Forest Service Museum, Buffalo Hump 8924', Salmon River, Conner, Medicine Tree, Warm Springs, Indian Trees, Lost Trail Pass 6995', Gibbonsville, 93, Chief Joseph Pass 7264', Pacific Time Mountain Time, Bitterroot Mtns, Anaconda Range, Big Hole National Battlefield, 274, 43, Wisdom, 278, Wise River, 43, Divide, Pipestone Pass 6453', Pigeon Creek, Silver Star, 41, Hollow Top Mtn. 10513', Jefferson River

Riggins, Spring Bar, Pollock, Hells Canyon Dam, Corn Creek, IDAHO, Greeley Mtn. 9243', Mt. McGuire 10082', Panther Creek, North Fork, Williams Lake, Salmon, Melrose, Twin Bridges, Sheridan, Ruby River, 15, 41, Mill Creek, 287

4 Packer John, New Meadows, Ponderosa, 55, Evergreen, McCall, Yellow Pine, Yellow Pine, Rainbow Pk. 9329', Big Baldy 9722', Middle Fork Salmon River, Taylor Mtn. 9960', Salmon River Gorge, 93, Iron Lake, Ellis, McFarland, Lemhi, Leadore, First Territorial Capitol, Bannack, Grant, Lewis & Clark Memorial, Bannock Pass 7681', 324, Clark Cyn. Reservoir, 29, Clark Canyon, Dell, 278, Dillon, Virginia City, Ruby Range, Beaverhead River, Lost River Range, Lemhi Range

4 Donnelly, Rainbow Point, Cascade Reservoir, Cascade Dam, Cascade, South Fork Salmon River, Bear Valley, Banner Creek, Twin Peaks 10328', Challis, Bayhorse, 21, Stanley, Flat Rock, 75, Clayton, 75, 93, Borah Peak 12662', Chilly, Park Creek, Mackay, Leslie, Garfield Mtn. 10961', Red Rock Lakes Natl. Wildlife Refuge & Wilderness, La, Red Rock River, Lima Reservoir, Monida Pass 6823', Scott Pk. 11393', Signal Pk. 8525', Payette Riv.

5 Banks, 52, Horseshoe Bend, Mountain View, 21, 55, Veterans Memorial, Idaho City, Grayback Gulch, 46, 20, Boise, Lucky Peak Lake, Arrowrock Reservoir, 84, 20, 55, 30, Boise Mtns, Sawtooth Range, Sawtooth National Recreation Area, Lowman, Sunny Gulch, Upper O'Brien, Castle Pk. 11815', Browns Pk. 9724', 75, Galena Pk. 11170', Galena, Galena Summit 8701', Ross Pk. 9773', Smoky Mtns, Ketchum, Sun Valley, Sun Valley Ski Area, Hyndman Peak 12078', Smiley Mtn. 11508', Pioneer Mtns, 93, John Day, Summit Creek, 28, 28, Howe, National Reactor Testing Station, 33, Mud Lake, Dubois, Terreton, 22, 33, 15, Rexbur, Henry's Fork, Rocky Mountains, Isl, 20

kilom. 20 40 60 80
miles 10 20 30 40 50

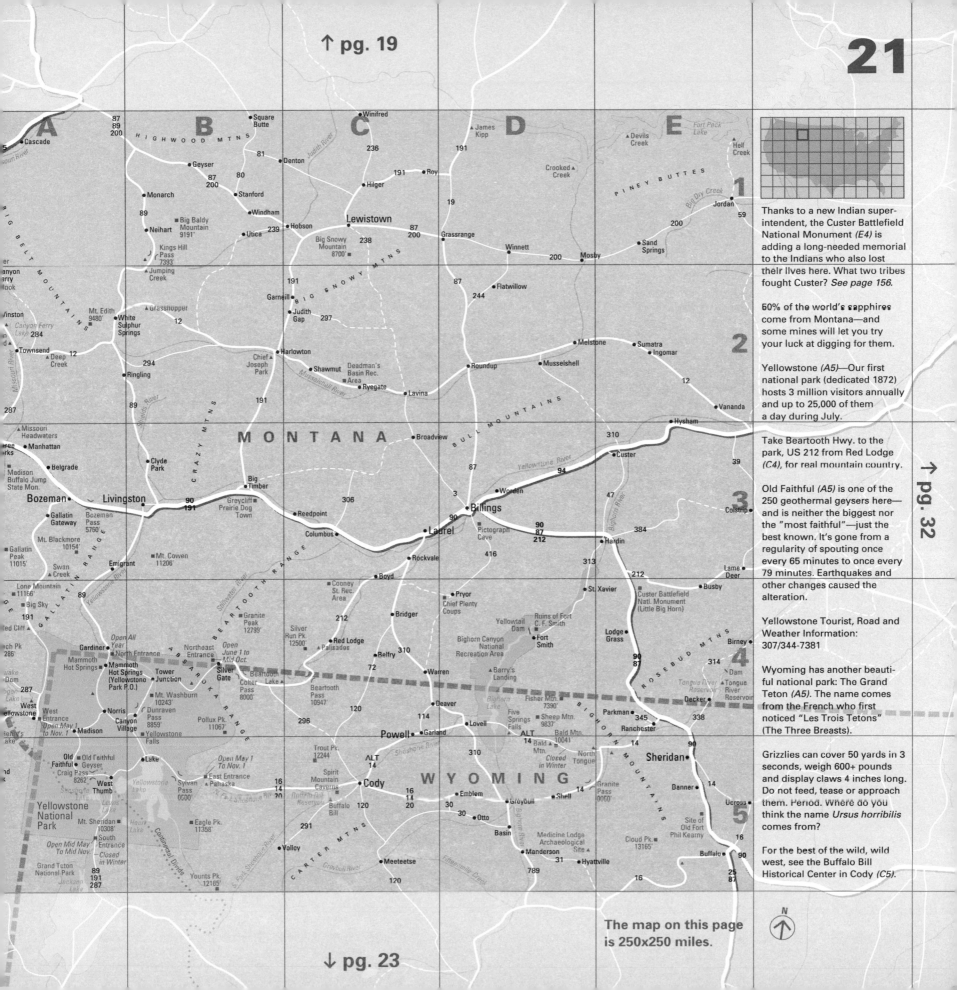

↑ pg. 32

Thanks to a new Indian superintendent, the Custer Battlefield National Monument (E4) is adding a long-needed memorial to the Indians who also lost their lives here. What two tribes fought Custer? *See page 156.*

60% of the world's sapphires come from Montana—and some mines will let you try your luck at digging for them.

Yellowstone (A5)—Our first national park (dedicated 1872) hosts 3 million visitors annually and up to 25,000 of them a day during July.

Take Beartooth Hwy. to the park, US 212 from Red Lodge (C4), for real mountain country.

Old Faithful (A5) is one of the 250 geothermal geysers here—and is neither the biggest nor the "most faithful"—just the best known. It's gone from a regularity of spouting once every 65 minutes to once every 79 minutes. Earthquakes and other changes caused the alteration.

Yellowstone Tourist, Road and Weather Information: 307/344-7381

Wyoming has another beautiful national park: The Grand Teton (A5). The name comes from the French who first noticed "Les Trois Tetons" (The Three Breasts).

Grizzlies can cover 50 yards in 3 seconds, weigh 600+ pounds and display claws 4 inches long. Do not feed, tease or approach them. Period. Where do you think the name *Ursus horribilis* comes from?

For the best of the wild, wild west, see the Buffalo Bill Historical Center in Cody (C5).

The map on this page is 250x250 miles.

← pg. 13

Not too surprisingly, Craters of the Moon National Monument (C1) was a training site for astronauts.

Johnny Potatoseed? Missionary Henry Harmon Spalding brought potatoes to Idaho in 1836 to enrich the diets of the Nez Percé Indians. The state now produces almost 5 million tons per year.

21 million of Idaho's acres are state or national park or forest —and much of that is not accessible by car.

Southern Idaho is home to the largest Basque population outside of the Pyrenees.

You'll figure out pretty quickly the border between Nevada and Utah. West Wendover, NV (B4) is the place with 5 casinos (in a town of 40).

The tumbleweed, which looks like a plant native to Nevada's deserts, arrived here via seeds carried in Russian immigrants' clothing.

The Central Pacific and Union Pacific railroads met at Promontory Point (D3) in 1869, the first rail line across the US.

A rocket-engined car called the Blue Flame set the world speed record at Bonneville Salt Flats (C4) in 1970. How fast did it go? *See page 156.*

22 July 1918—over 500 sheep were killed by a single bolt of lightning in the Wasatch Mountains (E5).

This corner of Utah is renowned for skiing. The best known areas are Robert Redford's Sundance (E5) and the Park City Ski Area (E5) runs just outside Salt Lake City.

The map on this page is 250x250 miles.

IDAHO

NEVADA

UTAH

SNAKE RIVER PLAIN

Mountain Home
Mountain Home A.F.B.
Bruneau
Three Island Crossing
Bliss
Gooding
Malad Gorge State Park
Hagerman
Wendell
Thousand Springs
Jerome
Balanced Rock
Buhl
Castleford
Twin Falls
Eden
Grasmere
Three Creek
Rogerson
Bear Gulch
Fathers and Sons
Oakley
Jarbidge
Jarbidge
North Wildhorse
Jackpot
Thousand Springs
Wells
Montello
Oasis
Pequop Summit 6967'
Pilot Peak 10716'
ALT 93
Silver Zone Pass 5940'
West Wendover
Wendover
Secret Pass 6457'
Snow Water Lake (Dry)
Ruby Dome 11387'
Spruce Mountain 10262'
Ruby Valley
Currie
Cherry Creek
Ibapah
White Horse Pass 6025'

Fairfield
Camus Creek
Twin Lakes Reservoir
Magic Reservoir
Dam
Shoshone Indian Ice Caves
Big Wood River
Richfield
Shoshone
Minidoka
Rupert
Burley
Delco
Albion
Malta
City of Rocks
Raft River
Almo
Strevell
Stone
Snowville
Park Valley
Golden Spike Natl. Hist. Site (Promontory Point)
Grouse Creek Mtns

Hailey
Bellevue
Carey
Lava Beds
Craters of the Moon National Monument
Arco
Butte City
National Reactor Testing Station (U.S. Atomic Energy Commission Reservation)
Atomic City
Idaho Falls
Shelley
Blackfoot
Springfield
American Falls Reservoir
Aberdeen
American Falls Dam
American Falls
Pocatello
Inkom
McCammon
Lava Hot Springs
Alexander
Soda Springs
Downey
Summit
Holbrook
Malad City
Preston
Weston
Smithfield
Logan
Hyrum Reservoir
Tremonton
Brigham City
Randolph
Woodru
Bear River Bay
Willard Bay
Willard Bay
Summit 9000'
Ogden
Roy
Sunset
Clearfield
Willows
Fremont Island
Carrington Island
Great Salt Lake St. Park
Antelope Island
Morgan
East Canyon
Summit 6850'
Eva
Hill Air Force Range
Bonneville Salt Flats
World Record Speedway
Site of World's Automobile Speed Record
Knolls
Wendover Bombing and Gunnery Range
Grantsville
Tooele
Bountiful
Murray
Midvale
Salt Lake City
pg. 90
Wanship
Rockport
Park City Ski Area
Kamas
Bingham Canyon Open Pit Copper Mine
Lehi
American Fork
Fairfield
Sundance Ski Area
Wildwood
Timpanogos Cave Natl. Mon.
Closed in Winter
Heber City
Currant Creek F.
10584'
Orem
Provo
Daniels Pass 8000'
Roads in this area closed to the public
Desert Test Center
Dugway Proving Ground
Dugway
Utah Lake

Rigby
Ririe
Juniper Point
Grays Lake Outlet
Blackfoot River
Grays Lake
Dam
Henr
Dixie Lake
Blackfoot River Reservoir
Alexander Reservoir
Bear River
Paris
Bear Lake
Garden City
Lake
Lodge
Pass 7805'
TEMP

Great Salt Lake Desert
Lakeside Mtns
Cedar Mtns
Dolphin Island
Spring Bay
Great Salt Lake
Stansbury Island

Bruneau River
Clover Creek
Salmon Falls Creek
Snake River
Salmon Falls Creek Res.
Humboldt River
N. Fork Humboldt River
Bishop Creek Reservoir
Butte Mountains
Toana Range
Pilot Range
Grouse Creek Range
Wasatch Range
Bannock Range
Jordan River
Weber River

kilom. 20 40 60 80
miles 10 20 30 40 50

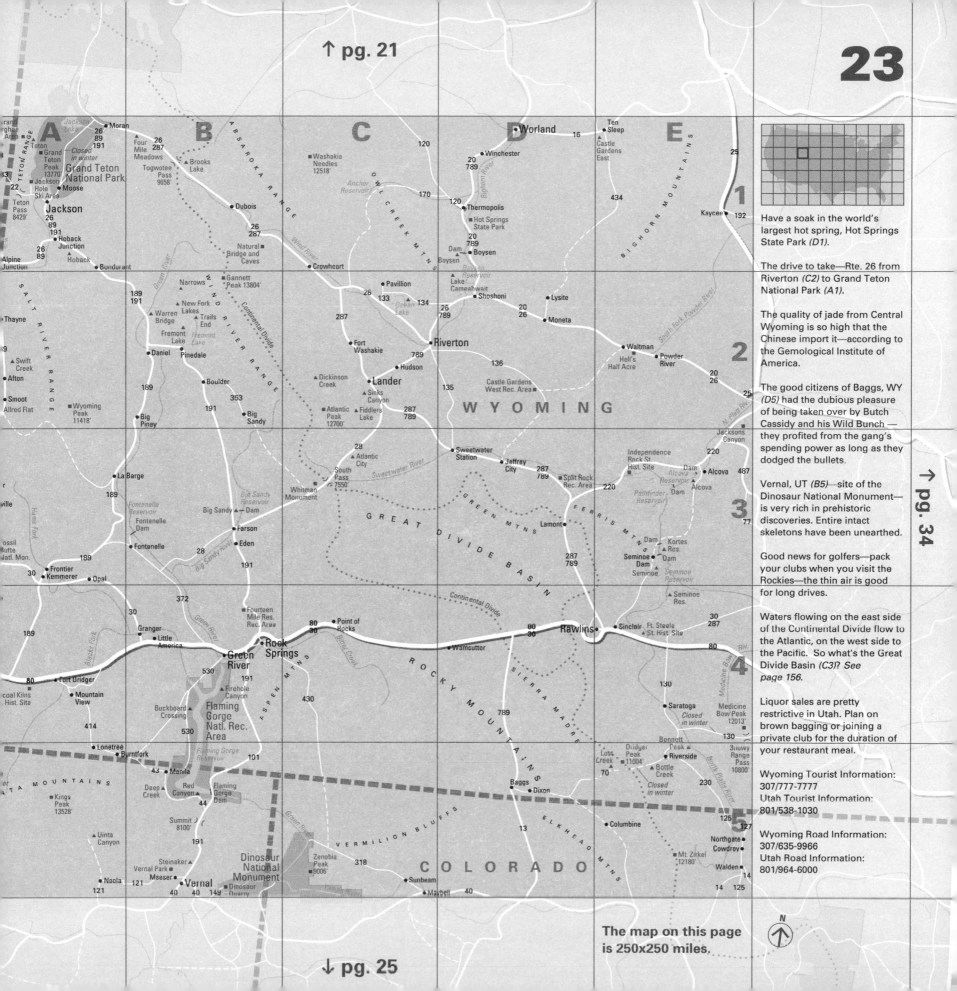

→ pg. 34

Have a soak in the world's largest hot spring, Hot Springs State Park (D1).

The drive to take—Rte. 26 from Riverton (C2) to Grand Teton National Park (A1).

The quality of jade from Central Wyoming is so high that the Chinese import it—according to the Gemological Institute of America.

The good citizens of Baggs, WY (D5) had the dubious pleasure of being taken over by Butch Cassidy and his Wild Bunch — they profited from the gang's spending power as long as they dodged the bullets.

Vernal, UT (B5)—site of the Dinosaur National Monument—is very rich in prehistoric discoveries. Entire intact skeletons have been unearthed.

Good news for golfers—pack your clubs when you visit the Rockies—the thin air is good for long drives.

Waters flowing on the east side of the Continental Divide flow to the Atlantic, on the west side to the Pacific. So what's the Great Divide Basin (C3)? See page 156.

Liquor sales are pretty restrictive in Utah. Plan on brown bagging or joining a private club for the duration of your restaurant meal.

Wyoming Tourist Information: 307/777-7777
Utah Tourist Information: 801/538-1030

Wyoming Road Information: 307/635-9966
Utah Road Information: 801/964-6000

The map on this page is 250x250 miles.

What's so special about the Bristlecone Pines on Wheeler Peak (B2)? *See page 156.*

Hwy. 50 *(A1)*—the so-called loneliest highway in America. If you want a really lonely experience, take nearly 20 hours to drive from Carson City to Ely— the old Pony Express route.

Nevada's Governor Bob Miller is also the Chairman of the Nevada Commission on Tourism. That's boosterism! Here are five things about Nevada he finds special:
*Las Vegas.
Reno.
Lake Tahoe.
Laughlin—a new resort on the Colorado River.
Historic sites of the Old West and Ghost Towns.*

Utah's National Parks:

Capitol Reef *(E3)*—Its dome-like rocks resemble the Capitol in Washington. There's a place here called "The Valley of the Goblins."

Zion *(C4)* owes its biblical-sounding name to the Mormons, who also christened individual rocks such as "Altar" and "Angel's Landing."

Bryce Canyon *(D4)*—Sedimentary rainbows of pink, orange, violet and blue.

Glen Canyon *(E4)*—Spectacular scenery plus vacation/ recreation amenities.

Canyonlands *(pg. 25, A3)*—The newest and largest national park. Check out the bird's eye view of the Colorado and Green Rivers.

Arches National Park *(pg. 25, B3)*—A 300-foot bridge is the world's longest natural arch.

The map on this page is 250x250 miles.

← pg. 15

← pg. 26

→ pg. 36

The driving in Canyonlands National Park (A3) is so treacherous that 4-wheel drive is recommended—and necessary.

Moab, UT (B3)—with its Biblical name and scenery—was the backdrop for "The Greatest Story Ever Told." Visitors these days are more interested in its mountain bike and river rafting adventures.

Look out the car window along Rte. 160. When you see people sprawled along the road, you're at "Four Corners" (B5). Which four states are they trying to touch? See page 156.

Monument Valley (A5), John Ford's home away from Hollywood, is on the Navajo Indian Reservation near the Arizona/Utah border.

Telluride Airport (C4), at 9086 feet above sea level, is the highest commercial airport in the US. You're in the clouds while you're still on the ground!

When the weatherman gives the lowest low for the day, it's most often in Gunnison (D3). Residents will assure you things warm up quickly once the sun comes up.

For ski information in this downhill wonderland—Colorado Ski Country USA: 303/837-0793. There are nearly 30 ski resorts in Colorado.

Get out of the snow and into the hot springs—try the 600-foot-long mineral water pool at Glenwood Springs (D2), or that favorite of the '50s Hollywood jet set, Durango (C5).

Another good reason to visit Durango—the annual playwrights' contest every summer.

The map on this page is 250x250 miles.

"Apache" is the Pueblo Indian word for "enemy," and the Apaches were indeed known for their fierceness.

There are 20 reservations and over 160,000 Native Americans in Arizona.

Watch your watch here. Arizona doesn't switch to Daylight Savings Time—no point in making a long hot day any longer.

The Grand Canyon (C1)—it recounts 2.5 billion years of geologic history to 3.5 million visitors per year.

Grand Canyon Best Views:
Mather Point.
Cape Royal.
Lipan Point.
Desert View.
Toroweap Point.

Grand Canyon Best Travel:
The newly restored steam-engine train from Williams.
Mule rides to the bottom.

The North Rim is only 14 miles, as the crow flies, from the South Rim—but the drive is nearly 200 miles! The trip is worth the trouble—it's much less crowded on the North Rim. The area is closed in the winter.

Grand Canyon Tourist Information:
602/638-2631

Oraibi, AZ *(E2)* is the oldest continuously habited site in the US. How long have people lived here? *See page 156.*

London Bridge is not falling down—it can be viewed in its reconstructed, theme-park splendor at Lake Havasu City *(A3).* (If you're thinking of Tower Bridge, you'll be disappointed—it's still in London!)

← pg. 17

The map on this page is 250x250 miles.

kilom. 20 40 60 80
miles 10 20 30 40 50

A B C D E

ARIZONA

Lake Mead
Lake Mead National Recreation Area
Temple Bar
South Cove
Natural Bridge
Mt. Dellenbaugh 6750'
Toroweap Point
Colorado River
Grand Canyon National Park
Open mid May to mid October
Closed in winter
North Rim Entrance Station
North Rim 8801'
Pt. Imperial
Cape Royal 7876'
Desert View
Hermits Rest
Grand Canyon Village
South Rim Entrance Station
Lipan Point
Ten-X
89
The Gap
Tuba City
Moenkopi
Elephant Feet
Red Lake
Zihi-Dus Jhini Pe 7100'
Hopi Indian Reservation
Inquire about road conditions before passing through area
Hotevilla
Bacobi
Hopi Indian Villages
Oraibi
Shongopovi
93
64
Cameron
264
160
160
98
56

Mt. Tipton 7364'
Windy Point
Chloride
Peach Springs
Grand Canyon Caverns
Valle
Kingman
BUS 40
40
93
Valentine
66
66
Mt. Floyd 7500'
64
Red Lake
Kaibab Lake
Kendrick Peak 10418'
Kendrick Park
Humphreys Peak 12670'
Wupatki National Monument
Bonito
Sunset Crater Natl. Mon.
Little Colorado River
Teas Toh
68
Seligman
Ash Fork
Williams
40
89
BUS 40
Flagstaff
Winona
15
15
Sunrise Trading Post
87

Yucca
Hualapai Mountain Park
Wild Cow
Cross Mountain 6443'
Mohon Peak 7499'
Hualapai Peak 8417'
40
89
Oak Cr. Canyon
Walnut Canyon Natl. Mon.
Lake View
40
180
99
Meteor Crater
Winslow
Holb

Lake Havasu City
London Bridge
Lake Havasu
Crossman Peak 5102'
Pine Peak 7068'
Wikieup
Bagdad
Burro Creek
95
93
Paulden
Tuzigoot National Monument
Clarkdale
Cottonwood
Cave Springs
Pine Grove
Double Springs
Mormon Lake
Sedona
ALT 89
179
Hutch Mountain 8650'
Happy Jack
87
99

Parker Dam
Buckskin Mountain
Earp
Parker
95
Bill Williams River
Santa Maria River
Alamo Lake
96
Yava
Hillside
Granite Basin
Chino Valley
Prescott Valley
The Playgrounds
279
Montezuma Castle Natl. Mon.
Clear Creek
Blue Ridge
Rock Crossing
Chevelon Crossing
Chevelon Lake
97
Prescott
Kirkland Junction
White Spar
Wolf Creek
Hilltop
Humboldt
Mayer
69
69
169
ALT 89
Powell Springs
Camp Verde
17
Clints Well
Kehl Springs

Cactus Plain
Bouse
Harcuvar Mtns
Hualapai Mtns
95
Congress (Ghost Town)
Yarnell
93
89
Bradshaw Mtns
Arcosanti
Mazatzal Mtns
Pine
Pine
Payson
87
Sycamore
Ponderosa
Tonto Creek
Mazatzal Peak 7888'
Woods
Canyon Point
Heber
277
Clay Springs
Snow

Quartzsite
La Posa
Merritt Pass
Aguila
71
Wenden
Salome
Hope
60
Wickenburg
Rock Springs
Waddell Dam
Lake Pleasant
W. Cedar Mountain 5512'
McDowell Mtns
Jakes Corner
188
260
Young
87
288
Aztec Peak 7730'
Blue House Mountain 6417'
60
77
72
60
Morristown
New River
Carefree
Punkin Center
Theodore Roosevelt Lake
Seneca
10

Big Horn Mtns
Surprise
60 89 93
74
17
Peoria pg. 91
Glendale
Phoenix
Scottsdale
Mesa
Tempe
Gilbert
Chandler
Phon D. Sutton
Roosevelt Dam
The Point
Tonto National Monument
Apache Junction
Acacia
Tortilla Flat
Apache Lake
Superstition Mtns
Jones Water
88

Polaris Mountain 3624'
Kofa Mtns
Wintersburg
Palo Verde
Buckeye
Avondale
10
85
17 10143
360
Sierra Estrella
Maricopa Mtns
587
Gilbert
10
Florence Junction
Boyce Thompson Arboretum St. Park
Superior
Oak Flat
Warnica Springs
Miami
Globe
San Carlos
Peridot
70 170
3

Castle Dome Peak 3793'
Yuma Proving Grounds (U.S. Army)
Mohawk Pass
Dateland
Sentinel
Gila River
Gila Bend
85
Maricopa Mtns
Santa Cruz River
Casa Grande
Coolidge
287
187 87
387
Casa Grande Ruins Natl. Mon.
84
287
Kelvin
77
Florence
Coolidge Dam
San Carlos Reservoir
Hayden
Winkelman
Bylas
Coolidge Dam
70

Mohawk
40
60
80
Aztec
8
85
8

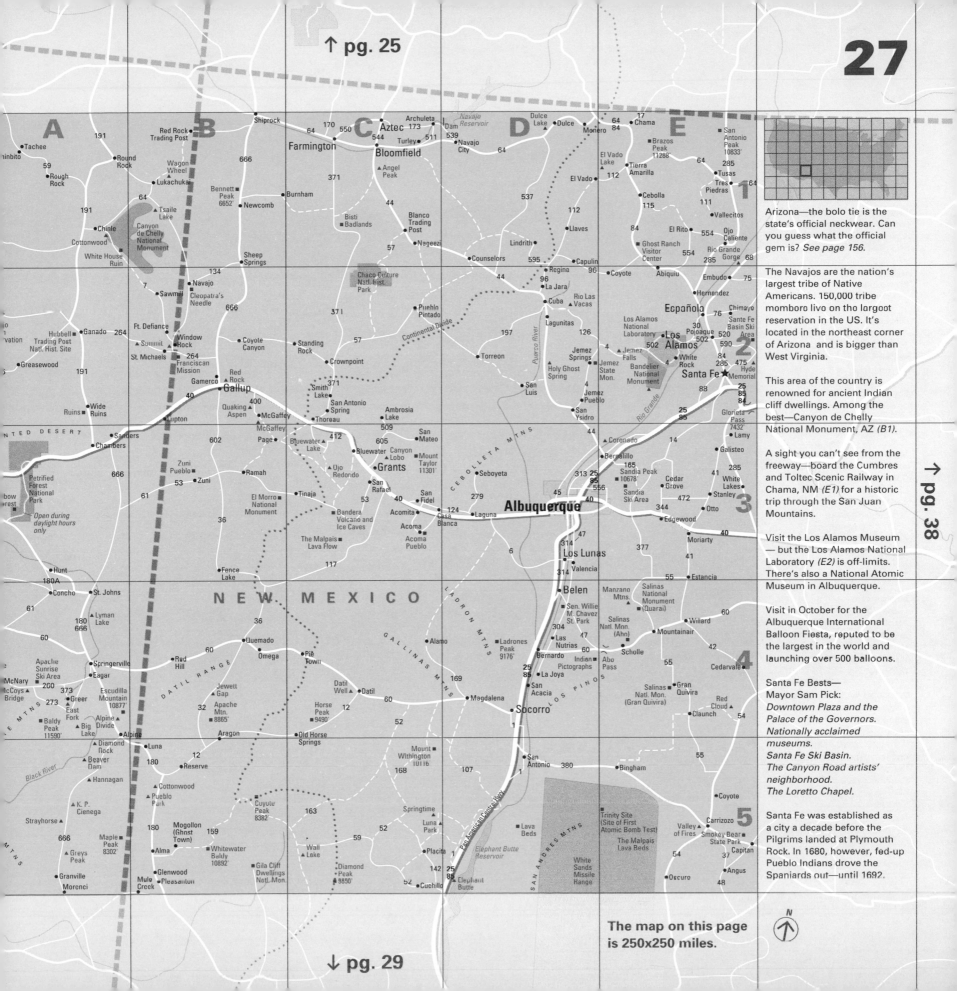

Arizona—the bolo tie is the state's official neckwear. Can you guess what the official gem is? *See page 156.*

The Navajos are the nation's largest tribe of Native Americans. 150,000 tribe members live on the largest reservation in the US. It's located in the northeast corner of Arizona and is bigger than West Virginia.

This area of the country is renowned for ancient Indian cliff dwellings. Among the best—Canyon de Chelly National Monument, AZ *(B1)*.

A sight you can't see from the freeway—board the Cumbres and Toltec Scenic Railway in Chama, NM *(E1)* for a historic trip through the San Juan Mountains.

Visit the Los Alamos Museum — but the Los Alamos National Laboratory *(E2)* is off-limits. There's also a National Atomic Museum in Albuquerque.

Visit in October for the Albuquerque International Balloon Fiesta, reputed to be the largest in the world and launching over 500 balloons.

Santa Fe Bests—
Mayor Sam Pick:
*Downtown Plaza and the Palace of the Governors. Nationally acclaimed museums.
Santa Fe Ski Basin.
The Canyon Road artists' neighborhood.
The Loretto Chapel.*

Santa Fe was established as a city a decade before the Pilgrims landed at Plymouth Rock. In 1680, however, fed-up Pueblo Indians drove the Spaniards out—until 1692.

The map on this page is 250x250 miles.

→ pg. 38

28

There was a Civil War battle fought in Arizona—at Picacho Pass *(D1)*, north of Tucson.

Kitt Peak National Observatory *(C2)* is home to the largest collection of large telescopes in the world.

Tucson sights—the Arizona-Sonora Desert Museum—which will provide you with 5 billion years' worth of Earth history; and the Center for Creative Photography—often called the best contemporary collection in the country.

Worth a visit is nearby Colossal Cave *(E2)*—whose many caverns were carved by nature. Interestingly, the temperature here is a comfortable and constant 72° F.

The saguaro cactus is found only in the southwest US/northwest Mexico. The Saguaro National Monument *(D1, E2)* is near Tucson. The "Grandaddy Cactus" (it's a 12-mile hike into the park) is 50 feet tall.

Breathe easy at the Titan Missile Museum in Green Valley *(D2)*—the missile is dismantled and the silo is open for tours.

What was the town motto of Tombstone *(E2)*? *See page 156.* It had its share of tough guys 100 years ago. There really was a shoot-out at the OK Corral and there's a Boot Hill Cemetery. Other Boot Hill Cemeteries are in Dodge City, KS; Pioche, NV; Billings, MT and Deadwood, SD.

Arizona Tourist Information: 602/542-8687

Arizona Road Information: 602/223-2000

Map labels

Grid columns: A B C D E
Grid rows: 1 2 3 4 5

Danger: Air Force Gunnery Range Area. Do not leave State Route 85 between Gila Bend and Ajo.

Barry M. Goldwater Air Force Range

BAUCEDA MTNS

Gibson
Rowood
Ajo
Kaka
Ventana
North Komelik
Hickiwan
Vaya Chin
34
Santa Rosa
Anegam
Organ Pipe Cactus Natl. Mon.
Tracy
86
Quijotoa
Gu Vo
Pisinimo
Lukeville
Sonoyta
Santa Cruz
86
Big Field
Sells
Fresnal
Pan Tak
386
Topawa
Kitt Peak National Observatory
Three Points (Robles Jct.)
286

ROSKRUGE MTNS

Chiu Chiuschu
Eloy
Picacho
Picacho Pass 1800'
Picacho Peak
84 287 10
8
87
89
77
15
Black Mtn. 5587'
Mammoth
Marana
Cortaro
Mt. Lemmon 9150'
77
76 San Manuel
Oracle
Peppersauce
Summerhaven
Bear Wallow
Soldiers Camp
General Hitchcock
Redington
Molino Basin
Jaynes
Tucson
Arizona-Sonora Desert Museum
Old Tucson
Mica Mtn. 8666'
Saguaro Natl. Mon. East
Mission San Xavier Del Bac
San Xavier
86
89
Twin Buttes
Green Valley
Colossal Cave
Vail
Mountain View
Pantono
Pomerene
Benson
10

GALIURO MTNS

Bonita
Aravaipa
Klondyke

A R I Z O N A

San Miguel
19 89
Madera Canyon
Bog Springs
Madera Canyon
90
80
Tumacacori Natl. Mon.
82 83
Sonoita
Elgin
Huachuca City
82
Fairbank
Tombsto
Tomb Cour St. H

DESIERTO DE ALTAR

2
Los Vidrios
8
2
San Emeterio
Parque Natural del Gran Desierto del Pinacate

Rio Sonoyta

Bahia del Adair
Puerto Peñasco

SIERRA DEL HUMO

Sasabe
El Sásabe
Thumb Rock 289
Calabasas Canyon
Patagonia
Patagonia Lake
Ft. Huachuca
Fort Huachuca Military Reservation
Sierra Vista
90
Lavender Open Pit Copper Mine
Bi
92
Coronado Natl. Mem.
Palominas
Naco
Dor

San Luisito
Nogales
Nogales
Saric
Cibuta

Bahia San Jorge
Est El Sahuaro
Campodónico
Las Enchilayas
Los Tajito

Gulf of California

Santo Tomás
Ramal La Alameda
El Desemboque
Caborca
Pitiquito
Altar
Oquitoa
Los Chacuales
El Ocuca
2
Tubutama
15
Cocóspera
Cananea
Imuris

Rio Asunción

Magdalena de Kino
El Nogal
Santa Ana
Bacoachi
Arizpe
Nacozar de Garcia

S O N O R A

Benjamin Hill
Querobabi
15
Huepac
Aconchi

Rio Sonora
Rio Moctezuma

Isla Angel de la Guarda

kilom. 20 40 60 80
miles 10 20 30 40 50

The map on this page is 250x250 miles.

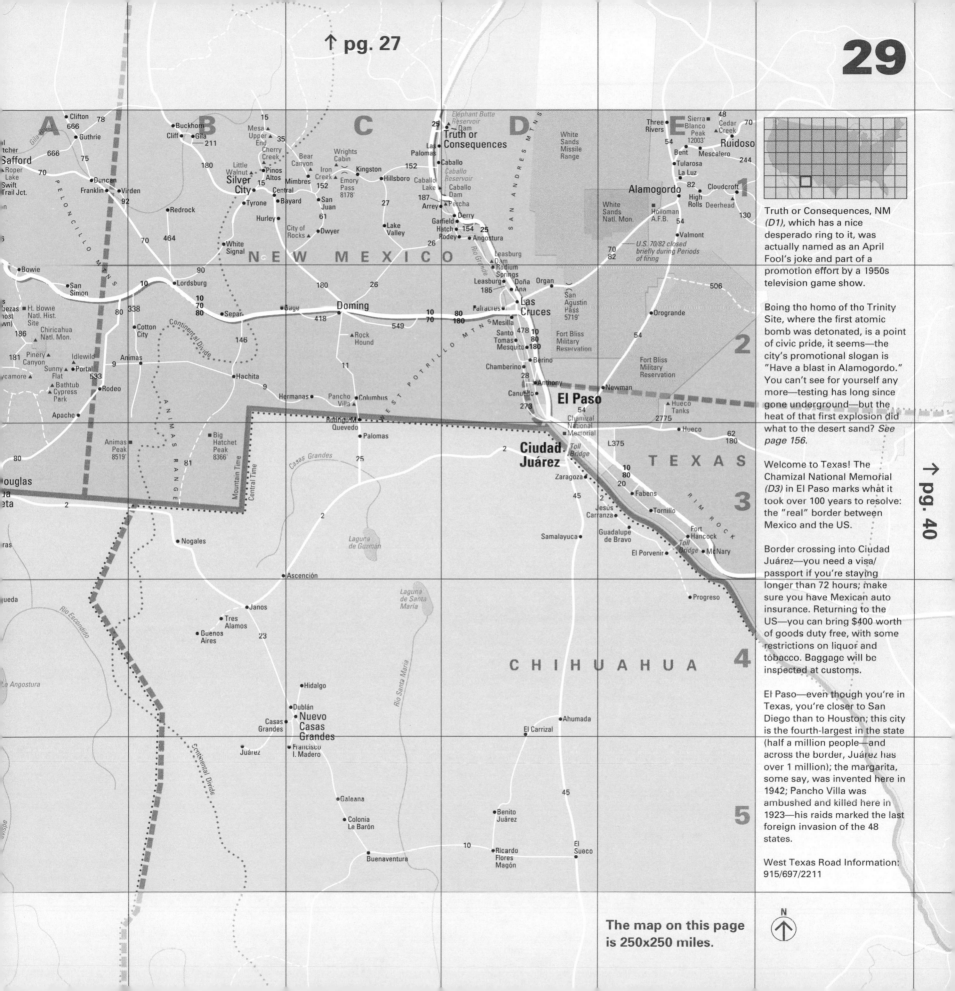

→ pg. 40

Truth or Consequences, NM *(D1)*, which has a nice desperado ring to it, was actually named as an April Fool's joke and part of a promotion effort by a 1950s television game show.

Being the home of the Trinity Site, where the first atomic bomb was detonated, is a point of civic pride, it seems—the city's promotional slogan is "Have a blast in Alamogordo." You can't see for yourself any more—testing has long since gone underground—but the heat of that first explosion did what to the desert sand? *See page 156.*

Welcome to Texas! The Chamizal National Memorial *(D3)* in El Paso marks what it took over 100 years to resolve: the "real" border between Mexico and the US.

Border crossing into Ciudad Juárez—you need a visa/passport if you're staying longer than 72 hours; make sure you have Mexican auto insurance. Returning to the US—you can bring $400 worth of goods duty free, with some restrictions on liquor and tobacco. Baggage will be inspected at customs.

El Paso—even though you're in Texas, you're closer to San Diego than to Houston; this city is the fourth-largest in the state (half a million people—and across the border, Juárez has over 1 million); the margarita, some say, was invented here in 1942; Pancho Villa was ambushed and killed here in 1923—his raids marked the last foreign invasion of the 48 states.

West Texas Road Information: 915/697/2211

The map on this page is 250x250 miles.

N

The Royal Canadian Mounties always get their man ... you can catch *them* in Regina.

Elbow Room in Montana—4th state in size, 44th in population; the entire state covers one time zone; one TV Guide covers all the state's programming; cattle outnumber people 3 to 1; and there is no traffic congestion— *none* (this in spite of the fact there are fewer paved roads here than in any other state.)

Before 1974, the speed limit for driving in Montana was defined as "reasonable and prudent"— residents will tell you that was a lot faster than 55 mph. Nowadays the fine for exceeding the speed limit is $5.

Stop and buy something while you're here—what shopping benefit do Montanans enjoy? *See page 156.*

The high plains were once home to a huge population of buffalo. We've all heard about their decimation, but the scale was nearly without historical precedent. In the space of 50 years, 30 million buffalo became a few hundred. Historians now say the wholesale slaughter of the buffalo destroyed more Indian populations than the cavalry did. Hungry railroad workers and "sporting" shooters leaning from train windows, as well as Indian foes, did the damage.

Sitting Bull, spiritual leader of the Sioux and their inspiration at Little Big Horn, eventually surrendered at the present day site of Fort Buford, ND *(C5).*

Montana Tourist Information: 1-800-548-3390

Montana Road Information: 406/444-6339

↑ pg. 19

The map on this page is 250x250 miles.

↓ pg. 32

A   B   C   D   E

Roblin

10 *Valley River*   276

Dauphin
Lake

*Lonely
Lake*

Ashern

Manigotagan River

Black
Island

Hecla
Island Hecla
Provincial
Park

8

Sandy River

5 • Grandview   • Gilbert
Plains 20   • Dauphin

Ste. Rose
du Lac   68

Fisher River

O'Hanly River

83

Squance
Lake

Ochre
River

Vermillion River

Ochre River

5

Riverton

1

276

8 • Arborg   68 • Hnausa

6

16 • Russell

Riding Mountain
National Park

Birdtail Creek

Mt. Agassiz
Ski Area

5

McCreary

50

Dog
Lake

68

68

*Lake
Winnipeg*

• Gimli

Grand
Beach   11

45

Assiniboine River

10

Kelwood

• Lundar

7

8

41

• Binscarth

• Oakburn

45

• Erickson

Minnedosa River

• Amaranth

6

• Gimli

Grand
Beach

Pine
Falls

St. Lazare

Shoal
Lake

16

• Newdale

*Lake
Manitoba*

50

Oak
Point

N. Shoal
Lake

• Birtle

21

16A

M A N I T O B A

• St. Laurent

E. Shoal
Lake

W. Shoal
Lake

Teulon

Netley
Lake

8

12

McAuley 83

• Minnedosa   • Neepawa

• Gladstone

6

• Woodlands

Lower Ft.
Garry Natl.
Hist. Park

• Selkirk

• Miniota

• Hamiota

24

• Westbourne

34

16

Stonewall

Lockport   44

Birds
Hill

Beauséjour

Assiniboine River

10

5

Austin

Portage
la Prairie

• Oakville

★ **Winnipeg**

12

1 • Hargrave

• Sidney

Yellowhead Hwy.

1

16

1

Anola   15

257 • Virden

1A • Brandon

Assiniboine River

Oak
Bluff   100

83

• Oak
Lake • Griswold

21

• Spruce
Woods
Heritage

• St. Claude   Elm
Creek

2

• Starbuck

59   Ste. Anne

Richer

2 • Souris

2

• Holland

13

3

75

52 • Steinbach

12

• Pipestone

• Hartney

23

• Glenboro

34

• Carman

3

18

Melita

• Minto

• Ninette

• Baldur

23

Jordan   • Morris

23

• St. Malo   12

21

Whitewater
Lake

10

Pelican
Lake

5

• Manitou

3

14

• Pierson   3

• Prehistoric
Mounds

• Boissevain

3 • Killarney

Pembina River

Rock
Lake

• Morden   • Winkler

Plum
Coulee

59

83

• Deloraine

Turtle
Mtn.

18

3

Cartwright

Crystal
City

31

32

75

N O R T H   D A K O T A

Westhope

Lake
Metigoshe

International
Peace
Garden

281

30

20

Maida

• Walhalla

Pembina Emerson

75 • Lancaster

4

5

Bottineau

Dunseith

Rolla

• Rocklake

5

Langdon

Icelandic

• Cavalier Hamilton

• Hallock

Lake
Bronson

83 14

3

281

• Munich

32

81

29

Lake
Bronson

• Upham

3

• Donaldson

• Karlstad

83

11

Minot
A.F.B.

Cando   17

• Starkweather

Edinburg Homme
Dam

• Grafton

Old
Mill   59

Rugby

• Ruthville

• Towner

• Knox

• Leeds

Lac Aux
Mortes

20

• Edmore

Webster

17   17

Park
River

Argyle

Newfolden

M N

5

• Minot

2

• Granville

Lake
Irvine

Church's
Ferry

Dry
Lake

Morrison
Lake

32

54

• Oslo   1

• Warren

14

Minnewaukan

Devils
Lake

Sweetwater
Lake

81

• Manvel

75

83

• Velva

19

• Esmond

Devils
Lake

E. Devils
Lake

1

29

E. Grand
Forks

• Euclid

41

• Balfour

Ft. Totten
Hist. Mon.

57 Fort
Totten

Devils
Lake

Lakota

2

Turtle
River

Grand
Forks

Red Lake River

52

3

281

20

Warwick

18

Sheyenne River

Larimore

Fisher

**The map on this page
is 250x250 miles.**

N
↑

The International Peace Garden
(B4) straddles the US and
Canada, celebrating the longest
undefended border in the
world. Not only that, its 2300
acres and more than 100,000
flowers and plants make it the
world's largest peace garden.

Cross that border and head to
Boissevain *(B4)* to see the
national (Canadian) turtle
races.

Where do the High Plains start?
See page 156.

The state with the greatest
percent of its population
working on farms is none other
than North Dakota (84%!). Not
that the population is that large
to begin with—this state of
70,703 square miles has fewer
people than San Francisco, a
city of 49 square miles.

Here's what George Sinner,
governor, would like you to
know about his state:
*It's home to the friendliest,
hardest-working, most honest
people in the world.
It boasts fresh, clean air and
water and a clear, blue, wide-
open sky.
It actually has four distinct and
wonderful seasons—"North
Dakota is not the freezer some
think it is."*

Indeed, on 6 July 1936 the
mercury hit a sultry 121° F.

The center of it all—Rugby, ND
(B5) is considered the geo-
graphical center of North
America.

The Red River of the North had
its share of trappers, traders,
settlers and riverboats. Board
the Delta Queen in Grand
Forks, ND *(E5)* for a 19th-
century–style river cruise.

→ pg. 44

Our first national monument, Devils Tower *(B5)* is the dormant core of a long-gone volcano.

Teddy Roosevelt claimed the Badlands of North Dakota *(D1)* had "a curious, fantastic beauty all their own." General Alfred Sully called them "a part of hell with the fires burned out." Decide for yourself in this wild, sculptural, solitary region.

"Dakota" was one of the names the Sioux Indians called themselves. By all accounts, they were the fiercest, most warlike tribe of the Plains. "Sioux" is a version of the name given them by their enemies and means "adders."

What feature gives the Black Hills *(C5)* their name? *See page 156.*

On 22 January 1943 the temperature in Spearfish, SD *(C5)* zoomed from -4° F to 45° F in two minutes; that 49° degree change is a US record.

The Mount Moriah Cemetery in Deadwood, SD *(C5)* is the final resting place of Wild Bill Hickok and Calamity Jane.

South Dakota and Nevada race neck and neck to lead the nation in gold production. George Hearst, father of William Randolph, made his fortune from the yellow gold of the Homestake Mine in Lead, SD *(C5)*—to this day, one of the largest producers of gold in the Western Hemisphere.

South Dakota Tourist Information:
605/773-3301

South Dakota Road Information:
605/773-3536

← pg. 21

The map on this page is 250x250 miles.

kilom. 20 40 60 80

miles 10 20 30 40 50

A B C D E

MONTANA

WYOMING

Miles City

Glendive

Sidney

Dickinson

Devils Tower Natl. Mon. 5117'

Black Hills

Spearfish   Sturgis

Gillette

Geographical Center of the United States

33

→ pg. 46

Max
83
Totten
Trail
rrison 41
Audubon
Lake
wea Coleharbor
200 Underwood
Knife River
Indian Villages
Natl. Hist. Site
on
200A

A Harvey B Sheyenne C Pekin D Northwood 18 15 Thompson E 2 Crookston
83 Fessenden New Rockford 15 Aneta 18 102
Egg Lake 15 Hatton 29 Climax 9
3 Hurdsfield 52 20 32 81 M N 1
Turtle Lake Mercer 200 281 Glenfield Cooperstown Finley 200 Mayville Hillsboro 200 Halstad Ada
Wilton 36 Carrington Arrowwood Lake 1 200 Blanchard 200
Arrowwood Natl. Wildlife Refuge Courtenay Lake Ashtabula Pillsbury 18 Gardner
NORTH DAKOTA Johns Lake Lake Williams Jim Lake Pingree 20 Rogers Bald Hill Dam Georgetown
Hannover 25 Horsehead Lake 36 52 281 Jamestown Reservoir Parkhurst 75 Moorhead 9
31 Mountain Time 83 BUS 94 Valley City Casselton Fargo 94 10
Central Time Menoken Indian Village Hist. Site 94 Jamestown 94 94
Mandan Bismarck 94 Steele Dawson Lake George Fingal
General Sibley Park Sterling Lake Etta 30 1 Leonard 75
Ft. Lincoln Moffit Long Lake Alkali Lake Claussen Springs 29
6 46 Gackle 46 Enderlin 81 9
Little Heart Round Lake 32 Sheyenne River
21 Cannon Ball Hazelton 34 Napoleon Lisbon 2
Flasher 83 30 13 La Moure Verona 18
Breien Linton 13 Beaver Lake Edgeley 13 Gwinner Wyndmere Breckenridge 210
Raleigh 24 Doyle Memorial 281 Oakes 32 Wahpeton Doran
Cannonball River Winona Strasburg 1 Silver Lake Lidgerwood 127 3
Ft. Yates 11 Ashley 11 Ellendale 11 Ludden 18 29 81
Selfridge 6 37 Havana 25 Rosholt
1 Mud Lake Reservoir 27 25 Claire City 127 75 Wheaton
McIntosh Walker 45 Britton 10 127 27
5 Herreid 10 10 Leola 10 Barnard Houghton Dam Roy Lake Lake City Buffalo Sisseton Browns Valley
Grand River Mound City Herreid Rec. Area Eureka 45 Columbia Rd. Reservoir Roy Lake Lake Traverse 28 Beardsley
63 Grand River Lake Hiddenwood 47 247 45 27 Pierpont 25 Piyas Lake Drywood Lakes Hartford Beach Big Stone Lake
20 Mobridge Selby Bowdle Roscoe Ipswich Mina Aberdeen Groton Pierpont Lake Rec. Area Waubay Lake Ortley Big Stone Lake
Timber Lake Grave of Sitting Bull Indian Creek 12 12 Bristol Wehster Bitter Lake 12 Milbank
63 Trail City Walth Bay 47 45 281 Ferney Bradley Florence 29 81 Crooked Lake 15
La Plant Dodge Draw 83 Onaka 20 Northville 37 20 Doland Rec. Area Two Woods Lake 212
Ridgeview Forest City West Whitlock's 212 Seneca Faulkton Fisher Grove Doland Clark Lake Kampeska Watertown
212 Gettysburg Rockham Redfield 37 Henry Lake Pelican Clear Lake 22
Lake Oahe Little Bend Onida 212 Doland 37 22 Ulven
Foster Bay 47 45 SOUTH DAKOTA 81 15
63 Blunt Highmore 14 Miller Hitchcock 28 Willow Lake Bryant Estelline 15
Cow Spring Creek 14 83 Harrold Wessington 25 Lake Poinsett Poinsett 29
Hayes Oahe Dam Pierre 34 Wolsey Huron De Smet Arlington
14 Fort Pierre Farm Island Mac's Corner 281 37 Huron Mem. Rec. Area Iroquois Lake Whitewood Brookings 14
34 1 Central Time Mountain Time

The map on this page is 250x250 miles.

N

Fort Lincoln (A2), now a state park, was under the command of General George Armstrong Custer; it was from here that he set forth for Little Big Horn. (North Dakotans have been known to raise billboards on the Montana border reading, "When Custer left North Dakota, he was still alive.")

The 46-foot-long statue in Jamestown, ND (C2) is indisputably the world's largest buffalo.

North Dakota and South Dakota were made states on the same day—nobody knows which came first because President Benjamin Harrison covered up the state names when he signed the official statehood documents, 100 years ago.

Although these Great Plains states claim a diversity of weather, it's a useful thing to know that it's possible for the temperature in Pierre, SD (B5) to hover right at 0° for well over a month in the winter.

Another capital fact: Local residents call the capital of South Dakota "Peer" not "Pee-Yare."

Do you recall the name of Lewis and Clark's Shoshone guide? See page 156. The only female on the expedition, she has more statues in her honor than any other woman in American history. She's reputedly buried at West Fort Manuel, SD (B3), not far from where she embarked, Mandan, ND (A2).

North Dakota Tourist Information: 1-800-437-2077

North Dakota Road Information: 1-800-472-2090

← pg. 23

Women first voted in an election in Wyoming 50 years before universal female suffrage was granted in the rest of the country. Also worth noting is the fact that the first woman governor in the US was elected here in 1924.

The ubiquitous Jackalope, that antlered rabbit found on every postcard rack in the West, was created in Douglas, WY (A2)—we know not why.

If you're around in July, join Cheyenne's renowned Frontier Days—the world's largest and oldest pro rodeo (B5).

236 people died in South Dakota's worst natural disaster ever—the flash flood in Rapid City (D1) 9/10 June 1972.

Long, long before you get to Wall, SD (E1), the Wall Drug is advertised by billboards. The big attraction? Free ice water—followed up by a buffalo burger and a nickel cup of coffee.

Of course the biggest attraction in this corner of the world is Mt. Rushmore (C1). If whole bodies had been carved to scale, you'd be looking at presidents standing 465 feet tall. Quick—no peeking—who are the presidents immortalized here? *See page 156.*

By 1890, the destruction of their way of life led many Indians to put their faith in the Ghost Dance, a ritual intended to resurrect the buffalo and remove the white man from the land. Fear of a Sioux uprising led the US Army to attack a village of dancers at Wounded Knee, SD (E2), where over 200 warriors, women and children were felled in a vengeful massacre. It was the last battle in the Indian Wars.

The map on this page is 250x250 miles.

kilom. 20 40 60 80
miles 10 20 30 40 50

WYOMING

COLORADO

A   **B**   **C**   **D**   **E**

63   Midland

Joe Creek   Lake Sharpe

34 / 47   North Shore

Iron Nation

281   37

Wessington Springs   Woonsocket

25

81   29

Winfred   Madison   Egan

83   Vivian   Presho

Big Bend Dam

34   Gannvalley

34   Howard

84   Lake Herman

Stamford   Murdo

47   50

American Creek   Chamberlain

45

37

81

19   Dell Rapids

Belvidere   Murdo Rec. Area

Big White River

90   Kimball

Plankinton   Mount Vernon   **Mitchell**

Corn Palace

38   25

Salem   Humboldt

115   Big Sioux River

63   Cedar Butte   44   White River

183

Elm Creek   Iona

45   Stickney

S O U T H   D A K O T A

Alexandria

Bridgewater

42   **Sioux Falls**   229

Rose Hill Rec. Area   Wood

44

Snake Creek

281

44   Parkston

44

115   18

83   18   Mission   Okreek

44   Winner

Duryanek   Platte

Armour

Olivet

81

18

29   Beresford

18   Colome   47

Lake Francis Case   50

Lake Andes   18 / 281

18

37   Scotland

46

83   Gregory   Burke

183   N. Wheeler

Ft. Randall Dam

Wagner

25

Union County

Mountain Time / Central Time

Wewela   Fairfax

Randall Creek

Missouri River

50   Tyndall

37

Lewis & Clark Lake

Yankton Dam   **Yankton**

50   48

Little White River

Nenzel   Crookston

12   Norden

281   Butte   Spencer

Lynch

Verdel

Vermillion

50

Cody

Valentine

Niobrara River

12   Niobrara

Crofton

Elk Point

11

Ponca   Ponca

S16F

Springview

Midway

Niobrara

Hartington

12

20   83

Merritt Res.

20   Wood Lake

183   Keller Park

11

281

Verdigre

81   15

Laurel   20

97

Bassett   Stuart

Atkinson   Atkinson

14

20

Randolph

Wakefield   35

Ainsworth

Atkinson Lake   Elkhorn River   O'Neill

Plainview

13   Pierce

Wayne

83   Moon Lake   7

Grove Lake

20

35

Long Lake   183

11

Orchard

Ewing

275   Neligh

Willow Creek

15

Elsmere

Purdum   7

Tilden

Norfolk   Wisner   51

Pilger   275

Mullen

Thedford

Halsey   91   Brewster   91

Calamus Res.

Bartlett

14

Petersburg

81   Madison

West Point

97

Cedars   Dunning

Almeria

Calamus Dam   Burwell

281

91

91

Tryon

Taylor   Sargent

Middle Loup River

N E B R A S K A

Albion

39

81

15

92   Stapleton   Arnold

2   Merna

183   Ord

70

14

Genoa   22

Schuyler   North Bend

07   83

Broken Bow

92

Arcadia

11

22

Fullerton

Columbus

30

Buffalo Bill Ranch State Hist. Park Home of Buffalo Bill

Ansley

Sherman Res.

Cotesfield

North Loup

Loup River

Silver Creek

David City   92

80   Sutherland

North Platte

Oconto

183   Litchfield

Bowman Lake   Loup City

St. Paul

92

Osceola   Stromsburg

Big Blue River

Sutherland Res.   Sutherland

Brady

Ravenna

Central City   Hord Lake

15

Lake Maloney

21   Miller

Ravenna Lake

2

Grand Island   Aurora   34

York

80   Seward

Wallace   Dickens   23

Gothenburg

South Platte River

Cheyenne

81

Lincoln ★   Milford

Jeffery Canyon Res.   30

Elm Creek   Gibbon

34 / 281

14

6   Blue River

Wellfleet

Farnam

Johnson Lake   Johnson Lake

80   **Kearney**

81

Fairmont   Friend   Crete   33

25

15

2

3

4

5

→ pg. 48

You've got to see the Corn Palace in Mitchell, SD (D1). The whole building is decked out in murals and decorations made entirely of corn and devoted to topics of an agrarian nature.

Moving into Nebraska—if you're on I-80, you're on The Oregon Trail, 20th century version. That huge covered wagon in Milford (E5) is a service station.

An early explorer called this land, "The Great American Desert." He would no doubt be surprised to learn that Nebraska sits on top of one of the largest underground seas in the world, the Ogallala Aquifer. Nebraska easily exceeds all our inland states in the plentitude of its water resources. The "desert" also produces millions upon millions of bushels of grain each year.

Nebraska National Forest near Halsey (B4) is the nation's largest manmade forest. What holiday do you think these tree-happy Nebraskans initiated? See page 156.

Lincoln, NE Bests— Mayor Bill Harris:
The State Capitol Building, one of the architectural wonders of the world.
The Haymarket District.
Folsom Children's Zoo.
The Arts and Entertainment District.
Holmes Park

Another Lincoln must-see: the National Museum of Roller Skating.

Nebraska Tourist Information: 1-800-228-4307

Nebraska Road Information: 402/471-4533

The map on this page is 250x250 miles.

N ↑

← pg. 25

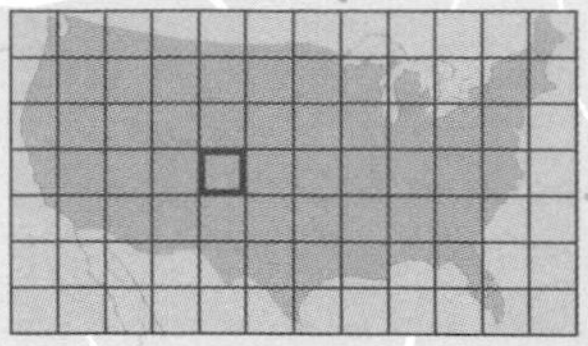

Rocky Mountain National Park *(A1)* is traversed by Trail Ridge Road, one of the highest highways in the US. The road is closed during the winter. It's crowded in the summer—but you won't be able to repeat this experience anywhere else.

More highs: The folks in Grand Lake *(A1)* say they have the highest yacht club in the world—8400 ft. above sea level.

What's it like to look down on a cloud while you're still on the ground? Drive Mt. Evans Hwy., the highest paved road in the US—at the Mt. Evans summit *(A2)* you're at 14,264 feet.

Boulder *(A1)* has its own glacier—uses it as a water supply.

Guinness says the largest single brewery building is Adolph Coors' in Golden, CO *(A2)*.

Zebulon Pike never made it to the top of the Peak named after him *(B3)*. Composer Katherine Lee Bates did, though. Name the tune she wrote as a result. *See page 156.*

Colorado Springs *(B3)* sights: The ProRodeo Hall of Champions and the Air Force Academy. The latter is Colorado's most-visited attraction, after the Rockies. See the academy's spectacular glass and aluminum chapel and you'll know why.

A reminder that the Great Plains were once the high seas: The Great Sand Dunes National Monument *(A4)*. The dunes soar to a height of 600 feet.

Colorado Tourist Information: 1-800-433-2656

Colorado Road Information: 303/639-1111

The map on this page is 250x250 miles.

↓ pg. 38

Map labels (grid A–E, rows 1–5):

A — Gould, Cameron Pass 10276', Milner Pass 10759', Trail Ridge High Point 12183', Estes Park, Rocky Mtn. Natl. Park, Grand Lake, Willow Creek Pass 9621', Lake Granby, Granby, Arapaho Natl. Rec. Area, Peaceful Valley, Boulder, Nederland, Eldora Ski Area, Winter Park Ski Area, Berthoud Pass 11314', Central City, Empire, Silver Plume, Idaho Springs, Golden, Lakewood, Eisenhower Mem. Tunnel, Loveland Pass 11992', Georgetown, Mt. Evans Highway Highest Auto Road in U.S., Mt. Evans 14264', Evergreen, Conifer, Jefferson, Como, Kenosha Pass 10001', Bailey, Pine Junction, Tarryall, Spruce Grove, Hartsel, Eleven Mile, Round Mountain, Eleven Mile Canyon Reservoir, Five Points, Royal Gorge, Cotopaxi, Texas Creek, Westcliffe, Mineral Hot Springs, Lake Isabel, Hooper, Great Sand Dunes Natl. Monument, Gardner, Mosca, Blanca Peak 14345', North La Veta Pass 9413', Alamosa, Fort Garland, Cuchara, San Luis, Blue Lake, Monument Park, Culebra Peak 14047', Segundo

B — Ft. Collins, Ault, Loveland, Greeley, Berthoud, Lyons, Longmont, Lafayette, Brighton, Marshall, pg. 93, Aurora, Denver, Englewood, Littleton, Kelsey, Deckers, Castle Rock, Franktown, Kiowa, Woodland Park, Garden of the Gods, Florissant Fossil Beds Natl. Mon., Manitou Springs, Colorado Springs, Pikes Peak 14110', Fort Carson, Security, Fountain, U.S. Air Force Academy, Cripple Creek, Canon City, Penrose, Lincoln Park, Florence, Wetmore, Pueblo, Colorado City, Hawley, Walsenburg, La Veta, Cuchara, Lathrop, Trinidad Lake, Trinidad, Beshoar Junction

C — Briggsdale, New Raymer, Stoneham, Lucerne, Barnesville, Goodrich, Weldona, Wiggins, Fort Morgan, Prospect Valley, Woodrow, Bennett, Watkins, Byers, Last Chance, Anton, Thurman, Matheson, Hugo, Peyton, Calhan, Falcon, Yoder, Punkin Center, Truckton, Limon, Arriba, Flagler, Delhi, Thatcher, Timpas

D — Sterling, Fleming, Atwood, Merino, Snyder, Akron, Yuma, Wray, Goodland, Seibert, Stratton, Burlington, Kanorado, Kit Carson, Cheyenne Wells, Cope, Joes, Idalia, Eads, Galatea, Chivington, Sheridan Lake, Arlington, McClave, Wiley, Ordway, Crowley, Fowler, Manzanola, Rocky Ford, La Junta, Las Animas, Lamar, Granada, Holly, Toonerville, Kim, Tobe, Andrix, Pritchett, Springfield, Walsh, Campo

E — Haxtun, Holyoke, Champion Lake, Clarkville, Abarr, Wheeler, Saint Francis, Bonny Reservoir, Goodland, Weskan, Towner, Bristol, Coolidge, Syracuse, Hamilton County, Cheney Center, Lycan, Saunders, Johnson City, Richfield

Rivers/features: Cache La Poudre River, Riverside Reservoir, Horsetooth Reservoir, S. Platte River, Continental Divide, Cheesman Lake, Sangre de Cristo Range, Arkansas River, Pueblo Reservoir, Huerfano River, Rio Grande, Purgatoire River, Big Sandy Creek, S. Fork Republican River, Frenchman River, John Martin Reservoir, Bent's Old Fort National Historic Site, Trout Creek Pass 9346'

Scale: kilom. 20 40 60 80 / miles 10 20 30 40 50

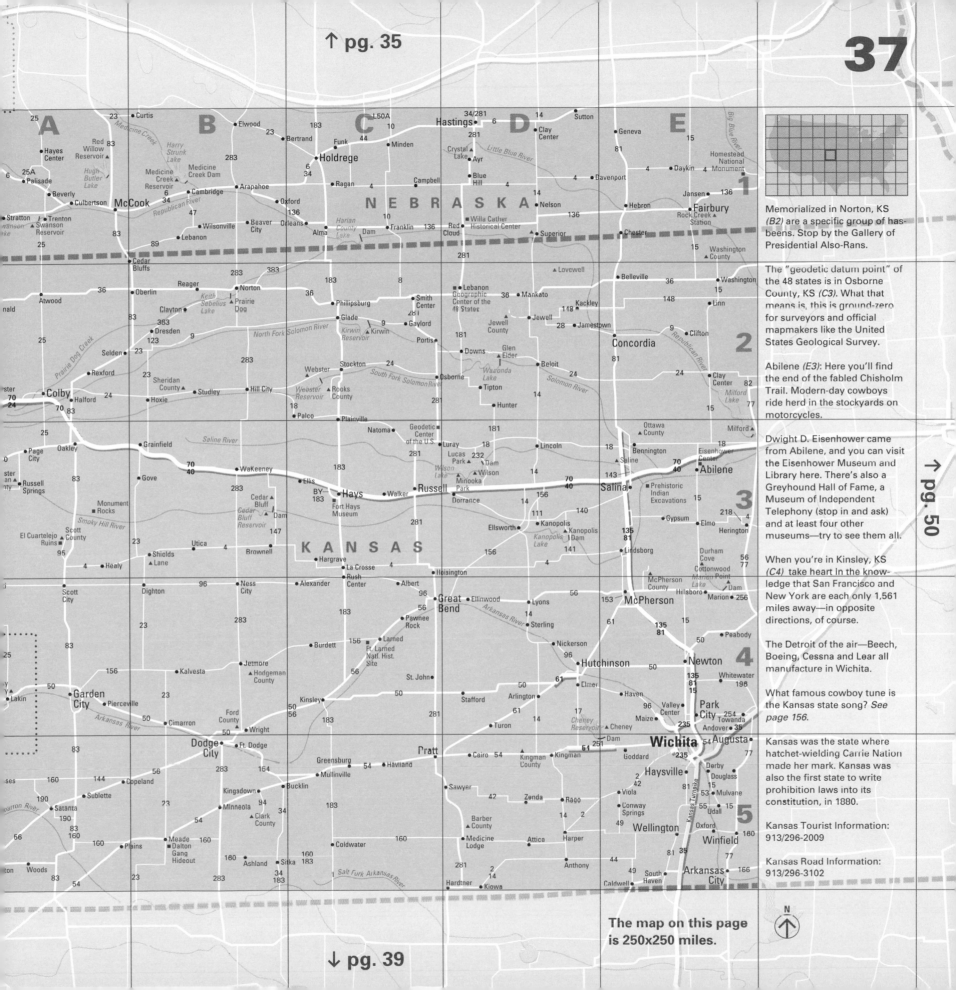

→ pg. 50

Memorialized in Norton, KS (B2) are a specific group of has-beens. Stop by the Gallery of Presidential Also-Rans.

The "geodetic datum point" of the 48 states is in Osborne County, KS (C3). What that means is, this is ground-zero for surveyors and official mapmakers like the United States Geological Survey.

Abilene (E3): Here you'll find the end of the fabled Chisholm Trail. Modern-day cowboys ride herd in the stockyards on motorcycles.

Dwight D. Eisenhower came from Abilene, and you can visit the Eisenhower Museum and Library here. There's also a Greyhound Hall of Fame, a Museum of Independent Telephony (stop in and ask) and at least four other museums—try to see them all.

When you're in Kinsley, KS (C4) take heart in the knowledge that San Francisco and New York are each only 1,561 miles away—in opposite directions, of course.

The Detroit of the air—Beech, Boeing, Cessna and Lear all manufacture in Wichita.

What famous cowboy tune is the Kansas state song? See page 156.

Kansas was the state where hatchet-wielding Carrie Nation made her mark. Kansas was also the first state to write prohibition laws into its constitution, in 1880.

Kansas Tourist Information: 913/296-2009

Kansas Road Information: 913/296-3102

The map on this page is 250x250 miles.

N

← pg. 27

The Rio Grande *(A1)* lives up to its name in New Mexico—the river is wild enough for white-water rafting. By the time it reaches the Gulf of Mexico, the rio is much slower and less grande.

Taos, NM *(A1)* is deservedly famed for its arts—there are 60 galleries in this town of less than 5,000. For a cultural overview, visit the Millicent Rogers Museum, home of an extensive collection of Southwestern and Spanish colonial art and craftwork.

A famous outlaw—reputed to have killed 21 men by the age of 21—was shot dead by Sheriff Pat Garrett in Fort Sumner, NM *(B4)*. Who? *See page 156.*

The most unusual crop in Texas—those Caddie tailfins "growing" out of the ground near Amarillo, courtesy of unusual art patron Stanley Marsh III.

The National Cowgirl Hall of Fame and Western Heritage Center in Hereford, TX *(D4)* honors Western women such as Annie Oakley, Georgia O'Keefe and Willa Cather.

The US Weather Bureau records show the first recorded "death by hail" happened in Lubbock, TX on 13 May 1930.

Lubbock sights: A statue of favorite native son Buddy Holly; and Prairie Dog Town, one of the last prairie dog colonies in the country.

New Mexico Tourist Information:
505/827-0291

New Mexico Road Information:
505/827-9300

The map on this page is 250x250 miles.

NEW MEXICO

Like Texas, in Oklahoma two things seem to really matter—cattle and oil. Learn a lot about the former at the Chisholm Trail Historical Museum (D4) in Waurika. You can see evidence of the latter everywhere—including on the grounds of the State Capitol in Oklahoma City, where you'll see what unusual site? See page 156.

This must be a friendly state—its official flower is the mistletoe.

If you're in Beaver (A1) in May, duck. The World Championship Cow Chip Throwing Contest is on.

Indian territory: The American Indian Hall of Fame in Anadarko (D3) salutes the accomplishments of outstanding Native Americans. Indian City USA is a museum depicting the daily lives of seven tribes.

Oklahoma City is one of those places chock-full of interesting and offbeat museums. Try the Cowboy Hall of Fame, the Softball Hall of Fame and Enterprise Square, USA—a monument to the glories of capitalism.

There ought to be a Storm Cellar Museum—the city has been struck by tornadoes 26 times since 1892.

The Sooner State is called that because eager settlers couldn't wait for the gun to go off during the homestead rush of 1889. Those who jumped the gun, of course, got there "sooner."

Oklahoma Tourist Information: 405/521-2409

Oklahoma Road Information: 405/425-2385

→ pg. 52

The map on this page is 250x250 miles.

N
↑

← pg. 29

Carlsbad Caverns *(B2)* is the site of spectacular, twice-daily flights of bats. About a quarter-million of them sweep out of the caves every day at dusk and in again at dawn.

You won't be able to miss Paisano Pete—he's a statue that's ranked as the world's largest roadrunner, in Fort Stockton, TX *(D4)*.

There are lots of statistics about Texas. Here are a few:

The state is just larger than France. The locals will tell you the food is a lot better, too. On the other hand, Texas is not even half the size of Alaska (don't remind any Texan of this, however).

The population density is about 64 people per square mile. As you travel about the country you'll feel more crowded in New Jersey— which crams nearly 1000 people to the square mile— and get a feel for even wider-open spaces in Alaska—where there's less than 1 person to the square mile.

Ranchers who are particularly boastful have been known to measure their ranches in "Rls." What does a Texas rancher mean when he says his spread is the size of 5 "Rls"? *See page 156.*

Expect geographic and clima-tological diversity here—it's a big place. The "flatlands" of west Texas are also home to the Davis Mountains *(B4)*, whose peaks can climb to 8000 feet. The land of sagebrush and windswept plains is subject to violent, unexpected flash floods. Be prepared to head for high ground in a heavy rainstorm.

NEW MEXICO

TEXAS

CHIH

Ruidoso Downs • Picacho • Sunset — Roswell — Caprock — Meadow — Slaton

James Canyon — Mayhill — Dexter — Tatum — Bronco — Plains — Brownfield — Tahoka

Piñon — Dunken — Hope — Artesia — Loco Hills — Maljamar — Buckeye — Denver City — Seagraves — Loop — Welch — O'Donnell

Lakewood — Lake McMillan Dam — Lovington — Hobbs — Seminole — Lamesa

Living Desert St. Park — Carlsbad — Lea — Andrews — Patricia

Sitting Bull Falls — Loving — Malaga — Black River Village — Eunice — Jal

Wind Mtn. 7278' — El Paso Gap — Whites City — Carlsbad Caverns Natl. Park

Dog Canyon — Red Bluff Lake — N. Cowden — Midland

Guadalupe Mountains Natl. Park — Pine Springs — Guadalupe Peak 8751' — Kermit — Notrees — Permian Basin Petroleum Museum — Odessa

Salt Flat — Orla — Arno — Wink — Penwell — Monahans Sandhills — Monahans

SIERRA DIABLO — Mentone — Pyote — Wickett

DELAWARE MTNS — Barstow — Pecos — Royalty — Grandfalls — Crane — Stiles

Sierra Blanca — Toyah — Lake Toyah — Pecos River

EAGLE MTNS — Van Horn — APACHE MTNS — Kent — Verhalen — Rankin

SIERRA VIEJA — Saragosa — Balmorhea — McCamey

Lonely Lee 6749' — DAVIS MTNS — Toyahvale — Balmorhea — Fort Stockton — Bakersfield — Iraan

McDonald Observatory — Davis Mtns. — Fort Davis — Fort Davis Natl. Hist. Site — Sheffield

Valentine — Alpine — Marathon — Sanderson

Rio Bravo del Norte — Ruidosa — Marfa — Cathedral Mountain 6860' — Dryden

Chinati Peak 7730' — Shafter

kilom. 20 40 60 80

miles 10 20 30 40 50

The map on this page is 250x250 miles.

A   B   C   D   E

1 **2** **3** **4** **5**

pg. 94

The really wild west—Sweetwater *(B2)* folks head out every March on the "World's Largest Rattlesnake Roundup," and will serve you said beast fried, if you so wish.

Austin—this town is renowned for the University of Texas, its great music scene and the fact that it's the capital city. In an attempt to avoid the oil boom and bust of other Texas cities, Austin has also encouraged a Silicon Gulch with over 250 high-tech companies.

Austin's State Capitol Building is taller than the US Capitol after which it was modeled. As a further snub to the Union, the statue atop the capitol faces south. The present Republican governor is only the second one of that party (and the first in over 100 years) to hold the state's highest office.

Do you know which six flags have in fact flown over Texas? *See page 156.*

More tornadoes have touched down in this state than any other in the past 25 years—but seldom in the same place twice.

If you're lucky enough to be driving along a Texas interstate in the spring, you'll be treated to an abundance of wildflowers. They're keeping the soil in place as part of a soil-erosion prevention program the state has run for 60 years.

By the way, it's the bluebonnet, not the yellow rose, that's the state flower.

Texas Tourist Information: 512/462-9191

Central Texas Road Information: 817/700 6261

→ pg. 54

The map on this page is 250x250 miles.

N

Place names (selection): Decatur, Bridgeport, Roanoke, Azle, Keller, Saginaw, Fort Worth, Weatherford, White Settlement, Kennedale, Burleson, Cresson, Granbury, Cleburne, Parker, Glen Rose, Walnut Springs, Whitney, Meridian, Clifton, Cranfills Gap, Valley Mills, McGregor, Mother Neff, Moody, Gatesville, Fort Hood, Adamsville, Copperas Cove, Killeen, Harker Hts., Temple, Belton, Nolanville, Salado, Lampasas, Briggs, Bartlett, Granger, Jarrell, Jonah, Taylor, Georgetown, Leander, Cedar Park, Round Rock, Jollyville, Elgin, Manor, Austin, Del Valle, Bastrop, Cedar Creek, McKinney Falls, Oak Hill, Dripping Springs, Kyle, Aquarena Springs, San Marcos, Lockhart.

Knox City, Munday, Olney, Jermyn, Jacksboro, Newcastle, Bryson, Joplin, Perrin, Springtown, Rhome, Jayton, Swenson, Aspermont, Old Glory, Rule, Haskell, Throckmorton, Graham, Woodson, Clairemont, Justiceburg, Snyder, Hermleigh, Ira, Dunn, Tuxedo, Stamford, Hamlin, Rotan, Roby, Anson, Lueders, Fort Griffin, Albany, Caddo, Breckenridge, Palo Pinto, Mineral Wells, Strawn, Mingus, Morgan Mill, Bluff Dale, Colorado City, Roscoe, Sweetwater, Merkel, Abilene, Baird, Cisco, Eastland, Ranger, Desdemona, Stephenville, Tuscola, Lawn, Blackwell, Happy Valley, Denton Community, Cross Plains, Rising Star, Carbon, Gorman, De Leon, Dublin, Alexander, Hico, Morton Valley, Sterling City, Robert Lee, Bronte, Winters, Burkett, Cross Cut, Coleman, Santa Anna, Bangs, Brownwood, Early, Zephyr, Priddy, Lamkin, Comanche, Hamilton, Evant, Sterling City, Carlsbad, San Angelo, Wall, Tankersley, Mertzon, Miles, Tennyson, Ballinger, Rockwood, Winchell, Goldthwaite, Barnhart, Eden, Rochelle, Richland Springs, San Saba, Lometa, Brady, Voca, Cherokee, Christoval, Eldorado, Menard, Hext, Camp Air, Fredonia, Field Creek, Valley Spring, Mason, Art, Llano, Buchanan Dam, Inks Lake, Burnet, Marble Falls, Oxford, London, Ozona, Sonora, Roosevelt, Junction, Teacup, Loyal Valley, Enchanted Rock, Johnson City, Telegraph, Harper, Fredericksburg, L.B.J. Ranch, L.B.J. St. Park, Blanco, Twin Sisters, Mountain Home, Camp Scenic, Kerrville, Cowboy Artists Museum, Comfort, Rocksprings, Juno, Loma Alta.

A quick culinary primer—local cuisine: Tex-Mex is chorizo, fajitas and chili. Try the best in Terlingua, TX *(C1)* at the World Championship Chili Cook-off.

Texan is barbecued rib-eye steak or a gravy-smothered chicken-fried steak. Beverage of choice: Lone Star Longnecks.

A famed Western justice and admirer of a certain English actress used to hold court at a gaming table in his Jersey Lilly Saloon in Langtry, TX *(E1)*. Name the judge and the lady. *See page 156.*

Big Bend *(C2)* is a Texas-sized park—it contains the entire Chisos Mountain range.

The path of the Rio Grande *(D1)* along this stretch of Texas has been chopped and channeled numerous times to keep from changing the US/Mexican Border.

If you're driving through Chihuahua, visit the extraordinary Barranca del Cobre—Copper Canyon *(off map)*. The canyon is deeper than Arizona's Grand.

Mexican driving rules and information:

The speed limit on highways is measured in kilometers. To translate into mph, multiply by 6 and drop the last digit.

Gas, while inexpensive, may be difficult to find outside the border towns.

Expect rugged roads. This may not be the place to test drive a brand-new car.

US insurance is invalid in Mexico. Buying Mexican insurance is easy, cheap and strongly advised.

The map on this page is 250x250 miles.

A 1
B
C T E X A S
D
E Lang
Judge
Roy Bean
Museum

Shafter
170
67
San Jacinto Mountain 4965'
385
Persimmon Gap 3771'
Rio Grande
Rio Bravo del Norte
Arroyo S

Coyame
Ojinaga
Toll Bridge
Presidio
El Camino del Rio
118
Rosillos Peak 5420'
S E R R A N I A S

Boquilla del Mezquite
170
Terlingua
Panther Jct. (Park Headquarters)
Boquillas del Carmen
Rio Grande Village

16
Rio Conchos
49
S I E R R A   P O N C E
The Basin
Emory Peak 7835'
Casa Grande 6129'
D E L   B U R R O

Castolon Ranger Station
Big Bend Natl. Park
Parque Internacional del Rio Bravo
El Milagro

2
Piedritas

Alamos de Márquez
San Miguel
La Cuesta

C H I H U A H U A
Santa Fé del Pino
La Babia

Julimes
San Guillermo

La Perla
El Tule

Los Garcia

La Rosetilla
La Rosita

Delicias
El Orranteño
49

3
El Alicante
Llano El Guaje

Saucillo
Norias del Caballo
La Mora
2

45
Cenzontle

Cuidad Camargo
Las Norias
C O A H U I L A

La Boquilla del Conchos
Le Boquilla
Rio Conchos
Melch Múzq

45
Nueva Reforma

4
B O L S O N   D E   M A P I M I
Ocampo
San Blas

Búfalo
Puertecitos

Sierra Mojada
La Esmeralda
El Magueyal

Jiménez
Estación El Oro
Buenaven

45
Nadadore

Salaices
Laguna del Rey
Cuatrociénegas de Carranza

Coronado
Laguna de las Palomas
30

5
Escalón
El Venado

Guadalupe de Bahues
Zavalsa

Ceballos

45
D U R A N G O

kilom. 20 40 60 80
miles 10 20 30 40 50

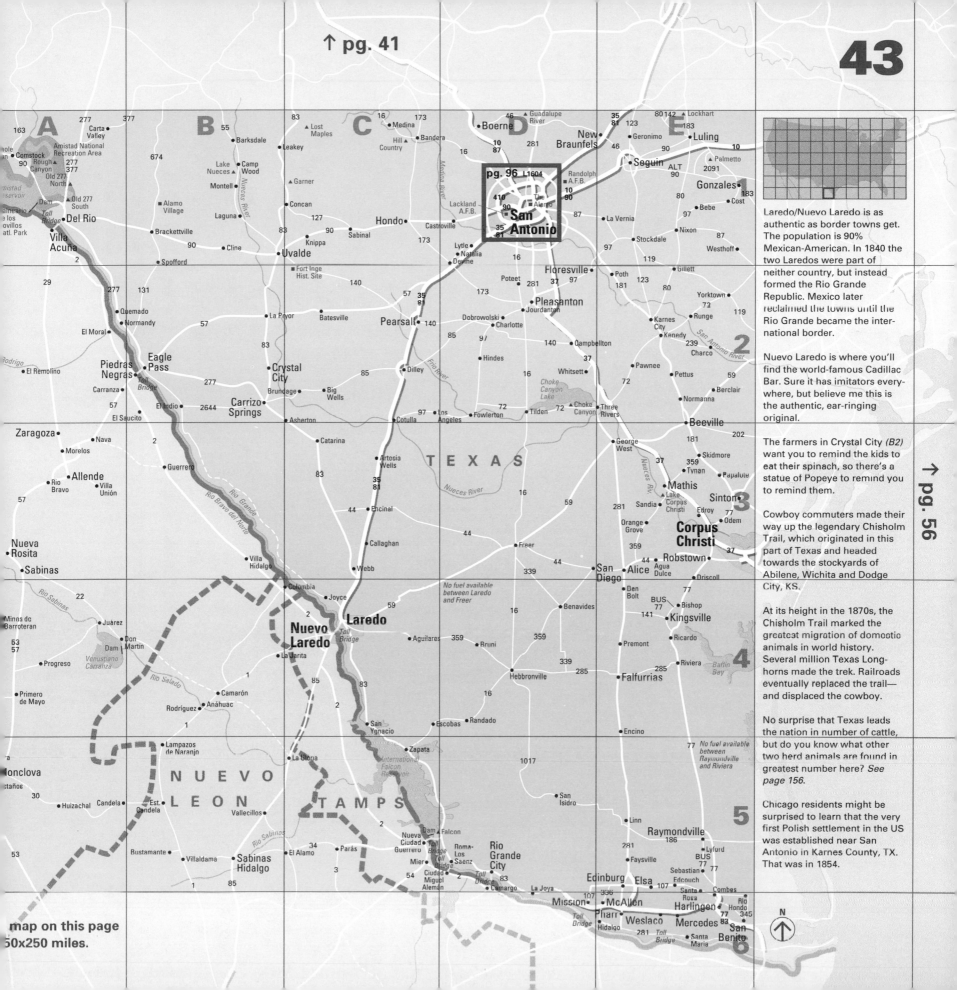

→ pg. 56

Laredo/Nuevo Laredo is as authentic as border towns get. The population is 90% Mexican-American. In 1840 the two Laredos were part of neither country, but instead formed the Rio Grande Republic. Mexico later reclaimed the towns until the Rio Grande became the international border.

Nuevo Laredo is where you'll find the world-famous Cadillac Bar. Sure it has imitators everywhere, but believe me this is the authentic, ear-ringing original.

The farmers in Crystal City (B2) want you to remind the kids to eat their spinach, so there's a statue of Popeye to remind you to remind them.

Cowboy commuters made their way up the legendary Chisholm Trail, which originated in this part of Texas and headed towards the stockyards of Abilene, Wichita and Dodge City, KS.

At its height in the 1870s, the Chisholm Trail marked the greatest migration of domestic animals in world history. Several million Texas Longhorns made the trek. Railroads eventually replaced the trail—and displaced the cowboy.

No surprise that Texas leads the nation in number of cattle, but do you know what other two herd animals are found in greatest number here? See page 156.

Chicago residents might be surprised to learn that the very first Polish settlement in the US was established near San Antonio in Karnes County, TX. That was in 1854.

map on this page
50x250 miles.

The license plates of Minnesota —"Land of 10,000 Lakes"— underestimate the total by more than 2000.

What's so special about Lake of the Woods, MN (B4)? See page 156.

Voyageurs National Park (D4) is not accessible by car. Once you get close, plan on finishing the journey by boat or floatplane. All the campsites are on islands.

Kettle Falls, MN (D4) is a border town in which you'll be looking south at Canada.

The Sioux had a word for it— "minisota" is how they described "sky-tinted water."

Minnesota Governor Rudy Perpich takes pride in these things:
Outdoors: Boundary Waters Canoe Area, the lakes, Bluff Country, Lake Superior.
The warmth and hospitality of the people.

Arts and theater in the Twin Cities.
High-tech industries and corporate headquarters moving in.
The weather—four proper seasons.

Water and winter have produced a prosperous mix here: hunting, fishing, tourism, etc. Also of note—both waterskis and the snowmobile were invented here.

Boise Cascade will show you their papermaking mill in International Falls (C4), if you're visiting in summer.

For a really big sight, cross the border to see Husky the Muskie in Kenora (B3)—40 feet high and 2-1/2 tons of fiberglass fish.

↑ pg. 31

ONTARIO

MINNESOTA

MB

Lake of the Woods

Voyageurs National Park

Quetico Provincial Park

Woodland Caribou Provincial Park

Atikaki Provincial Wilderness Park

Nopiming Provincial Park

Whiteshell Provincial Park

Fort Frances

International Falls

Kenora

Dryden

Sioux Lookout

Thief River Falls

MESABI IRON RANGE

The map on this page is 250×250 miles.

kilom. 20   40   60   80

miles 10   20   30   40   50

↓ pg. 46

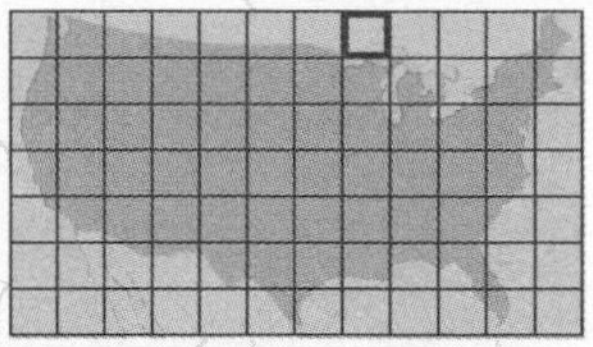

Map labels

A B C D E (column headers)

1 2 3 4 5 (row markers)

Wabakimi Lake
Wabakimi Provincial Park
Flint River
Allan Water
Pikitigushi River
Caribou Lake
Mojikit Lake
Ottertail River
Ara Lake
Meta Creek
Meta Lake
Abamasagi Lake
O'Sullivan Lake
Drowning River
Legarde River
Esnagami River
Esnagami Lake
Armstrong
Nipigon Provincial Forest
Auden
Jack River
Onaman River
Onaman Lake
Aroland
Cavell
643
Nakina
Twin Lakes
Kenogami River
Chipman Lake
Flint Lake
Flint River

Sesegonaga Lake
Kopka River
Wig Creek
Harmon Lake
etionga ke
Obonga Lake
Geikie Island
Kelvin Island
527
Murchison Island
Shakespeare Island
580
Sturgeon River Mine 801
Beardmore
584
Geraldton
Bankfield
Macleod
Longlac
11
025
Caramat
Stevens
McKay Lake
Pagwachuan River
Osawin River
11
Klotz Lake

Gull River
Chief Bay
Lake Nipigon
Grand Bay
Lake Nipigon
Orient Bay
Long Lake
Wintering Lake
Kanuck River
ONTARIO
Steel River

Pakashkan Lake
Mooseland Lake
Garden Lake
Lac des Îles
Eaglehead Lake
Black Sturgeon Lake
Pine Portage
585
11
Hydro
Kabimichigama Lake
Dickison Lake
Little Pic River
Killala Lake
Pic River
614
Manitouwadge
Zeum River
White Lake

Upsala
Muskeg Lake
Savanne
Argon Park
Raith
Dog River
Dog Lake
Nipigon
Red Rock
17
Cypress Park
Lookout
Nishin Lake Park
Nipigon Bay
Rossport Rainbow Falls
Cavers
Rossport
Schreiber
Terrace Bay
Santoy Lake
Jackfish
Neys
Marathon
17
Hemlo
White Lake
Heron Bay
627

Eastern Time Central Time
Hurkett
17
St. Ignace Island
Simpson Island
Mortimer Island
Slate Island
Tip Top Mtn. 2099' Highest point in Ontario

aham eel
Lac des Mille Lacs
17
Trout Lake Park
527
Dorion
Ouimet
Ouimet Canyon Prov. Park
Pearl
Loon
Pass Lake
Black Bay
Shehandowan
Mabella
Shabaqua Corners
Sistonens Corners
591
589
102
11
17
Sleeping Giant Prov. Park
587
Pukaskwa National Park

Shebandowan Lakes
Greenwater Lake
Kakabeka Falls
Kakaboka Falls
590
593
Silver Islet
Edward Island
Thunder Bay
Lake Superior
Michipicoten Island

Weikwabinonaw Lake
Suomi
61
Moose Hill
Jarvis River
Loch Lomond
Pie Island
Nolalu
588

Northern Light Lake
Whitefish Lake
Middle Falls
Pigeon River
Grand Portage
Grand Portage Natl. Mon.
Ferry
Natl. Park Service Headquarters
Rock Harbor Lodge
Ferry

Greenwood Lake
Judge C R Magney
Hovland
Isle Royale Natl. Park
Isle Royale (Michigan)
Ferry
Ferry

Brun Lake
Grand Marais
Grand Marais
Cascade River
Caribou ako
61
Lutsen
fte erance
Ferries run in the summer only, no autos carried
Copper Harbor
26
Eagle River
41
Phoenix
26
Fort Wilkins
Manitou Island
MI

Side text (right panel)

Upper Great Lakes facts: Superior, Huron and Michigan hold the largest concentration of fresh water in the world; goods sail from here to the Atlantic, the Gulf of Mexico and Canada; Lake states residents hold over 5 million fishing licenses.

The area near Thunder Bay is known for its huge supply of amethysts—you can literally pick them up right off the ground.

It was silver mining, however, which prompted Thunder Bay's most lasting legend. The harbor's Sleeping Giant rock is said by the Ojibways to be a giant spirit who protected the tribe but turned to stone when white men discovered the tribe's silver mine.

These days it's the lake that's the resource—Thunder Bay claims to be the world's largest grain-handling port.

Enjoy the view as you overlook Lake Superior. Besides its natural beauty, what's its other great claim to fame? *See page 156.*

The Isle Royale National Park *(B5)* is a perfect example of a near-perfect wilderness—99% of it is so designated. The ferry ride out to the largest island in Lake Superior takes about 5 hours. Embarkation points: Grand Portage, MN *(B5)*; Copper Harbor, MI *(C5)* and Houghton, MI *(pg. 47, C1).* (The park is officially part of the state of Michigan.)

Minnesota Tourist Information: 612/296-5029

Minnesota Road Information: 612/296-3076

↓ pg. 47

The map on this page is 250x250 miles.

N

← pg. 33

The Mighty Mississippi gets its humble start *(B1)* in Minnesota's Itasca State Park.

The world's largest open pit iron ore mine is the Hull-Rust Open Pit Mine in Hibbing, MN *(D1)*. The way the locals describe it: if the hole went down instead of across, it would open up on the other side of the world. The mine is open for visitors during the summer. This is a first-hand introduction to the history of American industry. The steel mills of Pittsburgh owe their existence to the iron ore of the Mesabi Iron Range *(C1)*.

You wouldn't expect to find the US Hockey Hall of Fame anywhere south of Eveleth, MN *(D1)*, would you?

In what city in Minnesota are you lucky enough to see the Northern Lights about 40 nights per year? *See page 156.*

Duluth *(E2)* is the largest freshwater inland port in the world. More grain is stored here than in the Plains states where it's grown.

Why you should be grateful on Thanksgiving: Most of the country's wild rice is grown in the lakes of northern Minnesota, harvested by hand by Chippewa Indians who then beat the grain loose on the sides of their canoes. Much of the rice is now carefully planted and tended. It may not be as "wild" as it once was—but the taste doesn't appear to have suffered.

February brings a horde of skiers to Hayward, WI *(E3)* for the American Birkebeiner, the largest cross-country ski race in the country and one of the most challenging in the world.

The map on this page is 250x250 miles.

A B C D E

Lake Superior

Lake Superior

MICHIGAN

WISCONSIN

Apostle Islands National Lakeshore
Red Cliff
Bayfield Madeline Island
Cat Island Outer Island Oak Island Stockton Island Michigan Island
Washburn Chequamegon Point
Bayview Park 13
Ashland 2 Cedar
13 169
Mellen Copper Falls 77
Bad River Rec. Area
Day Lake 77
Clam Lake 13 77
Ojibwa
E Fork Chippewa River
Stockfarm Bridge
Park Falls 70
Phillips 13
Ladysmith 73
27 73 Eastwood
Brunet Island
Cornell 64
27 73
Greenwood
Augusta
Osseo 12 27
53 94 95 Merrillan
Hixton
95
Black River Falls
53
Galesville 53 55
Sparta 16 71

Silver City 64 107
Porcupine Mountains 64
Bessemer Wakefield
Ironwood Hurley 2
51 Mercer Manitowish
Lac du Flambeau
Turtle Flambeau Flowage
Long Lake
Presque Isle W
Conover
Eagle River 51
Wabasso Lake Lac du Flambeau
Woodruff 17
Three Lakes
Smith Rapids
Willow Reservoir
Lake Nokomis 8
Rhinelander
Monico 55
Heafford Junction A
Tomahawk
Prentice 51
Westboro
Medford 64
Council Grounds
Merrill 64
Phlox
Wausau 29
Schofield Rothschild
Rib Mtn. 29
Mosinee
Big Eau Pleine Reservoir
Abbotsford 29
Marshfield 10
Stevens Point 10
Plover
Pittsville 54
Wisconsin Rapids
Hartman Creek
Necedah 21
Mill Bluff 90 80
New Lisbon 94

Ontonagon
Mass City 38
Courtney Lake
Lake Gogebic 45
Bergland
Bruce Crossing
Marenisco
Watersmeet 2
Presque Isle
Lac Vieux Desert
Nelma 73
Florence
Eagle River 70
Cranberry Lake
Armstrong Creek
Laona
Crandon
Richardson Lake
Wabeno Burnt Ridge
Elcho
Parrish 45 47
Langlade 64
Antigo 64
Rainbow Falls
Keshena Falls
Shawano Lake
Wittenberg 22
Gillett
Clintonville 49
New London 41
Waupaca 45
Menasha Neenah
Oshkosh
Berlin 73
Ripon
Princeton
Fond du Lac

Ferry to Isle Royale F.J. McLain 203 Laurium 26 Keweenaw Peninsula
Hancock Houghton
Portage Lake Point Abbaye
26 41 Keweenaw Bay
Twin Lakes Baraga
Baraga L'Anse
41
Sparrow Rapids 28 Lower Dam
Eastern Time / Central Time 141
Paulding Pond
Amasa
Michigamme Reservoir
Iron River Bewabic 2
Brule River 2 Florence
Iron Mountain
Kingsford B U
Niagara 8
Pembine
Goodman 8
141
Wausaukee
Crivitz
Menominee
Marinette
Pound Peshtigo
Stiles Jct. 22
Oconto Copper Culture Mound
Stiles
Howard Green Bay
De Pere 172
Black Creek
Denmark
Kaukauna
Appleton 55
High Cliff 32
Chilton 151
New Holstein Kiel
N. Fond du Lac
Plymouth 23
Sheboygan Falls
Kohler Andrae

Huron River Point
Big Bay
Perkins Park
Dead River Storage Basin
Marquette 41 Harvey
Ishpeming Negaunee BUS 28
Van Riper K.I. Sawyer A.F.B.
Covington 28 Republic 35
Lower Dam 95
Crystal Falls 69 Sagola
73 Peavy Pond
95
Gladstone
Bark River 2 41
Escanaba
Norway 2 Powers
Peninsula Point
Big Cedar River 141
Cedar River
J.W. Wells
Chambers Island
Washington Island
Gills Rock 42 Newport
Sister Bay
Peninsula
Baileys Harbor
Whitefish Dunes State Park 57
Sturgeon Bay
Brussels
Algoma
Kewaunee
Manitowoc
Two Rivers 310
Sheboygan

Grand Sable Dunes
Au Sable Point Grand Marais
Twelvemile Beach Hurricane River 77
Deer Lake Park 28 Munising
Grand Island
Bay Furnace
Chatham 94
Colwell Lake
Indian River 94
Palms Book St. Park
Shingleton
Flowing Well
Manistique 149 Indian Lake
Perkins 35
Rapid River 183
Thompson
Big Bay De Noc
Point Aux Barques
Fayette
Point Detour
Summer Island
St. Martin Island
Detroit Harbor
Detroit Island

→ pg. 58

Wisconsin Governor Tommy G. Thompson recommends:
Elroy-Sparta Bike Trail.
The House on the Rock.
Wisconsin Dells.
Door County.
Apostle Islands.

The Apostle Islands (A1) were so called because it was initially thought there were 12 of them. More thorough exploration yielded a total of 22.

Eagle River, WI (B2) is a good place to bring your snowmobile—the World Championship Derby is held here in January.

Wisconsin leads the nation in the production of dairy cows, milk, butter and cheese. So what would you expect its nickname to be? See page 156.

But there's more—various cities in Wisconsin boast the following:
World's Largest Loon—Mercer (B2).
World's Largest Talking Cow—Neillsville (A5).
World's Largest Muskie Fish—Hayward (pg. 46, E3).
World's Largest Six-Pack—La Crosse (pg. 49, A1).

"Winning isn't everything; it's the only thing." Easy for Vince Lombardi to say. His Green Bay Packers (D4) were Super Bowl champs in '66 and '67.

Not as famous as the Great Chicago Fire of the same year. Green Bay's fire of 1871 nonetheless killed 1000 residents.

Wisconsin Tourist Information:
608/266-2161

Wisconsin Road Information:
608/246-7580

The map on this page is 250x250 miles.

N ↑

↑ pg. 46

↑ pg. 35

The heartland: this is it all right—Iowa produces 10% of the nation's food. 95% of the land is dedicated to farming.

If you order a "tenderloin" here, expect pork. Most of the nation's pigs are from here.

There are a few sights you can't miss even if you try:
Blue Earth, MN (C1)—Soaring 55 feet into the air is the Jolly Green Giant.
Pocahontas, IA (B2)—If you're headed towards this town, you'll see a 25-foot statue of the Indian princess.
Stanton, IA (B5)—A huge water tower shaped like a coffee pot. "Mrs. Olson," of Folger's coffee fame, was born here.

Sgt. Charles Floyd died and was buried near Sioux City, IA (A3). He was the only member of the Lewis and Clark Expedition who died on the journey (appendicitis); he was the first American soldier to die west of the Mississippi; his monument was the country's first Registered Historic Landmark.

Who was the Duke from Winterset, IA (C4)? See page 156.

A place we hope is planning to convert its swords into ploughshares—the Strategic Air Command in Omaha, headquarters of the nation's nuclear arsenal since 1948. The museum will show you missiles, bombers and a red alert reenactment.

Nebraska has the nation's only unicameral legislature.

Iowa Tourist Information:
515/281-3100

Iowa Road Information:
515/288-1047

MINNESOTA   **IOWA**   **NEBRASKA (NE)**   **MISSOURI**

Grid columns: A B C D E — Rows: 1 2 3 4 5

Selected places: Pipestone, Pipestone Natl. Mon., Slayton, Windom, Fulda, Madelia, St. James, Stewartville, Chatfield, Rushf..., Geneva, Preston, Spring Valley, Niagara Cave, Decor..., Cresco, Split Rock Creek, Palisades, Blue Mounds, Luverne, Adrian, Worthington, Jackson, Kilen Woods, Fairmont, Blue Earth, Albert Lea, Helmer Myre, Austin, Lake Louise, Rock Rapids, Sibley, Marble Beach, Big Spirit Lake, Estherville, Armstrong, Buffalo Center, Lake Mills, Osage, Manly, Pioneer St. Park, Canton, Sheldon, Sanborn, Gull Pt., Milford, Fort Defiance, Bancroft, Britt, Forest City, Pilot Knob, Clear Lake, Mason City, Charles City, New Hampton, Newton Hills, Oak Grove, Mill Creek, Spencer, Emmetsburg, Algona, Ambrose A. Call, McIntosh Woods, Clear Lake, Sheffield, Greene, Heery Woods, Waverly, Oelw..., Hawarden, Paullina, Dog Creek Park, Laurens, Belmond, Beeds Lake, Hampton, Aplington, Cedar Falls, George Wyth Mem., Akron, Le Mars, Cherokee, Pocahontas, Humboldt, Clarion, Lake Cornelia, Parkersburg, Waterloo, Independ..., Silver Sioux, Storm Lake, Fort Dodge, Webster City, Iowa Falls, Pine Lake, Grundy Center, La Porte City, Stone, Sioux City, Ranney's Knob Peak, Holstein, Sac City, Rockwell City, Jewell, Eldora, Traer, Vinto..., South Sioux City, Moville, Ida Grove, Odebolt, Lake View, Dolliver Memorial, Union Grove, Brown's Lake, Winnebago, Sloan, Mapleton, Black Hawk Lake, Carroll, Scranton, Jefferson, Boone, Ames, Marshalltown, Toledo, Tama, Nevada, Lewis & Clark, Turin, Ute, Denison, Yellow Smoke, Swan Lake, Spring Lake, Ledges, Grinnell, Willia..., Decatur, Onawa, Toll Bridge, Dunlap, Manning, Springbrook, Perry, Jester Park, Rock Creek, Newton, Montezuma, Oakland, Tekamah, Woodbine, Dow House Natl. Hist. Site, Albert The Bull Statue, Audubon, Guthrie Center, Harlan, Badger Creek St. Park, Des Moines, Monroe, Elk Rock, New Sharon, Scribner, Winslow, Logan, Missouri Valley, Prairie Rose, Adair, Red Rock Reservoir, Pella, Blair, Fremont, Fremont Lakes, Omaha, Council Bluffs, Lake Anita, Atlantic, Oakland, Cold Springs, Winterset, Lake Ahquabi, Indianola, Knoxville, Oskaloosa, Lake Keomah, Boys Town, Offutt A.F.B., Glenwood, Green Valley, Creston, Afton, Osceola, Lucas, Chariton, Red Haw Lake, Albia, Ottumw..., Wahoo, Red Oak, Stanton, Corning, Lake Icaria, Greenfield, Pammel, Honey Creek, Lake Wapello, Bloomfield, Plattsmouth, Viking Lake, Shenandoah, Lake of Three Fires, Mount Ayr, Bobwhite, Corydon, Centerville, Lincoln, Sidney, Clarinda, Bedford, Lamoni, Nine Eagles, Leon, Nebraska City, Waubonsie, Hamburg, Eagleville, Syracuse, Unionville, Lancaster

Rivers: Des Moines River, Blue Earth River, Big Sioux River, Little Sioux River, Missouri River, Platte River, N. Raccoon River, Elkhorn River, Iowa River, Cedar River, Des Moines River, Charlton River

Scale: kilom. 20 40 60 80 — miles 10 20 30 40 50

The map on this page is 250x250 miles.

↓ pg. 50

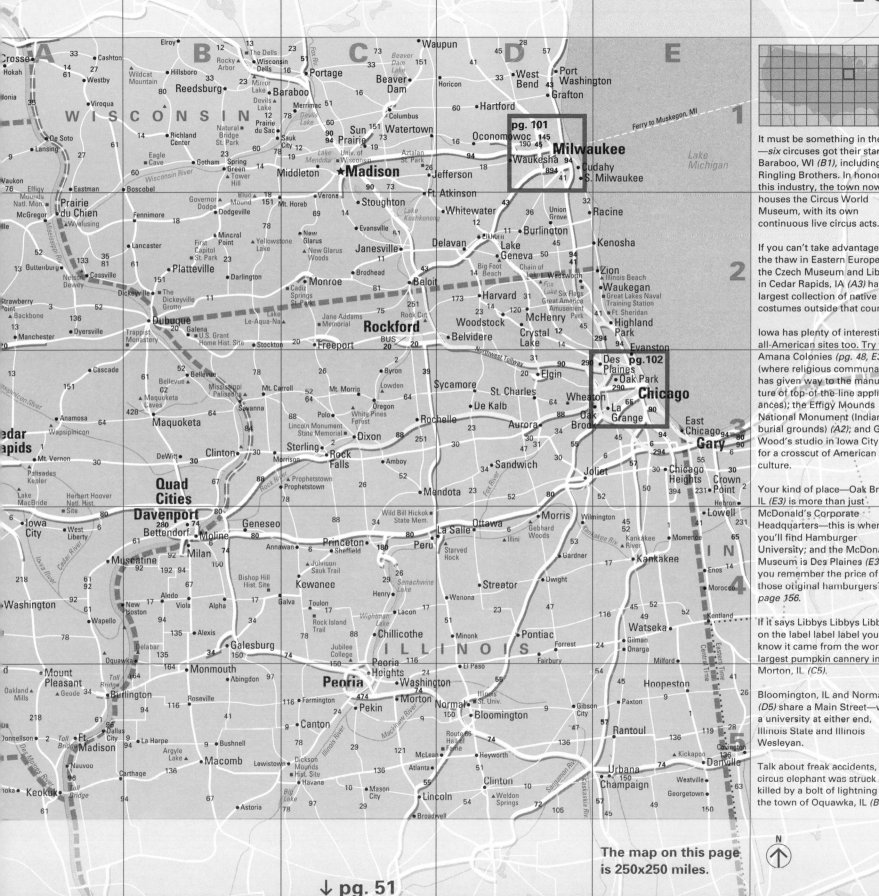

It must be something in the air —*six* circuses got their start in Baraboo, WI *(B1)*, including Ringling Brothers. In honor of this industry, the town now houses the Circus World Museum, with its own continuous live circus acts.

If you can't take advantage of the thaw in Eastern Europe yet, the Czech Museum and Library in Cedar Rapids, IA *(A3)* has the largest collection of native costumes outside that country.

Iowa has plenty of interesting all-American sites too. Try the Amana Colonies *(pg. 48, E3)* (where religious communal life has given way to the manufacture of top-of-the-line appliances); the Effigy Mounds National Monument (Indian burial grounds) *(A2)*; and Grant Wood's studio in Iowa City *(A4)* for a crosscut of American culture.

Your kind of place—Oak Brook, IL *(E3)* is more than just McDonald's Corporate Headquarters—this is where you'll find Hamburger University; and the McDonald's Museum is Des Plaines *(E3)*. Do you remember the price of those original hamburgers? *See page 156.*

If it says Libbys Libbys Libbys on the label label label you'll know it came from the world's largest pumpkin cannery in Morton, IL *(C5)*.

Bloomington, IL and Normal, IL *(D5)* share a Main Street—with a university at either end, Illinois State and Illinois Wesleyan.

Talk about freak accidents, a circus elephant was struck and killed by a bolt of lightning in the town of Oquawka, IL *(B4)*.

↓ pg. 51

→ pg. 60

The map on this page is 250x250 miles.

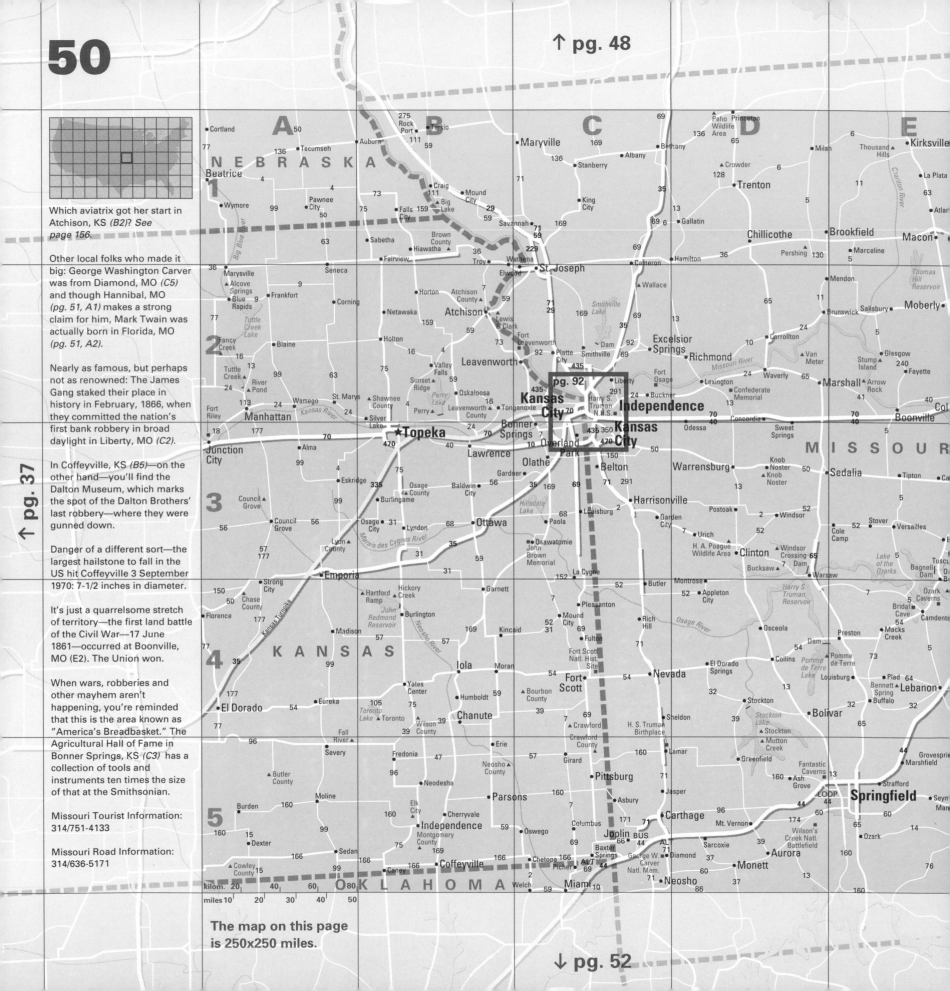

Which aviatrix got her start in Atchison, KS *(B2)? See page 156.*

Other local folks who made it big: George Washington Carver was from Diamond, MO *(C5)* and though Hannibal, MO *(pg. 51, A1)* makes a strong claim for him, Mark Twain was actually born in Florida, MO *(pg. 51, A2).*

Nearly as famous, but perhaps not as renowned: The James Gang staked their place in history in February, 1866, when they committed the nation's first bank robbery in broad daylight in Liberty, MO *(C2).*

In Coffeyville, KS *(B5)*—on the other hand—you'll find the Dalton Museum, which marks the spot of the Dalton Brothers' last robbery—where they were gunned down.

Danger of a different sort—the largest hailstone to fall in the US hit Coffeyville 3 September 1970: 7-1/2 inches in diameter.

It's just a quarrelsome stretch of territory—the first land battle of the Civil War—17 June 1861—occurred at Boonville, MO (E2). The Union won.

When wars, robberies and other mayhem aren't happening, you're reminded that this is the area known as "America's Breadbasket." The Agricultural Hall of Fame in Bonner Springs, KS *(C3)* has a collection of tools and instruments ten times the size of that at the Smithsonian.

Missouri Tourist Information: 314/751-4133

Missouri Road Information: 314/636-5171

↑ pg. 37

pg. 92

The map on this page is 250x250 miles.

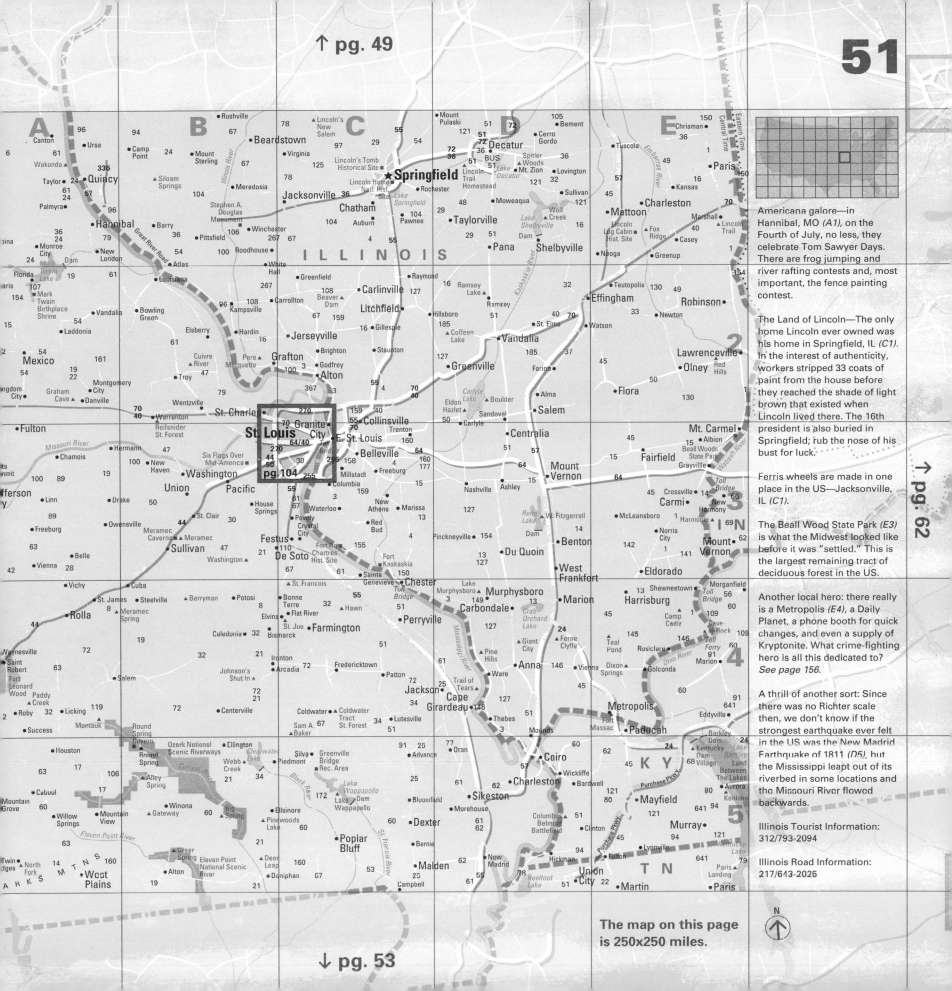

Americana galore—in Hannibal, MO (A1), on the Fourth of July, no less, they celebrate Tom Sawyer Days. There are frog jumping and river rafting contests and, most important, the fence painting contest.

The Land of Lincoln—The only home Lincoln ever owned was his home in Springfield, IL (C1). In the interest of authenticity, workers stripped 33 coats of paint from the house before they reached the shade of light brown that existed when Lincoln lived there. The 16th president is also buried in Springfield; rub the nose of his bust for luck.

Ferris wheels are made in one place in the US—Jacksonville, IL (C1).

The Beall Wood State Park (E3) is what the Midwest looked like before it was "settled." This is the largest remaining tract of deciduous forest in the US.

Another local hero: there really is a Metropolis (E4), a Daily Planet, a phone booth for quick changes, and even a supply of Kryptonite. What crime-fighting hero is all this dedicated to? See page 156.

A thrill of another sort: Since there was no Richter scale then, we don't know if the strongest earthquake ever felt in the US was the New Madrid Earthquake of 1811 (D5), but the Mississippi leapt out of its riverbed in some locations and the Missouri River flowed backwards.

Illinois Tourist Information: 312/793-2094

Illinois Road Information: 217/643-2026

The map on this page is 250x250 miles.

→ pg. 62

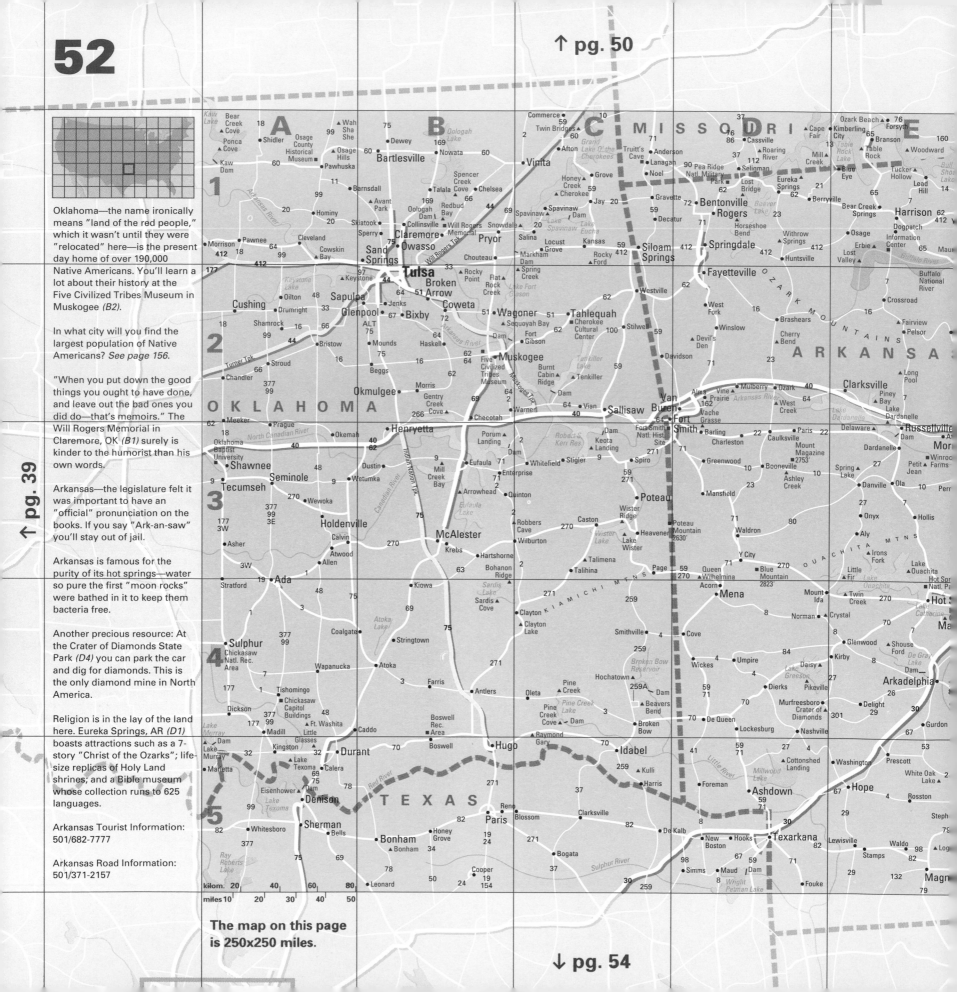

↑ pg. 39

Oklahoma—the name ironically means "land of the red people," which it wasn't until they were "relocated" here—is the present day home of over 190,000 Native Americans. You'll learn a lot about their history at the Five Civilized Tribes Museum in Muskogee (B2).

In what city will you find the largest population of Native Americans? *See page 156.*

"When you put down the good things you ought to have done, and leave out the bad ones you did do—that's memoirs." The Will Rogers Memorial in Claremore, OK (B1) surely is kinder to the humorist than his own words.

Arkansas—the legislature felt it was important to have an "official" pronunciation on the books. If you say "Ark-an-saw" you'll stay out of jail.

Arkansas is famous for the purity of its hot springs—water so pure the first "moon rocks" were bathed in it to keep them bacteria free.

Another precious resource: At the Crater of Diamonds State Park (D4) you can park the car and dig for diamonds. This is the only diamond mine in North America.

Religion is in the lay of the land here. Eureka Springs, AR (D1) boasts attractions such as a 7-story "Christ of the Ozarks"; life-size replicas of Holy Land shrines; and a Bible museum whose collection runs to 625 languages.

Arkansas Tourist Information: 501/682-7777

Arkansas Road Information: 501/371-2157

The map on this page is 250x250 miles.

→ pg. 64

There really was—and is—a "little rock"—it was a landmark for travelers along the Arkansas River. It rises just less than 20 feet above river level, near Little Rock, and extends about 40 feet along the river bank.

Davy Crockett called the men of Arkansas "half-horse, half-alligator" and meant it as a compliment. You still have to be tough to make it here—dollar for dollar the governor of Arkansas earns less than the 49 others.

Oxford, MS (D3)—the home of Ole' Miss—is also the county seat of William Faulkner's fictional Yoknapatawpha County—he called the town Jefferson and is still remembered, mostly fondly, by local residents.

The blues were born here too—and if you haven't heard Mississippi region blues, you can't know how deep and rich this music is. Do yourself a favor and visit the Delta Blues Museum, Clarksdale, MS (C4).

Travelling upriver brings you to Memphis. Beale St. is another shrine for music lovers.

How many people would you guess stream through *Graceland* each year? *See page 156.*

The modern self-service supermarket was born in Memphis—find out all about the Piggly Wiggly's start at the Pink Palace museum.

Andrew Jackson was responsible for Tennessee's nickname, when he led volunteer soldiers from the state in the Battle of New Orleans. Tennessee has henceforth been known as "the Volunteer State."

The map on this page is 250x250 miles.

↑ pg. 52

At one time it was the Mexicans who passed laws to keep out "illegal" aliens! In the 1830s, rowdy Anglos from Texas were not welcome to settle south of the border.

Texas gushed its way into history in 1901. The Spindletop, at Beaumont, marked the discovery of oil in the Lone Star State, 62 years after the world's first oil well was drilled in Titusville, PA.

Texas's most destructive tornado hit Waco 11 May 1953 and killed 114 people.

Long before there were Green Berets or "Special Forces," there were Texas Rangers—the nearly mythic lawmen of the Texas frontier. Their museum can be found in Waco.

Famed Texas Ranger Frank Hamer tracked Bonnie and Clyde to Gibsland, LA (E1), where he and other peace officers ended their crime spree with over 200 bullets.

Great Balls of Fire—the Brimstone Museum in Sulphur, LA (E5) is not a portent of things to come, but a reminder of the days when mining was this town's main industry.

Louisiana's laws are derived from the time when the state was a colony of France. What's the name for this legal system, unique among US states? See page 156.

Louisiana's bests, from Governor Buddy Roemer:
The variety and beauty of the land, from woods to bayous. Cuisine without rival. Homeland of jazz. Vibrant New Orleans. A people melded of many cultures.

↑ pg. 41

pg. 95

pg. 97

The map on this page is 250x250 miles.

kilom. 20   40   60   80

miles 10   20   30   40   50

TEXAS

ARKANSAS

Gulf of Mexico

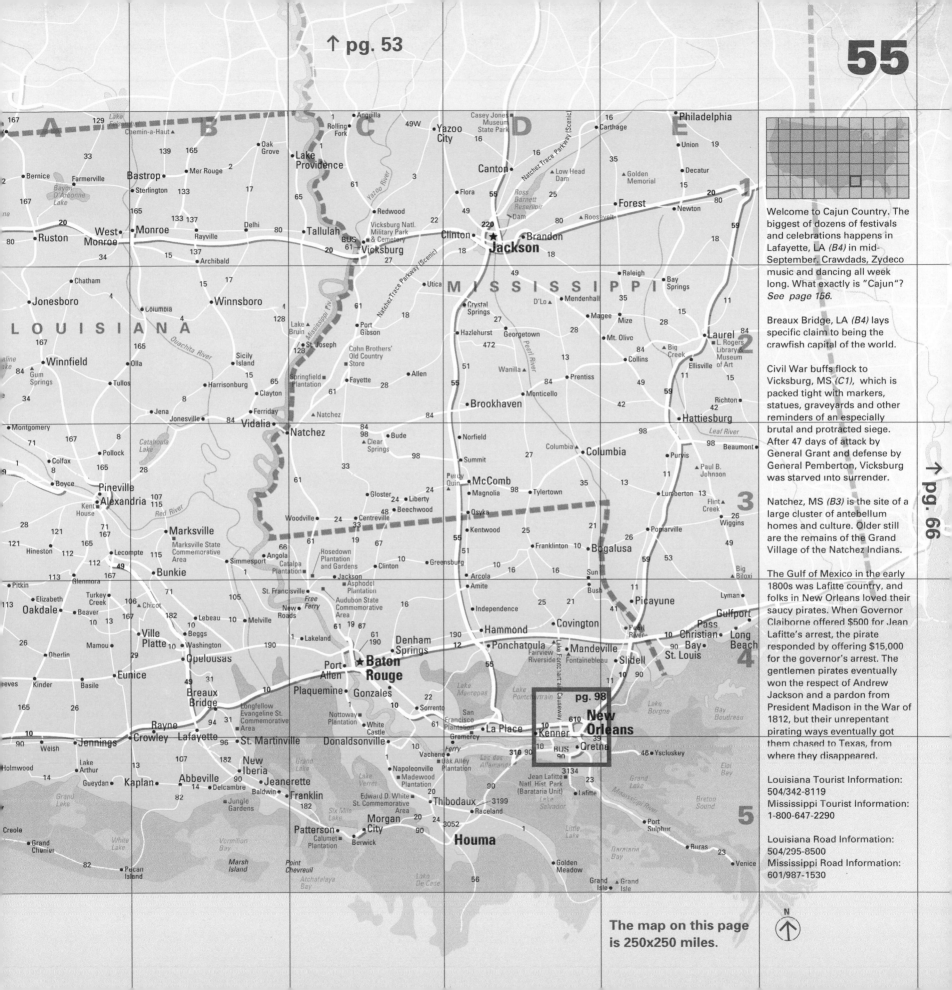

↑ pg. 66

Welcome to Cajun Country. The biggest of dozens of festivals and celebrations happens in Lafayette, LA *(B4)* in mid-September. Crawdads, Zydeco music and dancing all week long. What exactly is "Cajun"? *See page 156.*

Breaux Bridge, LA *(B4)* lays specific claim to being the crawfish capital of the world.

Civil War buffs flock to Vicksburg, MS *(C1),* which is packed tight with markers, statues, graveyards and other reminders of an especially brutal and protracted siege. After 47 days of attack by General Grant and defense by General Pemberton, Vicksburg was starved into surrender.

Natchez, MS *(B3)* is the site of a large cluster of antebellum homes and culture. Older still are the remains of the Grand Village of the Natchez Indians.

The Gulf of Mexico in the early 1800s was Lafitte country, and folks in New Orleans loved their saucy pirates. When Governor Claiborne offered $500 for Jean Lafitte's arrest, the pirate responded by offering $15,000 for the governor's arrest. The gentlemen pirates eventually won the respect of Andrew Jackson and a pardon from President Madison in the War of 1812, but their unrepentant pirating ways eventually got them chased to Texas, from where they disappeared.

Louisiana Tourist Information: 504/342-8119

Mississippi Tourist Information: 1-800-647-2290

Louisiana Road Information: 504/295-8500

Mississippi Road Information: 601/987-1530

The map on this page is 250x250 miles.

↑ pg. 54

← pg. 43

The worst natural disaster in US history was the Galveston Hurricane of September 1900 *(D1)*. At least 6000 people were killed and the same number injured or left homeless. Texas's hurricane belt runs north from Brownsville to Port Arthur. You are well advised to pay close attention to weather and news reports. What are the months commonly considered "hurricane season"? *See page 156.*

Not extinct, but nearly. At the Aransas National Wildlife Refuge *(A3)* you can see a flock of less than 100 whooping cranes who winter here. Even this small number is encouraging, since the birds were thought to be extinct.

Brownsville's Mayor Ygnacio D. Garza sends these reasons to visit:
It's less than five minutes from Matamaros, Mexico; South Padre Island and the unspoiled beaches of the Rio Grande.
Many historical buildings and sights.
One of the nicest zoos in the country.
Beautiful area and wonderful climate.

Padre Island National Seashore *(A5)* is a popular and scenic vacation destination. It got its start as a drop-off point for the stolen loot of the pirates who used to live here. Most of their millions have long since been lost at sea.

Fishing is the lucrative catch now—the bay from Port Isabel to Brownsville houses the world's largest shrimp fleet.

Those Texans flocking to the beach are vacationing on the shore of the world's largest gulf.

TEXAS

Houston
pg. 97
La Porte
Sugar Land
Rosenberg
Arcola
Alvin
Texas City
Galveston
Port Bolivar
Bolivar Peninsula
High Island
NASA L.B.J. Space Center
Rosharon
West Columbia
Angleton
Clute
Freeport
Bryan Beach State Park
Galveston Island
Brazos Bend
Columbus
Wallis
Flatonia
Schulenburg
Eagle Lake
Rock Island
Garwood
Hungerford
Wharton
Shiner
Hallettsville
Yoakum
El Campo
Ganado
Cuero
Edna
Lake Texana
Bay City
Matagorda
Victoria
Site of Fort St. Louis
Palacios
Palmetto Bend Dam
Goliad
Fannin Battleground State Park
Port Lavaca
Port Lavaca Fishing Pier State Park
Port O'Connor
Green Lake
Tivoli
Seadrift
Matagorda Island State Park
Refugio
Aransas National Wildlife Refuge
Goose Island
Rockport
Fulton Mansion State Park
Aransas Pass
Gregory
Port Aransas
Corpus Christi
Mustang Island
Naval Air Station Corpus Christi
Malaquite Beach
Griffins Pt.
Padre Island
Padre Island National Seashore
Laguna Madre
Port Mansfield
Port Isabel
Brazos Island St. Park
Brownsville
Matamoros

Colorado River
Lavaca River
San Antonio River
Brazos River
Galveston Bay
West Bay
Matagorda Bay
Matagorda Peninsula
Cavallo Pass
Aransas Pass
Corpus Christi Bay
San Antonio Bay
Matagorda Island
Gulf of Mexico

N ↑

The map on this page is 250x250 miles.

kilom. 20 40 60 80
miles 10 20 30 40 50

USAtlas **Food**

You can get good food (fast if you have to!) just off the road anywhere in America—and a longer detour could result in an unforgettable experience. These are just the *hors d'oeuvres* of America's culinary variety:

New England
A genuine, dig-a-pit-on-the-beach and dig your dinner while you're there—*clambake*.
Baked beans and brown bread.
Wild Maine blueberries—great Maine lobsters.
Portuguese specialties: linguiça sausage and spicy seafood stews.
Vermont cheddar.

New York City
We don't want to start any fights, but you probably will when you ask someone for the perfect New York cheesecake—heavy enough to weigh you down and *no*, we repeat, *no* fruit glaze topping.
The quintessential Jewish deli—and hot pastrami.
The Original Coney Island Hot Dog—the ultimate "ethnic food" of any ethnicity.

Pennsylvania Dutch
Lots (the phrase here is, "an elegant sufficiency").
Shoofly pie.
Scrapple.

Philadelphia
If we mention only the Philly Cheese Steak (with Cheez Whiz no less!) we'll have done this city proud—but we'll also mention hoagies and soft pretzels with mustard.

Chesapeake Bay
Crab—cakes, or hard-shell with a mallet.

The South
Virginia ham (we know of one family in Kentucky that cooks its hams in Coca-Cola).
Gallons of iced tea.
Southern fried chicken—tender, golden, to die for.
Soul food—"classics" that got their start as leftovers and scraps—chitlins, pig feet, collard greens.
Barbecue—the varieties and local subtleties cut a broad swath from North Carolina through Tennessee and on to St. Louis and Kansas City; every one is worth a taste.

Cajun
You've *seen* it everywhere, but you should *eat* it in Louisiana:
Red beans and rice.
Boudin sausage.
Jambalaya.
Gumbo.
... and look for three key ingredients:
Bell peppers, onions, celery.

Texas and Southwest
Rib-eye steaks.
Chili (another fight-starter—visit Terlingua in November for the Championship cook-off).
Blue corn tortillas.
Mexican food served hundreds of ways.

The Midwest
The place America loves to mock, but comes home to for dinner:
Salad bars with jello.
Deep dish fruit pies.
Bratwurst, sauerkraut—anything German.
The potato as a culinary art form.
Meat.

Chicago
This city is a one-horse food town—and the food is a deep dish pizza that is simply the best in the world.

The Great Plains and Beyond
Somewhere in America they had to specialize in "game" food—this is where you see buffalo, venison, rabbit and even antelope on the menu. Rattlesnake for the truly brave.

California
Not enough room in USAtlas for the food trends that are launched here—California's nouvelle cuisine has swept the world. "Pacific Rim" cuisines are still the rage here—Burmese is the newest favorite. Anything fresh, unusual and overpriced will be popular in Los Angeles and San Francisco. Don't forget the wine countries.

Hawaii
Mainlanders shouldn't miss:
An honestly prepared luau.
Local fish.
Maui onions and potato chips.
An Ono burger.

A craving for catfish?
Got to have garlic?
Look no further:

Apples—Wenatchee, WA

Apricots—Patterson, CA

Artichokes—Castroville, CA

Blueberries—South Haven, MI

Carrots—Holtville, CA

Catfish—Belzoni, MS

Cereal—Battle Creek, MI

Cherries—Traverse City, MI

Chili Peppers—Mesilla, NM

Cranberries—Cape Cod, MA

Crawfish—Breaux Bridges, LA

Eggs—Petaluma, CA

Garlic—Gilroy, CA

Milk—Harvard, IL

Popcorn—Van Buren, IN

Pumpkins—Morton, IL

Spinach—Crystal City, TX

Strawberries—Stilwell, OK

Swiss Cheese—Monroe, WI

Wheat—Wellington, KS

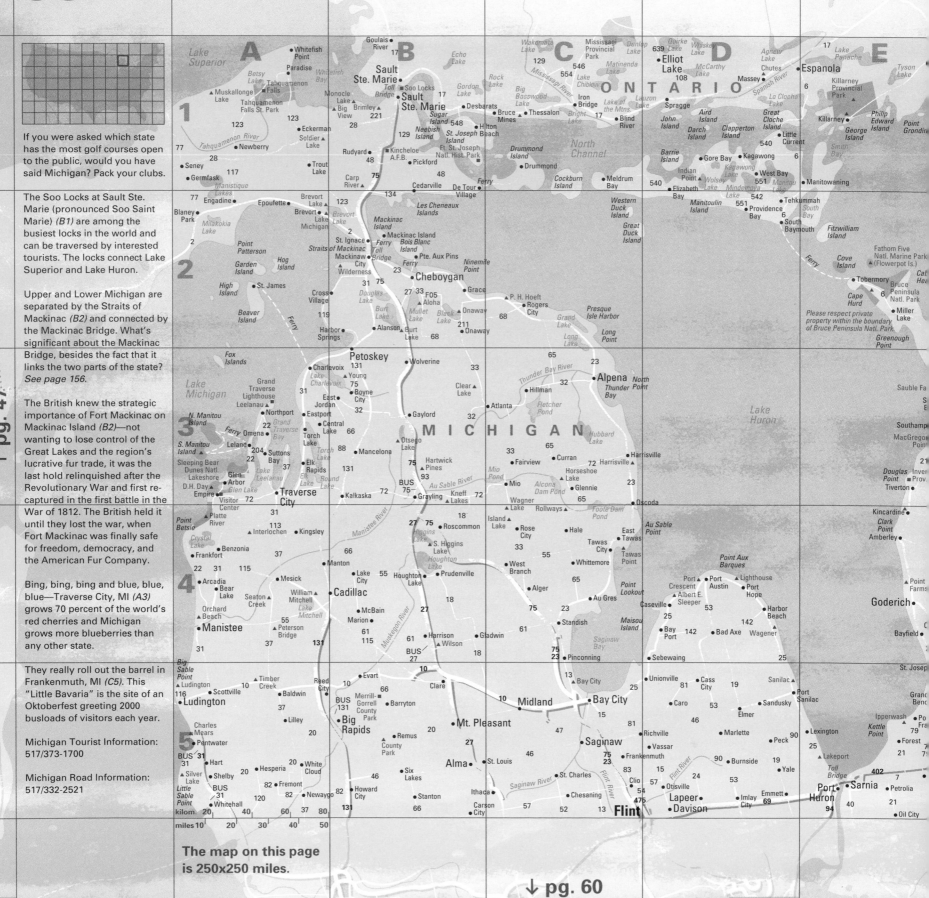

If you were asked which state has the most golf courses open to the public, would you have said Michigan? Pack your clubs.

The Soo Locks at Sault Ste. Marie (pronounced Soo Saint Marie) *(B1)* are among the busiest locks in the world and can be traversed by interested tourists. The locks connect Lake Superior and Lake Huron.

Upper and Lower Michigan are separated by the Straits of Mackinac *(B2)* and connected by the Mackinac Bridge. What's significant about the Mackinac Bridge, besides the fact that it links the two parts of the state? *See page 156.*

The British knew the strategic importance of Fort Mackinac on Mackinac Island *(B2)*—not wanting to lose control of the Great Lakes and the region's lucrative fur trade, it was the last hold relinquished after the Revolutionary War and first re-captured in the first battle in the War of 1812. The British held it until they lost the war, when Fort Mackinac was finally safe for freedom, democracy, and the American Fur Company.

Bing, bing, bing and blue, blue, blue—Traverse City, MI *(A3)* grows 70 percent of the world's red cherries and Michigan grows more blueberries than any other state.

They really roll out the barrel in Frankenmuth, MI *(C5)*. This "Little Bavaria" is the site of an Oktoberfest greeting 2000 busloads of visitors each year.

Michigan Tourist Information: 517/373-1700

Michigan Road Information: 517/332-2521

← pg. 47

The map on this page is 250x250 miles.

↓ pg. 60

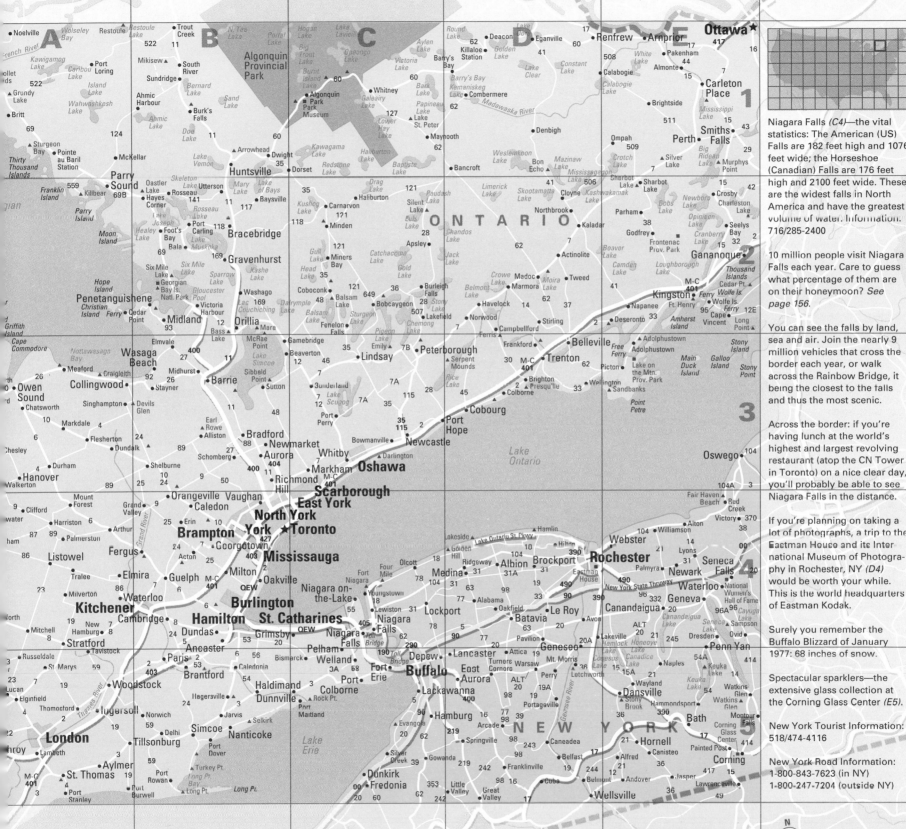

Niagara Falls (C4)—the vital statistics: The American (US) Falls are 182 feet high and 1076 feet wide; the Horseshoe (Canadian) Falls are 176 feet high and 2100 feet wide. These are the widest falls in North America and have the greatest volume of water. Information: 716/285-2400

10 million people visit Niagara Falls each year. Care to guess what percentage of them are on their honeymoon? See page 156.

You can see the falls by land, sea and air. Join the nearly 9 million vehicles that cross the border each year, or walk across the Rainbow Bridge, it being the closest to the falls and thus the most scenic.

Across the border: if you're having lunch at the world's highest and largest revolving restaurant (atop the CN Tower in Toronto) on a nice clear day, you'll probably be able to see Niagara Falls in the distance.

If you're planning on taking a lot of photographs, a trip to the Eastman House and its International Museum of Photography in Rochester, NY (D4) would be worth your while. This is the world headquarters of Eastman Kodak.

Surely you remember the Buffalo Blizzard of January 1977: 68 inches of snow.

Spectacular sparklers—the extensive glass collection at the Corning Glass Center (E5).

New York Tourist Information: 518/474-4116

New York Road Information: 1-800-843-7623 (in NY) 1-800-247-7204 (outside NY)

The map on this page is 250x250 miles.

→ pg. 72

↓ pg. 61

N

What Michigan city was the site of the first auto plant? *See page 156.*

Roadside trivia—we owe the following firsts to Michigan: *First 4-way traffic signal. First intercity superhighway. First concrete paved roads.*

Here's a surprise. The country's largest wooden shoe factory is in Holland, MI *(A1)*. What else is here? Fabulous tulip gardens, the Netherlands Museum and the only delft-ware factory in the country.

The unfortunate distinction of most deaths caused by a tornado goes to the city of Flint, MI where 116 died on 8 June 1953.

A fun factory tour—watch them make Kalamazoo Toy Trains in Bangor, MI *(A2)*.

Rebel with a memorial—the James Dean Museum is in Fairmount, IN *(B4)*.

Marblehead, OH *(E2)*, on Lake Erie, is the site of the oldest continuously operating lighthouse on the Great Lakes.

Ohio was where Cracker Jack was invented—one of the few things not invented by Thomas Edison, who was born in Milan, OH *(E3)*. Other places that lay claim to him: West Orange and Edison, NJ—where he worked; Fort Myers, FL—where he vacationed.

Columbus, OH is known by many consumer-products companies as "Test Market USA." It's renowned for being average.

No. Indiana Road Information: 317/232-8300

↑ pg. 49

The map on this page is 250x250 miles.

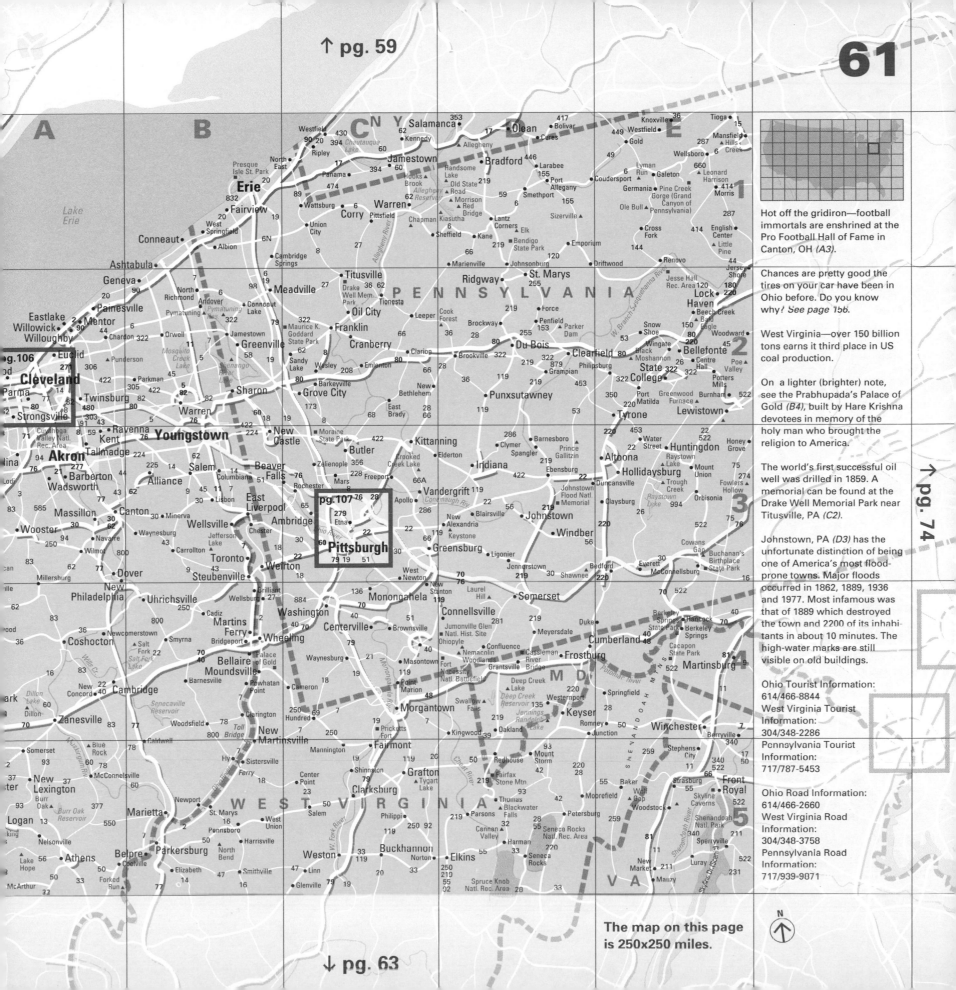

Hot off the gridiron—football immortals are enshrined at the Pro Football Hall of Fame in Canton, OH *(A3)*.

Chances are pretty good the tires on your car have been in Ohio before. Do you know why? *See page 156.*

West Virginia—over 150 billion tons earns it third place in US coal production.

On a lighter (brighter) note, see the Prabhupada's Palace of Gold *(B4)*, built by Hare Krishna devotees in memory of the holy man who brought the religion to America.

The world's first successful oil well was drilled in 1859. A memorial can be found at the Drake Well Memorial Park near Titusville, PA *(C2)*.

Johnstown, PA *(D3)* has the unfortunate distinction of being one of America's most flood-prone towns. Major floods occurred in 1862, 1889, 1936 and 1977. Most infamous was that of 1889 which destroyed the town and 2200 of its inhabitants in about 10 minutes. The high-water marks are still visible on old buildings.

Ohio Tourist Information:
614/466-8844
West Virginia Tourist Information:
304/348-2286

Pennsylvania Tourist Information:
717/787-5453

Ohio Road Information:
614/466-2660
West Virginia Road Information:
304/348-3758
Pennsylvania Road Information:
717/939-9071

The map on this page is 250x250 miles.

→ pg. 74

↑ pg. 60

← pg. 51

An infamous Indianan is remembered in Nashville, IN (B1). "Public Enemy Number One" came to a bloody end on 22 July 1934, after 14 months of mayhem. Who was he? *See page 156.*

Kentucky—born here, Abe Lincoln, near Hodgenville (C3); buried here, Daniel Boone, in Frankfort (C2).

On the first Saturday in May, mint julep consumption soars at Churchill Downs (C3) in Louisville. Welcome to the Kentucky Derby. Maybe this event contributes to the fact that Kentucky leads the nation in the distillation of whiskey.

Mammoth Cave National Park (B4) in Kentucky contains the world's most extensive cave system—300 winding miles.

America's first interstate highway was the Wilderness Road Daniel Boone and others cut through the Cumberland Gap (E4). 200,000 early Americans passed through on their way to settle the West.

Cumberland Falls (D4), in Daniel Boone National Forest is the only falls in America where moonbows—nighttime rainbows—can regularly be seen.

Oak Ridge, TN (E5) is the site of the oldest nuclear reactor in existence, built to fuel the Manhattan Project and still working.

Indiana Tourist Information:
317/232-8860
Tennessee Tourist Information:
615/741-2158

So. Indiana Road Information:
317/232-8298
Tennessee Road Information:
615/741-3181

The map on this page is 250x250 miles.

↓ pg. 64

pg. 105
pg. 108
pg. 99

INDIANA · KENTUCKY · TENNESSEE · OHIO

Indianapolis · Cincinnati · Louisville · Lexington · Frankfort · Evansville · Nashville · Knoxville · Terre Haute · Bloomington · Bowling Green · Hopkinsville · Clarksville · Owensboro · Henderson

A   B   C   D   E

WEST VIRGINIA

VIRGINIA

NORTH CAROLINA

Wellston Pomeroy Middleport Grantsville Huttonsville Brandywine Shenandoah Natl. Park Harrisonburg
Jackson Ripley Spencer Millstone Hacker Valley Holly River Island Harper Bridgewater Ruckersville
Point Pleasant Sutton Monterville Bartow Monterey
Gallipolis Waterloo Buffalo Webster Springs Cass Scenic Railroad State Park Dunmore Staunton Charlottesville Monticello Home of Thomas Jefferson
Vesuvius Clendenin Clay Cowen Linwood Tea Creek Frost Staunton Waynesboro
Ironton Hurricane Nitro Dunbar Charleston Summersville Cranberry Day Run Marlinton Rimel Goshen Greenville
Ashland Choctopoake St. Albans Belva Richwood Cranberry Glades Botanical Area Mill Point Pocahontas Warm Springs Lovingston
Huntington Milton West Hamlin Marmet Cedar Grove Hawks Nest Ansted Falling Spring Watoga Hot Springs Clifton Forge Lexington Buena Vista Buckingham
Wayne Beech Fork Racine Charmco Rupert Covington Longdale Amherst Appomattox Court House Natl. Hist. Park
Fort Gay Chapmanville Oak Hill Babcock Rainelle Lewisburg White Sulphur Springs Greenbrier Eagle Rock Natural Bridge Cave Mtn. Lake Lynchburg Appomattox Holliday Lake Pamplin
Louisa Chief Logan Naoma Sprague Alderson Organ Cave Sweet Springs Bedford
Dunlow Mabscott Beckley Pickaway Moncove Lake New Castle Salem
Kermit Man Shady Spring Hinton Union Pipestem
Williamson Mountain View Pineville Mullens Camp Creek Roanoke Altavista Brookneal Red Hill Patrick Henry Nat. Mem.
Jenny Wiley Prestonsburg Rich Creek Pearisburg Blacksburg Booker T. Washington Natl. Mon. Gretna
Pikeville Iaeger Welch Keystone Princeton Christiansburg Rocky Mount Staunton River J.H. Kerr Res.
Garrett Panther Bradshaw War Bluefield Radford Dublin Halifax S. Boston
Grundy Tazewell Bland Pulaski Clayton Lake Floyd Twin Ridge Chatham
Breaks Interstate Park Claypool Hill Wytheville Rocky Knob Fairy Stone Philpott Lake Martinsville Danville Roxboro
Jenkins Clintwood Hungry Mother Hillsville Woolwine Ridgeway Yanceyville
Whitesburg Pound Dante Marion Stuart Eden
Norton Lebanon St. Paul Hurricane Galax Madison Reidsville Marlow
Lynch Appalachia Bolton Mount Rogers Natl. Rec. Area Independence Mount Airy Hanging Rock Burlington Graham Hillsborough Durham Chapel Hill
Big Stone Gap Abingdon Beartree Grayson Highlands Dobson Walnut Cove Guilford Court House Natl. Military Park Greensboro pg. 118
Pennington Gap Bristol Damascus New River Twin Oaks Cherry Lane Pilot Mtn. Winston-Salem High Point Archdale Pittsboro Siler City
Jonesville Kingsport Gate City Jefferson Stone Mountain Elkin Lexington Thomasville Asheboro Sanford
Johnson City Elizabethton Boone North Wilkesboro Brooks Cross Roads Mocksville North Carolina Zoological Park
Erwin Roan Mtn. Elk Park Blowing Rock Taylorsville Statesville Salisbury Biscoe Carthage
Greeneville Andrew Johnson Natl. Hist. Site Bald Mtn. Ingalls Pineola Lenoir Lake Hickory High Rock Lake Troy Southern Pines Aberdeen
Morristown Swiss Spruce Pine Linville Falls Table Rock Mtn. Hickory Newton Mooresville Morrow Mountain World Golf Hall of Fame
Hot Springs Mt. Mitchell Crabtree Meadows Morganton Kannapolis Albemarle
Asheville Biltmore Estate Old Fort Black Mountain Lincolnton Concord Norwood Pee Dee River
Great Smoky Mtns. Natl. Park pg. 117 Charlotte

↑ pg. 76

Appalachian Facts:

The Appalachian Trail, running from Mt. Katahdin, ME to Springer Mountain, GA, is the most hiked trail in America.

The mountains truly are the backbone of the East. The range runs clear from the Gulf of St. Lawrence to Alabama.

Author Washington Irving (who lived when the westernmost boundary of the country was this mountain range) proposed the nation be named the United States of Appalachia.

Thomas Jefferson's beloved Monticello (E1) is also a monument to his genius. Besides writing the Declaration of Independence and designing the campus of the University of Virginia, our brilliant third president was an inventor, too.

Where Lee surrendered— Appomattox Court House (E2).

Peerless Drives—the 105-mile Skyline Drive in Shenandoah National Park (E1) and the Blue Ridge Parkway (D3) through Virginia and North Carolina. At 469 miles, the latter is considered the longest scenic drive in the world.

The Vanderbilts called it home; everyone else calls it the world's largest private residence. How many rooms does Biltmore (B5) have? See page 156.

Kentucky Tourist Information: 502/564-7281

Virginia Tourist Information: 804/786-4484

Kentucky Road Information: 502/564-4473

Virginia Road Information: 1-800-367-7623

The map on this page is 250x250 miles.

N

← pg. 53

Underground Tennessee—in Sweetwater you'll find the Craighead Caverns (E1). Go down 300 feet to see the Lost Sea, the world's largest underground lake.

Chattanooga Choo-Choo: The steepest passenger railway in the world (72.7% grade) climbs Lookout Mountain (D2).

The local lore says "When Lookout Mountain has its cap on, it will rain in six hours."

Near Lynchburg, TN (C2) you'll find a local landmark which has been operating since 1866. Tennessee passed the first prohibition laws in the US, making it a misdemeanor to sell alcoholic beverages in taverns and stores. No more, though some counties are dry. What's the landmark? See page 156.

Thou must see ... the world's largest Ten Commandments, laid out on a hill near Murphy, NC (E1).

Alabama still sings the blues—Florence (A2) hosts the W.C. Handy Festival each August.

The Alabama Space and Rocket Center in Huntsville is the planet's largest space museum, as well as the home of the famed summer Space Camp.

An awful lot of Alabama's success in agriculture can be traced to the Tuskegee Institute's celebrated alumnus, George Washington Carver, who found nearly 300 uses for the peanut and over 100 sweet potato products (D5).

Need a rug? Dalton, GA (D2) features over 200 carpet mills, earning it, naturally, the title "Carpet Capital of the World."

The map on this page is 250x250 miles.

↑ pg. 78

Charleston, SC *(E4)* is everybody's idea of the "Old South"; since 1931 historical preservation laws have been on the books and entire districts of the town recall an era of 150–200 years ago. Thankfully the city's southern charm survived not only the Civil War but the earthquake of 1886—strongest felt on the East Coast, and the 135-mph winds of Hurricane Hugo in October 1989.

America's only tea plantation is in South Carolina, off the coast of Charleston.

Tourists are welcome in Oyotunji *(D4)*—where villagers live and practice the ways of a Nigerian village.

Another strong reminder of the African heritage of local residents is the unique Gullah dialect, a kind of English spoken only by residents of the Sea Islands.

Want to send a gift that lasts … it seems forever? Stop by Claxton, GA *(C5)*. They've been baking fruitcake there since the early 1900s and now turn out over 6 million pounds a year.

Oliver Hardy was born in Harlem, GA *(C3)*. (Stan Laurel was born in England.)

Which state (no peeking!) is the largest east of the Mississippi? *See page 156.*

South Carolina Tourist Information:
803/734-0127
Georgia Tourist Information:
404/656-3590

South Carolina Road Information:
803/737-1030
Georgia Road Information:
404/656-5267

The map on this page is 250x250 miles.

↑ pg. 55

Ship Island (singular) (A4) has actually been plural (East and West) since 1969 thanks to Hurricane Camille.

Montgomery, AL was the home of Jefferson Davis and a logical choice for what honor? See page 156. The state nickname is "The Heart of Dixie."

A more recent local hero: Dr. Martin Luther King, Jr. began his involvement in the civil rights movement here at his Dexter Avenue Baptist Church.

In Enterprise, AL (D2) you'll see a Boll Weevil Monument—grateful farmers erected it in 1919 to thank the insect for destroying their cotton crops, forcing them to diversify into more profitable pursuits, especially growing tobacco.

A drive under the Mobile River in the Bankhead Tunnel (B3) will take you through the longest underwater vehicular tunnel in the US.

Slip across the border into Florida. Pensacola (C3) is a particularly historical site. It's been settled since 1559 and has seen 17 changes of government.

Maybe those settlers have stuck around because of what locals call the whitest beach in the world, along Gulf Islands National Seashore (B4).

Gulf goodies don't get better than the oysters at Apalachicola, FL (E4).

Alabama Tourist Information: 205/242-4169

Alabama Road Information: 205/242-4378

The map on this page is 250x250 miles.

ALABAMA

Gulf of Mexico

★ Montgomery

Meridian · Demopolis · Selma · Eufaula · Dothan · Mobile · Pensacola · Panama City · Biloxi · Pascagoula · Ocean Springs · Waynesboro · Jackson · Monroeville · Andalusia · Enterprise · Troy · Greenville · Brewton · Atmore · Crestview · De Funiak Springs · Marianna

kilom. 20 40 60 80

miles 10 20 30 40 50

Stunning coastal scenery—you'll never forget a visit to St. Simons Island, Jekyll Island or Cumberland Island National Seashore *(D1)*.

The Seminole Indians named the Okefenokee Swamp *(C2)*—it means "Land of the Trembling Earth" and, sure enough, there's not much here that's stable. Islands of peat float on the surface of the swamp. Native residents include hundreds of species of birds, as well as amphibians, fish, alligators, bears and bobcats.

Jacksonville, FL holds a US record. Care to guess? *See page 156.*

The Castillo de San Marcos *(E3)* near St. Augustine marks the northernmost reach of Spain's east coast empire in the New World. Another interesting local attraction is the Tragedy in US History Museum. If you like gruesome memorabilia, this is the place.

In any given year, there are at least 10 deaths by lightning in Florida.

The map on this page is 250x250 miles.

N

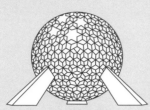

Spaceship Earth, at Walt Disney World's Epcot Center.

More than just "MOM"—survey the collection at the *Tattoo Art Museum,* San Francisco, CA.

A modern art masterpiece housing modern art masterpieces—the *Solomon R. Guggenheim Museum,* New York City—designed by Frank Lloyd Wright in 1956.

America's favorite pop plaything—visit the *Barbie Doll Hall of Fame,* Palo Alto, CA.

USAtlas Amusement Parks & Museums

Here's our highly selective list of reasons to stop the car, get out and walk around.

The Most Popular Amusement Parks
In a class by itself: *Walt Disney World,* Lake Buena Vista, FL—home of the Magic Kingdom, Epcot Center and Disney-MGM Studios.

Imagine the population of the entire state of California descending on the Orlando area—that's what happens year in and year out—over 25 million visitors. That means every day about 70,000 other people join you here. The record for one day was 92,000. Expect to spend several days (and several hundred dollars) and avoid Christmas, Easter and as much of summer vacation as possible.

Here are 10 other places at least one million people visit each year:
Coney Island, Brooklyn, NY
Marineland, Marineland, FL
Sea World, Orlando, FL
Busch Gardens, Tampa, FL
Cedar Point, Sandusky, OH
Six Flags Over Texas, Arlington, TX
Universal Studios, Universal City, CA
Knott's Berry Farm, Buena Park, CA
Disneyland, Anaheim, CA
Sea World, San Diego, CA

Local Color
Some are amusement parks, some are just amusing:
Hersheypark—a chocaholic fantasy—Hershey, PA
Sesame Place—your 2-year old can tell you all about it—Langhorne, PA
Paul Bunyan Amusement Center—if you like large lumberjacks—Brainerd, MN
Dollywood—owned and operated by Dolly Parton—Pigeon Forge, TN
Bedrock City—yabba dabba doo time—Custer, SD
Dogpatch, USA—in the heart of the Ozarks—Dogpatch, AR

For Purists
We turned up the following bone-rattling authentic wooden roller coasters:
The Cyclone, Coney Island, Brooklyn, NY
The Comet, Crystal Beach, Niagara Falls, NY

The Comet, Hersheypark, Hershey, PA
Thunderbolt, Kennywood Park, West Mifflin, PA
Gemini, Cedar Point, Sandusky, OH
The Beast, Kings Island, Cincinnati, OH
Mister Twister, Elitch Gardens, Denver, CO
The Giant Dipper, Santa Cruz Beach Boardwalk, Santa Cruz, CA

Enough Hot Dogs and Lemonade?
Museums offer their own excitement (and better food!)—ask the 4 million people a year who visit New York's Metropolitan Museum of Art. For an art adventure, though, try some of this country's smaller gems, like the Guggenheim in NYC, the Arthur Sackler Gallery in Washington, DC or the Isabella Stewart Gardner Museum in Boston.

If the kids are rebelling, go for science and industry instead:
Boston Children's Museum, Boston, MA
Computer Museum, Boston, MA
Corning Museum of Glass, Corning, NY
Longwood Gardens, Kennett Square, PA
Franklin Institute, Philadelphia, PA
Henry Ford Museum and Greenfield Village, Dearborn, MI
Children's Museum, Indianapolis, IN
Field Museum of Natural History, Chicago, IL
Museum of Science and Industry, Chicago, IL
The Exploratorium, San Francisco, CA
Pacific Science Center, Seattle, WA

For Specialists and Fanatics
Any old museum can display a $40 million Van Gogh, but how many contain complete sets of Tupperware?
Museum of Cartoon Art, Port Chester, NY
Mushroom Museum, Kennett Square, PA
Tupperware Museum, Orlando, FL
World of Rubber, Akron, OH
Popcorn Museum, Marion, OH
Museum of Magic, Marshall, MI
Circus World Museum, Baraboo, WI
McDonald's Museum, Des Plaines, IL
Bowling Hall of Fame, St. Louis, MO
Bible Museum, Eureka Springs, AR
Voodoo Museum, New Orleans, LA
Barbed Wire Museum, La Crosse, KS
Liberace Museum, Las Vegas, NV
Max Factor Museum, Los Angeles, CA
Barbie Doll Hall of Fame, Palo Alto, CA
Tattoo Art Museum, San Francisco, CA

A   B   C   D   E

Tarpon
Springs
ALT
19   Oldsmar
Dunedin
Clearwater
Largo   693 688 275 92
Indian Rocks Beach
Madeira Beach
St. Petersburg

pg. 122
Tampa

41— 275 301 39
Busch
Gardens
580
618
98
75

Winter 540
Haven Bok
Tower
Gardens
Bartow
17
Frostproof
—ALT

Lakeland
92 Plant
City 60
Brandon
Bradley

Lake
Kissimmee
Lake
Kissimmee 60
Lake
Wales

Lake
Weohyakapka

Riverview
Apollo
Beach
Ruskin
Piney Pt.

37

Fort
Meade
Bowling
Green
Wauchula
Pioneer
Park Zolfo
Springs 66

98
27
64
27
634
Highlands
Hammock

Avon
Park
17
Sebring
98
Lake
Istokpoga

1

De Soto
Natl. Mem.
Holmes Beach
Anna Maria Is.
Longboat Key
Longboat
Key 758

275 41
19   301
Parrish 62 Duette
Palmetto
Lake
Manatee 64
Bradenton
Ringling
Museums
Sarasota
Oscar
Scherer

17
Gardner

Myakka
City 70
Arcadia
72 Nocatee

Lake
Placid

70

F L O R I D A

2

Diesta Key
Casey Key
Laurel
Venice
41 North
775 Port
Englewood 776

681 75
17
Port
Charlotte
Punta
Gorda 31

Babcock

Caloosahatchee River
41
78

La
Belle
29
Tice
Fort
Myers
884
Lehigh
Acres
80
29
82

Toll
Bridge
Gasparilla Is.
Boca Grande
Bokeelia
Cayo
Costa
Island
Captiva
Island
Sanibel
Island

Charlotte
Harbor
767
Pine
Island Toll
Bridge
Sanibel

867
865
Cape
Coral
Koreshan St.
Hist. Site
Bonita
Springs
Bonita
Beach

Big
Cypress
Swamp

3

Naples
75
84
84 · 75
41
Collier-
Seminole
951
Marco
Island
Cape
Romano

*Gulf of
Mexico*

4

5

Dry
Tortugas

Fort Jefferson
Natl. Mon.

Marquesas
Keys

kilom. 20   40   60   80
miles 10   20   30   40   50

**The map on this page
is 250x250 miles.**

There are more species of fish in Florida's rivers, lakes, everglades and coastal waters than anywhere else in the world.

You'll understand the influence the Greek sponge fishers had on Tarpon Springs *(C1)* when you see the Saint Nicholas Greek Orthodox Cathedral, a replica of the Hagia Sophia in Instabul.

Tampa, FL is humid all right. In August, average humidity levels exceed 90%. When it's also 80°-plus F, this is one place you don't want to be caught with a busted air conditioner in your car.

Art in Sarasota *(D2)*—the world's most important collection of Rubens and other priceless works in the Ringling Museum of Art. Lest you think John Ringling forgot those who made him his fortune, there is a Circus Museum here too.

Maybe Thomas Edison came up with his famous quote about genius, inspiration and perspiration here. He "wintered" in which town? *See page 156.*

The beach in Fort Myers *(E2)* is renowned simply for being so pleasant—no undertow, no steep coastal shelf and home to schools of friendly porpoises.

Sanibel and Captiva Islands *(E3)* are justly famous for their spectacular natural attractions and apparently endless variety of seashells.

Florida Tourist Information:
904/487-1462

Florida Road Information:
813/272-2211

→ pg. 80

N

It's only been about 225 years since the British conquered the province and the French settlers. That explains the Québecois license plate—"Je me souviens"—"I remember." The Meech Lake Accord was only the latest in a series of bids by Québec for some semblance of independence from English-speaking Canada.

Canada's oldest city, the city of Québec, was founded by Samuel de Champlain in 1608. Its residents are 95% French-speaking, and this is the only walled city in North America.

Montreal is Canada's largest and the world's second-largest what? *See page 156.* (Hint: Only Paris is larger.) The town is as much fun to visit in the winter as it is in the summer, thanks to nearly 80 miles of underground shopping/pedestrian passageways.

Vieux Montreal (the old quarter) is probably the densest concentration of 17th- and 18th-century architecture in North America. The beautiful Notre Dame de Montreal cathedral is worth a special visit.

Only New York has a busier port on the Eastern seaboard—ships come to Montreal via the St. Lawrence Seaway.

The coldest it ever got in New England: A bone-chilling -50° F on 30 December 1933 in Bloomfield, VT *(D5)*.

Québec Tourist Information:
514/873-2015

Québec Road Information:
514/873-4121

The map on this page is 250x250 miles.

↓ pg. 72

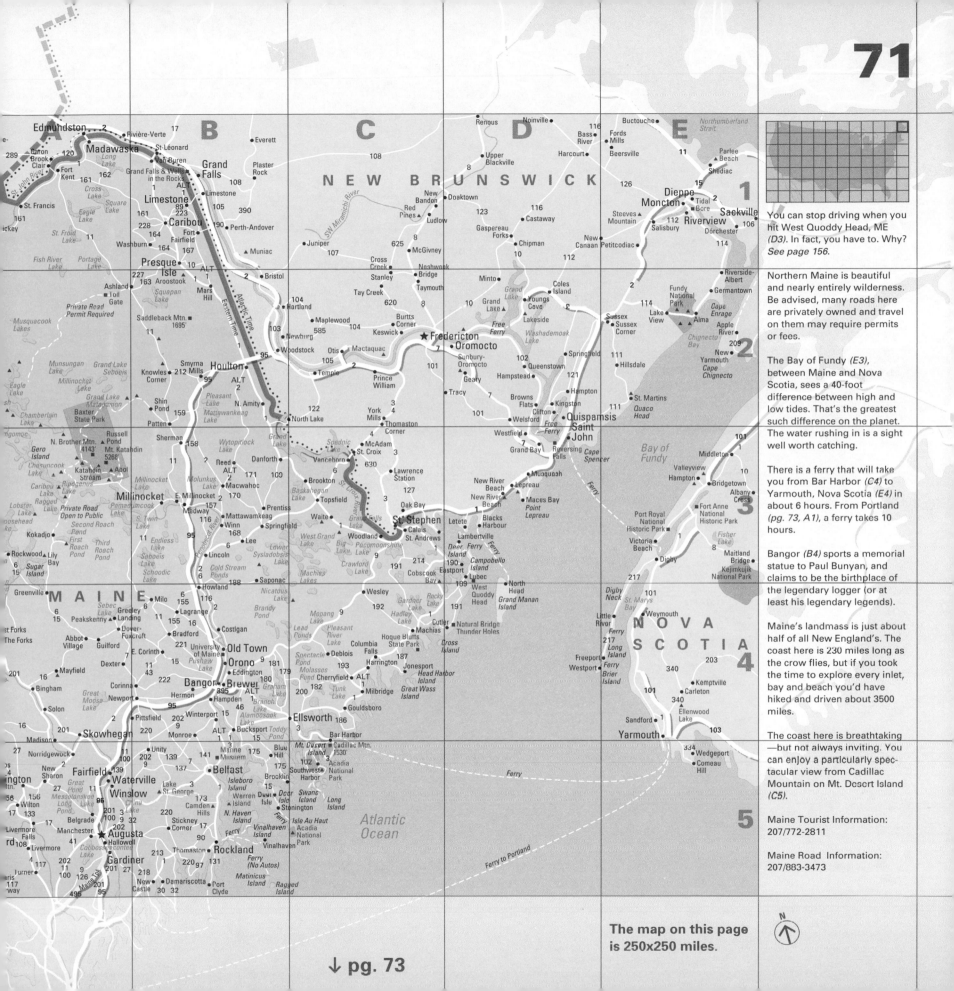

You can stop driving when you hit West Quoddy Head, ME (*D3*). In fact, you have to. Why? *See page 156.*

Northern Maine is beautiful and nearly entirely wilderness. Be advised, many roads here are privately owned and travel on them may require permits or fees.

The Bay of Fundy (*E3*), between Maine and Nova Scotia, sees a 40-foot difference between high and low tides. That's the greatest such difference on the planet. The water rushing in is a sight well worth catching.

There is a ferry that will take you from Bar Harbor (*C4*) to Yarmouth, Nova Scotia (*E4*) in about 6 hours. From Portland (*pg. 73, A1*), a ferry takes 10 hours.

Bangor (*B4*) sports a memorial statue to Paul Bunyan, and claims to be the birthplace of the legendary logger (or at least his legendary legends).

Maine's landmass is just about half of all New England's. The coast here is 230 miles long as the crow flies, but if you took the time to explore every inlet, bay and beach you'd have hiked and driven about 3500 miles.

The coast here is breathtaking —but not always inviting. You can enjoy a particularly spectacular view from Cadillac Mountain on Mt. Desert Island (*C5*).

Maine Tourist Information: 207/772-2811

Maine Road Information: 207/883-3473

The map on this page is 250x250 miles.

↓ **pg. 73**

↑ **pg. 70**

← **pg. 59**

An excellent art collection—the Munson-Williams Proctor Institute in Utica.

The National Baseball Hall of Fame and Museum in Cooperstown, NY (B4) is the mecca for fans of our national pasttime.

Every New England state can boast about its fall foliage, but Vermont in late September or early October is special.

Stowe, VT (D1), opened in the 1920s, was the first major ski resort in the US.

Which of the New England states were not among the original 13 colonies? See page 156.

Loons and tourists flock to the New Hampshire Lakes Region—even more popular since On Golden Pond.

Mt. Washington (E1) has claimed to be the windiest spot in the world since 1934, when the fastest winds on record, 231 mph, were clocked here.

Slow down—Connecticut had the nation's first speed limits in 1901: 12 mph in town, 15 mph in the country.

New Hampshire Tourist Information:
603/271-2343
Vermont Tourist Information:
802/828-3236
Connecticut Tourist Information:
203/258-4290

New Hampshire Road Information:
603/485-9526
Vermont Road Information:
802/828-2648
Connecticut Road Information:
203/566-5900

The map on this page is 250x250 miles.

↓ **pg. 74**

pg. 113

A   **B**   **C**   **D**   **E**

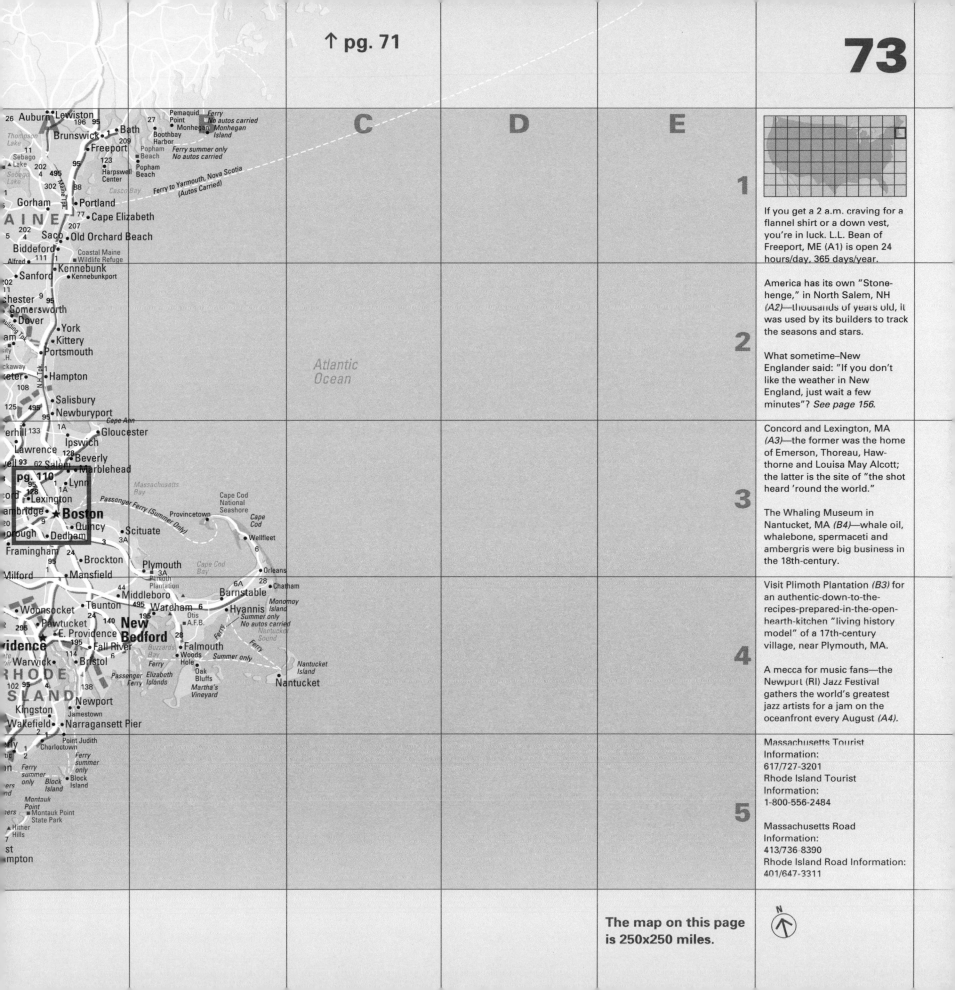

1

26 • Auburn • Lewiston
196 • 95
• Bath
Brunswick • 1
209
• Freeport
Pemaquid   Ferry
Point   No autos carried
27 • Boothbay   • Monhegan
Harbor   Island
Popham   Ferry summer only
• Beach   No autos carried
• Popham
Beach
95   123
• Harpswell
Center
Thompson
Lake
11
Sebago
▲Lake   202
4   495
Sebago
Lake
1
302   88
Casco Bay
Ferry to Yarmouth, Nova Scotia
(Autos Carried)

• Gorham
MAINE
77 • Portland
• Cape Elizabeth
202
4   207
• Saco • Old Orchard Beach
5
Biddeford •
Alfred • 111   1
• Sanford   Coastal Maine
• Kennebunk ■ Wildlife Refuge
• Kennebunkport

Atlantic
Ocean

2

02
11
chester   9   95
• Somersworth
• Dover • York
am   • Kittery
sity • Portsmouth
N.H.
ckaway
ter • Hampton
108
• Salisbury
• 495 • Newburyport
95
Cape Ann

3

erhill 133
1A • Gloucester
• Ipswich
Lawrence 128
ll 93   62 Salem • Beverly
• Marblehead
pg. 110
95   1 • Lynn
128   1A
ord • Lexington
ambridge • ★Boston
Passenger Ferry (Summer Only)
• Quincy
ough • Dedham   • Scituate
3   3A
Massachusetts
Bay
Cape Cod
National
Seashore
• Provincetown
Cape
Cod
• Wellfleet
6

Concord and Lexington, MA
(A3)—the former was the home
of Emerson, Thoreau, Haw-
thorne and Louisa May Alcott;
the latter is the site of "the shot
heard 'round the world."

The Whaling Museum in
Nantucket, MA *(B4)*—whale oil,
whalebone, spermaceti and
ambergris were big business in
the 18th-century.

4

Framingham
95   24
1 • Brockton
Milford • Mansfield
• Plymouth
Plimoth
3A
Plantation
Cape Cod
Bay
• Orleans
44
• Middleboro   6A   28
• Taunton   495 • Wareham   • Barnstable
• Woonsocket
24   140   195   6 • Chatham
• Pawtucket
295
• E. Providence   New
idence   195   Bedford
• Fall River   28
Warwick • Bristol   114 • Falmouth
RHODE
ISLAND
102 95   4   138
• Kingston
• Newport
Ferry
Hyannis
Otis
A.F.B.
Monomoy
Island
Summer only
No autos carried
Nantucket
Sound
Buzzards
Bay   • Woods
• Hole
Ferry   Summer only
Passenger   Elizabeth
Ferry   Islands
• Oak
Bluffs
Martha's
Vineyard
Nantucket
Island
• Nantucket
• Jamestown
• Wakefield
• Narragansett Pier
2

Visit Plimoth Plantation *(B3)* for
an authentic-down-to-the-
recipes-prepared-in-the-open-
hearth-kitchen "living history
model" of a 17th-century
village, near Plymouth, MA.

A mecca for music fans—the
Newport (RI) Jazz Festival
gathers the world's greatest
jazz artists for a jam on the
oceanfront every August *(A4)*.

5

ly
tip
on
ers
nd
Point Judith
• Charlootown
Ferry
summer
only
Ferry
summer
only • Block
Island
Block
Island
Montauk
Point
■ Montauk Point
State Park
▲ Hither
Hills
st
mpton

If you get a 2 a.m. craving for a
flannel shirt or a down vest,
you're in luck. L.L. Bean of
Freeport, ME *(A1)* is open 24
hours/day, 365 days/year.

America has its own "Stone-
henge," in North Salem, NH
(A2)—thousands of years old, it
was used by its builders to track
the seasons and stars.

What sometime–New
Englander said: "If you don't
like the weather in New
England, just wait a few
minutes"? *See page 156.*

Massachusetts Tourist
Information:
617/727-3201
Rhode Island Tourist
Information:
1-800-556-2484

Massachusetts Road
Information:
413/736-8390
Rhode Island Road Information:
401/647-3311

**The map on this page
is 250x250 miles.**

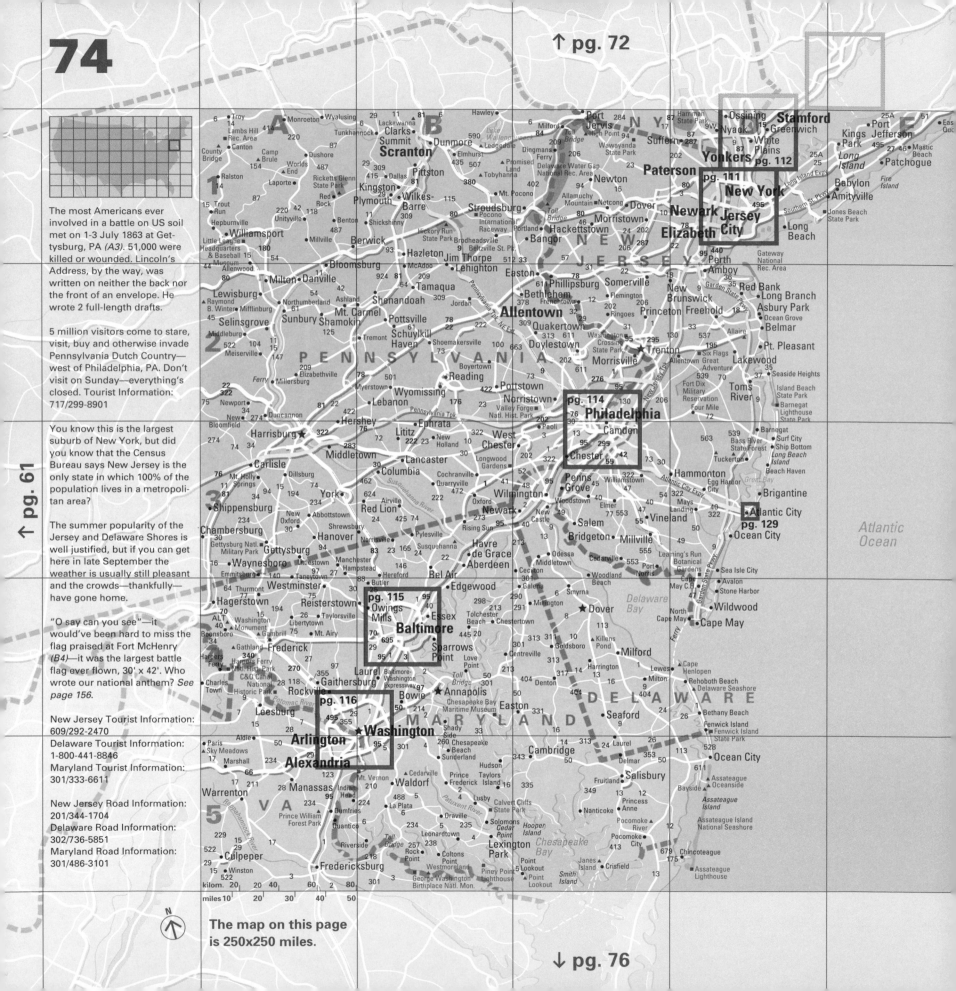

The most Americans ever involved in a battle on US soil met on 1-3 July 1863 at Gettysburg, PA (A3). 51,000 were killed or wounded. Lincoln's Address, by the way, was written on neither the back nor the front of an envelope. He wrote 2 full-length drafts.

5 million visitors come to stare, visit, buy and otherwise invade Pennsylvania Dutch Country—west of Philadelphia, PA. Don't visit on Sunday—everything's closed. Tourist Information: 717/299-8901

You know this is the largest suburb of New York, but did you know that the Census Bureau says New Jersey is the only state in which 100% of the population lives in a metropolitan area?

The summer popularity of the Jersey and Delaware Shores is well justified, but if you can get here in late September the weather is usually still pleasant and the crowds—thankfully—have gone home.

"O say can you see"—it would've been hard to miss the flag praised at Fort McHenry (B4)—it was the largest battle flag ever flown, 30' x 42'. Who wrote our national anthem? See page 156.

New Jersey Tourist Information: 609/292-2470

Delaware Tourist Information: 1-800-441-8846
Maryland Tourist Information: 301/333-6611

New Jersey Road Information: 201/344-1704
Delaware Road Information: 302/736-5851
Maryland Road Information: 301/486-3101

← pg. 61

pg. 72

pg. 111

pg. 112

pg. 114

pg. 115

pg. 116

pg. 129

↓ pg. 76

The map on this page is 250x250 miles.

USAtlas Architecture

Few countries match the US for diversity of architecture. Herewith, a few examples that are worth a stop on your travels:

Excess

How better to represent the wealth and power of "The Gilded Age"? The Vanderbilt railroad fortune built at least two of America's most spectacular mansions—the *Biltmore Estate* near Asheville, NC; and the *Breakers*, a palatial "summer cottage" in Newport, RI.

Of course, there's *Hearst Castle* in San Simeon, CA—to this day not all the furnishings have been unpacked and placed. The splendid buildings were designed by Julia Morgan, who left more modest but equally significant houses and buildings all over Berkeley and San Francisco.

Peculiarities

America's love affair with royalty—or maybe fairy tales—can be found in Logan County, OH, where 2 brothers built castles over 100 years ago; and at *Vikingsholm Castle* near South Lake Tahoe, CA—a spectacular rendition of Scandinavian architecture.

The *House on the Rock* in Spring Green, WI, well, redefines "house." Built within and atop a chimney rock, the house features a 140-foot glass "Infinity Room" jutting out over the landscape that is emphatically *not* for those who fear heights.

Beauties

The Victorian "painted ladies" of San Francisco are topped only by the town of Cape May, NJ—all of which, deservedly so, is designated a historical landmark. Visit for Victorian Week in October.

Mission San Xavier del Bac, near Tucson, AZ—a near-perfect vision of mission simplicity and Spanish Baroque. Santa Barbara, CA boasts similar simple dignity.

Thomas Jefferson's tributes to classicism: *Monticello* and the *University of Virginia*.

The Chrysler Building, NYC.

The Art Deco hotels of Miami Beach.

Modern Marvels

How it should be done—I have high praise and warm thoughts for these buildings designed by Louis I. Kahn:
Library, Phillips Exeter Academy, Exeter, NH.
Yale Center for British Art, New Haven, CT.
Richards Laboratory for Research, University of Pennsylvania, Philadelphia, PA.
Kimbell Art Museum, Fort Worth, TX.
Salk Institute, La Jolla, CA.

High praise, too, for Cummins Engine Corp. of Columbus, IN which has funded the design of public buildings, furthered the idea of corporate civic-mindedness and yielded architecture by I.M. Pei, Eero Saarinen, Eliel Saarinen, Cesar Pelli and others.

Significant Scrapers

The 20th century skyline is summarized in buildings like Mies van der Rohe's *Seagram's Building*, NYC—the original "glass tower"; the *John Hancock Tower* in Chicago and San Francisco's peculiar *Transamerica Pyramid*—which sprouted ears when it was discovered the elevator shafts had to go somewhere! One of my favorites—the 1932 *Philadelphia Savings Fund Society* building, a classic example of "form follows function," built decades before International became the skyscraper style of choice.

Tallest Towers

Chicago's got most of them: the *First National Bank*—world's tallest bank building at 850 feet; world's tallest "multi-use skyscraper"—1127 feet—*John Hancock Center*; and the *Sears Tower*—the world's tallest building, period (not counting radio antennas!), at 1454 feet.

The *US Capitol Building* is 287 feet high. By law no building in Washington, DC can stand taller.

Old World Architecture

All of America is not steel and glass; consider: "Little Bavaria" in Frankenmuth, MI; and on the palm of Michigan's mitten, Holland.
The *Old Globe Theatre* brought back for a command performance in Odessa, TX.
London Bridge standing tall in Lake Havasu, AZ.
Solvang, CA—a postcard-perfect miniature re-creation of Denmark.

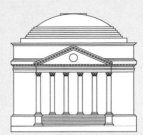

America's Classic Architect—Thomas Jefferson's *Rotunda* at the University of Virginia is acclaimed as architecturally perfect.

Mission San Xavier del Bac, near Tucson, AZ

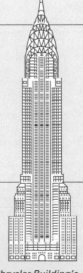

The *Chrysler Building's* distinctive steel crown was the topper which won it the title of world's tallest building in 1930—for a few short months.

A state legislature has been active in Virginia longer than anywhere else in the Western Hemisphere. Can you dust off that fourth grade social studies text and recall the name of the ruling body of Colonial Virginia? *See page 156*.

When it comes to living history, you just can't beat Colonial Williamsburg *(B2)*: 1.2 million visitors annually, and authentic down to the doorknobs, flower beds and herb gardens. Don't rush; see it all.

Virginian settlers celebrated the first Thanksgiving at Berkeley Plantation *(B2)* almost two years before the Pilgrims landed.

The coast of North Carolina is infamous for bad weather and nefarious locals. The Cape Hatteras Lighthouse *(D4)*, at 208 feet, is the tallest in the US. It wasn't standing to greet Blackbeard—he of the 13 wives and the unaccounted-for millions in plundered treasure—who literally lost his head nearby in 1718. Today's would-be pirates can learn dastardly-doing at Captain Sinbad's Pirate School in nearby Beaufort *(C5)*.

Set a better example for the kids by taking them to the Wright Brothers Memorial *(D3)* at Kitty Hawk instead.

For the best of the Cape Hatteras experience, ferry to Ocracoke Island *(D4)* and take in the incredible beauty of the first US National Seashore.

North Carolina Tourist Information:
1-800-847-4862

North Carolina Road Information:
919/733-3861

← pg. 63

VIRGINIA

NORTH CAROLINA

Richmond

Atlantic Ocean

The map on this page is 250×250 miles.

N

USAtlas **Calendar of Events— A Selective List for Travelers**

Thirty days hath September ...
And here's even more stuff to try to remember.
Whether days twenty-eight, three-oh or thirty-one,
each month has events we hope you'll find fun.

Call ahead and confirm all information. Dates,
times and events are subject to change.

January
The Winter Carnival, Saint Paul, MN: The snow
sculpture contest is great!

February
Daytona 500, Daytona Beach, FL: Fanatics flock to
this grandaddy of stock car races.

Mardi Gras, New Orleans, LA: Lots of cities have
Mardi Gras celebrations—but why consider
anywhere else?

National Date Festival, Indio, CA: *Arabian Nights*
style—ostrich and camel races, and plenty of dates.

March
Buzzard Day, in Hinkley, OH; and the swallows
return to the Mission—San Juan Capistrano, CA.

April
Boston Marathon, Boston, MA: Patriots Day
celebrates the footsore heroes of Heartbreak Hill.

National Whistling Convention, Lewisburg, NC:
You know how to whistle, don't you?

May
The Kentucky Derby, Louisville, KY: Once in your
life, run for the roses—you'll never forget it.

Cinco de Mayo Celebrations, Los Angeles, CA: The
Mexican Revolution is celebrated here and in other
Hispanic centers across the country. Olé.

June
Superman Festival, Metropolis, IL: What else when
the newspaper is The Daily Planet and where a
phone booth accepts calls to the Man of Steel?

National Ragtime and Traditional Jazz Festival, St.
Louis, MO: Music doesn't get better than this.

July
Fourth of July Parade, Bristol, RI: The oldest
Independence Day parade in the US. .

Harbor Festival, New York, NY: Fabulous fireworks,
the world's greatest ethnic food and even the
occasional Tall Ship.

Hemingway Days Festival, Key West, FL: They
imitate his writing, his fishing, his beard—but
mostly his legendary ability to enjoy himself.

August
Elvis International Tribute Week—Memphis, TN:
The ultimate *Graceland* visit. Stay 'til the end for
the culminating candlelight procession.

National Hot Air Balloon Races, Indianola, IA: The
prettiest sight in a blue summer sky.

September
Festival Acadiens, Lafayette, LA: Celebrate the
delicious, exciting, spicy history of the Bayou.

October
*National Wild Turkey Calling Contest and Turkey
Trot*, Yellville, AR: The name of the town alone
should convince you this is the real McCoy.

Whole Enchilada Fiesta, Las Cruces, NM: You gotta
have a gimmick—this one claims the world's
biggest enchilada.

November
Macy's Thanksgiving Day Parade, New York, NY:
Don't you want to see the Rockettes in person once
in your life?

Doo Dah Parade, Pasadena, CA: A Briefcase Drill
Team and a Lawn Chair Squad, too—a far cry from
the Tournament of Roses Parade it spoofs.

December
If you can't be or plan not to be home for
Christmas, the lights and delights of the following
are especially suited to the season:
New York, NY
Cape May, NJ
Savannah, GA
Santa Fe, NM
and, believe it or not,
Niagara Falls, NY

Talkin' turkey in Yellville, AR,
in October.

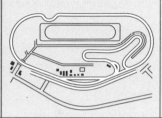

The Daytona 500 is the world's
largest stock car race.

National Hot Air Balloon Races,
Indianola, IA; if you can't make
it in August, capture some of the
color at the *National Balloon
Museum.*

Frigates, fireworks, festivals
and food—Fourth of July in
New York Harbor.

↑ pg. 65

The insect-eating Venus flytrap, a blood cousin of the carnivore of Little Shop of Horrors fame, grows wild one place in the world—near Hampstead, NC (B1).

Since Calabash, NC (B2) has only 200 residents and over 22 sea-food restaurants, you can bet that most diners are coming in from out of town, drawn to the Calabash-style fried seafood famed up and down the entire East Coast.

Myrtle Beach, SC (A2) is a prime vacation destination. It won't swallow you whole like Disney World or Atlantic City. There are boardwalk attractions, beaches galore and amusement parks here—this is the home of the world's greatest concentration of miniature golf courses.

A cultural stop—Brookgreen Gardens (A2) features over 400 sculptures by top 19th- and 20th-century artists.

South Carolina was the first state to secede from the Union—doing so in 1860. Not too surprisingly then, the first battle of the Civil War, which resulted in a Union defeat and retreat, happened at Fort Sumter (A4) in Charleston Harbor 12 April 1861. The Confederacy held onto the fort until the end of the war.

Farther east than the harbor, somewhere off the coast in the Atlantic, the SS Central America sank in 1857 in one of those infamous East Coast hurricanes. It's now known as the US's richest shipwreck— already yielding $1 billion in gold with more still to come up.

Do you know the nickname of this sweet Southern state? See page 156.

Map labels

A B C D E

NORTH CAROLINA

211 301 87 242 ▲ Jones 41 701 421 ● Burgaw ● Folkstone
● Lumberton 41 ● Elizabethtown Currie 210 40 50 ● Surf City
74 701 ● Singletary Lake ● Moores Creek Natl. Battlefield ● Hampstead
95 ● Clarkton 87 17 ● Topsail Beach
● Rowland 41 74 74 ● Bolton ● Delco Wilmington 76 ● Wrightsville Beach
501 76 ● Chadbourn ● Whiteville Lake Waccamaw
● Dillon 76 211 ● Masonboro
● Little Pee Dee 701 421 ● Carolina Beach
9 ● Nichols 133 ● Fort Fisher
501 ● Mullins 17 ● Southport
76 Shallotte 130 ● Long Beach Smith Island
● Marion ● Loris 9 179 ● Holden Beach Cape Fear
576 Little River ● Calabash

SOUTH CAROLINA

● Kingsburg 378 ● Conway 17 North Myrtle Beach
● Hemingway 501 ● Myrtle Beach
41 Myrtle Beach ● Surfside Beach
● Murrells Inlet ● Garden City
701 ● Huntington Beach
51 ▲ Brookgreen Gardens
● Andrews 521 Pawleys Island
41 Georgetown
ALT 17 ● Belle Isle Gardens North Island
701 Santee River Cat Island
● Jamestown Cedar Island Cape Island
Buck Hall Bulls Bay
● Awendaw

Fort Moultrie (Fort Sumter Natl. Mon.)
■ Fort Sumter (Fort Sumter Natl. Mon.)

Atlantic Ocean

Onslow Bay

kilom. 20 40 60 80
miles 10 20 30 40 50

N

The map on this page is 250x250 miles.

USAtlas **Geographic & Weather Extremes**

Farthest Flung

For the record—Alaska is, in fact, our northern-most, easternmost and westernmost state; Hawaii is the southernmost—for the other 48:
Northernmost point: Lake of the Woods, MN
Westernmost point: Cape Flattery, WA
Southernmost point: Key West, FL
Easternmost point: West Quoddy Head, ME

Water Words

Most miles of coast: Alaska
Wettest point in the world: Mt. Waialeale, Kauai, HI—over 500 inches of rain per year.
Greatest difference between low and high tide: The Bay of Fundy, between Maine and Nova Scotia—40-foot difference between tides.
Largest beach: Those 28 sun-soaked miles of Virginia Beach.
Hottest water: The mineral pools in Hot Springs State Park, WY bubble along at about 110° F and have done so for about 50 million years.

Lakes—

Deepest: Crater Lake, OR—1932 feet
Oldest: Mono Lake, CA—no one knows how old, really; at least 730,000 years is the best guess.
Lowest: Salton Sea, CA
Largest (surface area): Lake Superior—it's bigger than the state of Maine.

Waterfalls—

Greatest volume: Niagara Falls, NY
Widest: Niagara Falls, again
Highest: Ribbon Creek, CA
Longest: Yosemite Falls, CA

How low can you go?

Deepest canyon: Grand Canyon, AZ
Deepest gorge: Hell's Canyon, OR
Longest, deepest rift: Craters of the Moon, ID

How high?

Highest state: Colorado—more than 75% of the land is 10,000 feet above sea level.
Highest mountain: Mt. McKinley, AK—in fact, 17 of the country's 20 highest peaks are in Alaska.
Highest mountain (total height): Mauna Loa, HI—measuring from its ocean floor base, the volcano is 33,476 feet high, 4448 feet taller than Mt. Everest.

Hurricanes

Every region has its distinctive disaster, but the all-American weather phenomenon is the hurricane, which affects millions of people every year from Maine to Texas.

Hurricane comes from the Spanish "huracan," which is likely a corruption of the name of the Mayan storm god—Hunraken.

Each year sees about 6 full-blown hurricanes and, unfortunately, about 100 deaths and $100 million in property damage. Hugo, however, did $4.5 *billion* worth of damage alone.

Everyone gets nervous when they hear "100 mph winds," but it's the rain and the huge "storm surge" waves that cause the most destruction.

The official list of hurricane names—alphabetical, alternating genders since 1973—repeats every six years ... except for hurricanes that will go down in history. There'll never be another hurricane named Camille.

Where do you go for ...

Dinosaur digging?
Dinosaur National Monument, Vernal, UT
"Biggest living thing?"
Sequoia National Park, CA
Most extensive cave system?
Mammoth Cave National Park, Mammoth, KY
Active volcanoes?
Kilauea, HI
Windiest spot in the world?
Mt. Washington, NH
Hottest, driest spot on earth?
Death Valley, CA

And don't forget

The San Andreas fault, clearly visible for the most part, extends for 600 miles through California.

The lowest high is Florida—where the highest elevation is 345 feet above sea level.

Despite the fact all the Great Lakes flow into it, Lake Ontario is the smallest Great Lake.

The states with most tornadoes, in order, are: Texas, Oklahoma, Florida and Kansas.

For extremists—the points that are the northernmost, the southernmost, the eastern-most, the westernmost, and the center of the 48 states.

The Greek version of "Hunra-ken" is Boreas—the old man responsible for calling up a strong north wind by blowing on his conch shell.

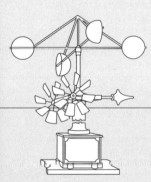

How do we know Mt. Washington, NH is so windy? For over a century instruments like this anemometer, circa 1867, have been supplying meterologists with such data.

Save the museums for another trip. You can see complete dinosaur skeletons, intact and on-site, at the Dinosaur National Monument in Vernal, UT.

← pg. 69

How the other 1/2 of 1% lives: Palm Beach *(B2)* somehow manages to fit 20 private polo clubs within its 14-mile city limits. Probably was the favorite stop for Prince Charles on his US tour.

MAJOR TABLOID TAKES OVER ONE-HORSE TOWN—it's true, the National Enquirer is head-quartered in otherwise quiet Lantana, FL *(B2)*. You'll find a Christmas tree here larger than the one at the White House or at Rockefeller Plaza. Just one of those claim-to-fame things.

Butterfly World *(B2)*: Learn all about the winged beauties, then watch three thousand of them flying through giant aviaries. It's the largest park devoted to butterflies in the world.

With about 165 miles of canals hereabouts, Ft. Lauderdale is properly called the Venice of America. It's probably "traffic" jammed too—the area is called the yacht capital of America.

The operative word for Florida is wet. Only Alaska has more shoreline; the Everglades *(A3)* occupy a million and a half acres of swampland; and the nation's only submerged national park is here. The Biscayne National Park *(B4)*, south of Miami, is almost entirely underwater and protects part of the only living coral reef in the US.

Key West *(A5)* is the southern-most city in the continental US. Pity the poor residents; the mean (terrible!) January temperature here is 70° F. No wonder the author of Cat on a Hot Tin Roof wrote here. Who was he, by the way? *See page 156.*

The map on this page is 250x250 miles.

Map labels:

A B C D E

FLORIDA

Atlantic Ocean

Gulf of Mexico

Kenansville, Gifford, Vero Beach, Yeehaw Junction, North Hutchinson Island, Fort Drum, Sunland Gardens, Fort Pierce, Hutchinson Island, Port St. Lucie, Basinger, Whispering Pines, Stuart, Okeechobee, Hobe Sound, Jonathan Dickinson, Brighton, Upthegrove Beach, Buckhead Ridge, Jupiter, Port Mayaca, Palm Beach Gardens, Palmdale, Canal Point, West Palm Beach, Palm Beach, Moore Haven, Pahokee, Croquet Hall of Fame, Lake Okeechobee, Ortona Lock, Clewiston, Belle Glade, Lantana, Lake Worth, Lake Harbor, South Bay, Boynton Beach, Delray Beach, Caloosahatchee, Boca Raton, Deerfield Beach, Butterfly World, Hillsboro Beach, Margate, Pompano Beach, Hugh Taylor Birch Rec. Area, Immokalee, Sawgrass Expy., Plantation, Fort Lauderdale, Big Cypress Swamp, Bear Island, Everglades Pkwy. (Alligator Alley), Dania, Hollywood, The Everglades, Miles City, Big Cypress National Preserve, pg. 123, North Miami, Hialeah, Miami Beach, Burns Lake, Fifty Mile Bend, Miami, Carnestown Visitor Center, Ochopee, Midway, Coral Gables, Key Biscayne, Everglades City, Shark Valley Visitor Center, Perrine, Ten Thousand Islands, Lopez River, Everglades National Park, Homestead, Biscayne Bay, Boca Chita Key, Visitor Center, Florida City, Elliott Key, Biscayne Natl. Park, Broad River, Long Pine Key, Key Largo, John Pennekamp Coral Reef State Park, Graveyard Creek, Joe River, Hells Bay, Lard Can, Key Largo, Middle Cape, Cape Sable, Flamingo, Flamingo Lodge, Tavernier, Florida Bay, Islamorada, Long Key, Layton, FLORIDA KEYS, Grassy Key, Marathon, Big Pine Key, Bahia Honda, Boot Key, Ramrod Key, Big Pine, Spanish Harbor, Sugarloaf Key, Key West

Route numbers: 60, 441, 95, 1, A1A, 68, 70, 98, 76, 710, 706, 786, 78, 715, 802, 441, 806, 808, 84, 27, 75, 29, 41, 821, 836, 826, 997, 9336

kilom. 20 40 60 80
miles 10 20 30 40 50

N

USAtlas City & Town Names

Ever thought of travelling around the world and not leaving the country? how about some space travel? or a quick course in American history? We found these places to make your trips even more of an adventure ... many city names appear in more than one state.

A European Vacation

Dublin—5	Paris—11
London—4	Versailles—5
Oxford—7	Orleans—2
Manchester—10	Lisbon—3
Cambridge—8	Geneva—7
Aberdeen—7	Vienna—4
Glasgow—3	Milan—5
Oslo—1	Rome—3
Amsterdam—1	Naples—4
Munich—1	Venice—4
Berlin—3	Athens—6
Hamburg—5	Malta—3
Warsaw—5	

'Round the World

Cuba—3	Cairo—4
Havana—3	Bethlehem—1
Jamaica—1	Nazareth—1
Trinidad—2	Lebanon—10
Panama—1	Turkey—1
Peru—3	Bagdad—2
Brazil—1	Melbourne—2
Patagonia—1	Sidney—5
Morocco—1	
Carthage—7	

The Great Beyond

Apollo, PA	Luna, NM
Venus, TX	Star, NC
Mars, PA	Sunrise, WY
Jupiter, FL	Sunset, UT
Neptune, OR	Cosmos, MN

Presidential Top Ten

Our research uncovered a number of towns with presidential names—these were most popular:

Jackson—22	Jefferson—14
Madison—18	Grant—9
Washington—15	Cleveland—9
Lincoln—18	Harrison—11
Monroe—16	Roosevelt—6

Just Plain Fun

Defiance, OH— Settled by General Mad Anthony Wayne who "defied the Indians and all the devils in Hell to take this fort."

Difficult, TN—Local residents couldn't come up with a name, telling the post office it was just too difficult.

Fiddletown, CA—The miners who settled here included a lot of fiddle players from Missouri.

La Push, WA—The French settlers called it "La Bouche," for the mouth of the nearby river. That was a mouthful for the Americans who followed. They pronounced the place "la push."

Ninety Six, SC—It was about that many miles to the nearest Cherokee town, according to early traders.

Pie Town, NM—The local baker (so says his grandson) advertised his trade with a billboard and travellers paid enough attention that the town was soon known, officially and on the map, by its pies.

Other Origins

Portland, OR—Two Easterners flipped a coin. The winner was from Portland, ME. The loser was from Boston.

Seattle, WA—Sealth, chief of the Duwamish Indians, promised to roll over in his grave every time his name was spoken and charged $16,000 for the privilege of using it. Settlers paid up and Seattle it is.

Yazoo City, MS—Sounds more fun than it is—it comes from a local Indian tribe's word for "River of Death."

Wink, TX—Lucky Colonel Winkler already had a town named after him, so these local residents shortened their town moniker to "wink."

Bliss, ID and Boring, OR—We wish the origin of these town names were more interesting than the fact that both are named after local families.

Why, AZ—Routes 85 and 86 intersect at a "Y." But residents of the nearby city thought "Why" would be easier to map and remember.

If these cities are any indication, we appreciate our native fauna more than our former presidents:

Beaver Falls, PA
Beaverdam, OH
Beaver Dam, KY
Beaver Dam, WI
Beaver, OK
Beaver City, NE
Beaver, UT

Eagle Lake, ME
Eagle Rock, VA
Eagle River, MI
Eagle Lake, TX
Eagle Pass, TX
Eagle Nest, NM
Eagleville, CA

Buffalo, NY
Buffalo, WV
Buffalo, SD
Buffalo, MO
Buffalo, OK
Buffalo, TX
Buffalo, WY

Wolf Hole, AZ
Wolf Creek, MT
Wolf Point, MT
Wolf Creek, OR

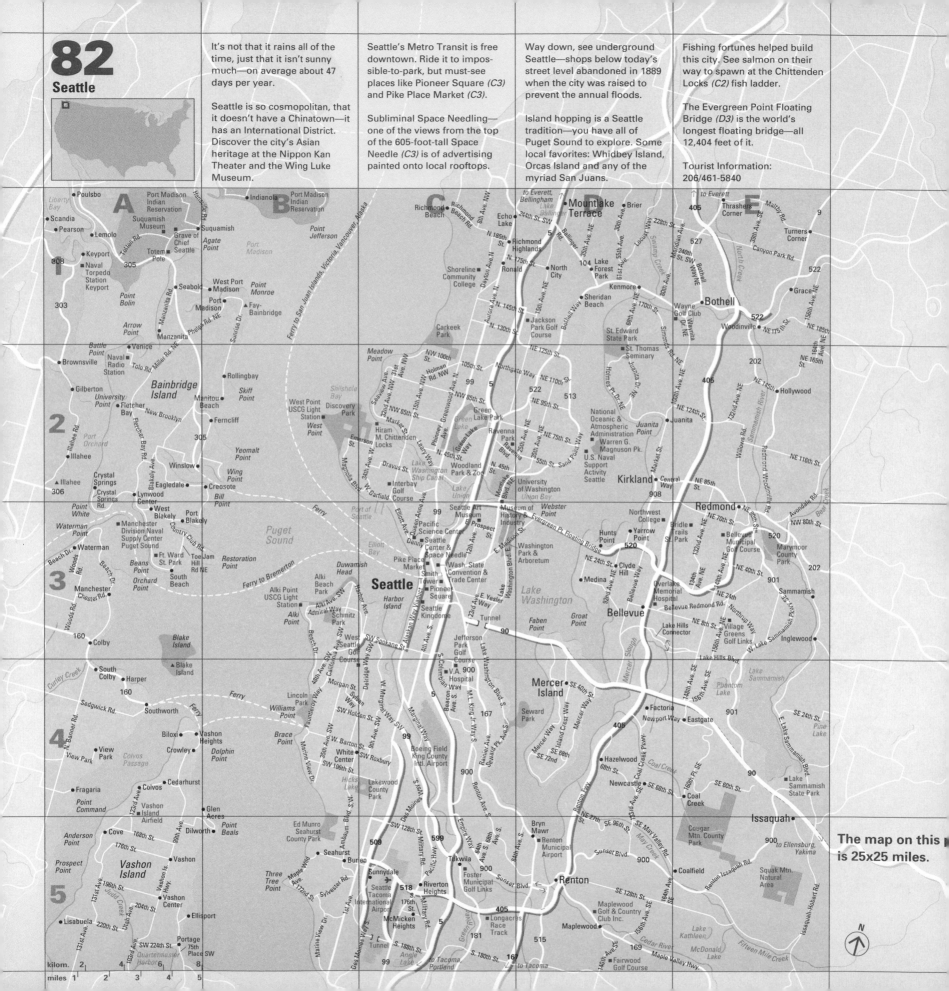

82

Seattle

It's not that it rains all of the time, just that it isn't sunny much—on average about 47 days per year.

Seattle is so cosmopolitan, that it doesn't have a Chinatown—it has an International District. Discover the city's Asian heritage at the Nippon Kan Theater and the Wing Luke Museum.

Seattle's Metro Transit is free downtown. Ride it to impossible-to-park, but must-see places like Pioneer Square (C3) and Pike Place Market (C3).

Subliminal Space Needling—one of the views from the top of the 605-foot-tall Space Needle (C3) is of advertising painted onto local rooftops.

Way down, see underground Seattle—shops below today's street level abandoned in 1889 when the city was raised to prevent the annual floods.

Island hopping is a Seattle tradition—you have all of Puget Sound to explore. Some local favorites: Whidbey Island, Orcas Island and any of the myriad San Juans.

Fishing fortunes helped build this city. See salmon on their way to spawn at the Chittenden Locks (C2) fish ladder.

The Evergreen Point Floating Bridge (D3) is the world's longest floating bridge—all 12,404 feet of it.

Tourist Information: 206/461-5840

The map on this page is 25x25 miles.

Portland mayor J.E. Bud Clark's favorite things:
That the city is planned to be on a human scale.
Its beautiful setting on the confluence of the Columbia and Willamette Rivers.
That it's one hour from the Cascades and Pacific Ocean.
That it's the home of the world acclaimed Goose Hollow Inn (which he owns).

Take advantage—the buses downtown are free.

This city is park crazy—one of its 160 parks is only four feet square.

Macleay Park *(B2)* doesn't permit scooters, skates or bicycles, much less cars—"no wheeled vehicle ever to enter the premises" was the stipulation on

Donald Macleay's turn-of-the-century bequest.

Crystal Springs Garden *(C3)* is the place to go to see azaleas and rhododendrons blooming in April and May.

But roses are the town favorite. This city has enough rose bushes to line the coast to Pasadena. See the Rose Festi-

val in June, but bring an umbrella because it always rains.

The Oregon Museum of Science and Industry *(B3)* is the product of the largest "barn raising" in the US: in 1957 400 volunteers laid 102,000 bricks in one day.

Tourist Information:
503/378-4423

83
Portland

map on this page
x25 miles.

If you thought the Carrington estate shown on the opening shots of Dynasty was in Denver, you're off by 1300 miles. It's the Filoli Estate in Woodside (D2).

West Coast Ivy League: Start your tour of Stanford (C3) at the Main Quadrangle to see the several hundred acre campus. The Stanford Linear Accelera-tor Center will try to help you understand quarks; the Stanford Art Museum is diverse, its Rodin Garden excellent.

Macintosh apples are grown in Washington; Apple Macin-toshes, here in Cupertino (B4).

Silicon Valley residents have more than just microchips— Great America (C4) has roller coasters, rides and the world's tallest carousel—two decks and 100 horses and beasts.

The most bizarre Victorian mansion you'll ever see—the Winchester Mystery House (B4)—built by the heir to the rifle fortune when she was convinced by a medium that 24-hour building on the house would appease spirits of those killed by the rifles and allow her to live forever. (Thirty eight years and 160 rooms later, the latter proved false.)

Japanese and American auto partnerships started here at NUMMI in Fremont.

Tourist Information:
415/348-7600 (San Mateo Cnty.)
408/295-9600 (San Jose)

The map on this page is 25x25 miles.

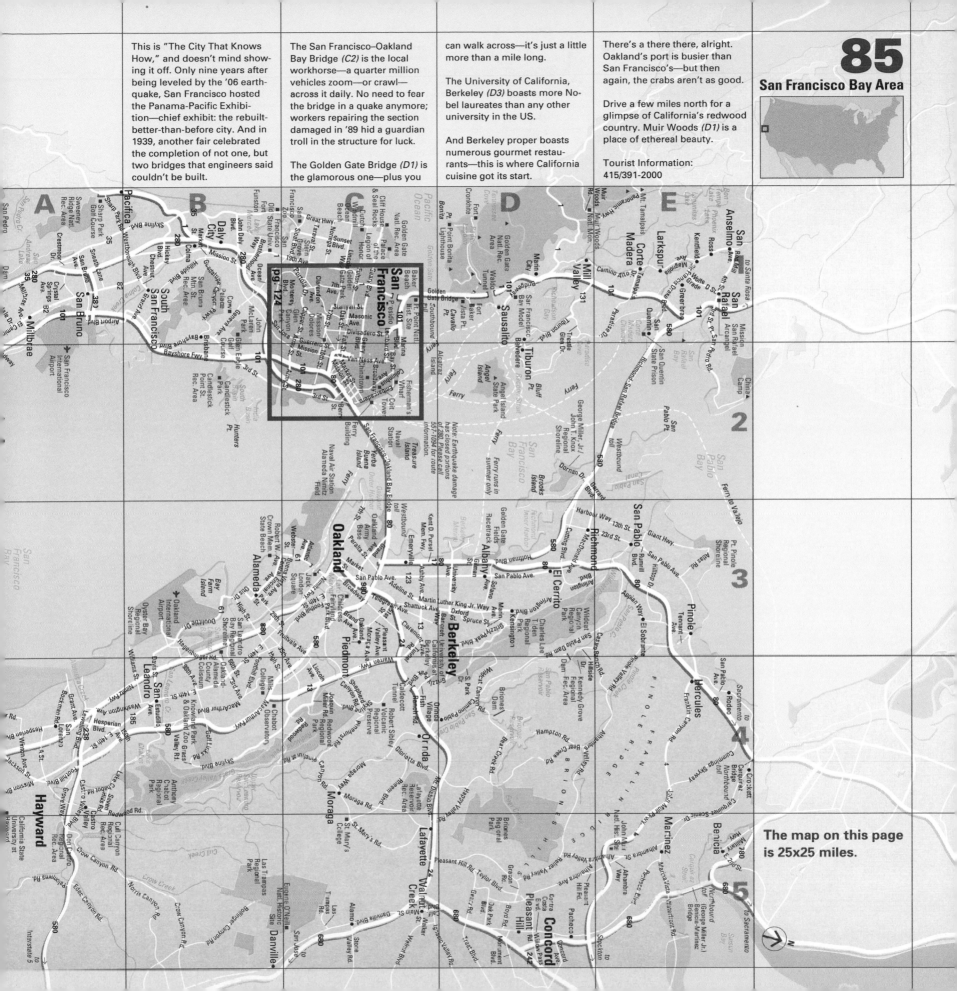

This is "The City That Knows How," and doesn't mind showing it off. Only nine years after being leveled by the '06 earthquake, San Francisco hosted the Panama-Pacific Exhibition—chief exhibit: the rebuilt-better-than-before city. And in 1939, another fair celebrated the completion of not one, but two bridges that engineers said couldn't be built.

The San Francisco–Oakland Bay Bridge (C2) is the local workhorse—a quarter million vehicles zoom—or crawl—across it daily. No need to fear the bridge in a quake anymore; workers repairing the section damaged in '89 hid a guardian troll in the structure for luck.

The Golden Gate Bridge (D1) is the glamorous one—plus you can walk across—it's just a little more than a mile long.

The University of California, Berkeley (D3) boasts more Nobel laureates than any other university in the US.

And Berkeley proper boasts numerous gourmet restaurants—this is where California cuisine got its start.

There's a there there, alright. Oakland's port is busier than San Francisco's—but then again, the crabs aren't as good.

Drive a few miles north for a glimpse of California's redwood country. Muir Woods (D1) is a place of ethereal beauty.

Tourist Information:
415/391-2000

The map on this page is 25x25 miles.

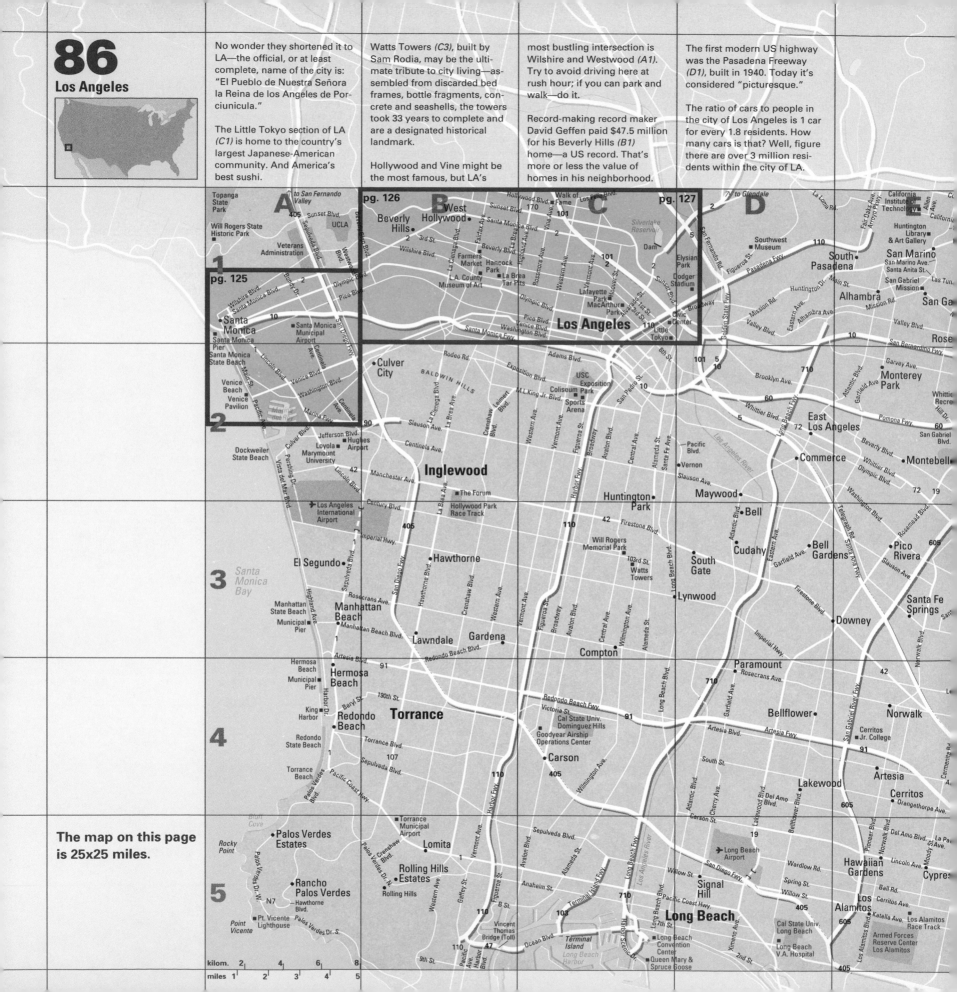

86

Los Angeles

No wonder they shortened it to LA—the official, or at least complete, name of the city is: "El Pueblo de Nuestra Señora la Reina de los Angeles de Porciuncula."

The Little Tokyo section of LA (C1) is home to the country's largest Japanese-American community. And America's best sushi.

Watts Towers (C3), built by Sam Rodia, may be the ultimate tribute to city living—assembled from discarded bed frames, bottle fragments, concrete and seashells, the towers took 33 years to complete and are a designated historical landmark.

Hollywood and Vine might be the most famous, but LA's most bustling intersection is Wilshire and Westwood (A1). Try to avoid driving here at rush hour; if you can park and walk—do it.

Record-making record maker David Geffen paid $47.5 million for his Beverly Hills (B1) home—a US record. That's more or less the value of homes in his neighborhood.

The first modern US highway was the Pasadena Freeway (D1), built in 1940. Today it's considered "picturesque."

The ratio of cars to people in the city of Los Angeles is 1 car for every 1.8 residents. How many cars is that? Well, figure there are over 3 million residents within the city of LA.

The map on this page is 25x25 miles.

Blame the auto-happy population and the pollutant-trapping San Gabriel Mountains—LA and Orange counties are the smoggiest in the nation.

The worst smog attack in the city's history was 35 years ago—closing the airport and harbor. Despite eye-popping growth—and all those cars!—it hasn't been that bad since.

And new, even tougher laws—"Use a barbecue, go to jail"—demand more improvement.

Earlier travelers reached the end of the Santa Fe Trail on the outskirts of Los Angeles (which didn't consist of much at the time) in El Monte *(A2)*.

One of the best county fairs in the country is held in this over-urbanized metropolis: The LA County Fair in September at the Pomona Fairplex *(D2)*.

Every place has its claim to fame—Yorba Linda's *(C5)* is the Richard Nixon birthplace.

Anaheim—famous since 1955 for one thing: Disneyland *(A5)!* Nikita Khrushchev wouldn't leave the US without seeing it.

Just a freeway away: Knott's Berry Farm *(A5)*; Six Flags Magic Mountain *(off map)*; and beaches everywhere. It's all within range— mountains, forests and desert. Some day trips to consider: Angeles National Forest, Lake Arrowhead, Palm Springs.

Tourist Information: 213/624-7300

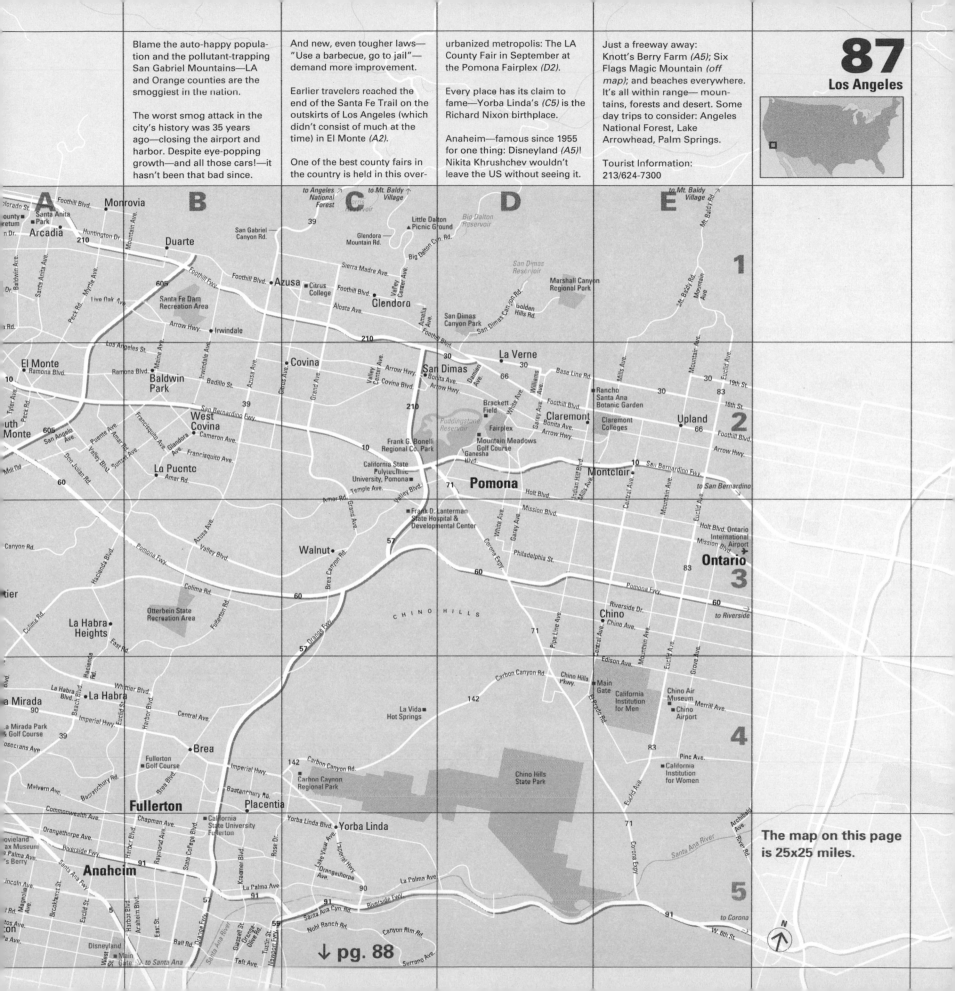

The map on this page is 25x25 miles.

↓ pg. 88

88

Orange County

20% of the nation's swimming pools are found in greater Los Angeles and most of the nation's surfers cluster on the beaches of Orange County.

Henry Huntington started the craze in the early 1900s. To get people to take his train to his new namesake development, he hired a Hawaiian surfer as an attraction. It worked.

These days, 146,000 bathers are watched over by 300 lifeguards each summer day.

Every dollar you spend here goes toward the 4 billion Orange County makes in tourism each year.

Whether or not you've seen it on religious TV, you'll want to see Garden Grove's Crystal

Cathedral in person. Get the full effect of the enormous cathedral with its 90-ft. doors for drive-in worshippers (C1).

One of the more beautiful terminals for whale-watching cruises and Catalina Island ferries is the Victorian-style Balboa Pavilion (B3).

Another attraction—many

claim the frozen banana was invented on Balboa Island.

How's this for growth? 20 years ago, Irvine, Orange County's second most populous city, did not even exist (as a chartered city, anyway).

Tourist Information:
714/999-8999

The map on this p
is 25x25 miles.

kilom. 2 4 6 8
miles 1 2 3 4 5

The first European to sail to California was fortunate to drop anchor in beautiful San Diego Bay. Juan Rodriguez Cabrillo staked his claim for Spain in 1542. Well over a million people rediscover Cabrillo—Cabrillo National Monument (A3) is as visited as the Statue of Liberty and the whalewatching is much better.

The USA's best: The astounding San Diego Zoo (B2) has more animals and birds than any other. Just north of here in Escondido, sister zoo The Wild Animal Park is the largest (in acreage) in the country.

San Diego has successfully recaptured a downbeat downtown. The Gaslamp Quarter (B3) is the new center for the arts—shoppers and diners head for the extraordinary and playful Horton Plaza.

The US Navy relocated its Pacific headquarters here after the bombing of Pearl Harbor. It's still a sizeable presence, but tourism is a bigger employer.

The statistic that converts tourists to residents: San Diego's mean annual temperature is 71°.

Tijuana trip tips: Buy Mexican auto insurance in San Ysidro. On weekends, take the San Diego Trolley and walk over the border, or drive across at less-crowded Otay Mesa (D5).

Tourist Information: 619/236-1212

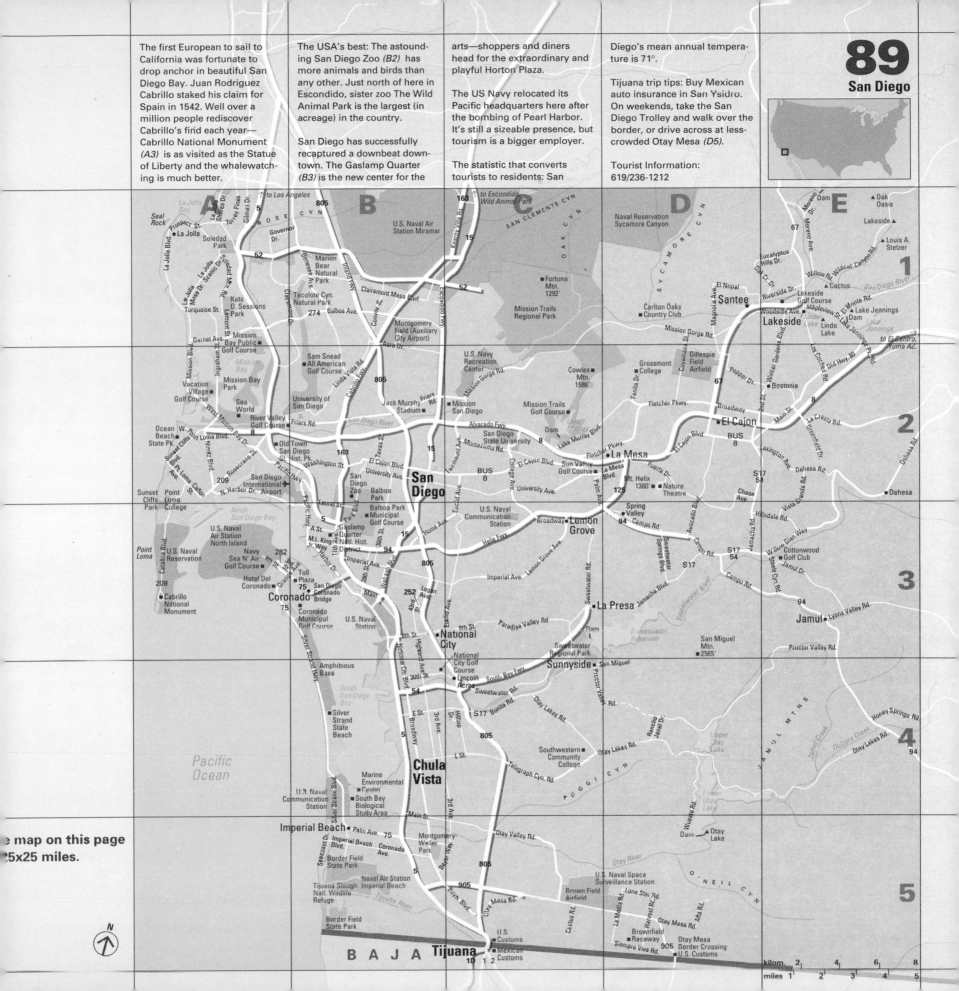

e map on this page
25x25 miles.

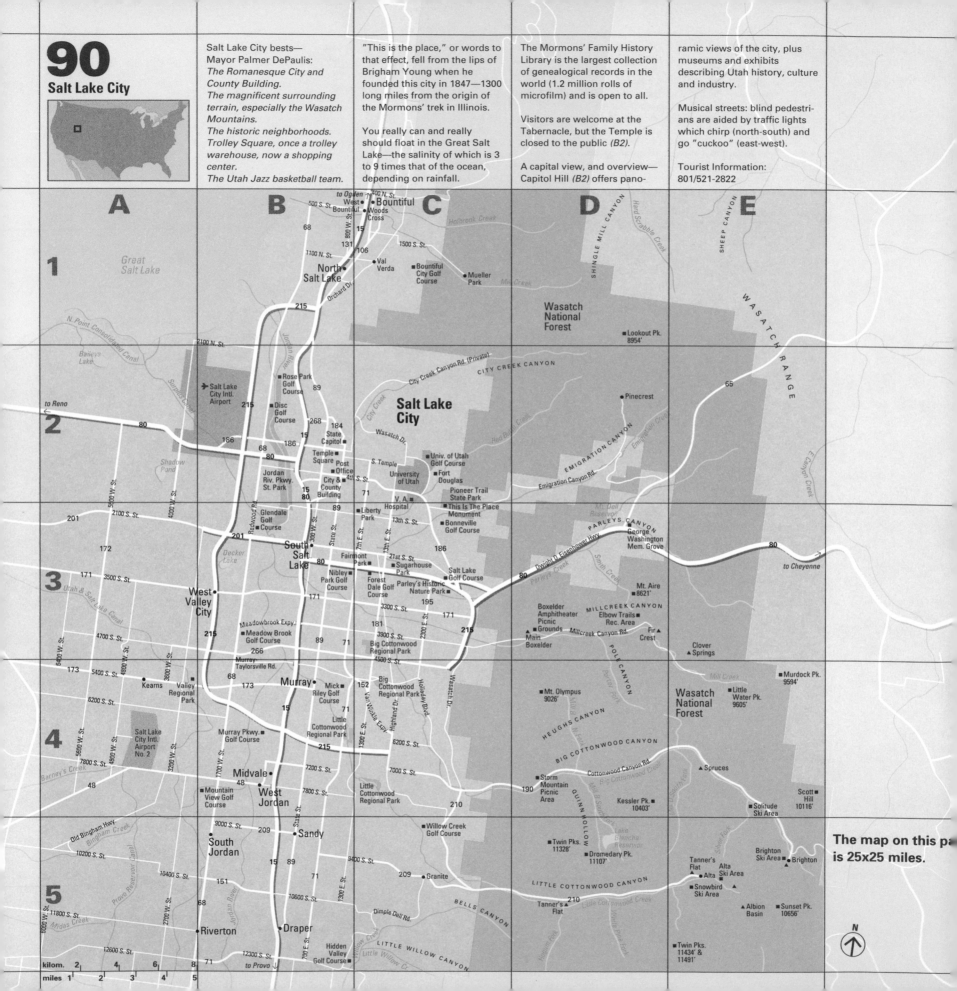

90

Salt Lake City

Salt Lake City bests—
Mayor Palmer DePaulis:
The Romanesque City and County Building.
The magnificent surrounding terrain, especially the Wasatch Mountains.
The historic neighborhoods.
Trolley Square, once a trolley warehouse, now a shopping center.
The Utah Jazz basketball team.

"This is the place," or words to that effect, fell from the lips of Brigham Young when he founded this city in 1847—1300 long miles from the origin of the Mormons' trek in Illinois.

You really can and really should float in the Great Salt Lake—the salinity of which is 3 to 9 times that of the ocean, depending on rainfall.

The Mormons' Family History Library is the largest collection of genealogical records in the world (1.2 million rolls of microfilm) and is open to all.

Visitors are welcome at the Tabernacle, but the Temple is closed to the public *(B2)*.

A capital view, and overview—Capitol Hill *(B2)* offers pano-

ramic views of the city, plus museums and exhibits describing Utah history, culture and industry.

Musical streets: blind pedestrians are aided by traffic lights which chirp (north-south) and go "cuckoo" (east-west).

Tourist Information:
801/521-2822

The map on this pa[ge]
is 25x25 miles.

Risen again like its namesake, Phoenix is built on the irrigation canal system of a 1000-year-old city.

"Desert Rats" are the folks who somehow can stay here even in the summer. The temperature hovers right around 92° in mid-July. Local literature claims 300 sunny days a year and only 7 inches of rain.

You'd expect to find one of the world's finest collections of cactus here—visit the Desert Botanical Gardens (D4) to discover how vibrant and varied drylands flora really is.

There are 50,000 Indians living on 23 reservations in the Phoenix area. To experience Southwest Indian culture, ask the Native American Tourism

Center for tour and event information: 602/945-0771.

Appropriately, the Heard Museum of Anthropology and Primitive Art (B3) includes an extensive collection of Native American Art.

Frank Lloyd Wright had a propensity for well-to-do clients. His winter home, Taliesin West

(E2), is located in Scottsdale— the "Beverly Hills" of Phoenix. Still under debate is whether he designed the trés cher Arizona Biltmore (C3).

A good reason to come: Phoenix boasts more 5-star resorts than any other US city.

Tourist Information: 602/254-6500

map on this page
5x25 miles.

City Hall sends along this list of bests:

Country Club Plaza.

Kansas City jazz—this is the only city in the world with a Municipal Jazz Commission. (Charlie Parker came from here.)

Barbecue—Calvin Trillin (and he's not alone) calls Arthur Bryant's Barbecue the world's best restaurant.

The Nelson-Atkins Museum of Art—a famous collection of Asian Art and a new Henry Moore Sculpture Garden.

The Kansas City Royals.

Everything's not only up-to-date here, this city can also one-up Paris (more boulevards) and Rome (more fountains).

The Kansas City most people expect to find—heads of cattle and thick strip steaks—that's out by the Stockyards (C3).

This is a shopping kind of town—Country Club Plaza (C3), the nation's first drive-to shopping center (1922), boasts statuary, fountains and reproductions from Seville, Spain. Other hot spots: Hallmark Cards' huge down-town complex that locals call a city within the city, Crown Center (C3); and Westport Square, where pioneers used to outfit themselves for the journey West, now restored to outfit urbanites (C3).

Some suburb—Independence is Missouri's fourth-largest city.

Tourist Information: 816/221-5242

The map on this p is 25x25 miles.

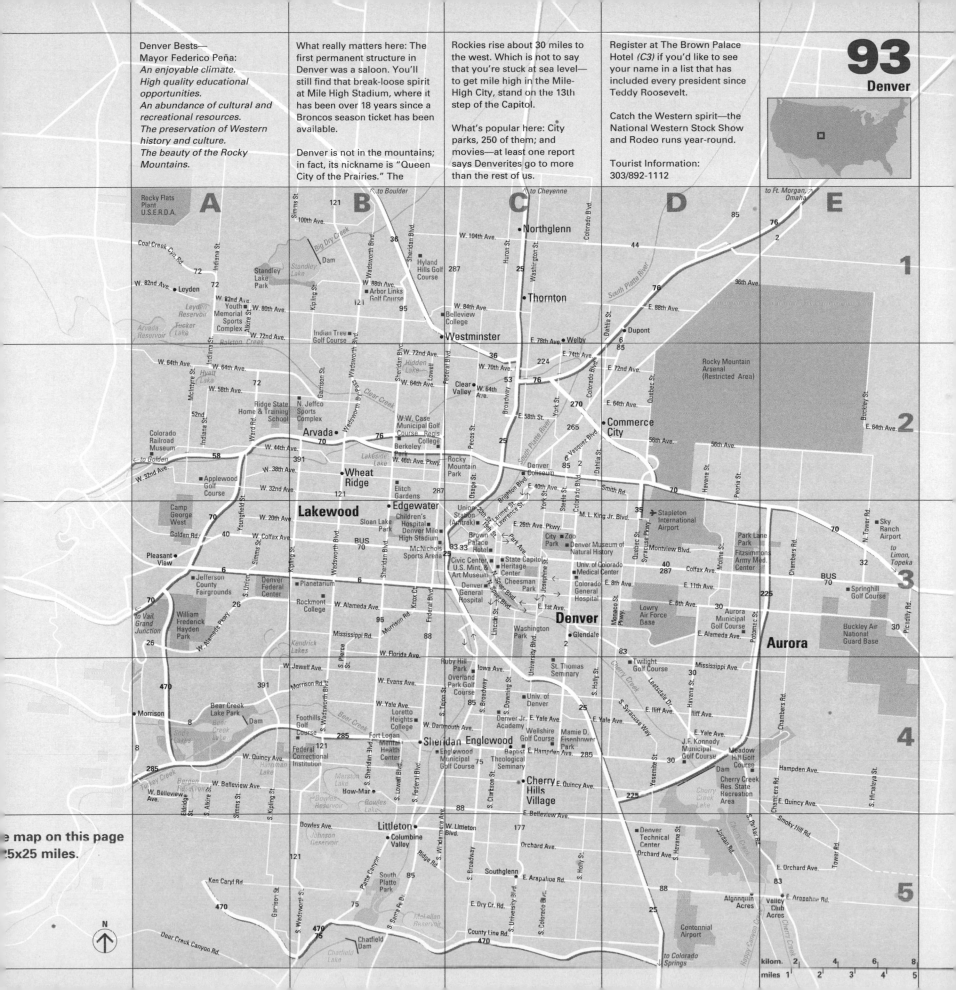

Denver Bests—
Mayor Federico Peña:
An enjoyable climate.
High quality educational
opportunities.
An abundance of cultural and
recreational resources.
The preservation of Western
history and culture.
The beauty of the Rocky
Mountains.

What really matters here: The
first permanent structure in
Denver was a saloon. You'll
still find that break-loose spirit
at Mile High Stadium, where it
has been over 18 years since a
Broncos season ticket has been
available.

Denver is not in the mountains;
in fact, its nickname is "Queen
City of the Prairies." The

Rockies rise about 30 miles to
the west. Which is not to say
that you're stuck at sea level—
to get mile high in the Mile-
High City, stand on the 13th
step of the Capitol.

What's popular here: City
parks, 250 of them; and
movies—at least one report
says Denverites go to more
than the rest of us.

Register at The Brown Palace
Hotel *(C3)* if you'd like to see
your name in a list that has
included every president since
Teddy Roosevelt.

Catch the Western spirit—the
National Western Stock Show
and Rodeo runs year-round.

Tourist Information:
303/892-1112

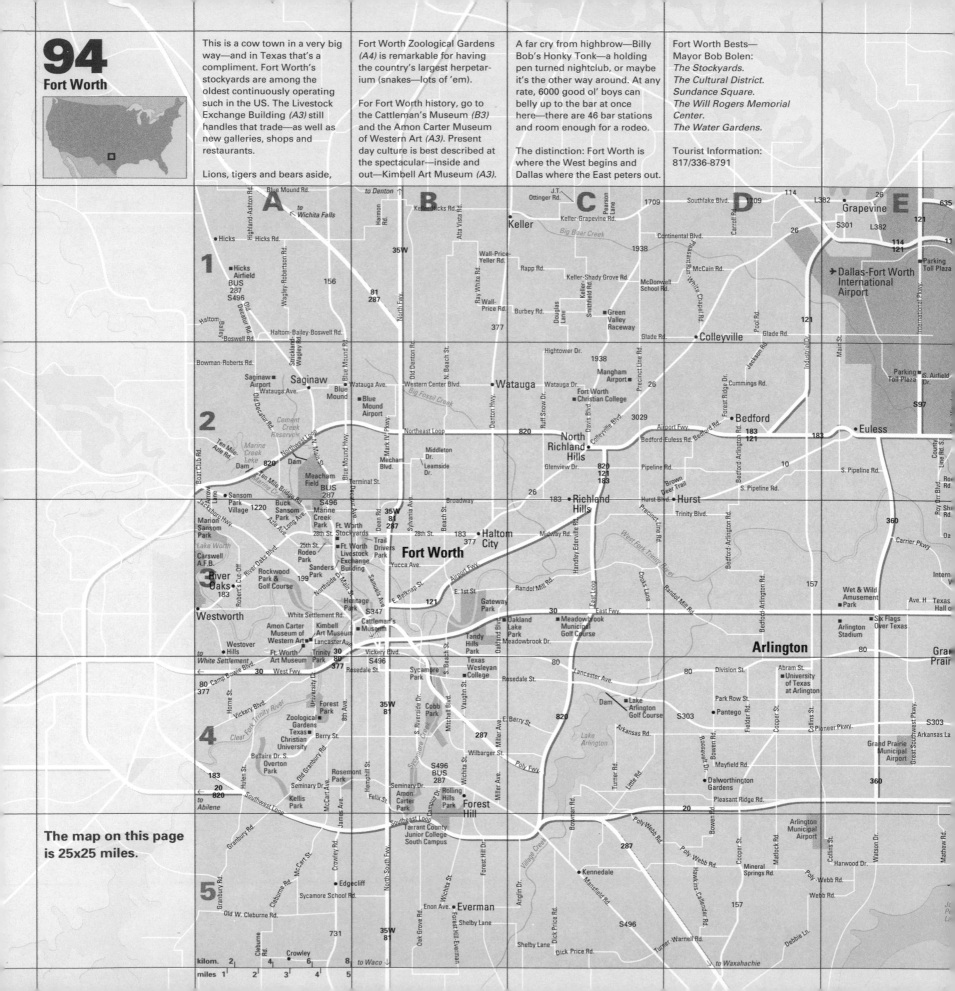

This is a cow town in a very big way—and in Texas that's a compliment. Fort Worth's stockyards are among the oldest continuously operating such in the US. The Livestock Exchange Building (A3) still handles that trade—as well as new galleries, shops and restaurants.

Lions, tigers and bears aside,

Fort Worth Zoological Gardens (A4) is remarkable for having the country's largest herpetarium (snakes—lots of 'em).

For Fort Worth history, go to the Cattleman's Museum (B3) and the Amon Carter Museum of Western Art (A3). Present day culture is best described at the spectacular—inside and out—Kimbell Art Museum (A3).

A far cry from highbrow—Billy Bob's Honky Tonk—a holding pen turned nightclub, or maybe it's the other way around. At any rate, 6000 good ol' boys can belly up to the bar at once here—there are 46 bar stations and room enough for a rodeo.

The distinction: Fort Worth is where the West begins and Dallas where the East peters out.

Fort Worth Bests—
Mayor Bob Bolen:
The Stockyards.
The Cultural District.
Sundance Square.
The Will Rogers Memorial Center.
The Water Gardens.

Tourist Information:
817/336-8791

The map on this page is 25x25 miles.

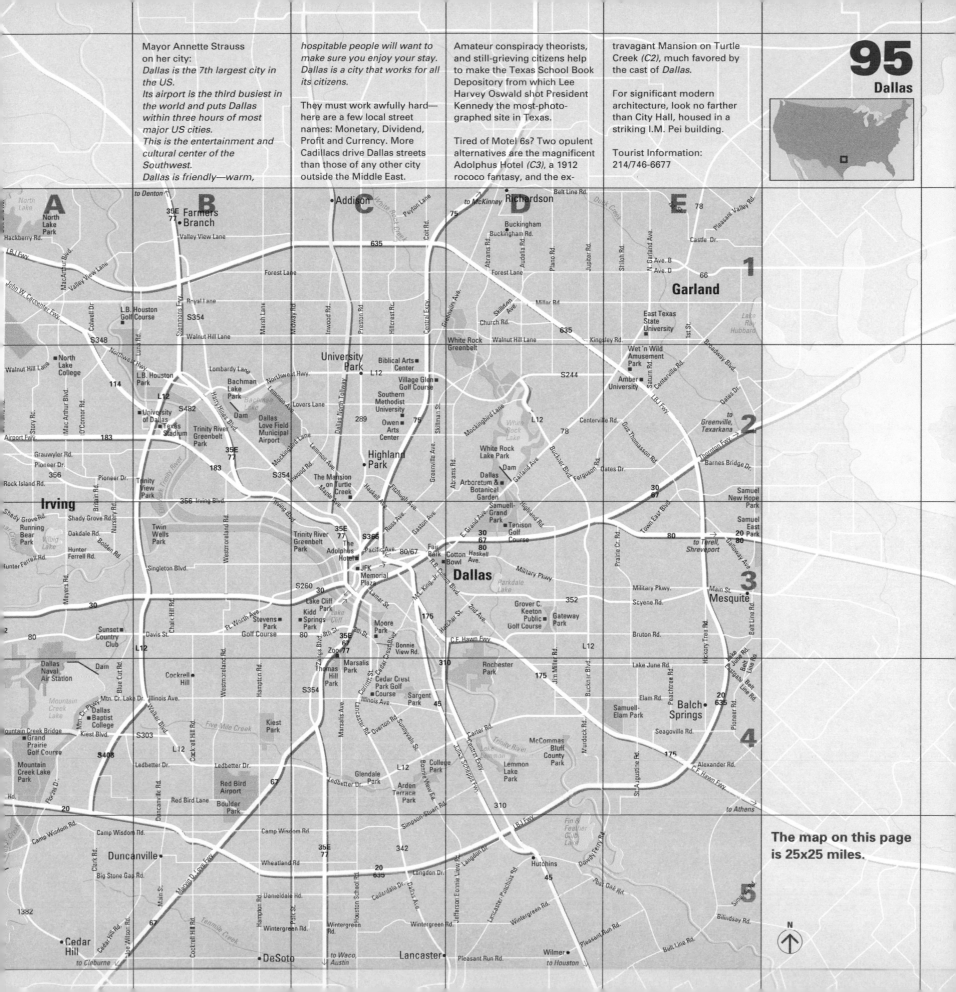

Mayor Annette Strauss on her city:
Dallas is the 7th largest city in the US.
Its airport is the third busiest in the world and puts Dallas within three hours of most major US cities.
This is the entertainment and cultural center of the Southwest.
Dallas is friendly—warm, hospitable people will want to make sure you enjoy your stay. Dallas is a city that works for all its citizens.

They must work awfully hard—here are a few local street names: Monetary, Dividend, Profit and Currency. More Cadillacs drive Dallas streets than those of any other city outside the Middle East.

Amateur conspiracy theorists, and still-grieving citizens help to make the Texas School Book Depository from which Lee Harvey Oswald shot President Kennedy the most-photographed site in Texas.

Tired of Motel 6s? Two opulent alternatives are the magnificent Adolphus Hotel (C3), a 1912 rococo fantasy, and the extravagant Mansion on Turtle Creek (C2), much favored by the cast of Dallas.

For significant modern architecture, look no farther than City Hall, housed in a striking I.M. Pei building.

Tourist Information:
214/746-6677

The map on this page is 25x25 miles.

96

San Antonio

Alamo Facts *(C3)*:

It's the most visited tourist attraction in Texas (which might explain why it's surrounded by hotels, motels and fast-food joints).

It marks perhaps the most significant lost battle in Texan/American history—188 Texans tried to stave off 5000 Mexican soldiers in a siege that lasted nearly 2 weeks and ended in a wholesale massacre of the defenders of the Alamo.

Davey Crockett, Jim Bowie and William Travis—Texas-size heroes all—died here.

Another Texas landmark—the amazing collection of horns, antlers and stuffed animals in the Hall of Horns at the Lone Star Brewery *(C3)*.

You might also note this city has prominent German-American and Polish-American populations and the great ethnic festivals you might therefore expect.

A stroll along the Paseo del Rio *(C3)* is the finishing touch of civility in this sophisticated city. Tourists, commuters and residents alike make use of taxi-boats in the canals.

San Antonio's cluster of five well-preserved missions is the largest such collection in the country.

Tourist Information:
512/270-8748

The map on this page is 25x25 miles.

"Houston" was the first word spoken on the moon, 20 July 1969. The astronauts were communicating with Mission Control at the Johnson Space Center (E5).

Architecture and such of note:

Stop in and meditate at Rothko Chapel (B3), an elegant octagonal prayer space with 14 blue/ black paintings by the building's designer.

A 51-foot wall of water cascades down the front of the Transco Tower (A3).

Houston likes to consider the Astrodome (B4) the "eighth wonder of the world." Is it big? Prince Rainier was asked if he wanted an Astrodome in Monaco. His answer: "Marvelous. We could be the world's only indoor country." No rained out games, ever, and it's always a comfortable 72° inside.

Houston is connected by 240 miles of the country's most tortuous freeways. Fortunate pedestrians make do with a tunnel system that saves them from summer heat and humidity.

Although 50 miles inland from the Gulf of Mexico, Houston is the world's third largest port. It connects via The Houston Ship Channel (D3).

Would you have guessed? The second-largest Indochinese population in the US is here.

Tourist Information: 713/523-5050

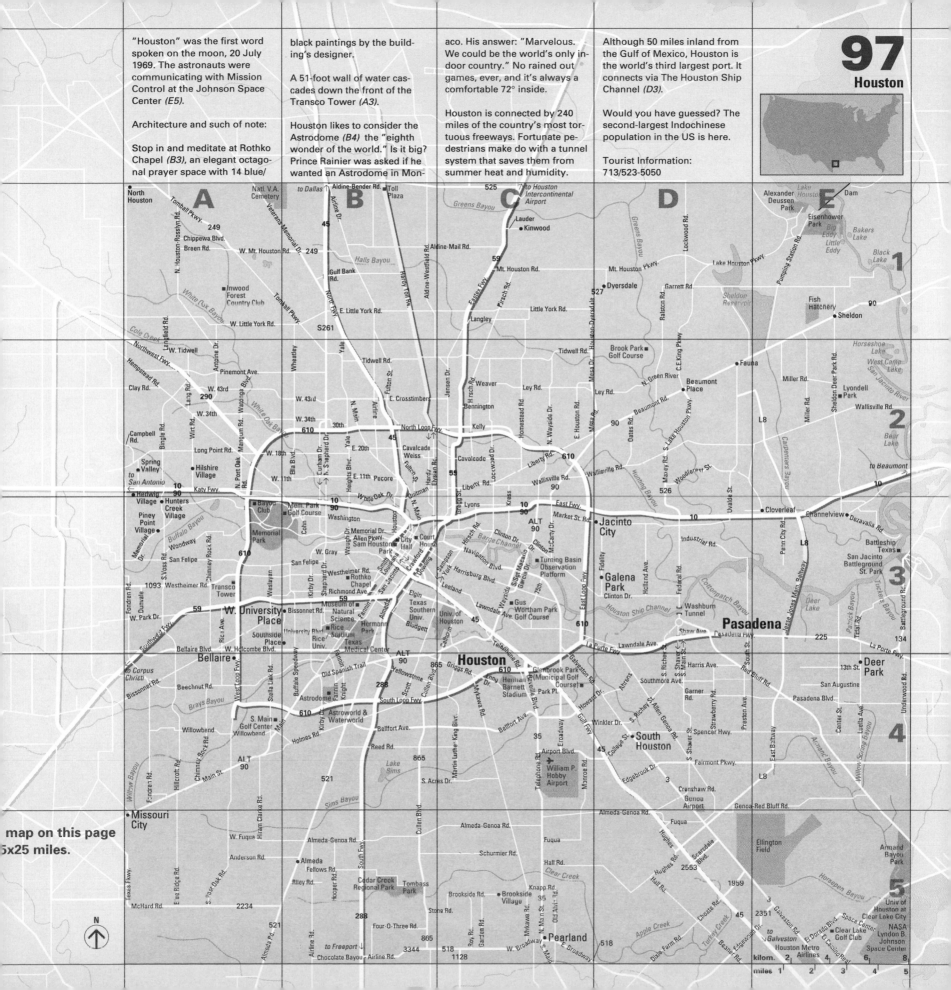

map on this page
5x25 miles.

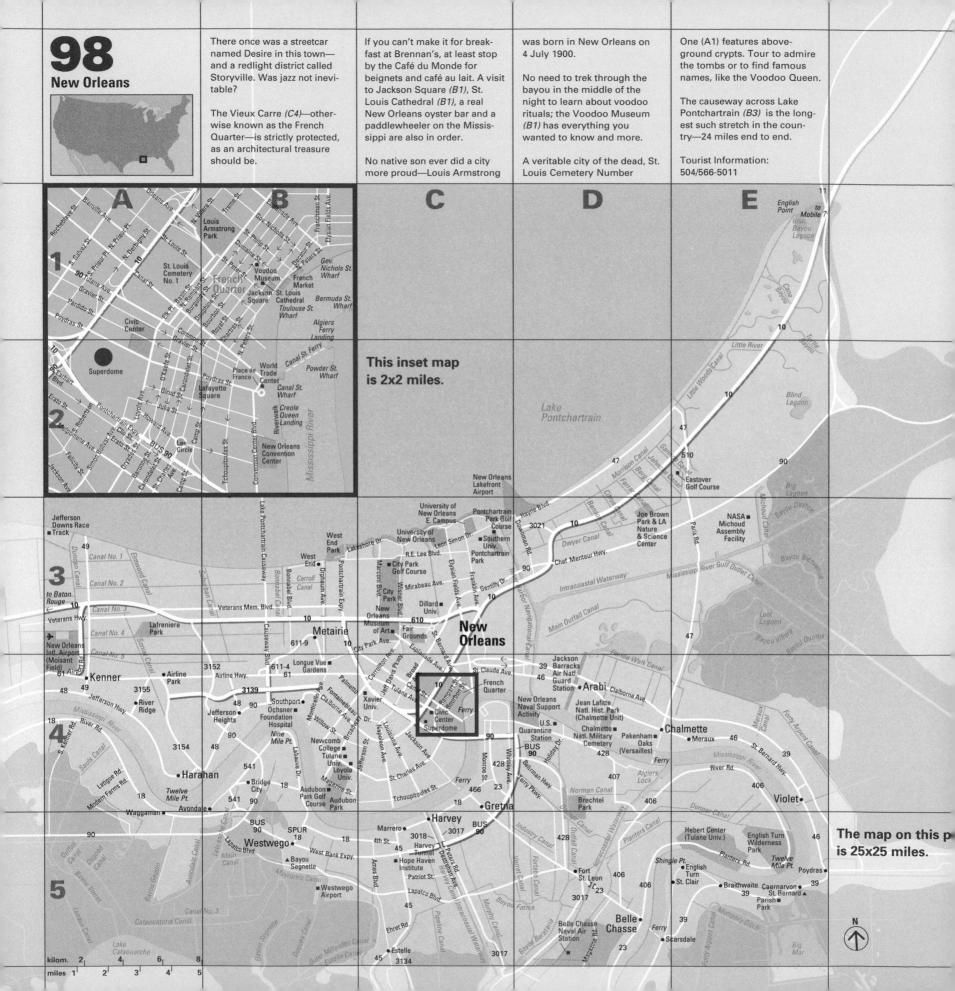

There once was a streetcar named Desire in this town—and a redlight district called Storyville. Was jazz not inevitable?

The Vieux Carre (C4)—otherwise known as the French Quarter—is strictly protected, as an architectural treasure should be.

If you can't make it for breakfast at Brennan's, at least stop by the Café du Monde for beignets and café au lait. A visit to Jackson Square (B1), St. Louis Cathedral (B1), a real New Orleans oyster bar and a paddlewheeler on the Mississippi are also in order.

No native son ever did a city more proud—Louis Armstrong

was born in New Orleans on 4 July 1900.

No need to trek through the bayou in the middle of the night to learn about voodoo rituals; the Voodoo Museum (B1) has everything you wanted to know and more.

A veritable city of the dead, St. Louis Cemetery Number

One (A1) features above-ground crypts. Tour to admire the tombs or to find famous names, like the Voodoo Queen.

The causeway across Lake Pontchartrain (B3) is the longest such stretch in the country—24 miles end to end.

Tourist Information:
504/566-5011

This inset map is 2x2 miles.

The map on this p is 25x25 miles.

Nashville Bests—
Mayor Bill Boner:
*Christie Cookies—the tastiest I've ever encountered.
Fountain Square.
Music Row and Opryland.
The revitalized downtown: a new mall, Church St. Centre, historic Second Ave. and the Nashville Convention Center.
The June Summer Lights Festival.*

"Print City USA" doesn't have quite the same ring, but that industry is bigger here than country music.

The "Athens of the South" does indeed boast not only several institutions of higher learning, but also a full-scale replica of the Parthenon *(B3)*, originally constructed for the Tennessee centennial in 1897.

Nashville boasts more churches per capita than any other major US city.

Opryland USA *(C2)* has replaced Ryman Auditorium *(C3)* as the home of the Grand Ole Opry, but diehards can still visit the auditorium; thousands do every year. Families who enjoy an amusement park with their music best head to Opryland.

… And you ain't nothin' but a hound dog if you don't tour RCA's Studio B *(B3)*.

Andrew Jackson lived here, at the Hermitage *(D2)*. Visit to discover the devoted family man behind the seventh president's "Old Hickory" persona.

Tourist Information: 615/259-4755

99
Nashville

map on this page 5x25 miles.

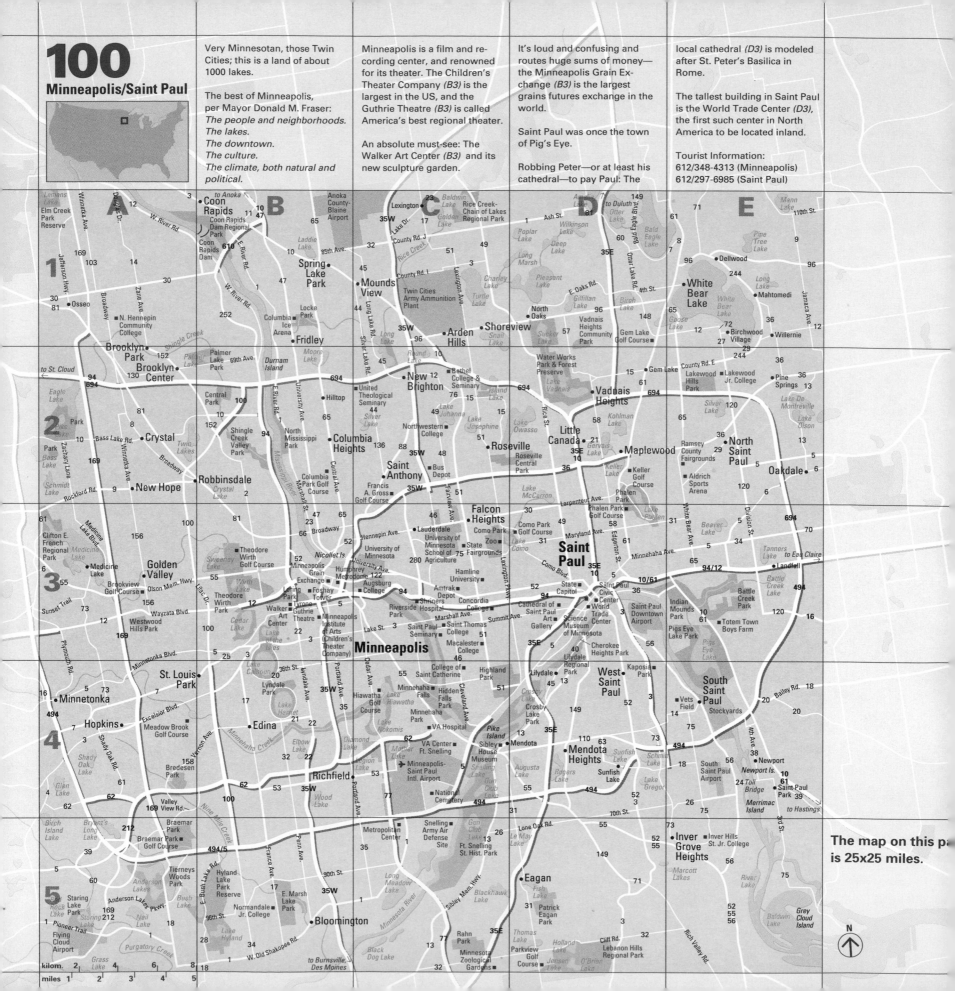

100
Minneapolis/Saint Paul

Very Minnesotan, those Twin Cities; this is a land of about 1000 lakes.

The best of Minneapolis, per Mayor Donald M. Fraser:
*The people and neighborhoods.
The lakes.
The downtown.
The culture.
The climate, both natural and political.*

Minneapolis is a film and recording center, and renowned for its theater. The Children's Theater Company (B3) is the largest in the US, and the Guthrie Theatre (B3) is called America's best regional theater.

An absolute must-see: The Walker Art Center (B3) and its new sculpture garden.

It's loud and confusing and routes huge sums of money—the Minneapolis Grain Exchange (B3) is the largest grains futures exchange in the world.

Saint Paul was once the town of Pig's Eye.

Robbing Peter—or at least his cathedral—to pay Paul: The local cathedral (D3) is modeled after St. Peter's Basilica in Rome.

The tallest building in Saint Paul is the World Trade Center (D3), the first such center in North America to be located inland.

Tourist Information:
612/348-4313 (Minneapolis)
612/297-6985 (Saint Paul)

The map on this page is 25x25 miles.

Statistically Milwaukeeans do indeed consume the most beer per capita in the US—also the most popcorn.

Immigration was such that by the end of the 19th century, two out of three daily newspapers were printed in German.

This town is renowned (no surprise) for superlative ethnic festivals. Come any weekend in the summer for a guaranteed good time.

Year-round fun is found at the Milwaukee Public Museum (D3), famed for its incredible walk-through exhibits.

You don't have to ask for the time in Milwaukee—the world's largest four-faced clock is on the Allen-Bradley Co. (D3). Each face is 40 feet high.

Milwaukee bests—the town as it appeals to Mayor John A. Norquist's 5 senses:
Sight: Lake Michigan's beaches and parkland, especially during summer festivals; European spires; new office towers.
Sound: The roar of fans at Brewers and Bucks games; the Milwaukee Symphony Orchestra.
Touch: The exhibits at the Milwaukee Public Museum.
Taste: The foods of different cuisines in the many ethnic neighborhoods.
Smell: Ambrosia chocolates and the nearby Spice House.

Tourist Information:
414/273-3950

101
Milwaukee

You'd expect "the city that works" to have a town motto that says, simply, "I will."

Second City Nothing—
Busiest airport.
Biggest post office.
Largest commodity futures exchange.
Tallest building
Largest bank building.
Largest water filtration plant.

The Chicago River used to run from the Mississippi to Lake Michigan—that was God's plan. It's run the other way since 1900—see the town motto above.

In an unkind and ungentle era, Jane Addams' Hull House was a haven of social services for tenement dwellers. You can tour the relocated and restored house at the University of Illinois at Chicago (D3).

The Great Chicago Fire of 1871 destroyed 65 acres per hour, and caused $125,000 worth of damage per minute.

The Lincoln Park Zoo (D2) is the most visited zoo in the country, with over 12,000 visitors a day—maybe because it's free.

The building currently housing the outstanding collections of the Museum of Contemporary Art (D3) was once home to the offices of Playboy Magazine.

You'll have to go to Warsaw to find more Poles than you'll find in Chicago.

Tourist Information:
312/280-5740

The map on this pa
is 25x25 miles.

The Motown Museum (Barry Gordy's former home) is a state historical site (C3).

Hello, Central? Detroit residents were the first to get their own phone numbers.

In this city of autos, an excellent people mover provides covered, elevated mass transit around the downtown core.

Henry Ford may as well have invented the suburb—not only did he invent the car, he came up with the idea of charcoal briquettes. Could backyard barbecues be far behind? You will take time, I hope, to visit Greenfield Village (B4), and Ford's Fairlane mansion, where he and good friend Thomas Edison puttered and invented.

Do you remember "If it's good for GM, it's good for the country"? Still the largest manufacturing company in the world. Motor City indeed.

Should you cross (south!) to Canada, you'll find more of the same: American auto plants.

You wouldn't think of this city as a garden center, but it is.

The Eastern Market has been in the flower bedding business for nearly 100 years and Detroit produces the seeds that grow up in over half the gardens in the US.

Detroit claims to have opened the world's first Convention and Visitors Bureau, in 1896. These days they can be reached at: 313/567-1170

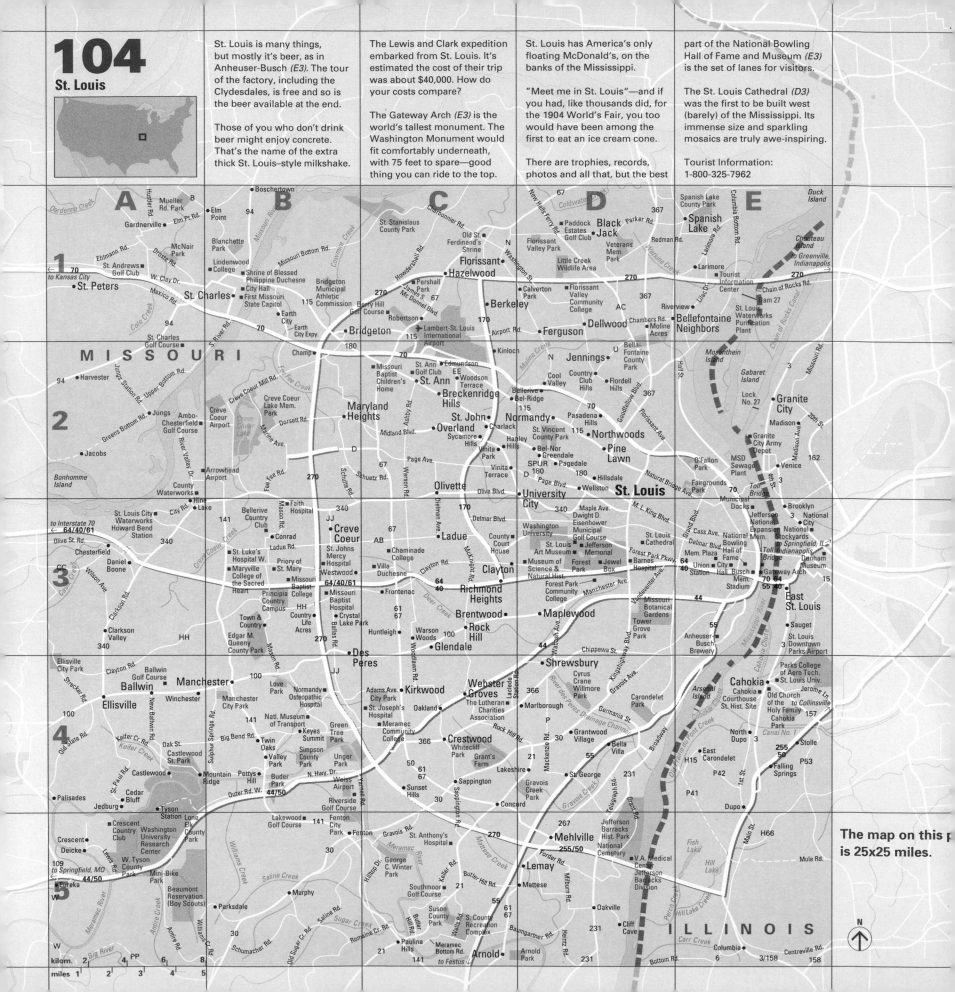

St. Louis is many things, but mostly it's beer, as in Anheuser-Busch (E3). The tour of the factory, including the Clydesdales, is free and so is the beer available at the end.

Those of you who don't drink beer might enjoy concrete. That's the name of the extra thick St. Louis–style milkshake.

The Lewis and Clark expedition embarked from St. Louis. It's estimated the cost of their trip was about $40,000. How do your costs compare?

The Gateway Arch (E3) is the world's tallest monument. The Washington Monument would fit comfortably underneath, with 75 feet to spare—good thing you can ride to the top.

St. Louis has America's only floating McDonald's, on the banks of the Mississippi.

"Meet me in St. Louis"—and if you had, like thousands did, for the 1904 World's Fair, you too would have been among the first to eat an ice cream cone.

There are trophies, records, photos and all that, but the best part of the National Bowling Hall of Fame and Museum (E3) is the set of lanes for visitors.

The St. Louis Cathedral (D3) was the first to be built west (barely) of the Mississippi. Its immense size and sparkling mosaics are truly awe-inspiring.

Tourist Information:
1-800-325-7962

The map on this p is 25x25 miles.

One way to become a major city—in 1969 most of the surrounding county was merged with Indianapolis. The city's population (and tax base) jumped instantly from 485,000 to 745,000.

Who'd have thought the '60s would be forever immortalized here? But this is where, at the Indianapolis Museum of Art (C2), you'll find Robert Indiana's original LOVE sculpture.

Love might make the world go 'round, but here it's sports that makes things hum. Of course, there's the Indy 500—the world's largest single day sporting event—but Indianapolis also hosted the 1987 Pan Am Games; and the Hoosier Dome (C3), these days, is the Hoosier home of the Indianapolis Colts. In the US, only Los Angeles equals Indianapolis as a center of world-class sports facilities.

Indianapolis had the first Union Station (serving more than one railroad) in the country, a Romanesque Revival beauty built in 1888. It's still a train depot, but you can also steam in for shopping and dining (C3).

This town is understandably proud of its Children's Museum (C3), the largest in the world—five floors of trains, dinosaurs, touchy-feely stuff and even a 23,000 year-old mummy.

Tourist Information:
317/237-5200

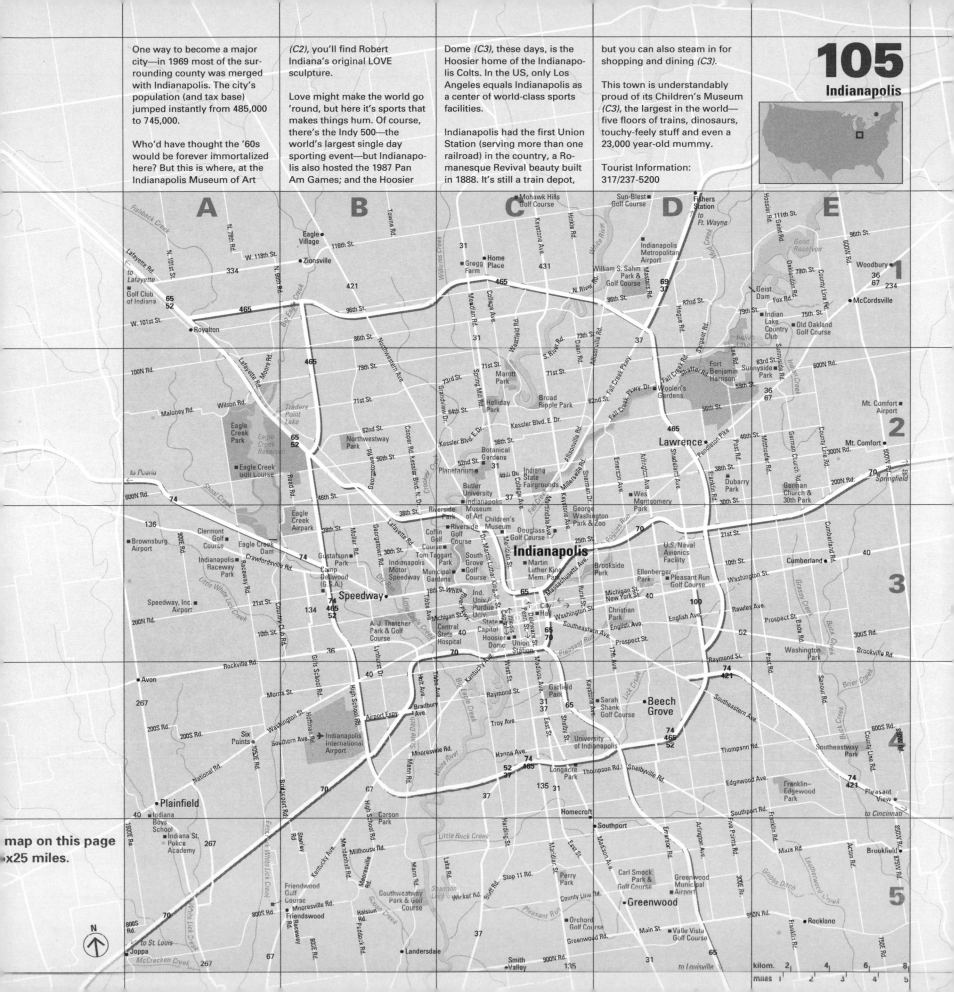

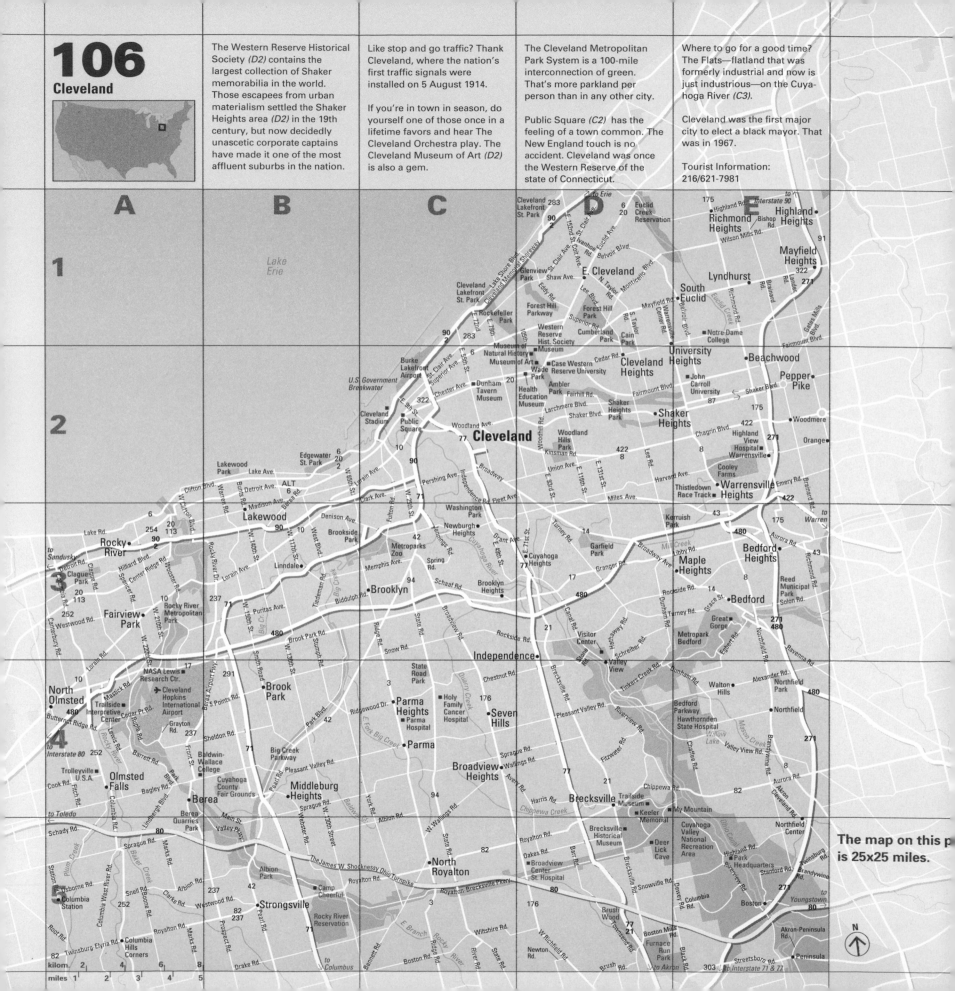

106

Cleveland

The Western Reserve Historical Society (D2) contains the largest collection of Shaker memorabilia in the world. Those escapees from urban materialism settled the Shaker Heights area (D2) in the 19th century, but now decidedly unascetic corporate captains have made it one of the most affluent suburbs in the nation.

Like stop and go traffic? Thank Cleveland, where the nation's first traffic signals were installed on 5 August 1914.

If you're in town in season, do yourself one of those once in a lifetime favors and hear The Cleveland Orchestra play. The Cleveland Museum of Art (D2) is also a gem.

The Cleveland Metropolitan Park System is a 100-mile interconnection of green. That's more parkland per person than in any other city.

Public Square (C2) has the feeling of a town common. The New England touch is no accident. Cleveland was once the Western Reserve of the state of Connecticut.

Where to go for a good time? The Flats—flatland that was formerly industrial and now is just industrious—on the Cuyahoga River (C3).

Cleveland was the first major city to elect a black mayor. That was in 1967.

Tourist Information: 216/621-7981

The map on this p is 25x25 miles.

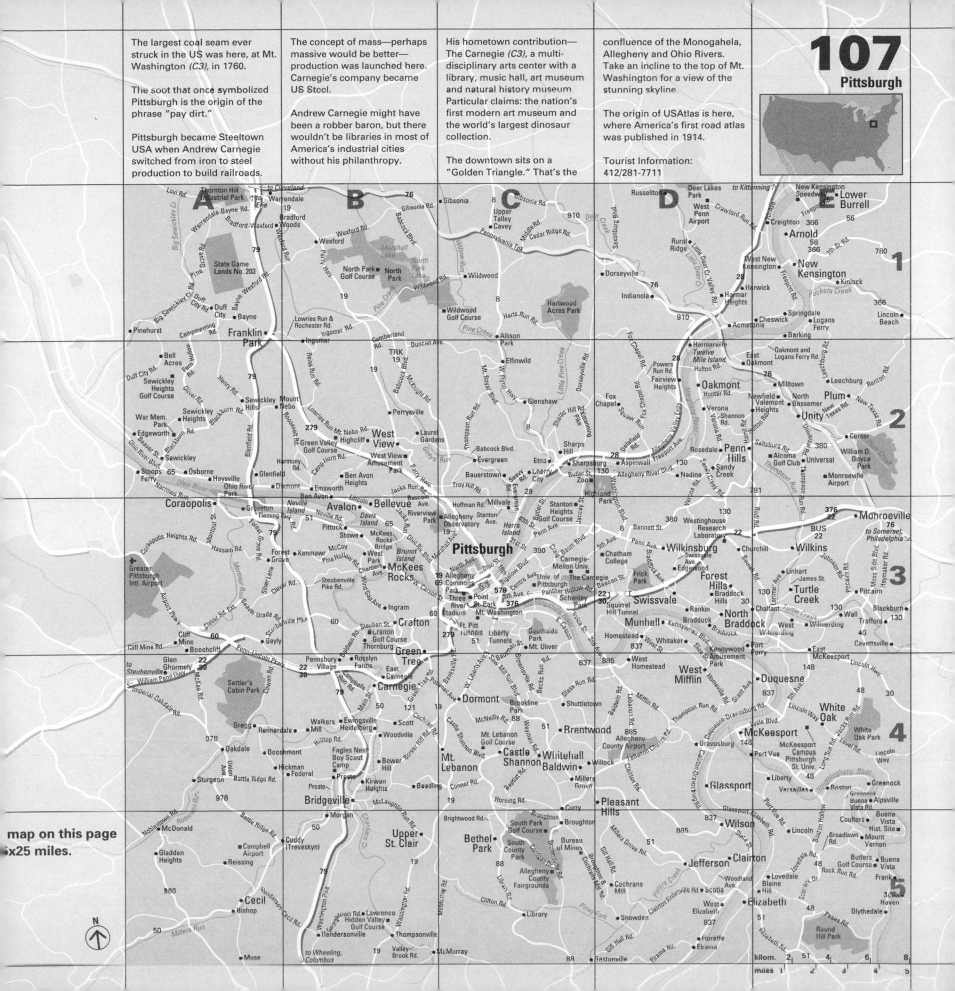

The largest coal seam ever struck in the US was here, at Mt. Washington (C3), in 1760.

The soot that once symbolized Pittsburgh is the origin of the phrase "pay dirt."

Pittsburgh became Steeltown USA when Andrew Carnegie switched from iron to steel production to build railroads.

The concept of mass—perhaps massive would be better—production was launched here. Carnegie's company became US Steel.

Andrew Carnegie might have been a robber baron, but there wouldn't be libraries in most of America's industrial cities without his philanthropy.

His hometown contribution—The Carnegie (C3), a multi-disciplinary arts center with a library, music hall, art museum and natural history museum. Particular claims: the nation's first modern art museum and the world's largest dinosaur collection.

The downtown sits on a "Golden Triangle." That's the confluence of the Monogahela, Allegheny and Ohio Rivers. Take an incline to the top of Mt. Washington for a view of the stunning skyline

The origin of USAtlas is here, where America's first road atlas was published in 1914.

Tourist Information:
412/281-7711

map on this page
5x25 miles.

108
Cincinnati

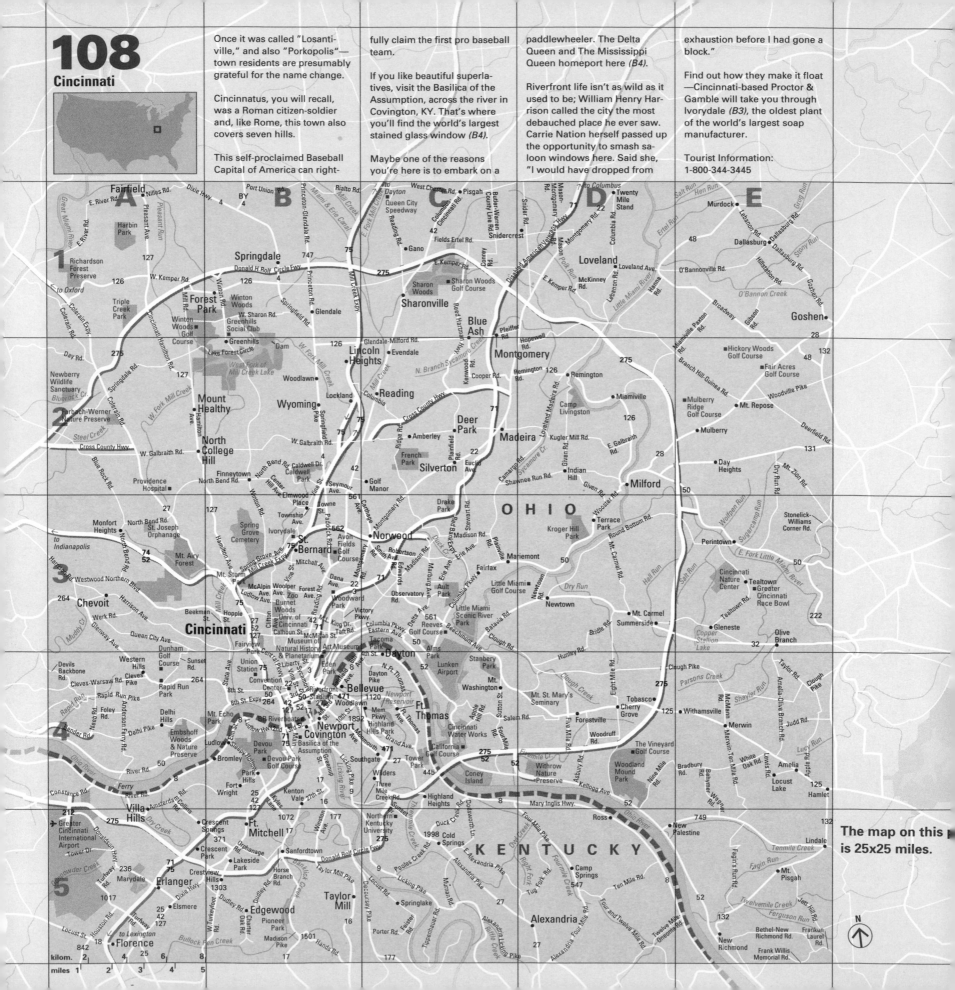

Once it was called "Losantiville," and also "Porkopolis"— town residents are presumably grateful for the name change.

Cincinnatus, you will recall, was a Roman citizen-soldier and, like Rome, this town also covers seven hills.

This self-proclaimed Baseball Capital of America can right-fully claim the first pro baseball team.

If you like beautiful superlatives, visit the Basilica of the Assumption, across the river in Covington, KY. That's where you'll find the world's largest stained glass window (B4).

Maybe one of the reasons you're here is to embark on a paddlewheeler. The Delta Queen and The Mississippi Queen homeport here (B4).

Riverfront life isn't as wild as it used to be; William Henry Harrison called the city the most debauched place he ever saw. Carrie Nation herself passed up the opportunity to smash saloon windows here. Said she, "I would have dropped from exhaustion before I had gone a block."

Find out how they make it float —Cincinnati-based Proctor & Gamble will take you through Ivorydale (B3), the oldest plant of the world's largest soap manufacturer.

Tourist Information: 1-800-344-3445

A capital capitol—the Columbus Statehouse (C3) is famed as the purest example of Greek Revival architecture in the US.

For modern architecture, try the Wexner Center (C3) home to much of the city's visual and performing arts, and a striking piece of visual art itself.

The first lowland gorilla to be born in captivity was born in the Columbus Zoo (B1). Now there are four generations amusing the public.

You've seen plenty of historic neighborhoods restored by their cities—what makes German Village (C4) unique is that it is the country's largest National Historic District restored by *private* funds.

The first Saturday evening of every month, Columbus art patrons and general party-goers descend upon the Short North neighborhood, between 670 and Third Ave. (C3), for the Gallery Hop—gallery openings, food, drink and live music.

The Brewery District is one of those preserved-architecture—condo/office/restaurant developments now, but it's still the home to the Columbus Brewing Company, if you fancy a micro-brewery tour (C4).

Bring your walking shoes—Ohio State University (C3) has the largest main campus of any US university.

Tourist Information:
614/221-2489

109
Columbus

map on this page
5x25 miles.

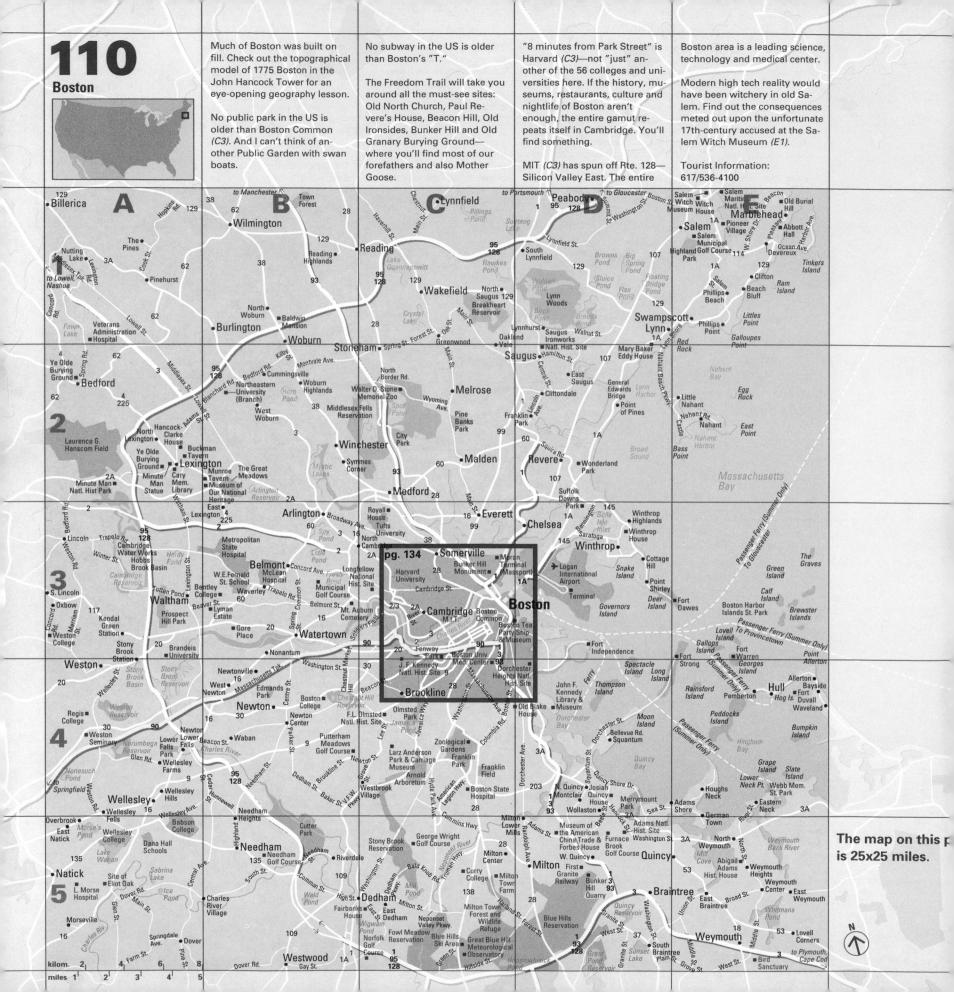

110

Boston

Much of Boston was built on fill. Check out the topographical model of 1775 Boston in the John Hancock Tower for an eye-opening geography lesson.

No public park in the US is older than Boston Common (C3). And I can't think of another Public Garden with swan boats.

No subway in the US is older than Boston's "T."

The Freedom Trail will take you around all the must-see sites: Old North Church, Paul Revere's House, Beacon Hill, Old Ironsides, Bunker Hill and Old Granary Burying Ground— where you'll find most of our forefathers and also Mother Goose.

"8 minutes from Park Street" is Harvard (C3)—not "just" another of the 56 colleges and universities here. If the history, museums, restaurants, culture and nightlife of Boston aren't enough, the entire gamut repeats itself in Cambridge. You'll find something.

MIT (C3) has spun off Rte. 128— Silicon Valley East. The entire

Boston area is a leading science, technology and medical center.

Modern high tech reality would have been witchery in old Salem. Find out the consequences meted out upon the unfortunate 17th-century accused at the Salem Witch Museum (E1).

Tourist Information:
617/536-4100

The map on this p[...]
is 25x25 miles.

111
New York

The five boroughs of Manhattan, Brooklyn, Queens, Staten Island and the Bronx united to form New York City in 1898. With a population of three million, the new city instantly qualified as the largest city in the world.

Join the fun. You and nearly 18 million other folks will visit the Big Apple this year.

New York is no place to learn how to drive—in fact, if you're under 18 you're forbidden to drive, by law. You cannot turn right on red here, you know.

The city is just over 300 miles square; the population density is about 26,000 people per square mile. Does that help explain New Yorkers?

A tough town with a heart: nearly 1/5 of the land in New York is devoted to parks and playgrounds. Visit the Brooklyn Botanic Garden (C4) for some beautiful greenery.

There's over three-quarters of a million college students here. Only 10 cities in the US have entire populations as large.

Want a great deal? The Staten Island Ferry costs a *quarter*, with an incomparable view of the world's most famous skyline—and lady Liberty, too.

The Verrazano Narrows Bridge (B5), is the world's longest suspension bridge.

Tourist Information:
212/397-8222

map on this page
x25 miles.

Taking the *Hudson River Day-liner* up the Hudson River to West Point? You're on the world's oldest scheduled passenger steamer route—established by Robert Fulton in 1807.

A favorite expression of American culture is memorialized in Port Chester, NY *(D4)*—the Museum of Cartoon Art, which houses over 60,000 original cartoons. Stop in Sundays for animated films.

The choice of any generation in Purchase, NY—Pepsi's hometown—is the exceptional sculpture garden at the company's headquarters *(C3)*.

Washington Irving's home Sunnyside is in Tarrytown, NY *(A3)*, in the middle of the Sleepy Hollow Country he made famous.

Golf was introduced to the US in Yonkers *(B5)* at—where else—St. Andrew's Golf Course.

An unusual architectural fancy—the First Presbyterian Church in Stamford, CT *(E3)* is shaped like a fish.

Long Island Sound fishing and trade built this area of Connecticut. Explore the area's history and marine life through exhibits, films, demonstrations and an aquarium at the Maritime Center at Norwalk *(F2)*.

Damning themselves with faint praise—the Connecticut state nickname is "The Land of Steady Habits."

The map on this page is 25x25 miles.

↓ pg. 111

Coming and going—plenty of top Broadway productions start out at the Shubert Theatre in New Haven; others end up at the Westport Country Playhouse (pg. 112, F1).

More traditionally, it's no surprise that there is an American Shakespeare Theatre (modeled after the Old Globe, of course) in Connecticut's Stratford (B3).

Those business commuters aren't just escaping the press of urban New York. Connecticut levies no state income tax.

If it's good enough for them … Eli Whitney, William Howard Taft and Noah Webster all studied at Yale (D1). So did George Bush, Jodie Foster and Garry Trudeau. And yes, there is ivy on the walls.

Yale museum sights not to be missed:

The Beinecke Rare Book and Manuscript Library, whose Vermont marble walls are cut so thin they're transluscent.

A striking Louis I. Kahn building houses the Yale Center for British Art, the finest such collection outside of England.

Did you know you could win a Pulitzer Prize for a mural? This one did: the Peabody Museum of Natural History's giant depiction of North America as it looked millions of years ago.

Just for fun: Bridgeport's P.T. Barnum Museum (B3).

Tourist Information: 203/258-4290

The map on this page is 25x25 miles.

114

Philadelphia

Yes, that is a giant clothespin (by Claes Oldenberg) downtown. Classicists may prefer the Rodin Museum *(B3)*, home of the largest collection of his sculpture outside France.

A unique landscaping idea—the Moon Tree is a sycamore grown from seeds taken to the moon on Apollo 14.

Philly firsts: America's oldest zoo, medical college, bank, stock exchange, art school, fire-fighting company, and the oldest lending library and hospital—both founded by the unstoppable Benjamin Franklin.

To him we also owe: the postal service, our country's first designated university (U Penn) and first newspaper. See his inventions at Franklin Court *(C3)*, and his final resting place at Christ Church Cemetery *(C3)*—along with four other signers of the Declaration of Independence.

Don't forget the Ben Franklin Cribbage Tournament in May.

In a city replete with Americana, the Norman Rockwell Museum *(C3)* is right at home.

Every one of his covers for The Saturday Evening Post is on display.

Cross to Camden, NJ *(C3)* for the Campbell Museum, memorializing cozy soup days of yore, and housing an astounding collection of soup tureens.

Tourist Information: 215/636-1666

The map on this p is 25x25 miles.

The Inner Harbor (C3) is probably where you'll head—and rightly so. This area is anchored by The National Aquarium—very definitely worth a visit—the building (designed by Cambridge 7 Associates) is striking. A rain forest, a coral reef and other aquatic habitats await you inside.

The Roland Park Shopping Center, opened in 1896, is designated America's first shopping center (C3).

Then again there's Lexington Market (C3)—it's been open as a city-operated market longer than any other in the US ... since 1782. What you buy there, of course, are crabs. Enough are caught in

Chesapeake Bay each year to provide 100 pounds' worth to every Baltimorean.

George Herman Ruth was judged "incorrigible" at the age of 7, but a monk at St. Mary's Industrial School for Boys taught him what he was born to learn. The Babe never played for the home team—but Baltimore proudly claims him.

A whole different ballgame—check out the Lacrosse Hall of Fame. If you want to catch a live game, head over to Johns Hopkins University (C3).

Baltimore built the first Washington Monument (C3); Climb it for a great view.

Tourist Information: 301/837-4636

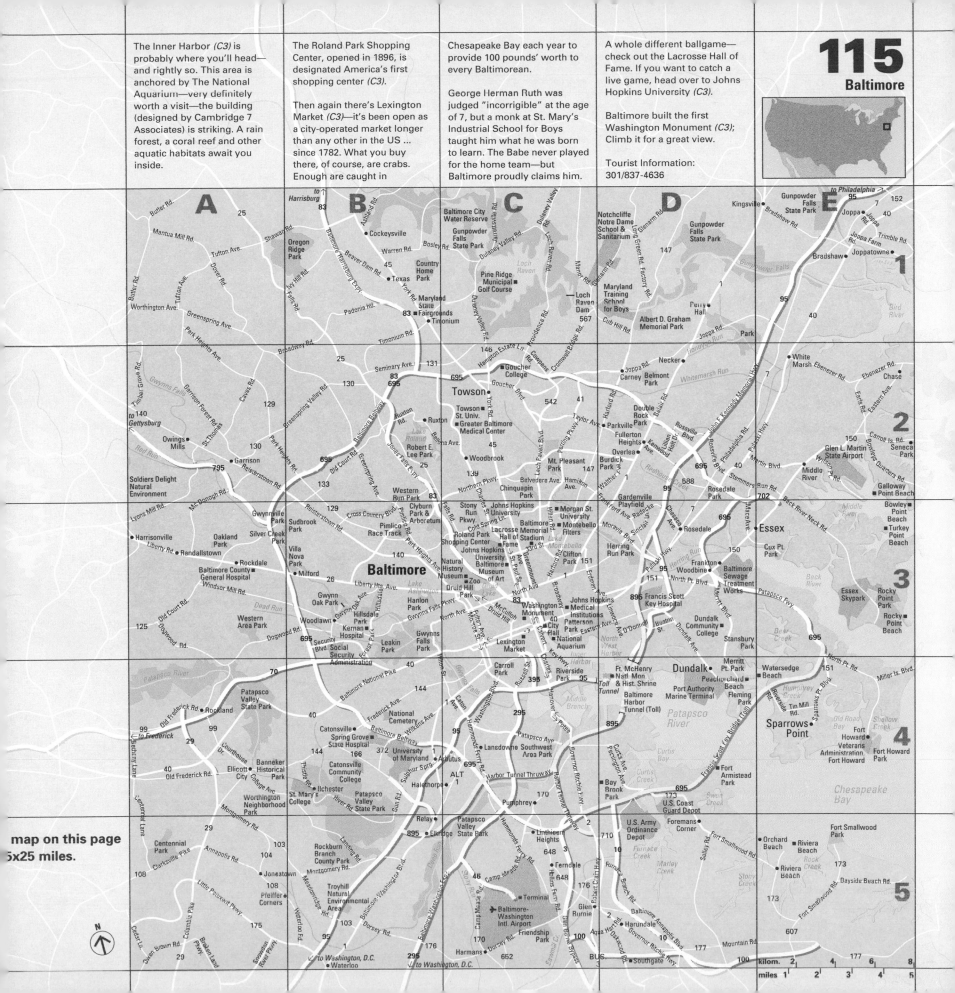

map on this page
5x25 miles.

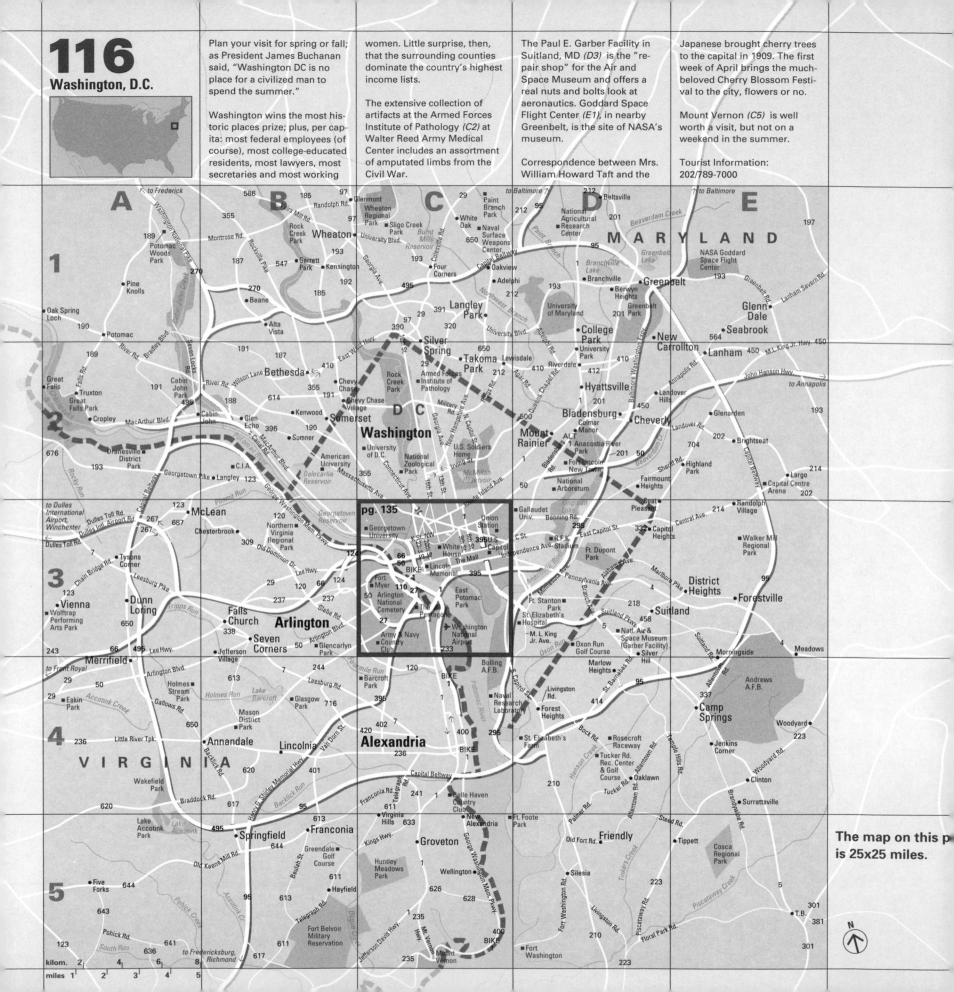

116

Washington, D.C.

Plan your visit for spring or fall; as President James Buchanan said, "Washington DC is no place for a civilized man to spend the summer."

Washington wins the most historic places prize; plus, per capita: most federal employees (of course), most college-educated residents, most lawyers, most secretaries and most working women. Little surprise, then, that the surrounding counties dominate the country's highest income lists.

The extensive collection of artifacts at the Armed Forces Institute of Pathology (C2) at Walter Reed Army Medical Center includes an assortment of amputated limbs from the Civil War.

The Paul E. Garber Facility in Suitland, MD (D3) is the "repair shop" for the Air and Space Museum and offers a real nuts and bolts look at aeronautics. Goddard Space Flight Center (E1), in nearby Greenbelt, is the site of NASA's museum.

Correspondence between Mrs. William Howard Taft and the Japanese brought cherry trees to the capital in 1909. The first week of April brings the much-beloved Cherry Blossom Festival to the city, flowers or no.

Mount Vernon (C5) is well worth a visit, but not on a weekend in the summer.

Tourist Information: 202/789-7000

The map on this p is 25x25 miles.

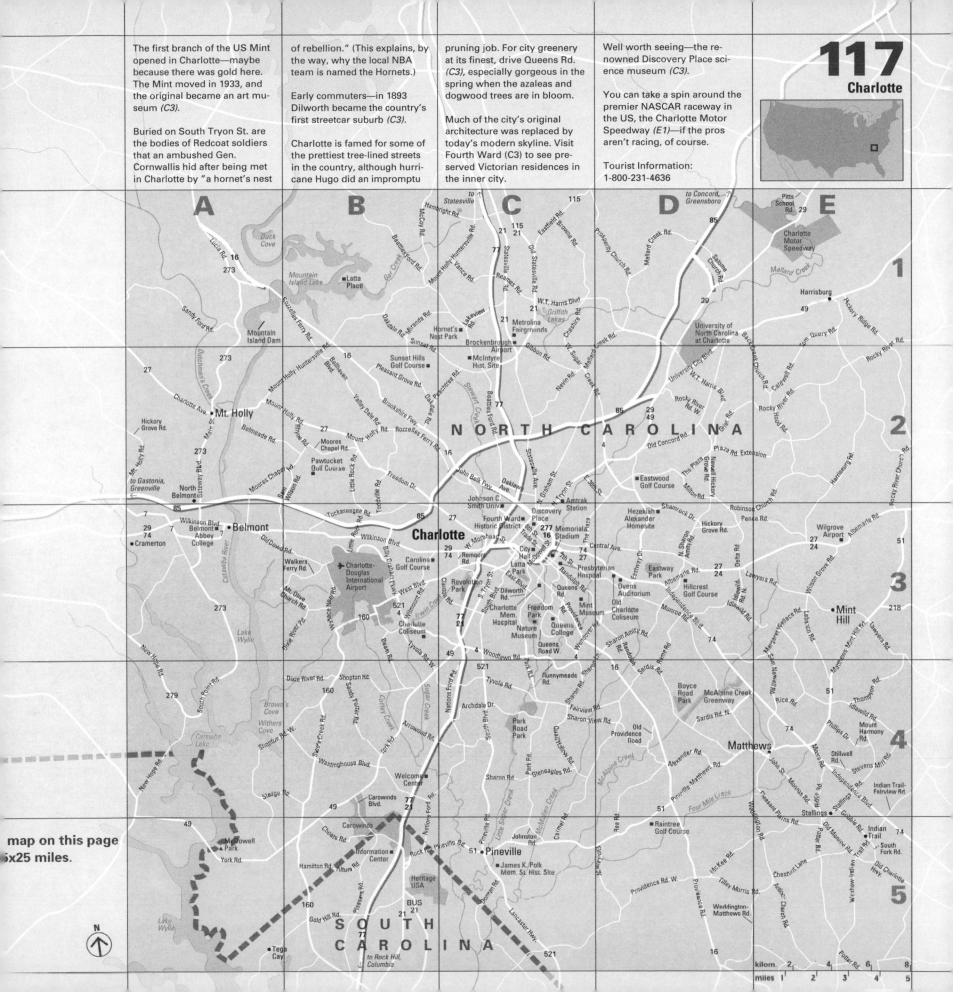

The first branch of the US Mint opened in Charlotte—maybe because there was gold here. The Mint moved in 1933, and the original became an art museum (C3).

Buried on South Tryon St. are the bodies of Redcoat soldiers that an ambushed Gen. Cornwallis hid after being met in Charlotte by "a hornet's nest of rebellion." (This explains, by the way, why the local NBA team is named the Hornets.)

Early commuters—in 1893 Dilworth became the country's first streetcar suburb (C3).

Charlotte is famed for some of the prettiest tree-lined streets in the country, although hurricane Hugo did an impromptu pruning job. For city greenery at its finest, drive Queens Rd. (C3), especially gorgeous in the spring when the azaleas and dogwood trees are in bloom.

Much of the city's original architecture was replaced by today's modern skyline. Visit Fourth Ward (C3) to see preserved Victorian residences in the inner city.

Well worth seeing—the renowned Discovery Place science museum (C3).

You can take a spin around the premier NASCAR raceway in the US, the Charlotte Motor Speedway (E1)—if the pros aren't racing, of course.

Tourist Information:
1-800-231-4636

map on this page
6x25 miles.

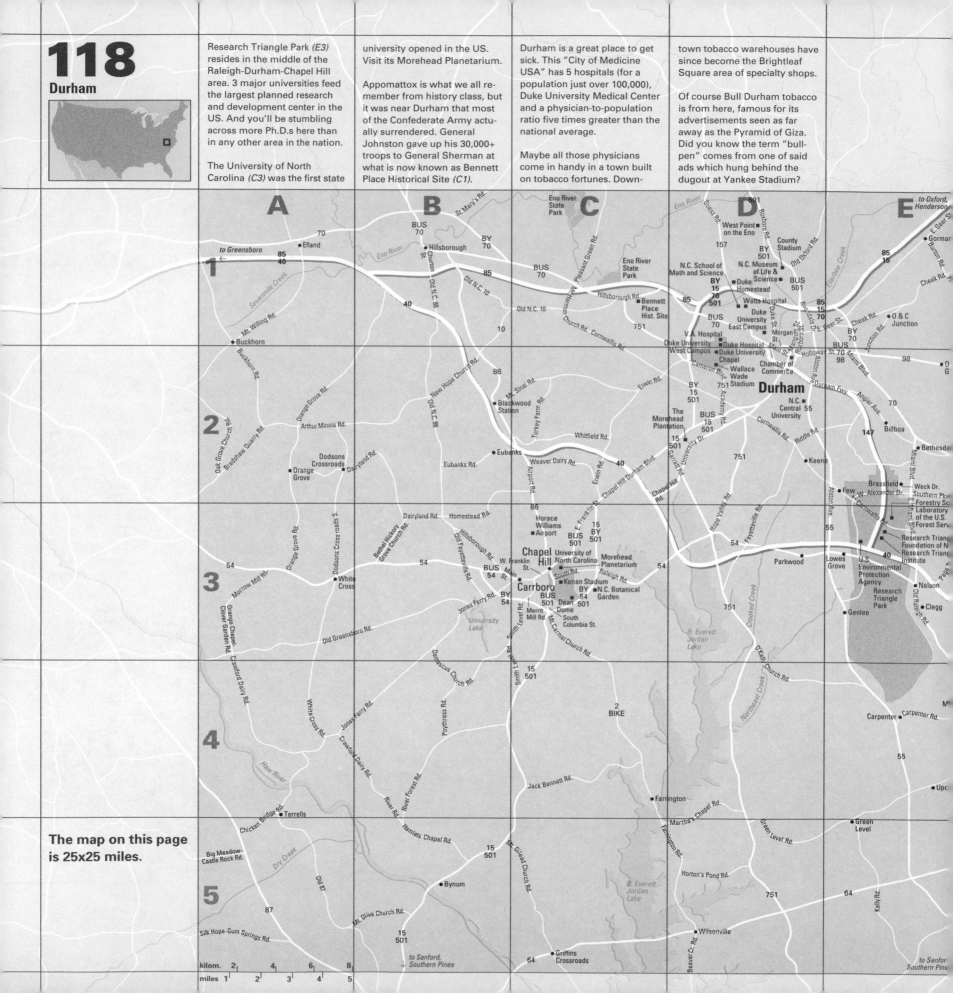

Research Triangle Park (E3) resides in the middle of the Raleigh-Durham-Chapel Hill area. 3 major universities feed the largest planned research and development center in the US. And you'll be stumbling across more Ph.D.s here than in any other area in the nation.

The University of North Carolina (C3) was the first state university opened in the US. Visit its Morehead Planetarium.

Appomattox is what we all remember from history class, but it was near Durham that most of the Confederate Army actually surrendered. General Johnston gave up his 30,000+ troops to General Sherman at what is now known as Bennett Place Historical Site (C1).

Durham is a great place to get sick. This "City of Medicine USA" has 5 hospitals (for a population just over 100,000), Duke University Medical Center and a physician-to-population ratio five times greater than the national average.

Maybe all those physicians come in handy in a town built on tobacco fortunes. Down-town tobacco warehouses have since become the Brightleaf Square area of specialty shops.

Of course Bull Durham tobacco is from here, famous for its advertisements seen as far away as the Pyramid of Giza. Did you know the term "bull-pen" comes from one of said ads which hung behind the dugout at Yankee Stadium?

The map on this page is 25x25 miles.

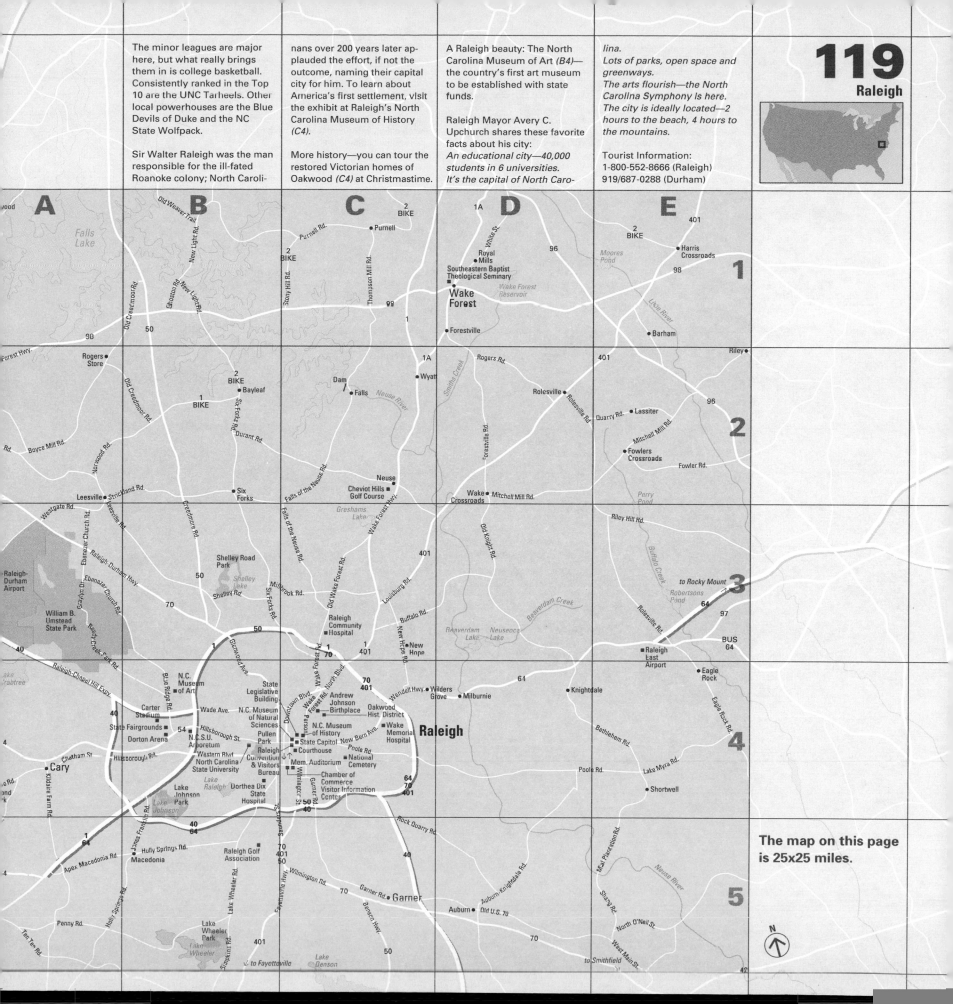

The minor leagues are major here, but what really brings them in is college basketball. Consistently ranked in the Top 10 are the UNC Tarheels. Other local powerhouses are the Blue Devils of Duke and the NC State Wolfpack.

Sir Walter Raleigh was the man responsible for the ill-fated Roanoke colony; North Caroli-nans over 200 years later applauded the effort, if not the outcome, naming their capital city for him. To learn about America's first settlement, visit the exhibit at Raleigh's North Carolina Museum of History (C4).

More history—you can tour the restored Victorian homes of Oakwood (C4) at Christmastime.

A Raleigh beauty: The North Carolina Museum of Art (B4)—the country's first art museum to be established with state funds.

Raleigh Mayor Avery C. Upchurch shares these favorite facts about his city:
An educational city—40,000 students in 6 universities.
It's the capital of North Caro-lina.
Lots of parks, open space and greenways.
The arts flourish—the North Carolina Symphony is here.
The city is ideally located—2 hours to the beach, 4 hours to the mountains.

Tourist Information:
1-800-552-8666 (Raleigh)
919/687-0288 (Durham)

119
Raleigh

The map on this page is 25x25 miles.

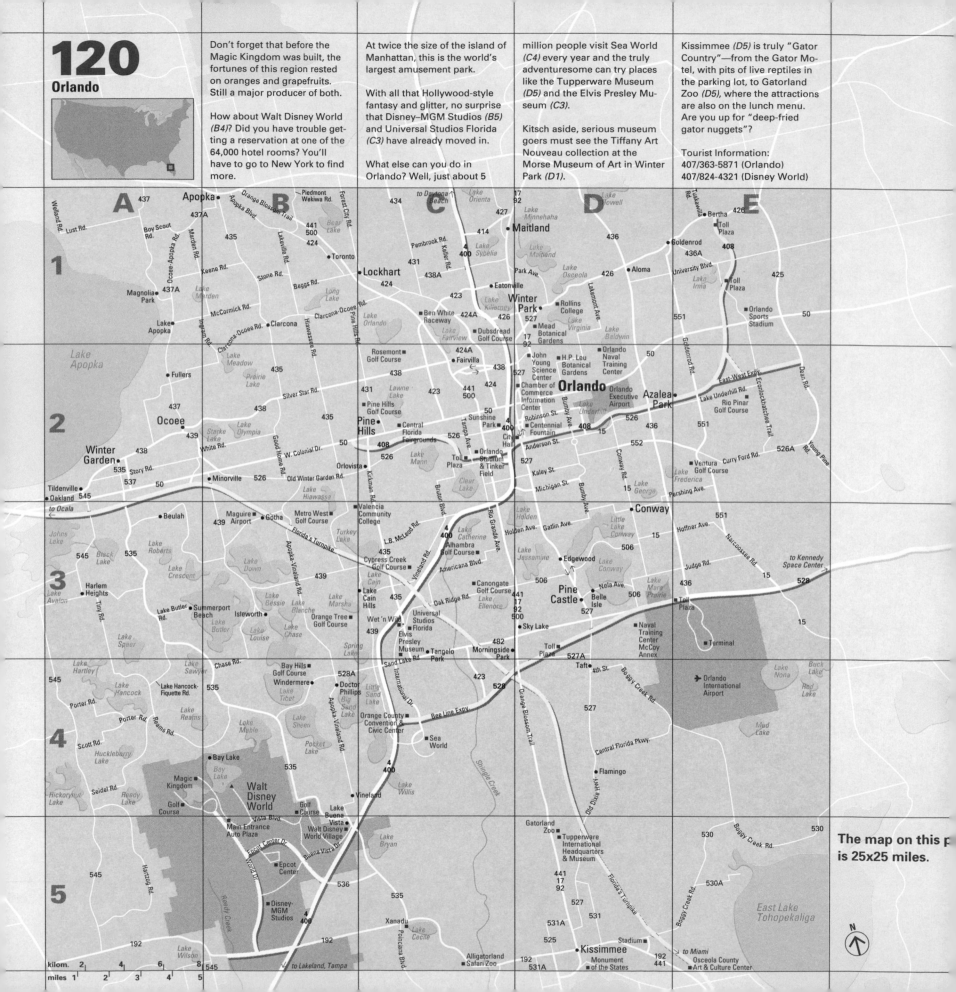

120

Orlando

Don't forget that before the Magic Kingdom was built, the fortunes of this region rested on oranges and grapefruits. Still a major producer of both.

How about Walt Disney World (B4)? Did you have trouble getting a reservation at one of the 64,000 hotel rooms? You'll have to go to New York to find more.

At twice the size of the island of Manhattan, this is the world's largest amusement park.

With all that Hollywood-style fantasy and glitter, no surprise that Disney–MGM Studios (B5) and Universal Studios Florida (C3) have already moved in.

What else can you do in Orlando? Well, just about 5 million people visit Sea World (C4) every year and the truly adventuresome can try places like the Tupperware Museum (D5) and the Elvis Presley Museum (C3).

Kitsch aside, serious museum goers must see the Tiffany Art Nouveau collection at the Morse Museum of Art in Winter Park (D1).

Kissimmee (D5) is truly "Gator Country"—from the Gator Motel, with pits of live reptiles in the parking lot, to Gatorland Zoo (D5), where the attractions are also on the lunch menu. Are you up for "deep-fried gator nuggets"?

Tourist Information:
407/363-5871 (Orlando)
407/824-4321 (Disney World)

The map on this p
is 25x25 miles.

Sherman did not mess around here—not only was the city burned to the ground in 1864, even the railroad tracks for getting here were destroyed. Naturally the city's symbol is the phoenix; its town motto: *resurgens.*

Atlanta was not one to lose gracefully—The Stone Mountain Monument *(E1)* dwarfs "the North's" Mt. Rushmore; it's the largest mural sculpture in the world and honors Robert E. Lee, Stonewall Jackson and Jefferson Davis.

Yes, Margaret Mitchell lived and wrote *Gone With the Wind* here. Miss Mitchell's Miss Pittypat lived on one of the 26 roads hereabouts named Peachtree.

Downtown's Peachtree Street was originally an Indian trail to the Chattahoochee River.

The medical community's FBI for germs—the Centers for Disease Control *(D2)*—is here, tirelessly fighting new and deadly diseases.

Atlanta's excellent rapid rail and bus system, MARTA, can get you where you want to go. Downtown hotel guests often opt for horse and carriage rides, instead.

Coca Cola has been the real thing in Atlanta since 1886. Sip one at the Varsity, "The World's Largest Drive-In Restaurant."

Atlanta Tourist Information: 404/521-6688

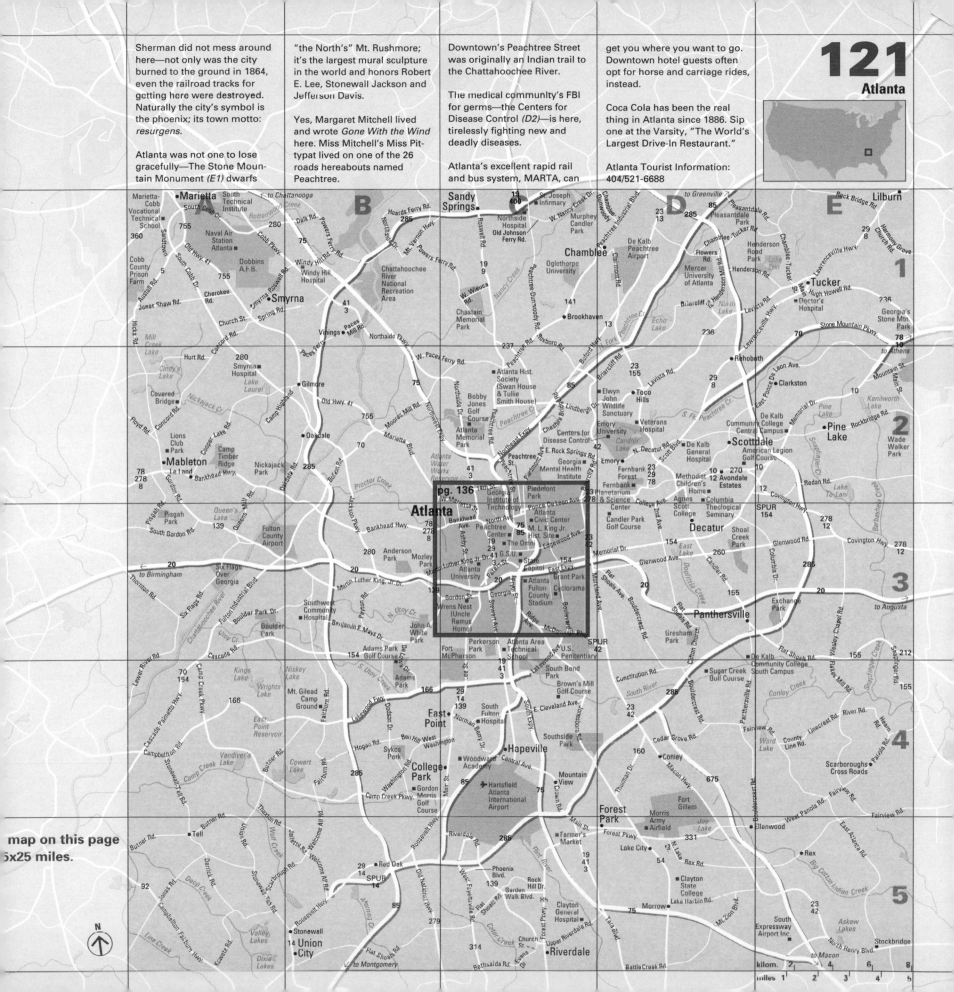

map on this page
5x25 miles.

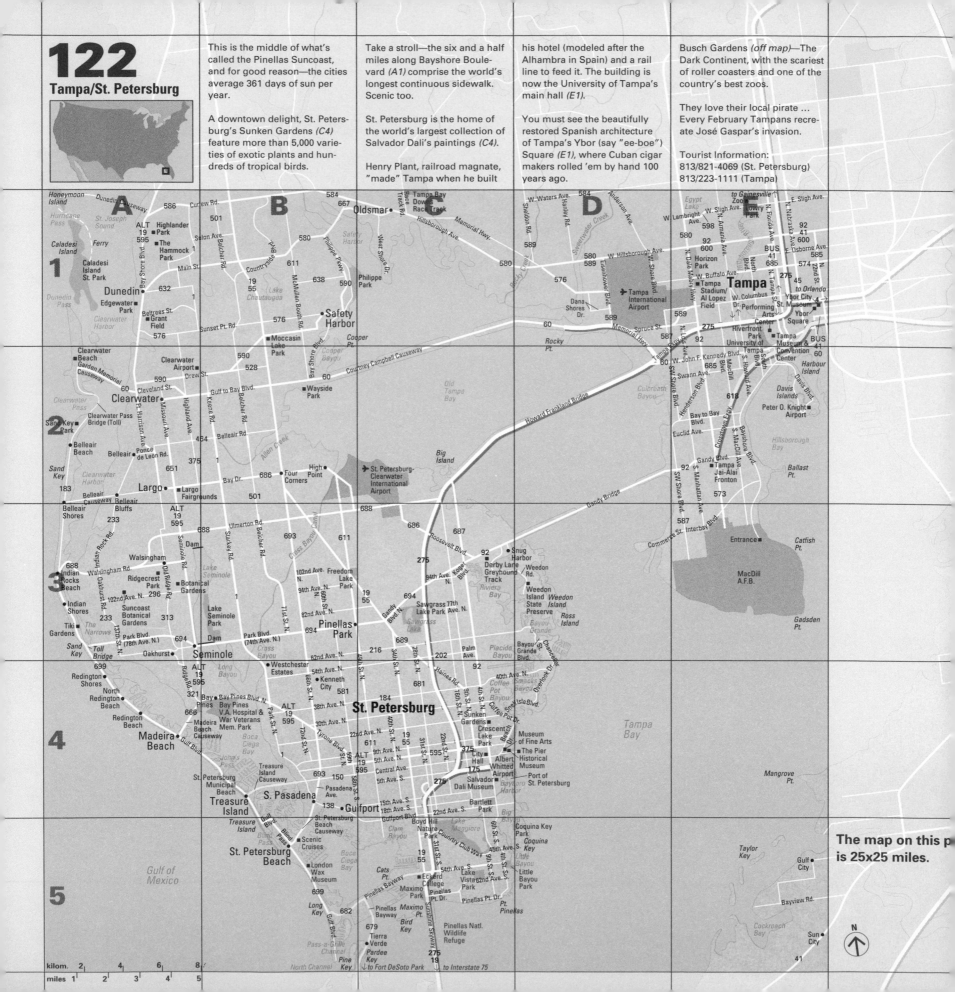

122

Tampa/St. Petersburg

This is the middle of what's called the Pinellas Suncoast, and for good reason—the cities average 361 days of sun per year.

A downtown delight, St. Petersburg's Sunken Gardens (C4) feature more than 5,000 varieties of exotic plants and hundreds of tropical birds.

Take a stroll—the six and a half miles along Bayshore Boulevard (A1) comprise the world's longest continuous sidewalk. Scenic too.

St. Petersburg is the home of the world's largest collection of Salvador Dali's paintings (C4).

Henry Plant, railroad magnate, "made" Tampa when he built his hotel (modeled after the Alhambra in Spain) and a rail line to feed it. The building is now the University of Tampa's main hall (E1).

You must see the beautifully restored Spanish architecture of Tampa's Ybor (say "ee-boe") Square (E1), where Cuban cigar makers rolled 'em by hand 100 years ago.

Busch Gardens (off map)—The Dark Continent, with the scariest of roller coasters and one of the country's best zoos.

They love their local pirate ... Every February Tampans recreate José Gaspar's invasion.

Tourist Information:
813/821-4069 (St. Petersburg)
813/223-1111 (Tampa)

The map on this p[age]
is 25x25 miles.

You'll quickly figure out that Miami and Miami Beach are very distinct. Miami Beach (E4) is the one with the art deco hotels ... so many that the area comprises the largest national historic district in the US.

Still, you can have a great time in Miami, too. Come for Carnaval and get attached to the world's longest conga line.

Miami is famous for palm trees, but can you imagine over 500 species? Go see for yourself at Fairchild Tropical Garden (off map), the largest tropical garden in the country.

Would you expect to find North America's oldest building here? It's the Ancient Spanish Monastery (D2), built in the 12th century, dismantled and shipped to the US by William Randolph Hearst (yes, the one who obviously wasn't satisfied with a castle in California) and reassembled here.

You'll find more pieces of Europe here at Villa Vizcaya (D5), whose designer transplanted whole rooms from grand European houses.

"Little" Havana and "Little" Haiti are home of Cuban and Haitian populations of about half a million. Nothing little about that.

More passengers cruise out of the Port of Miami (E4) than anywhere else in the world.

Tourist Information:
1-800-283-2707

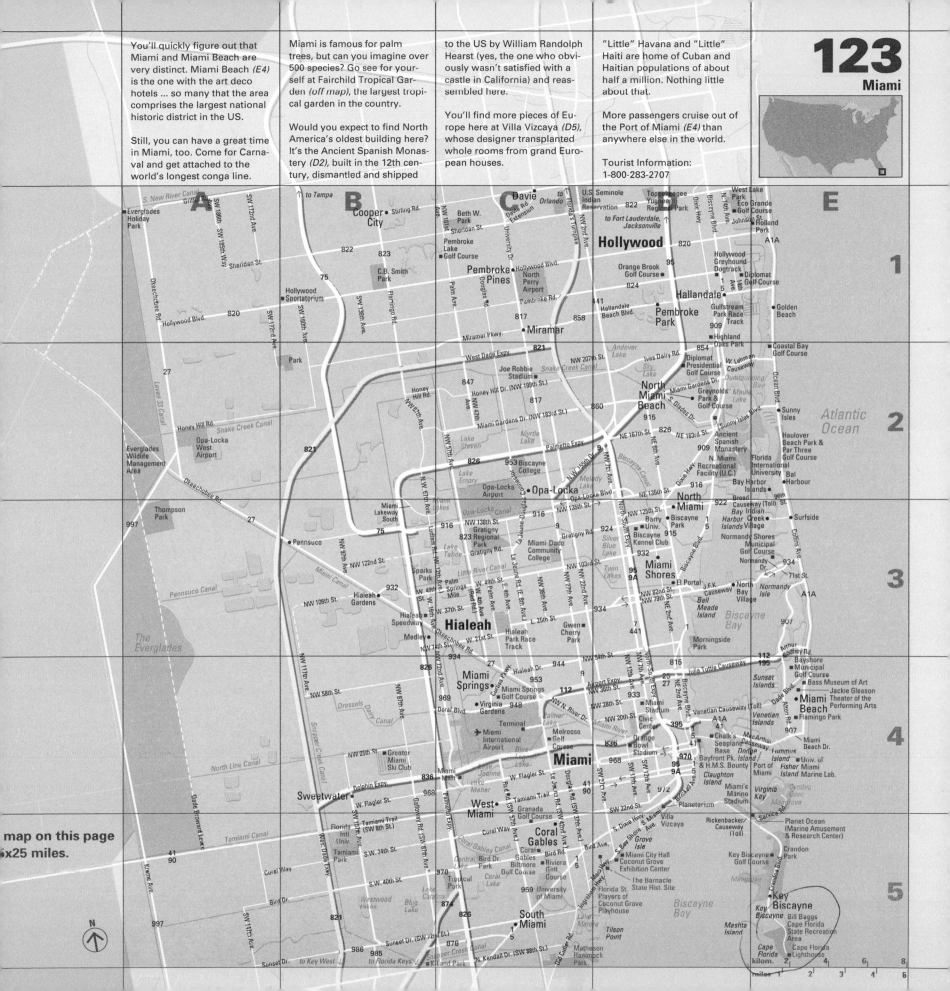

The 1989 Quake was nothing compared to the Big One, 18 April 1906. No other earthquake in US history cost as many lives.

Driving the world's steepest grades is not for amateurs. Why not park the car (if you can find a space) and explore Alamo Square (C3), Union Square (D3), Jackson Square (E2) and even Square One (as representative of SF haute cuisine as any of dozens of fun restaurants.)

Nob Hill (D3) was nowhere hill until the cable car climbed it. Still a hard climb to get here—by foot, car or socially. Yes, up at the top is the hotel you've seen on TV. But don't call it the St. Gregory; it's the Fairmont.

The only curved escalators in the world are those in the San Francisco Centre (D3).

In the dark about what to visit? Try the Tactile Dome at The Exploratorium (B1) (a don't-miss museum). You can only negotiate by touch.

Golden Gate Park (A4) is one of the country's great city parks.

The park's fragile-looking Conservatory of Flowers withstood the 1906 quake (and 1989's).

San Francisco average daily high temperatures:

J	56.1°	J	64.0°
F	59.4°	A	65.0°
M	60.0°	S	68.9°
A	61.1°	O	68.3°
M	62.5°	N	62.9°
J	64.3°	D	56.9°

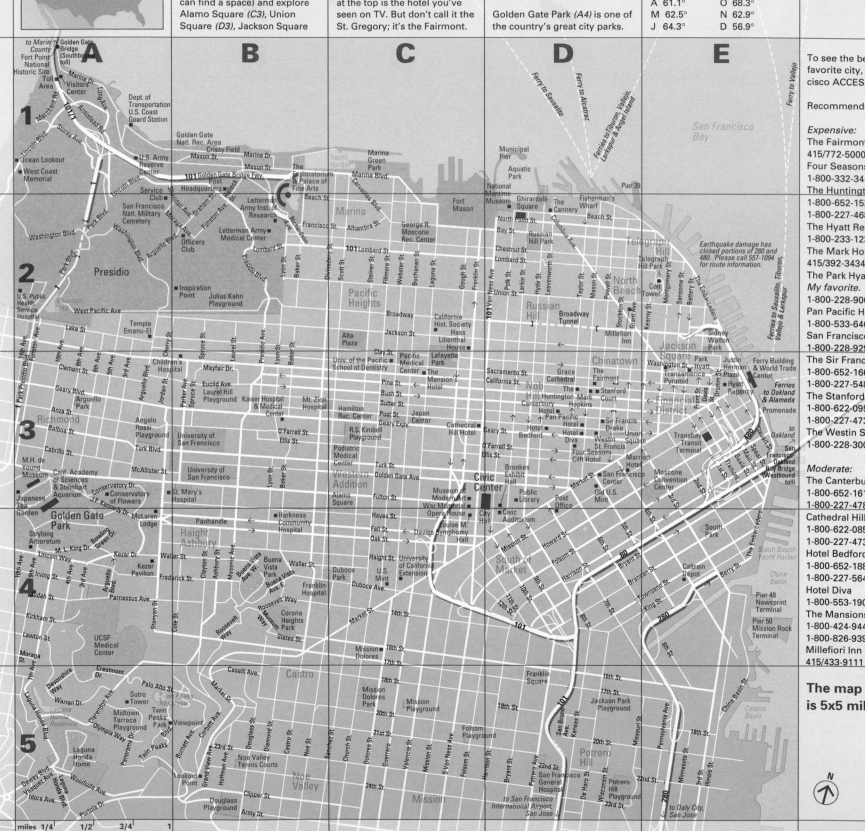

To see the best of America's favorite city, use my San Francisco ACCESS Guide.

Recommended hotels:

Expensive:
The Fairmont
415/772-5000
Four Seasons Clift Hotel
1-800-332-3442
The Huntington
1-800-652-1539 (CA)
1-800-227-4683 (outside CA)
The Hyatt Regency
1-800-233-1234
The Mark Hopkins
415/392-3434
The Park Hyatt
My favorite.
1-800-228-9000
Pan Pacific Hotel
1-800-533-6465
San Francisco Marriott
1-800-228-9290

The Sir Francis Drake
1-800-652-1668 (CA)
1-800-227-5480 (outside CA)
The Stanford Court
1-800-622-0957 (CA)
1-800-227-4736 (outside CA)
The Westin St. Francis
1-800-228-3000

Moderate:
The Canterbury Hotel
1-800-652-1614 (CA)
1-800-227-4788 (outside CA)
Cathedral Hill Hotel
1-800-622-0855 (CA)
1-800-227-4730 (outside CA)
Hotel Bedford
1-800-652-1889 (CA)
1-800-227-5642 (outside CA)
Hotel Diva
1-800-553-1900
The Mansions Hotel
1-800-424-9444 (CA)
1-800-826-9398 (outside CA)
Millefiori Inn
415/433-9111

The map on this page is 5x5 miles.

Los Angelenos used to endure a day-long stagecoach ride to visit the beach here. Shouldn't take you that long, even when traffic is horrendous.

Where the seaside action is: the 75-year-old Santa Monica Pier (A3). A long-favorite attraction is the Carousel, which still offers rides, and a chance to catch the brass ring, for 25¢.

For that postcard-perfect seaside sunset, head to Palisades Park (A1).

Douglas Aircraft used to be based at the Santa Monica Airport (D3). See some classics, including WW II fighters, at the airport's Museum of Flying.

A turn-of-the-century developer created a fantasy town of canals, complete with gondola and camel rides on opening day. Oil leakage and other problems caused most of Venice's waterways to be filled in, but a sort of outrageous carnival atmosphere prevailed. It's still as wild as ever; come join the roller skaters, body builders, bikers, street performers and other fun seekers on Ocean Front Walk (B4).

Despite the plethora of tony galleries, the mural seems to be the art form favored in the Santa Monica/Venice area. There are at least 25.

It's not hard to believe that Marina del Rey (C5) is the world's largest man-made small boat harbor. Or that there are moorings for 10,000 private pleasure craft.

125
Santa Monica

mmended hotels:

pensive:
w's Santa Monica Beach el
00-223-0888
angri-La Hotel
/394-2791
eraton Miramar Hotel
00-325-3535

derate:
mel Hotel
/451-2469
iday Inn Bayview Plaza
00-465-4329
ific Shore Hotel
00-241-3848
vereign Hotel
/395-9921

map on this page
5 miles.

miles 1/4 1/2 3/4 1

126

Los Angeles

William Mulholland built the aqueduct from Northern California that allowed this dusty town to bloom (eventually) to a population of several million. If the water goes—so long LA.

Even before there were real estate agents in Los Angeles, there were mastodons and sabre-tooth tigers. To find out more about them, visit the La Brea Tar Pits *(D3)*.

Tourists looking for stars show up for afternoon cocktails at the Beverly Hills Hotel's Polo Lounge *(A1)*. Stars looking for contracts show up for breakfast.

When those stars make it big, they get their footprints in front of Mann's Chinese Theatre *(E1)*. Rumor has it, though, that if they lose it big there are stacks of slabs of concrete in Mann's basement with the prints of has-beens.

HOLLYWOODLAND, the sign once said. It was originally put up to advertise (what else?) real estate. The letters are 50 feet high.

Los Angeles boasts of some wonderful museums—LA County *(C3)* and the Museum of Contemporary Art *(pg. 127, D5)*, for openers—but the indigenous culture is that of the car. LA has some of the best urban drives in the world: Mulholland Drive, Sunset Blvd., Wilshire Blvd. (from downtown to the beach) and the Pacific Coast Highway to Malibu.

For a place with "no downtown," Los Angeles is doing all right. Its Civic Center *(D5)* is the largest collection of government offices outside of Washington, DC.

Fearless Angelenos voted out their 13-story height limit in 1926 to make way for their 27-story city hall *(E5)*. A landmark by any architectural standard and the tallest building in town for decades after.

Who are these people? And how did they get stars on the Hollywood Walk of Fame? Money, and an assertive press agent. Of the 1800 or so stars laid out we'll bet there are quite a few names you won't recognize.

Just over a quarter of the Los Angeles population is Hispanic. The city's roots are at El Pueblo de Los Angeles Historic Park and Olvera Street *(E5)*. A little touristy, but closer than Tijuana.

If you have to be buried, you could do worse than Forest Lawn *(E1)*—Mary Pickford, Clark Gable and Carole Lombard, Nat King Cole and even Walt Disney are all here now.

Los Angeles average daily high temperatures:

J	66.6°	J	83.8°
F	68.5°	A	84.1°
M	68.7°	S	83.0°
A	70.9°	O	78.5°
M	73.2°	N	72.7°
J	77.9°	D	68.1°

To get to the heart of Los Angeles, get a copy of my Los Angeles ACCESS Guide.

Recommended hotels—

Expensive:
The Beverly Hills Hotel
1-800-283-8885
The Beverly Wilshire Hotel
1-800-427-4354
The Biltmore
1-800-252-0175 (CA)
1-800-421-8000 (outside CA)
The Century Plaza Hotel
1-800-228-3000
The Four Seasons
213/273-2222
The Hotel Bel-Air
213/472-1211
1-800-648-4097 (outside CA)
The Huntington Hotel and Cottages
1-800-822-1777
The Los Angeles Airport Hilton
1-800-445-8667
The Los Angeles Airport Marriott
1-800-228-9290
The Sheraton Grande Hotel
1-800-325-3535
The Westin Bonaventure
1-800-228-3000
The Wilshire Towers Hotel
213/385-7281

Moderate:
The Beverly Crest Hotel
1-800-247-6432
Holiday Inn—Los Angeles Convention Center
1-800-465-4329
The Hollywood Roosevelt Hotel
1-800-950-7667
The Park Plaza Hotel
213/384-5281

The map on this page is 5x5 miles.

Big in Las Vegas:

Caesars Palace's Omnimax Theatre is said to be the largest theatre in the world (B4).

The Golden Nugget (D1) does indeed house a 63-pound, $1 million gold nugget.

McCarran International Airport (off map) is the busiest per cap-ita in the country. (It has slot machines too.)

The Four Queens Hotel and Casino (D1) is the home of Big Bertha, the world's largest slot machine.

Serious gambling—Binion's Horseshoe Hotel and Casino (D1) will take on a bet of $1 million. They also host the World Series of Poker. Blackjack play-ers frequent the Las Vegas Club (D1), which claims the most liberal 21 rules in the world.

Important to know when travel-ing with kids—everyone under 18 is barred from casino floors. Good to know—Circus Circus (B3) has a place for kids to en-tertain themselves, with high-wire acts and clowns all year.

When not on tour, the US Air Force Thunderbirds nest at Nellis Air Force Base (off map).

Las Vegas average daily high temperatures:

J	56.0°	J	104.5°
F	62.4°	A	101.9°
M	68.3°	S	94.7°
A	77.2°	O	81.5°
M	87.4°	N	66.0°
J	98.6°	D	57.1°

Hotel/Casinos—
Aladdin
1-800-634-3424
Bally's Las Vegas
1-800-634-3434
Caesars Palace
1-800-634-6001
Continental
1-800-634-6641
Circus Circus
1-800-634-3450
Dunes
1-800-634-6971
Flamingo Hilton
1-800-732-2111
The Golden Nugget
1-800-634-3454
Hacienda Resort
1-800-634-6713
Holiday Casino/Holiday Inn
1-800-634-6765
Imperial Palace
1-800-634-6441
The Landmark
1-800-634-6777
Las Vegas Hilton
1-800-732-7117
Marina
1-800-634-6169
Mirage
1-800-627-6667
Palace Station
1-800-634-3101
The Park
1-800-782-9909
Riviera
1-800-634-6753
Sahara
1-800-634-6666
The Sands
1-800-634-6901
The Tropicana
1-800-634-4000
Union Plaza
1-800-634-6575
Vegas World
1-800-634-6277

The map on this p is 5x5 miles.

miles 1/4   1/2   3/4   1

Take a look at the map. You can see why this town has been America's best-known boardwalk since 1870—the current stretch is just over 4 miles long.

Put plenty of hotel casinos on your *Monopoly* properties. When gambling was made legal in Atlantic City, property values increased by 2000%.

You know that the board game uses Atlantic City street names.

12 million visitors are discharged from tour buses here every year. The total number of visitors is 32 million. They gamble away about $3.2 billion.

It's the third of his casinos, but by far the most famous. Donald

Trump's Taj Mahal *(D2)* cost $1 billion, is New Jersey's tallest building (42 stories) and houses the world's largest casino.

The most famous winner in America is crowned here and has been since 1921. Here she comes, Miss America.

Wish you were here. Picture

postcards—and compressed correspondence—were first sent from Atlantic City.

Atlantic City average daily high temperatures:

J	40.3°	J	79.9°
F	41.8°	A	79.5°
M	47.7°	S	73.8°
A	57.7°	O	64.4°
M	65.7°	N	54.3°
J	74.5°	D	44.8°

tel/Casinos—
lly's Grand
00-257-8677
lly's Park Place
00-772-7777
esars
00-257-8555
ridge
00-257-8585
rrah's Marina
00-242-7724
sorts International
9/344-6000
nds
00-257-8580
owboat
00-621-0200
j Mahal
9/449-1000
opWorld
00-843-8767
imp Castle
00-777-1177
imp Plaza
00-677-7378

map on this page
5 miles.

N

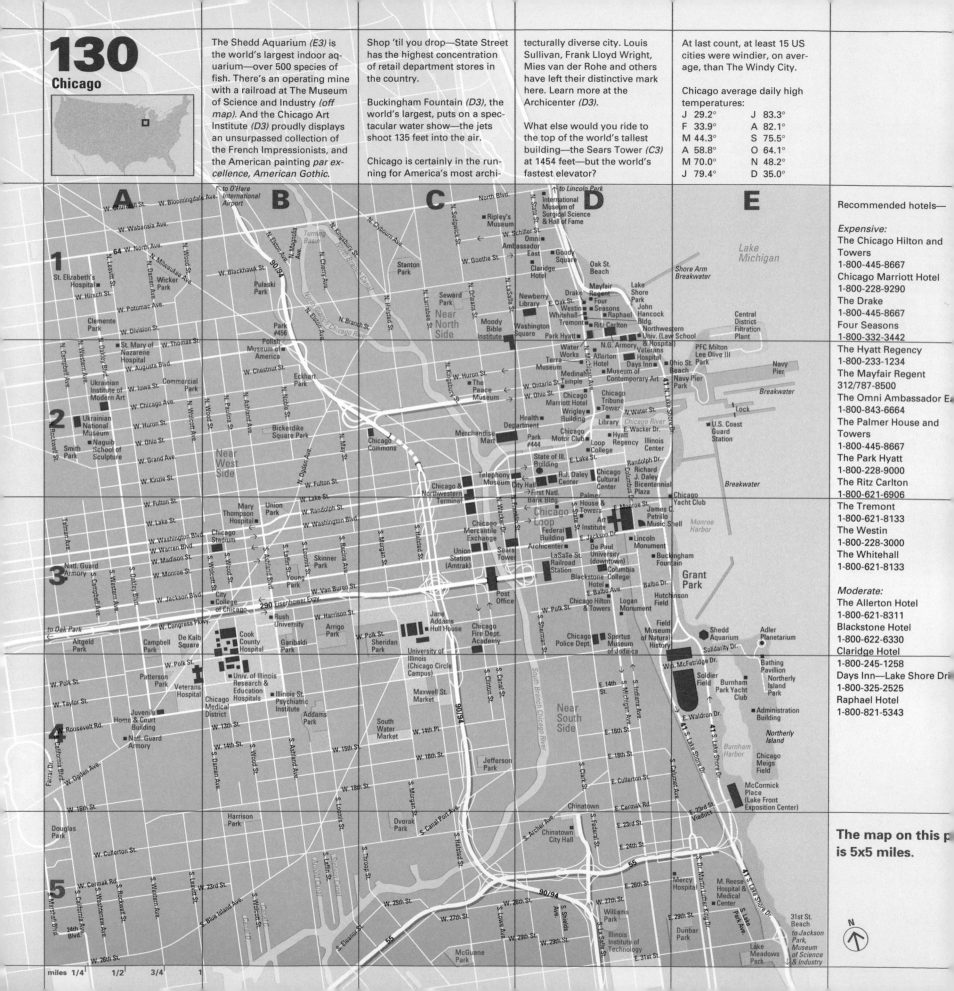

The Shedd Aquarium *(E3)* is the world's largest indoor aquarium—over 500 species of fish. There's an operating mine with a railroad at The Museum of Science and Industry *(off map)*. And the Chicago Art Institute *(D3)* proudly displays an unsurpassed collection of the French Impressionists, and the American painting *par excellence, American Gothic.*

Shop 'til you drop—State Street has the highest concentration of retail department stores in the country.

Buckingham Fountain *(D3),* the world's largest, puts on a spectacular water show—the jets shoot 135 feet into the air.

Chicago is certainly in the running for America's most archi-tecturally diverse city. Louis Sullivan, Frank Lloyd Wright, Mies van der Rohe and others have left their distinctive mark here. Learn more at the Archicenter *(D3).*

What else would you ride to the top of the world's tallest building—the Sears Tower *(C3)* at 1454 feet—but the world's fastest elevator?

At last count, at least 15 US cities were windier, on average, than The Windy City.

Chicago average daily high temperatures:

J	29.2°	J	83.3°
F	33.9°	A	82.1°
M	44.3°	S	75.5°
A	58.8°	O	64.1°
M	70.0°	N	48.2°
J	79.4°	D	35.0°

Recommended hotels—

Expensive:
The Chicago Hilton and Towers
1-800-445-8667
Chicago Marriott Hotel
1-800-228-9290
The Drake
1-800-445-8667
Four Seasons
1-800-332-3442

The Hyatt Regency
1-800-233-1234
The Mayfair Regent
312/787-8500
The Omni Ambassador Ea
1-800-843-6664
The Palmer House and Towers
1-800-445-8667
The Park Hyatt
1-800-228-9000
The Ritz Carlton
1-800-621-6906

The Tremont
1-800-621-8133
The Westin
1-800-228-3000
The Whitehall
1-800-621-8133

Moderate:
The Allerton Hotel
1-800-621-8311
Blackstone Hotel
1-800-622-6330
Claridge Hotel
1-800-245-1258
Days Inn—Lake Shore Dri
1-800-325-2525
Raphael Hotel
1-800-821-5343

The map on this p is 5x5 miles.

miles 1/4   1/2   3/4   1

Philadelphia sits on the Delaware River. That makes it the world's largest freshwater port.

Philadelphia takes its maritime role seriously. Penn's Landing (E3)—on the river—is a delightful mix of history, shopping, open-air entertainment and ships: from wooden sail boats to submarines—all open for tours.

The fabulous Mummers' Parade happens on New Year's Day. 300,000 spectators watch 30,000 participants marching in one of three brigades: the clowns, the fancy brigade or the string bands. There's a Mummers' Museum too (D4).

"The most historic square mile in America" (D3)—Independence Hall, Congress Hall, City Tavern …. The bell that rings in Independence Hall was a bicentennial gift of the British. The original Liberty Bell, of course, Is cracked and has been since the first time it was rung.

The US Mint (D3) in Philadelphia is the one where coins are made. Come watch. As you'd expect, the metal detectors here are very sensitive.

Incredibly scenic: Approaching the city via West River Drive through Fairmount Park (A2).

Philadelphia average daily high temperatures:

J	38.6°	J	86.1°
F	41.1°	A	84.6°
M	50.5°	S	77.8°
A	63.2°	O	66.5°
M	73.0°	N	54.5°
J	81.7°	D	43.0°

Recommended hotels—

Expensive:
The Barclay,
Rittenhouse Square
800-421-6662
The Four Seasons
800-332-3442
Hotel Top of The Bellevue
215/893-1776
The Latham
800-528-4261
The Rittenhouse
800-635-1042
Sheraton Society Hill
800-325-3535
The Warwick
800-523-4210
The Wyndham-Franklin Plaza
800-822-4200

Moderate:
Chestnut Hill Hotel
215/242-5905
The Comfort Inn
800-221-2222
The Holiday Inn
(downtown locations)
800-465-4329
The Quality Inn
(downtown locations)
800-221-2222

map on this page
5 miles.

132
New York City

Learn all the essentials about this great, confusing, exhilarating city in my New York ACCESS Guide.

Recommended hotels—

Expensive:
The Grand Hyatt
1-800-233-1234
The Helmsley Park Lane
1-800-221-4982
Hotel Parker Meridien
1-800-543-4300
Hotel Pierre
1-800-332-3442
The Mayfair Regent
1-800-223-0542
New York Hilton and Towers
1-800-445-8667
The Plaza
1-800-228-3000
The Regency Hotel
1-800-233-2356
The Waldorf Astoria
1-800-445-8667
The United Nations Plaza Hotel
1-800-233-1234

Moderate:
The Algonquin
1-800-548-0345
The Dorset
1-800-227-2348
The Empire
1-800-545-7400
The Gramercy Park Hotel
1-800-221-4083
The Mayflower Hotel
1-800-223-4164
The Milford Plaza
1-800-528-1234
The Roosevelt
1-800-223-1870
The Royalton
1-800-635-9013
Sheraton Centre
1-800-325-3535
The Warwick Hotel
1-800-223-4099

The map on this page is 5x5 miles.

Peter Minuit, we all know, bought Manhattan for $24—a good deal that a successor of his blew when the Dutch accepted a colony in South America from the British in trade for the magic isle.

The "Wall" on Wall Street was constructed to keep the Indians out—doesn't do much good against modern-day hostiles.

When kids draw a skyscraper, inevitably the result is the Chrysler Building *(E3)* ... a beautiful caricature of a tall building.

Another old favorite, the Empire State Building *(E2)*, hosts the Run Up every February. Racers climb all 1,575 steps to the top of the building as fast as possible (about 14 minutes). Whew!

You want great food? Try the Fulton Fish Market *(B2)*—the catch of the day is you have to be there by 6 a.m.

There's more to shopping here than Saks; you want to shop like a New Yorker, go to Canal Street *(C2)*. Ready, set, haggle!

A real shopping adventure is Chinatown *(C2)*. Shop the produce stands and sample things you've never heard of—like 100-year-old eggs.

Only China has more Chinese. And Athens more Greeks, San Juan more Puerto Ricans, Dublin more Irish and Israel more Jews. Where else could they have put the United Nations *(E3)*?

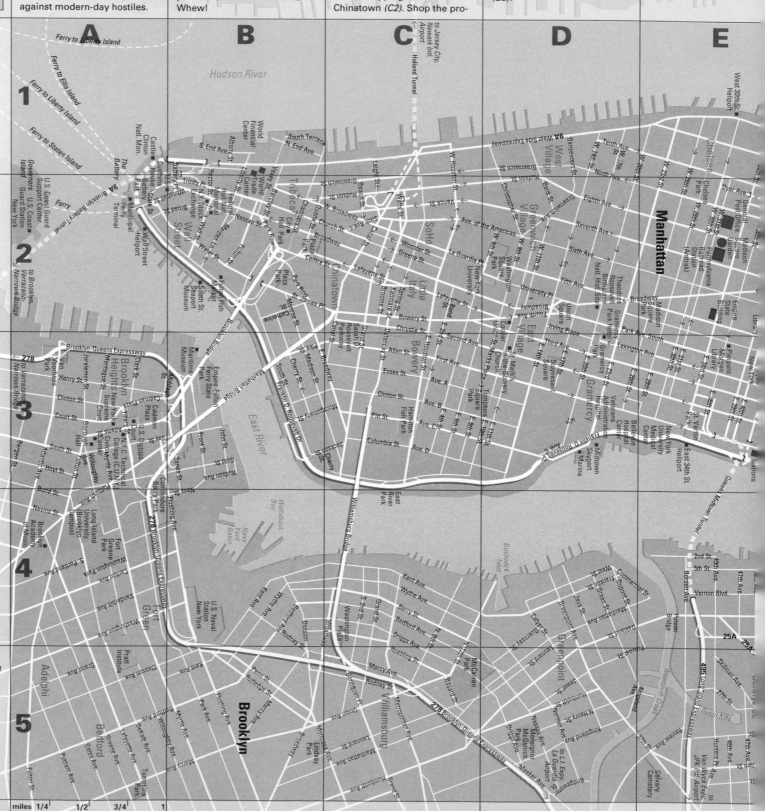

miles 1/4   1/2   3/4   1

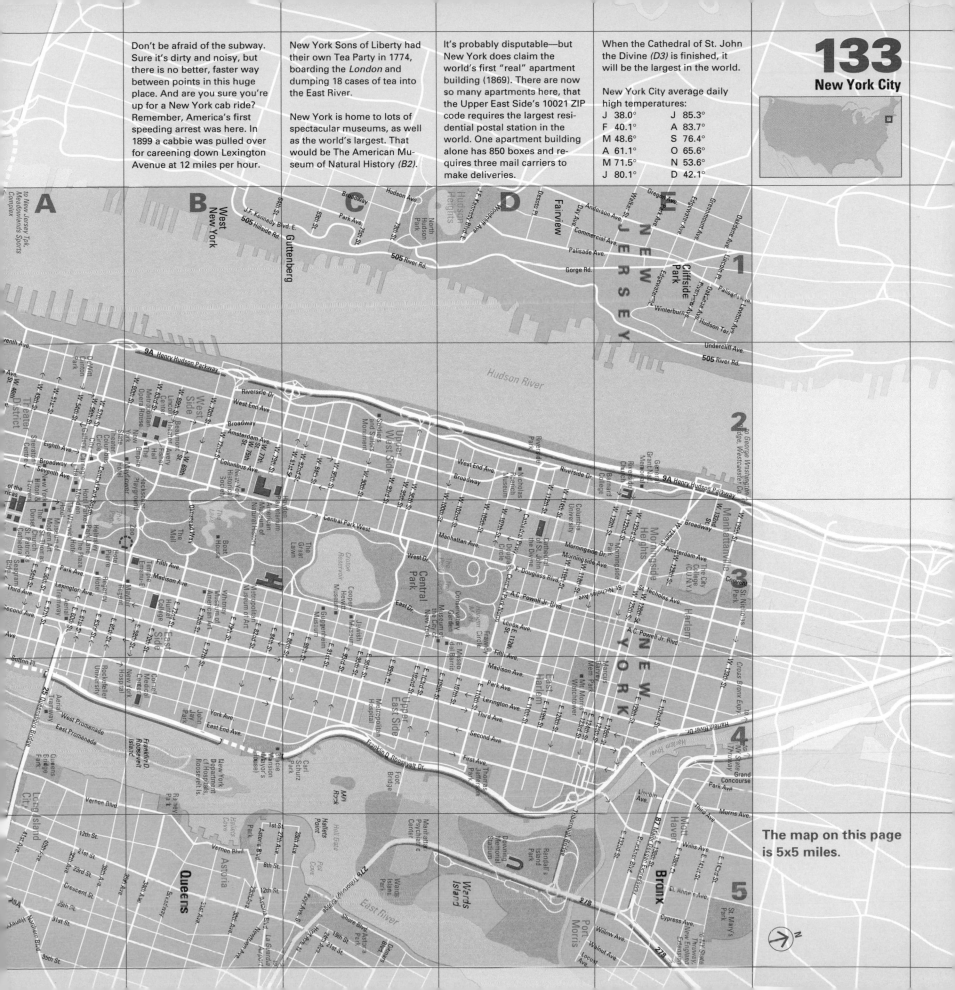

Don't be afraid of the subway. Sure it's dirty and noisy, but there is no better, faster way between points in this huge place. And are you sure you're up for a New York cab ride? Remember, America's first speeding arrest was here. In 1899 a cabbie was pulled over for careening down Lexington Avenue at 12 miles per hour.

New York Sons of Liberty had their own Tea Party in 1774, boarding the *London* and dumping 18 cases of tea into the East River.

New York is home to lots of spectacular museums, as well as the world's largest. That would be The American Museum of Natural History *(B2)*.

It's probably disputable—but New York does claim the world's first "real" apartment building (1869). There are now so many apartments here, that the Upper East Side's 10021 ZIP code requires the largest residential postal station in the world. One apartment building alone has 850 boxes and requires three mail carriers to make deliveries.

When the Cathedral of St. John the Divine *(D3)* is finished, it will be the largest in the world.

New York City average daily high temperatures:

J	38.0°	J	85.3°
F	40.1°	A	83.7°
M	48.6°	S	76.4°
A	61.1°	O	65.6°
M	71.5°	N	53.6°
J	80.1°	D	42.1°

133
New York City

The map on this page is 5x5 miles.

MIT (B3), Harvard (A2), BU (B4), Tufts and Boston College are some of the more than 50 colleges and universities here. It's bred in the bone—the country's first compulsory grammar school education was established in Boston in 1636.

Boston has three irresistible museums: The MFA (C4), The Isabella Stewart Gardner (an Italian palazzo) (B4) and The Institute of Contemporary Art (a 19th century police station reborn) (C4). There's even more in Cambridge.

More Cambridge culture—the 2 dozen bookstores around Harvard Square are considered to make up the Bookstore Capital of the World.

If you're in Boston for the holidays, join the annual re-enactment of that famous Tea Party — every 15 December (E3).

You won't get much argument that Boston's drivers are the worst—and insurance rates the highest.

Massachusetts' first railroad was built to transport the granite for the Bunker Hill Monument (D1). But the battle was actually fought on Breed's Hill.

Boston average daily high temperatures:

J	36.4°	J	81.8°
F	37.7°	A	79.8°
M	45.0°	S	72.3°
A	56.6°	O	62.5°
M	67.0°	N	51.6°
J	76.6°	D	40.3°

Recommended hotels—

Expensive:
Boston Marriott Copley Place
1-800-228-9290
The Boston Sheraton
1-800-325-3535
The Colonnade
1-800-962-3030
Copley Plaza Hotel
1-800-826-7539
The Four Seasons
1-800-332-3442
Hyatt Regency Cambridge
1-800-228-9000
The Marriott at Long Wharf
1-800-228-9290
The Meridien
1-800-543-4300
The Ritz Carlton
1-800-241-3333
Royal Sonesta Cambridge
1-800-343-7170

Moderate:
The Copley Square Hotel
1-800-225-7062
The Eliot Hotel
617/267-1607
The Harvard Manor House
617/864-5200
The Midtown Hotel
1-800-343-1177

The map on this page is 5x5 miles.

The President's Palace was whitewashed to cover burns from the British in the War of 1812. Teddy Roosevelt was first to call it the White House (C2).

There are caves underneath the Lincoln Memorial (C3)—open for exploration spring and fall.

The Pentagon (B4)—the world's largest administrative building needs the world's largest parking lot.

The Tombs of the Unknowns, of John F. Kennedy and of over 210,000 service men and women are in Arlington National Cemetery (B4). The Iwo Jima Memorial is also here.

The Sunset Parade at Arlington (7:30 p.m. Tuesdays in the summer) is among the capital's most moving ceremonies.

The Smithsonian (D3) operates 14 buildings for its exhibits and can display only 1% of its inventory at a time.

The National Air and Space Museum—you have to go—is the world's most popular museum (D3).

The Library of Congress (E2) collections increase by 400 items per hour!

Washington DC average daily high temperatures:

J	40.9°	J	87.0°
F	43.9°	A	85.8°
M	53.5°	S	79.3°
A	65.7°	O	68.0°
M	74.6°	N	55.9°
J	82.6°	D	44.9°

[You] want to know what's [the]re in Washington, get a [co]py of my Washington DC [AC]CESS.

[Re]commended hotels—

[Ex]pensive:
[Th]e Four Seasons
[8]00-332-3442
[Th]e Hay Adams
[8]00-424-5054
[Th]e Hyatt Regency
[8]00-228-9000
[Th]e J.W. Marriott Hotel at
[Na]tional Place
[8]00-228-9290
[Vi]ews L'Enfant Plaza
[8]00-223-0888
[Th]e Madison
[8]00-424-8577
[Th]e Ritz Carlton
[8]00-241-3333
[Th]e Sheraton Carlton
[8]00-562-5661
[Wa]shington Hilton Hotel
[8]00-445-8667
[Th]e Watergate
[8]00-424-2736

[M]oderate:
[Du]pont Plaza Hotel
[8]00-421-6662
[Th]e Intrigue Hotel
[8]00-426-4455
[Om]ni Georgetown Hotel
[8]00-843-6664
[Th]e Savoy Suites
[8]00-426-4455

[This] map on this page [is] 5 miles.

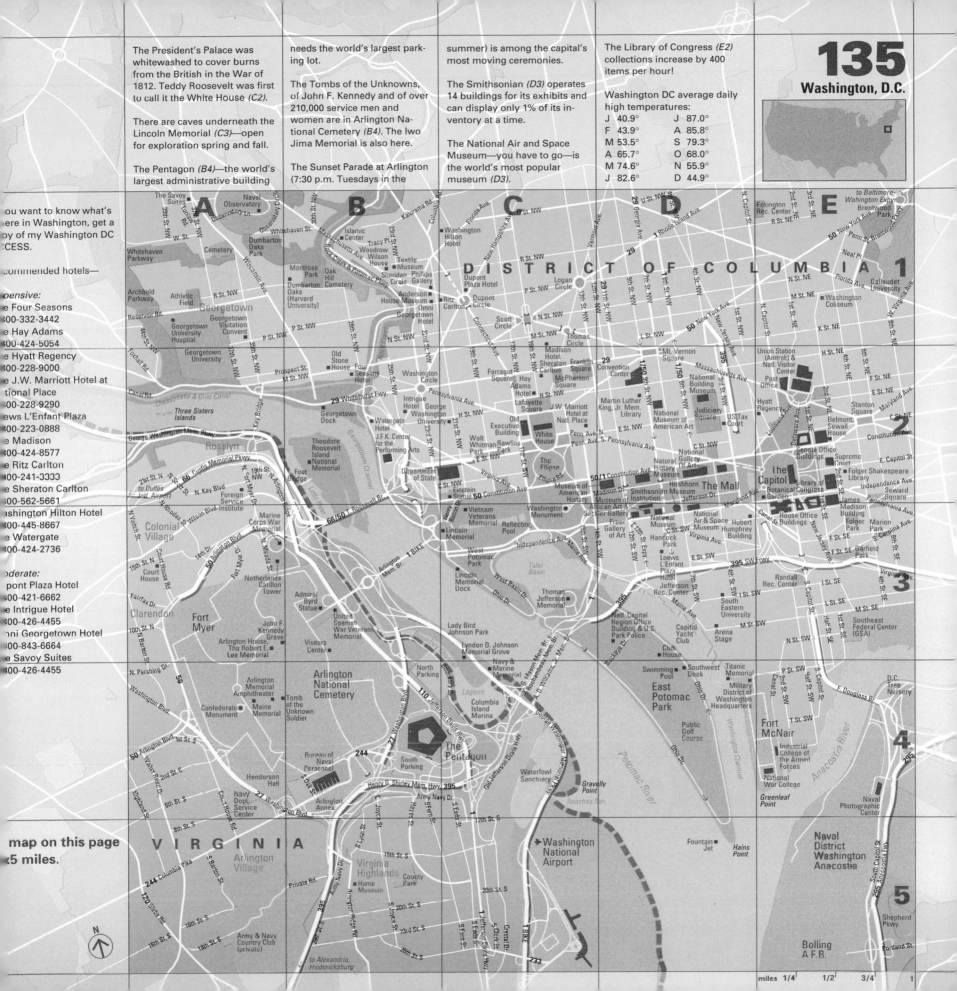

Such grandiosity—the Fabulous Fox Theatre (C1) is a 1929 Moorish fantasy—one of the last great movie palaces, second in size only to Radio City Music Hall.

There are plenty of other big sights here. CNN Center (C3) is home to a major hotel, shops and restaurants, in addition to CNN Studios. Come by for a tour to see how television news is gathered and aired.

Stay on the 73rd floor of the Westin Peachtree Plaza (C2) and no guest in any hotel anywhere is further up than you are.

Atlanta out of sight: the old railroad terminal in the city's center has come back to life as Underground Atlanta (C3)—shops, restaurants, comedy clubs and night clubs, many below street level.

Significant Georgians: The Carter Presidential Center is here (E2), as well as the Dr. Martin Luther King, Jr. National Historic Site (D3). Dr. King was born, preached and is buried here.

Peachtree Street's Salute 2 America claims to be the largest July 4th parade in the country.

Atlanta average daily high temperatures:

J	51.2°	J	87.9°
F	55.3°	A	87.6°
M	63.2°	S	82.3°
A	73.2°	O	72.9°
M	79.8°	N	62.6°
J	85.6°	D	54.1°

Atlanta

Recommended hotels—

Expensive:
Atlanta Marriott Marquis
1-800-228-9290
Ritz Carlton Buckhead
404/237-2700
Atlanta Hilton & Towers
404/659-2000
Hyatt Regency Atlanta
1-800-228-9000
Omni International
1-800-241-5500
Stouffers Waverly Hotel
404/953-4500
Westin Peachtree Plaza
1-800-228-3000

Moderate:
Comfort Inn
404/524-5555
Days Inn Downtown
1-800-325-2525
Quality Inn Habersham
1-800-241-4288
Holiday Inn Downtown
404/659-2727
Stone Mountain Inn
404/469-3311

The map on this p
is 5x5 miles.

miles 1/4 1/2 3/4 1

Bold type indicates cities with 100,000 population or more.

Place Name / Page Number / Grid Number
Stantonburg **118** C5

A

Abarr, CO 36 D2
Abbeville, AL 66 E1
Abbeville, GA 65 B5
Abbeville, LA 55 B5
Abbeville, SC 65 B2
Abbey, SK 19 D1
Abbot Village, ME 71 A4
Abbotsford, BC 9 A1
Abbotsford, WI 47 B4
Abbottstown, PA 74 A3
Aberdeen, ID 22 D2
Aberdeen, MD 74 B3
Aberdeen, MS 53 E4
Aberdeen, NC 63 E5
Aberdeen, OH 62 E1
Aberdeen, SD 33 D4
Aberdeen, WA 8 D4
Abernathy, TX 38 E5
Abilene, KS 37 E3
Abilene, TX 41 C2
Abingdon, VA 63 B4
Abington, IL 49 B5
Abington, PA 114 C1
Abiquiu, NM 27 E2
Ackerman, MS 53 E5
Acmetonia, PA 107 D1
Acoma, NM 27 C3
Acoma, NV 24 A4
Aconchi, SON 28 E4
Acorn, AR 52 D4
Acton Vale, PQ 70 C4
Ada, MN 33 E1
Ada, OK 52 A4
Adair, IA 48 C4
Adak, AK 4 E5
Adams, MA 72 D3
Adams, NY 72 A3
Adams, WI 47 B5
Adams Shore, MA 110 E4
Adamsville, TX 41 D4
Addison, IL 102 A3
Addison, TX 95 C1
Addison, VT 72 C2
Adel, GA 67 B2
Adel, OR 13 A1
Adelanto, CA 17 B2
Adelphi, MD 116 C1
Adin, CA 12 E2
Adirondack Center, NY 72 C1
Admiralty Is. Natl. Mon., AK 5 E5
Adrian, MI 60 C2
Adrian, MN 48 A1
Adrian, TX 38 D3
Advance, MO 51 C5
Advance, OR 83 B5
Afton, IA 48 C5
Afton, OK 52 C1
Afton, WY 23 A2
Agate, NE 34 C3
Agate Fossil Beds Natl. Mon., NE 34 C3
Agnes, OR 10 B5
Agua Dulce, TX 43 E3
Agua Fria, NM 38 A1
Agua Prieta, SON 29 A3
Aguadilla, PR 6 A3
Aguanga, CA 17 B4
Aguila, AZ 26 B4
Aguilares, TX 43 C4
Ahoskie, NC 76 B3
Ahumada, CHIH 29 D4
Aiken, SC 65 C3
Aiken, TX 54 D3
Ainsworth, NE 35 B3
Airline Park, LA 98 A4
Airville, PA 74 B3
Aitkin, MN 46 C2
Ajo, AZ 28 B1
Akeley, MN 46 B1
Aklavik, NT 5 E2
Akron, CO 36 D1
Akron, IA 48 A2
Akron, IN 60 B4
Akron, OH 61 A3
Akutan, AK 4 G5
Alabama, NY 59 D4
Alakanuk, AK 5 A3
Alameda, CA 85 B3
Alamo, CA 85 C5
Alamo, NM 27 C4
Alamo, NV 15 E4
Alamo Heights, TX 96 C2
Alamogordo, NM 29 E1
Alamos de Marquez, COAH 42 C2
Alamosa, CO 36 A5
Alanson, MI 58 B2
Alapaha, GA 67 B1
Albany, CA 85 D3
Albany, GA 67 A1
Albany, IN 60 C4
Albany, KY 62 D4
Albany, MN 46 B3
Albany, MO 50 C1
Albany, NY 72 C4
Albany, OR 10 D2
Albany, TX 41 C2
Albany Cross, NS 71 F3
Albemarle, NC 63 D5
Albert, KS 37 C4
Albert Lea, MN 48 D1
Albertville, AL 64 C3
Albia, IA 48 E5
Albin, WY 34 C4
Albion, ID 22 C2
Albion, IL 51 E3
Albion, MI 60 C2
Albion, NE 35 D4
Albion, NJ 114 F5
Albion, NY 59 D4
Albion, PA 61 B1
Albuquerque, NM 27 D3
Alcoa, TN 64 E1
Alcova, WY 23 E3
Alder Creek, NY 72 B3
Alderson, WV 63 C2
Aldersyde, AB 18 D1
Aldie, VA 74 A5
Aledo, IL 49 B4
Alexander, ID 22 E2
Alexander, KS 37 C4
Alexander, ND 30 C5
Alexander, TX 41 D2
Alexander City, AL 64 D5
Alexandria, IN 60 B5
Alexandria, KY 108 D5
Alexandria, LA 55 A3
Alexandria, MN 46 B3
Alexandria, SD 35 D1
Alexandria, VA 74 A5
Alexandria Bay, NY 72 A2
Alexis, IL 49 B4
Alford, FL 66 E3
Alfred, ME 73 A1
Alfred, NY 59 E5
Alger, MI 58 C4
Algoma, WI 47 E4
Algona, IA 48 C2
Algonac, MI 60 E1
Algonquin Acres, CO 93 D5
Algood, TN 62 C5
Alhambra, AZ 91 B3
Alhambra, CA 86 E1
Alibates Flint Quarries Natl. Mon., TX 38 E3
Alice, TX 43 E3
Aliceville, AL 64 A5
Allagash, ME 71 A1
Allegan, MI 60 A2
Allen, MS 55 C2
Allen, OK 52 A3
Allen, TN 64 E1
Allen Park, MI 103 C5
Allendale, SC 65 D4
Allende, COAH 43 A3
Allentown, PA 74 B2
Allenwood, PA 74 A2
Allerton, MA 110 E4
Alliance, NE 34 D4
Alliance, OH 61 B3
Allison Park, PA 107 C1
Alma, AR 52 D2
Alma, GA 67 C1
Alma, IL 51 D2
Alma, KS 50 A3
Alma, MI 58 B5
Alma, NB 71 E2
Alma, NE 37 C1
Alma, NM 27 B5
Alma, WI 46 E5
Almeda, TX 97 B5
Almeria, NE 35 C4
Almira, WA 9 D4
Almo, ID 22 C3
Almonesson, NJ 114 D5
Aloha, OR 83 A3
Aloma, FL 120 D1
Alpena, MI 58 C3
Alpha, IL 49 B4
Alpine, AZ 27 A4
Alpine, CA 17 B5
Alpine, NJ 112 A5
Alpine, TX 40 C5
Alpine Junction, WY 23 A1
Alpsville, PA 107 E4
Alsea, OR 10 D2
Alta, UT 90 C5
Alta Vista, MD 116 B1
Altamont, TN 64 C1
Altar, SON 28 C3
Altavista, VA 63 E3
Altheimer, AR 53 B4
Alto, TX 54 C3
Alton, IL 51 C2
Alton, MO 51 B5
Alton, NH 72 E2
Alton, NY 59 E4
Altoona, PA 61 E3
Alturas, CA 13 A2
Altus, OK 39 C4
Alva, OK 39 D1
Alvin, TX 56 C1
Alvord Ranch, OR 13 C1
Aly, AR 52 E3
Alzada, MT 32 C4
Amaranth, MB 31 C1
Amargosa Valley, NV 15 D5
Amarillo, TX 38 E3
Amasa, MI 47 C2
Amberly, OH 108 C2
Amboy, CA 17 D3
Amboy, IL 49 C3
Ambridge, PA 61 C3
Ambrosia Lake, NM 27 C2
Amelia, OH 108 E4
Amelia Court House, VA 76 A2
Amenia, NY 72 D4
American Falls, ID 22 D2
American Fork, UT 22 D5
American River, WA 9 B4
Americus, GA 67 A1
Ames, IA 48 D3
Amherst, MA 72 E4
Amherst, VA 63 E2
Amidon, ND 32 D2
Amistad, NM 38 D2
Amite, LA 55 D4
Amityville, NY 74 E1
Amlin, OH 109 A2
Amory, MS 53 E4
Amsterdam, NY 72 C3
Anaconda, MT 20 D2
Anacortes, WA 9 A2
Anadarko, OK 39 D3
Anaheim, CA 17 A3
Anáhuac, NL 43 B4
Anahuac, TX 54 D5
Anamosa, IA 49 A3
Anatone, WA 11 E1
Ancaster, ON 59 B4
Anchorage, AK 5 C4
Andalusia, AL 66 C2
Anderson, CA 12 C3
Anderson, IN 60 B5
Anderson, MO 52 A1
Anderson, SC 65 B2
Andover, KS 37 E4
Andover, ME 70 E5
Andover, NY 59 E5
Andover, OH 61 B2
Andrade, CA 17 E5
Andrews, SC 78 A3
Andrews, TX 40 D2
Andrix, CO 36 D5
Anegam, AZ 28 C1
Aneroid, SK 19 E3
Aneta, ND 33 D1
Angels Camp, CA 14 E2
Angleton, TX 56 C1
Angola, IN 60 C3
Angora, NE 34 D3
Angostura, NM 29 D1
Anguilla, MS 55 C1
Angus, NM 27 E5
Ann Arbor, MI 60 C1
Anna, IL 51 D4
Annandale, MN 46 C4
Annandale, VA 116 B4
Annapolis, MD 74 B4
Annawan, IL 49 C4
Anniston, AL 64 C4
Anoka, MN 46 D4
Anola, MB 31 E3
Anoskie, NC 76 B3
Ansley, NE 35 C5
Anson, TX 41 B1
Ansonia, CT 113 B1
Ansted, WV 63 B2
Antelope, OR 11 A2
Antelope, MT 30 C4
Anthony, KS 37 D5
Anthony, NM 29 D2
Antigo, WI 47 C4
Antimony, UT 24 D3
Antioch, CA 14 C1
Antioch, NE 34 D4
Antioch Park, KS 92 B4
Antlers, OK 52 B4
Anton, CO 36 D2
Anton, TX 38 E5
Antonito, CO 25 E5
Antrim, NH 72 E2
Antwerp, NY 72 A2
Apache, AZ 29 A2
Apache, OK 39 D3
Apache Junction, AZ 26 D5
Apache Springs, NM 38 A3
Apalachicola, FL 66 E4
Apex, NC 118 E5
Aplington, IA 48 D2
Apollo, PA 61 C3
Apollo Beach, FL 69 D1
Apopka, FL 67 E5
Appalachia, VA 63 A4
Apple River, NB 71 E2
Apple Valley, CA 17 B2
Appleton, MN 46 A4
Appleton, WI 47 D5
Appleton City, MO 50 D4
Appomattox, VA 63 E2
Aptos, CA 14 C3
Arab, AL 64 C3
Arabela, NM 38 A5
Arabi, LA 98 D4
Aragon, NM 27 B5
Aransas Pass, TX 56 A3
Arapahoe, NE 37 B1
Aravaipa, AZ 28 E1
Arborg, MB 31 D1
Arbutus, MD 115 B4
Arcade, NY 59 D5
Arcadia, CA 87 A1
Arcadia, FL 69 E2
Arcadia, LA 55 A1
Arcadia, MI 58 A4
Arcadia, MO 51 B4
Arcadia, NE 35 C4
Arcadia, WI 47 A5
Arcata, CA 12 B2
Archdale, NC 63 D4
Archer, FL 67 C4
Archer City, TX 39 D5
Arches Natl. Park, UT 25 B3
Archibald, LA 55 B1
Archuleta, NM 27 C1
Archville, NY 112 A3
Arco, ID 22 C1
Arcola, LA 55 D3
Arcola, TX 56 C1
Arctic Red River, NT 5 E2
Arden Hills, MN 100 C1
Ardill, SK 30 B2
Ardmore, OK 39 E4
Ardmore, PA 114 A3
Ardmore, SD 34 C2
Ardsley, NY 112 B4
Arecibo, PR 6 A3
Argo, IL 102 C5
Argos, IN 60 A3
Argyle, MN 31 E5
Arietta, NY 72 B3
Ariton, AL 66 D1
Arizpe, SON 28 E4
Arkadelphia, AR 52 E4
Arkansas City, AR 53 B5
Arkansas City, KS 37 E5
Arlington, CO 36 C4
Arlington, GA 66 E1
Arlington, KS 37 D4
Arlington, MA 110 B3
Arlington, MS 53 E5
Arlington, OR 11 B1
Arlington, SD 33 E5
Arlington, TX 54 A1
Arlington, VA 74 A4
Arlington, VT 72 D3
Arlington, WA 9 A3
Armonk, NY 112 C2
Armour, SD 35 D2
Armstrong, IA 48 C1
Armstrong Creek, WI 47 C3
Arnett, OK 39 B2
Arno, TX 40 C3
Arnold, MO 104 C5
Arnold, NE 35 B4
Arnold, PA 107 E1
Arnprior, ON 59 E1
Arrey, NM 29 C1
Arriba, CO 36 D2
Arroyo Grande, CA 16 D1
Arroyo Hondo, NM 38 A1
Arroyo Seco, NM 38 A1
Art, TX 41 C4
Artesia, CA 86 E4
Artesia, NM 40 B1
Artesia Wells, TX 43 C3
Arthabaska, PQ 70 D4
Arthur, NE 34 E4
Arundel, PQ 70 A4
Arvada, CO 93 B2
Asbestos, PQ 70 D4
Asbury, MO 50 C5
Asbury Park, NJ 74 D2
Ascencion, CHIH 29 B3
Ascutney, VT 72 D2
Ash Flat, AR 53 B1
Ash Fork, AZ 26 C2
Ash Grove, MO 50 D5
Ash Lake, MN 44 D5
Ash Springs, NV 15 E4
Ashbourne, PA 114 C1
Ashburn, GA 67 A1
Ashdown, AR 52 D5
Asheboro, NC 63 E5
Asher, OK 52 A3
Ashern, MB 31 C1
Asherton, TX 43 C2
Asheville, NC 63 B5
Ashford, AL 66 E2
Ashland, AL 64 D4
Ashland, KS 37 B5
Ashland, KY 63 A2
Ashland, ME 71 B2
Ashland, MT 32 A4
Ashland, NH 72 E2
Ashland, NJ 114 D4
Ashland, OH 60 E3
Ashland, OR 12 D1
Ashland, PA 74 D2
Ashland, VA 76 A1
Ashland, WI 47 A2
Ashley, IL 51 D3
Ashley, ND 33 C3
Ashtabula, OH 61 B1
Ashville, AL 64 C3
Ashwood, OR 11 A3
Aspen, CO 25 E2
Aspermont, TX 41 B1
Aspinwall, PA 107 D2
Assiniboia, SK 30 A3
Astoria, IL 49 B5
Astoria, OR 8 D5
Atascadero, CA 14 D5
Atchison, KS 50 B2
Athens, AL 64 B2
Athens, GA 65 A3
Athens, MI 60 B2
Athens, OH 61 A5
Athens, TN 64 D1
Athens, TX 54 D2
Atherton, CA 84 D3
Athol, MA 72 E3
Atka, AK 4 F5
Atkins, AR 52 E3
Atkinson, NE 35 C3
Atlanta, GA 64 E3
Atlanta, IL 49 C5
Atlanta, MI 58 C3
Atlanta, MO 50 E1
Atlanta, TX 54 D1
Atlantic, IA 48 B4
Atlantic, NC 76 D5
Atlantic Beach, FL 67 D2
Atlantic City, NJ 74 D3
Atlas, IL 51 B1
Atmore, AL 66 B3
Atoka, OK 52 B4
Atomic City, ID 22 D1
Attalla, AL 64 C3
Attica, IN 60 A5
Attica, KS 37 D5
Attica, NY 59 D5
Attica, OH 60 F3
Attogok, AK 5 A4
Attu, AK 4 D3
Atwater, CA 14 D3
Atwater, MN 46 B4
Atwood, CO 36 C1
Atwood, KS 37 A2
Atwood, OK 52 A3
Au Gres, MI 58 C4
Au Sable Forks, NY 72 C1
Auburn, AL 64 D5
Auburn, CA 12 D5
Auburn, IL 51 C1
Auburn, IN 60 C3
Auburn, KY 62 B4
Auburn, ME 73 A1
Auburn, NC 119 D5
Auburn, NE 50 B1
Auburn, NY 72 A4
Auburn, WA 9 A4
Auburndale, FL 67 E5
Audubon, IA 48 B4
Audubon, NJ 114 D4
Augusta, AR 53 B2
Augusta, GA 65 C3
Augusta, KS 37 E5
Augusta, ME 71 A5
Augusta, MT 18 E5
Augusta, WI 47 A4
Ault, CO 36 B1
Aurora, CO 36 D2
Aurora, IL 49 D3
Aurora, IN 62 C1
Aurora, KY 51 E5
Aurora, ME 71 B4
Aurora, MN 46 D1
Aurora, MO 50 D5
Aurora, NC 76 C4
Aurora, NE 35 D5
Aurora, ON 59 B3
Ausable Chasm, NY 72 C1
Austin, MB 31 C2
Austin, MN 48 D1
Austin, NV 15 D1
Austin, TX 41 E5
Ava, MO 50 F5
Ava, NY 72 A3
Avalon, CA 17 A4
Avalon, NJ 74 D4
Avalon, PA 107 B3
Avenal, CA 14 D5
Avon, IN 105 A4
Avon, NC 76 D4
Avon, NY 59 D4
Avon Park, FL 69 E1
Avondale, AZ 26 C5
Avondale, CO 36 B4
Avondale, LA 98 B4
Avondale, PA 74 B3
Avondale Estates, GA 121 D2
Avonlea, SK 30 B2
Awendaw, SC 78 A3
Awin, AL 66 C1
Axial, CO 25 D1
Axtell, UT 24 D2
Ayer, MA 72 E3
Aylmer, ON 59 A5
Ayr, NE 36 D1
Azalea Park, FL 120 E2
Azle, TX 41 E1
Aztec, NM 27 C1
Azusa, CA 87 B2

B

Babbitt, NV 15 B2
Babcock, FL 69 E2
Babylon, NY 74 E1
Bacoachi, SON 28 D4
Bacobi, AZ 26 E1
Bad Axe, MI 58 D4
Badlands Natl. Park, SD 34 D1
Bado, OK 39 C2
Bagdad, AZ 26 B3
Bagdad, CA 17 D3
Baggs, WY 23 D5
Bagley, MN 46 A1
Baie-du-Febvre, PQ 70 C4
Baie-St.-Paul, PQ 70 D1
Bailey, CO 36 A2
Baileys Harbor, WI 47 E3
Bainbridge, GA 67 A2
Bainbridge, NY 72 B5
Bainbridge, OH 62 E1
Bainville, MT 30 C5
Baird, TX 41 C2
Baker, CA 17 D1
Baker, FL 66 C3
Baker, MT 32 C3
Baker, NV 24 B2
Baker, OR 11 D3
Baker, WV 61 E5
Bakersfield, CA 16 E1
Bakersfield, MO 53 A1
Bakersfield, TX 40 D4
Bal Harbor, FL 123 E2
Bala-Cynwyd, PA 114 B2
Balcarres, SK 30 D1
Balch Springs, TX 95 E4
Balcones Heights, TX 96 B2
Bald Knob, AR 53 B2
Baldur, MB 31 C3
Baldwin, FL 67 D2
Baldwin, LA 55 B5
Baldwin, MI 58 A5
Baldwin, PA 107 C4
Baldwin, WI 46 E4
Baldwin City, KS 50 C3
Baldwin Park, CA 87 B2
Baldwinsville, NY 72 A4
Baldwyn, MS 53 E3
Balfour, BC 18 A2
Balfour, ND 31 A5
Ballinger, TX 41 B3
Ballston Spa, NY 72 C3
Ballwin, MO 104 A4
Balmorhea, TX 40 C4
Baltimore, MD 74 B4
Bamberg, SC 65 D3
Bamfield, BC 8 D1
Bancroft, IA 48 C2
Bandelier Natl. Mon., NM 27 E2
Bandera, TX 43 C1
Bandon, OR 10 B4
Bangor, ME 71 B4
Bangor, MI 60 A2
Bangor, PA 74 C1
Bangs, TX 41 C3
Banks, AL 66 D1
Banksville, NY 112 C2
Banner, WY 21 E5
Bar Harbor, ME 71 C4
Baraboo, WI 49 B1
Baraga, MI 47 C1
Barberton, OH 61 A3
Barberton, WA 83 D1
Barberville, FL 67 E4
Barboursville, WV 63 A2
Barco, NC 76 C3
Bardstown, KY 62 C3
Bardwell, KY 51 D5
Barham, NC 119 E1
Bark River, MI 47 D2
Barkeyville, PA 61 C2
Barking, PA 107 E1
Barksdale, TX 43 B1
Barling, AR 52 D3
Barnard, SD 33 C3
Barnegat, NJ 74 D3
Barnegat Light, NJ 74 D3
Barnesboro, PA 61 D3
Barnesville, CO 36 B1
Barnesville, GA 65 A4
Barnesville, MN 46 A2
Barnesville, OH 61 B4
Barnet, VT 72 D1
Barneveld, NY 72 B3
Barnhart, TX 41 A4
Barnsdall, OK 52 A1
Barnstable, MA 73 B4
Barnwell, AL 66 B3
Barnwell, SC 65 D3
Barre, MA 72 E3
Barre, VT 72 D1
Barrie, ON 59 B3
Barron, WI 46 E3
Barrow, AK 5 C1
Barry, IL 51 B1
Barryton, MI 58 B5
Barstow, CA 17 C2
Barstow, TX 40 C3
Bartel, CA 12 D2
Bartlesville, OK 52 B1
Bartlett, NE 35 D4
Bartlett, TN 53 D2
Bartlett, TX 41 E4
Barton, OR 83 E5
Barton, VT 70 D5
Bartow, FL 69 E1
Bartow, WV 63 D1
Basalt, NV 15 B2
Basile, LA 55 A4
Basin, WY 21 D5
Basinger, FL 80 A1
Basque, OR 13 D2
Bass Lake, CA 14 E3
Bass Lake, IN 60 A3
Bassano, AB 19 A1
Bassett, NE 35 C3
Bastican, PQ 70 C3
Bastrop, LA 55 B1
Bastrop, TX 41 E5
Bat Cave, NC 65 B1
Batavia, NY 59 D4
Batesburg, SC 65 C2
Batesland, SD 34 E2
Batesville, AR 53 B2
Batesville, MS 53 D4
Batesville, TX 43 C2
Bath, ME 73 A1
Bath, NC 76 C4
Bath, NY 59 E5
Bathurst Inlet, NT 5 G2
Baton Rouge, LA 55 C4
Battens Crossroads, AL 66 D2
Battle Creek, MI 60 B2
Battle Mountain, NV 13 D4
Baudette, MN 44 B4
Bauerstown, PA 107 C2
Bavon, VA 76 C1
Baxley, GA 67 C1
Baxter Springs, KS 50 C5
Bay City, MI 58 C5
Bay City, TX 56 B2
Bay Harbor Islands, FL 123 E2
Bay Lake, FL 120 B4
Bay Minette, AL 66 B3
Bay Pines, FL 122 B4
Bay Port, MI 58 D4
Bay St. Louis, MS 55 E4
Bay Springs, MS 55 E2
Bayard, NE 34 D4
Bayard, NM 29 B1
Bayboro, NC 76 C4
Bayfield, CO 25 D5
Bayfield, WI 47 A1
Bayleaf, NC 119 B2
Bayne, PA 107 A1
Bayonet Point, FL 67 C5
Bayonne, NJ 111 A5
Bayou La Batre, AL 66 A4
Bayside, MA 110 E4
Bayside, WI 101 D1
Baytown, TX 54 C5
Beach, ND 32 C2
Beach Bluff, MA 110 E1
Beach Haven, NJ 74 D3
Beachwood, OH 106 E2
Beacon, NY 72 D5
Beacon Hill, FL 6 F4
Beadling, PA 107 B4
Beane, MD 116 B1
Bear Creek Springs, AR 52 E1
Bear Lake, MI 58 A4
Bearden, AR 53 A5
Beardsley, MN 33 E4
Beardstown, IL 51 B1
Beatrice, AL 66 B2
Beatrice, NE 50 A1
Beatty, NV 15 C4
Beatty, OR 12 E1
Beauceville, PQ 70 E3
Beaufort, NC 76 C5
Beaufort, SC 65 E4
Beauharnois, PQ 70 B5
Beaumont, CA 17 B3
Beaumont, MS 55 E3
Beaumont, TX 54 D5
Beaumont Place, TX 97 D2
Beauport, PQ 70 D2
Beaupre, PQ 70 D2
Beausejour, MB 31 E2
Beaver, LA 55 A4
Beaver, OK 39 B1
Beaver, UT 24 C3
Beaver City, NE 37 B1
Beaver Dam, KY 62 B4
Beaver Dam, WI 49 C1
Beaver Falls, PA 61 C3
Beaver Marsh, OR 10 E5
Beaverdam, OH 60 D4
Beaverdell, BC 9 D1
Beaverton, OR 10 E1
BeBe, TX 43 E1
Becancour, PQ 70 C3
Beckley, WV 63 C2
Bedford, IA 48 C5
Bedford, IN 62 B2
Bedford, KY 62 C2
Bedford, MA 110 A2
Bedford, NY 72 D5
Bedford, OH 106 E3
Bedford, PA 61 E3
Bedford, PQ 70 C5
Bedford, TX 94 D2
Bedford, VA 63 D2
Bedford Center, NY 112 C1
Bedford Heights, OH 106 E3
Bedford Hills, NY 112 B2
Bedford Park, IL 102 C5
Bedrock, CO 25 B3
Beebe, AR 53 B4
Beech Creek, PA 61 E2
Beech Grove, IN 105 D4
Beechcliff, PA 107 A4
Beecher Falls, VT 70 D5
Beechey Point, AK 5 C1
Beechmont, PA 107 A4
Beechwood, MS 55 C3
Beegum, CA 12 C3
Beersville, NB 71 E1
Beeville, TX 43 E2
Beggs, OK 52 B2
Begs, LA 55 B4
Bel Air, MD 74 B3
Bel-Nor, MO 104 D2
Bel-Ridge, MO 104 C2
Belden, CA 12 D4
Belding, MI 60 B1
Belen, NM 27 D4
Belfair, WA 8 E3
Belfast, ME 71 B5
Belfast, NY 59 D5
Belfield, ND 32 D2
Belfrey, MT 21 C4
Belgrade, ME 71 A5
Belgrade, MN 46 B4
Belgrade, MT 21 A3
Belhaven, NC 76 C4
Beliot, KS 37 D2
Belknap Springs, OR 10 E3
Bell, CA 86 D3
Bell Acres, PA 107 A2
Bell Gardens, CA 86 D3
Bella Coola, BC 5 G6
Bella Villa, MO 104 D4
Bellaire, OH 61 B4
Bellaire, TX 97 A4
Belle Chasse, LA 98 D5
Belle Fourche, SD 32 C5
Belle Glade, FL 80 A2
Belle Isle, FL 120 D3
Belle Meade, TN 99 B4
Belleair, FL 122 A2
Belleair Beach, FL 122 A2
Belleair Bluffs, FL 122 A2
Belleair Shores, FL 122 A2

Place Name · Page Number · Grid Number
Stantonburg **118** C5

C

Bellefontaine, OH 60 D4
Bellefontaine Neighbors, MO 104 D1
Bellefonte, PA 61 E2
Bellerive, MO 104 D2
Belleview, FL 67 D4
Belleville, IL 51 C3
Belleville, IN 62 A1
Belleville, KS 37 E2
Belleville, NJ 111 A3
Belleville, ON 59 D3
Bellevue, IA 49 B3
Bellevue, ID 22 B1
Bellevue, KY 108 B4
Bellevue, OH 60 E3
Bellevue, PA 107 B3
Bellevue, TN 99 A5
Bellevue, TX 39 D5
Bellevue, WA 9 A3
Bellflower, CA 86 D4
Bellingham, WA 9 A2
Bellmawr, NJ 114 D4
Bellows Falls, NH 72 D3
Bells, TN 53 E1
Bells, TX 52 A5
Bellville, TX 54 B5
Bellwood, IL 102 B3
Belmar, NJ 74 D2
Belmond, IA 48 D2
Belmont, CA 84 E2
Belmont, MA 110 B3
Belmont, NC 117 A3
Belmont, NY 59 D5
Belmont Corner, ME 71 B5
Belmont Hills, PA 114 B2
Beloit, WI 49 C2
Belpre, OH 61 B5
Belton, MO 50 C3
Belton, SC 65 B2
Belton, TX 41 E4
Beltsville, MD 116 D1
Belvedere, CA 85 D1
Belvedere, WA 9 E3
Belvidere, IL 49 D2
Belvidere, SD 35 A1
Belzoni, MS 53 C5
Bement, IL 51 D1
Bemidji, MN 46 B1
Ben Avon, PA 107 B2
Ben Avon Heights, PA 107 B2
Ben Bolt, TX 43 E4
Bena, MN 46 C1
Benavides, TX 43 D4
Bend, OR 11 A3
Bengough, SK 30 B3
Benicia, CA 85 E5
Benito Juárez, CHIH 29 D5
Benjamin, TX 39 B5
Benjamin Hill, SON 28 D4
Benkelman, NE 36 E1
Benndale, MS 66 A3
Bennett, CO 36 B2
Bennettsville, SC 65 E1
Bennington, KS 37 E3
Bennington, VT 72 D3
Bensenville, IL 102 A2
Benson, AZ 28 E2
Benson, MN 46 A4
Benson, SK 30 D3
Bent, NM 29 E1
Benton, AR 53 A3
Benton, CA 15 B3
Benton, IL 51 D3
Benton, PA 74 A1
Benton Harbor, MI 60 A2
Bentonville, AR 52 D1
Benzonia, MI 58 A4
Beowawe, NV 13 E4
Berclair, TX 43 E2
Berea, KY 62 D3
Berea, OH 106 A4
Bergenfield, NJ 111 B1
Bergland, MI 47 B2
Berino, NM 29 D2
Berkeley, CA 14 C2
Berkeley, MO 104 C1
Berkeley Springs, WV 61 E4
Berkley, IL 102 B3
Berkley, MI 103 B2
Berlin, NH 70 E5
Berlin, NJ 114 E5
Berlin, WI 47 C5
Bernalillo, NM 27 E3
Bernardo, NM 27 D4
Berne, IN 60 C4
Bernice, LA 55 A1
Bernie, KS 51 C5
Berrien Springs, MI 60 A2
Berry Hill, TN 99 C4
Berrydale, FL 66 C3
Berryville, AR 52 D1
Berryville, VA 61 E4
Bertha, FL 120 E1
Berthierville, PQ 70 C4
Berthoud, CO 36 B1
Bertrand, KS 37 C1
Berwick, LA 55 C5
Berwick, PA 74 B1
Berwyn, IL 102 C4
Berwyn Heights, MD 116 D1
Beryl Junction, UT 24 B4
Beshoar Junction, CO 36 B5
Bessemer, AL 64 B4
Bessemer, MI 47 B2
Bethany, MO 50 C1
Bethany, OR 83 A2
Bethany Beach, DE 74 D4
Bethayres, PA 114 C1
Bethel, AK 5 B3
Bethel, ME 70 E5
Bethel, NC 76 B4
Bethel, OH 62 D1
Bethel, VT 72 D2
Bethel Park, PA 107 C5
Bethlehem, PA 74 C2
Bethesda, MD 116 B2
Bethesda, NC 118 E2
Bettendorf, IA 49 D2
Bettles, AK 5 C2
Beulah, FL 120 A3
Beulah, ND 32 E1
Beulah, WY 32 C5
Beulaville, NC 76 B5
Beverley, SK 19 E2
Beverly, MA 73 A3
Beverly, NE 36 A1
Beverly, NJ 114 E1
Beverly Hills, CA 86 B1
Beverly Hills, MI 103 A1
Bexley, IN 60 E4
Bexley, OH 109 D3
Bicknell, IN 62 A2
Biddeford, ME 73 A1
Bieber, CA 12 E2
Bienfait, SK 30 D4
Big Bar, CA 12 C2
Big Bay, MI 47 D1
Big Bear Lake, CA 17 C3
Big Beaver, SK 30 B4
Big Bend, WI 101 B5
Big Bend Natl. Park, TX 42 C2
Big Creek, WV 63 A1
Big Falls, MN 44 C5
Big Field, AZ 28 C2
Big Lake, MN 46 C4
Big Lake, TX 40 E4
Big Pine, CA 15 B3
Big Pine, FL 80 A5
Big Piney, WY 23 B2
Big Point, MS 66 A3
Big Rapids, MI 58 B5
Big Sandy, MT 19 B5
Big Sandy, WY 23 B2
Big Spirit Lake, IA 48 B1
Big Spring, TX 40 E2
Big Stone Gap, VA 63 A4
Big Sur, CA 14 C4
Big Timber, MT 21 B3
Big Trees, CA 14 E2
Big Water, UT 24 D5
Big Wells, TX 43 C2
Bigford, MN 44 C5
Bigfork, MT 18 D4
Biggs, OR 11 B1
Bill, WY 34 A2
Billboa, NC 118 E2
Billerica, MA 110 A1
Billings, MT 21 D3
Billsburg, SD 32 E5
Biloxi, MS 66 A4
Biloxi, WA 82 A4
Binger, OK 39 D3
Bingham, ME 71 A4
Bingham, NE 34 E4
Bingham, NM 27 E5
Bingham Farms, MI 103 A2
Binghamton, NY 72 A5
Binscarth, MB 31 A2
Birchdale, MN 44 C4
Birchwood Village, MN 100 E1
Bird City, KS 36 E2
Bird Is., MN 46 B5
Birmingham, AL 64 B4
Birmingham, MI 103 B1
Birmingham, MO 92 D1
Birney, MT 21 E4
Birtle, MB 31 A2
Bisbee, AZ 28 E3
Biscayne Park, FL 123 D3
Biscoe, NC 63 E5
Bishop, CA 15 B3
Bishop, PA 107 A5
Bishop, TX 43 E4
Bishopton, PQ 70 D4
Bishopville, SC 65 E2
Bismarck, ND 33 A2
Bismark, KS 51 B4
Bitter Springs, AZ 24 D5
Bixby, OK 52 B2
Black Canyon of the Gunnison Natl. Mon., CO 25 D3
Black Creek, WI 47 D4
Black Diamond, AB 18 D1
Black Jack, MO 104 D1
Black Lake, NM 38 A1
Black Mountain, NC 63 B5
Black River, NY 72 A2
Black River Falls, WI 47 A5
Black River Village, NM 40 B2
Black Rock, UT 24 C2
Black-Lake, PQ 70 D3
Blackburn, PA 107 E3
Blackduck, MN 44 B5
Blackfoot, ID 22 D1
Blackfoot, MT 18 E4
Blacklick, OH 109 E3
Blacks Harbour, NB 71 D3
Blacksburg, VA 63 C3
Blackshear, GA 67 C1
Blacksher, AL 66 B2
Blackstone, VA 76 A2
Blackwell, OK 39 E1
Blackwell, TX 41 B2
Blackwood, NJ 114 D5
Blackwood Station, NC 118 B2
Blackwood Terrace, NJ 114 D5
Bladensburg, MD 116 D2
Blaine, KS 50 A2
Blaine Hill, PA 107 E5
Blair, NE 48 A4
Blairsville, GA 64 E2
Blairsville, PA 61 D3
Blakely, GA 66 E2
Blanchard, ND 33 E1
Blanchard, OK 39 E3
Blanche, PQ 70 A5
Blanchester, OH 62 D1
Blanco, TX 41 D5
Blanco Trading Post, NM 27 C1
Bland, VA 63 C3
Blanding, UT 25 B4
Blaney Park, MI 58 A2
Bledsoe, TX 38 D5
Blenheim, NJ 114 D5
Blewett, WA 9 B4
Blichton, GA 65 D5
Bliss, ID 22 B1
Blissfield, MI 60 D2
Block Is., RI 73 A5
Bloome, WI 47 A4
Bloomer, WI 46 E4
Bloomfield, IA 48 E5
Bloomfield, IN 62 A2
Bloomfield, KS 51 C5
Bloomfield, KY 62 C3
Bloomfield, MT 32 B1
Bloomfield, NM 27 C1
Bloomfield, VT 70 D5
Bloomfield Hills, MI 103 A1
Bloomington, IL 49 D5
Bloomington, IN 62 B1
Bloomington, MN 100 B5
Bloomsburg, PA 74 A2
Blossom, TX 52 C5
Blountstown, FL 66 E3
Blowing Rock, NC 63 B4
Bloxham, FL 67 A3
Blue Ash, OH 108 C2
Blue Bell, PA 114 A1
Blue Earth, MN 48 C1
Blue Eye, AR 52 E1
Blue Hill, ME 71 B5
Blue Hill, NE 37 D1
Blue Lake, CA 12 B2
Blue Mound, TX 94 A2
Blue Mountain Lake, NY 72 B2
Blue Rapids, KS 50 A2
Blue Ridge, GA 64 E2
Blue Summit, MO 92 D3
Bluefield, WV 63 C3
Blues Old Stand, AL 66 D1
Bluewater, NM 27 C3
Bluff, UT 25 A5
Bluff City, TN 63 B4
Bluff Dale, TX 41 E2
Bluffton, IN 60 C4
Blunt, SD 33 B5
Bly, OR 12 E1
Blythe, CA 17 E4
Blythedale, PA 107 E5
Blytheville, AR 53 D1
Boca Grande, FL 69 D2
Boca Raton, FL 80 A2
Bodega Bay, CA 14 B1
Boerne, TX 43 D1
Bogalusa, LA 55 D3
Bogata, TX 52 C5
Boise, ID 20 A5
Boise City, OK 38 D1
Boissevain, MB 31 B4
Bokeelia, FL 69 E2
Bolinger, AL 66 A2
Bolivar, MO 50 D4
Bolivar, NY 61 D1
Bolivar, TN 53 E2
Bolton, NC 78 B1
Bombay Beach, CA 17 D4
Bonair, PA 107 D2
Bonanza, UT 25 B1
Bondad, CO 25 C5
Bondurant, WY 23 A1
Bondville, VT 72 D3
Bonham, TX 52 B5
Bonifay, FL 66 D3
Bonita, AZ 28 E1
Bonita Beach, FL 69 E3
Bonita Springs, FL 69 E3
Bonne Terre, MO 51 C4
Bonner Springs, KS 50 C3
Bonners Ferry, ID 18 B3
Bonny Slope, OR 83 B2
Booker, TX 39 A1
Booker T. Washington Natl. Mon., VA 63 D3
Boone, CO 36 B4
Boone, IA 48 C3
Boone, NC 63 B4
Booneville, AR 52 D3
Booneville, KY 62 E3
Booneville, MS 53 E3
Boonsboro, MD 74 A4
Boonville, CA 12 B5
Boonville, IN 62 A3
Boonville, MO 50 E2
Boonville, NY 72 B3
Boothbay Harbor, ME 73 B1
Boquilla del Mezquite, CHIH 42 B1
Boquillas del Carmen, COAH 42 D1
Bordeaux, TN 99 B3
Border, WY 23 A3
Borger, TX 39 A2
Boring, OR 10 E1
Boscawen, NH 72 E2
Boschertown, MO 104 B1
Boscobel, WI 49 B1
Bosler, WY 34 A4
Bossier City, LA 54 E1
Boston, MA 73 A3
Boston, PA 107 E4
Boston Mills, OH 106 E5
Bostonia, CA 89 E2
Boswell, BC 18 B2
Boswell, OK 52 B5
Bothell, WA 82 E1
Bottineau, ND 31 B4
Boulder, CO 36 A1
Boulder, MT 20 E2
Boulder, UT 24 E4
Boulder, WY 23 B2
Boulder City, NV 17 E1
Boundary, AK 5 D3
Bountiful, UT 22 D4
Bouse, AZ 26 A4
Bovill, ID 20 A1
Bovina, TX 38 D4
Bow Is., AB 19 B2
Bow-Mar, CO 93 B4
Bowbells, ND 30 E4
Bowdle, SD 33 B4
Bower Hill, PA 107 B4
Bowie, AZ 29 A2
Bowie, MD 74 B4
Bowie, TX 39 E5
Bowling Green, FL 69 E1
Bowling Green, IN 62 A1
Bowling Green, KY 62 B4
Bowling Green, MO 51 B2
Bowling Green, OH 60 D3
Bowling Green, VA 76 A1
Bowman, ND 32 D3
Boyce, LA 55 A3
Boyce, MS 66 A2
Boyd, MT 21 C3
Boyds, WA 9 E3
Boyertown, PA 74 B2
Boyne City, MI 58 B3
Boynton Beach, FL 80 B2
Boys Town, NE 48 A5
Boysen, WY 23 D1
Bozeman, MT 21 A3
Bracebridge, ON 59 B2
Bracketville, TX 43 B1
Brad, TX 41 D1
Braddock, PA 107 D3
Braddock Hills, PA 107 D3
Bradenton, FL 69 D1
Bradford, ME 71 B4
Bradford, ON 59 B3
Bradford, PA 61 D1
Bradford, VT 72 D1
Bradford Woods, PA 107 A1
Bradley, FL 69 D1
Bradley, SD 33 D4
Bradshaw, MD 115 E1
Bradshaw, WV 63 B3
Brady, NE 35 B5
Brady, TX 41 C4
Braham, MN 46 D3
Brainerd, MN 46 C2
Braintree, MA 110 D5
Braintree Five Corners, MA 110 D5
Braithwaite, LA 98 E5
Brampton, ON 59 B4
Branchville, MD 116 D1
Branchville, SC 65 D3
Brandenburg, KY 62 B3
Brandon, FL 69 D1
Brandon, MB 31 B3
Brandon, MS 55 D1
Brandon, VT 72 D2
Branford, CT 113 E1
Branford, FL 67 C3
Branson, CO 38 C1
Branson, MO 52 E1
Brantford, ON 59 B5
Brantley, AL 66 C2
Brashears, AR 52 D2
Brassfield, NC 118 E2
Brawley, CA 17 D5
Brazil, IN 62 A1
Brea, CA 87 B4
Breakabeen, NY 72 C4
Breaux Bridge, LA 55 B4
Breckenridge, MN 33 E3
Breckenridge, TX 41 C1
Breckenridge Hills, MO 104 C2
Brecksville, OH 106 D4
Bredenbury, SK 30 E1
Breien, ND 33 A3
Bremen, GA 64 D3
Bremerton, WA 8 E3
Bremond, TX 54 A4
Brenham, TX 54 B5
Brentwood, MO 104 C3
Brentwood, PA 107 C4
Brentwood, TN 99 C5
Brevard, NC 65 B1
Brevort, MI 58 A2
Brewer, ME 71 B4
Brewster, WA 9 C3
Brewster, KS 37 A2
Brewster, NE 35 B4
Brewster, NY 72 D5
Brewton, AL 66 C2
Briarcliff Manor, NY 112 B2
Brice, OH 109 E4
Bridge City, LA 98 B4
Bridge City, TX 54 E5
Bridgeboro, GA 67 A1
Bridgeboro, NJ 114 E2
Bridgeford, SK 30 A1
Bridgehampton, NY 72 E5
Bridgeport, AL 64 C2
Bridgeport, CA 15 A2
Bridgeport, CT 72 E5
Bridgeport, NE 34 D4
Bridgeport, NJ 114 A5
Bridgeport, OH 61 B4
Bridgeport, TX 41 E1
Bridgeport, WA 9 C3
Bridger, MT 21 C4
Bridgeton, MO 104 B1
Bridgeton, NJ 74 C3
Bridgetown, NS 71 E3
Bridgeview, IL 102 C5
Bridgeville, CA 12 B3
Bridgeville, PA 107 B4
Bridgewater, ME 71 B2
Bridgewater, NY 72 B4
Bridgewater, PA 114 E1
Bridgewater, SD 35 E1
Bridgton, ME 73 A1
Brier, WA 82 D1
Brigantine, NJ 74 D3
Briggs, TX 41 E4
Briggsdale, CO 36 C1
Briggsdale, OH 109 B4
Brigham City, UT 22 D4
Brighton, CO 36 B1
Brighton, FL 80 A1
Brighton, MI 60 C1
Brighton, UT 90 E5
Brightseat, MD 116 E2
Brilliant, OH 61 B4
Brinkley, AR 53 B3
Brisbane, CA 85 B1
Bristol, CO 36 E4
Bristol, CT 72 E5
Bristol, FL 66 E3
Bristol, NB 71 B2
Bristol, RI 73 A4
Bristol, SD 33 D4
Bristol, TN 63 B4
Bristol, VA 63 B4
Bristow, OK 52 A2
Britt, IA 48 C2
Britton, SD 33 D3
Broad Axe, PA 114 A1
Broadalbin, NY 72 C3
Broaddus, TX 54 D3
Broadus, MT 32 B4
Broadview, IL 102 B3
Broadview, MT 21 C3
Broadview, SK 30 E2
Broadview Heights, OH 106 C4
Broadwell, IL 49 C5
Brocket, AB 18 D2
Brockport, NY 59 D4
Brockton, MA 73 A3
Brockton, MT 30 B5
Brockville, ON 72 A1
Brockway, MT 32 A1
Brockway, PA 61 D2
Brockwell, AR 53 A1
Brodhead, WI 49 C2
Brodheadsville, PA 74 B1
Brogan, OR 11 D4
Broken Arrow, OK 52 B2
Broken Bow, NE 35 B4
Broken Bow, OK 52 C4
Bromley, KY 108 B4
Bromont, PQ 70 C5
Bromptonville, PQ 70 D4
Bronco, TX 40 D1
Bronson, MI 60 B2
Bronte, TX 41 B3
Bronxville, NY 112 B5
Brook Park, OH 106 B4
Brookfield, IL 102 B4
Brookfield, IN 105 E5
Brookfield, MO 50 E1
Brookfield, WI 101 B3
Brookhaven, GA 121 C1
Brookhaven, MS 55 D2
Brookhaven, PA 114 A5
Brookings, OR 10 B5
Brookings, SD 33 E5
Brooklawn, NJ 114 C4
Brookline, MA 110 C4
Brookline, PA 114 A3
Brooklyn, IL 104 E3
Brooklyn, ME 71 C5
Brooklyn, OH 106 C3
Brooklyn Center, MN 100 A2
Brooklyn Heights, OH 106 C3
Brooklyn Park, MN 100 A2
Brookneal, VA 63 E3
Brooks, AB 19 A1
Brooks, ME 71 B5
Brooks Cross Roads, NC 63 C4
Brookside Village, TX 97 C5
Brookston, IN 60 A4
Brooksville, FL 67 D5
Brooksville, MS 53 E5
Brookton, ME 71 C3
Brookville, IN 62 C1
Brookville, PA 61 D2
Broomall, PA 114 A3
Brothers, OR 11 A4
Broughton, PA 107 C5
Browmell, KS 37 B3
Brown Deer, WI 101 C1
Brownfield, TX 40 E1
Browning, MT 18 E4
Browns, AL 66 B1
Browns Flats, NB 71 C2
Browns Valley, MN 33 E4
Brownstown, IN 62 B2
Brownsville, KY 62 B4
Brownsville, PA 61 C4
Brownsville, TN 53 D2
Brownsville, TX 56 A6
Brownsville, WA 82 A2
Brownwood, TX 41 C3
Broxton, GA 67 B1
Bruce, MS 53 E4
Bruce, WI 47 A3
Bruce Crossing, MI 47 B2
Brule, WI 46 E2
Brundage, TX 43 C2
Brundidge, AL 66 D1
Bruneau, ID 22 A1
Bruni, TX 43 D4
Bruno, MN 46 D2
Brunswick, GA 67 D1
Brunswick, ME 73 A1
Brunswick, MO 50 D2
Brush, CO 36 C1
Brussels, WI 47 D4
Bryan, OH 60 C3
Bryan, TX 54 B4
Bryant, IN 60 C4
Bryant, SD 33 E5
Bryce Canyon Natl. Park, UT 24 D4
Bryn Mawr, PA 114 A2
Bryn Mawr, WA 82 D5
Bryson, TX 41 D1
Bryson City, NC 65 A1
Buchanan Dam, TX 41 D4
Buck Is. Reef Natl. Mon., VI 6 D4
Buck Meadows, CA 14 E2
Buckatunna, MS 66 A2
Buckeye, AZ 26 B5
Buckhannon, WV 61 C5
Buckhead Ridge, FL 80 A1
Buckhorn, NC 118 A1
Buckhorn, NM 29 B1
Buckingham, PQ 70 A5
Buckingham, TX 95 D1
Buckingham, VA 63 E2
Buckland, PQ 70 E2
Buckley, WA 9 A4
Bucklin, KS 37 B5
Buckner, MO 50 C2
Bucksport, ME 71 B4
Bucksville, AL 64 B4
Buctouche, NB 71 E1
Bucyrus, OH 60 E3
Bude, MS 55 C3
Buena, WA 9 B5
Buena Park, CA 87 A5
Buena Vista, CO 25 E3
Buena Vista, PA 107 E5
Buena Vista, VA 63 D2
Buenaventura, CHIH 29 C5
Buenos Aires, CHIH 29 B4
Bueyeros, NM 38 C2
Búfalo, CHIH 42 A4
Buffalo, AB 19 B1
Buffalo, MN 46 C4
Buffalo, MO 50 E4
Buffalo, NY 59 C5
Buffalo, OK 39 B1
Buffalo, SD 32 D4
Buffalo, TX 54 B3
Buffalo, WV 63 A1
Buffalo, WY 21 E5
Buford, CO 25 D1
Buford, GA 64 E3
Buford, WY 34 A5
Buhl, ID 22 B2
Buna, TX 54 E4
Bunkie, LA 55 B3
Bunnell, FL 67 E3
Buras, LA 55 E5
Burbank, CA 17 A2
Burbank, IL 102 D5
Burden, KS 50 A5
Burdett, KS 37 C4
Burgaw, NC 78 B1
Burien, WA 82 B5
Burkburnett, TX 39 D5
Burke, SD 35 C2
Burkesville, KY 62 C4
Burkett, TX 41 C3
Burkeville, TX 54 E4
Burkeville, VA 76 A2
Burley, ID 22 C2
Burlingame, CA 85 A2
Burlingame, KS 50 B3
Burlington, CO 36 E2
Burlington, IA 49 A5
Burlington, IN 60 A4
Burlington, KS 50 B4
Burlington, MA 110 B1
Burlington, NC 63 E4
Burlington, ON 59 B4
Burlington, OR 83 B1
Burlington, PA 114 E1
Burlington, VT 72 C1
Burlington, WI 49 D2
Burnet, TX 41 D4
Burney, CA 12 D3
Burnham, NM 27 B1
Burnham, PA 61 E2
Burns, OR 11 C5
Burns Junction, OR 13 D1
Burnside, KY 62 D4
Burnside, MI 58 D5
Burnsville, MN 46 D5
Burnt Ft., GA 67 D2
Burnt Ranch, OR 11 B3
Burntfork, WY 23 A5
Burr Ridge, IL 102 B5
Burtts Corner, NB 71 C2
Burwell, NE 35 C4
Busby, MT 21 E4
Bush, LA 55 D4
Bushland, TX 38 E3
Bushnell, IL 49 B5
Bustamente, NL 43 B5
Butler, AL 66 A1
Butler, MD 74 B4
Butler, MO 50 C4
Butler, PA 61 C3
Butler, WI 101 C1
Butte, MT 20 E2
Butte, NE 35 C2
Butte City, ID 22 D1
Butte Falls, OR 10 D5
Buxton, NC 76 D4
Buxton, OR 10 D1
Buyck, MN 44 D5
Byers, CO 36 B2
Bylas, AZ 26 E5
Bynum, MT 18 E5
Bynum, NC 118 B5
Byram, CT 112 D4
Byron, IL 49 C3
Caballo, NM 29 C1
Cabin John, MD 116 A2
Cable, MN 46 E2
Cable, WI 47 A2
Cabool, MO 51 A5
Caborca, SON 28 B3
Cabot, AR 53 A3
Cabri, SK 19 D1
Cabrillo Natl. Mon., CA 89 A3
Cactus, TX 38 E2
Caddo, OK 52 B4
Caddo, TX 41 D2
Cadillac, MI 58 B4
Cadillac, SK 19 E3
Cadiz, CA 17 D3
Cadiz, KY 62 A5
Cadiz, OH 61 B4
Cadott, WI 47 A4
Caernarvon, LA 98 E5
Caguas, PR 6 B3
Cahokia, IL 104 E4
Cahuilla, CA 17 B4
Cairo, GA 67 A2
Cairo, IL 51 D5
Cairo, KS 37 D5
Cairo, NY 72 C4
Cajon, CA 17 B3
Calabash, NC 78 B2
Calais, ME 71 C3
Caldwell, ID 11 E5
Caldwell, KS 37 E5
Caldwell, OH 61 B4
Caldwell, TX 54 A4
Caledon, ON 59 B4
Caledonia, MI 60 B1
Caledonia, MN 49 A1
Caledonia, MO 51 B4
Calera, AL 64 C5
Calera, OK 52 A5
Calexico, CA 17 D5
Calhan, CO 36 B3
Calhoun, GA 64 D2
Calhoun City, MS 53 E4
Calhoun Falls, SC 65 B2
Calico Rock, AR 53 A1
Caliente, CA 17 A1
Caliente, NV 24 A4
California, MO 50 E3
California City, CA 17 B1
Calipatria, CA 17 D5
Calistoga, CA 14 C1
Callaghan, TX 43 C3
Callahan, CA 12 C2
Callahan, FL 67 D2
Callao, UT 24 B1
Callicoon, NY 72 C5
Calmar, IA 48 E2
Calvary, GA 67 A2
Calverton Park, MO 104 D1
Calvin, OK 52 A3
Camargo, TAMPS 43 D5
Camarrón, NL 43 B4
Camas, WA 10 E1
Camas Valley, OR 10 C4
Cambria, CA 14 C5
Cambridge, ID 11 E4
Cambridge, MA 73 A3
Cambridge, MD 74 C5
Cambridge, MN 46 D3
Cambridge, NE 37 B1

Bold type indicates cities with 100,000 population or more.

Place Name / Page Number / Grid Number
Stantonburg **118** C5

Cambridge, NJ .. **114** D1
Cambridge, OH ... **61** A4
Cambridge, ON ... **59** A4
Cambridge City, IN ... **60** C5
Cambridge Springs, PA ... **61** B1
Camden, AL ... **66** B1
Camden, AR ... **53** A5
Camden, ME ... **71** B5
Camden, NC ... **76** C3
Camden, NJ ... **74** C3
Camden, NY ... **72** A3
Camden, SC ... **65** D2
Camden, TN ... **64** A1
Camdenton, MO . **50** E4
Cameron, AZ ... **26** D1
Cameron, LA ... **54** E5
Cameron, MO ... **50** C1
Cameron, TX ... **54** A4
Cameron, WI ... **46** E3
Cameron, WV ... **61** C4
Camilla, GA ... **67** A2
Camp Air, TX ... **41** C4
Camp Crook, SD . **32** C4
Camp Houston, OK ... **39** C1
Camp Point, IL ... **51** B1
Camp Scenic, TX **41** C5
Camp Springs, KY ... **108** D5
Camp Springs, MD ... **116** E4
Camp Verde, AZ . **26** C3
Camp Wood, TX . **43** B1
Campbell, CA ... **84** A4
Campbell, MO ... **51** C5
Campbell, NE ... **36** C1
Campbell Corner, MD ... **116** A2
Campbellsville, KY ... **62** C4
Campbellton, TX . **43** D2
Campo, CO ... **36** D5
Campodonico, SON ... **28** A3
Campti, LA ... **54** E2
Canaan, CT ... **72** D4
Canaan, NH ... **72** E2
Canada Lake, NY **72** B3
Canadian, TX ... **39** B2
Canajoharie, NY . **72** B4
Canal Point, FL ... **80** A2
Canal Winchester, OH ... **109** E5
Canandaigua, NY **59** E4
Cananea, SON ... **28** E3
Canby, CA ... **12** E2
Canby, MN ... **46** A5
Candela, COAH ... **43** A5
Cando, ND ... **31** C5
Candor, NY ... **72** A5
Cane Ridge, TN .. **99** E5
Caneadea, NY ... **59** D5
Caney, KS ... **50** B5
Caneyville, KY ... **62** B4
Canisteo, NY ... **59** E5
Cannelton, IN ... **62** B3
Cannon Falls, MN **46** D5
Cannonville, UT .. **24** D4
Canon City, CO ... **36** A4
Cantitoe Corners, NY ... **112** C1
Canton, GA ... **64** E3
Canton, IL ... **49** C5
Canton, MO ... **51** A1
Canton, MS ... **55** D1
Canton, NC ... **65** A1
Canton, NY ... **72** A1
Canton, OH ... **61** A3
Canton, OK ... **39** D2
Canton, PA ... **74** A1
Canton, SD ... **48** A2
Canton, TX ... **54** B2
Cantwell, AK ... **5** C3
Canutillo, TX ... **29** D2
Canyon, TX ... **38** E3
Canyon de Chelly Natl. Mon., AZ ... **27** B1
Canyon Ferry, MT **21** A2
Canyon Village, WY ... **21** B4
Canyonlands Natl. Park, UT ... **25** A3
Canyonville, OR .. **10** C5
Cap-de-la-Madeleine, PQ ... **70** C3
Cape Canaveral, FL ... **67** F5
Cape Charles, VA **76** C1
Cape Coral, FL ... **69** E2
Cape Elizabeth, ME ... **73** A1
Cape Girardeau, MO ... **51** D4
Cape Krusenstern Natl. Mon., AK ... **5** B2
Cape May, NJ ... **74** D4
Cape May C. H., NJ ... **74** D4
Cape Vincent, NY **59** E2
Capitan, NM ... **27** E5
Capitol Heights, MD ... **116** D3
Capitol Reef Natl. Park, UT ... **24** E3
Capitola, CA ... **14** C3
Capps, FL ... **67** B3
Caprock, NM ... **40** C1
Captain Cook, HI .. **7** D5
Capulin, NM ... **38** C1
Capulin Mountain Natl. Mon., NM ... **38** C1
Carbon, TX ... **41** D2
Carbon Hill, AL ... **64** B4
Carbondale, CO .. **25** D2
Carbondale, IL ... **51** D4
Carbondale, PA ... **72** B5
Cardston, AB ... **18** E3
Carefree, AZ ... **26** C4
Carey, ID ... **22** C1
Carey, OH ... **60** D3
Caribou, ME ... **71** B1
Carievale, SK ... **30** E4
Carleton, NS ... **71** E4
Carleton Place, ON ... **59** E1
Carlin, NV ... **13** E4
Carlinville, IL ... **51** C2
Carlisle, AR ... **53** B3
Carlisle, KY ... **62** D2
Carlisle, PA ... **74** A3
Carlsbad, NM ... **40** B2
Carlsbad, TX ... **41** A3
Carlsbad Caverns Natl. Park, NM ... **40** B2
Carlstadt, NJ ... **111** A2
Carlyle, IL ... **51** D3
Carlyle, SK ... **30** E3
Carmacks, YT ... **5** F4
Carman, MB ... **31** D3
Carmel, CA ... **14** C3
Carmel Valley, CA ... **14** C4
Carmi, IL ... **51** E3
Carnegie, PA ... **107** B4
Carnestown, FL ... **80** A3
Carney, MD ... **115** D2
Caro, MI ... **58** D5
Carolina Beach, NC ... **78** B1
Carp, NV ... **24** A4
Carpenter, NC ... **118** E4
Carpinteria, CA ... **16** D2
Carrabelle, FL ... **67** A4
Carranza, COAH .. **43** B2
Carrboro, NC ... **118** C3
Carrington, ND ... **33** C1
Carrizo, AZ ... **26** E4
Carrizo Springs, TX ... **43** B2
Carrizozo, NM ... **27** E5
Carroll, IA ... **48** B3
Carrollton, GA ... **64** D4
Carrollton, IL ... **51** B2
Carrollton, KY ... **62** C2
Carrollton, MO ... **50** D2
Carrollton, OH ... **61** B3
Carson, CA ... **86** B4
Carson, OR ... **11** E3
Carson City, MI ... **58** B5
Carson City, NV .. **13** A5
Carta Valley, TX .. **43** A1
Cartersville, GA .. **64** D3
Carthage, IL ... **49** B5
Carthage, MO ... **50** C5
Carthage, MS ... **55** D1
Carthage, NC ... **63** E5
Carthage, NY ... **72** A2
Carthage, TN ... **62** C5
Carthage, TX ... **54** D2
Cartwright, MB ... **31** C4
Caruthersville, MO ... **53** D1
Carver, OR ... **83** D5
Carway, AB ... **18** E3
Cary, NC ... **119** A4
Casa Blanca, NM **27** C3
Casa Grande, AZ **26** C5
Casa Grande Ruins Natl. Mon., AZ .. **26** D5
Casas Grandes, CHIH ... **29** B4
Cascade, IA ... **49** A3
Cascade, ID ... **20** A4
Cascade, MT ... **21** A1
Caseville, MI ... **58** D4
Casey, IL ... **51** E1
Cashton, WI ... **49** A1
Casper, WY ... **34** A2
Cass City, MI ... **58** D5
Cass Lake, MN ... **46** B1
Casselman, ON ... **70** A5
Casselton, ND ... **33** E2
Cassopolis, MI ... **60** A2
Cassville, MO ... **52** D1
Cassville, WI ... **49** A2
Castaic, CA ... **17** A2
Castaños, COAH . **43** A5
Castaway, NB ... **71** D1
Castillo de San Marcos Natl. Mon., FL ... **67** E3
Castle Clinton Natl. Mon., NY ... **132** A1
Castle Dale, UT .. **24** E2
Castle Danger, MN ... **46** E1
Castle Hills, TX ... **96** C2
Castle Rock, CO .. **36** B2
Castle Rock, SD .. **32** D4
Castle Rock, WA ... **8** E5
Castle Shannon, PA ... **107** C4
Castleberry, AL ... **66** C2
Castleford, ID ... **22** B2
Castlegar, BC ... **18** A2
Castlewood, MO ... **104** A4
Castolon, TX ... **42** C2
Caston, OK ... **52** C3
Castro Valley, CA **85** A4
Castroville, CA ... **14** C3
Castroville, TX ... **43** D1
Cataldo, ID ... **18** A5
Catarina, TX ... **43** C3
Catawaba Is., OH **60** E2
Catherine, AL ... **66** B1
Cathlamet, WA ... **8** D5
Catonsville, MD **115** B4
Catskill, NY ... **72** C4
Caulksville, AR ... **52** D3
Causey, NM ... **38** C5
Cavalier, ND ... **31** D4
Cave Junction, OR ... **10** C5
Cavettsville, PA **107** E3
Cayce, SC ... **65** D2
Cayton, CA ... **12** D2
Cayucos, CA ... **14** C5
Cazenovia, NY ... **72** A4
Ceballos, DGO ... **42** B5
Cebolla, NM ... **27** E1
Cecil, PA ... **107** A5
Cecilton, MD ... **74** C3
Cecilville, CA ... **12** C2
Cedar, WI ... **47** A2
Cedar Bluff, MO **104** A4
Cedar Bluffs, KS . **37** B2
Cedar Breaks Natl. Mon., UT ... **24** C4
Cedar Butte, SD .. **35** A1
Cedar City, UT ... **24** C4
Cedar Creek, AZ . **26** E4
Cedar Creek, TX .. **41** E5
Cedar Falls, IA ... **48** E2
Cedar Grove, CA . **15** A4
Cedar Grove, NM **27** E3
Cedar Grove, WV **63** B2
Cedar Hill, TX ... **95** A5
Cedar Hills, OR ... **83** B3
Cedar Key, FL ... **67** C4
Cedar Mill, OR ... **83** B2
Cedar Park, TX ... **41** E5
Cedar Point, ON .. **59** A2
Cedar Rapids, IA ... **49** A3
Cedar River, MI .. **47** D3
Cedar Springs, MI **60** B1
Cedarbrook, PA . **114** B1
Cedaredge, CO ... **25** C3
Cedarhurst, WA .. **82** A4
Cedartown, GA ... **64** D3
Cedarvale, NM ... **27** E4
Cedarville, CA ... **13** A2
Cedarville, MI ... **58** B1
Cedarville, NJ ... **74** C3
Cedoux, SK ... **30** C3
Celina, OH ... **60** C4
Celina, TN ... **62** C5
Centennial, WY ... **34** A4
Center, CO ... **25** E4
Center, PA ... **107** E2
Center, TX ... **54** D2
Center City, NJ .. **114** C5
Center Line, MI . **103** D2
Center Ossipee, NH ... **72** E1
Center Point, WV **61** C5
Center Ridge, AR **53** A2
Center Valley, PA **74** C2
Centerville, IA ... **48** E5
Centerville, MO ... **51** B4
Centerville, PA ... **61** C4
Centerville, TN ... **64** A1
Central, AZ ... **29** A1
Central, NM ... **29** B1
Central, UT ... **24** B4
Central Butte, SK **30** A1
Central City, CO .. **36** A2
Central City, KY .. **62** A4
Central City, NE .. **35** D5
Central College, OH ... **109** D1
Central Lake, MI . **58** A3
Central Lakes, MN ... **46** D1
Centralia, IL ... **51** D3
Centralia, MO ... **51** A2
Centralia, WA ... **8** E4
Centre, AL ... **64** D3
Centre Hall, PA ... **61** E2
Centre Is., NY ... **112** E5
Centreville, AL ... **64** B5
Centreville, MD .. **74** B4
Centreville, MS .. **55** C3
Cenzontle, COAH **42** E3
Ceres, NY ... **61** D1
Cerritos, CA ... **86** E4
Cerro Gordo, IL ... **51** D1
Ceylon, SK ... **30** C3
Chacon, NM ... **38** A2
Chadbourn, NC ... **78** A1
Chadron, NE ... **34** D2
Chalfant, PA ... **107** E3
Challis, ID ... **20** C4
Chalmette, LA ... **98** D4
Chama, NM ... **27** E1
Chamberino, NM **29** D2
Chamberlain, SD **35** C1
Chamberlain, SK . **30** B1
Chambers, AZ ... **27** A3
Chambersburg, PA ... **74** A3
Chamblee, GA .. **121** D1
Chamois, KS ... **51** A3
Champ, MO ... **104** B2
Champaign, IL ... **49** E5
Champlain, NY ... **70** C5
Chandler, AZ ... **26** C5
Chandler, OK ... **52** A2
Channel Islands Natl. Park, CA ... **16** E3
Channelview, TX **97** E3
Channing, TX ... **38** D2
Chanute, KS ... **50** B4
Chapel Hill, NC ... **63** E4
Chaplin, SK ... **30** A2
Chapmanville, WV ... **63** B2
Chappaqua, NY **112** C1
Chappell, NE ... **34** D5
Charco, TX ... **43** E2
Chardon, OH ... **61** A2
Chariton, IA ... **48** D5
Charlack, MO ... **104** C2
Charlemagne, PQ **70** B4
Charles City, IA .. **48** E2
Charles River Village, MA ... **110** B5
Charles Town, WV ... **74** A4
Charlesbourg, PQ **70** D2
Charleston, AR ... **52** D3
Charleston, IL ... **51** E1
Charleston, MO ... **51** D5
Charleston, MS .. **53** D4
Charleston, SC ... **65** E4
Charleston, WV .. **63** B1
Charlestown, IN . **62** C2
Charlestown, NH **72** D2
Charlestown, RI .. **73** A5
Charlevoix, MI ... **58** A3
Charlotte, MI ... **60** B1
Charlotte, NC ... **65** D1
Charlotte, TN ... **62** A5
Charlotte, TX ... **43** D2
Charlotte, VT ... **72** C1
Charlottesville, VA ... **63** E1
Charmco, WV ... **63** C2
Charny, PQ ... **70** D2
Chase, MD ... **115** E2
Chase City, VA ... **76** A3
Chateaugay, NY . **72** B1
Chatfield, MN ... **48** E1
Chatham, IL ... **51** C1
Chatham, LA ... **55** A2
Chatham, MA ... **73** B4
Chatham, MI ... **47** E2
Chatham, VA ... **63** E3
Chatom, AL ... **66** A2
Chatsworth, GA .. **64** D2
Chattahoochee, FL ... **66** E3
Chattanooga, TN **64** D2
Cheam View, BC ... **9** B1
Cheboygan, MI ... **58** B2
Checotah, OK ... **52** B2
Chehalis, WA ... **8** E5
Chelan, WA ... **9** C3
Chelsea, MA ... **110** D3
Chelsea, OK ... **52** B1
Chelten Hills, PA ... **114** B1
Cheltenham, PA **114** C1
Chemainus, BC ... **8** E1
Chemult, OR ... **10** E4
Cheneville, PQ ... **70** A5
Cheney, WA ... **9** E4
Cheny Center, CO **36** E4
Chepachet, RI ... **73** A4
Cheraw, SC ... **65** E1
Cherokee, IA ... **48** B2
Cherokee, NC ... **65** A1
Cherokee, OK ... **39** D1
Cherokee, TX ... **41** D4
Cherry City, PA .. **107** C2
Cherry Creek, NV **22** A4
Cherry Grove, OH ... **108** D4
Cherry Hills Village, CO ... **93** C4
Cherry Lane, NC . **63** C4
Cherryfield, ME .. **71** C4
Cherryvale, KS ... **50** B5
Chertsey, PQ ... **70** B4
Chesaning, MI ... **58** C5
Chesapeake, OH . **63** A1
Chesapeake, VA **76** C2
Chesapeake Beach, MD ... **74** B5
Chesnee, SC ... **65** C1
Chester, CA ... **12** D4
Chester, IL ... **51** C4
Chester, MA ... **72** D4
Chester, MT ... **19** B4
Chester, NE ... **36** E1
Chester, PA ... **74** C3
Chester, SC ... **65** C1
Chester, VT ... **72** D2
Chester, WV ... **61** B3
Chesterbrook, VA ... **116** B3
Chesterfield, MO ... **104** A3
Chesterfield, SC . **65** E1
Chestertown, MD **74** B4
Chestertown, NY **72** C2
Cheswick, PA ... **107** E1
Chetopa, KS ... **50** C5
Cheverly, MD ... **116** D2
Cheviot, OH ... **108** A3
Chevy Chase, MD ... **116** B2
Chevy Chase Village, MD ... **116** B2
Chewalah, WA ... **9** E3
Chews Landing, NJ ... **114** D4
Cheyenne, OK ... **39** B3
Cheyenne, WY ... **34** B5
Cheyenne Wells, CO ... **36** E3
Chicago, IL ... **49** E3
Chicago Heights, IL ... **49** E3
Chickasaw, AL ... **66** A3
Chickasha, OK ... **39** D3
Chico, CA ... **12** D4
Chiefland, FL ... **67** C4
Chignik, AK ... **5** B5
Chilchinbito, AZ .. **27** A1
Childersburg, AL . **64** C4
Childress, TX ... **39** B4
Chillicothe, TX ... **39** C4
Chillicothe, IL ... **49** C4
Chillicothe, MO ... **50** D1
Chillicothe, OH ... **60** E5
Chilliwack, BC ... **9** B1
Chilly, ID ... **20** C5
Chiloquin, OR ... **10** E5
Chilton, WI ... **47** D5
Chimayo, NM ... **27** E2
China, ME ... **71** B5
China Grove, TX .. **96** E4
China Lake, CA ... **17** B1
Chincoteague, VA ... **74** D5
Chinese Camp, CA ... **14** E2
Chinle, AZ ... **27** A1
Chino, CA ... **87** E3
Chino Valley, AZ . **26** C3
Chinook, MT ... **19** C4
Chipley, FL ... **66** D3
Chipman, NB ... **71** D1
Chippewa Falls, WI ... **47** A4
Chiricahua Natl. Mon., AZ ... **29** A2
Chisholm, MN ... **46** D1
Chitwood, OR ... **10** C2
Chiu Chiushu, AZ **28** C1
Chivington, CO ... **36** D4
Chloride, AZ ... **26** A2
Choate, BC ... **9** B1
Chocowinity, NC . **76** C4
Cholame, CA ... **14** D5
Choteau, MT ... **18** E5
Chouteau, OK ... **52** B1
Chowchilla, CA ... **14** E3
Chrisman, IL ... **51** E1
Christiansburg, VA ... **63** D3
Christiansted, VI .. **6** D4
Christmas Valley, OR ... **11** A5
Christoval, TX ... **41** B4
Chromo, CO ... **25** D5
Chrysler, AL ... **66** B2
Chugwater, WY .. **34** D4
Chula Vista, CA **17** B5
Church Wells, UT **24** D5
Churchbridge, SK **30** E1
Churchill, PA ... **107** D3
Churchs Ferry, ND ... **31** C5
Cibuta, SON ... **28** D3
Cicero, IL ... **102** C4
Cicero, NY ... **72** A4
Cima, CA ... **17** D2
Cimarron, CO ... **25** D2
Cimarron, KS ... **37** B4
Cimarron, NM ... **38** B1
Cincinnati, OH . **62** D1
Cincinnatus, NY .. **72** A4
Cinnaminson, NJ ... **114** D2
Circle, AK ... **5** D2
Circle, MT ... **32** B1
Circleville, OH ... **60** E5
Circleville, UT ... **24** D3
Cisco, TX ... **41** C2
Citra, FL ... **67** D4
Citronelle, AL ... **66** A3
Ciudad Camargo, CHIH ... **42** A3
Ciudad Juárez, CHIH ... **29** D3
Ciudad Miguel Aleman, TAMPS ... **43** D5
Clair, NB ... **71** A1
Claire City, SD ... **33** E3
Clairemont, TX ... **41** A1
Clairton, PA ... **107** D5
Clallam Bay, WA .. **8** D2
Clam Lake, WI ... **47** A2
Clanton, AL ... **64** C5
Clara City, MN ... **46** B4
Clarcona, FL ... **120** B1
Clare, MI ... **58** B5
Claremont, CA ... **87** D2
Claremont, NH ... **72** D2
Claremore, OK .. **52** B1
Clarence, LA ... **55** A2
Clarence, MO ... **50** E1
Clarenceville, MI ... **103** A3
Clarendon, AR ... **53** B3
Clarendon, TX ... **39** A3
Clarendon Hills, IL ... **102** A5
Claresholm, AB ... **18** E2
Clarinda, IA ... **48** B5
Clarington, OH ... **61** B4
Clarion, IA ... **48** D2
Clarion, PA ... **61** C2
Clark, SD ... **33** D5
Clark Fork, ID ... **18** B4
Clarkdale, AZ ... **26** C3
Clarkesville, GA .. **65** A2
Clarkfield, MN ... **46** A5
Clarkrange, TN ... **62** D5
Clarks Summit, PA ... **74** B1
Clarksboro, NJ .. **114** B5
Clarksburg, WV .. **61** C5
Clarksdale, MS ... **53** C4
Clarkson Valley, MO ... **104** A3
Clarkston, GA ... **121** E2
Clarkston, WA ... **11** E1
Clarksville, AR ... **52** E2
Clarksville, IN ... **62** B2
Clarksville, NY ... **72** C4
Clarksville, TN ... **62** A5
Clarksville, TX ... **52** C5
Clarksville, VA ... **76** A3
Clarkton, NC ... **78** A1
Clarkville, CO ... **36** D1
Clarno, OR ... **11** B3
Claude, TX ... **39** A3
Claunch, NM ... **27** E4
Clawson, MI ... **103** B1
Claxton, GA ... **65** C5
Clay, KY ... **62** A4
Clay, WV ... **63** B1
Clay Center, KS .. **37** E2
Clay Center, NE .. **37** D1
Clay City, KY ... **62** E3
Clay Springs, AZ . **26** E4
Claycomo, MO ... **92** D1
Clayhatchee, AL ... **66** D2
Claypool Hill, VA **63** B3
Claysburg, PA ... **61** E3
Clayton, AL ... **66** D1
Clayton, GA ... **65** A2
Clayton, ID ... **20** C5
Clayton, KS ... **37** B2
Clayton, LA ... **55** B2
Clayton, MO ... **104** C3
Clayton, NM ... **38** D1
Clayton, NY ... **72** A2
Clayton, OK ... **52** C4
Cle Elum, WA ... **9** B4
Clear Creek, CA .. **12** C1
Clear Lake, IA ... **48** D2
Clear Lake, MN .. **46** C4
Clear Lake, SD ... **33** E5
Clear Lake, UT ... **24** C2
Clear Valley, CO . **93** C2
Clearcreek, UT ... **24** E1
Clearfield, PA ... **61** D2
Clearfield, UT ... **22** D4
Clearlake, CA ... **12** C5
Clearmont, WY ... **32** A5
Clearwater, FL ... **69** C1
Clearwater, MT ... **20** D1
Cleburne, TX ... **41** E2
Clegg, NC ... **118** E3
Clementon, NJ .. **114** E4
Clemson, SC ... **65** B2
Clendenin, WV ... **63** B1
Cleo Springs, OK **39** D1
Clermont, FL ... **67** D5
Clermont, PQ ... **70** D1
Cleveland, GA ... **65** A2
Cleveland, ID ... **22** E3
Cleveland, MS ... **53** C4
Cleveland, OH .. **61** A2
Cleveland, OK ... **52** A1
Cleveland, TN ... **64** D1
Cleveland, TX ... **54** C5
Cleveland, WA ... **11** B1
Cleveland Heights, OH ... **106** D2
Clewiston, FL ... **80** A2
Cliff, NM ... **29** B1
Cliff Cave, MO .. **104** D5
Cliff Mine, PA ... **107** A3
Cliffdell, WA ... **9** B5
Cliffside Park, NJ ... **111** B2
Clifton, AZ ... **29** A1
Clifton, CO ... **25** C2
Clifton, KS ... **36** E2
Clifton, MA ... **110** E1
Clifton, NB ... **71** C2
Clifton, NJ ... **111** A2
Clifton, TX ... **41** E3
Clifton Forge, VA **63** D2
Clifton Heights, PA ... **114** A4
Cliftondale, MA **110** D2
Climax, CO ... **25** E2
Climax, MN ... **33** E1
Climax, SK ... **19** D3
Cline, TX ... **43** B1
Clines Corners, NM ... **38** A3
Clinton, AR ... **53** A2
Clinton, IA ... **49** B3
Clinton, IL ... **49** D5
Clinton, IN ... **62** A1
Clinton, KY ... **51** D5
Clinton, LA ... **55** C3
Clinton, MA ... **72** E3
Clinton, MD ... **116** E4
Clinton, MI ... **60** D2
Clinton, MO ... **50** D3
Clinton, MS ... **55** D1
Clinton, NC ... **76** A5
Clinton, OK ... **39** C3
Clinton, SC ... **65** C2
Clinton, TN ... **62** E5
Clintonville, WI .. **47** C4
Clintwood, VA ... **63** A3
Clio, AL ... **66** D1
Clio, MI ... **58** C5
Clo-oose, BC ... **8** D1
Cloquet, MN ... **46** D2
Closter, NJ ... **112** A5
Cloudcroft, NM ... **29** E1
Cloverdale, CA ... **12** B5
Cloverdale, IN ... **62** A1
Cloverleaf, TX ... **97** E3
Cloverport, KY ... **62** B3
Clovis, CA ... **14** F4
Clovis, NM ... **38** C4
Clute, TX ... **56** C1
Clyattville, GA ... **67** B2
Clyde Hill, WA ... **82** D3
Clyde Park, MT ... **21** B3
Clymer, PA ... **61** D3
Coachella, CA ... **17** C4
Coahoma, TX ... **41** A2
Coal Creek, WA .. **82** E4
Coaldale, AB ... **18** E2
Coaldale, NV ... **15** B2
Coalfield, WA ... **82** E5
Coalgate, OK ... **52** A4
Coalinga, CA ... **14** D4
Coatesville, PA ... **74** B3
Coaticook, PQ ... **70** D5
Cobleskill, NY ... **72** C4
Cobourg, ON ... **59** D3
Coburn Gore, PQ . **70** E4
Cochran, GA ... **65** B5
Cochrans Mill, PA ... **107** D5
Cochranville, PA . **74** B3
Cockeysville, MD ... **115** B1
Cockrell Hill, TX .. **95** B4
Cocoa, FL ... **67** F5
Cocoa Beach, FL . **67** F5
Cocolalla, ID ... **18** A4
Cocospera, SON .. **28** D3
Cody, NE ... **35** A2
Cody, WY ... **21** C5
Coeur d'Alene, ID **18** A4
Coffeeville, AL ... **66** A2
Coffeeville, MS .. **53** D4
Coffeyville, KS ... **50** B5
Coffins Corner, NJ ... **114** E4
Cohagen, MT ... **32** A1
Cohasset, MA ... **73** A3
Cokeville, WY ... **23** A3
Colby, KS ... **37** A2
Colby, WA ... **82** A3
Colchester, CT ... **72** E5
Cold Bay, AK ... **5** A5
Cold Point, PA ... **114** A1
Cold Springs, MI **108** C5
Coldfoot, AK ... **5** C2
Coldwater, KS ... **37** C5
Coldwater, MI ... **60** B2
Coldwater, MO ... **51** C4
Cole Camp, MO ... **50** E3
Colebrook, NH ... **70** E5
Coleharbor, ND ... **33** A1
Coleman, FL ... **67** D5
Coleman, TX ... **41** C3
Colemantown, NJ ... **114** E3
Coles Is., NB ... **71** C2
Colfax, CA ... **12** D5
Colfax, LA ... **55** A3
Colfax, WA ... **9** E5
Colgate, WI ... **101** A1
Colina, OH ... **60** C4
Collbran, CO ... **25** C2
College Park, GA ... **121** B4
College Park, MD ... **116** D1
College Station, TX ... **54** B4
Colleyville, TX ... **94** D1
Colliersville, NY .. **72** B4
Collierville, TN ... **53** D2
Collingdale, PA . **114** B4
Collingswood, NJ ... **114** D3
Collingwood, ON **59** A3
Collins, MO ... **50** D4
Collins, MS ... **55** E2
Collinsville, IL ... **51** C2
Collinsville, OK ... **52** B1
Colma, CA ... **85** B1
Colmar Manor, MD ... **116** D2
Colmesneil, TX ... **54** D4
Coloma, CA ... **14** D1
Coloma, WI ... **47** C5
Colombia, NL ... **43** C4
Colome, SD ... **35** B2
Colon, MI ... **60** B2
Colonia Le Baron, CHIH ... **29** C5
Colorado City, AZ **24** C5
Colorado City, CO **36** B4
Colorado City, TX **41** A2
Colorado Natl. Mon., CO ... **25** C2
Colorado Springs, CO ... **36** B3
Colquitt, GA ... **66** E2
Colstrip, MT ... **21** E3
Colton, NY ... **72** A1
Coltons Point, MD ... **74** B5
Columbia, AL ... **66** E2
Columbia, IL ... **104** E5
Columbia, KY ... **62** C4
Columbia, LA ... **55** B2
Columbia, MO ... **50** E2
Columbia, MS ... **55** D3
Columbia, NC ... **76** C3
Columbia, PA ... **74** B3
Columbia, SC ... **65** D2
Columbia, TN ... **64** B1
Columbia City, IN **60** B3
Columbia Falls, ME ... **71** C4
Columbia Falls, MT ... **18** D4
Columbia Heights, MN ... **100** B2
Columbia Hills Corners, OH ... **106** A5
Columbia Station, OH ... **106** A5
Columbiana, AL .. **64** C4
Columbiana, OH . **61** B3
Columbine, CO ... **23** E5
Columbine Valley, CO ... **93** B5
Columbus, GA .. **64** E5
Columbus, IN ... **62** B1
Columbus, KS ... **50** C5
Columbus, MS ... **64** A4
Columbus, MT ... **21** C3
Columbus, NE ... **35** F4
Columbus, NM ... **29** C2
Columbus, OH .. **60** E4
Columbus, TX ... **56** B1
Columbus, WI ... **49** C1
Colusa, CA ... **12** C5
Colville, WA ... **9** E3
Colvos, WA ... **82** A4
Comanche, OK ... **39** D4
Comanche, TX ... **41** D3
Combes, TX ... **43** F6
Combs, KY ... **62** E3
Comeau Hill, NS . **71** E5
Comfort, TX ... **41** D5
Commerce, CA ... **86** D2
Commerce, GA ... **65** A2
Commerce, OK ... **52** C1
Commerce, TX ... **54** B1
Commerce City, CO ... **93** D2
Como, CO ... **36** A2
Compton, CA ... **86** C3
Comstock, NY ... **72** C2
Comstock, TX ... **43** A1
Concan, TX ... **43** C1
Conchas, NM ... **38** B3
Concho, AZ ... **27** A4

Place Name / Page Number / Grid Number
Stantonburg 118 C5

Conconully, WA 9 C3
Concord, CA 14 C1
Concord, MA 73 A3
Concord, MO 104 C4
Concord, NC 63 D5
Concord, NH 72 E2
Concordia, KS 37 E2
Concordia, MO 50 D2
Concrete, WA 9 A2
Condon, OR 11 B2
Cone, TX 39 A5
Confluence, PA ... 61 D4
Congress, AZ 26 B4
Conifer, CO 36 A2
Conley, GA 121 D4
Conneaut, OH 61 B1
Conneaut Lake, PA 61 B2
Connell, WA 9 D5
Connellsville, PA 61 D4
Conner, MT 20 C2
Connersville, IN .. 60 C5
Conover, WI 47 B2
Conrad, MO 104 B3
Conrad, MT 19 A4
Conroe, TX 54 C5
Conshohocken, PA 114 A2
Constableville, NY 72 A3
Constantia, NY ... 72 A3
Consul, SK 19 C3
Contrecoeur, PQ .. 70 C4
Converse, TX 96 E2
Conway, AR 53 A3
Conway, FL 120 D3
Conway, NH 72 E1
Conway, SC 78 A2
Conway, TX 39 A3
Conway Springs, KS 37 E5
Conyers, GA 65 A3
Cook, MN 44 D5
Cookeville, TN 62 C5
Cooks Hammock, FL 67 B3
Cookshire, PQ 70 D4
Cool Valley, MO 104 D2
Coolidge, AZ 26 D5
Coolidge, KS 36 E3
Coolidge Dam, AZ 26 E5
Coolville, OH 61 A5
Coon Rapids, MN 100 B1
Cooper, TX 52 B5
Cooper City, FL .. 123 B1
Coopers Mills, ME 71 B5
Cooperstown, ND 33 D1
Cooperstown, NY 72 B4
Coopersville, MI .. 60 A1
Coos Bay, OR 10 C4
Cope, CO 36 D2
Copeland, KS 37 A5
Copeland, ID 18 B3
Copenhagen, NY 72 A2
Copper Harbor, MI 45 C5
Copperas Cove, TX 41 E4
Coppermine, NT ... 5 G2
Coquille, OR 10 C4
Coral Gables, FL .. 80 B3
Coraopolis, PA .. 107 A3
Corbin, KY 62 E4
Corcoran, CA 14 E5
Cordele, GA 67 A1
Cordell, OK 39 C3
Cordova, AK 5 D4
Corinna, ME 71 B4
Corinne, SK 30 C2
Corinth, MS 53 E2
Corinth, NY 72 C3
Cornelia, GA 65 A2
Cornelius Pass, OR 83 A1
Cornell, WI 47 A4
Corning, AR 53 C1
Corning, CA 12 C4
Corning, IA 48 C5
Corning, KS 50 A2
Corning, NY 59 E5
Cornish, ME 73 A1
Cornucopia, WI ... 46 E1
Cornwall, ON 72 A1
Cornwall Bridge, CT 72 D5
Corona Del Mar, CA 88 B3
Coronado, CA 17 B5
Coronado, CHIH .. 42 A5
Corpus Christi, TX 43 E3
Corrigan, TX 54 C4
Corry, PA 61 C1
Corsicana, TX 54 A2
Cortaro, AZ 28 D1
Corte Madera, CA 85 E1
Cortes, AZ 26 C3
Cortez, CO 25 C5
Cortez Gold Mines, NV 13 E5
Cortland, NE 50 A1
Cortland, NY 72 A4
Corvallis, OR 10 D2
Corydon, IA 48 D5
Corydon, IN 62 B3
Cos Cob, CT 112 D3
Coshocton, OH 61 A4
Cosmos, MN 46 B4
Cost, TX 43 E1
Costa Mesa, CA .. 17 A3
Costigan, ME 71 B4
Costilla, NM 38 A1
Cotati, CA 14 B1
Coteau-du-Lac, PQ 70 B5
Cotesfield, NE 35 C5
Cotopaxi, CO 36 A4
Cottage Grove, OR 10 D3
Cottage Hill, MA 110 D3
Cotton City, NM .. 29 B2
Cotton Plant, AR .. 53 B3
Cottondale, FL 66 E3
Cottonwood, AL .. 66 E2
Cottonwood, AZ .. 26 C3
Cottonwood, ID ... 20 A2
Cottonwood, SD ... 34 E1
Cotulla, TX 43 C2
Coudersport, PA .. 61 D1
Cougar, WA 8 E5
Coulee, ND 30 E4
Coulee City, WA 9 D4
Coulters, PA 107 E5
Coulterville, CA ... 14 E2
Council Bluffs, IA 48 A5
Council Grove, KS 50 A3
Counselors, NM .. 27 D1
Country Club Hills, MO 104 D2
Country Life Acres, MO 104 B3
Countryside, IL .. 102 B5
Courtenay, ND 33 C1
Courtland, VA 76 B2
Coushatta, LA 54 E2
Coutts, AB 19 A3
Cove, AR 52 D4
Cove, OR 11 D2
Cove, WA 82 A5
Cove Ft., UT 24 C3
Covelo, CA 12 B4
Covina, CA 87 C2
Covington, GA 65 A3
Covington, IN 49 E5
Covington, KY ... 108 B4
Covington, LA 55 D4
Covington, MI 47 C2
Covington, OH 62 D1
Covington, OK 39 E1
Covington, TN 53 D2
Covington, VA 63 D2
Cowansville, PQ .. 70 C5
Cowdrey, CO 23 E5
Cowen, WV 63 C1
Coweta, OK 52 B2
Cowley, AB 18 D2
Coyame, CHIH 42 A1
Coyote, NM 27 E2
Coyote Canyon, NM 27 B2
Crafton, PA 107 B3
Craig, CO 25 D1
Craig, MO 50 B1
Craigmont, ID 20 A1
Cramerton, NC .. 117 A3
Cranberry, PA 61 C2
Cranberry Lake, NY 72 B2
Cranbrook, BC 18 B2
Crandon, WI 47 C3
Crane, MT 32 C1
Crane, OR 11 C5
Crane, TX 40 D3
Crane Lake, MN .. 44 D5
Crane Valley, SK . 30 B3
Cranfills Gap, TX 41 E3
Crater Lake Natl. Park, OR 10 D5
Craters of the Moon Natl. Mon., ID 22 C1
Crawford, NE 34 C3
Crawfordsville, IN 60 A5
Crawfordville, FL 67 A3
Creede, CO 25 E4
Creedmoor, NC ... 76 A4
Creighton, PA 107 E1
Creola, AL 66 B3
Creole, LA 55 A5
Creosote, WA 82 B2
Crescent, MO 104 A5
Crescent, OR 10 E4
Crescent Beach, FL 67 E3
Crescent City, CA 12 B1
Crescent City, FL . 67 E4
Crescent Junction, UT 25 A2
Crescent Park, KY 108 A5
Crescent Springs, KY 108 A5
Cresco, IA 48 E1
Cresskill, NJ 112 A5
Cresson, TX 41 E2
Crested Butte, CO 25 E3
Crestline, OH 60 E3
Creston, BC 18 B2
Creston, IA 48 C5
Creston, SD 34 D1
Crestview, FL 66 C3
Crestview Hills, KY 108 B5
Crestwood, MO 104 C4
Crete, NE 35 E5
Creve Coeur, MO 104 B3
Cripple Creek, CO 36 A3
Crisfield, MD 74 C5
Crivitz, WI 47 D3
Crockett, CA 85 C4
Crockett, TX 54 C3
Crofton, NE 35 E3
Croghan, NY 72 A2
Crook, CO 34 D5
Crookston, MN ... 33 E1
Crookston, NE 35 A2
Cropley, MD 116 A2
Cropwell, NJ 114 E3
Crosby, MN 46 C2
Crosby, ND 30 D4
Crosbyton, TX 39 A5
Cross City, FL 67 C4
Cross Creek, NB .. 71 C2
Cross Cut, TX 41 C3
Cross Fork, PA ... 61 E1
Cross Plains, TX .. 41 C2
Cross Village, MI 58 A2
Crossett, AR 53 B5
Crossville, IL 51 E3
Crossville, TN 62 D5
Croton Lake, NY 112 B1
Croton Heights, NY 112 B1
Croton-on-Hudson, NY 112 A2
Crowell, TX 39 B5
Crowey, TX 94 A5
Crowheart, WY ... 23 C1
Crowley, CO 36 C4
Crowley, LA 55 B4
Crowley, OR 11 D5
Crowley, WA 82 A4
Crown Point, IN .. 49 E3
Crownpoint, NM . 27 C2
Crowsnest Pass, AB 18 D2
Croydon, PA 114 E1
Crump, TN 53 E2
Cruz Bay, VI 6 D3
Crystal, MN 100 A2
Crystal City, MB .. 31 C4
Crystal City, MO .. 51 C3
Crystal City, TX .. 43 B2
Crystal Falls, MI .. 47 C2
Crystal Lake, IL ... 49 D2
Crystal Lake Park, MO 104 B3
Crystal River, FL .. 67 C5
Crystal Springs, MS 55 D2
Crystal Springs, WA 82 A2
Cuatrociénegas de Carranza, COAH 42 E5
Cuba, MO 51 B4
Cuba, NM 27 D2
Cuba, NY 59 D5
Cuchara, CO 36 A5
Cuchillo, NM 27 C5
Cuckoo, VA 76 A1
Cudahy, CA 86 D3
Cudahy, WI 49 D1
Cuddy, PA 107 B5
Cuero, TX 56 A2
Cuervo, NM 38 B3
Cuidad Camargo, CHIH 42 A3
Culbertson, MT ... 30 C5
Culbertson, NE ... 37 A1
Culebra [Dewey], PR 6 C3
Cullman, AL 64 B3
Culpeper, VA 74 A5
Culver, OR 11 A3
Culver City, CA ... 86 B2
Cumberland, IN 105 E3
Cumberland, KY .. 63 A4
Cumberland, MD 61 D4
Cumberland, VA . 76 A2
Cumberland, WI .. 46 E3
Cumberland Gap, TN 62 E4
Cumming, GA 64 E3
Cummingsville, MA 110 B2
Cunningham, TN . 62 A5
Cupar, SK 30 C1
Cupertino, CA 84 B4
Curlew, WA 9 E2
Curran, MI 58 C3
Currant, NV 15 E2
Currie, NC 78 B1
Currie, NV 22 A5
Curry, PA 107 C4
Curtis, NE 37 B1
Cushing, OK 52 A2
Cusseta, GA 64 E5
Custer, MT 21 E3
Custer, SD 34 C1
Custer Battlefield Natl. Mon. [Little Big Horn], MT 21 E4
Cut Bank, MT 18 E4
Cuthbert, GA 66 E1
Cutler, ME 71 D4
Cuyahoga Heights, OH 106 D3
Cuyama, CA 16 E1
Cynthiana, KY 62 D2
Cypress, CA 86 E5
Cyriac, PQ 70 C1

D

Dade City, FL 67 D5
Dadeville, AL 64 D5
Dahlonega, GA ... 64 E2
Daingerfield, TX .. 54 C1
Dairyland, MN 46 E2
Dalark, AR 52 E4
Dale, IN 62 A3
Dale, OR 11 C3
Dales, CA 12 D3
Daleville, AL 66 D2
Dalhart, TX 38 D2
Dallas, GA 64 E3
Dallas, OR 10 D2
Dallas, PA 74 A1
Dallas, TX 54 A1
Dallas City, IL 49 A5
Dallasburg, OH .. 108 E1
The Dalles, OR 11 A1
Dalton, GA 64 D2
Dalton, NE 34 D4
Dalworthington Gardens, TX 94 D4
Daly City, CA 14 B2
Damariscotta, ME 71 B5
Damascus, OR 83 E5
Damascus, VA 63 B4
Damascus Heights, OR 83 D5
Danbury, CT 72 D5
Danbury, WI 46 D3
Danby, CA 17 D2
Danby, VT 72 D2
Danforth, ME 71 B3
Dania, FL 80 B3
Daniel, WY 23 B2
Daniel Boone, MO 104 A3
Danielson, CT 73 A4
Dannemora, NY .. 72 C1
Danner, OR 13 D1
Dansville, NY 59 E5
Danta, VA 63 B3
Danville, AR 52 E3
Danville, CA 85 B5
Danville, IL 49 E5
Danville, KS 51 A2
Danville, KY 62 D3
Danville, PA 74 A2
Danville, PQ 70 D4
Danville, VA 63 E3
Danville, VT 72 D1
Danville, WA 9 E2
Daphne, AL 66 B3
Darby, MT 20 C2
Darby, PA 114 B4
Darbydale, OH .. 109 A5
Dardanelle, AR ... 52 E3
Dardanelle, CA ... 14 E2
Darien, CT 112 E2
Darien, GA 67 D1
Darien, IL 102 A5
Darlington, SC 65 E1
Darlington, WI 49 B2
Darrington, WA 9 B3
Dassel, MN 46 C4
Dateland, AZ 26 A5
Datil, NM 27 C4
Dauphin, MB 31 B1
Davenport, IA ... 49 B4
Davenport, NE 36 D1
Davenport, WA 9 E4
David City, NE 35 E5
Davidson, AR 52 C2
Davidson, OK 39 C4
Davidson, SK 30 B1
Davie, FL 123 C1
Davis, AZ 26 A2
Davis, CA 14 C1
Davis, OK 39 E4
Davis Creek, CA .. 13 A2
Davison, MI 58 D5
Dawson, GA 66 E1
Dawson, ND 33 B2
Dawson, YT 5 D3
Dawson Creek, BC 5 G5
Dawson Springs, KY 62 A4
Dawsonville, GA . 64 E2
Day Heights, OH 108 E2
Daykin, NE 36 E1
Dayton, KY 108 C4
Dayton, OH 60 D5
Dayton, TN 64 D1
Dayton, TX 54 C5
Dayton, WA 11 E1
Daytona Beach, FL 67 E4
Dayville, OR 11 C3
De Beque, CO 25 C2
De Borgia, MT 18 B5
De Funiak Springs, FL 66 D3
De Kalb, IL 49 D3
De Kalb, MS 64 A5
De Kalb, NY 72 A2
De Kalb, TX 52 C5
De Land, FL 67 E4
De Leon, TX 41 D2
De Leon Springs, FL 67 E4
De Pere, WI 47 D4
De Queen, AR 52 D4
De Quincy, LA 54 E4
De Ridder, LA 54 E4
De Smet, SD 33 D5
De Soto, GA 67 A1
De Soto, IA 49 A1
De Soto, MO 51 C3
De Soto, TX 95 B5
De Tour Village, MI 58 B1
De Witt, AR 53 B4
Deadhorse, AK 5 D1
Deadwood, SD 32 C5
Dearborn, MI 60 D1
Dearborn Heights, MI 103 B4
Deary, ID 20 A1
Death Valley Junction, CA 15 D5
Death Valley Natl. Mon., CA 15 C5
Deaver, WY 21 C4
DeBary, FL 67 E4
Deblois, ME 71 C4
Decatur, AL 64 B3
Decatur, AR 52 C1
Decatur, GA 121 D3
Decatur, IL 51 D1
Decatur, IN 60 C4
Decatur, MI 60 A2
Decatur, MS 55 E1
Decatur, NE 48 A4
Decatur, TN 64 D1
Decatur, TX 41 E1
Decker, MT 21 E4
Deckers, CO 36 A2
Decorah, IA 48 E1
Dedham, MA 73 A3
Deep River, CT ... 72 E5
Deer Isle, ME 71 B5
Deer Lodge, MT .. 20 E2
Deer Park, NJ ... 114 E3
Deer Park, OH .. 108 C2
Deer Park, TX 97 E4
Deer Park, WA 9 E4
Deer River, MN ... 46 C1
Deerfield, IN 60 C4
Deerfield, MA 72 E3
Deerfield Beach, FL 80 B2
Defiance, OH 60 C3
Dehesa, CA 89 E2
Deicke, MO 104 A5
Del Bonita, AB 18 E3
Del Mar, CA 17 B4
Del Norte, CO 25 E5
Del Rio, TX 43 A1
Del Valle, TX 41 E5
Delanco, NJ 114 D1
Delano, CA 14 E5
Delavan, WI 49 D2
Delaware, OH 60 E4
Delcambre, LA 55 B5
Delco, ID 22 C2
Delco, NC 78 B1
Delebar, IL 49 B4
Delhi, CO 36 C5
Delhi, LA 55 B1
Delhi, NY 72 B4
Delhi Hills, OH .. 108 A4
Delicias, CHIH 42 A3
Delight, AR 52 E4
Dell, MT 20 D4
Dell Rapids, SD ... 35 E1
Dellwood, MN ... 100 E1
Dellwood, MO ... 104 D1
Delmar, MD 74 C5
Delmont, NJ 74 D3
Deloraine, MB 31 B4
Delphi, IN 60 A4
Delphos, OH 60 C4
Delran, NJ 114 D2
Delray Beach, FL . 80 B2
Delta, CO 25 C3
Delta, UT 24 D2
Delta Junction, AK 5 D3
Deming, NM 29 C2
Deming, WA 9 A2
Demopolis, AL 66 A1
Denali, AK 5 D3
Denali Natl. Park and Preserve, AK 5 C3
Denham Springs, LA 55 C4
Denio Junction, NV 13 C2
Denison, IA 48 B3
Denison, TX 52 A5
Denmark, NY 72 A2
Denmark, OR 10 B4
Denmark, SC 65 D3
Denmark, WI 47 D4
Denton, MD 74 C4
Denton, MT 21 C1
Denton, TX 54 A1
Denton Community, TX 41 C2
Denver, CO 36 B2
Denver City, TX .. 40 D1
Departure Bay, BC 8 E1
Depew, NY 59 C5
Depoe Bay, OR ... 10 C2
Deposit, NY 72 B5
Deptford, NJ 114 C5
Derby, CT 72 D5
Derby, KS 37 E5
Dermott, AR 53 B5
Derry, NM 29 D1
Des Arc, AR 53 B3
Des Moines, IA 48 D4
Des Peres, MO .. 104 B3
Des Plaines, IL ... 49 E3
Deschaillons-sur-St.-Laurent, PQ 70 C3
Desdemona, TX .. 41 D2
Deseret, UT 24 C2
Desert Center, CA 17 D4
Desert Hot Springs, CA 17 C3
Desert View, AZ .. 26 D1
Detroit, MI 60 D1
Detroit, OR 10 E2
Detroit Harbor, WI 47 E3
Detroit Lakes, MN 46 A2
Devenport, AL 66 C1
Devereau, MA ... 110 E1
Devers, TX 54 D5
Devils Den, CA ... 14 D5
Devil's Hole Natl. Mon., CA 15 D5
Devils Lake, ND .. 31 C5
Devil's Postpile Natl. Mon., CA 15 A3
Devils Tower Junction, WY 32 B5
Devils Tower Natl. Mon., WY 32 B5
Devine, CO 36 B4
Devine, TX 43 D1
Dewey, OK 52 B1
DeWitt, IA 49 B3
Dexter, KS 50 A5
Dexter, ME 71 A4
Dexter, MO 51 C5
Dexter, NM 40 B1
Dexter, OR 10 D3
Diamond, MO 50 C5
Diamond Lake, OR 10 E4
Diboll, TX 54 C3
Dickens, NE 35 A5
Dickens, TX 39 A5
Dickey, ME 71 A1
Dickeyville, WI 49 B2
Dickinson, ND 32 D2
Dickson, OK 52 A4
Dickson, TN 64 A1
Dieppe, NB 71 E1
Dierks, AR 52 D4
Difficult, TN 62 C5
Digby, NS 71 E3
Dighton, KS 37 B4
Dilley, TX 43 C2
Dillia, NM 38 A3
Dillingham, AK 5 B4
Dillon, MT 20 E3
Dillon, SC 78 A1
Dillsboro, IN 62 C1
Dillsburg, PA 74 A3
Dilworth, WA 82 B5
Dimmitt, TX 38 D4
Dingmans Ferry, PA 74 C1
Dinosaur, CO 25 C1
Dinosaur Natl. Mon., UT 23 B5
Discovery Bay, WA 8 E3
Disraeli, PQ 70 D4
District Heights, MD 116 E3
Divide, MT 20 E3
Dixfield, ME 71 A5
Dixie Valley, NV .. 13 C5
Dixmont, ME 71 B4
Dixmont, PA 107 A2
Dixon, IL 49 C3
Dixon, KY 62 A4
Dixon, MT 18 C5
Dixon, WY 23 D5
Dixons Mill, AL 66 B1
Doaktown, NB 71 D1
Dobbs Ferry, NY 112 A4
Dobson, NC 63 C4
Doctor Phillips, FL 120 B4
Dodge, WA 11 E1
Dodge Center, MN 46 D5
Dodge City, KS ... 37 B5
Dodgeville, WI 49 B2
Dodson, MT 19 D4
Dodsons Crossroads, NC 118 A2
Dogpatch, AR 52 E1
Doland, SD 33 D5
Dolgeville, NY 72 B3
Don Luis, AZ 28 E3
Don Martin, COAH 43 A4
Dona Ana, NM 29 D2
Donaldson, MN .. 31 E4
Donaldsonville, LA 55 C5
Donalsonville, GA 66 E2
Donavan, MA 73 A2
Donelson, TN 99 D3
Doniphan, MO 51 B5
Donnacona, PQ .. 70 D3
Donnellson, IA 49 A5
Donnelly, ID 20 A4
Dora, NM 38 C5
Doran, MN 33 E3
Dorchester, NB ... 71 E1
Dorion, PQ 70 B5
Dormont, PA 107 C4
Dorrance, KS 37 D3
Dorris, CA 12 D1
Dorset, VT 72 D3
Dorseyville, PA . 107 D1
Dorton, KY 63 A3
Dos Cabezas, AZ 29 A2
Dos Rios, CA 12 B4
Dosquet, PQ 70 D3
Dothan, AL 66 D2
Dotsero, CO 25 D2
Double Springs, AL 64 B3
Douglas, AZ 29 A3
Douglas, GA 67 B1
Douglas, NM 29 A3
Douglas, WY 34 A3
Douglass, KS 37 E5
Dove Creek, CO .. 25 B4
Dover, DE 74 C4
Dover, MA 110 A5
Dover, NC 76 B5
Dover, NH 73 A2
Dover, NJ 74 C1
Dover, OH 61 A3
Dover, TN 62 A5
Dover-Foxcroft, ME 71 B4
Dowagiac, MI 60 A2
Dowbrowski, TX . 43 D2
Dowd, CO 25 E2
Downey, CA 86 D3
Downey, ID 22 D2
Downieville, CA .. 12 E5
Downing, AL 66 D1
Downs, KS 37 D2
Downsville, NY ... 72 B5
Doylestown, PA .. 74 C2
Drain, OR 10 D4
Drake, MO 51 A3
Draper, UT 90 B5
Dravosburg, PA . 107 D4
Dresden, KS 36 B2
Dresden, NY 59 E4
Dresden, TN 53 E1
Drew, MS 53 C4
Drexel Hill, PA .. 114 A3
Driftwood, PA 61 E1
Driggs, ID 23 A1
Dripping Springs, TX 41 E5
Driscoll, TX 43 E3
Drummond, MI 58 C1
Drummond, MT ... 20 D1
Drummondville, PQ 70 C4
Drumright, OK 52 A2
Dryden, NY 72 A5
Dryden, ON 44 D2
Dryden, TX 40 E5
Du Bois, PA 61 D2
Du Quoin, IL 51 D3
Duanesburg, NY . 72 C4
Duarte, CA 87 B2
Dublán, CHIH 29 C4
Dublin, CA 14 C2
Dublin, GA 65 B5
Dublin, OH 109 A2
Dublin, TX 41 D2
Dublin, VA 63 C3
Dubois, ID 20 E5
Dubois, WY 23 B1
Dubuque, IA 49 B2
Duchesne, UT 25 A1
Ducktown, TN 64 E1
Duckwater, NV ... 15 E2
Dudley, GA 65 B5
Duette, FL 69 D1
Duff City, PA 107 A1
Dugway, UT 22 C5
Duhamel, PQ 70 A4
Duke, PA 61 E4
Dulce, NM 27 D1
Duluth, MN 46 E2
Dumas, AR 53 B4
Dumas, TX 38 E2
Dumfries, VA 74 A5
Dunbar, WV 63 B1
Duncan, AZ 29 A1
Duncan, BC 8 E1
Duncan, OK 39 D4
Duncannon, PA ... 74 A2
Duncansville, PA 61 E3
Duncanville, TX .. 95 B5
Dundalk, MD 115 D4
Dundas, ON 59 B4
Dundee, MI 60 D2
Dunedin, FL 69 C1
Dunham, PQ 70 C5
Dunken, NM 40 A1
Dunkirk, MT 19 A4
Dunkirk, NY 59 C5
Dunlap, IA 48 B4
Dunlap, TN 64 D1
Dunlap, TX 39 B5
Dunlow, WV 63 A2
Dunmore, PA 74 B1
Dunmore, WV 63 D1
Dunn Loring, VA 116 A3
Dunn, NC 76 A5
Dunn, TX 41 A2
Dunnellon, FL 67 D4
Dunnigan, CA 12 C5
Dunning, NE 35 B4
Dunnville, ON 59 B5
Dunraven, NY 72 C5
Dunseith, ND 31 B4
Dunsmuir, CA 12 D2
Dunvilla, MN 46 A2
Duplainville, WI 101 A3
Dupo, IL 104 E4
Dupont, CO 93 D1
Dupree, SD 32 E4
Dupuyer, MT 18 E4
Duquesne, PA ... 107 E4
Duran, NM 38 A4
Durand, WI 46 E5
Durango, CO 25 C5
Durant, MS 53 D5
Durant, OK 52 A5
Durham, NC 63 E4
Durham, NH 73 A2
Durham, OR 83 B4
Durham, WI 101 C5
Durkee, OR 11 E4
Dushore, PA 74 A1
Dustin, OK 52 B3
Dusty, WA 9 E5
Dutch Harbor, AK . 4 G5
Dutton, MT 19 A5
Duval Mine, NV .. 13 D4
Dwarf, KY 63 A3
Dwight, IL 49 D4
Dwyer, NM 29 C1
Dyer, NV 15 B3
Dyersburg, TN 53 D1
Dyersdale, TX 97 D1
Dyersville, IA 49 A2
Dysart, SK 30 C1

E

Eads, CO 36 D4
Eagan, MN 100 D5
Eagle, AK 5 D3
Eagle Lake, ME ... 71 A1
Eagle Lake, MN .. 46 C5
Eagle Lake, TX ... 56 B1
Eagle Nest, NM .. 38 A1
Eagle Pass, TX ... 43 B2
Eagle Picher, NV . 13 B4
Eagle River, MI ... 45 C5
Eagle River, WI .. 47 B3
Eagle Rock, NC . 119 E4
Eagle Rock, VA ... 63 D2
Eagle Village, IN 105 B1
Eagledale, WA 82 A2
Eagleville, CA 13 A2
Eagleville, MO 48 C5

Bold type indicates cities with 100,000 population or more.

Place Name — Page Number — Grid Number

Stantonburg **118** C5

Earl, CO **36** B5
Earl Grey, SK ...**30** C1
Earlimart, CA ...**14** E5
Earlington, KY ...**62** A4
Early, TX **41** C3
Earp, CA **26** A3
Earth, TX **38** D4
Earth City, MO ...**104** B1
Easley, SC **65** B1
East Angus, PQ ...**70** D4
East Aurora, NY ...**59** D5
East Bethel, MN ..**46** D4
East Brady, PA ...**61** C2
East Braintree, MA **110** E5
East Brewton, AL **66** C2
East Broughton Station, PQ **70** D3
East Burke, VT ...**70** D5
East Carbon City, UT **25** A2
East Carnegie, PA **107** B4
East Carondelet, IL **104** E4
East Chicago, IN .**49** E3
East Cleveland, OH **106** D1
East Corinth, ME **71** B4
East Dedham, MA **110** C5
East Detroit, MI **103** E1
East Dorset, VT ...**72** D2
East Glacier Park, MT **18** E4
East Grand Forks, MN **31** E5
East Hampton, NY **73** A5
East Haven, CT **113** E1
East Helena, MT .**20** E2
East Jorden, MI ..**58** B3
East Lexington, MA **110** B3
East Liverpool, OH **61** B3
East Los Angeles, CA **86** D2
East McKeesport, PA **107** E3
East Millinocket, ME **71** B3
East Natick, MA **110** A5
East Oakmont, PA **107** D2
East Palatka, FL .**67** C2
East Palo Alto, CA **84** D3
East Point, GA **64** E3
East Quogue, NY **74** E1
East Rutherford, NJ **111** A2
East St. Louis, IL .**51** C4
East Sooke, BC ...**8** E2
East Stoneham, ME **72** E1
East Tawas, MI ..**58** C4
East Waterboro, ME **73** A1
East Weymouth, MA **110** E5
East Windham, NY **72** C4
East York, ON ...**59** C4
Eastend, SK **19** D3
Eastern Neck, MA **110** E4
Eastgate, WA ...**82** E4
Eastland, TX **41** D2
Eastman, GA **65** B5
Eastman, WI **49** A1

Easton, MD **74** C4
Easton, PA **74** C2
Eastport, ID **18** B3
Eastport, ME **71** D3
Eastport, MI **58** A1
Eastview, NY **112** B3
Eastview, TN **53** E2
Eastville, VA **76** C1
Eaton, OH **60** C5
Eaton Rapids, MI **60** C1
Eatonton, GA **65** A4
Eatonville, FL **120** C1
Eau Claire, WI **47** A4
Ebensburg, PA **61** D3
Echo, AL **66** D2
Echo Lake, WA ...**82** C1
Eckerman, MI **58** A1
Ecorse, MI **103** C5
Edcouch, TX **43** E5
Eddington, ME ...**71** B4
Eddington, PA ...**114** D1
Eddy, FL **67** C2
Eddystone, PA ..**114** A5
Eddyville, KY **51** E4
Eddyville, OR **10** C2
Eden, AL **66** D2
Eden, ID **22** B2
Eden, NC **63** D4
Eden, TX **41** B4
Eden, VT **72** D1
Eden, WY **23** B3
Edenton, NC **76** C3
Edenwold, TN **99** C1
Edgecliff, TX **94** A5
Edgefield, SC **65** C3
Edgeley, ND **33** C3
Edgemont, AR ...**53** A2
Edgemont, SD ...**34** C2
Edgerton, WY **34** A2
Edgewater, NJ ..**111** B2
Edgewater Park, NJ
Edgewood, FL ...**120** D3
Edgewood, KY ..**108** B5
Edgewood, MD ...**74** B4
Edgewood, NM ...**27** E3
Edgewood, PA ..**107** D3
Edgeworth, PA ..**107** B2
Edina, MN **100** B4
Edina, MO **50** E1
Edinburg, ND **31** D5
Edinburg, TX **43** E5
Edison, GA **66** E1
Edisto Beach, SC **65** E4
Edisto Is., SC **65** E4
Edmonds, WA ...**9** A3
Edmonton, KY ...**62** C4
Edmore, ND **31** C5
Edmundson, MO **104** C2
Edmundston, NB .**71** A1
Edna, TX **56** B1
Edroy, TX **43** E3
Edwall, WA **9** E4
Edwards, CA **17** B2
Edwards, NY **72** A2
Eek, AK **5** B4
Effie, MN **44** C5
Effigy Mounds Natl. Mon., IA **49** A2
Effingham, IL **51** D2
Effingham, SC ...**65** E2
Efland, NC **118** A1
Egan, SD **35** E1
Egegik, AK **5** B4
Egg Harbor City, NJ
Egnar, CO **25** B4
Egypt, WA **9** L4
Eholt, BC **9** E2
Ehrenberg, AZ ...**17** E4

Ehrhardt, SC **65** D3
Ekalaka, MT **32** C2
El Alamo, NL **43** C5
El Alicante, COAH **42** C5
El Cajon, CA **17** B5
El Campo, TX **56** B1
El Carrizal, CHIH .**29** C4
El Cerrito, CA **85** D3
El Centro, CA **17** D5
El Descanso, BC ..**17** B5
El Desemboque, SON **28** A4
El Dorado, AR ...**53** A5
El Dorado, KS **50** A4
El Dorado Springs, MO **50** A4
El Indio, TX **43** B2
El Magueyal, COAH **42** D4
El Milagro, COAH **42** D2
El Monte, CA **87** A2
El Moral, COAH **43** A2
El Morro Natl. Mon., NM **27** B3
El Nogal, SON ...**28** D4
El Ocuca, SON ...**28** D4
El Orranteño, CHIH **42** A3
El Paso, TX **29** C2
El Paso Gap, NM **40** A2
El Portal, CA **14** E2
El Portal, FL **123** D3
El Porvenir, CHIH **29** E3
El Remolino, COAH **43** A2
El Reno, OK **39** D3
El Rito, NM **27** E1
El Sásabe, SON ..**28** C2
El Sauzito, COAH **43** B2
El Segundo, CA ..**86** A3
El Sobrante, CA ..**85** E3
El Sueco, CHIH ..**29** C5
El Tule, COAH ...**42** E3
El Vado, NM **27** E1
El Venado, COAH **42** E5
Elamville, AL **66** D1
Elba, AL **66** D2
Elbe, WA **9** A5
Elberton, GA **65** B2
Elbow, WI **47** C3
Elbow Lake, MN .**46** A3
Elcho, WI **47** C3
Elderton, PA **61** D3
Eldon, MO **50** E3
Eldora, IA **48** D3
Eldorado, IL **51** E3
Eldorado, OK **39** B4
Eldorado, TX **41** A4
Electra, TX **39** C5
Electric Mills, MS **64** A5
Eleva, WI **47** A5
Elfinwild, PA **107** C2
Elfros, SK **30** E4
Elgin, AZ **28** E2
Elgin, IL **49** D3
Elgin, ND **32** E3
Elgin, NV **24** A4
Elgin, OR **11** D2
Elgin, TX **56** A1
Elicott City, MD ..**74** B4
Elida, NM **38** C5
Elizabeth, IL **108** B2
Elizabethton, IN .**63** B4
Elizabethtown, KY **62** C3

Elizabethtown, NC **78** A1
Elizabethtown, NY **72** C1
Elizabethville, PA **74** A2
Elk City, ID **20** B2
Elk City, OK **39** C3
Elk Creek, CA **12** C4
Elk Grove Village, IL **102** A2
Elk Park, NC **63** B5
Elk Point, NE **35** E3
Elk Rapids, MI ..**58** A3
Elk River, MN ...**46** C4
Elk Springs, CO ..**25** C1
Elkhart, KS **38** E5
Elkhart, IN **60** B3
Elkhorn, WI **49** D2
Elkin, NC **63** C4
Elkins, NM **38** B5
Elkins, WV **61** D5
Elko, BC **18** C2
Elko, NV **13** E4
Elkridge, MD ...**115** B5
Elkton, KY **62** A5
Elkton, OR **10** C3
Elkwater, AB **19** B2
Ellaville, GA **64** E2
Ellendale, ND **33** C3
Ellensburg, WA ..**9** B5
Ellenville, NY **72** C5
Ellenwood, GA ..**121** D5
Ellijay, GA **64** E2
Ellington, MO **51** B5
Ellinwood, KS ...**37** D4
Elliot Lake, ON ..**58** D1
Ellis, KS **37** C3
Ellisport, WA **82** A5
Elliston, MT **20** E2
Ellisville, FL **67** C2
Ellisville, MO ...**104** A4
Ellisville, MS **64** B3
Ellsworth, KS **37** D3
Ellsworth, ME ...**71** C4
Ellsworth, NE **34** E4
Ellsworth, WA ...**83** D2
Ellsworth, WI **46** E4
Elm Creek, MB ..**31** E5
Elm Creek, NE ...**35** C5
Elm Grove, WI ..**101** C3
Elm Point, MO ..**114** E1
Elm Springs, SD .**32** D5
Elma, WA **8** E4
Elmer, KS **37** D4
Elmer, MI **58** D5
Elmer, NJ **74** C3
Elmhurst, IL **102** A3
Elmhurst, PA **74** B1
Elmira, NY **72** A5
Elmo, KS **37** E3
Elmo, MT **18** C5
Elmonica, OR ...**83** A2
Elmore, OH **60** D3
Elmore, SK **30** E4
Emory, GA **121** D2
Elmsford, NY ...**121** B4
Elmwood, OK **39** A1
Elmwood Park, IL **102** B3
Elmwood Park, NJ **111** A1
Elmwood Place, OH **108** B2
Elnora, IN **62** A2
Eloy, AZ **28** D1
Elrama, PA **107** D5
Elrose, SK **19** E1
Elroy, WI **49** B1
Elsa, TX **43** E5
Elsa, YT **5** E3
Elsberry, MO **51** B2

Elsinore, MO **51** B5
Elsmere, KY **108** A5
Elsmere, NE **35** B3
Eltopia, WA **11** D1
Elvins, KS **51** B4
Elwood, IN **60** B5
Elwood, NE **37** B1
Elwood, UT **24** D1
Ely, MN **44** E5
Ely, NV **24** A1
Elyria, OH **61** A2
Emblem, PA **107** E4
Emblem, WY **21** D5
Embudo, NM **27** E2
Emerson, MN **31** E4
Emery, UT **24** E2
Emeryville, CA ...**85** C3
Emigrant, MT **21** A3
Emily, MN **46** C2
Eminence, IN **62** A1
Emlenton, PA **61** C2
Emmetsburg, IA .**48** B2
Emmett, ID **11** E5
Emmett, MI **60** D3
Emmitsburg, MD .**74** A3
Emory, TX **54** B1
Empire, CO **36** A2
Empire, MI **58** A3
Emporia, KS **50** A3
Emporia, VA **76** B3
Emporium, PA **61** D1
Emsworth, PA ..**107** B2
Encinal, TX **43** C3
Encino, NM **38** A4
Encino, TX **43** E4
Enderlin, ND **33** D2
Enfield, NC **76** B3
Engadine, MI **58** A2
Engelhard, NC ...**76** D4
England, AR **53** A3
Englewood, CO ..**36** B2
Englewood, FL ...**69** D2
Englewood, NJ ..**60** D5
Englewood, NJ .**111** B1
Englewood Cliffs, NJ **111** B1
English Center, PA **61** E1
English Turn, LA .**98** E5
Enid, OK **39** D1
Enigma, GA **67** B1
Enning, SD **32** D5
Ennis, MT **20** E3
Ennis, TX **54** A2
Enochs, TX **38** D5
Enos, IL **51** B1
Enos, IN **49** E4
Enosburg Falls, VT **70** C5
Enterprise, AL ...**66** D2
Enterprise, NT ...**5** G3
Enterprise, OR ..**52** B3
Enterprise, OR ..**11** E2
Enterprise, UT ..**24** B4
Enumclaw, WA ..**9** A4
Eola, TX **41** A4
Epes, AL **64** A4
Ephraim, UT **24** E2
Ephrata, PA **74** B3
Ephrata, WA **9** C4
Epoufette, MI ...**58** A2
Epping, ND **30** D5
Erdenheim, PA .**114** B1
Erial, NJ **114** E5
Erick, OK **39** B3
Erickson, MB **31** B2
Erie, KS **50** B5
Erie, PA **61** B1
Erin, TN **62** A5
Erlanger, KY ...**108** A5
Erlton, NJ **114** D3
Ernest, PA **114** A1
Errol, NH **70** E5
Erskine, MN **46** A1

Erwin, AR **53** B2
Erwin, TN **63** B5
Escalante, UT **24** D4
Escalón, CHIH ...**42** B5
Escanaba, MI **47** E2
Escatawpa, MS ..**66** A4
Escobas, TX **43** E4
Escondido, CA ...**17** B4
Eskridge, KS **50** A3
Esmond, ND **31** B5
Espanola, NM ...**27** E2
Espanola, ON ...**58** D1
Essex, CA **17** E2
Essex, CT **72** E5
Essex, MT **18** D4
Essex, NY **72** C1
Essex Junction, VT **72** C1
Essington, PA ..**114** B4
Est. Candela, NL .**43** B5
Est. El Sahuaro, SON **28** A3
Estacada, OR **10** E2
Estacion El Oro, COAH **42** A4
Estancia, NM **27** E3
Estelle, LA **98** C5
Esterhazy, SK ...**30** E1
Estes Park, CO ..**36** A1
Estevan, SK **30** D4
Estherville, IA ...**48** B1
Estill, SC **65** D4
Eston, SK **19** D1
Etna, CA **12** C2
Etna, PA **61** C3
Etna Green, IN ..**60** B3
Etowah, TN **64** E1
Etzikom, AB **19** B3
Eubank, KY **62** D4
Eubanks, NC **118** B2
Eucha, OK **52** C5
Euclid, MN **31** E5
Euclid, OH **61** A2
Eudora, AR **53** B5
Eudora, MS **53** F4
Eufaula, AL **66** E1
Eufaula, OK **52** B3
Eugene, OR **10** D3
Euless, TX **94** E2
Eulonia, GA **67** D1
Eunice, LA **55** A4
Eunice, NM **40** C2
Eupora, MS **53** F4
Eureka, CA **12** A2
Eureka, KS **50** A4
Eureka, MO **104** A4
Eureka, MT **18** C3
Eureka, NV **15** E1
Eureka, SD **33** B3
Eureka Springs, AR **52** D1
Eustace, TX **54** B2
Eustis, FL **67** E4
Eustis, ME **70** E4
Eutaw, AL **64** A4
Eva, OK **38** E1
Evan, TN **63** A5
Evanston, IL **49** E2
Evanston, WY **22** E4
Evansville, IN ...**62** A3
Evansville, MN ..**46** A3
Evansville, WI ..**49** C2
Evant, TX **41** D3
Evart, MI **58** B5
Eveleth, MN **46** D1
Evendale, OH ..**108** B2
Everett, MA **110** C3
Everett, NB **71** B1
Everett, PA **61** E3
Everett, WA **9** A3

Everglades City, FL **80** A3
Everglades Natl. Park, FL **80** A4
Evergreen, AL ...**66** C2
Evergreen, CO ...**36** A2
Evergreen, PA ..**107** C2
Evergreen Park, IL **102** D5
Everman, TX **94** A2
Evesboro, NJ ...**114** E3
Ewan, WA **9** E5
Ewing, NE **35** D3
Ewingsville, PA .**107** B4
Excelsior Springs, MO **50** C2
Exeter, CA **15** A4
Exeter, NH **73** A2
Exmore, VA **76** C1
Eyebrow, SK **30** A1

Fabens, TX **29** E3
Fabius, NY **72** A4
Factoria, WA **82** D4
Fair Haven, VT ..**72** D2
Fair Lawn, NJ ..**111** A1
Fair Oaks, GA ..**121** A1
Fair Play, CA **14** E1
Fairacres, NM ...**29** D2
Fairbank, AZ **28** E3
Fairbanks, AK ...**5** D3
Fairburn, GA **64** E4
Fairburn, SD **32** D5
Fairbury, IL **49** D4
Fairbury, NE **37** E1
Fairfax, CA **14** C1
Fairfax, OH **108** C3
Fairfax, SC **65** D4
Fairfax, VA **76** A2
Fairfield, CA **14** C1
Fairfield, CT ...**113** A4
Fairfield, IA **49** A5
Fairfield, ID **22** B1
Fairfield, IL **51** E3
Fairfield, MT **18** E5
Fairfield, ND **32** D1
Fairfield, OH ..**108** A1
Fairfield, TX **54** B3
Fairfield, UT **22** D5
Fairhope, AL **66** B3
Fairlee, VT **72** D1
Fairmont, MN ...**48** C1
Fairmont, NE ...**35** E5
Fairmont, WV ...**61** C5
Fairmount, GA ..**64** E2
Fairmount Heights, MD **116** D2
Fairview, CA **15** A5
Fairview, KS **50** B1
Fairview, MI **58** C4
Fairview, MT **30** C3
Fairview, NJ ...**111** B2
Fairview, OK **39** D2
Fairview, OR **83** D1
Fairview, PA **61** B1
Fairview, TN **62** B5
Fairview, UT **24** E1
Fairview Heights, PA **107** D2
Fairview Park, OH **106** A3
Fairvilla, FL **120** C2
Fairway, KS **92** B4
Faith, SD **32** E4

Fajardo, PR **6** C3
Falcon, CO **36** B3
Falcon Heights, MN **100** C3
Falfurrias, TX ...**43** E4
Fall City, WA ...**9** A4
Fall River, RI ...**73** A4
Fall River Mills, CA **12** E3
Falls, NC **119** C2
Falls City, NE ...**50** B1
Fallon, NV **13** B5
Falls, NC **119** C2
Faltwillow, MT ...**21** D2
Fargo, GA **67** C2
Fargo, ND **33** E2
Fargo, NY **72** A2
Faribault, MN ...**46** D5
Farina, IL **51** D2
Farmer, WA **9** C4
Farmers Branch, TX **95** B1
Farmersville, TX ..**54** A1
Farmerville, LA ..**55** A1
Farmingdale, SD .**34** D1
Farmington, IL ...**49** C5
Farmington, ME ..**71** A5
Farmington, MI .**103** A4
Farmington, MO .**51** C4
Farmington, NM .**27** C1
Fleming, CO **36** D1
Farmville, NC **76** B4
Farmville, VA **76** A2
Farnam, NE **35** B5
Farnham, PQ ...**70** C5
Farrington, NC ..**118** C4
Farris, OK **52** B4
Farson, WY **23** B3
Farthing, WY **34** B4
Farwell, TX **38** D4
Faulkton, SD **33** C4
Fauna, TX **97** C3
Fauquier, BC **9** E1
Fayette, AL **64** A2
Fayette, MO **50** E2
Fayette, MS **55** C2
Fayetteville, AR .**52** D2
Fayetteville, GA .**64** E4
Fayetteville, NC ..**76** A5
Fayetteville, NY ..**72** A4
Fayetteville, OH **62** D1
Fayetteville, TN ..**64** B2
Faysville, TX **43** E5
Federal, PA **107** B4
Fellowship, NJ .**114** E3
Fence Lake, NM .**27** B3
Fennimore, WI ...**49** B2
Fenton, MI **60** D1
Fenton, MO **104** B5
Fenwick Is., DE ..**74** D4
Fergus, ON **59** A4
Fergus Falls, MN **46** A3
Ferguson, MO ..**104** D1
Fernandina Beach, FL **67** D2
Ferncliff, WA **82** B2
Ferndale, CA **12** B2
Ferndale, MD ...**115** C5
Ferndale, MI **103** C2
Ferney, SD **33** D4
Fernley, NV **13** B5
Ferriday, LA **55** B2
Ferron, UT **24** E2
Fertile, MN **46** A1
Fertile, MO **51** B3
Fessenden, ND ..**33** B1

Festus, MO **51** C3
Few, NC **118** E2
Fiddletown, CA ..**14** E1
Field, NM **38** C4
Field Creek, TX ..**41** D4
Fields, OR **13** C2
Fieldsburg, SC ..**65** D2
Fillmore, CA **15** A4
Fillmore, SK **30** D3
Fillmore, UT **24** D2
Findlay, OH **60** D3
Fine, NY **72** A2
Fingal, ND **33** D2
Finley, ND **33** D1
Finneytown, OH **108** B2
Firebaugh, CA ..**14** D3
Fish Camp, CA ..**14** E3
Fisher, MN **31** E5
Fishers Station, IN **105** D1
Fitchburg, MA ...**72** E3
Fitzgerald, GA ...**67** B1
Fitzwatertown, PA **114** B1
Five Forks, VA ..**116** A5
Five Points, PA .**114** A1
Flagler, CO **36** D2
Flagler Beach, FL **67** E3
Flagstaff, AZ ...**26** D2
Flamingo, FL **80** B4
Flandreau, SD ...**35** E1
Flat River, MO ..**51** C4
Flat Rock, MI ...**60** D2
Flatonia, TX **56** A1
Flatwillow, MT ..**21** D2
Flaxville, MT **30** B4
Fleming, CO **36** D1
Flemingsburg, KY **62** E2
Flemington, NJ ..**74** C2
Fletcher Bay, WA **82** A2
Flint, MI **58** C5
Flomaton, AL **66** B3
Floodwood, MN ..**46** D1
Flora, IL **51** D2
Flora, IN **51** D1
Flora, MS **55** D1
Florala, AL **66** C2
Floreffe, PA **107** D5
Florence, AZ **26** D5
Florence, CO **36** A4
Florence, KS **50** A4
Florence, KY ...**108** A5
Florence, MN ...**46** A5
Florence, MT **20** C1
Florence, OH **62** D1
Florence, OR **10** C3
Florence, SC **65** E2
Florence, SD **33** E4
Florence, WI **47** C2
Florence Junction, AZ **26** D5
Floresville, TX ..**43** D2
Florida City, FL ..**80** B4
Floridana Beach, FL **67** F5
Florissant, MO ..**104** C1
Florissant Fossil Beds Natl. Mon., CO ..**36** A3
Flourtown, PA ..**114** B1
Floyd, NM **38** C4
Floyd, VA **63** D3
Floydada, TX **39** A5
Fly, OH **61** B5
Folcroft, PA **114** B4
Foley, AL **66** B3
Foley, MN **46** C3
Folkenberg, OR .**83** A1
Folkston, GA **67** D2
Folkstone, NC ...**78** B1
Folly Beach, SC .**65** E4
Folsom, NM **38** G1
Folsom, PA **114** A4

Ft. Macleod, AB ..**18** E2
Ft. Madison, IA ..**49** A5
Ft. Matanzas Natl. Mon., FL **67** E3
Ft. McPherson, NT **5** E2
Ft. Meade, FL ...**69** E1
Ft. Mitchell, KY .**108** B5
Ft. Morgan, CO ..**36** C1
Ft. Moultrie [Ft. Sumter] Natl. Mon., SC ..**78** A3
Ft. Mudge, GA ..**67** C1
Ft. Myers, FL ...**69** E2
Ft. Nelson, BC ...**5** G4
Ft. Payne, AL **64** C2
Ft. Peck, MT **30** A5
Ft. Pierce, FL **80** B2
Ft. Pierre, SD ...**33** B5
Ft. Pulaski Natl. Mon., GA **65** E4
Ft. Ripley, MN ..**46** B3
Ft. Rock, OR **11** A4
Ft. St. Leon, LA .**98** C5
Ft. Scott, KS **50** C4
Ft. Simpson, NT .**5** G3
Ft. Smith, AR **52** C2
Ft. Smith, MT ...**21** D4
Ft. Steele, BC ...**18** C2
Ft. Stockton, TX .**40** D4
Ft. Sumner, NM .**38** B4
Ft. Sumter, SC ..**78** A4
Ft. Supply, OK ..**39** C1
Ft. Thomas, AZ ..**26** E5
Ft. Thomas, KY **108** C4
Ft. Totten, ND ...**31** C5
Ft. Union Natl. Mon., NM **38** A2
Ft. Valley, GA ...**65** A5
Ft. Walton Beach, FL **66** C3
Ft. Washakie, WY **23** C2
Ft. Washington, PA **114** B1
Ft. Wayne, IN ..**60** C3
Ft. Worth, TX ..**41** E1
Ft. Wright, KY ..**108** B4
Ft. Bragg, CA ...**12** A4
Ft. Bridger, WY .**23** A4
Ft. Yukon, AK ...**5** D2
Fortine, MT **18** C3
Fortuna, CA **12** B2
Fortuna, ND **30** C4
Fortuna Ledge, AK **5** B3
Fossil, OR **11** B2
Fossil Butte Natl. Mon., WY **23** A3
Fosston, MN **46** A1
Foster City, CA ..**84** E2
Fosterdale, NY ..**72** C5
Fostoria, OH **60** D3
Fouke, AR **52** D5
Fountain, CO **36** B3
Fountain Valley, CA **88** B2
Four Corners, FL **122** B2
Four Corners, MD **116** C1
Four Corners, OK **38** E1
Four Mile, NV ...**14** A1
Fourtown, MN ...**44** A5
Fowler, CO **36** C4
Fowlers Crossroads, NC **119** C2
Fowlerton, TX ...**43** D2
Fowlerville, MI ..**60** D1
Fox, MN **44** A4
Fox Chapel, PA .**107** D2
Fox Point, WI ...**101** D1
Fox Valley, SK ..**19** C2
Foxholm, ND **30** E5

Place Name / Page Number / Grid Number
Stantonburg 118 C5

Fragaria, WA ... 82 A4
Framingham, MA 73 A3
Francis, SK ... 30 C2
Francisco I. Madero, CHIH ... 29 B5
Franconia, VA ... 116 A5
Frank, PA ... 107 E5
Frankenmuth, MI 58 C5
Frankfort, IN ... 60 A5
Frankfort, KS ... 50 A2
Frankfort, KY ... 62 C2
Frankfort, MI ... 58 A4
Franklin, AL ... 66 B2
Franklin, AZ ... 29 A1
Franklin, GA ... 64 D4
Franklin, IN ... 62 B1
Franklin, KY ... 62 B5
Franklin, LA ... 55 C5
Franklin, ME ... 71 C4
Franklin, MI ... 103 A1
Franklin, NC ... 65 A1
Franklin, NE ... 37 C1
Franklin, NH ... 72 E2
Franklin, OH ... 60 D5
Franklin, PA ... 61 C2
Franklin, TN ... 64 B1
Franklin, TX ... 54 A4
Franklin, VA ... 76 B3
Franklin, WI ... 101 C5
Franklin Park, IL 102 B3
Franklin Park, MA ... 110 D2
Franklin Park, PA ... 107 A1
Franklinton, LA ... 55 D3
Franklinville, NY . 59 D5
Frankston, TX ... 54 C2
Frankton, MD ... 115 D3
Franktown, CO ... 36 B2
Fraser, MI ... 103 D1
Frazee, MN ... 46 A2
Frazer, MT ... 30 A5
Frederick, MD ... 74 A4
Frederick, OK ... 39 C4
Fredericksburg, TX ... 41 B5
Fredericksburg, VA ... 74 A5
Fredericton, NB . 71 C2
Fredericktown, MO ... 51 C4
Fredericktown, OH ... 60 E4
Frederiksted, PR ... 6 D4
Frederiksted, VI ... 6 D4
Fredonia, AZ ... 24 C5
Fredonia, KS ... 50 B5
Fredonia, NY ... 59 C5
Fredonia, TX ... 41 C4
Freeburg, IL ... 51 C3
Freeburg, MO ... 51 A3
Freehold, NJ ... 74 D2
Freeport, FL ... 66 D3
Freeport, IL ... 49 C2
Freeport, ME ... 73 A1
Freeport, NS ... 71 E4
Freeport, PA ... 61 C3
Freeport, TX ... 56 C2
Freer, TX ... 43 D3
Fremont, CA ... 14 C2
Fremont, MI ... 58 A5
Fremont, NE ... 48 A4
Fremont, OH ... 60 D3
French Lick, IN ... 62 B2
Frenchburg, KY ... 62 E2
Frenchglen, OR ... 13 C1
Frenchman, NV ... 15 B1
Frenchtown, NJ .. 74 C2
Fresnal, AZ ... 28 C2
Fresno, CA ... 14 E4
Fresno, MT ... 19 C4
Fridley, MN ... 100 B1
Friend, NE ... 35 E5
Friendly, MD ... 116 D5
Friendship, WI ... 47 B5
Friendswood, IN 105 B5
Friona, TX ... 38 D4
Frisco City, AL ... 66 B2
Fritch, TX ... 38 E2
Front Royal, VA ... 61 E5
Frontenac, MO .. 104 C3
Fronteras, SON ... 29 A3
Frontier, WY ... 23 A3
Frost, WV ... 63 D1
Frostburg, MD ... 61 D4
Frostproof, FL ... 69 E1
Fruita, CO ... 25 C2
Fruitland, MD ... 74 C5
Fruitland, UT ... 25 A1
Fryeburg, NH ... 72 E1
Fulda, MN ... 48 A1
Fullers, FL ... 120 A2
Fullerton, CA ... 87 B4
Fullerton, NE ... 35 D4
Fullerton Heights, MD ... 115 D2
Fulton, KS ... 51 A3
Fulton, KY ... 51 E5
Fulton, MO ... 51 A2
Fulton, MS ... 64 A3
Fulton, NY ... 72 A3
Fundy Natl. Park, NB ... 71 E2
Funk, NE ... 36 C1
Fuquay-Varina, NC ... 76 A5
Furnace Creek, CA ... 15 C5

G

Gabbs, NV ... 15 C1
Gabriola, BC ... 8 E1
Gackle, ND ... 33 C2
Gadsden, AL ... 64 C3
Gaffney, SC ... 65 C1
Gage, NM ... 29 B2
Gail, TX ... 40 E1
Gainesboro, TN .. 62 C5
Gainesville, FL ... 67 D3
Gainesville, GA .. 65 A2
Gainesville, MO .. 53 A1
Gainesville, TX ... 39 E5
Gaithersburg, MD ... 74 A4
Galatea, CO ... 36 D4
Galax, VA ... 63 C4
Galeana, CHIH ... 29 C5
Galena, ID ... 20 B5
Galena, MD ... 74 C4
Galena, WI ... 49 B2
Galena Park, TX .. 97 D3
Galesburg, IL ... 49 B4
Galesville, WI ... 47 A5
Galeton, PA ... 61 E1
Galion, OH ... 60 E3
Galisteo, NM ... 27 E3
Gallatin, MO ... 50 D1
Gallatin, TN ... 62 B5
Gallatin Gateway, MT ... 21 A3
Gallipolis, OH ... 63 A1
Galloway, OH ... 109 A4
Gallup, NM ... 27 B2
Galva, IL ... 49 C4
Galveston, IN ... 60 B4
Galveston, TX ... 56 D1
Gambell, AK ... 5 A2
Gamerco, NM ... 27 B2
Ganado, AZ ... 27 A2
Ganado, TX ... 56 B1
Gandy, UT ... 24 B1
Gannvalley, SD ... 35 C1
Gano, OH ... 108 C1
Gantt, AL ... 66 C2
The Gap, AZ ... 26 D1
Gap, PA ... 74 B3
Garberville, CA ... 12 B3
Garden City, KS .. 37 A4
Garden City, MI 103 A4
Garden City, MO . 50 C3
Garden City, SC .. 78 A2
Garden City, TX ... 40 E3
Garden City, UT .. 22 E3
Garden Grove, CA ... 88 B1
Garden Home, OR 83 B3
Garden Ridge, TX 96 E1
Gardena, CA ... 86 B3
Gardens Corner, SC ... 65 E4
Gardiner, ME ... 71 A5
Gardiner, MT ... 21 A4
Gardner, CO ... 36 A4
Gardner, FL ... 69 E1
Gardner, IL ... 49 D4
Gardner, KS ... 50 C3
Gardner, ND ... 33 E1
Gardnerville, MO ... 104 A1
Gardnerville, NV . 15 A1
Garfield, CO ... 25 E3
Garfield, NJ ... 111 A2
Garfield, NM ... 29 D1
Garibaldi, OR ... 10 D1
Garland, MT ... 32 A3
Garland, TX ... 95 E1
Garland, WY ... 21 C4
Garneill, MT ... 21 C2
Garner, NC ... 119 C5
Garnett, KS ... 50 B4
Garon Brook, NB . 71 A1
Garrett, KY ... 63 A3
Garrett Park, MD ... 116 B1
Garrison, MD ... 115 A2
Garrison, MN ... 46 C2
Garrison, MT ... 20 E2
Garrison, ND ... 33 A1
Garrison, UT ... 24 B2
Garwood, TX ... 56 B1
Gary, IN ... 49 E3
Gas City, IN ... 60 B4
Gaspereau Forks, NB ... 71 D1
Gasquet, CA ... 12 B1
Gastonia, NC ... 65 C1
Gastonville, PA . 107 C5
Gate City, VA ... 63 A4
Gates of the Arctic Natl. Park and Preserve, AK ... 5 C2
Gatesville, TX ... 41 E3
Gateway, CO ... 25 B3
Gatlinburg, TN ... 64 E1
Gautier, MS ... 66 A4
Gaylord, KS ... 36 C2
Gaylord, MI ... 58 B3
Gayly, PA ... 107 A3
Gazelle, CA ... 12 B2
Geary, NB ... 71 C2
Geary, OK ... 39 D2
Gee Brook, NY ... 72 A4
Gem Lake, MN .. 100 D2
Geneseo, IL ... 49 B4
Geneseo, NY ... 59 D4
Geneva, AL ... 66 D2
Geneva, GA ... 64 E5
Geneva, ID ... 23 A3
Geneva, MN ... 48 D1
Geneva, NE ... 37 E1
Geneva, NY ... 59 E4
Geneva, OH ... 61 B2
Genlee, NC ... 118 E3
Genoa, NE ... 35 D4
Genoa, NY ... 72 A4
George West, TX 43 E3
Georgesville, OH ... 109 A5
Georgetown, CO . 36 A2
Georgetown, GA . 66 E1
Georgetown, ID .. 22 E2
Georgetown, IL ... 49 E5
Georgetown, KY . 62 D2
Georgetown, MN 33 E2
Georgetown, MS 55 D2
Georgetown, OH . 62 D1
Georgetown, SC . 78 A3
Georgetown, TX . 41 E4
Georgiana, AL ... 66 C2
Geraldine, MT ... 19 B4
Gering, NE ... 34 C4
Gerlach, NV ... 13 B4
German Town, MA ... 110 E4
Germania, PA ... 61 E1
Germantown, NB 71 E2
Germantown, OH 60 D5
Germantown, TN 99 A2
Germfask, MI ... 58 A1
Geronimo, TX ... 43 E1
Gettysburg, PA ... 74 A3
Gettysburg, SD ... 33 B4
Geyser, MT ... 21 B1
Geyserville, CA ... 12 B5
Ghent, KY ... 62 C2
Giant Forest, CA . 15 A4
Gibbon, NE ... 35 C5
Gibbonsville, ID .. 20 C3
Gibbsboro, NJ ... 114 B4
Gibbstown, NJ .. 114 B5
Gibsland, LA ... 54 E1
Gibson, AZ ... 28 B1
Gibson City, IL ... 49 D5
Gibsonia, PA ... 107 C1
Gibsons, BC ... 8 E1
Giddings, TX ... 54 A5
Gifford, FL ... 80 A1
Gifford, WA ... 9 E3
Gila, NM ... 29 B1
Gila Bend, AZ ... 26 B5
Gila Cliff Dwellings Natl. Mon., NM 27 B5
Gilbert, AZ ... 91 E5
Gilbert, MN ... 46 D1
Gilbert, OR ... 83 D4
Gilbert Plains, MB ... 31 B1
Gilberton, WA ... 82 A2
Gillespie, IL ... 51 C2
Gillett, AR ... 53 B4
Gillett, TX ... 43 E2
Gillett, WI ... 47 D4
Gillette, WY ... 32 B5
Gills Rock, WI ... 47 E3
Gilman, IL ... 49 E4
Gilmer, TX ... 54 C1
Gilmore, GA ... 121 B2
Gilmore, ID ... 20 D4
Gilroy, CA ... 14 C3
Gimli, MB ... 31 E1
Girard, KS ... 50 C5
Glacier Bay Natl. Park and Preserve, AK 5 E4
Glacier Natl. Park, MT ... 18 D3
Glad Valley, SD .. 32 E4
Gladden Heights, PA ... 107 A5
Gladewater, TX .. 54 C2
Gladstone, MB ... 31 C2
Gladstone, MI ... 47 E2
Gladstone, MO ... 92 C1
Gladstone, OR ... 83 C5
Gladwin, MI ... 58 B4
Gladwyne, PA ... 114 A2
Glasgow, KY ... 62 C4
Glasgow, MO ... 50 E2
Glasgow, MT ... 30 A5
Glasnevin, SK ... 30 B3
Glassport, PA ... 107 D4
Glen, NH ... 72 E1
Glen Acres, WA .. 82 B4
Glen Arbor, MI ... 58 A3
Glen Burnie, MD ... 115 C5
Glen Echo, MD .. 116 B2
Glen Ghormely, PA ... 107 A4
Glen Rose, TX ... 41 E2
Glen Ullin, ND ... 32 E2
Glenaire, MO ... 92 D1
Glenarden, MD . 116 E2
Glenboro, MB ... 31 C3
Glencoe, MN ... 46 C5
Glendale, AZ ... 26 C5
Glendale, CA ... 17 A3
Glendale, CO ... 93 C3
Glendale, MO ... 104 C3
Glendale, NJ ... 114 E4
Glendale, NV ... 24 A5
Glendale, OH ... 108 B1
Glendale, WI ... 101 D1
Glendive, MT ... 32 B1
Glendo, WY ... 34 B3
Glendora, CA ... 87 C1
Glendora, NJ ... 114 D4
Gleneste, OH ... 108 E3
Glenfield, ND ... 33 C1
Glenfield, PA ... 107 A2
Glenmont, MD .. 116 B1
Glenmora, LA ... 55 A3
Glenn Dale, MD 116 E1
Glennallen, AK ... 5 C3
Glennie, MI ... 58 C3
Glennville, GA ... 65 C5
Glenolden, PA ... 114 B4
Glenpool, OK ... 52 B2
Glenrio, NM ... 38 D3
Glenrock, WY ... 34 A2
Glens Falls, NY .. 72 C3
Glenshaw, PA ... 107 C2
Glenside, PA ... 114 B1
Glenville, CT ... 112 C3
Glenville, WV ... 61 C5
Glenwood, AR ... 52 E4
Glenwood, IA ... 48 B5
Glenwood, MN ... 46 B3
Glenwood, NM ... 27 B5
Glenwood Springs, CO ... 25 D2
Globe, AZ ... 26 E5
Glorieta, NM ... 38 A2
Gloster, MS ... 55 C3
Gloucester, MA .. 73 A3
Gloucester, VA ... 76 C1
Gloucester City, NJ ... 114 C4
Gloversville, NY .. 72 C3
Goddard, KS ... 37 E5
Goderich, ON ... 58 E4
Goerkes Corner, WI ... 101 B3
Goffstown, NH ... 72 E2
Golconda, IL ... 51 E4
Golconda, NV ... 13 D4
Gold, PA ... 61 E1
Gold Bar, WA ... 9 A3
Gold Beach, OR .. 10 B5
Gold Hill, OR ... 10 C5
Golden, CO ... 36 A2
Golden, ID ... 20 B2
Golden Beach, FL ... 123 E1
Golden Meadow, LA ... 55 D5
Golden Valley, MN ... 100 A3
Goldendale, WA . 11 B1
Goldenrod, FL ... 120 D1
Goldfield, NV ... 15 C3
Goldsboro, MD ... 74 C4
Goldsboro, NC ... 76 B5
Goldthwaite, TX . 41 D3
Golf Manor, OH 108 C2
Goliad, TX ... 56 A2
Golondrinas, NM 38 A2
Gonzales, LA ... 55 C4
Gonzales, TX ... 43 E1
Gooding, ID ... 22 B1
Goodland, KS ... 36 E2
Goodlettsville, TN ... 62 B5
Goodman, WI ... 47 C3
Goodrich, CO ... 36 C1
Goodridge, MN ... 44 A5
Goodview, MN ... 46 E5
Goodwater, AL ... 64 C5
Goodwell, OK ... 38 E1
Gordon, AK ... 5 D5
Gordon, NE ... 34 E3
Gordonsville, VA . 76 A1
Gorham, ME ... 73 A1
Gorman, NC ... 118 E1
Gorman, TX ... 41 D2
Goshen, IN ... 60 B3
Goshen, NY ... 72 C5
Goshen, OH ... 108 E1
Goshen, VA ... 63 D1
Gosport, IN ... 62 A1
Gotha, FL ... 120 B3
Gotham, WI ... 49 B1
Gothenburg, NE ... 35 B5
Gould, CO ... 36 A1
Gould, PQ ... 70 D4
Gould Park, OH . 109 D2
Gouldsboro, ME .. 71 C4
Gouverneur, NY .. 72 A2
Gove, KS ... 37 B3
Govenlock, SK ... 19 C3
Government Camp, OR ... 11 A2
Gowanda, NY ... 59 C5
Gower, TN ... 99 A4
Gowers Corner, FL ... 67 D5
Grace, MI ... 58 B2
Grace, WA ... 82 E1
Graceville, FL ... 66 D2
Graceville, MN ... 46 A4
Grady, NM ... 38 C4
Grafton, IL ... 51 B2
Grafton, ND ... 31 D5
Grafton, WI ... 49 D1
Grafton, WV ... 61 C5
Graham, NC ... 63 E4
Graham, TX ... 41 D1
Grahanna, OH ... 109 D3
Grainfield, KS ... 37 B3
Grainton, NE ... 35 A5
Gramercy, LA ... 55 D5
Grampian, PA ... 61 D2
Gran Quivira, NM 27 E4
Granada, CO ... 36 E4
Granbury, TX ... 41 E2
Granby, CO ... 36 A1
Grand Bay, NB ... 71 D3
Grand Beach, MB 31 E2
Grand Canyon Natl. Park, AZ ... 26 C1
Grand Canyon Village, AZ ... 26 C1
Grand Chenier, LA ... 55 A5
Grand Coulee, WA 9 D4
Grand Falls, MN . 44 C5
Grand Falls, NB .. 71 B1
Grand Forks, BC ... 9 E2
Grand Forks, ND . 31 E5
Grand Gorge, NY 72 C4
Grand Haven, MI 60 A1
Grand Is., NE ... 35 D5
Grand Isle, LA ... 55 E5
Grand Isle, ME ... 71 A1
Grand Junction, CO ... 25 C2
Grand Junction, TN ... 53 E2
Grand Lake, CO ... 36 A1
Grand Ledge, MI . 60 B1
Grand Marias, MI 47 E1
Grand Marias, MN ... 45 A5
Grand Mere, PQ .. 70 C3
Grand Portage, MN ... 45 B5
Grand Prairie, TX 94 E3
Grand Rapids, MI ... 60 B1
Grand Rapids, MN ... 46 C1
Grand Teton Natl. Park, WY ... 23 A1
Grand View, ID ... 13 E1
Grandfalls, TX ... 40 D3
Grandfield, OK ... 39 D4
Grandin, FL ... 67 D3
Grandview, MB ... 31 A1
Grandview, MO ... 92 D5
Grandview, UT ... 13 E1
Grandview, WA ... 11 C1
Grandview Heights, OH ... 109 C3
Granger, TX ... 41 E4
Granger, WY ... 23 B4
Grangeville, ID ... 20 A2
Granite, CO ... 25 E3
Granite, OK ... 39 C3
Granite, OR ... 11 D3
Granite, UT ... 90 C5
Granite City, IL ... 51 C3
Granite Falls, MN ... 46 A5
Grant, MT ... 20 D4
Grant, NE ... 34 E5
Grants, NM ... 27 C3
Grants Pass, OR .. 10 C5
Grantsburg, WI ... 46 D3
Grantsdale, MT ... 20 C2
Grantsville, UT ... 22 D5
Grantsville, WV ... 63 B1
Grantville, MD ... 61 D4
Grantwood Village, MO ... 104 D4
Granville, AZ ... 27 A5
Granville, ND ... 31 A5
Granville, NY ... 72 C2
Granville, PQ ... 70 C5
Grapevine, CA ... 16 E1
Grapevine, TX ... 94 D1
Grasmere, ID ... 22 A2
Grass Valley, CA . 12 D5
Grass Valley, OR . 11 B2
Grasslands Natl. Park, SK ... 19 E4
Grassrange, MT .. 21 D1
Grassy Butte, ND 32 D1
Gravelbourg, SK . 30 A2
Gravenhurst, ON . 59 B2
Gravette, AR ... 52 C1
Gray, ME ... 73 A1
Grayland, WA ... 8 D4
Grayling, MI ... 58 B3
Grays River, WA ... 8 D5
Grayson, KY ... 62 E2
Grayville, IL ... 51 E3
Greasewood, AZ . 27 A2
Great Barrington, MA ... 72 D4
Great Bend, KS ... 37 C4
Great Falls, MD 116 A2
Great Falls, MT ... 19 A5
Great Falls, SC ... 65 D1
Great Neck, NY 111 E2
Great Neck Estates, NY ... 111 E2
Great Sands Dunes Natl. Mon., CO . 36 A4
Great Smoky Mountains Natl. Park, NC . 63 A5
Great Valley, NY . 59 D5
Greeley, CO ... 36 B1
Greeley Landing, ME ... 71 A4
Green Bay, WI ... 47 D4
Green Cove Springs, FL ... 67 D3
Green Farms, CT 113 A4
Green Hill, TN ... 99 E2
Green Lake, TX ... 56 A2
Green Level, NC 118 E5
Green River, UT .. 25 A2
Green River, WY . 23 B4
Green Tree, PA . 107 B3
Green Valley, AZ 28 D2
Greenbelt, MD .. 116 D1
Greenbrae, CA ... 85 E1
Greenbrier, AR ... 53 A2
Greenbush, MN .. 44 A4
Greencastle, IN ... 62 A1
Greendale, MO . 104 D2
Greendale, WI .. 101 D4
Greene, IA ... 48 D2
Greene, NY ... 72 B5
Greeneville, TN .. 99 A2
Greenfield, CA ... 14 C4
Greenfield, IA ... 48 C4
Greenfield, IL ... 51 C2
Greenfield, IN ... 60 B5
Greenfield, MA ... 72 D3
Greenfield, MO ... 50 D5
Greenfield, OH ... 60 E5
Greenfield, TN ... 53 E1
Greenfield, WI .. 101 D4
Greenfield Hill, CT ... 113 A4
Greenhills, OH .. 108 B2
Greenleaf City, OR ... 10 C3
Greenock, PA ... 107 E4
Greenport, NY ... 72 E5
Greensboro, AL .. 64 B5
Greensboro, GA .. 65 B3
Greensboro, NC 63 E4
Greensburg, IN ... 62 C1
Greensburg, KS .. 37 C5
Greensburg, KY .. 62 C4
Greensburg, LA ... 55 C3
Greensburg, PA .. 61 C3
Greenup, IL ... 51 E1
Greenup, KY ... 63 A1
Greenville, AL ... 66 C1
Greenville, CA ... 12 E4
Greenville, FL ... 67 B3
Greenville, GA ... 64 E4
Greenville, IL ... 51 D2
Greenville, KY ... 62 A4
Greenville, ME ... 71 A4
Greenville, MI ... 60 B1
Greenville, MS ... 53 C5
Greenville, NC ... 76 B4
Greenville, OH ... 60 C5
Greenville, PA ... 61 B2
Greenville, SC ... 65 B1
Greenville, TX ... 54 B1
Greenville, VA ... 63 E1
Greenwich, CT .. 112 D3
Greenwich, NJ .. 114 B5
Greenwich, OH ... 60 E3
Greenwood, AR .. 52 D3
Greenwood, BC ... 9 E2
Greenwood, GA .. 67 A2
Greenwood, IN . 105 D5
Greenwood, MA 110 C1
Greenwood, MS .. 53 D5
Greenwood, SC .. 65 B2
Greenwood, WI .. 47 A4
Greer, AZ ... 27 A4
Greer, ID ... 20 A1
Gregg, PA ... 107 A4
Gregory, MI ... 60 C1
Gregory, SD ... 35 C2
Gregory, TX ... 56 A3
Grenada, MS ... 53 D4
Grenfell, SK ... 30 D2
Grenloch, NJ ... 114 D5
Grenville, NM ... 38 C1
Grenville, PQ ... 70 A5
Gresham, OR ... 83 E4
Gretna, LA ... 55 D5
Gretna, VA ... 63 E3
Grey Forest, TX ... 96 A1
Greybull, WY ... 21 D5
Gridley, CA ... 12 D5
Grier, NM ... 38 C4
Griffin, GA ... 64 E4
Griffin, NY ... 72 C3
Griffins Crossroads, NC ... 118 C5
Grimsby, ON ... 59 B4
Grinnell, IA ... 48 E4
Griswold, MB ... 31 B3
Groesbeck, TX ... 54 A3
Groom, TX ... 39 A3
Grosse Pointe City, MI ... 103 E3
Grosse Pointe Farms, MI ... 103 E2
Grosse Pointe Park, MI ... 103 E3
Grosse Pointe Shores, MI ... 60 D1
Grosse Pointe Woods, MI ... 103 E2
Groton, CT ... 73 A5
Groton, SD ... 33 D4
Grotto, WA ... 9 B3
Grove, OK ... 52 C1
Grove City, IN ... 60 E5
Grove City, OH .. 109 B5
Grove City, PA ... 61 C2
Grove Hill, AL ... 66 B2
Groveland, CA ... 14 E2
Groveland, FL ... 67 D5
Groveport, OH ... 109 D5
Grovespring, MO 50 E5
Groveton, NH ... 70 E5
Groveton, PA ... 107 A3
Groveton, TX ... 54 C4
Groveton, VA ... 116 C5
Grundy, VA ... 63 B3
Grundy Center, IA 48 E3
Gruver, TX ... 38 E2
Grygla, MN ... 44 A5
Gu Vo, AZ ... 28 B1
Guadalupe, AZ ... 91 C5
Guadalupe, CA ... 16 D1
Guadalupe de Bahues, CHIH ... 42 A5
Guadalupe de Bravo, CHIH ... 29 D3
Guadalupe Mountains Natl. Park, TX ... 40 A3
Guadalupita, NM 38 A2
Gualala, CA ... 12 B5
Guelph, ON ... 59 B4
Guerette, ME ... 71 A1
Guerneville, CA .. 14 B1
Guernsey, WY ... 34 B3
Guerrero, COAH .. 43 B3
Gueydan, LA ... 55 A5
Guilford, ME ... 71 A4
Guin, AL ... 64 A4
Gulf Beach, FL ... 66 B4
Gulf City, FL ... 122 E5
Gulf Shores, AL .. 66 B3
Gulfport, FL ... 122 B4
Gulfport, MS ... 55 E4
Gull Lake, SK ... 19 D2
Gum Spring, VA .. 76 A1
Gunnison, CO ... 25 D3
Gunnison, UT ... 24 D2
Guntersville, AL .. 64 C3
Gurdon, AR ... 52 E4
Gusher, UT ... 25 B1
Gustine, CA ... 14 D3
Guthrie, AZ ... 29 A1
Guthrie, KY ... 62 A5
Guthrie, OK ... 39 E2
Guthrie, TX ... 39 B5
Guthrie, WI ... 101 B5
Guthrie Center, IA ... 48 C4
Guttenberg, NJ . 111 B2
Guttenberg, IA ... 49 A2
Guymon, OK ... 38 E1
Gwinn, MI ... 47 D2
Gwinner, ND ... 33 D3
Gypsum, KS ... 37 E3

H

Hachita, NM ... 29 B2
Hackberry, LA ... 54 E5
Hackensack, NJ 111 B1
Hacker Valley, WV ... 63 C1
Hackettstown, NJ ... 74 C1
Haddon Heights, NJ ... 114 D4
Haddonfield, NJ 114 D3
Haena, HI ... 6 D1
Hageman, ID ... 22 B1
Hagerman, NM ... 40 B1
Hagerstown, MD 74 A4
Hague, NY ... 72 C2
Hahira, GA ... 67 B2
Haigler, NE ... 36 E1
Hailey, ID ... 22 B1
Haines, AK ... 5 E4
Haines, OR ... 11 D3
Haines City, FL ... 67 E5
Haines Junction, YT ... 5 E4
Halawa, HI ... 7 C2
Haldimand, ON ... 59 B5
Hale, MI ... 58 C4
Hale Center, TX .. 38 E5
Haleakala Natl. Park, HI ... 7 D3
Haleiwa, HI ... 7 A2
Hales Corners, WI ... 101 C4
Halethorpe, MD 115 C4
Haley, OR ... 83 E4
Haleyville, AL ... 64 A3
Half Moon Bay, CA ... 14 B2
Halford, KS ... 36 A2
Halfway, OR ... 11 E3
Halifax, VA ... 63 E3
Hallandale, FL .. 123 D1
Halletsville, TX ... 56 A1
Halliday, ND ... 32 E1
Hallock, MN ... 31 E4
Hallowell, ME ... 71 A5
Hallstead, PA ... 72 B5
Halsey, NE ... 35 B4
Halsey, OR ... 10 D3
Halstad, MN ... 33 E1
Haltom City, TX .. 94 B3
Halton Hills, ON .. 59 B4
Hamburg, AR ... 53 B5
Hamburg, CA ... 12 C1
Hamburg, IA ... 48 B5
Hamburg, NY ... 59 C5
Hamburg, PA ... 74 B2
Hamilton, AL ... 64 A3
Hamilton, CO ... 25 D1
Hamilton, MO ... 50 D1
Hamilton, MT ... 20 C2
Hamilton, ND ... 31 D4
Hamilton, NY ... 72 B4
Hamilton, OH ... 62 D1
Hamilton, ON ... 59 B4
Hamilton, TX ... 41 E3
Hamilton City, CA 12 D4
Hamiota, MB ... 31 A2
Hamler, OH ... 60 D3
Hamlet, NC ... 65 E1
Hamlet, OH ... 108 E4
Hamlin, TX ... 41 B1
Hamlin, WV ... 63 A2
Hammon, OK ... 39 C2
Hammond, LA ... 55 D4
Hammond, MT ... 32 B4
Hammondsport, NY ... 59 E5
Hammondville, AL ... 64 D2
Hammonton, NJ . 74 D3
Hampden, ME ... 71 B4
Hampshire, WY .. 34 B1
Hampstead, MD .. 74 A3
Hampstead, NB .. 71 C2
Hampstead, NC .. 78 B1
Hampton, AR ... 53 A5
Hampton, IA ... 48 D2
Hampton, NB ... 71 C2
Hampton, NH ... 73 A2
Hampton, NS ... 71 E3
Hampton, OR ... 11 B4
Hampton, SC ... 65 D4
Hampton, VA ... 76 C2
Hampton Springs, FL ... 67 B3
Hamtramck, MI . 103 D3
Hana, HI ... 7 D3
Hanalei, HI ... 6 D1
Hanapepe, HI ... 6 D1
Hancock, MD ... 61 E4
Hancock, MI ... 47 C1
Hancock, NY ... 72 B5
Hanford, CA ... 14 E4
Hanksville, UT ... 24 E3
Hanley Hills, MO ... 104 C2
Hannibal, MO ... 51 A1
Hanover, ND ... 33 A2
Hanover, NH ... 72 D2
Hanover, ON ... 59 A3
Hanover, PA ... 74 A3
Hapeville, GA ... 121 C4
Happy, TX ... 38 E4
Happy Camp, CA 12 C1
Happy Jack, AZ .. 26 D3
Happy Valley, OR 83 D4
Happy Valley, TX 41 B2
Harahan, LA ... 98 A4

Bold type indicates cities with 100,000 population or more.

Place Name / Page Number / Grid Number: Stantonburg **118** C5

Harbor Beach, MI 58 D4
Harbor Springs, MI 58 B2
Harborton, OR 83 B1
Harborton, VA 76 C1
Harcourt, NB 71 D1
Hardeeville, SC 65 D5
Hardesty, OK 39 A1
Hardin, IL 51 B1
Hardin, MT 21 E3
Hardtner, KS 37 D5
Hardwick, VT 72 D1
Hardy, AR 53 B1
Hargrave, KS 37 C3
Hargrave, MB 31 A3
Harker Heights, TX 41 E4
Harlan, IA 48 B4
Harlan, KY 62 E4
Harlem, GA 65 C3
Harlem, MT 19 D4
Harlem, OH 109 D1
Harlem Heights, FL 120 A3
Harley Dome, UT 25 B2
Harlingen, TX 43 E6
Harlowton, MT 21 B2
Harman, WV 61 D5
Harmans, MD 115 C5
Harmar Heights, PA 107 D1
Harmarville, PA 107 D2
Harmonville, PA 114 A1
Harmony, CA 14 C5
Harmony, ME 71 A4
Harned, KY 62 B3
Harper, KS 37 D5
Harper, TX 41 C5
Harper, WA 82 A4
Harper, WV 63 D1
Harper Woods, MI 103 E2
Harpers Ferry, WV 74 A4
Harpersville, AL 64 C4
Harpster, ID 20 A2
Harpswell Center, ME 73 A1
Harriet, AR 53 A1
Harriman, TN 62 D5
Harrington, DE 74 C4
Harrington, ME 71 C4
Harrington, WA 9 E4
Harris, OK 52 C5
Harris Crossroads, NC 119 E1
Harrisburg, AR 53 C2
Harrisburg, IL 51 E4
Harrisburg, NC 117 E1
Harrisburg, NE 34 C4
Harrisburg, PA 74 A3
Harrison, AR 52 E1
Harrison, MI 58 B4
Harrison, MT 20 E3
Harrison, NJ 111 A3
Harrison, NY 112 C5
Harrison, OH 62 C1
Harrison, NE 34 C3
Harrisonburg, LA 55 B2
Harrisonburg, VA 63 E1
Harrisonville, MD 115 A3
Harrisonville, MO 50 C3
Harrisville, MI 58 C3
Harrisville, NY 72 A2
Harrisville, WV 61 B5
Harrodsburg, KY 62 D3
Harrold, SD 33 B5
Harstel, CO 36 A3
Hart, MI 58 A5
Hart, SK 30 B4
Hart, TX 38 E4
Hartell, AB 18 D1
Hartford, AL 66 D2
Hartford, CT 72 E4
Hartford, NJ 114 E2
Hartford, WI 49 D1
Hartford City, IN 60 B4
Hartington, NE 35 E3
Hartland, NB 71 B2
Hartley, TX 38 D2
Hartline, WA 9 D4
Hartney, MB 31 A3
Hartsdale, NY 112 B4
Hartselle, AL 64 B3
Hartshorne, OK 52 B3
Hartsville, SC 65 E1
Hartville, MO 50 E5
Hartville, WY 34 B3
Hartwell, GA 65 B2
Harundale, MD 115 D5
Harvard, IL 49 D2
Harvester, MO 104 A2
Harvey, LA 98 C5
Harvey, MI 47 D1
Harvey, ND 33 B1
Harwick, PA 107 D1
Harwood Heights, IL 102 B2
Hasbrouck Heights, NY 111 A2
Haskell, OK 52 B2
Haskell, TX 41 C1
Hastings, MI 60 B1
Hastings, MN 46 D5
Hastings, NE 37 D1
Hastings-on-Hudson, NY 112 A5
Hat Creek, CA 12 D3
Hatch, NM 29 D1
Hatch, UT 24 C4
Hathaway, MT 32 A3
Hatteras, NC 76 D4
Hattiesburg, MS 55 E2
Hatton, ND 33 D1
Havana, FL 67 A3
Havana, IL 49 C5
Havana, ND 33 D3
Havelock, NC 76 C5
Havelock, PQ 70 B5
Haven, KS 37 F4
Haverford, PA 114 A2
Haverhill, MA 73 A3
Haviland, KS 37 C5
Havre, MT 19 C4
Havre de Grace, MD 74 B3
Hawaii Volcanoes Natl. Park, HI 7 D5
Hawaiian Gardens, CA 86 E5
Hawarden, IA 48 A2
Hawesville, KY 62 A3
Hawi, HI 7 D4
Hawk Springs, WY 34 C4
Hawkesbury, PQ 70 A5
Hawkins, TX 54 C1
Hawkins, WI 47 A3
Hawkinsville, GA 65 B5
Hawley, CO 36 C4
Hawley, PA 74 B1
Hawthorne, CA 86 B3
Hawthorne, FL 67 D3
Hawthorne, NV 15 B2
Haxtun, CO 36 D1
Hay Springs, NE 34 D3
Hayden, AZ 26 D5
Hayden, CO 25 D1
Hayes, SD 33 A5
Hayes Center, NE 37 A1
Hayesville, NC 64 E1
Hayfield, VA 116 A5
Hayfork, CA 12 C3
Haynesville, LA 54 E1
Haynesville, ME 71 B3
Hayneville, AL 66 C1
Hays, KS 37 C3
Haysville, KS 37 E5
Haysville, PA 107 A2
Hayti, MO 53 D1
Hayward, CA 14 C2
Hayward, WI 46 E3
Hazard, KY 63 A3
Hazel Dell, WA 83 C1
Hazel Green, AL 64 B2
Hazel Park, MI 103 C2
Hazeldale, OR 83 A3
Hazelia, OR 83 B5
Hazelton, ND 33 B2
Hazelton, PA 74 B1
Hazelwood, MO 104 C1
Hazelwood, WA 82 D4
Hazen, AR 53 B3
Hazen, ND 32 E1
Hazen, NV 13 B5
Hazlehurst, GA 65 C5
Hazlehurst, MS 55 D2
Hazlet, SK 19 D2
Headland, AL 66 E2
Heafford Junction, WI 47 B3
Healdsburg, CA 12 B5
Healdton, OK 39 E4
Healy, KS 37 A3
Hearne, TX 54 A4
Heath, OH 61 A4
Heavener, OK 52 C3
Hebbronville, TX 43 D4
Heber, AZ 26 E4
Heber City, UT 22 E5
Heber Springs, AR 53 A2
Hebo, OR 10 D1
Hebron, IN 49 E3
Hebron, NE 37 E1
Hebron, OH 61 A4
Hector, MN 46 B5
Hedley, BC 9 C1
Hedley, TX 39 A4
Hedwig Village, TX 97 A2
Heflin, AL 64 D4
Heidelberg, PA 107 B4
Helena, AR 53 C3
Helena, AZ 91 D5
Helena, MT 20 E2
Helotes, TX 96 A1
Helper, UT 24 E1
Helvetia, OR 83 A1
Hemet, CA 17 B3
Hemingford, NE 34 D3
Hemingway, SC 78 A2
Hemlock, OR 10 D1
Hemphill, TX 54 E3
Hempstead, TX 54 B5
Henderson, KY 62 A3
Henderson, NC 78 A3
Henderson, NV 17 E1
Henderson, TN 53 F2
Henderson, TX 54 C2
Hendersonville, NC 65 B1
Hendersonville, PA 107 B5
Hendersonville, TN 99 D1
Hendy Woods, CA 12 B5
Hennessey, OK 39 D2
Henniker, NH 72 E2
Henning, MN 46 A2
Henrietta, TX 39 D5
Henry, ID 22 E2
Henry, IL 49 C4
Henry, SD 33 E5
Henryetta, OK 52 B3
Hensley, AR 53 A4
Hentown, GA 66 E2
Hepburnville, PA 74 A1
Heppner, OR 11 C2
Herbert, SK 19 E2
Hercules, CA 85 E3
Hereford, MD 74 B3
Hereford, OR 11 D4
Hereford, TX 38 D4
Herington, KS 37 E3
Herkimer, NY 72 B3
Herman, MN 46 A3
Hermanas, NM 29 C2
Hermann, MO 51 A3
Hermantown, MN 46 D2
Hermiston, OR 11 C1
Hermitage, AR 53 A5
Hermitage, TN 99 D3
Hermleigh, TX 41 A2
Hermon, ME 71 B4
Hermosa, CO 25 C5
Hermosa, SD 34 D1
Hermosa Beach, CA 86 A4
Hernandez, NM 27 E2
Hernando, MS 53 D3
Herreid, SD 33 B3
Hershey, PA 74 A3
Hertford, NC 76 C3
Hesperia, MI 58 A5
Hettinger, ND 32 D3
Hewitt, MN 46 B2
Hext, TX 41 C4
Heyworth, IL 49 D5
Hialeah, FL 123 D3
Hialeah Gardens, FL 123 B3
Hiawatha, KS 50 B1
Hibbing, MN 46 D1
Hickiwan, AZ 28 B1
Hickman, KY 51 D5
Hickman, PA 107 A4
Hickory, NC 63 C5
Hickory Flat, MS 53 E3
Hickory Hills, IL 102 C5
Hickorytown, PA 114 A1
Hicks, TX 94 A1
Hico, TX 41 E2
Hidalgo, CHIH 29 C4
Hidalgo, TX 43 E6
Higgins, TX 39 B2
High Is., TX 56 D1
High Point, FL 122 B2
High Point, NC 63 D4
High Rolls, NM 29 E1
High Springs, FL 67 C3
Highcliff, PA 107 B2
Highland, NY 72 D5
Highland Heights, KY 108 C4
Highland Heights, OH 106 E1
Highland Home, AL 66 C1
Highland Park, IL 49 E2
Highland Park, MD 116 E2
Highland Park, MI 103 C3
Highland Park, PA 114 A3
Highland Park, TX 95 C2
Highlands, NC 65 A1
Highmore, SD 33 C5
Hiko, NV 15 E4
Hilger, MT 21 C1
Hilham, TN 62 C5
Hill City, KS 37 B2
Hill City, MN 46 C1
Hill City, SD 34 C1
Hill Country Village, TX 96 C1
Hilliard, OH 109 A3
Hillman, MI 58 C3
Hillsboro, KS 37 E4
Hillsboro, ND 33 E1
Hillsboro, NM 29 C1
Hillsboro, OH 62 E1
Hillsboro, TX 54 A2
Hillsboro, WI 49 B1
Hillsboro Beach, FL 80 D2
Hillsborough, CA 85 A1
Hillsborough, NC 63 E4
Hillsborough, NH 72 E2
Hillsdale, MI 60 C2
Hillsdale, MO 104 D2
Hillsdale, NB 71 D2
Hillsdale, NY 72 D4
Hillshire Village, TX 97 A2
Hillside, AZ 26 B3
Hillside, IL 102 B3
Hillsview, OR 83 E4
Hillsville, VA 63 C3
Hilltop, MN 100 B2
Hilo, HI 7 E4
Hilton, NY 59 D4
Hinausa, MB 31 E1
Hinckley, UT 24 C2
Hine, MO 104 A3
Hineston, LA 55 A3
Hinesville, GA 65 D5
Hingham, MT 19 B4
Hinsdale, IL 102 B5
Hinsdale, MT 19 E5
Hinton, OK 39 D3
Hinton, WV 63 C2
Hitchcock, SD 33 D5
Hixton, WI 47 A5
Hoback Jct., WY 23 A1
Hobart, OK 39 C3
Hobbs, NM 40 D2
Hobe Sound, FL 80 B1
Hoboken, NJ 111 B3
Hobson, MT 21 C1
Hobucken, NC 76 C4
Hodgekins, IL 102 B5
Hodgenville, KY 62 C3
Hodgeville, SK 30 A2
Hodgkins, IL 102 B5
Hoffmeister, NY 72 B3
Hogansville, GA 64 E4
Hohenwald, TN 64 A1
Hoisington, KS 37 C3
Hokah, MN 49 A1
Holbrook, AZ 26 E3
Holbrook, ID 22 D3
Holcomb, MS 53 D4
Holden, UT 24 D2
Holden Beach, NC 78 B2
Holdenville, OK 52 A3
Holdrege, NE 37 C1
Holland, MB 31 C3
Holland, MI 60 A1
Hollandale, MS 53 C5
Hollidaysburg, PA 61 E3
Hollis, AR 52 E3
Hollis, OK 39 B4
Hollister, CA 14 C3
Holloway, MN 46 A4
Holly, CO 36 E4
Holly Beach, LA 54 E5
Holly Hill, SC 65 E3
Holly Springs, MS 53 D3
Hollywood, CA 126 D1
Hollywood, FL 80 B3
Hollywood, WA 82 E2
Hollywood Park, TX 96 C1
Holmes Beach, FL 69 D1
Holmwood, LA 55 A5
Holopaw, FL 67 F5
Holstein, IA 48 B3
Holton, KS 50 B2
Holts Summit, KS 51 A3
Holy Cross, AK 5 B3
Holyoke, CO 36 E1
Holyoke, MA 72 E4
Home Place, IN 105 C1
Homecroft, IN 105 C4
Homedale, ID 11 E5
Homer, AK 5 C4
Homer, LA 54 E1
Homer, MI 60 C2
Homerville, GA 67 C2
Homestead, FL 80 B4
Homestead, PA 107 D3
Hometown, IL 102 D5
Homewood, AL 64 B4
Hominy, OK 52 A1
Homosassa, FL 67 C5
Hondo, NM 38 A5
Hondo, TX 43 C1
Honea Path, SC 65 B2
Honesdale, PA 72 B5
Honey Brook, PA 74 B3
Honey Grove, PA 61 E3
Honey Grove, TX 52 B5
Honey Moon Bay, BC 8 D1
Honeydew, CA 12 A3
Honokaa, HI 7 D4
Honokohau, HI 7 C2
Honolulu, HI 7 A2
Honomu, HI 7 E4
Hood River, OR 11 A1
Hood View, OR 83 A5
Hoodsport, WA 8 E3
Hooker, OK 39 A1
Hooks, TX 52 D5
Hoolehua, HI 7 B2
Hoonah, AK 5 E5
Hoopa, CA 12 B2
Hooper, CO 36 A4
Hooper Bay, AK 5 A3
Hoopeston, IL 49 E5
Hoosick Falls, NY 72 D3
Hope, AR 52 E5
Hope, AZ 26 A4
Hope, BC 9 B1
Hope, IN 62 B1
Hope, NM 40 B1
Hope Hull, AL 66 C1
Hopewell, TN 99 D2
Hopewell, VA 76 B2
Hopkins, MN 100 A4
Hopkinsville, KY 62 A5
Hopland, CA 12 B5
Hoquiam, WA 8 D4
Horicon, WI 49 D1
Hornbeck, LA 54 E3
Hornell, NY 59 E5
Horning, PA 107 C4
Horse Cave, KY 62 C4
Horseheads, NY 72 A5
Horseshoe Bend, ID 20 A5
Horton, KS 50 B2
Hosford, FL 66 F3
Hot Springs, AR 52 E4
Hot Springs, MT 18 E5
Hot Springs, SD 34 C2
Hot Springs, VA 63 D2
Hot Springs Natl. Park, AR 52 E3
Hotchkiss, CO 25 D3
Hotevilla, AZ 26 E1
Houghs Neck, MA 110 E4
Houghton, MI 47 C1
Houghton, SD 33 D3
Houghton Lake, MI 58 B4
Houlton, ME 71 B2
Houma, LA 55 D5
Houston, MO 51 A5
Houston, MS 53 E4
Houston, TX 54 C5
Houston Lake, MO 92 B1
Hovland, MN 45 B5
Howard, SD 35 E1
Howard, WI 47 D4
Howard City, MI 58 B5
Howard Lake, MN 46 C4
Howe, ID 20 D5
Howell, MI 60 C1
Howes, SD 32 E5
Howland, ME 71 B4
Howser, BC 18 B1
Hoxie, AR 53 B1
Hoxie, KS 37 B2
Huachuca City, AZ 28 E2
Hubbard, TX 54 A3
Hudson, FL 67 C5
Hudson, MD 74 B5
Hudson, MI 60 C2
Hudson, NY 72 D4
Hudson, WI 46 D4
Hudson, WY 23 C2
Hudson Falls, NY 72 C3
Hudson Heights, NY 133 D1
Hueco, TX 29 E3
Huepac, SON 28 E4
Hughes, AK 5 C2
Hughes, AR 53 C3
Hugo, CO 36 C3
Hugo, OK 52 B5
Hugoton, KS 37 A5
Huizachal, COAH 43 A5
Hulett, WY 32 B5
Hull, MA 110 E4
Humacao, PR 6 C4
Humble, TX 54 C5
Humboldt, AZ 28 C3
Humboldt, IA 48 C2
Humboldt, KS 50 B4
Humboldt, SD 35 E1
Humboldt, TN 53 E1
Hungerford, TX 56 B1
Hunt, AZ 27 A3
Hunter, KS 36 D2
Hunter, NY 72 C4
Hunters, WA 9 E4
Hunters Creek Village, TX 97 A3
Huntingburg, IN 62 A3
Huntingdon, PA 61 E3
Huntingdon, PQ 70 B5
Huntingdon, TN 53 E1
Huntington, CT 113 B2
Huntington, IN 60 B4
Huntington, MA 72 D4
Huntington, OR 11 E4
Huntington, UT 24 E2
Huntington, WV 63 A2
Huntington Beach, CA 17 A3
Huntington Park, CA 86 C2
Huntington Woods, MI 103 B2
Huntleigh, MO 104 C3
Hunts Point, WA 82 D3
Huntsville, AL 64 B2
Huntsville, AR 52 D1
Huntsville, ON 54 B1
Huntsville, TX 54 C4
Hurdsfield, ND 33 B1
Hurffville, NJ 114 D5
Hurley, NM 29 B1
Hurley, WI 47 B2
Huron, OH 60 E3
Huron, SD 33 D5
Hurricane, UT 24 B4
Hurricane, WV 63 A1
Hurst, TX 94 D3
Hurtsboro, AL 66 D1
Huson, MT 20 C1
Hutchins, TX 95 D5
Hutchinson, KS 37 D4
Hutchinson, MN 46 C4
Huttonsville, WV 63 D1
Hyak, WA 9 B4
Hyannis, MA 73 B4
Hyannis, NE 34 E4
Hyattsville, MD 116 D2
Hyattville, WY 21 D5
Hyden, KY 62 E3
Hye, TX 99 D1
Hysham, MT 21 E2

I

Iaeger, WV 63 B3
Ibapah, UT 22 B5
Iberia, MO 51 A4
Iberville, PQ 70 C5
Ida Grove, IA 48 B3
Idabel, OK 52 C5
Idaho City, ID 20 A5
Idaho Falls, ID 22 E1
Idaho Springs, CO 36 A2
Idalia, CO 36 E2
Idalou, TX 38 E5
Idington, MN 44 D5
Idleyld Park, OR 10 D4
Ilchester, MD 115 B4
Ile-Perrot, PQ 70 B5
Ilgen City, MN 46 E1
Illahee, WA 82 A2
Imbler, OR 11 D2
Imboden, AR 53 B1
Imlay City, MI 58 D5
Immokalee, FL 80 A3
Imnaha, OR 11 E2
Imperial, CA 17 D5
Imperial, NE 36 E1
Imperial Beach, CA 17 B5
Imuris, SON 28 D3
Inchelium, WA 9 E3
Independence, CA 15 B4
Independence, IA 48 E3
Independence, KS 50 B5
Independence, LA 55 D4
Independence, MN 46 D1
Independence, MO 50 C2
Independence, OH 106 D3
Independence, VA 63 C4
Indiahoma, OK 39 D4
Indian Creek Village, FL 123 E3
Indian Falls, CA 12 E4
Indian Head, MD 74 A5
Indian Head, SK 30 D2
Indian Head Park, IL 102 B5
Indian Hill, OH 108 D2
Indian Lake, NY 72 B2
Indian Neck, CT 113 E1
Indian Pass, FL 66 E4
Indian River, NY 72 A2
Indian Rocks Beach, FL 69 C1
Indian Shores, FL 122 A3
Indian Springs, NV 15 E5
Indian Trail, NC 117 E5
Indian Wells, AZ 27 A2
Indiana, PA 61 D3
Indianapolis, IN 60 B5
Indianol, WA 82 B1
Indianola, IA 48 D4
Indianola, MS 53 C5
Indianola, PA 107 D1
Indio, CA 17 C4
Indus, MN 44 C4
Ingalls, NC 63 B5
Ingersoll, ON 59 A5
Inglewood, CA 86 B2
Inglewood, TN 99 C2
Inglewood, WA 82 E3
Inglis, FL 67 C4
Ingomar, MT 21 E2
Ingomar, PA 107 B2
Ingram, PA 107 B3
Inkom, ID 22 D2
Inkster, MI 103 A5
Inlet, NY 72 B2
Instow, SK 19 D3
Intake, MT 32 C1
Interior, SD 34 E1
International Falls, MN 44 C4
Inuvik, NT 5 E2
Inver Grove Heights, MN 100 E5
Inverness, FL 67 D5
Inverness, MS 53 C5
Inwood, NY 111 E4
Inyokern, CA 17 B1
Iola, KS 50 D4
Iona, SD 35 C1
Ione, NV 15 C1
Ionia, MI 60 B1
Iowa City, IA 49 A4
Iowa Falls, IA 48 D3
Iowa Park, TX 39 D5
Ipswich, MA 73 A3
Ipswich, SD 33 C4
Ira, TX 41 A2
Iraan, TX 40 E4
Irasburg, VT 70 D5
Iron Mountain, MI 47 D2
Iron River, MI 47 C2
Ironside, OR 11 D4
Ironton, KS 51 B4
Ironton, OH 63 A1
Ironwood, MI 47 B2
Iroquois, SD 33 D5
Irvine, AB 19 C2
Irvine, KY 62 E3
Irving, TX 95 A2
Irvington, NY 112 A4
Irwindale, CA 87 B1
Irwinton, GA 65 B4
Irwinville, GA 67 B1
Isabel, SD 33 A4
Isabella, MN 44 E5
Ishpeming, MI 47 D1
Islamorada, FL 80 B4
Island Grove, FL 67 D4
Island Park, ID 21 A5
Island Pond, VT 70 D5
Isle Royale Natl. Park, MI 45 B5
Isleworth, FL 120 B3
Issaquah, WA 82 E5
Italy, TX 54 A2
Ithaca, MI 58 C5
Ithaca, NY 72 A5
Ituna, SK 30 D1
Iuka, MS 64 A3
Ivy Rock, PA 114 A1

J

Jacinto City, TX 97 D3
Jack Creek, NV 13 E3
Jackman, ME 70 E4
Jackpot, NV 22 B3
Jacksboro, TX 41 D1
Jackson, AL 66 B2
Jackson, CA 14 D1
Jackson, GA 65 A4
Jackson, KY 62 E3
Jackson, LA 55 C3
Jackson, MI 60 C2
Jackson, MN 48 B1
Jackson, MO 51 C4
Jackson, MS 55 D1
Jackson, MT 20 D3
Jackson, OH 63 A1
Jackson, TN 53 E1
Jackson, WY 23 A1
Jacksonboro, SC 65 E4
Jacksonville, AL 64 D3
Jacksonville, AR 53 A3
Jacksonville, FL 67 D2
Jacksonville, GA 67 D1
Jacksonville, IL 51 C1
Jacksonville, NC 76 B5
Jacksonville, TX 54 C2
Jacksonville Beach, FL 67 D2
Jacob Lake, AZ 24 C5
Jacobs, MO 104 A2
Jacobson, MN 46 C1
Jacumba, CA 17 C5
Jacume, BC 17 B5
Jakes Corner, AZ 26 D4
Jal, NM 40 C2
Jalama, CA 16 D2
Jamaica, VT 72 D3
James Is., SC 65 E4
Jamestown, KS 36 D2
Jamestown, KY 62 D4
Jamestown, ND 33 C2
Jamestown, NY 61 C1
Jamestown, OH 60 D5
Jamestown, PA 61 B2
Jamestown, RI 73 A4
Jamestown, SC 78 A3
Jamestown, TN 62 D5
Jamul, CA 89 E3
Janesville, WI 49 C2
Janos, CHIH 29 B4
Jansen, NE 36 F1
Jarbidge, NV 22 A3
Jarrell, TX 41 E4
Jasonville, IN 62 A1
Jasper, AL 64 B4
Jasper, FL 67 C2
Jasper, GA 64 E2
Jasper, IN 62 A2
Jasper, MO 50 C5
Jasper, NY 59 E5
Jasper, TN 64 C2
Jasper, TX 54 D4
Jay, NY 72 C1
Jay, OK 52 C1
Jay Em, WY 34 B3
Jaynes, AZ 28 D1
Jayton, TX 41 B1
Jean, NV 17 E1
Jeanerette, LA 55 B5
Jedburg, MO 104 A4
Jefferson, CO 30 A2
Jefferson, GA 65 A3
Jefferson, IA 48 C3
Jefferson, NC 63 C4
Jefferson, PA 107 D5
Jefferson, SC 65 D1
Jefferson, TX 54 D1
Jefferson, WI 49 C1
Jefferson City, MO 51 A3
Jefferson City, TN 62 F5
Jefferson Heights, LA 98 B4
Jefferson Village, VA 116 B3
Jeffersonville, IN 62 C2
Jeffersonville, VT 72 C1
Jeffrey City, WY 23 D3
Jellico, TN 62 E4
Jemez Pueblo, NM 27 D2
Jemez Springs, NM 27 D2
Jemison, AL 64 C5
Jena, LA 55 B2
Jenkins, KY 63 A3
Jenkins Corner, MD 116 E4
Jenkintown, PA 114 C1
Jenks, OK 52 B2
Jenner, AB 19 B1
Jenner, CA 14 B1
Jennerstown, PA 61 D3
Jennings, LA 55 A5
Jennings, MO 104 D2
Jennings Lodge, OR 83 C5
Jensen, UT 25 B1
Jermyn, TX 41 D1
Jerome, ID 22 B2
Jersey City, NJ 74 D1
Jersey Shore, PA 61 E2
Jerseyville, IL 51 C2
Jesup, GA 67 D1
Jesús Carranza, CHIH 29 E3
Jet, OK 39 D1
Jetmore, KS 37 B4
Jewel Cave Natl. Mon., SD 34 C1
Jewell, IA 48 D3
Jewell, KS 37 D2
Jiggs, NV 13 E5
Jim Thorpe, PA 74 A1
Jiménez, CHIH 42 A4
Joelton, TN 99 A1
Joes, CO 36 D2
John Day, OR 11 C3
John Day Fossil Beds Natl. Mon., OR 11 B2
Johnson City, OR 83 C5

Place Name / Page Number / Grid Number
Stantonburg 118 C5

Johnson City, KS 36 E5
Johnson City, NY 72 A5
Johnson City, TN 63 B4
Johnson City, TX 41 C5
Johnsonburg, PA 61 D1
Johnstown, NY 72 C3
Johnstown, OH 60 E4
Johnstown, PA 61 D3
Joliet, IL 49 D3
Joliette, PQ 70 B4
Jollyville, TX 41 E5
Jolon, CA 14 C4
Jonah, TX 41 E4
Jonesboro, AR 53 C1
Jonesboro, IN 60 B4
Jonesboro, LA 55 A2
Jonesboro, TX 41 E3
Jonesport, ME 71 C4
Jonestown, MD 115 A5
Jonesville, LA 55 B2
Jonesville, MI 60 C2
Jonesville, SC 65 C1
Jonesville, VA 63 A4
Joplin, MO 50 C5
Joplin, MT 19 B4
Joplin, TX 41 D1
Joppa, IN 105 A5
Joppa, MD 115 E1
Joppatowne, MD 115 E1
Jordan, MB 31 D3
Jordan, MN 46 C5
Jordan, MT 21 E1
Jordan, PA 74 B2
Jordan River, BC 8 D2
Jordan Valley, OR 13 E1
Joseph, OR 11 E2
Joseph City, AZ 26 E3
Joshua Tree, CA 17 C3
Joshua Tree Natl. Mon., CA 17 D3
Jourdanton, TX 43 D2
Joyce, TX 43 C4
Juanita, WA 82 D2
Juárez, CHIH 29 B5
Juárez, COAH 43 A4
Judith Gap, MT 21 C2
Julesburg, CO 34 E5
Julian, CA 17 C4
Julimes, CHIH 42 A2
Junction, TX 41 B5
Junction, UT 24 D3
Junction, WV 61 D4
Junction City, AR 55 A1
Junction City, KS 50 A3
Junction City, OR 10 D3
Juneau, AK 5 E4
Jungs, MO 104 A2
Juniper, NB 71 C2
Juno, TX 41 A5
Juntura, OR 11 D5
Jupiter, FL 80 B2
Justice, IL 102 C5
Justiceburg, TX 41 A1

K

Kackley, KS 36 D2
Kadoka, SD 34 E1
Kahlotus, WA 9 D5
Kahoka, IA 49 A5
Kahului, HI 7 C3
Kaibab, AZ 24 C5
Kailua, HI 7 A2
Kailua-Kona, HI 7 D4
Kaka, AZ 28 C1
Kake, AK 5 E5
Kalama, WA 8 E5
Kalamazoo, MI 60 B2
Kalispell, MT 18 C4
Kalkaska, MI 58 B3
Kalvesta, KS 37 B4
Kamas, UT 22 E5
Kamiah, ID 20 A1
Kampsville, IL 51 B2
Kanab, UT 24 C5
Kane, PA 61 D1
Kaneohe, HI 7 A2
Kankakee, IL 49 E4
Kannapolis, NC 63 D5
Kanopolis, KS 37 D3
Kansas, IL 51 E1
Kansas, OK 52 C1
Kansas City, KS 50 C2
Kansas City, MO 50 C2
Kapaa, HI 6 D1
Kapalua, HI 7 C2
Kaplan, LA 55 B5
Karlstad, MN 31 E4
Karluk, AK 5 B5
Karnes City, TX 43 E2
Kashega, AK 4 G5
Kashegelok, AK 5 B4
Kaslo, BC 18 B1
Kasson, MN 46 D5
Katalla, AK 5 D4
Katevale, PQ 70 D5
Katmai Natl. Park and Preserve, AK 5 B4
Katonah, NY 112 C1
Kaufman, TX 54 B2
Kaukauna, WI 47 D5
Kaunakakai, HI 7 B2
Kawaihae, HI 7 D4
Kaycee, WY 23 E1
Kayenta, AZ 25 A5
Keaau, HI 7 E4
Keams Canyon, AZ 27 A2
Kearney, NE 35 C5
Kearns, UT 90 A4
Kearny, NJ 111 A3
Keaton Beach, FL 67 B3
Keene, NC 118 D2
Keene, NH 72 E3
Keene, NY 72 C1
Keeseville, NY 72 C1
Keewatin, MN 46 D1
Kejimkujik Natl. Park, NS 71 E3
Keller, TX 94 C1
Kelliher, MN 44 B5
Kellogg, ID 18 B5
Kelowna, BC 9 D1
Kelso, CA 17 D2
Kelso, WA 8 E5
Kelvin, AZ 26 D5
Kelwood, MB 31 B2
Kemmerer, WY 23 A3
Kemp, TX 54 B1
Kemptville, NS 71 E4
Kenai, AK 5 C4
Kenai Fjords Natl. Park, AK 5 C4
Kenansville, FL 80 A1
Kendal Green Station, MA 110 A3
Kendallville, IN 60 B3
Kendrick, ID 20 A1
Kenedy, TX 43 E2
Kenly, NC 76 A4
Kenmare, ND 30 E4
Kenmawr, PA 107 B3
Kenmore, WA 82 D1
Kenna, NM 38 C5
Kennebunk, ME 73 A2
Kennebunkport, ME 73 A2
Kennedale, TX 94 C5
Kennedy, NY 61 C1
Kennedy, SK 30 E2
Kenner, LA 55 D4
Kenneth City, FL 122 B4
Kennett, MO 53 C1
Kennewick, WA 11 C1
Keno, OR 12 D1
Kenora, ON 44 B3
Kenosha, WI 49 E2
Kensington, CA 85 D3
Kensington, MD 116 B1
Kent, OH 61 A3
Kent, OR 11 B2
Kent, TX 40 B4
Kent, WA 9 A4
Kent City, MI 60 A1
Kentfield, CA 85 E1
Kentland, IN 49 E4
Kenton, OH 60 D4
Kenton, OK 38 D1
Kenton Vale, KY 108 B4
Kentwood, LA 55 D3
Kenwood, MD 116 B2
Keokea, HI 7 D5
Keokuk, IA 49 A5
Keosauqua, IA 49 A5
Keremeos, BC 9 D2
Kerens, TX 54 B2
Kerhonkson, NY 72 C5
Kerkhoven, MN 46 B4
Kerman, CA 14 E4
Kermit, TX 40 C3
Kermit, WV 63 A2
Kerrick, TX 38 E1
Kerrville, TX 41 C5
Kershaw, SC 65 D1
Keswick, NB 71 C2
Ketchikan, AK 5 F5
Ketchum, ID 20 B5
Ketik, AK 5 B3
Kettering, OH 60 D5
Kettle Falls, MN 44 D4
Kettle Falls, WA 9 E3
Kettleman City, CA 14 E5
Kewanee, IL 49 C4
Kewaunee, WI 47 E4
Key Biscayne, FL 80 B3
Key Largo, FL 80 B4
Key West, FL 80 A5
Keyes Summit, MO 104 B4
Keyport, WA 82 A1
Keyser, WV 61 D4
Keystone, SD 34 D1
Keystone, WV 63 B3
Keystone Heights, FL 67 D3
Keysville, VA 76 A2
Kiel, WI 47 D5
Kihei, HI 7 C3
Kildonan, BC 8 D1
Kilgore, TX 54 C2
Kill Devil Hill, NC 76 D3
Killarney, MB 31 B4
Killdeer, SK 30 A4
Killeen, TX 41 E4
Kim, CO 36 C5
Kimball, MN 46 C4
Kimball, NE 34 C5
Kimball, SD 35 C1
Kimberley, BC 18 B2
Kimberling City, MO 52 E1
Kimberly, OR 11 B3
Kimbro, TN 99 E5
Kincaid, KS 50 B4
Kincardine, ON 58 E4
Kinder, LA 55 A4
King City, CA 14 C4
King City, MO 50 C1
King City, OR 83 A4
King Ferry, NY 72 A4
Kingdom City, MO 51 A2
Kingfield, ME 71 A4
Kingfisher, OK 39 D2
Kingman, AZ 26 A2
Kingman, KS 37 D5
Kings Canyon Natl. Park, CA 15 A4
Kings Mountain, NC 65 C1
Kings Park, NY 74 E1
Kings Point, NY 111 E2
Kingsburg, SC 78 A2
Kingsdown, KS 37 B5
Kingsford, WI 47 D3
Kingsgate, BC 18 B3
Kingsland, GA 67 D2
Kingsley, FL 67 D3
Kingsley, MI 58 A4
Kingsley, PA 72 B5
Kingsport, TN 63 A4
Kingston, NB 71 C2
Kingston, NM 29 C1
Kingston, NY 72 C5
Kingston, OK 52 A5
Kingston, ON 59 E2
Kingston, PA 74 B1
Kingston, RI 73 A4
Kingston, UT 24 D3
Kingstree, SC 65 E2
Kingsville, MD 115 E1
Kingsville, TX 43 E4
Kingwood, WV 61 D4
Kinloch, MO 104 C2
Kinlock, PA 107 E1
Kinsley, KS 37 C4
Kinston, NC 76 B5
Kinton, OR 83 A4
Kinwood, TX 97 C1
Kiowa, CO 36 B2
Kiowa, KS 37 D5
Kiowa, MT 18 E4
Kiowa, OK 52 B4
Kipahulu, HI 7 D3
Kipnuk, AK 5 A4
Kiptopeke, VA 76 C2
Kirby, AR 52 E4
Kirby, TX 96 D3
Kirbyville, TX 54 E4
Kirk, OR 10 E5
Kirkland, TX 39 B4
Kirkland, WA 9 A3
Kirkland Junction, AZ 26 C3
Kirklin, IN 60 A5
Kirklyn, PA 114 A3
Kirksville, MO 50 E1
Kirkwood, MO 104 C4
Kirkwood, NJ 114 E4
Kirwan Heights, PA 107 B4
Kisbey, SK 30 E3
Kissimmee, FL 67 E5
Kit Carson, CO 36 D3
Kitchawan, NY 112 B1
Kitchener, ON 59 A4
Kitimat, BC 5 F6
Kittanning, PA 61 C3
Kittery, ME 73 A2
Kitty Hawk, NC 76 D3
Kivalina, AK 5 B1
Klamath, CA 12 B1
Klamath Falls, OR 12 E1
Klamath River, CA 12 D1
Klondyke, AZ 28 E1
Knightdale, NC 119 D4
Knippa, TX 43 C1
Knob Noster, MO 50 D3
Knolls, UT 22 C5
Knowles Corner, ME 71 B2
Knox, IN 60 A3
Knox, ND 31 B5
Knox City, TX 41 B1
Knoxville, IA 48 D4
Knoxville, PA 61 E1
Knoxville, TN 62 E5
Kobuk Valley Natl. Park, AK 5 B2
Kodiak, AK 5 C5
Kohls Ranch, AZ 26 D4
Kokomo, IN 60 B4
Kooskia, ID 20 A2
Kootenay Bay, BC 18 B2
Kosciusko, MS 53 D5
Kotlick, AK 5 B3
Kotzebue, AK 5 B2
Kountze, TX 54 D4
Koyuk, AK 5 B2
Krebs, OK 52 B3
Kremmling, CO 25 E1
Kress, TX 38 E4
Kresson, NJ 114 E4
Kronau, SK 30 C2
Kukuihaele, HI 7 D4
Kupaahu, HI 7 E5
Kye, IL 102 B2
Kyle, SD 34 E2
Kyle, SK 19 E1
Kyle, TX 41 E5

L

La Babia, COAH 42 E2
La Barge, WY 23 A3
La Belle, FL 69 E2
La Boquilla del Conchos, CHIH 42 A4
La Crosse, KS 37 C3
La Crosse, MN 49 A1
La Cuesta, COAH 42 D2
La Cueva, NM 38 A2
La Cygne, KS 50 C3
La Esmeralda, COAH 42 C4
La Fayette, GA 64 D2
La Fayette, NY 72 A4
La Follette, TN 62 E5
La Galette, PQ 70 D1
La Gloria, NL 43 C5
La Grande, OR 11 D2
La Grange, GA 64 E4
La Grange, IL 49 E3
La Grange, TX 54 A5
La Grange Park, IL 102 B4
La Guadeloupe, PQ 70 E3
La Habra, CA 87 A4
La Habra Heights, CA 87 A3
La Harpe, IL 49 B5
La Honda, CA 84 B2
La Jara, CO 25 E5
La Jara, NM 27 D2
La Jarita, NL 43 B4
La Jolla, CA 17 B5
La Joya, NM 27 D4
La Joya, TX 43 D6
La Junta, CO 36 C4
La Luz, NM 29 E1
La Malbaie, PQ 70 E1
La Mesa, CA 17 B5
La Mirada, CA 87 A4
La Mora, COAH 42 D3
La Moure, ND 33 D3
La Passe, PQ 70 C1
La Perade, PQ 70 C3
La Perla, CHIH 42 B3
La Pine, OR 10 E4
La Plant, SD 33 A4
La Plata, MD 74 B5
La Plata, MO 50 E1
La Pocatiere, PQ 70 E1
La Porte, IN 60 A3
La Porte, TX 56 C1
La Porte City, IA 48 E3
La Presa, CA 89 C3
La Pryor, TX 43 B2
La Puente, CA 87 B2
La Push, WA 8 D3
La Rosetilla, CHIH 42 A3
La Rosita, COAH 42 E3
La Rumorosa, BC 17 C5
La Sal, UT 25 B3
La Sal Junction, UT 25 B3
La Salle, IL 49 D4
La Salle, ON 103 D5
La Tuque, PQ 70 B2
La Verdin, UT 24 B4
La Vergne, TN 99 E5
La Verne, CA 87 D2
La Vernia, TX 43 E1
La Veta, CO 36 B5
Labelle, PQ 70 A4
Lac-aux-Sables, PQ 70 C3
Lac Bouchette, PQ 70 B1
Lac du Flambeau, WI 47 B3
Lac-Etchemin, PQ 70 E3
Lac-Megantic, PQ 70 E4
Lac-Remi, PQ 70 A4
Lachine, PQ 70 B5
Lachute, PQ 70 B5
Lackawanna, NY 59 C5
Lacolle, PQ 70 C5
Lacon, IL 49 C4
Laconia, NH 72 E2
Lacoste, PQ 70 A4
Laddonia, MO 51 A2
Ladue, MO 104 C3
Ladysmith, BC 8 E1
Ladysmith, WI 47 A3
Lafayette, AL 64 D5
Lafayette, CA 85 C5
Lafayette, CO 36 B1
Lafayette, IN 60 A5
Lafayette, LA 55 B4
Lafayette Hill, PA 114 A1
Lafitte, LA 55 D5
Lafleche, SK 30 A3
Lagrange, IN 60 B3
Lagrange, ME 71 B4
Laguna, NM 27 D3
Laguna, TX 43 B1
Laguna Beach, CA 17 A3
Laguna Niguel, CA 88 D3
Lagunitas, NM 27 D2
Lahaina, HI 7 C3
Laie, HI 7 A2
Lake, ID 21 A4
Lake, MO 104 A3
Lake, WY 21 B5
Lake Alma, SK 30 C4
Lake Andes, SD 35 D2
Lake Apopka, FL 120 A1
Lake Arrowhead, CA 17 B3
Lake Arthur, LA 55 A5
Lake Benton, MN 46 A5
Lake Bronson, MN 31 E4
Lake Buena Vista, FL 120 B5
Lake Butler, FL 67 C3
Lake Chain Hill, FL 120 C3
Lake Charles, LA 54 E5
Lake City, CO 25 D4
Lake City, FL 67 C3
Lake City, GA 121 D5
Lake City, MI 58 B4
Lake City, MN 46 E5
Lake City, SC 65 E2
Lake City, SD 33 E3
Lake City, TN 62 E5
Lake Clark Natl. Park and Preserve, AK 5 C4
Lake Clear Junction, NY 72 B1
Lake Cowichan, BC 8 E1
Lake Elsinore, CA 17 B3
Lake End, LA 54 E2
Lake Forest Park, WA 82 D1
Lake Geneva, WI 49 D2
Lake George, CO 36 A3
Lake George, NY 72 C3
Lake Harbor, FL 80 A2
Lake Havasu City, AZ 26 A3
Lake Isabella, CA 17 A1
Lake Itasca, MN 46 B1
Lake Junaluska, NC 65 A1
Lake Luzerne, NY 72 C3
Lake Mills, IA 48 D1
Lake Orion, MI 60 D1
Lake Oswego, OR 83 C4
Lake Park, MN 46 A2
Lake Parlin, ME 71 A4
Lake Placid, FL 69 E1
Lake Placid, NY 72 B1
Lake Providence, LA 55 C1
Lake Quivera, KS 92 A4
Lake View, IA 48 B3
Lake View, NB 71 E2
Lake Village, AR 53 B5
Lake Wales, FL 69 E1
Lake Waukomis, MO 92 B1
Lake Worth, FL 80 B2
Lakecreek, OR 10 D5
Lakehurst, NJ 74 D2
Lakeland, FL 69 D1
Lakeland, GA 67 B2
Lakeland, LA 55 C4
Lakeport, CA 12 B5
Lakeshire, MO 104 D4
Lakeshore, CA 15 A3
Lakeside, BC 9 E1
Lakeside, CA 89 E1
Lakeside Park, KY 108 B5
Laketown, UT 22 E3
Lakeview, MT 20 E4
Lakeview, OR 13 A1
Lakeville, MN 46 D5
Lakeville, NY 59 D4
Lakewood, CA 86 D4
Lakewood, CO 93 B3
Lakewood, NJ 74 D2
Lakewood, NM 40 B2
Lakewood, OH 61 A2
Lakewood, TN 99 D2
Lakin, KS 37 A4
Lakota, ND 31 D5
Lamar, CO 36 D4
Lamar, MO 50 C5
Lambert, MS 53 C4
Lamberton, MN 46 B5
Lambertville, NJ 74 C2
Lame Deer, MT 21 E3
Lamesa, TX 40 E1
Lamkin, TX 41 D3
Lamoni, IA 48 D5
Lamont, FL 67 B3
Lamont, WY 23 D3
Lampasas, TX 41 D4
Lampazos de Naranjo, NL 43 B5
Lamy, NM 27 E3
Lanagan, MO 52 C1
Lanai City, HI 7 C3
Lanark Village, FL 67 A4
Lancaster, CA 17 A2
Lancaster, KY 62 D3
Lancaster, MN 31 E4
Lancaster, MO 48 E5
Lancaster, NH 70 E5
Lancaster, NY 59 D5
Lancaster, OH 61 A5
Lancaster, PA 74 B3
Lancaster, SC 65 D1
Lancaster, TX 95 C5
Lancaster, WI 49 B2
Lancasterville, PA 114 A1
Lance Creek, WY 34 B2
Lander, WY 23 C2
Landersdale, IN 105 B5
Landfall, MN 100 E3
Landover Hills, MD 116 D2
Landrum, SC 65 B1
Landsdowne, PA 114 B3
Lanett, AL 64 D5
Langdon, ND 31 B4
Langenburg, SK 30 E1
Langford Cove, TN 99 E2
Langlade, WI 47 C3
Langley, BC 9 A1
Langley, VA 116 B2
Langley Park, MD 116 C1
Langtry, TX 42 E1
Lanham, MD 116 E2
Lannon, WI 101 B2
L'Annonciation, PQ 70 A4
Lansdowne, MD 115 C4
L'Anse, MI 47 C1
Lansing, IA 49 A1
Lansing, MI 60 C1
Lansing, NY 72 A5
Lantana, FL 80 B2
Lantier, PQ 70 B4
Lantz Corners, PA 61 D1
Laona, WI 47 C3
Lapeer, MI 58 D5
Laporte, PA 74 A1
Larabee, PA 61 D1
Laramie, WY 34 A4
Larchmont, NY 112 C5
Laredo, TX 43 C4
Largo, MD 116 E2
Larimore, MO 104 E1
Larimore, ND 31 D5
Larkspur, CA 85 E1
Larned, KS 37 C4
Las Animas, CO 36 D4
Las Bostonnais, PQ 70 B2
Las Cruces, CA 16 D2
Las Cruces, NM 29 D2
Las Enchilayas, SON 28 B3
Las Norias, COAH 42 C4
Las Nutrias, NM 27 D4
Las Palomas, NM 29 C1
Las Vegas, NM 38 A2
Las Vegas, NV 15 E5
L'Ascension, PQ 70 A4
Lassen Volcanic Natl. Park 12 E3
Lassiter, NC 119 E2
L'Assomption, PQ 70 B4
Last Chance, CO 36 C2
Lathrop, MI 47 D2
Lathrup Village, MI 103 B2
Latta, SC 65 E1
Lauderdale, MN 100 C3
Lauderdale, MS 66 A1
Laurel, DE 74 C5
Laurel, FL 69 D2
Laurel, MD 74 B4
Laurel, MS 55 E2
Laurel, MT 21 C3
Laurel, NE 35 E3
Laurel Gardens, PA 107 B2
Laurelville, OH 60 E5
Laurens, IA 48 B2
Laurens, SC 65 C2
Laurier, WA 9 E2
Laurinburg, NC 65 E1
Laurium, MI 47 C1
Lauzon, PQ 70 D2
Lava Beds Natl. Mon., CA 12 E1
Laval, PQ 70 B5
Lavaltrie, PQ 70 B4
Laveen, AZ 91 A5
Laverne, OK 39 B1
Laverock, PA 114 B1
Lavina, MT 21 C2
Lavonia, GA 65 A2
Lawn, TX 41 C2
Lawndale, CA 86 B3
Lawrence, IN 105 D2
Lawrence, KS 50 B3
Lawrence, MA 73 A3
Lawrence, PA 107 B5
Lawrence Station, NB 71 C3
Lawrenceburg, IN 62 C1
Lawrenceburg, KY 62 D3
Lawrenceburg, TN 64 A2
Lawrenceville, GA 65 A3
Lawrenceville, IL 51 E2
Lawrenceville, NY 72 B1
Lawrenceville, PA 59 E5
Lawrenceville, VA 76 A3
Lawson, SK 30 A1
Lawtey, FL 67 D3
Lawton, OK 39 D4
Laytonville, CA 12 B4
Le Center, MN 46 C5
Le Gite-du-Berger, PQ 70 C1
Le Land, GA 121 A2
Le Mars, IA 48 A2
Le Roy, NY 59 D4
Le Sueur, MN 46 C5
Lea, NM 40 C2
Leachville, AR 53 C1
Lead, SD 32 C5
Lead Hill, AR 52 E1
Leader, SK 19 C1
Leadore, ID 20 D4
Leadville, CO 25 E2
Leahy, WA 9 D4
Leakesville, MS 66 A3
Leakey, TX 43 B1
Leander, TX 41 E4
Leary, GA 66 E1
Leasburg, NM 29 D2
Leavenworth, KS 50 C2
Leavenworth, WA 9 B4
Leawood, KS 92 C4
Lebam, WA 8 D5
Lebanon, IN 60 B5
Lebanon, KS 37 D2
Lebanon, KY 62 C3
Lebanon, MO 50 E4
Lebanon, NE 36 B1
Lebanon, NH 72 D2
Lebanon, OR 10 D2
Lebanon, PA 74 B2
Lebanon, TN 62 B5
Lebanon, VA 63 B4
Lebanon Station, FL 67 C4
Lebeau, LA 55 B4
Lebec, CA 16 E2
Lebret, SK 30 D1
Lecompte, LA 55 A3
Lee, MA 72 D4
Lee, ME 71 B3
Lee Vining, CA 15 A2
Lee's Summit, MO 92 E5
Leechburg, PA 107 E2
Leedey, OK 39 C2
Leeds, AL 64 C4
Leeds, ND 31 B5
Leeper, PA 61 C2
Lees, TX 40 E2
Lees Ferry, AZ 24 D5
Leesburg, FL 67 D4
Leesburg, GA 67 A1
Leesburg, OH 62 E1
Leesburg, VA 74 A4
Leesville, LA 54 E3
Leesville, NC 119 A2
Leggett, CA 12 B3
Lehi, UT 22 D5
Lehigh Acres, FL 69 E2
Lehighton, PA 74 B2
Lehman, TX 38 D5
Lehr, ND 33 C3
Leithchfield, KY 62 B4
Leland, MI 58 A3
Leland, MS 53 C5
Lemay, MO 104 D5
Lemhi, ID 20 C4
Lemmon, SD 32 E3
Lemolo, WA 82 A1
Lemon Grove, CA 89 C3
Lenexa, KS 92 A5
Lennoxville, PQ 70 D4
Lenoir, NC 63 C5
Lenoir City, TN 64 E1
Lenola, NJ 114 D2
Lenox, MA 72 D4
Leola, SD 33 C3
Leominster, MA 72 E3
Leon, IA 48 D5
Leon Valley, TX 96 B2
Leonard, ND 33 E2
Leonard, TX 52 B5
Leonardtown, MD 74 B5
Leonia, NJ 111 B2
Leoti, KS 37 A4
Lepreau, NB 71 D3
Les-Becquets, PQ 70 C3
Les Chenaux, PQ 70 D2
Leslie, AR 53 A2
Leslie, ID 20 C5
Leslie, MI 60 C1
Letete, NB 71 D3
Lethbridge, AB 18 E2
Leucadia, CA 17 B4
Levan, UT 24 D1
Levelland, TX 38 D5
Levis, PQ 70 D2
Lewellen, NE 34 E5
Lewes, DE 74 C4
Lewisburg, PA 61 E2
Lewisburg, TN 64 B1
Lewisburg, WV 63 C2
Lewisdale, MD 116 C2
Lewiston, ID 20 A1
Lewiston, ME 73 A1
Lewiston, MT 21 C1
Lewiston, NY 59 C4
Lewiston, PA 61 E2
Lewistown, IL 49 B5
Lewisville, AR 52 E5
Lewisville, TX 54 A1
Lexington, GA 65 A3
Lexington, KY 62 D2
Lexington, MA 110 A2
Lexington, MI 58 E5
Lexington, MN 100 C1
Lexington, MO 50 D2
Lexington, MS 53 D5
Lexington, NC 63 D5
Lexington, NE 35 B5
Lexington, OR 11 C2
Lexington, SC 65 D2
Lexington, TN 53 E1
Lexington, VA 63 D2
Lexington Park, MD 74 B5
Leyden, CO 93 A1
Leyendecker, NV 24 B1
Libby, MN 46 C2
Libby, MT 18 B4
Liberal, OK 39 A1
Liberty, IN 60 C5
Liberty, KY 62 D4
Liberty, ME 71 B5
Liberty, MO 50 C2
Liberty, MS 55 C3
Liberty, NC 63 E4
Liberty, NY 72 C5
Liberty, PA 107 E4
Liberty, SC 65 B2
Liberty, TX 54 D5
Libertytown, MD 74 A4
Libertyville, AL 66 C2
Library, PA 107 C5
Licking, MO 51 A4
Lickton, TN 99 B1
Lida, NV 15 C3
Lidgerwood, ND 33 E3
Ligonier, IN 60 B3
Ligonier, PA 61 D3
Lihue, HI 6 D1
Likely, CA 13 A2
Lilburn, GA 121 E1
Lilley, MI 58 A5
Lillington, NC 76 A5
Lilydale, MN 100 D4
Lima, OH 60 D4
Limestone, ME 71 B1
Limestone, NB 71 B1
Limon, CO 36 C2
Lincoln, CA 12 D5
Lincoln, IL 49 C5
Lincoln, KS 37 D3
Lincoln, MA 110 A3
Lincoln, ME 71 B3
Lincoln, MT 20 E1

Bold type indicates cities with 100,000 population or more.

Place Name / Page Number / Grid Number
Stantonburg **118** C5

Lincoln, NE **35** E5
Lincoln, NM **38** A5
Lincoln, PA **107** E5
Lincoln Acres, CA **89** C4
Lincoln Beach, PA **107** E1
Lincoln City, OR .. **10** C2
Lincoln Heights, OH **108** B2
Lincoln Park, CO . **36** A4
Lincoln Park, MI **103** C5
Lincolnia, VA **116** B4
Lincolnton, GA **65** B3
Lincolnton, NC **63** C5
Lind, WA **9** D5
Lindale, OH **108** E5
Linden, AL **66** B1
Linden, NJ **74** D1
Linden, TN **64** A1
Linden, TX **54** D1
Lindenwold, NJ **114** E4
Lindrith, NM **27** D1
Lindsay, MI **32** B1
Lindsay, OK **39** E2
Lindsay, ON **59** C3
Lindsborg, KS **37** E3
Lindstrom, MN **46** D4
Lingle, WY **34** C3
Lingo, NM **38** C5
Linhart, PA **107** E3
Liniera [St.-Come], PQ **70** E3
Linn, KS **37** E2
Linn, MO **51** A3
Linn, TX **43** E5
Linn, WV **61** C5
Linndale, OH **106** B3
Linthicum Heights, MD **115** C5
Linton, IN **62** A2
Linton, ND **33** B3
Linwood, WV **63** C1
Linworth, OH **109** B2
Lipton, SK **30** C1
Lisabuela, WA **82** A5
Lisbon, ND **33** D2
Lisbon, NH **72** E1
Lisbon, OH **61** B3
Lisbon Falls, ME . **73** A1
Lisco, NE **34** D4
L'Islet, PQ **70** F2
Lisman, AL **66** A1
Listowel, ON **59** A4
Litchfield, CA **12** E4
Litchfield, CT **72** D5
Litchfield, IL **51** C2
Litchfield, MN **46** B4
Litchfield, NE **35** C5
Lithopolis, OH ... **109** E5
Lititz, PA **74** B3
Little America, WY **23** B4
Little Canada, MN **100** D2
Little Creek, TN .. **99** B2
Little Falls, MN ... **46** C3
Little Falls, NY **72** B3
Little Fork, MN **44** C4
Little Lake, CA **15** B5
Little Nahant, MA **110** E2
Little River, NS ... **71** E4
Little River, SC **78** B2
Little Rock, AR . **53** A3
Little Shasta, CA **12** D1
Little Valley, NY . **59** D5
Littlefield, AZ **24** B5
Littlefield, TX **38** D5
Littlestown, PA ... **74** A3
Littleton, CO **93** B5
Littleton, NH **72** E1
Live Oak, CA **12** D5
Live Oak, FL **67** C3
Live Oak, TX **96** E2
Livengood, AK **5** C2
Livermore, CA **14** C2
Livermore, ME **71** A5
Livermore Falls, ME **71** A5
Livingston, AL **66** A1
Livingston, MT **21** B3
Livingston, TN **62** C5
Livingston, TX **54** C4
Livingstonville, NY **72** C4
Livonia, MI **60** D1
Lizton, IN **60** A5
Llanerch, PA **114** A3
Llano, TX **41** D4
Llaves, NM **27** D1
Loa, UT **24** D3
Lobitos, CA **84** D1
Lock Haven, PA ... **61** E2
Lockbourne, OH **109** C5
Locke, NY **72** A4
Lockes, NV **15** E2
Lockesburg, AR ... **52** D4
Lockhart, FL **120** C1
Lockhart, MS **66** A1
Lockhart, TX **41** E5
Lockland, OH **108** B2
Lockport, MB **31** E2
Lockport, NY **59** C4
Loco Hills, NM **40** B1
Locust Grove, AR **53** A2
Locust Grove, OH **62** E1
Locust Grove, OK **52** C1
Locust Lake, OH **108** E4
Lodge Grass, MT **21** E4
Lodgepole, NE **34** D5
Lodgepole, SD **32** D3
Lodi, CA **14** D2
Lodi, NJ **111** A2
Lodi, OH **61** A3
Lodoga, CA **12** C5
Logan, IA **48** A4
Logan, NM **38** C3
Logan, OH **61** A5
Logan, UT **22** E3
Logan, WV **63** B2
Logans Ferry, PA **107** E1
Logansport, IN **60** A4
Logansport, LA **54** D2
Loganville, GA **65** A3
Loleta, CA **12** B2
Lolo, MT **20** C1
Lolo Hot Springs, MT **20** C1
Loma, CO **25** C2
Loma, MI **19** B4
Loma Alta, TX **41** A5
Loma Mar, CA **84** B1
Loman, MN **44** C4
Lometa, TX **41** D4
Lomita, CA **86** B5
Lompoc, CA **16** D1
London, KY **62** E4
London, OH **60** E5
London, ON **59** A5
London, TX **41** C4
Londonderry, VT . **72** D3
Lone Pine, CA **15** B4
Lonetree, WY **23** A5
Long Beach, CA **17** A3
Long Beach, MS .. **55** E4
Long Beach, NC .. **78** B2
Long Beach, NY .. **74** E1
Long Beach, WA ... **8** D5
Long Branch, NJ . **74** D2
Long Creek, OR ... **11** C3
Long Hill, CT **113** A2
Long Key, FL **80** B5
Long Lake, NY **72** B2
Long Prairie, MN **46** B3
Long Valley, SD .. **34** E2
Long Valley Junction, UT **24** C4
Longboat Key, FL **69** D2
Longmire, WA **9** A5
Longmont, CO **36** B1
Longueuil, PQ .. **70** C5
Longview, TX **54** C2
Longview, WA **8** E5
Lonoke, AR **53** A3
Lonsdale, MN **46** D5
Loogootee, IN **62** A2
Lookout, CA **12** E2
Lookout Mountain, TN **64** D2
Loop, TX **40** D1
Lordsburg, NM **29** B2
Loreburn, SK **30** A1
Loring, MT **19** E4
Loris, SC **78** A2
Los Alamitos, CA **86** E5
Los Alamos, CA .. **16** D1
Los Alamos, NM . **27** E2
Los Algodnes, BC **17** B5
Los Altos, CA **84** C3
Los Altos Hills, CA **84** C3
Los Angeles, CA **16** A3
Los Angeles, TX .. **43** C2
Los Banos, CA **14** D3
Los Chacuales, SON **28** C4
Los Garcia, CHIH **42** A3
Los Gatos, CA **14** C2
Los Le Febres, NM **38** A2
Los Lunas, NM **27** D3
Los Molinos, CA . **12** D4
Los Montoyas, NM **38** A3
Los Nietos, CA **86** E3
Los Serranos, CA **87** D4
Los Tajito, SON ... **28** B3
Los Vidrios, SON **28** A1
Lost Hills, CA **14** E5
Lostine, OR **11** E2
Lothair, MT **19** B4
Loudonville, OH .. **61** A3
Louisa, KY **63** A2
Louisa, VA **76** A1
Louisburg, KS **50** C3
Louisburg, MO **50** E4
Louise, MS **53** C5
Louisiana, MO **51** B2
Louisville, GA **65** C4
Louisville, KY ... **62** C2
Louisville, MS **53** E5
Louisville, PQ **70** C4
Loup City, NE **35** C5
Love Point, MD ... **74** B4
Lovedale, PA **107** E5
Lovelady, TX **54** C3
Loveland, CO **36** B1
Loveland, OH **108** D1
Lovell, WY **21** D4
Lovell Corners, MA **110** E5
Lovelock, NV **13** B4
Loving, NM **40** B2
Lovington, VA **63** E2
Lovington, IL **51** D1
Lovington, NM **40** C1
Lowell, ID **20** B2
Lowell, IN **49** F4
Lowell, MA **73** A3
Lower Burrell, PA **107** E1
Lowes Grave, NC **118** E3
Lowman, ID **20** A5
Lowville, NY **72** A3
Loyal Valley, TX .. **41** C5
Loysville, PA **74** A3
Luara Lynn, AZ ... **27** A5
Lubbock, TX **38** E5
Lubec, ME **71** D3
Lucas, IA **48** D5
Lucedale, MS **66** A3
Lucerne, CO **36** B1
Lucerne, WA **9** B3
Lucerne Valley, CA **17** C2
Lucia, CA **14** C4
Ludden, ND **33** D3
Ludington, MI **58** A5
Ludlow, CA **17** D2
Ludlow, KY **108** B4
Ludlow, NB **71** C2
Ludlow, SD **32** D3
Ludlow, VT **72** D2
Ludowici, GA **65** D5
Lueders, TX **41** C1
Lufkin, TX **54** D3
Lukachukai, AZ ... **27** B1
Luling, TX **43** E1
Lumberton, MS ... **55** E3
Lumberton, NC ... **78** A1
Lumpkin, GA **66** E1
Lumsden, SK **30** C1
Luna, NM **27** B5
Lund, BC **5** G7
Lund, NV **24** A2
Lund, UT **24** B3
Lundar, MB **31** D1
Lunenburg, VT **72** F1
Luning, NV **15** B2
Lupton, AZ **27** B2
Luray, KS **37** D3
Luray, VA **61** E5
Lusby, MD **74** B5
Lusk, WY **34** B3
Lutesville, MO **51** C4
Lutie, TX **39** B3
Lutzen, MN **44** A5
Luverne, AL **66** C1
Luverne, MN **48** A1
Lycan, CO **36** E5
Lyeffion, AL **66** C2
Lyford, TX **43** E5
Lykens, PA **74** A2
Lynch, KY **63** A4
Lynch, NE **35** D2
Lynchburg, TN **64** C2
Lynchburg, VA **63** F2
Lyndhurst, NJ **111** A3
Lyndhurst, OH ... **106** E1
Lyndon, KS **50** B3
Lyndonville, VT ... **72** D1
Lynn, IN **60** C5
Lynn, MA **73** A3
Lynn Haven, FL ... **66** D3
Lynndyl, UT **24** D1
Lynnfield, MA **110** C1
Lynnhurst, MA **110** C1
Lynnville, KY **51** E5
Lynwood, CA **86** C3
Lynwood Center, WA **82** A2
Lynn Mountain, NY **72** B1
Lyons, CO **36** A1
Lyons, GA **65** C5
Lyons, IL **102** C4
Lyons, KS **37** D4
Lyons, NY **59** F4
Lyons Falls, NY ... **72** A3
Lysite, WY **23** D2
Lytle, TX **43** D1

M

Maalaea, HI **7** C3
Mabelle, TX **39** C5
Mableton, GA **121** A2
Mabscott, WV **63** B2
Mabton, WA **11** C1
Macclenny, FL **67** D3
Macdoel, CA **12** D1
Macdona, TX **96** A4
Macedonia, NC **119** B5
Maceo, KY **62** A3
Maces Bay, NB ... **71** D3
Machias, ME **71** C4
Mack, CO **25** B2
Mackay, ID **20** C5
Mackinac Island, MI **58** B2
Mackinaw City, MI **58** B2
Macks Creek, MO **50** E4
Macomb, IL **49** B5
Macon, GA **65** A4
Macon, MO **50** E1
Mac's Corner, SD **33** C5
Macwahoc, ME .. **71** B3
Mad River, CA **12** B3
Madawaska, ME **71** A1
Madeira Beach, FL **69** C1
Madelia, MN **46** C5
Madeline, CA **12** E3
Madera, CA **14** E3
Madera Canyon, AZ **28** D2
Madiera, OH **108** C2
Madill, OK **52** A4
Madison, FL **67** B3
Madison, GA **65** A3
Madison, IL **104** E2
Madison, IN **62** C2
Madison, KS **50** A4
Madison, ME **71** A4
Madison, MN **46** A4
Madison, NC **63** D4
Madison, NE **35** E4
Madison, SD **35** E1
Madison, TN **99** C2
Madison, WI **49** C1
Madison, WV **63** D2
Madison, WY **21** A4
Madison Heights, MI **103** C1
Madisonville, KY **62** A4
Madisonville, TN **64** E1
Madisonville, TX **54** B4
Madras, OR **11** A3
Maeser, UT **23** B5
Magdalena, NM .. **27** D4
Magdalena de Kino, SON **28** D4
Magee, MS **55** D2
Magnolia, AR **52** E5
Magnolia, MS **55** D3
Magnolia, NJ **114** D4
Magnolia Park, FL **120** A1
Magog, PQ **70** D5
Magrath, AB **18** E3
Mahnomen, MN . **46** A1
Mahtomedi, MN **100** E1
Maida, ND **31** C4
Main Street Station, MA **110** A1
Maitland, FL **120** C1
Maize, KS **37** E4
Major's Place, NV **24** A2
Malabar, FL **67** F5
Malad City, ID **22** D3
Malaga, NJ **74** C3
Malaga, NM **40** B2
Malden, MA **110** C2
Malden, MO **51** C5
Malibu, CA **16** E3
Maljamar, NM **40** C1
Malo, WA **9** E3
Malone, FL **66** E2
Malone, NY **72** B1
Malta, CO **25** E2
Malta, ID **22** C2
Malta, MT **19** E5
Malvern, AR **52** F4
Mamaroneck, NY **112** C5
Mammoth, AZ **28** E1
Mammoth Cave Natl. Park, KY **62** B4
Mammoth Hot Springs, WY **21** A4
Mammoth Lakes, CA **15** A3
Mammoth Spring, AR **53** B1
Mamou, LA **55** A4
Man, WV **63** B2
Manahawkin, NJ **74** D3
Mancelona, MI ... **58** B3
Manchester, GA . **64** F4
Manchester, IA ... **49** A2
Manchester, KY .. **62** E4
Manchester, MD **74** A3
Manchester, ME . **71** A5
Manchester, MO **104** B4
Manchester, NH . **72** E2
Manchester, OH . **62** E1
Manchester, TN . **64** C1
Manchester, WA **82** A3
Manchester Depot, VT **72** D3
Mancos, CO **25** C5
Mandan, ND **33** A2
Manderson, WY . **21** D5
Mandeville, LA ... **55** D4
Mangum, OK **39** C4
Manhasset, NY **111** E2
Manhattan, KS **50** A2
Manhattan, MT ... **21** A3
Manhattan, NV ... **15** C2
Manila, AR **53** C1
Manila, UT **23** B5
Manistee, MI **58** A4
Manistique, MI ... **47** E2
Manitou, MB **31** C3
Manitou Beach, WA **82** B2
Manitou Springs, CO **36** B3
Manitowoc, WI .. **47** D5
Manitowish, WI . **47** B2
Mankato, KS **37** D2
Mankato, MN **46** C5
Mankota, SK **19** E3
Manley Hot Springs, AK **5** C3
Manlius, NY **72** A4
Manly, IA **48** D2
Manning, IA **48** B4
Manning, ND **32** D1
Manning, OR **10** D1
Manning, SC **65** E2
Mannington, WV **61** C5
Manns Harbor, NC **76** D3
Manor, TX **41** E5
Manorhaven, NY **111** E1
Manouane, PQ **70** A3
Mansfield, AR **52** D3
Mansfield, LA **54** E2
Mansfield, MA ... **73** A3
Mansfield, MO **50** E5
Mansfield, OH **60** E3
Mansfield, PA **61** E1
Mansfield, WA **9** C4
Manson, WA **9** C3
Manteca, CA **14** D2
Manteo, NC **76** D3
Manti, UT **24** E2
Manton, MI **58** A4
Mantua, NJ **114** C5
Manvel, ND **31** E5
Manville, WY **34** B3
Many, LA **54** E3
Manyberries, AB **19** B3
Manzanita, WA .. **82** A1
Manzanita Lake, CA **12** D3
Manzanola, CO ... **36** C4
Maple Creek, SK **19** C2
Maple Grove, PQ **70** D3
Maple Heights, OH **106** E3
Maple Shade, PA **114** D3
Maple Valley, WA **9** A4
Maple View, NY . **72** A3
Maplesville, AL .. **64** C5
Mapleton, IA **48** A3
Maplewood, MN **100** D2
Maplewood, MO **104** D3
Maplewood, NB . **71** C2
Maplewood, WA **82** D5
Maquoketa, IA **49** B3
Marana, AZ **28** D1
Marathon, FL **80** A5
Marathon, TX **40** C5
Marble Canyon, AZ **24** D5
Marble Cliff, OH **109** B3
Marble Falls, TX . **41** D4
Marblehead, MA **73** A3
Marceline, MO **50** E1
Marcell, MN **46** C1
Marcellus, MI **60** A2
Marcoux, MN **46** A1
Marenisco, MI **47** B2
Marfa, TX **40** B5
Margaretville, NY **72** C4
Marianna, AR **53** C3
Marianna, FL **66** E3
Maricopa, CA **16** E1
Mariemont, OH . **108** C3
Marienville, PA ... **61** D1
Marietta, GA **64** E3
Marietta, OH **61** B5
Marietta, OK **39** E5
Marieville, PQ **70** C5
Marin City, CA **85** D1
Marine City, MI .. **60** E1
Marineland, FL **67** E3
Marinette, WI **47** D3
Marion, AL **64** B5
Marion, AR **53** C2
Marion, IL **51** D4
Marion, IN **60** B4
Marion, KS **37** E4
Marion, KY **51** F4
Marion, MI **58** B4
Marion, NC **63** B5
Marion, OH **60** E4
Marion, SC **78** A2
Marion, VA **63** B3
Mariposa, CA **14** E3
Marissa, IL **51** C3
Marked Tree, AR **53** C2
Markham, ON **59** C3
Markleeville, CA . **15** A1
Marks, MS **53** C4
Marksville, LA **55** B3
Marlborough, MA **73** A3
Marlborough, MO **104** D4
Marlette, MI **58** D5
Marlin, TX **54** A3
Marlinton, WV **63** D1
Marlow, NC **63** E4
Marlow Heights, MD **116** D4
Marlton, NJ **114** E3
Marmarth, ND **32** C3
Marmet, WV **63** B2
Marquette, MI **47** D1
Marrero, LA **98** C5
Mars, PA **61** C3
Mars Hill, ME **71** B2
Marshall, AR **52** E2
Marshall, CO **36** A1
Marshall, IL **51** E1
Marshall, MI **60** B2
Marshall, MN **46** A5
Marshall, MO **50** D2
Marshall, TX **54** D1
Marshall, VA **74** A5
Marshalltown, IA **48** D3
Marshfield, MO .. **50** E5
Marshfield, VT ... **72** D1
Marshfield, WI ... **47** B4
Marsland, NE **34** D3
Martin, SD **34** E2
Martin, TN **51** E5
Martinez, CA **85** E5
Martins Beach, NJ **114** E2
Martins Ferry, CA **12** B2
Martins Ferry, OH **61** B4
Martinsburg, WV **61** E4
Martinsville, IN ... **62** B1
Martinsville, VA . **63** D3
Marvel, AR **53** C3
Maryhill, WA **11** B1
Maryland Heights, MO **104** B2
Marys Corner, WA **8** E5
Marysvale, UT **24** D3
Marysville, WA **9** A3
Marysville, CA **12** D5
Marysville, KS **50** A2
Marysville, OH **60** E4
Maryville, MO **50** C1
Maryville, TN **64** E1
Masardis, ME **71** B2
Masefield, SK **19** E3
Mason, MI **60** C1
Mason, TN **53** D2
Mason, TX **41** C4
Mason City, IA **48** D2
Masontown, PA .. **61** C4
Masonville, NJ .. **114** E2
Masouche, PQ **70** B4
Mass City, MI **47** C1
Massadona, CO .. **25** C1
Massena, NY **72** A1
Massillon, OH **61** A3
Masson, PQ **70** A5
Masterson, TX **38** E2
Mastic Beach, NY **74** E1
Matador, TX **39** A5
Matagorda, TX ... **58** B2
Matamoros, TAMPS **56** A6
Matawin, PQ **70** B3
Matheson, CO **36** C3
Mathis, TX **43** E3
Mathison, MS **53** E4
Mattawamkeag, ME **71** B3
Mattese, MO **104** D5
Matthews, NC .. **117** E4
Mattoon, IL **51** E1
Maud, TX **52** D5
Maumee, AR **52** E1
Maumee, OH **60** D2
Maunaloa, HI **7** B2
Maupin, OR **11** A2
Maurine, SD **32** D4
Mauston, WI **47** B5
Mauvella, MS **66** A3
Mauzy, VA **61** E5
Max, ND **33** A1
Maxwell, CA **12** C5
Maxwell, NM **38** B1
Mayaguez, PR **6** A4
Maybell, CO **23** C5
Mayer, AZ **26** C3
Mayfield, KY **51** E5
Mayfield, ME **71** A4
Mayfield Heights, OH **106** E1
Mayhill, NM **40** A1
Mayo, FL **67** B3
Mays Landing, NJ **74** D3
Mays Lick, KY **62** E2
Maysville, KY **62** E2
Mayville, ND **33** C1
Maywood, CA **86** D2
Maywood, IL **102** B3
Maywood, NJ ... **111** A1
Maywood Park, OR **83** D3
Mazama, WA **9** C2
McAdam, NB **71** C3
McAdoo, PA **74** B2
McAlester, OK **52** B3
McAlister, NM **38** C4
McAllaster, KS **37** A3
McAllen, TX **43** E6
McArthur, OH **61** A5
McAuley, MB **31** A2
McBain, MI **58** B4
McBee, SC **65** E1
McCall, ID **20** A3
McCamey, TX **40** E4
McCammon, ID ... **22** D2
McCloud, CA **12** D2
McColl, SC **65** E1
McColloms, NY ... **72** B1
McComb, MS **55** D3
McConnells, SC .. **65** C1
McConnellsburg, PA **61** E3
McConnellsville, OH **61** A5
McCook, IL **102** B4
McCook, NE **37** A1
McCordsville, IN **105** E1
McCormick, SC ... **65** B3
McCreary, MB **31** B1
McCredie Springs, OR **10** E4
McCrory, AR **53** B2
McDaniels, KY **62** B3
McDermitt, NV ... **13** D2
McDonald, KS **37** A2
McDonald, NM **40** C1
McDonald, PA .. **107** A5
McDonough, GA . **64** F4
McGehee, AR **53** B5
McGill, NV **24** A1
McGivney, NB **71** C2
McGregor, IA **49** A2
McGregor, MN **46** C2
McGregor, ND **30** D4
McGregor, TX **41** E3
McHenry, IL **49** D2
McHenry Natl. Mon., MD **115** D4
McIntosh, FL **67** D4
McIntosh, SD **33** A3
McKees Rocks, PA **107** B3
McKeesport, PA **107** D4
McKeever, NY **72** B3
McKenney, VA **76** A2
McKenzie, AL **66** C2
McKenzie, TN **53** E1
McKinney, TX **54** A1
McKittrick, CA **16** F1
McLain, MS **66** A3
McLaughlin, SD .. **33** A3
McLean, IL **49** D5
McLean, TX **39** B3
McLean, VA **116** A3
McLeansboro, IL . **51** E3
McMicken Heights, WA **82** C5
McMinnville, OR **10** D1
McMinnville, TN **64** C1
McMurray, PA .. **107** B5
McNary, AZ **27** A4
McNary, TX **29** E3
McNeal, AZ **29** A2
McPherson, KS ... **37** E4
McRae, GA **65** B5
Meacham, OR **11** D2
Meade, KS **37** B5
Meadow, SD **32** E4
Meadow, TX **40** E1
Meadowhurst, OR **83** A2
Meadows, MD .. **116** E3
Meadville, PA **61** B2
Mechanic Falls, ME **73** A1
Mechanicsburg, OH **60** D4
Mechanicville, NY **72** C3
Medart, FL **67** A3
Medford, MA **110** C2
Medford, OK **39** E1
Medford, OR **10** D5
Medford, WI **47** B4
Medical Springs, OR **11** E3
Medicine Bow, WY **34** A4
Medicine Hat, AB **19** B2
Medicine Lake, MN **100** A3
Medicine Lake, MT **30** C5
Medicine Lodge, KS **37** D5
Medina, NY **59** D4
Medina, OH **61** A3
Medina, TX **43** C1
Medina, WA **82** D3
Medley, FL **123** B3
Medora, ND **32** D2
Medway, ME **71** B3
Meeker, CO **25** D1
Meeker, OK **52** A2
Meeteetse, WY .. **21** C5
Megargel, TX **39** C5
Megler, WA **8** D5
Mehlville, MO .. **104** D5
Meigs, GA **67** A2
Meiserville, PA ... **74** A2
Melbourne, AR ... **53** A1
Melbourne, FL **67** F5
Melbourne, PQ **70** D4
Melchor Múzquiz, COAH **42** E3
Melita, MB **31** A3
Mellen, WI **47** A2
Melocheville, PQ **70** B5
Melrose, AR **53** A2
Melrose, MA **110** C2
Melrose, MT **20** E3
Melrose, NM **38** C4
Melrose Park, IL **102** B3
Melrose Park, PA **114** C1
Melstone, MT **21** D2
Melville, LA **55** B4
Melville, SK **30** D1
Melvindale, MI . **103** C5
Memphis, MO **48** E6
Memphis, TN **53** D2
Memphis, TX **39** B4
Mena, AR **52** D4
Menahga, MN **46** B2
Menard, TX **41** B4
Menasha, WI **47** D5
Mendenhall, MS **55** D2
Mendocino, CA .. **12** B4
Mendon, MO **50** D2
Mendota, CA **14** D4
Mendota, IL **49** C3
Mendota, MN ... **100** D4
Mendota Heights, MN **100** D4
Menlo Park, CA .. **84** D3
Meno, OK **39** D1
Menominee, MI .. **47** D3
Menomonee Falls, WI **101** B1
Menomonie, WI . **46** E4
Mentone, TX **40** C3
Mentor, OH **61** A2
Mer Rouge, LA **55** B1
Meraux, LA **98** E4
Merced, CA **14** D3
Mercedes, TX **43** E6
Mercer, ND **33** A1
Mercer, OH **60** C4
Mercer Is., WA ... **82** D4
Merchantville, NJ **114** D3
Mercier, PQ **70** D2
Meredith, NH **72** D1
Meredosia, IL **51** B1
Meriden, CT **72** E5
Meridian, MS **66** A1
Meridian, TX **41** E3
Merino, CO **36** C1
Merkel, TX **41** B2
Merna, NE **35** B4
Merriam, IN **60** B3
Merriam, KS **92** B4
Merrifield, MN **46** C2
Merrifield, VA ... **116** A4
Merrill, OR **12** E1
Merrill, WI **47** B4
Merrillan, WI **47** A5
Merrimac, WI **49** C1
Merriman, NE **34** E2
Merritt Is., FL **67** F5
Merryville, LA **54** E4
Mertzon, TX **41** A4
Merwin, OH **108** E4
Mesa, AZ **26** C5
Mesa, CO **25** C2
Mesa, NM **38** B5
Mesa Verde Natl. Park, CO **25** C5
Mescalero, NM ... **28** E1
Meshik, AK **5** B5
Mesick, MI **58** A4

Place Name / Page Number / Grid Number
Stantonburg 118 C5

Mesilla, NM ... 29 D2
Mesquite, NM ... 29 D2
Mesquite, NV ... 24 A5
Mesquite, TX ... 95 E3
Metairie, LA ... 98 B3
Metaline Falls, WA ... 18 A3
Metropolis, IL ... 51 E4
Mexia, AL ... 66 B2
Mexia, TX ... 54 A3
Mexicali, BC ... 17 D5
Mexican Hat, UT ... 25 A5
Mexico, ME ... 71 A5
Mexico, MO ... 51 A2
Mexico, NY ... 72 A3
Mexico Beach, FL ... 66 E4
Meyersdale, PA ... 61 D4
Miami, AZ ... 26 D5
Miami, FL ... 80 B3
Miami, OK ... 50 C5
Miami, TX ... 39 A2
Miami Beach, FL ... 80 B3
Miami Shores, FL ... 123 D3
Miami Springs, FL ... 123 C4
Miamiville, OH ... 108 D2
Mianus, CT ... 112 D3
Michigan City, IN ... 60 A3
Mickleton, NJ ... 114 B5
Midale, SK ... 30 D3
Midas, NV ... 13 D3
Middle Fork, IN ... 60 A5
Middle River, MD ... 115 E2
Middleboro, MA ... 73 A4
Middleburg, PA ... 74 A2
Middleburg Heights, OH ... 106 B4
Middleburgh, NY ... 72 C4
Middlebury, VT ... 72 C2
Middlegate, NV ... 15 A1
Middleport, OH ... 63 A1
Middlesboro, KY ... 62 E4
Middleton, NS ... 71 E3
Middleton, WI ... 49 C1
Middletown, CT ... 72 E5
Middletown, DE ... 74 C3
Middletown, NY ... 72 C5
Middletown, OH ... 60 D5
Middletown, PA ... 74 A3
Midland, MI ... 58 C5
Midland, ON ... 59 B2
Midland, SD ... 35 A1
Midland, TX ... 40 E3
Midland City, AL ... 66 D2
Midlothian, TX ... 54 A2
Midvale, UT ... 22 D5
Midville, GA ... 65 C4
Midway, AL ... 66 D1
Midway, GA ... 65 D5
Midway, NE ... 35 C3
Midway, TX ... 96 A5
Midwest City, OK ... 39 E3
Mier, TAMPS ... 43 C5
Mifflinburg, PA ... 74 A2
Mifflintown, PA ... 74 A2
Milaca, MN ... 46 C3
Milam, LA ... 54 E3
Milan, IL ... 49 B4
Milan, MI ... 60 D2
Milan, MO ... 50 D1
Milan, OH ... 60 E3
Milan, TN ... 53 E1
Milano, TX ... 54 A4
Milbank, SD ... 33 E4
Milbridge, ME ... 71 C4
Milburnie, NC ... 119 D4
Miles, TX ... 41 B3
Miles City, FL ... 80 A3
Miles City, MT ... 32 A2
Milford, CA ... 12 E4
Milford, CT ... 72 E5
Milford, DE ... 74 C4
Milford, IA ... 48 B2
Milford, IL ... 49 E4
Milford, MA ... 73 A3
Milford, MD ... 115 B3
Milford, NE ... 35 E5
Milford, NH ... 72 E3
Milford, OH ... 62 D1
Milford, PA ... 74 C1
Milford, UT ... 24 C3
Milk River, AB ... 19 A3
Mill City, NV ... 13 C4
Mill City, OR ... 10 E2
Mill Point, WV ... 63 C1
Millbrae, CA ... 85 A1
Milledgeville, GA ... 65 B4
Millen, GA ... 65 C4
Miller, CA ... 17 B4
Miller, NE ... 35 C5
Miller, OR ... 83 B1
Miller, SD ... 33 C5
Millers Grove, PA ... 107 C4
Millersburg, OH ... 61 A3
Millersburg, PA ... 74 A2
Millerton, NY ... 72 D4
Millican, OR ... 11 A4
Milligan, FL ... 66 C3
Millington, MD ... 74 C4
Millington, TN ... 53 D2
Millinocket, ME ... 71 B3
Millstadt, IL ... 51 C3
Millstone, WV ... 63 B1
Milltown, PA ... 107 E2
Millvale, PA ... 107 C3
Millville, NJ ... 74 C3
Millville, PA ... 74 A1
Millwood, NY ... 112 B2
Millwood, OH ... 61 A4
Milnesand, NM ... 38 C5
Milo, ME ... 71 B4
Milpitas, CA ... 14 C2
Milton, DE ... 74 C4
Milton, FL ... 66 C3
Milton, IA ... 48 E5
Milton, MA ... 110 D5
Milton, ON ... 59 B4
Milton, PA ... 74 A2
Milton, WV ... 63 A1
Milton Center, MA ... 110 C5
Milton Freewater, OR ... 11 D1
Milton Lower Mills, MA ... 110 D5
Milwaukee, WI ... 49 D1
Milwaukie, WA ... 10 E1
Mimbres, NM ... 29 C1
Mina, NV ... 15 B2
Minam, OR ... 11 E2
Minas de Barroteran, COAH ... 43 A4
Minden, LA ... 54 E1
Minden, NE ... 37 C1
Mineola, TX ... 54 C1
Mineral, CA ... 12 D3
Mineral, VA ... 76 A1
Mineral Hill, NM ... 38 A2
Mineral Hot Springs, CO ... 36 A4
Mineral Point, WI ... 49 B2
Mineral Wells, TX ... 41 D1
Minersville, UT ... 24 C3
Minerva, OH ... 61 B3
Minerva Park, OH ... 109 C2
Mingus, TX ... 41 D2
Minidoka, ID ... 22 C2
Miniota, MB ... 31 A2
Minneapolis, MN ... 46 D4
Minnedosa, MB ... 31 B2
Minnekahta, SD ... 34 C2
Minneola, KS ... 37 B5
Minneota, MN ... 46 A5
Minnetonka, MN ... 100 A4
Minnewaukan, ND ... 31 C5
Minong, WI ... 46 E2
Minonk, IL ... 49 D4
Minorville, FL ... 120 B2
Minot, ND ... 31 A5
Mint Hill, NC ... 117 E3
Minto, MB ... 31 B3
Minton, NB ... 71 C2
Minton, SK ... 30 C4
Minturn, CO ... 25 E2
Mio, MI ... 58 C3
Miramar, FL ... 123 C1
Mishawaka, IN ... 60 A3
Mission, BC ... 9 A1
Mission, KS ... 92 B3
Mission, SD ... 35 A2
Mission, TX ... 43 D6
Mission Beach, CA ... 17 B5
Mission Hills, KS ... 92 C4
Mission Viejo, CA ... 88 E4
Mission Woods, KS ... 92 C3
Mississauga, ON ... 59 B4
Mississippi State, MS ... 53 E5
Missoula, MT ... 20 D1
Missouri City, TX ... 97 A5
Missouri Valley, IA ... 48 A4
Misty Fjords Natl. Mon., AK ... 5 F5
Mitchell, IN ... 62 B2
Mitchell, NE ... 34 C4
Mitchell, OR ... 11 B3
Mitchell, SD ... 35 D1
Mize, MS ... 55 E2
Mizpah, MN ... 44 B5
Moab, UT ... 25 B3
Moberly, MO ... 50 E2
Mobile, AL ... 66 A3
Mobridge, SD ... 33 B4
Moccasin, AZ ... 24 C5
Mocksville, NC ... 63 D5
Modena, UT ... 24 B3
Modesto, CA ... 14 D2
Modoc Point, OR ... 12 E1
Moenkopi, AZ ... 26 D1
Moffit, ND ... 33 B2
Mogollon, NM ... 27 B5
Mohall, ND ... 31 A4
Mohawk, AZ ... 26 A5
Mohawk, CA ... 12 E4
Mohler, OR ... 10 D1
Mojave, CA ... 17 A1
Moline, IL ... 49 B4
Moline, KS ... 50 A5
Moline Acres, MO ... 104 D1
Momence, IL ... 49 E4
Monahans, TX ... 40 D3
Monarch, MT ... 21 B1
Monchy, SK ... 19 E4
Moncks Corner, SC ... 65 E3
Monclova, COAH ... 43 A5
Moncriefs Store, GA ... 67 A2
Moncton, NB ... 71 E1
Mondovi, WI ... 46 E5
Monero, NM ... 27 D1
Moneta, WY ... 23 D2
Monett, MO ... 50 D5
Monette, AR ... 53 C1
Monfort Heights, OH ... 108 A3
Monhegan, ME ... 73 B1
Monico, WI ... 47 C3
Monmouth, IL ... 49 B5
Monmouth, OR ... 10 D2
Monon, IN ... 60 A4
Monongahela, PA ... 61 C4
Monroe, CT ... 113 A1
Monroe, GA ... 65 A3
Monroe, IA ... 48 D4
Monroe, LA ... 55 B1
Monroe, ME ... 71 B4
Monroe, MI ... 60 D2
Monroe, NC ... 65 D1
Monroe, NY ... 72 C5
Monroe, OR ... 10 D3
Monroe, UT ... 24 D3
Monroe, WA ... 9 A3
Monroe, WI ... 49 C2
Monroe City, MO ... 51 A1
Monroeton, PA ... 74 A1
Monroeville, AL ... 66 B2
Monroeville, PA ... 107 E3
Monrovia, CA ... 87 A1
Monson, ME ... 71 A4
Mont St.-Hilaire, PQ ... 70 C4
Mont-Tremblant, PQ ... 70 A4
Montague, CA ... 12 D1
Montague, TN ... 99 C2
Montclair, CA ... 87 E2
Montclair, MA ... 110 D4
Monte Vista, CO ... 25 E5
Monteagle, TN ... 64 C2
Montebello, CA ... 86 E2
Montebello, PQ ... 70 A5
Montell, TX ... 43 B1
Montello, NV ... 22 B4
Monterey, CA ... 14 C3
Monterey, TN ... 62 D5
Monterey, VA ... 63 D1
Monterey Park, CA ... 86 E2
Monterville, WV ... 63 C1
Montesano, WA ... 8 D4
Montevideo, MN ... 46 A4
Montezuma, GA ... 65 A5
Montezuma, NM ... 38 A2
Montezuma Castle Natl. Mon., AZ ... 26 D3
Montgomery, AL ... 66 C1
Montgomery, LA ... 55 A3
Montgomery, OH ... 108 C2
Montgomery, TX ... 54 B5
Montgomery City, MO ... 51 A2
Monticello, AR ... 53 B5
Monticello, FL ... 67 B3
Monticello, GA ... 65 A4
Monticello, IN ... 60 A4
Monticello, KY ... 62 D4
Monticello, ME ... 71 B2
Monticello, MN ... 46 C4
Monticello, MS ... 55 D2
Monticello, NY ... 72 C5
Monticello, UT ... 25 B4
Montmagny, PQ ... 70 E2
Montmartre, SK ... 30 D2
Montour Falls, NY ... 59 E5
Montpelier, ID ... 22 E3
Montpelier, IN ... 60 C4
Montpelier, VT ... 72 D1
Montpellier, PQ ... 70 A5
Montreal, PQ ... 70 B5
Montreal Nord, PQ ... 70 B5
Montrose, AR ... 53 B5
Montrose, CO ... 25 D2
Montrose, MO ... 50 D4
Montrose, PA ... 72 B5
Montross, VA ... 76 B1
Monument, OR ... 11 C3
Monument Park, CO ... 36 A5
Moody, TX ... 41 E3
Moorcroft, WY ... 32 B5
Moore Haven, FL ... 80 A2
Moorefield, WV ... 61 D5
Moorestown, NJ ... 114 E2
Mooresville, IN ... 62 B1
Moorhead, MN ... 33 E2
Moorseville, NC ... 63 D5
Moose, WY ... 23 A1
Moose Jaw, SK ... 30 B2
Moose Lake, MN ... 46 D2
Moosomin, SK ... 30 E2
Mora, MN ... 46 D3
Mora, NM ... 38 A2
Moraga, CA ... 83 C4
Moran, KS ... 50 B4
Moran, TX ... 41 C2
Moran, WY ... 23 A1
Morden, MB ... 31 C4
Morehead, KY ... 62 E2
Morehead City, NC ... 76 C5
Morehouse, MO ... 51 D5
Moreland, GA ... 64 E4
Morenci, AZ ... 27 A5
Morelos, COAH ... 43 A3
Morgan, NC ... 76 A5
Morgan, PA ... 107 B5
Morgan, UT ... 22 E4
Morgan City, LA ... 55 C5
Morgan Hill, CA ... 14 C3
Morgan Mill, TX ... 41 D2
Morganfield, KY ... 51 E4
Morgans Corner, NC ... 76 C3
Morganton, NC ... 63 C5
Morgantown, IN ... 62 B1
Morgantown, KY ... 62 B4
Morgantown, WV ... 61 C4
Moriarty, NM ... 27 E3
Morley, CO ... 38 B1
Morningside, MD ... 116 E4
Morningside Park, FL ... 120 C3
Morny, TN ... 99 A2
Morocco, IN ... 49 E4
Moroni, UT ... 24 E1
Morovis, PR ... 6 B3
Morrilton, AR ... 52 E3
Morris, IL ... 49 D4
Morris, MB ... 31 D3
Morris, MN ... 46 A4
Morris, NY ... 72 B4
Morris, OK ... 52 B2
Morris, PA ... 61 E1
Morrison, CO ... 93 A4
Morrison, IL ... 49 B3
Morrison, OK ... 52 A1
Morristown, AZ ... 26 B4
Morristown, NJ ... 74 C1
Morristown, NY ... 72 A2
Morristown, SD ... 32 E3
Morristown, TN ... 63 A5
Morrisville, NC ... 118 E4
Morrisville, NY ... 72 A4
Morrisville, PA ... 74 C2
Morrisville, VT ... 72 D1
Morro Bay, CA ... 14 C5
Morrow, GA ... 121 D5
Morse, SK ... 19 E2
Morseville, MA ... 110 A5
Mortlach, SK ... 30 A2
Morton, IL ... 49 C5
Morton, MN ... 46 B5
Morton, PA ... 114 A4
Morton, TX ... 38 D5
Morton, WA ... 8 E5
Morton Grove, IL ... 102 C1
Morton Valley, TX ... 41 D2
Mosby, MT ... 21 D1
Mosca, CO ... 36 A5
Moscow, ID ... 20 A1
Moses, NM ... 38 D1
Moses Lake, WA ... 9 D5
Mosinee, WI ... 47 B4
Mosquero, NM ... 38 C2
Moss Point, MS ... 66 A4
Mossbank, SK ... 30 A2
Motley, MN ... 46 B2
Mott, ND ... 32 E3
Moulton, AL ... 64 B3
Moultrie, GA ... 67 A2
Mound Bayou, MS ... 53 C4
Mound City, KS ... 50 C4
Mound City, MO ... 50 B1
Mound City, SD ... 33 B3
Mound City Group Natl. Mon., OH ... 60 E5
Mounds, IL ... 51 D4
Mounds, OK ... 52 B2
Mounds View, MN ... 100 C1
Moundsville, WV ... 61 B4
Mount Air, OH ... 109 B1
Mount Airy, MD ... 74 A4
Mount Airy, NC ... 63 D4
Mount Ayr, IA ... 48 C5
Mount Baker Lodge, WA ... 9 B2
Mount Carmel, IL ... 51 E3
Mount Carmel, OH ... 108 D3
Mount Carmel, PA ... 74 A2
Mount Carmel Junction, UT ... 24 C4
Mount Carroll, IL ... 49 B3
Mount Clemens, MI ... 60 D1
Mount Comfort, IN ... 105 E2
Mount Enterprise, TX ... 54 D2
Mount Ephraim, NJ ... 114 D4
Mount Gilead, OH ... 60 E4
Mount Healthy, OH ... 108 A2
Mount Holly, NC ... 117 A2
Mount Holly Springs, PA ... 74 A3
Mount Horeb, WI ... 49 C2
Mount Ida, AR ... 52 D4
Mount Juliet, TN ... 99 E2
Mount Kisco, NY ... 112 B1
Mount Laurel, NJ ... 114 E3
Mount Lebanon, PA ... 107 C4
Mount Morris, IL ... 49 C3
Mount Morris, NY ... 59 D5
Mount Nebo, PA ... 107 A2
Mount Olive, MS ... 55 E2
Mount Oliver, PA ... 107 C3
Mount Pisgah, OH ... 108 E5
Mount Pleasant, IA ... 49 A5
Mount Pleasant, MI ... 58 B5
Mount Pleasant, TN ... 64 B1
Mount Pleasant, TX ... 54 C1
Mount Pleasant, UT ... 24 E1
Mount Pocono, PA ... 74 B1
Mount Prospect, IL ... 102 A1
Mount Pulaski, IL ... 51 D1
Mount Ranier, MD ... 116 D2
Mount Repose, OH ... 108 E2
Mount Royal, NJ ... 114 C5
Mount Rushmore Natl. Mon., SD ... 34 C1
Mount Shasta, CA ... 12 D2
Mount Sterling, IL ... 51 B1
Mount Sterling, KY ... 62 E2
Mount Sterling, OH ... 60 E5
Mount Storm, WV ... 61 D5
Mount Trumbull, AZ ... 24 B5
Mount Union, PA ... 61 E3
Mount Vernon, AL ... 66 B3
Mount Vernon, IA ... 49 A3
Mount Vernon, IL ... 51 D3
Mount Vernon, IN ... 51 E3
Mount Vernon, KY ... 62 D3
Mount Vernon, MO ... 50 D5
Mount Vernon, NY ... 111 D1
Mount Vernon, OH ... 60 E4
Mount Vernon, OR ... 11 C3
Mount Vernon, PA ... 107 E5
Mount Vernon, SD ... 35 D1
Mount Vernon, TX ... 54 C1
Mount Vernon, WA ... 9 A2
Mount View, TN ... 99 E4
Mount Washington, KY ... 62 C3
Mount Washington, OH ... 108 C4
Mount Zion, IL ... 51 D1
Mountain City, NV ... 13 E3
Mountain City, TN ... 63 B4
Mountain Grove, MO ... 51 A5
Mountain Home, AR ... 53 A1
Mountain Home, ID ... 22 A1
Mountain Home, TX ... 41 C5
Mountain Iron, MN ... 46 D1
Mountain Ridge, MO ... 104 A4
Mountain View, AR ... 53 A2
Mountain View, AZ ... 28 D2
Mountain View, CA ... 14 C2
Mountain View, GA ... 121 C4
Mountain View, MO ... 51 A5
Mountain View, OK ... 39 C3
Mountain View, WV ... 63 B3
Mountain View, WY ... 23 A4
Mountainair, NM ... 27 E4
Mountlake Terrace, WA ... 82 D1
Moville, IA ... 48 A3
Moweagua, IL ... 51 D1
Moyie, BC ... 18 B2
Moyie Springs, ID ... 18 B3
Mt. Rainier Natl. Park, WA ... 9 A4
Mt. St. Helens Natl. Volcanic Mon., WA ... 8 E5
Mud Butte, SD ... 32 D4
Mueller Park, UT ... 90 C1
Muir Woods Natl. Mon., CA ... 85 E1
Mulberry, AR ... 52 D2
Mulberry, OH ... 108 E2
Muldraugh, KY ... 62 B3
Mule Creek, NM ... 27 B5
Mule Creek Jct., WY ... 34 C2
Muleshoe, TX ... 38 D4
Mullan, ID ... 18 B5
Mullen, NE ... 35 A4
Mullens, WV ... 63 B2
Mullins, SC ... 78 A2
Mullinville, KS ... 37 C5
Mulloy, OR ... 83 A5
Muncie, IN ... 60 C5
Muncy, PA ... 74 A1
Munday, TX ... 41 C1
Munfordville, KY ... 62 C4
Munhall, PA ... 107 D3
Munich, ND ... 31 C4
Munising, MI ... 47 E1
Munsonville, NH ... 72 E3
Murdo, SD ... 35 A1
Murdock, OH ... 108 E1
Murfreesboro, AR ... 52 D4
Murfreesboro, NC ... 76 B3
Murfreesboro, TN ... 64 B1
Murphy, GA ... 67 A2
Murphy, MO ... 104 B5
Murphy, NC ... 64 E1
Murphy, OR ... 10 C5
Murphys, CA ... 14 E2
Murphysboro, IL ... 51 D4
Murray, KY ... 51 E5
Murray, UT ... 22 D5
Murrells Inlet, SC ... 78 A2
Muscatine, IA ... 49 A4
Muscle Shoals, AL ... 64 A3
Muse, PA ... 107 A5
Muskego, WI ... 101 B5
Muskegon, MI ... 60 A1
Muskogee, OK ... 52 B2
Musquash, NB ... 71 D3
Musselshell, MT ... 21 D2
Myakka City, FL ... 69 D2
Myerstown, PA ... 74 B2
Myrtle Beach, SC ... 78 A2
Myrtle Creek, OR ... 10 C4
Myrtle Point, OR ... 10 C4
Mystic, CT ... 73 A5
Myton, UT ... 25 A1

N

Naalehu, HI ... 7 D5
Naco, SON ... 28 E3
Nacogdoches, TX ... 54 D3
Nacozari de Garcia, SON ... 28 E4
Nadadores, COAH ... 42 E5
Nadine, PA ... 107 D2
Nageezi, NM ... 27 C1
Nags Head, NC ... 76 D3
Nahanni Natl. Park Reserve, NT ... 5 F3
Nahant, MA ... 110 E2
Nahunta, GA ... 67 D1
Naknek, AK ... 5 B4
Nakusp, BC ... 18 A1
Nampa, ID ... 11 E5
Namur, PQ ... 70 A5
Nanaimo, BC ... 8 E1
Nanticoke, MD ... 74 C5
Nanticoke, ON ... 59 B5
Nanton, AB ... 18 D1
Nantucket, MA ... 73 B4
Naoma, WV ... 63 B2
Napa, CA ... 14 C1
Naples, FL ... 69 E3
Naples, ID ... 18 B3
Naples, ME ... 73 A1
Naples, NY ... 59 E5
Napoleon, ND ... 33 B2
Napoleon, OH ... 60 C3
Napoleonville, LA ... 55 C5
Nappanee, IN ... 60 B3
Nara Vista, NM ... 38 D3
Narcissa, PA ... 114 A1
Narragansett Pier, RI ... 73 A4
Narrows, OR ... 11 C5
Narrowsburg, NY ... 72 C5
Nashua, MT ... 30 A5
Nashua, NH ... 73 A3
Nashville, AR ... 52 D4
Nashville, GA ... 67 B2
Nashville, IL ... 51 D3
Nashville, IN ... 62 B1
Nashville, NC ... 76 A4
Nashville, TN ... 62 B5
Nashwaak Bridge, NB ... 71 C2
Nashwauk, MN ... 46 C1
Natal, BC ... 18 C2
Natchez, MS ... 116 C5
Natchitoches, LA ... 54 E2
Natick, MA ... 110 A5
National City, CA ... 89 B3
National City, IL ... 104 E3
National Park, NJ ... 114 C4
Natoma, KS ... 37 C3
Natural Bridges Natl. Mon., UT ... 25 A4
Naturita, CO ... 25 C4
Naukan, AK ... 5 A2
Nauvoo, IA ... 49 A5
Nava, COAH ... 43 A3
Navajo, NM ... 27 B2
Navajo City, NM ... 27 D1
Navajo Natl. Mon., AZ ... 24 E5
Navarre, OH ... 61 A3
Navarre Beach, FL ... 66 C3
Navarro, CA ... 12 B5
Navasota, TX ... 54 B5
Nazareth, PA ... 74 C2
Neah Bay, WA ... 8 D2
Nebo, MO ... 92 E1
Nebraska City, NE ... 48 A5
Necanicum, OR ... 8 D5
Necedah, WI ... 47 B5
Necker, MD ... 115 D2
Needham, MA ... 110 B5
Needham Heights, MA ... 110 B5
Needles, BC ... 9 E1
Needles, CA ... 17 E2
Needmore, TN ... 99 E2
Needmore, TX ... 38 D5
Neenah, WI ... 47 D5
Neepawa, MB ... 31 B2
Neeses, SC ... 65 D3
Neguanee, MI ... 47 D1
Nehalem, OR ... 10 D1
Neihart, MT ... 21 B1
Neilsville, WI ... 47 A5
Neilton, WA ... 8 D3
Neligh, NE ... 35 D3
Nellsville, WI ... 47 A5
Nelma, WI ... 47 C2
Nelson, BC ... 18 A2
Nelson, NC ... 118 E3
Nelson, NE ... 37 D1
Nelson, NV ... 17 E1
Nelsonville, OH ... 61 A5
Nelway, BC ... 18 A2
Nemah, WA ... 8 D4
Nenana, AK ... 5 C3
Nenzel, NE ... 35 A2
Neodesha, KS ... 50 B5
Neoga, IL ... 51 E1
Neola, UT ... 23 A5
Neosho, MO ... 50 C5
Nephi, UT ... 24 D1
Neptune, OR ... 10 C3
Nespelem, WA ... 9 D3
Ness City, KS ... 37 B4
Netawaka, KS ... 50 B2
Netcong, NJ ... 74 C1
Neuse, NC ... 119 C2
Nevada, IA ... 48 D3
Nevada, MO ... 50 C4
Nevada City, CA ... 12 D5
Neville, SK ... 19 E2
New Albany, IN ... 62 B2
New Albany, MS ... 53 E3
New Albany, OH ... 109 E2
New Alexandria, PA ... 61 D3
New Alexandria, VA ... 116 C5
New Athens, IL ... 51 C3
New Bandon, NB ... 71 C2
New Bedford, MA ... 73 A4
New Berlin, NY ... 72 B4
New Berlin, WI ... 101 C4
New Bern, NC ... 76 C5
New Bethlehem, PA ... 61 C2
New Bloomfield, PA ... 74 A2
New Boston, IL ... 49 B4
New Boston, OH ... 62 E1
New Boston, TX ... 52 D5
New Braunfels, TX ... 43 D1
New Bremen, OH ... 60 C4
New Brighton, MN ... 100 C2
New Britain, CT ... 72 E5
New Brunswick, NJ ... 74 C2
New Buffalo, MI ... 60 A3
New Canaan, CT ... 72 D5
New Canaan, NB ... 71 D1
New Carrollton, MD ... 116 D1
New Castle, DE ... 74 C3
New Castle, IN ... 60 C5
New Castle, KY ... 62 C2
New Castle, ME ... 71 B5
New Castle, PA ... 61 B3
New Castle, VA ... 63 D2
New Concord, OH ... 61 A4
New Cuyama, CA ... 16 E1
New Denver, BC ... 18 A1
New England, ND ... 32 D2
New Glarus, WI ... 49 C2
New Hampton, IA ... 48 E2
New Harmony, IN ... 51 E3
New Hartford, NY ... 72 B3
New Haven, CT ... 72 E5
New Haven, MO ... 51 B3
New Holland, PA ... 74 B3
New Holstein, WI ... 47 D5
New Hope, MN ... 100 A2
New Hope, NC ... 119 C3
New Hundred, WV ... 61 C4
New Iberia, LA ... 55 B5
New Kensington, PA ... 107 E1
New Lebanon, NY ... 72 D4
New Leipzig, ND ... 32 E3
New Lexington, OH ... 61 A5
New Lisbon, WI ... 47 B5
New London, CT ... 72 E5
New London, MN ... 46 B4
New London, MO ... 51 A1
New London, WI ... 47 C4
New Madrid, MO ... 51 D5
New Market, VA ... 61 E5
New Martinsville, WV ... 61 B5
New Meadows, ID ... 20 A3
New Milford, CT ... 72 D5
New Milford, PA ... 72 B5
New Orleans, LA ... 55 D4
New Oxford, PA ... 74 A3
New Palestine, OH ... 108 D5
New Paltz, NY ... 72 C5
New Philadelphia, OH ... 61 A4
New Pine Creek, OR ... 13 A1
New Port Richey, FL ... 67 C5

Bold type indicates cities with 100,000 population or more.

Place Name / Page Number / Grid Number
Stantonburg 118 C5

New Prague, MN 46 C5
New Princeton, OR 11 C5
New Raymer, CO 36 C1
New Richmond, OH 108 E5
New Richmond, WI 46 D4
New River, AZ 26 C4
New River Beach, NB 71 D3
New Roads, LA 55 C4
New Rockford, ND 33 C1
New Rome, OH 109 B4
New Sharon, IA 48 E4
New Sharon, ME 71 A5
New Smyrna Beach, FL 67 E4
New Stanton, PA 61 C4
New Topsail Beach, NC 78 B1
New Town, ND 30 E5
New Ulm, MN 46 C5
New Vienna, OH 62 D1
New Waverly, TX 54 C4
New Westminster, BC 9 A1
New Yarmouth, NB 71 E2
New York, NY 74 D1
Newark, CA 84 D4
Newark, DE 74 C3
Newark, NJ 74 D1
Newark, NY 59 E4
Newark, OH 61 A4
Newaygo, MI 58 A5
Newberg, OR 10 D1
Newberry, FL 67 C3
Newberry, MI 58 A1
Newberry, SC 65 C2
Newburg, NB 71 D2
Newburgh, NY 72 D5
Newburgh Heights, OH 106 C3
Newburyport, MA 73 A2
Newcastle, ON 59 C3
Newcastle, TX 41 D1
Newcastle, WA 82 D4
Newcastle, WY 34 C1
Newcomb, NM 27 B1
Newcomb, NY 72 C2
Newcomerstown, OH 61 A4
Newdale, MB 31 B2
Newell, SD 32 D5
Newfield, PA 107 E2
Newfolden, MN 31 E5
Newhalem, WA 9 B2
Newhalen, AK 5 B4
Newington, GA 65 D4
Newkirk, NM 38 B3
Newkirk, OK 39 E1
Newman, NM 29 E2
Newmarket, ON 59 B3
Newnan, GA 64 E4
Newport, AR 53 B2
Newport, FL 67 A3
Newport, KY 108 B4
Newport, ME 71 D4
Newport, MN 100 E4
Newport, NH 72 E2
Newport, OH 61 B5
Newport, OR 10 C2
Newport, PA 74 A2
Newport, RI 73 A4
Newport, TN 63 A5
Newport, TX 39 D5
Newport, VT 70 D5
Newport, WA 18 A4
Newport Beach, CA 17 A3
Newport News, VA 76 C2
Newry, ME 70 E5
Newton, GA 67 A2
Newton, IA 48 D4
Newton, IL 51 E2
Newton, KS 37 E4
Newton, MA 110 B4
Newton, MS 55 E1
Newton, NC 63 C5
Newton, NJ 74 C1
Newton, TX 54 E4
Newton Center, MA 110 B4
Newton Grove, NC 76 A5
Newton Lower Falls, MA 110 A4
Newtonville, MA 110 B4
Newtown, OH 108 D3
Niagara, WI 47 D3
Niagara Falls, NY 59 C4
Niagara Falls, ON 59 C4
Niagara on-the-Lake, ON 59 C4
Nice, CA 12 B5
Niceville, FL 66 C3
Nicholasville, KY 62 D3
Nichols, NC 78 B1
Nichols, SC 78 A1
Nicholville, NY 72 B1
Nickerson, KS 37 D4
Nicolet, PQ 70 C3
Nikolski, AK 4 G5
Niland, CA 17 D4
Niles, IL 102 C1
Niles, MI 60 A3
Ninette, MB 31 B3
Ninety-Six, SC 65 C2
Niobrara, NE 35 D3
Nipton, CA 17 E1
Nitro, WV 63 B1
Nixon, NV 13 A5
Nixon, TX 43 E1
Noble, KY 62 C2
Nobleford, AB 18 E2
Noblesville, IN 60 B5
Nocatee, FL 69 E2
Nocona, TX 39 E5
Node, WY 34 C3
Noel, MO 52 A1
Nogales, AZ 28 D3
Nogales, CHIH 29 B3
Nogales, SON 28 D3
Noinville, NB 71 D1
Nolanville, TX 41 E4
Nome, AK 5 B2
Nonantum, MA 110 B3
Nonaville, TN 99 E1
Nondalton, AK 5 B4
Noonan, ND 30 D4
Norden, NE 35 B2
Nordman, ID 18 A3
Norfield, MS 55 D3
Norfolk, CT 72 D4
Norfolk, NE 35 F4
Norfolk, NY 72 A1
Norfolk, VA 76 C2
Norias del Caballo, COAH 42 D3
Norlina, NC 76 A3
Normal, IL 49 D5
Norman, AR 52 D4
Norman, OK 39 F3
Normandy, MO 104 D2
Normandy, TX 43 A2
Normanna, TX 43 E2
Noroton Heights, CT 112 E2
Norridge, IL 102 B2
Norridgewock, ME 71 A5
Norris, MT 20 E3
Norris, TN 62 E5
Norris, WY 21 A4
Norris City, IL 51 E3
Norristown, PA 74 C2
Norrisville, MD 74 B3
North, SC 65 D3
North Adams, MA 72 D3
North Amity, ME 71 B2
North Anson, ME 71 A4
North Arlington, NY 111 A3
North Bay, NY 72 A3
North Bay Village, FL 123 D3
North Belmont, NC 117 A2
North Bend, NE 35 E4
North Bend, OR 10 C4
North Bend, WA 9 A4
North Bennington, VT 72 D3
North Bessemer, PA 107 E2
North Bonneville, WA 10 E1
North Braddock, PA 107 D3
North Branch, MN 46 D3
North Cambridge, MA 110 C3
North Cape May, NJ 74 D4
North Cascades Natl. Park, WA 9 B2
North City, WA 82 D1
North College Hill, OH 108 A2
North Cowden, TX 40 D3
North Creek, NY 72 C2
North Dupo, IL 104 E4
North East, PA 61 C1
North East Carry, ME 71 A3
North Edwards, CA 17 B1
North English, IA 48 E4
North Fork, ID 20 C3
North Greenwich, CT 112 C3
North Head, NB 71 D4
North Hero, NY 72 C1
North Houston, TX 97 A1
North Hudson, NY 72 C2
North Kansas City, MO 92 C2
North Komelik, AZ 28 C1
North Lake, NB 71 B2
North Las Vegas, NV 15 E5
North Lexington, MA 110 A2
North Little Rock, AR 53 A3
North Lucy, NM 38 A3
North Miami, FL 80 B3
North Miami Beach, FL 123 D2
North Oaks, MN 100 D1
North Olmstead, OH 106 A4
North Pelton, ON 103 E4
North Platte, NE 35 A5
North Pole, AK 5 D3
North Port, FL 69 D2
North Powder, OR 11 D3
North Quincy, MA 110 D4
North Redington Beach, FL 122 A4
North Richland Hills, TX 94 C2
North Richmond, OH 61 B2
North Rim, AZ 26 C1
North Riverside, IL 102 C4
North Royalton, OH 106 B5
North Saint Paul, MN 100 E2
North Salt Lake, UT 90 B1
North Saugus, MA 110 C1
North Shore, CA 17 C4
North Stratford, NH 70 D5
North Tarrytown, NY 112 A3
North Troy, VT 70 D5
North Vancouver, BC 9 A1
North Vernon, IN 62 C1
North Weymouth, MA 110 E5
North Wilkesboro, NC 63 C4
North Wilton, CT 112 E1
North Woburn, MA 110 B1
North Woodbury, NJ 114 C4
North Woodstock, NH 72 E1
North York, ON 59 B4
Northampton, MA 72 E4
Northern Yukon Natl. Park, YT 5 D2
Northfield, MA 72 E3
Northfield, MN 46 D5
Northfield, OH 106 E4
Northfield, VT 72 D1
Northfield Center, OH 106 E5
Northgate, CO 23 E5
Northgate, ND 30 E4
Northgate, SK 30 E4
Northglenn, CO 93 C1
Northlake, IL 102 A3
Northmoor, MO 92 B1
Northome, MN 44 B5
Northport, AL 64 B5
Northport, MI 58 A3
Northport, NE 34 D4
Northport, WA 9 E3
Northumberland, PA 74 A2
Northvale, NJ 112 A4
Northville, NY 72 C3
Northville, SD 33 C4
Northway Jct., AK 5 D3
Northwood, ND 33 D1
Northwood, NH 73 A2
Northwoods, MO 104 D2
Norton, CT 112 E3
Norton, KS 37 B2
Norton, VA 63 A4
Norton, VT 70 D5
Norton, WV 61 C5
Nortonville, KY 62 A4
Norwalk, CA 86 E4
Norwalk, CT 72 D5
Norwalk, OH 60 E3
Norway, ME 71 A5
Norway, MI 47 D2
Norwich, CT 72 E5
Norwich, NY 72 B4
Norwich, VT 72 D2
Norwood, CO 25 C4
Norwood, MN 46 C5
Norwood, NC 63 D5
Norwood, NJ 112 A5
Norwood, OH 108 C3
Norwood, PA 114 A4
Notre-Dame-de-la-Merci, PQ 70 B4
Notrees, TX 40 D3
Novato, CA 14 B1
Nowata, OK 52 B1
Nubieber, CA 12 E3
Nucla, CO 25 C4
Nueva Ciudad Guerrero, TAMPS 43 C5
Nueva Reforma, COAH 42 E4
Nueva Rosita, COAH 43 A3
Nuevo Casas Grandes, CHIH 29 C4
Nuevo Laredo, TAMPS 43 C4
Nulato, AK 5 B3
Nutley, NJ 111 A2
Nutting Lake, MA 110 A1
Nyack, NY 74 D1
Nyssa, OR 11 E5

O

O & C Junction, NC 118 E1
Oak Bay, NB 71 C3
Oak Bluff, MB 31 D3
Oak Bluffs, MA 73 B4
Oak Brook, IL 102 A4
Oak City, UT 24 D2
Oak Creek, CO 25 E1
Oak Creek, WI 101 E5
Oak Grove, LA 55 B1
Oak Grove, NC 118 E2
Oak Grove, OR 83 C4
Oak Harbor, WA 9 A2
Oak Hill, AL 66 B1
Oak Hill, FL 67 F4
Oak Hill, OH 63 A1
Oak Hill, TN 99 C4
Oak Hill, WV 63 C2
Oak Lake, MB 31 A3
Oak Lawn, IL 102 C5
Oak Park, GA 65 C5
Oak Park, IL 49 E3
Oak Park, MI 103 B2
Oak Point, MB 31 D2
Oak Ridge, TN 62 E5
Oak Spring Lock, MD 116 A1
Oak Valley, NJ 114 C5
Oakbrook Terrace, IL 102 A4
Oakburn, MB 31 A2
Oakdale, CA 14 D2
Oakdale, GA 121 B2
Oakdale, LA 55 A4
Oakdale, MN 100 E2
Oakdale, PA 107 A4
Oakes, ND 33 D3
Oakfield, NY 59 D4
Oakhurst, CA 14 E3
Oakhurst, FL 122 A3
Oakland, CA 14 C2
Oakland, FL 120 A2
Oakland, IA 48 B4
Oakland, MD 61 D5
Oakland, MO 104 C4
Oakland, MS 53 D4
Oakland, NE 48 A4
Oakland City, IN 62 A3
Oakland Vale, MA 110 C1
Oaklawn, MD 110 D4
Oakley, ID 22 C2
Oakley, KS 37 A3
Oaklyn, NJ 114 D3
Oaklyn, PA 114 D3
Oakmont, PA 107 D2
Oakridge, OR 10 D4
Oakview, MD 116 C1
Oakville, MB 31 D2
Oakville, MO 104 D5
Oakville, ON 59 B4
Oakville, WA 8 F4
Oasis, CA 17 C4
Oasis, NV 22 B4
Oberlin, KS 37 B2
Oberlin, LA 55 A4
Oberlin, OH 60 E3
Obetz, OH 109 D4
Obion, TN 53 D1
Ocala, FL 67 D4
Ocampo, COAH 42 D4
Ocate, NM 38 A2
Ocean City, MD 74 D5
Ocean City, NJ 74 D3
Ocean City, WA 8 D4
Ocean Grove, NJ 74 D2
Ocean Park, WA 8 D4
Ocean Shores, WA 8 D4
Ocean Springs, MS 66 A4
Ocean View, NJ 74 D3
Oceanside, CA 17 B4
Ochopee, FL 80 A3
Ochre River, MB 31 B1
Ocilla, GA 67 B1
Ocoee, FL 120 A2
Oconomowoc, WI 49 D1
Oconto, NE 35 B5
Oconto, WI 47 D4
Ocracoke, NC 76 D4
Odell, IN 60 A5
Odessa, DE 74 C3
Odessa, MO 50 D3
Odessa, TX 40 D3
Odessa, WA 9 D4
O'Donnell, TX 40 D1
Oelrichs, SD 34 D2
Oelwein, IA 48 E2
Ogallala, NE 34 E5
Ogden, UT 22 D4
Ogden Center, UT 25 B4
Ogdensburg, NY 72 A1
Oglala, SD 34 D2
Ogontz, PA 114 C1
Oil City, PA 61 C2
Oilton, OK 52 A2
Ojai, CA 16 E2
Ojibwa, WI 47 A3
Ojinaga, CHIH 42 B1
Ojo Caliente, NM 27 E1
Okanagan Falls, BC 9 D2
Okanogan, WA 9 D3
Okeechobee, FL 80 A1
Okemah, OK 52 A3
Oklahoma City, OK 39 E2
Oklaunion, TX 39 C5
Okmulgee, OK 52 B2
Okolona, MS 53 E4
Okreek, SD 35 B2
Ola, AR 52 E3
Olancha, CA 15 B5
Olar, SC 65 D3
Olatha, CO 25 C3
Olathe, KS 50 C3
Olcott, NY 59 C4
Old Crow, YT 5 D2
Old Faithful, WY 21 A5
Old Forge, NY 72 B3
Old Fort, NC 63 B5
Old Glory, TX 41 B1
Old Greenwich, CT 112 E3
Old Hickory, TN 99 D2
Old Horse Springs, NM 27 C4
Old Houlka, MS 53 E4
Old Orchard Beach, ME 73 A1
Old Saybrook, CT 72 E5
Old Station, CA 12 D3
Old Town, ID 18 A4
Old Town, ME 71 B4
Oldsmar, FL 69 D1
Olean, NY 61 D1
Oleta, OK 52 C4
Olive Branch, MS 53 D3
Olive Branch, OH 108 E3
Olive Hill, KY 62 E2
Olivehurst, CA 12 D5
Oliver, BC 9 D2
Oliver, CO 25 D3
Olivet, SD 35 D2
Olivette, MO 104 C2
Olivia, MN 46 B5
Olla, LA 55 A2
Olmos Park, TX 96 C3
Olmsted Falls, OH 106 A4
Olney, IL 51 E2
Olney, MT 18 C4
Olney, TX 41 D1
Olton, TX 38 E4
Olustee, FL 67 C3
Olympia, WA 8 E4
Olympic Natl. Park, WA 8 D3
Omaha, NE 48 A4
Omaha, TX 54 C1
Omak, WA 9 D3
Omega, NM 27 B4
Omena, MI 58 A3
Onaka, SD 33 C4
Onamia, MN 46 C3
Onancock, VA 76 C1
Onarga, IL 49 E4
Onawa, IA 48 A3
Onaway, MI 58 B2
Oneida, NY 72 A4
Oneida, TN 62 D5
O'Neill, NE 35 C3
Oneonta, AL 64 C3
Oneonta, NY 72 B4
Onida, SD 33 B5
Onion Valley, CA 15 B4
Ono, CA 12 C3
Ontario, CA 17 A3
Ontario, OR 11 E4
Ontonagon, MI 47 B1
Onyx, AR 52 E3
Opa-Locka, FL 123 C2
Opal, WY 23 A3
Opelika, AL 64 D5
Opelousas, LA 55 B4
Opheim, MT 30 A4
Opihikao, HI 7 E5
Opp, AL 66 D2
Oppello, AR 52 E3
Opportunity, WA 18 A4
Option, PA 107 C4
Oquitoa, SON 28 C3
Oraibi, AZ 26 E2
Oran, MO 51 D5
Orange, CA 88 C1
Orange, CT 113 C1
Orange, MA 72 E3
Orange, OH 106 E2
Orange, TX 54 E5
Orange, VA 76 A1
Orange Grove, NC 118 A2
Orange Grove, TX 43 E3
Orange Park, FL 67 D3
Orangeburg, NY 112 A4
Orangeburg, SC 65 D3
Orangeville, ON 59 B4
Orangeville, UT 24 E2
Oraville, MD 74 B5
Orbisonia, PA 61 E3
Orchard, NE 35 D3
Orchard Beach, MD 115 E5
Orchard City, CO 25 C3
Orchards, WA 83 D1
Ord, NE 35 C4
Ordway, CO 36 C4
Oregon, IL 49 C3
Oregon City, OR 10 E1
Oreland, PA 114 B1
Orem, UT 22 E5
Orenco, OR 83 A2
Orford, NH 72 D1
Organ, NM 29 D2
Orick, CA 12 A2
Orient Point, NY 72 E5
Oriental, NC 76 C5
Orillia, ON 59 B2
Orin, WY 34 B3
Orinda, CA 85 C4
Orinda Village, CA 83 D2
Orion, AB 19 B3
Orland, CA 12 C4
Orlando, FL 67 E5
Orleans, MA 73 B3
Orleans, NE 37 C1
Orlovista, FL 120 C2
Ormond Beach, FL 67 E4
Ormond-by-the-Sea, FL 67 E4
Orofino, ID 20 A1
Orogrande, NM 29 E2
Oromocto, NB 71 D2
Orono, ME 71 B4
Oronoque, CT 113 B2
Orovada, NV 13 C3
Oroville, CA 12 D5
Oroville, WA 9 D2
Orr, MN 44 D5
Ortley, SD 33 E4
Ortonville, MN 46 A4
Orwell, OH 61 B2
Osage, AR 52 E1
Osage, IA 48 D1
Osage, WY 34 C1
Osage Beach, MO 50 E3
Osage City, KS 50 B3
Osawatomie, KS 50 C3
Osborne, KS 37 C2
Osborne, PA 107 A2
Osceola, AR 53 D2
Osceola, IA 48 D5
Osceola, MO 50 D4
Osceola, NE 35 E5
Osceola, WI 46 D4
Oscoda, MI 58 C3
Osgood, IN 62 C1
Oshawa, ON 59 C3
Oshkosh, NE 34 E4
Oshkosh, WI 47 D5
Oskaloosa, IA 48 E4
Oskaloosa, KS 50 B2
Oslo, MN 31 E5
Osoyoos, BC 9 D2
Osseo, MN 100 A1
Osseo, WI 47 A5
Ossining, NY 74 D1
Oswego, KS 50 C5
Oswego, NY 59 E3
Osyka, MS 55 D3
Otego, NY 72 B4
Otis, MA 72 D4
Otisville, MI 58 D5
Otselic, NY 72 A4
Ottawa, IL 49 D4
Ottawa, KS 50 B3
Ottawa, OH 60 D3
Ottawa, ON 59 E1
Otter Creek, FL 67 C4
Otter Lake, NY 72 B3
Otto, WY 21 D5
Ottumwa, IA 48 E5
Ouray, CO 25 D4
Ouray, UT 25 B1
Outlook, OR 83 D5
Ovando, MT 20 D1
Overbrook, MA 110 A5
Overland, MO 104 C2
Overland Park, KS 50 C3
Overlea, MD 115 D2
Overton, NV 24 A5
Ovid, NY 59 E4
Owasso, OK 52 B1
Owatonna, MN 46 D5
Owego, NY 72 A5
Owen, WI 47 A4
Owen Sound, ON 59 A3
Owensboro, KY 62 A3
Owensville, MO 51 A3
Owenton, KY 62 C2
Owings Mills, MD 74 B4
Owingsville, KY 62 E2
Owosso, MI 60 C1
Owyhee, NV 13 E2
Oxbow, MA 110 A3
Oxbow, ME 71 B2
Oxbow, SK 30 E4
Oxford, AL 64 D4
Oxford, KS 37 E5
Oxford, MS 53 D3
Oxford, NC 76 A3
Oxford, NE 37 B1
Oxford, NY 72 B4
Oxford, PA 74 B3
Oxnard, CA 16 E2
Ozark, AL 66 D2
Ozark, AR 52 D2
Ozark, MO 50 E5
Ozona, TX 41 A4

P

Pacheco, CA 85 D5
Pacific, MO 51 B3
Pacific Grove, CA 14 C3
Pacifica, CA 14 B2
Packwood, WA 9 A5
Paducah, KY 51 E4
Paducah, TX 39 B5
Page, AZ 24 D5
Page, NM 27 B3
Page, OK 52 C3
Page City, KS 37 A3
Pagedale, MO 104 D2
Pageland, SC 65 D1
Pagosa Springs, CO 25 D5
Pahala, HI 7 D5
Pahoa, HI 7 E5
Pahokee, FL 80 A2
Pahrump, NV 15 D5
Paicines, CA 14 C3
Painesville, OH 61 A2
Paint Rock, AL 64 C2
Paint Rock, TX 41 B3
Painted Post, NY 59 E5
Paintsville, KY 63 A2
Paisley, OR 11 A5
Palacios, TX 56 B2
Palatka, FL 67 D3
Palau, COAH 43 A3
Palco, KS 37 C2
Palestine, TX 54 B3
Palisade, CO 25 C2
Palisade, NE 37 A1
Palisades, MO 104 A4
Palisades Park, NJ 111 B2
Palm Bay, FL 67 F5
Palm Beach, FL 80 B2
Palm Beach Gardens, FL 80 B2
Palm Desert, CA 17 C4
Palm Springs, CA 17 C3
Palmdale, CA 17 A2
Palmdale, FL 80 A2
Palmer, AK 5 C4
Palmer, MA 72 E4
Palmerton, PA 74 B2
Palmetto, FL 69 D1
Palmetto, GA 64 E4
Palmyra, IN 62 B2
Palmyra, MO 51 A1
Palmyra, NJ 114 D2
Palmyra, NY 59 E4
Palmyra, VA 76 A1
Palo Alto, CA 14 B2
Palo Pinto, TX 41 D1
Palo Verde, AZ 26 B5
Palo Verde, CA 17 E4
Palomas, CHIH 29 C3
Palominas, AZ 28 E3
Palos Verdes Estates, CA 86 A5
Palouse, WA 18 A5
Pampa, TX 39 A3
Pamplin, VA 63 E2
Pan Tak, AZ 28 C2
Pana, IL 51 D1
Panaca, NV 24 A3
Panama, NY 61 C1
Panama City, FL 66 D3
Panama City Beach, FL 66 D3
Pangman, SK 30 C3
Panguitch, UT 24 C4
Panhandle, TX 39 A3
Pansy, AR 53 A4
Pantego, TX 94 D4
Panthersville, GA 121 D3
Pantono, AZ 28 E2
Paola, KS 50 C3
Paoli, IN 62 B2
Paoli, PA 74 C3
Paonia, CO 25 D3
Papalote, TX 43 E3
Papineauville, PQ 70 A5
Parachute, CO 25 C2
Paradise, CA 12 D4
Paradise, MI 58 A1
Paradise, WA 9 A5
Paradise Valley, AZ 91 D3
Paradise Valley, NV 13 D3
Paradox, CO 25 B3
Paragould, AR 53 C1
Paramount, CA 86 D4
Paramus, NJ 111 A1
Parás, NL 43 C5
Parc de Frontenac, PQ 70 D4
Parc D'Oka, PQ 70 B5
Parc Natl. de la Mauricie, PQ 70 B3
Paris, AR 52 D3
Paris, AZ 52 D3
Paris, ID 22 E3
Paris, IL 51 E1
Paris, KY 62 D2
Paris, ME 71 A5
Paris, MO 51 A2
Paris, ON 59 B5
Paris, TN 51 E5
Paris, TX 52 B5
Paris, VA 74 A5
Parish, WI 47 B3
Park City, KS 37 E4
Park Falls, WI 47 A3
Park Hills, KY 108 B4
Park Place, OR 83 D5
Park Rapids, MN 46 B2
Park Ridge, IL 102 B1
Park River, ND 31 D5
Park Valley, UT 22 C3
Parkdale, AR 53 B5
Parker, AZ 26 A3
Parker, NJ 74 C1
Parker, TX 41 E2
Parkers Lake, KY 62 D4
Parkersburg, IA 48 D2
Parkersburg, WV 61 B5
Parkfield, CA 14 D5
Parkman, OH 61 B2
Parkman, WY 21 E4
Parkrose, OR 83 D2
Parksdale, MO 104 B5
Parkside, PA 114 A5
Parkston, SD 35 D2
Parksville, BC 8 D1
Parkville, MD 115 D2
Parkville, MO 92 B1
Parkwood, NC 118 D3
Parlin, CO 25 E3
Parma, ID 11 E5
Parma, OH 106 C4
Parma Heights, OH 106 C4
Parowan, UT 24 C4
Parrish, FL 69 D1
Parry Sound, ON 59 A1
Parshall, ND 30 E5
Parsons, KS 50 B5
Parsons, TN 64 A1
Parsons, WV 61 D5

Place Name / Page Number / Grid Number

Stantonburg 118 C5

Partoun, UT 24 B1
Pasadena, CA .. 17 A3
Pasadena, TX ... 97 D3
Pasadena Hills, MO 104 D2
Pascagoula, MS .. 66 A4
Pasco, WA 11 D1
Paskenta, CA 12 C4
Paso Robles, CA . 14 D5
Pasqua, SK 30 B2
Pass Christian, MS 55 E4
Passaic, NJ 111 A2
Pastura, NM 38 A4
Patagonia, AZ 28 D3
Patchogue, NY 74 E1
Pateros, WA 9 C3
Paterson, NJ 74 D1
Paterson, WA 11 C1
Patricia, TX 40 E2
Patten, ME 71 B2
Patterson, CA 14 D2
Patterson, LA 55 C5
Patton, MO 51 C4
Paulden, AZ 26 C3
Paulding, OH 60 C3
Paulina, IA 48 A2
Paulina, OR 11 B4
Paulina Hills, MO 104 C5
Pauls Valley, OK . 39 E4
Paulsboro, NJ ... 114 B5
Paulson, BC 9 E2
Pavilion, NY 59 D4
Pavillion, WY 23 C2
Pavo, GA 67 B2
Paw Paw, MI 60 B2
Pawhuska, OK 52 A1
Pawleys Is., SC ... 78 A3
Pawling, NY 72 D5
Pawnee, IL 51 C1
Pawnee, OK 52 A1
Pawnee, TX 43 E2
Pawnee City, NE . 50 A1
Pawnee Rock, KS 37 C4
Pawtucket, RI 73 A4
Paxson, AK 5 D3
Paxton, IL 49 E5
Paxton, NE 35 A5
Payette, ID 11 E4
Paynes Corner, NY 112 C2
Paynesville, MN . 46 B4
Payson, AZ 26 D4
Payson, UT 24 E1
Peabody, KS 37 E4
Peabody, MA 110 D1
Peach Springs, AZ 26 B2
Pearisburg, VA ... 63 C3
Pearl River, LA 55 E4
Pearland, TX 97 C5
Pearsall, TX 43 C2
Pearson, GA 67 C1
Pearson, WA 82 A1
Pecan City, GA 67 A1
Peck, MI 58 D5
Pecos, NM 38 A2
Pecos, TX 40 C3
Peebles, OH 62 E1
Peekskill, NY 72 D5
Peetz, CO 34 D5
Pekin, IL 49 C5
Pekin, ND 33 D1
Pelham, GA 67 A2
Pelham, NY 112 B5
Pelham, ON 59 C4
Pelican Rapids, MN 46 A2
Pelion, SC 65 D3
Pell City, AL 64 C4
Pella, IA 48 E4
Pelly Crossing, YT . 5 E3
Pelsor, AR 52 E2
Pelton, ON 103 E4
Pemaquid Point, ME 73 B1
Pemberton, MA 110 E4
Pembina, ND 31 E4
Pembine, WI 47 D3
Pembroke, GA 65 D5
Pembroke Park, FL 123 D1
Pembroke Pines, FL 123 C1
Pendleton, IN 60 B5
Pendleton, OR 11 D2
Penetanguishene, ON 59 A2
Penfield, PA 61 D2
Peninsula, OH ... 106 E5
Penland, NC 63 B5
Penn Hills, PA ... 107 D2
Penn Square, PA 114 A1
Penn Valley, PA 114 A2
Penn Wynne, PA 114 A3
Penn Yan, NY 59 E5
Pennant, SK 19 D1
Pennington Gap, VA 63 A4
Penns Grove, NJ . 74 C3
Pennsauken, PA 114 D3
Pennsboro, WV ... 61 B5
Pennsbury Village, PA 107 B4
Pennsuco, FL 123 B3
Penrose, CO 36 B4
Pensacola, FL 66 C3
Penticton, BC 9 D1
Pentwater, MI 58 A5
Penwell, TX 40 D3
Peonia, KY 62 B4
Peoria, AZ 26 C4
Peoria, IL 49 C5
Peoria Heights, IL 49 C5
Pep, NM 38 C5
Pepper Pike, OH 106 E2
Perez, CA 12 E2
Perham, MN 46 A2
Peridot, AZ 26 E5
Perintown, OH .. 108 E3
Perkins, MI 47 E2
Perrin, TX 41 D1
Perrine, FL 80 B3
Perris, CA 17 B3
Perry, FL 67 B3
Perry, GA 65 A5
Perry, IA 48 C4
Perry, ME 71 C3
Perry, MI 60 C1
Perry, NY 59 D5
Perry, OK 39 E1
Perry, OR 11 D2
Perry Hall, MD .. 115 D1
Perrysburg, OH ... 60 D2
Perrysville, PA .. 107 B2
Perryton, TX 39 A1
Perryville, AK 5 A5
Perryville, AR 52 E3
Perryville, MO 51 C4
Perth, ON 59 E1
Perth Amboy, NJ 74 D2
Perth-Andover, NB 71 B1
Peru, IL 49 C4
Peru, IN 60 B4
Peru, VT 72 D3
Peshtigo, WI 47 D3
Petaluma, CA 14 B1
Peterborough, NH 72 E3
Peterborough, ON 59 C3
Petersburg, AK 5 E5
Petersburg, IN 62 A2
Petersburg, NE 35 D4
Petersburg, NY 72 D3
Petersburg, VA 76 B2
Petersburg, WV .. 61 D5
Petitcodiac, NB .. 71 E1
Petoskey, MI 58 B3
Petrified Forest Natl. Park, AZ 27 A3
Petrolia, CA 12 A3
Pettus, TX 43 E2
Pettys Hill, MO . 104 B4
Pevely, MO 51 C3
Pewaukee, WI .. 101 A3
Peyton, CO 36 B3
Pfeiffer Corners, MD 115 A5
Pharr, TX 43 E6
Phenix City, AL ... 64 E5
Phil Campbell, AL 64 A3
Philadelphia, NY 72 A2
Philadelphia, MS 55 E1
Philadelphia, PA 74 C2
Philip, SD 34 E1
Philippi, WV 61 C5
Philipsburg, MT .. 20 D2
Philipsburg, PA .. 61 E2
Phillips, ME 71 A5
Phillips, WI 47 A3
Phillips Beach, MA 110 E1
Phillips Point, MA 110 E1
Phillipsburg, KS .. 37 C2
Phillipsburg, NJ .. 74 C2
Phillipsburg, OH .. 60 D5
Phippsburg, CO ... 25 E1
Phlox, WI 47 C4
Phoenicia, NY 72 C4
Phoenix, AZ 26 C5
Phoenix, MI 45 C5
Picacho, AZ 28 D1
Picacho, CA 17 E5
Picacho, NM 40 A1
Picayune, MS 55 E4
Picher, OK 50 C5
Pickerington, OH 109 E4
Pickford, MI 58 B1
Pico Rivera, CA .. 86 E2
Pie Town, NM 27 C4
Piedmont, AL 64 D3
Piedmont, CA 83 C3
Piedmont, MO 51 B5
Piedmont, PQ 70 B4
Piedra, CO 25 D5
Piedras Negras, COAH 43 B2
Piedritas, COAH .. 42 D2
Pierce, ID 20 B1
Pierce, NE 35 E3
Pierceville, KS 37 A4
Piermont, NY 112 A4
Pierpont, SD 33 D4
Pierre, SD 33 B5
Pierrefonds, PQ ... 70 B5
Pierreville, PQ ... 70 C4
Pierson, FL 67 E4
Pierson, MB 31 A4
Piggott, AR 53 C1
Piketon, OH 62 E1
Pikeville, KY 63 A3
Pikeville, TN 64 D1
Pilger, NE 35 E4
Pillsbury, ND 33 D1
Pilot Rock, OR ... 11 D2
Pincher Creek, AB 18 D2
Pinckneyville, IL .. 51 D3
Pinconning, MI ... 58 C4
Pine, AZ 26 D4
Pine Bluff, AR 53 A4
Pine Bluffs, WY .. 34 C5
Pine Castle, FL .. 120 D3
Pine Falls, MB 31 E2
Pine Hill, AL 66 B1
Pine Hill, NJ 114 E5
Pine Hills, FL 120 C2
Pine Junction, CO 36 A2
Pine Knolls, MD 116 A1
Pine Knot, KY 62 D4
Pine Lake, GA ... 121 E2
Pine Lawn, MO . 104 D2
Pine Level, AL 66 D1
Pine Mountain, GA 64 E5
Pine Ridge, SD 34 D2
Pine River, MN ... 46 B2
Pine Springs, MN 100 E2
Pine Springs, TX . 40 A3
Pinecreek, MN 44 A4
Pinecrest, UT 90 D2
Pinedale, WY 23 B2
Pinehurst, MA .. 110 A1
Pinehurst, OR 12 D1
Pinehurst, PA 107 A1
Pinellas Park, FL 122 B3
Pineola, NC 63 B5
The Pines, MA .. 110 A1
Pinetta, FL 67 B2
Pineville, KY 62 E4
Pineville, LA 55 A3
Pineville, NC 65 D1
Pineville, WV 63 B2
Piney Point, FL 69 D1
Piney Point Village, TX 97 A3
Pingree, ND 33 C1
Pinole, CA 85 E3
Pinon, AZ 27 A1
Pinon, NM 40 A2
Pinos Altos, NM . 29 B1
Pintlala, AL 66 C1
Pioche, NV 24 A3
Pipe Spring Natl. Mon., AZ 24 C5
Pipestone, MB 31 A3
Pipestone, MN 48 A1
Pipestone Natl. Mon., MN 48 A1
Piqua, OH 60 D5
Pisgah, OH 108 C1
Pisinimo, AZ 28 C2
Pismo Beach, CA 16 D1
Pistol River, OR .. 10 B5
Pitcairn, PA 107 E3
Pitiquito, SON 28 B4
Pitkin, LA 55 A4
Pittock, PA 107 B3
Pittsboro, NC 63 E4
Pittsburg, KS 50 C5
Pittsburg, TX 54 C1
Pittsburgh, PA .. 62 C3
Pittsfield, IL 51 B1
Pittsfield, MA 72 D4
Pittsfield, ME 71 B4
Pittsfield, NH 72 E2
Pittsfield, PA 61 C1
Pittston, PA 74 B1
Pittsville, WI 47 B5
Placentia, CA 87 B4
Placerville, CA 14 E1
Placerville, CO 25 C4
Placita, NM 27 C5
Placitas, NM 38 A2
Plad, MO 50 E4
Plain Dealing, LA 54 E1
Plainfield, CT 73 A4
Plainfield, IN 105 A4
Plains, GA 66 E1
Plains, KS 37 A5
Plains, MT 18 C5
Plains, TX 40 D1
Plainview, NE 35 D3
Plainview, SD 32 E5
Plainview, TX 38 E4
Plainville, KS 37 C2
Plainwell, MI 60 B2
Plankinton, SD 35 D1
Plano, TX 54 A1
Plant City, FL 69 D1
Plantation, FL 80 B3
Plaquemine, LA .. 55 C4
Plaster Rock, NB . 71 B1
Platina, CA 12 C3
Platinum, AK 5 A4
Platte, SD 35 C2
Platte City, MO .. 50 C2
Platte Woods, MO 92 B1
Platteville, CO 36 B1
Platteville, WI 49 B2
Plattsburgh, NY .. 72 C1
Plattsmouth, NE .. 48 A5
Pleasant Hill, CA 85 D5
Pleasant Hill, KY . 62 D3
Pleasant Hill, NM 38 C4
Pleasant Hills, PA 107 D4
Pleasant Plains, AR 53 B2
Pleasant Ridge, MI 103 C2
Pleasant Valley, MO 92 D1
Pleasant View, CO 25 B4
Pleasant View, IN 105 E4
Pleasanton, KS ... 50 C4
Pleasanton, NM .. 27 B5
Pleasanton, TX ... 43 D2
Pleasantville, NJ 74 D3
Pleasantville, NY 112 B2
Plentywood, MT . 30 C4
Plessisville, PQ .. 70 D3
Plevna, MT 32 C2
Plover, WI 47 C5
Plum, PA 107 E2
Plum Coulee, MB 31 C4
Plummer, ID 18 A5
Plummer, MN 44 A5
Plush, OR 13 A1
Plymouth, CA 14 D1
Plymouth, IN 60 A3
Plymouth, MA 73 A3
Plymouth, ME 71 B4
Plymouth, NC 76 C4
Plymouth, NH 72 E1
Plymouth, PA 74 B1
Plymouth, WI 47 D5
Plymouth Meeting, PA 114 A1
Plymouth Valley, PA 114 A1
Poca, WV 63 B1
Pocahontas, AR .. 53 B1
Pocatello, ID 22 D2
Pocomoke City, MD 74 C5
Pohenegamook, PQ 70 E1
Point Arena, CA .. 12 A5
Point Harbor, NC 76 D3
Point Hope, AK 5 B1
Point Judith, RI ... 73 A5
Point Lookout, MD 74 C5
Point Marion, PA 61 C4
Point of Pines, MA 110 D2
Point of Rocks, WY 23 C4
Point Pelee Natl. Park, ON 60 E2
Point Pleasant, NJ 74 D2
Point Pleasant, WV 63 A1
Point Shirley, MA 110 D3
Pointe-au-Pic, PQ 70 E1
Pointe Aux Pins, MI 58 B2
Pte.-Claire, PQ 70 B5
Pojoaque, NM 27 E2
Poland, NY 72 B3
Poland Springs, ME 73 A1
Pollock, ID 20 A3
Pollock, LA 55 A3
Pollocksville, NC . 76 C5
Polo, IL 49 C3
Polson, MT 18 C5
Pomerene, AZ 28 E2
Pomeroy, OH 63 A1
Pomeroy, WA 11 E1
Pomona, CA 17 A3
Pompano Beach, FL 80 B2
Ponca, NE 35 E3
Ponca City, OK 39 E1
Ponce, PR 6 B4
Ponce de Leon, FL 66 D3
Poncha Springs, CO 25 E3
Ponchatoula, LA .. 55 D4
Pond Creek, OK ... 39 D1
Pontiac, IL 49 D4
Pontiac, MI 60 D1
Pontotoc, MS 53 E3
Popham Beach, ME 73 B1
Poplar, MT 30 B5
Poplar Bluff, MO . 51 C5
Poplarville, MS 55 E3
Port Alberni, BC 8 D1
Port Allegany, PA 61 D1
Port Allen, LA 55 C4
Port Angeles, WA . 8 E2
Port Aransas, TX . 56 A3
Port Arthur, TX 54 E5
Port Austin, MI 58 D4
Port Blakely, WA 82 A3
Port Bolivar, TX 56 D1
Port Charlotte, FL 69 E2
Port Clinton, OH .. 60 E2
Port Clyde, ME 71 B5
Port Colburne, ON 59 C5
Port Elgin, ON 58 E3
Port Gamble, WA .. 9 A3
Port Gibson, MS .. 55 C2
Port Hardy, BC 5 G6
Port Henry, NY 72 C2
Port Hope, MI 58 D4
Port Hope, ON 59 D3
Port Hueneme, CA 16 E2
Port Huron, MI 58 E5
Port Isabel, TX 56 A6
Port Jefferson, NY 74 E1
Port Jervis, NY 74 C1
Port Kent, NY 72 C1
Port Lavaca, TX ... 56 A2
Port Madison, WA 82 B1
Port Mansfield, TX 56 A5
Port Matilda, PA . 61 E2
Port Mayaca, FL .. 80 A2
Port Norris, NJ 74 C3
Port O'Conner, TX 56 B2
Port Ontario, NY . 72 A3
Port Orford, OR 10 B4
Port Perry, PA 107 D3
Port Radium, NT 5 G2
Port Renfrew, BC .. 8 D2
Port St. Joe, FL 66 E4
Port St. Lucie, FL . 80 B1
Port Sanilac, MI .. 58 D5
Port Spencer, AK .. 5 A2
Port Sulphur, LA .. 55 E5
Port Townsend, WA 8 E3
Port Vue, PA 107 E4
Port Washington, NY 111 E1
Port Washington, WI 49 D1
Portage, ME 71 A1
Portage, WA 82 A5
Portage, WI 49 C1
Portage la Prairie, MB 31 D2
Portageville, NY .. 59 D5
Portair, NM 38 C4
Portal, ND 30 E4
Portala, AZ 29 A2
Portales, NM 38 C4
Porters Corners, MT 20 D2
Porterville, CA 15 A5
Porthill, ID 18 B3
Portis, KS 36 C2
Portland, IN 60 C4
Portland, ME 73 A1
Portland, MI 60 B1
Portland, OR 10 E1
Portland, PA 74 C1
Portland, TN 62 B5
Portneuf, PQ 70 C3
Portola, CA 12 E4
Portola Valley, CA 84 C2
Portsmouth, NH .. 73 A2
Portsmouth, OH .. 62 E1
Portsmouth, VA 76 C2
Post, OR 11 B4
Post, TX 41 A1
Post Falls, ID 18 A4
Postoak, MO 50 D3
Postville, IA 49 A2
Potato Creek, SD 34 E2
Poteau, OK 52 C3
Poteet, TX 43 D2
Poth, TX 43 E2
Potlatch, ID 18 A5
Potomac, MD 116 A1
Potomac, MT 20 D1
Potosi, MO 51 B4
Potsdam, NY 72 A1
Potter, NE 34 D5
Potters Mills, PA 61 E2
Pottstown, PA 74 B2
Pottsville, PA 74 B2
Poughkeepsie, NY 72 D5
Poulsbo, WA 82 A1
Poultney, VT 72 D2
Pound, VA 63 A3
Pound, WI 47 D3
Pound Ridge, NY 112 D1
Powder River, WY 23 E2
Powderville, MT . 32 B3
Powell, OH 109 B1
Powell, WY 21 C4
Powellhurst, OR .. 83 D3
Powers, MI 47 D3
Powers, OR 10 C4
Powhatan Point, OH 61 B4
Poydras, LA 98 E5
Prague, OK 52 A3
Prairie City, OR ... 11 C3
Prairie City, SD ... 32 D4
Prairie du Chien, WI 49 A2
Prairie du Sac, WI 49 B1
Prairie Village, KS 92 B4
Prairieville, AL 66 B1
Pratt, KS 37 D5
Prattsville, NY 72 C4
Prattville, AL 64 C5
Premont, TX 43 E4
Prentice, WI 47 B3
Prentiss, ME 71 B3
Prentiss, MS 55 D2
Prescott, AR 52 E5
Prescott, AZ 26 C3
Prescott, WA 11 D1
Prescott, WI 46 D4
Prescott Valley, AZ 26 C3
Presho, SD 35 B1
Presidio, TX 42 B1
Presque Isle, ME 71 B1
Presque Isle, WI . 47 B2
Presto, PA 107 B4
Preston, ID 22 E3
Preston, MN 48 E1
Preston, MO 50 E4
Prestonburg, KY .. 63 A3
Price, UT 24 E1
Prichard, AL 66 B3
Priddy, TX 41 D3
Priest River, ID 18 A4
Primero de Mayo, COAH 43 A4
Primos, PA 114 A4
Prince Frederick, MD 74 B5
Prince George, BC . 5 G5
Prince Rupert, BC .. 5 F6
Prince William, NB 71 C2
Princess Anne, MD 74 C5
Princeton, AR 53 A4
Princeton, BC 9 C1
Princeton, IL 49 C4
Princeton, IN 62 A3
Princeton, KY 62 A4
Princeton, MN 46 C3
Princeton, MO 50 D1
Princeton, NJ 74 C2
Princeton, SC 65 B2
Princeton, WI 47 C5
Princeton, WV 63 C3
Prineville, OR 11 A3
Pringle, SD 34 C1
Pringle, TX 38 E2
Prior Lake, MN 46 D5
Pritchett, CO 36 D5
Proctor, MN 46 D2
Proebstel, WA 83 E1
Progreso, CHIH .. 29 E4
Progreso, COAH .. 43 A4
Progress, OR 83 B3
Prophetstown, IL 49 C3
Prospect, OR 10 D5
Prospect Park, PA 114 A4
Prospect Valley, CO 36 B1
Prosperity, FL 66 D3
Prosser, WA 11 C1
Providence, AL 66 B1
Providence, KY 62 A4
Providence, RI . 73 A4
Provincetown, MA 73 B3
Provo, SD 34 C2
Provo, UT 22 E5
Prudenville, MI 58 B4
Prudhoe Bay, AK ... 5 C1
Pryor, MT 21 D4
Pryor, OK 52 B1
Pueblo, CO 36 B4
Pueblo Pintado, NM 27 C2
Puertecitos, COAH 42 D4
Puerto De Luna, NM 38 B4
Puerto Peñasco, SON 28 A2
Pukaskwa Natl. Park, ON 45 E4
Pulaski, NY 72 A3
Pulaski, TN 64 B2
Pulaski, VA 63 C3
Pullman, WA 11 E1
Pumphrey, MD .. 115 C4
Punkin Center, AZ 26 D4
Punkin Center, CO 36 C3
Punta Gorda, FL .. 69 E2
Punxsutawney, PA 61 D2
Purcell, OK 39 E3
Purchase, NY 112 C4
Purdum, NE 35 B4
Purdy, WA 8 E4
Purisima, CA 84 D1
Purnell, NC 119 C1
Purple Springs, AB 19 A2
Purvis, MS 55 E3
Putnam, AL 66 A1
Putnam, CT 72 E4
Puuwai, HI 6 C1
Puyallup, WA 9 A4
Pylesville, MD 74 B3
Pyote, TX 40 C3

Q

Quakertown, PA . 74 C2
Quanah, TX 39 B4
Quantico, VA 74 A5
Qu' Appelle, SK .. 30 C2
Quarryville, PA 74 B3
Quartzsite, AZ 26 A4
Quatre Chemins, PQ 70 E3
Quay, NM 38 C3
Quebec, PQ 70 D2
Queenstown, NB 71 C2
Queets, WA 8 D3
Quemado, NM 27 B4
Quemado, TX 43 A2
Querobabi, SON .. 28 D4
Questa, NM 38 A1
Quijotoa, AZ 28 C1
Quilcene, WA 8 E3
Quincey, MA 110 D5
Quincy, CA 12 E4
Quincy, FL 67 A3
Quincy, IL 51 A1
Quincy, MA 73 A3
Quincy, WA 9 C4
Quinton, OK 52 B3
Quispamsis, NB .. 71 D2
Quitaque, TX 39 A4
Quitman, GA 67 B2
Quitman, MS 66 A1
Quitman, TX 54 C1

R

Raceland, LA 55 D5
Racine, WI 49 E2
Racine, WV 63 B2
Radcliff, KY 62 B3
Radford, VA 63 C3
Radisson, WI 47 A3
Radium Springs, NM 29 D2
Radville, SK 30 C3
Raeford, NC 76 A5
Ragland, NM 38 C4
Rago, KS 37 D5
Rainbow Bridge Natl. Mon., AZ 24 E5
Rainelle, WV 63 C2
Rainier, OR 8 E5
Raleigh, MS 55 E2
Raleigh, NC 76 A4
Raleigh, ND 33 A3
Raleigh Hills, OR 83 B3
Ralls, TX 39 A5
Ralston, PA 74 A1
Ramah, NM 27 B3
Ramal La Alameda, SON 28 B3
Ramon, NM 38 A4
Ramsey, IL 51 D2
Ranchester, WY . 21 E4
Rancho Palos Verdes CA 86 A5
Ranchos de Taos, NM 38 A1
Randallstown, MD 115 A3
Randle, WA 9 A5
Randolph, MO 92 D2
Randolph, NE 35 E3
Randolph, UT 22 E4
Randolph, VT 72 D2
Randolph Village, MD 116 E3
Randsburg, CA 17 B1
Rangeley, ME 70 E5
Rangely, CO 25 C1
Ranger, TX 41 D2
Rankin, PA 107 D3
Rankin, TX 40 E4
Rantoul, IL 49 E5
Rapid City, SD 34 D1
Rapid River, MI ... 47 E2
Ratcliff, TX 54 C3
Ratliff City, OK 39 E4
Raton, NM 38 B1
Raub, ND 32 E1
Rauch, MN 44 C5
Ravalli, MT 18 C5
Ravena, NY 72 C4
Ravenna, NE 35 C5
Ravenna, OH 61 A3
Rawdon, PQ 70 B4
Rawlins, WY 23 D4
Ray, MN 44 C4
Ray, ND 30 D5
Raymond, AB 18 E3
Raymond, CA 14 E3
Raymond, CO 36 A1
Raymond, IL 51 C2
Raymond, WA 8 D4
Raymondville, TX 43 E5
Rayne, LA 55 B4
Rayon City, TN 99 D2
Raytown, MO 92 D4
Rayville, LA 55 B1
Reading, MA 110 C1
Reading, OH 108 C2
Reading, PA 74 B2
Reading Highlands, MA 110 B1
Reager, KS 37 B2
Reardan, WA 9 E4
Rebecca, GA 67 B1
Rector, AR 53 C1
Red Bank, NJ 74 D2
Red Bay, AL 64 A3
Red Bluff, CA 12 C4
Red Boiling Springs, TN 62 C5
Red Bud, IL 51 C3
Red Cloud, NE 37 D1
Red Creek, NY 59 E4
Red Elm, SD 32 E4
Red Hill, NM 27 B4
Red Hook, NY 72 D4
Red Lake, AZ 26 E1
Red Lake Falls, MN 44 A5
Red Lion, PA 74 B3
Red Lodge, MT 21 C4
Red Mountain, CA 17 B1
Red Oak, GA 121 B5
Red Oak, IA 48 B5
Red River, NM 38 A1
Red Rock, PA 74 A1
Red Rock Trading Post, AZ 27 B1
Red Wing, MN 46 D5
Redcliff, AB 19 B2
Redding, CA 12 C3
Redfield, SD 33 C5
Redford, NY 72 B1
Redford Township, MI 103 A3
Redig, SD 32 C4
Redington, AZ 28 E1
Redington Beach, FL 122 A4
Redington Shores, FL 122 A4
Redkey, IN 60 C4
Redlake, MN 44 B5
Redlands, CA 17 B3
Redmond, OR 11 A3
Redmond, WA 82 E2
Redondo Beach, CA 86 A4
Redrock, NM 29 B1
Redstone, CO 25 D2
Redstone, MT 30 B4
Redvers, SK 30 E3
Redwood, MS 55 C1
Redwood, NC 119 A1
Redwood, NY 72 A2
Redwood Falls, MN 46 B5
Redwood Natl. Park, CA 12 B2
Reed, ME 71 B3
Reed City, MI 58 A5
Reeder, ND 32 D3
Reedpoint, MT 21 C3
Reedsburg, WI 49 B1
Reedsport, OR 10 C3
Reedville, OR 83 A3
Reedville, VA 76 C1
Reeves, LA 55 A4
Reform, AL 64 A4
Refugio, TX 56 A3
Regina, NM 27 D2
Regina, SK 30 C2

Bold type indicates cities with 100,000 population or more.

Place Name / Page Number / Grid Number
Stantonburg 118 C5

Regway, SK 30 C4
Rehoboth, GA 121 D2
Rehoboth Beach, DE 74 D4
Rehouse, MS 61 D5
Reidsville, GA 65 C5
Reidsville, NC 63 E4
Reissing, PA 107 A5
Reisterstown, MD 74 B4
Relay, MD 115 B5
Remer, MN 46 C1
Remington, OH 108 D2
Remus, MI 58 B5
Renfrew, ON 59 E1
Rennerdale, PA 107 B4
Reno, NV 13 A5
Reno, TX 52 B5
Renous, NB 71 D1
Renoyo, PA 61 C1
Rensselaer, IN 60 A4
Renton, WA 9 A4
Repaupo, NJ 114 B5
Repton, AL 66 B2
Republic, MI 47 D2
Republic, WA 9 D3
Reserve, NM 27 B5
Reva, SD 32 D4
Revere, MA 110 D2
Rex, GA 121 E5
Rexburg, ID 20 E5
Rexford, KS 36 A2
Rexford, MT 18 C3
Reynolds, IN 60 A4
Reynoldsburg, OH 109 E3
Rhinelander, WI 47 B3
Rhome, TX 41 E1
Rhyolite, NV 15 C4
Ribera, NM 38 A3
Ricardo, TX 43 E4
Ricardo Flores Magon, CHIH 29 D5
Rice, CA 17 E3
Rice, WA 9 E3
Rice Lake, WI 46 E3
Rich Creek, WV 63 C3
Rich Hill, MO 50 C4
Rich Square, NC 76 B3
Richardson, OR 10 C3
Richardson, TX 95 D1
Richardton, ND 32 E2
Richer, MB 31 E3
Richey, MT 32 B1
Richfield, ID 22 B1
Richfield, KS 36 E5
Richfield, MN 100 B4
Richfield, UT 24 D2
Richfield Springs, NY 72 B4
Richford, NY 72 A5
Richford, VT 70 C5
Richland, GA 66 E1
Richland, MI 60 B2
Richland, MT 30 A4
Richland, OR 11 E3
Richland, TX 54 A2
Richland, WA 11 C1
Richland Center, WI 49 B1
Richland Hills, TX 94 C3
Richland Springs, TX 41 D4
Richlands, NC 76 B5
Richmond, CA 85 D3
Richmond, IN 60 C5
Richmond, KY 62 D3
Richmond, MI 60 D1
Richmond, MO 50 D2
Richmond, PQ 70 D4
Richmond, VA 76 B2
Richmond Beach, WA 82 C1
Richmond Heights, MO 104 C3
Richmond Heights, OH 106 E1
Richmond Highlands, WA 82 C1
Richmond Hill, ON 59 B3
Richmondville, NY 72 C4
Richton, MS 55 E2
Richville, MI 58 C5
Richwood, WV 63 C1
Ridgecrest, CA 17 B1
Ridgefield, CT 72 D5
Ridgefield, NJ 111 B2
Ridgefield Park, NJ 111 B2
Ridgeland, SC 65 D4
Ridgeview, SD 33 A4
Ridgeway, CO 25 D4
Ridgeway, NY 76 B3
Ridgeway, PA 61 D2
Ridgeway, VA 63 D3
Riding Mtn. Natl. Park, MB 31 B1
Ridley Park, PA 114 A4
Rifle, CO 25 D2
Rigaud, PQ 70 B5
Rigby, ID 22 E1
Riggins, ID 20 A3
Riley, AL 66 B2
Riley, NC 119 E2
Rimel, WV 63 D1
Ringgold, LA 54 E2
Ringling, MT 21 B2
Ringoes, NJ 74 C2
Rio Blanco, CO 25 D2
Rio Bravo, COAH 43 A3
Rio Dell, CA 12 A3
Rio Grande City, TX 43 D5
Rio Hondo, TX 43 E6
Rio Vista, CA 14 C1
Ripley, MS 53 E3
Ripley, NY 61 C1
Ripley, OH 62 E1
Ripley, TN 53 D1
Ripley, WV 63 B1
Ripon, WI 47 C5
Ririe, ID 22 E1
Rising Star, TX 41 C2
Rising Sun, IN 62 C1
Rising Sun, MD 74 B3
Rison, AR 53 A4
Ritzville, WA 9 D5
River Edge, NJ 111 B1
River Falls, AL 66 C2
River Forest, IL 102 B3
River Grove, IL 102 B2
River Hills, WI 101 D1
River Oaks, TX 94 A3
River Ridge, LA 98 A4
River Rouge, MI 103 C5
Riverdale, GA 121 C5
Riverdale, MA 110 B5
Riverdale, MD 116 D2
Rivergrove, OR 83 B4
Riverhead, NY 72 E5
Riverhurst, SK 30 A1
Riverside, CA 17 B3
Riverside, CT 112 D3
Riverside, IL 102 C4
Riverside, MD 74 B5
Riverside, MO 92 B2
Riverside, NJ 114 D1
Riverside, WY 23 E5
Riverside-Albert, NB 71 E2
Riverton, MB 31 E1
Riverton, NJ 114 D2
Riverton, UT 90 B5
Riverton, WY 23 C2
Riverton Heights, WA 82 C5
Riverview, FL 69 D1
Riverview, MO 104 E1
Riverview, NB 71 E1
Riviera, TX 43 E4
Riviera Beach, MD 115 E5
Riviere-a-Pierre, PQ 70 C2
Riviere Bleue, PQ 71 A1
Riviere-Verte, NB 71 B1
Roan Mountain, TN 63 B5
Roanoke, AL 64 D4
Roanoke, TX 41 E1
Roanoke, VA 63 D3
Roanoke Rapids, NC 76 B3
Roaring Springs Ranch, CA 13 C1
Robbinsdale, MN 100 B2
Robert Lee, TX 41 B3
Roberta, GA 65 A5
Robertsdale, AL 66 B3
Robertson, MO 104 C1
Robinson, IL 51 E2
Robinsons Ranch, UT 24 B2
Roblin, MB 31 A1
Robsart, SK 19 C3
Robstown, TX 43 E3
Roby, MO 51 A4
Roby, TX 41 B1
Rocanville, SK 30 E2
Rochelle, GA 67 B1
Rochelle, IL 49 C3
Rochelle, TX 41 C4
Rochelle Park, NJ 111 A1
Rochester, IL 51 C1
Rochester, IN 60 A4
Rochester, MN 46 E5
Rochester, NH 73 A2
Rochester, NY 59 D4
Rochester, PA 61 C3
Rochester, VT 72 D2
Rock Creek, BC 9 D2
Rock Creek, MN 46 D3
Rock Creek, OR 83 A1
Rock Creek Corner, OR 83 D5
Rock Falls, IL 49 C3
Rock Harbor Lodge, MI 45 C4
Rock Hill, MO 104 C3
Rock Hill, SC 65 D1
Rock Is., PQ 70 D5
Rock Is., TX 56 A1
Rock Point, MD 74 B5
Rock Port, MO 50 B1
Rock Rapids, IA 40 A2
Rock River, WY 34 A4
Rock Springs, AZ 26 C4
Rock Springs, MT 32 A2
Rock Springs, WY 23 B4
Rockdale, MD 115 A3
Rockdale, TX 54 A4
Rockford, AL 64 C5
Rockford, IL 49 C2
Rockglen, SK 30 A3
Rockham, SD 33 C5
Rockingham, NC 65 E1
Rocklake, ND 31 C4
Rockland, MD 115 A4
Rockland, ME 71 B5
Rockland, ON 70 A5
Rockland Lake, NY 112 A3
Rocklane, IN 105 E5
Rockledge, FL 64 F5
Rockledge, PA 114 C1
Rockmart, GA 64 D3
Rockport, CO 34 B5
Rockport, TX 56 A3
Rockport, WA 9 B2
Rocksprings, TX 41 B5
Rockvale, MT 21 C3
Rockville, IN 62 A1
Rockville, MD 74 A4
Rockwell City, IA 48 C3
Rockwood, ME 71 A3
Rockwood, OR 83 E3
Rockwood, TN 64 D1
Rockwood, TX 41 C3
Rocky Ford, CO 36 C4
Rocky Mount, NC 76 B4
Rocky Mount, VA 63 D3
Rocky Mtn. Natl. Park, CO 36 A1
Rocky River, OH 106 A3
Rodeo, CA 85 C4
Rodeo, NM 29 A2
Rodey, NM 29 D1
Rodrigo M. Quevedo, CHIH 29 C2
Rodriguez, NL 43 B4
Roeland Park, KS 92 B3
Roger, ND 33 D2
Rogers, AR 52 D1
Rogers, TX 54 A4
Rogers City, MI 58 C2
Rogers Store, NC 119 A2
Rogerson, ID 22 B2
Rogersville, AL 64 B2
Rogersville, TN 63 A4
Rohwer, AR 53 B4
Rolesville, NC 119 D2
Roll, OK 39 B2
Rolla, KS 36 E5
Rolla, MO 51 A4
Rolla, ND 31 B4
Rolling Fork, MS 55 C1
Rolling Hills, CA 86 B5
Rolling Hills Estates, CA 86 B5
Rollingbay, WA 82 B2
Rollins, MT 18 C4
Roma los Saenz, TX 43 D5
Rome, GA 64 D3
Rome, NY 72 B3
Rome, OR 13 D1
Romeo, MI 60 D1
Romeoville, NM 38 A3
Romney, IN 60 A5
Romney, WV 61 E4
Romulus, MI 103 A5
Ronald, WA 82 C1
Ronan, MT 18 D5
Roodhouse, IL 51 B1
Roosevelt, AZ 26 D4
Roosevelt, MN 44 B4
Roosevelt, OK 39 C4
Roosevelt, TX 41 B5
Roosevelt, UT 25 A1
Rooseveltown, NY 72 B1
Roosville, BC 18 C3
Rosalia, WA 9 E5
Rosamond, CA 17 A2
Rosarito, BC 17 B5
Roscoe, NY 72 C5
Roscoe, SD 33 C4
Roscoe, TX 41 B2
Roscommon, MI 58 B4
Rose City, MI 58 C4
Rose Valley, PA 114 A4
Roseau, MN 44 A4
Rosebud, MT 32 A3
Rosebud, TX 54 A4
Roseburg, OR 10 C4
Rosedale, MD 115 D3
Rosedale, MS 53 C4
Rosedale, PA 107 D2
Roseland, ON 103 E4
Rosemead, CA 86 E1
Rosemont, IL 102 B2
Rosemount, MN 46 D5
Rosenberg, TX 56 B1
Roseville, CA 14 D1
Roseville, IL 49 B5
Roseville, MI 103 E1
Roseville, MN 100 C2
Rosharon, TX 56 C1
Rosholt, SD 33 E3
Rosiclare, IL 51 E4
Rosinville, SC 65 E3
Roslyn, PA 114 B1
Rosman, NC 65 A1
Ross, CA 85 E1
Ross, KY 108 D5
Ross, ND 30 D5
Ross River, YT 5 E3
Rossland, BC 9 E2
Rosslyn Farms, PA 107 B4
Rosston, AR 52 E5
Rosston, OK 39 B1
Rossville, IN 60 A5
Roswell, GA 64 E3
Roswell, NM 40 B1
Rotan, TX 41 D1
Rothschild, WI 47 B4
Rotterdam, NY 72 C3
Rouleau, SK 30 B2
Round Hill, CT 112 C3
Round Mountain, CA 12 D3
Round Mountain, NV 15 D2
Round Rock, AZ 27 A1
Round Rock, TX 41 E5
Round Spring, MO 51 B5
Roundhead, OH 60 D4
Roundup, MT 21 D2
Rouses, NY 70 C5
Rowayton, CT 112 F5
Rowe, NM 38 A3
Rowland, NC 78 A1
Rowood, AZ 28 B1
Roxboro, NC 63 E3
Roxton Falls, PQ 70 C4
Roy, MT 21 C1
Roy, NM 38 B2
Roy, UT 22 D4
Royal Mills, NC 119 D1
Royal Oak, MI 103 B1
Royalton, IN 105 A1
Royalton, MN 46 C3
Royalton, VT 72 D2
Royalty, TX 40 D3
Royston, GA 65 A2
Rozet, WY 32 B5
Ruby, WA 18 A3
Ruby Valley, NV 22 A5
Rubys Inn, UT 24 D4
Ruch, OR 10 C5
Ruckersville, VA 63 E1
Rudyard, MI 58 B1
Ruffin, SC 65 D3
Rugby, ND 31 B5
Ruggs, OR 11 C2
Ruidosa, NM 29 E1
Ruidosa, TX 40 A5
Ruidoso Downs, NM 40 A1
Rule, TX 41 B1
Ruleville, MS 53 C4
Rumford, ME 71 A5
Runge, TX 43 E2
Runnemede, NJ 114 D4
Rupert, ID 22 C2
Rupert, WV 63 C2
Rural Hill, TN 99 D4
Rural Ridge, PA 107 D1
Rush Center, KS 37 C3
Rush Springs, OK 39 D4
Rushford, MN 48 E1
Rushville, IL 51 B1
Rushville, IN 62 C1
Rushville, NE 34 D3
Rusk, TX 54 C3
Ruskin, FL 69 D1
Russell, KS 37 C3
Russell, KY 63 A1
Russell, MB 31 A1
Russell Cave Natl. Mon., AL 64 C2
Russell Springs, KS 37 A3
Russell Springs, KY 62 D4
Russellton, PA 107 D1
Russellville, AL 64 A3
Russellville, AR 52 E3
Russellville, KY 62 B5
Russellville, OR 83 D3
Rustic, CO 34 A5
Ruston, LA 55 A1
Ruth, NV 24 A1
Rutherford, NJ 111 A2
Rutherfordton, NC 65 B1
Ruthville, ND 31 A5
Rutland, VT 72 D2
Ruxton, MD 115 B2
Ryan, CA 15 C5
Ryan, OK 39 D5
Rye, NY 112 C4
Rye Brook, NY 112 C4
Ryegate, MT 21 C2

S

Sabetha, KS 50 B1
Sabinal, TX 43 C1
Sabinas, COAH 43 A3
Sabinas Hidalgo, NL 43 B5
Sabine Pass, TX 54 E5
Sac City, IA 48 B3
Sackets Harbor, NY 72 A3
Sackville, NB 71 E1
Saco, ME 73 A1
Saco, MT 19 E4
Sacramento, CA 14 D1
Safety Harbor, FL 122 B1
Safford, GA 66 E2
Safford, AL 66 B1
Safford, AZ 29 A1
Sag Harbor, NY 72 E5
Saginaw, MI 58 C5
Saginaw, TX 94 A2
Sagola, MI 47 D2
Saguache, CO 25 E4
Saguaro Natl. Mon. East, AZ 28 E2
Saguaro Natl. Mon. West, AZ 28 D1
St.-Agathe, PQ 70 D3
Ste.-Agathe-Sud, PQ 70 A4
St. Albans, VT 72 C1
St. Albans, WV 63 B1
St. Alexandre, PQ 70 E1
St.-Alexis-des-Monts, PQ 70 B3
St. Andrews, NB 71 D3
St. Ann, MO 104 C2
Ste. Anne, MB 31 E3
Ste.-Anne-de-Beaupre, PQ 70 D2
St.-Anselme, PQ 70 D2
St. Anthony, ID 20 E5
St. Anthony, MN 100 C2
St.-Antoine, PQ 70 B4
St. Augustine, FL 67 E3
St. Bernard, OH 108 B3
St.-Casimir, PQ 70 C3
St. Catharines, ON 59 B4
St. Celestin, PQ 70 C3
St. Charles, IL 49 D3
St. Charles, MI 58 C5
St. Charles, MN 46 E5
St. Charles, MO 51 B2
St.-Charles, PQ 70 D2
St.-Chrysostome, PQ 70 B5
St. Clair, LA 98 E5
St. Clair, MO 51 B3
St. Clair Shores, MI 103 E1
St. Claude, MB 31 D3
St. Cloud, FL 67 E5
St. Cloud, MN 46 C3
St.-Come, PQ 70 B4
St. Croix, IN 62 B3
St.-Croix, NB 71 C3
Ste. Croix, PQ 70 D3
St. Croix Falls, WI 46 D4
St.-Cyrille, PQ 70 C4
St.-Denis, PQ 70 C4
St.-Didace, PQ 70 B4
St.-Donat, PQ 70 A4
St. Elmo, IL 51 D2
Ste.-Emelie-de-l'Energie, PQ 70 B4
Ste. Famille, PQ 70 D2
St.-Felix-de-Valois, PQ 70 B4
St. Ferdinand, PQ 70 D3
Ste.-Foy, PQ 70 D2
St. Francis, KS 36 E2
St. Francis, ME 71 A1
St. Francis, MN 46 D4
St. Francis, WI 101 E3
St. Francisville, LA 55 C4
St.-Franscois-du-Lac, PQ 70 C4
St. Gabriel, PQ 70 B4
St.-Gedeon, PQ 70 E3
Ste. Genevieve, MO 51 C3
St. George, GA 67 D2
St. George, MO 104 D4
St. George, SC 65 E3
St. George, UT 24 B4
St.-Georges, PQ 70 E3
St.-Georges-Ouest, PQ 70 E3
St.-Gerard, PQ 70 D4
St.-Germain-de-Grantham, PQ 70 C4
St.-Guillaume-Nord, PQ 70 B3
St. Helena, CA 14 C1
St. Helens, OR 10 E1
St.-Henri, PQ 70 D2
St.-Hyacinthe, PQ 70 C4
St. Ignace, MI 58 B2
St. Ignace-du-Lac, PQ 70 B3
St.-Jacques-de-Leeds, PQ 70 D3
St. James, MI 58 A2
St. James, MN 48 B1
St. James, MO 51 A4
St.-Jean-Chrysostome, PQ 70 D2
St.-Jean-Port-Joli, PQ 70 E1
St.-Jean-sur-Richelieu, PQ 70 C5
St.-Jerome, PQ 70 B4
St. Jo, TX 39 E5
St. John, KS 37 C4
St. John, MO 104 C2
St. John, NB 71 D3
St. Johns, AZ 27 A4
St. Johns, MI 60 C1
St. Johnsbury, VT 72 D1
St. Johnsville, NY 72 B3
St. Joseph, LA 55 C2
St. Joseph, MI 60 A2
St. Joseph, MN 46 B3
St. Joseph, MO 50 C2
St.-Jovite, PQ 70 A4
St. Laurent, MB 31 D2
St. Lazare, MB 31 A2
St.-Leonard, NB 71 B1
St. Louis, MI 58 B5
St. Louis, MO 51 C3
St. Louis Park, MN 100 B4
St. Malo, MB 31 E3
St.-Malo, PQ 70 D5
St.-Marcel, PQ 70 E2
Ste. Marie, PQ 70 D3
St. Maries, ID 18 A5
St. Martins, NB 71 E2
St. Martinville, LA 55 B5
St. Mary, MT 18 D3
St. Marys, GA 67 D2
St. Marys, KS 50 A2
St. Marys, OH 60 C4
St. Marys, PA 61 D2
St. Marys, WV 61 B5
St. Matthews, SC 65 D3
St. Michael, AK 5 B3
St. Michaels, AZ 27 B2
St.-Michel-des-Saints, PQ 70 B3
St.-Pacome, PQ 70 E1
St.-Pamphile, PQ 70 E2
St.-Pascal, PQ 70 E1
Saint Paul, MN 46 D4
St. Paul, NE 35 D5
St. Paul, VA 63 B4
St.-Paul-de-Montminy, PQ 70 E2
Saint Paul Park, MN 100 E4
St. Pauls, NC 78 A1
Ste.-Perpetue, PQ 70 E2
St. Peter, MN 46 C5
St. Peters, MO 104 A1
St. Petersburg, FL 69 D1
St. Petersburg Beach, FL 122 B4
St.-Pierre-de-Verone, PQ 70 C5
St.-Raphael, PQ 70 D2
St.-Raymond, PQ 70 C2
St. Regis, MT 18 C5
St. Regis Falls, NY 72 B1
St. Robert, KS 51 A4
St.-Roch-de-Mekinac, PQ 70 C3
Ste. Rosalie, PQ 70 C4
Ste.-Rose, PQ 70 E3
Ste. Rose du Lac, MB 31 B1
St.-Simeon, PQ 70 E1
St.-Stephen, NB 71 C3
St. Stephen, SC 65 E3
St. Teresa, FL 67 A4
Ste.-Thecle, PQ 70 C3
Ste.-Therese, PQ 70 B5
St. Thomas, ON 59 A5
St.-Tite, PQ 70 C3
St. Xavier, MT 21 D4
St.-Urbain, PQ 70 D1
St. Zacharie, PQ 70 E3
Salaberry-de-Valleyfield, PQ 70 B5
Salado, TX 41 E4
Salaises, CHIH 42 A5
Salamanca, NY 61 C1
Salem, AR 53 A1
Salem, FL 67 B3
Salem, IL 51 D2
Salem, IN 62 B2
Salem, MA 73 A3
Salem, MO 51 A4
Salem, NJ 74 C3
Salem, NY 72 D3
Salem, OH 61 B3
Salem, OR 10 D2
Salem, SD 35 E1
Salem, VA 63 D3
Salem, WV 61 C5
Salina, KS 37 E3
Salina, UT 24 D2
Salinas, CA 14 C3
Salinas Natl. Mon. [Abo], NM 27 E4
Salinas Natl. Mon. [Gran Quivira], NM 27 E4
Salinas Natl. Mon. [Quarai], NM 27 E4
Salisbury, MD 74 C5
Salisbury, MO 50 E2
Salisbury, NB 71 E1
Salisbury, NC 63 D5
Sallisaw, OK 52 C2
Salmo, BC 18 A2
Salmon, ID 20 C3
Salome, AZ 26 A4
Salt Flat, TX 40 A3
Salt Lake City, UT 22 D5
Saltcoats, SK 30 E1
Saluda, SC 65 C2
Saluda, VA 76 B1
Salvo, NC 76 D4
Salyersville, KY 62 F3
Samalayuca, CHIH 29 D3
Sammamish, WA 82 E3
Samson, AL 66 D2
San Acacia, NM 27 D4
San Andreas, CA 14 E2
San Angelo, TX 41 B3
San Anselmo, CA 84 E1
San Antonio, NM 27 D5
San Antonio, TX 43 D1
San Antonio Spring, NM 27 C2
San Augustine, TX 54 D3
San Benito, TX 43 E6
San Bernardino, CA 17 B3
San Blas, COAH 42 E4
San Bruno, CA 85 A1
San Buenaventura, COAH 42 E4
San Carlos, CA 84 E2
San Clemente, CA 17 B4
San Diego, CA 17 B5
San Diego, TX 43 D3
San Dimas, CA 87 C2
San Emeterio, SON 28 B2
San Fernando, CA 17 A2
San Fidel, NM 27 C3
San Francisco, CA 14 B2
San Gabriel, CA 86 E1
San German, PR 6 A4
San Gregorio, CA 84 C1
San Guillermo, COAH 42 D2
San Isidro, TX 43 D5
San Jon, NM 38 C3
San Jose, CA 14 C2
San Juan, NM 29 C1
San Juan, PR 6 B3
San Juan Capistrano, CA 17 B4
San Leandro, CA 85 B4
San Lorenzo, CA 85 A4
San Luis, CO 36 A5
San Luis Obispo, CA 16 D1
San Luisito, SON 28 B3
San Manuel, AZ 28 E1
San Marcos, TX 41 E5
San Marino, CA 86 E1
San Mateo, CA 14 B2
San Mateo, NM 27 C3
San Miguel, AZ 28 C2
San Miguel, CA 14 D5
San Miguel, COAH 42 D2
San Pablo, CA 85 E3
San Pierre, IN 60 A4
San Rafael, CA 14 B1
San Rafael, NM 27 C3
San Saba, TX 41 D4
San Sebastian, PR 6 A3
San Simeon, CA 14 C5
San Simon, AZ 29 A2
San Xavier, AZ 28 D2
San Ygnacio, TX 43 C4
San Ysidro, NM 27 D2
Sanborn, IA 40 A2
Sand Hill, MS 66 A2
Sand Springs, MT 21 E1
Sand Springs, OK 52 B1
Sanders, AZ 27 A3
Sanderson, TX 40 D5
Sandersville, GA 65 B4
Sandford, NS 71 E4
Sandia, TX 43 E3
Sandoval, IL 51 D2
Sandpoint, ID 18 A4
Sands Point, NY 111 F1
Sandusky, MI 58 D5
Sandusky, OH 60 E2
Sandwich, IL 49 D3
Sandy, OR 10 E1
Sandy, UT 90 B5
Sandy Creek, NY 72 A3
Sandy Creek, PA 107 D2
Sandy Hook, CT 72 D5
Sandy Hook, KY 62 E2
Sandy Lake, PA 61 C2
Sandy Springs, GA 121 C1
Sanford, FL 67 E4
Sanford, ME 73 A2
Sanford, NC 63 E5
Sanfordtown, KY 108 B5
Sanibel, FL 69 E3
Sansom Park Village, TX 94 A2
Santa Ana, CA 17 A3
Santa Ana, SON 28 D4
Santa Anna, TX 41 C3
Santa Barbara, CA 16 D2
Santa Clara, CA 14 C2
Santa Cruz, AZ 28 B2
Santa Cruz, CA 14 C3
Santa Fe, NM 27 E2
Santa Fé del Pino, COAH 42 C2
Santa Fe Springs, CA 86 E3
Santa Margarita, CA 14 D5
Santa Maria, CA 16 D1
Santa Maria, TX 43 E6
Santa Monica, CA 17 A3
Santa Paula, CA 16 E2
Santa Rita, MT 18 E4
Santa Rosa, AZ 28 C1
Santa Rosa, CA 14 B1
Santa Rosa, NM 38 B3
Santa Rosa, TX 43 E5
Santa Rosa Beach, FL 66 D3
Santaquin, UT 24 D1
Santee, CA 89 D1
Santiam Junction, OR 10 E3
Santo Tomas, SON 28 A3
Santo Tomas, NM 29 D2
Sapello, NM 38 A2
Saponac, ME 71 B3
Sappho, WA 8 D2
Sappington, MO 104 C4
Sapulpa, OK 52 B2
Saragosa, TX 40 C4
Saralano, AL 66 A3
Saranac, NY 72 C1
Saranac Lake, NY 72 B1
Sarasota, FL 69 D2
Saratoga, CA 84 A4
Saratoga, TX 54 D5
Saratoga, WY 23 E4
Saratoga Springs, NY 72 C3
Sarcoxie, MO 50 D5
Sardis, AL 66 B1
Sardis, GA 65 C4
Sardis, MS 53 D3
Sargent, NE 35 C4
Saric, SON 28 C3
Sarnia, ON 58 E5
Sasabe, AZ 28 C2
Satanta, KS 37 A5
Satellite Beach, FL 67 F5
Saucillo, CHIH 42 A3
Saugatuck, CT 112 F1
Saugatuck, MI 60 A1
Sauget, IL 104 E3
Saugus, CA 17 A2
Saugus, MA 110 D2
Sauk Centre, MN 46 B3
Sauk City, WI 49 C1
Sauk Rapids, MN 46 C3

Place Name / Page Number / Grid Number

Stantonburg **118** C5

Sault Ste. Marie, MI **58** B1
Sault Ste. Marie, ON **58** B1
Saunders, KS **36** E5
Saundersville, TN **99** E1
Sausalito, CA **14** B1
Savage, MT **32** C1
Savanna, IA **49** B3
Savannah, GA **65** D5
Savannah, MO **50** C1
Savannah, TN **64** A2
Sawmill, AZ **27** B2
Sawyer, KS **37** D5
Sayers, TX **96** E4
Sayre, OK **39** B3
Sayre, PA **72** A5
Scandia, WA **82** A1
Scarborough, NY **112** A3
Scarborough, ON **59** C4
Scarboroughs Cross Roads, GA **121** E4
Scarsdale, LA **98** D5
Scarsdale, NY **112** B4
Scenic, SD **34** D1
Schellbourne, NV **24** A1
Schenectady, NY **72** C3
Schertz, TX **96** E2
Schiller Park, IL **102** B2
Schofield, WI **47** B4
Scholle, NM **27** E4
Schroon Lake, NY **72** C2
Schulenburg, TX **56** A1
Schurtz, NV **15** B1
Schuyler, NE **35** E4
Schuylerville, NY **72** C3
Schuylkill Haven, PA **74** B2
Scipio, UT **24** D2
Scituate, MA **73** B3
Scobey, MT **30** B4
Scotia, PA **107** D5
Scotland Neck, NC **76** B3
Scotstown, PQ **70** E4
Scott, NY **72** A4
Scott, PA **107** B4
Scott, PQ **70** D3
Scott City, KS **37** A4
Scott Haven, PA **107** E5
Scottdale, GA **121** D2
Scotts Bluff Natl. Mon., NE **34** C4
Scotts Corner, NY **112** D1
Scottsbluff, NE **34** C4
Scottsboro, AL **64** C2
Scottsboro, TN **99** A3
Scottsburg, IN **62** B2
Scottsdale, AZ **26** C5
Scottsmoor, FL **67** F4
Scottsville, KY **62** B5
Scottville, MI **58** A5
Scout Lake, SK **30** A3
Scranton, IA **48** C3
Scranton, PA **74** B1
Scribner, NE **48** A4
Sea Is., FL **67** D1
Sea Isle City, NJ **74** D3
Sea Ranch, CA **12** B5
Seabold, WA **82** A1
Seabrook, MD **116** E1
Seadrift, TX **56** A2
Seaford, DE **74** C4
Seagraves, TX **40** D1
Seahurst, WA **82** B5
Seal Cove, ME **71** C5
Seal Rock, WA **8** E3
Seale, AL **64** E5
Sealy, TX **54** B5
Searchlight, NV **17** E1
Searcy, AR **53** B2
Searsport, ME **71** B5
Seaside, CA **14** C3
Seaside, OR **8** D5
Seaside Heights, NJ **74** D2
Seat Pleasant, MD **116** D3
Seattle, WA **9** A3
Sebastian, TX **43** E5
Sebastopol, CA **14** B1
Sebeka, MN **46** B2
Sebewaing, MI **58** D4
Seboyetta, NM **27** D3
Sebree, KY **62** A4
Sebring, FL **69** E1
Secaucus, NJ **111** B3
Second Mesa, AZ **26** E2
Section Thirty, MN **44** D5
Security, CO **36** B3
Sedalia, MO **50** E3
Sedan, KS **50** A5
Sedan, NM **38** D2
Sedgwick, CO **34** D5
Sedona, AZ **26** D3
Sedro Woolley, WA **9** A2
Seeley Lake, MT **20** D1
Seguin, TX **43** E1
Segundo, CO **36** B5
Seibert, CO **36** D2
Seiling, OK **39** C2
Sekiu, WA **8** D2
Selawik, AK **5** B2
Selby, SD **33** B4
Selden, KS **37** A2
Seldovia, AK **5** C4
Selfridge, ND **33** A3
Seligman, AZ **26** B2
Seligman, MO **52** D1
Selinsgrove, PA **74** A2
Selkirk, MB **31** E2
Sellersburg, IN **62** C2
Sells, AZ **28** C2
Selma, AL **66** B1
Selma, CA **14** E4
Selma, TX **96** E1
Selmer, TN **53** E2
Seminoe Dam, WY **23** E3
Seminole, FL **122** A3
Seminole, OK **52** A3
Seminole, TX **40** D2
Sena, NM **38** A3
Senath, MO **53** C1
Senatobia, MS **53** D3
Seneca, AZ **26** E4
Seneca, KS **50** A1
Seneca, OR **11** C4
Seneca, SC **65** A2
Seneca, SD **33** C4
Seneca Falls, NY **59** E4
Seneca Park, MD **115** E2
Seneca Rocks, WV **61** D5
Seney, MI **58** A1
Sentinel, AZ **26** B5
Separ, NM **29** B2
Sept-Iles, PQ **70** D1
Sequim, WA **8** E3
Sequoia Natl. Park, CA **15** A4
Service Creek, OR **11** B3
Seven Corners, VA **116** B3
Seven Hills, OH **106** C4
Seven Persons, AB **19** B2
Severy, KS **50** A5
Sevey, NY **72** B2
Sevier, UT **24** D3
Sevierville, TN **62** E5
Seward, AK **5** C4
Seward, NE **35** E5
Sewickley, PA **107** A2
Sewickley Heights, PA **107** A2
Sewickley Hills, PA **107** A2
Seymour, IN **62** B2
Seymour, MO **50** E5
Seymour, TX **39** C5
Shadehill, SD **32** E3
Shadeville, OH **109** C5
Shady Side, MD **74** B4
Shady Spring, WV **63** C2
Shafter, TX **42** B1
Shaker Heights, OH **106** D2
Shakopee, MN **46** C4
Shallotte, NC **78** B2
Shamokin, PA **74** A2
Shamrock, OK **52** A2
Shamrock, TX **39** B3
Shaniko, OR **11** B2
Shannon, MS **53** E4
Sharon, PA **61** B2
Sharon Hill, PA **114** B4
Sharon Springs, KS **36** E3
Sharonville, OH **108** C1
Sharps Corner, SD **34** D2
Sharps Hill, PA **107** C2
Sharpsburg, PA **107** C2
Shattuck, OK **39** B2
Shaunavon, SK **19** D3
Shavano Park, TX **96** B1
Shaver Lake, CA **15** A3
Shawano, WI **47** C4
Shawinigan, PQ **70** B3
Shawinigan Sud, PQ **70** C3
Shawmut, MT **21** C2
Shawnee, KS **92** B4
Shawnee, OK **52** A3
Shawnee, WY **34** B3
Shawnee Hills, OH **109** A1
Shawneetown, IL **51** E4
Sheaville, OR **13** E1
Sheboygan, WI **47** D5
Sheboygan Falls, WI **47** D5
Shediac, NB **71** E1
Sheds, NY **72** A4
Sheep Springs, NM **27** B1
Sheffield, IA **48** D2
Sheffield, IL **49** C4
Sheffield, PA **61** C1
Sheffield, TX **40** E4
Shelbina, MO **51** A1
Shelby, MI **58** A5
Shelby, MS **53** C4
Shelby, MT **19** A4
Shelby, NC **65** C1
Shelbyville, IL **51** D1
Shelbyville, IN **62** B1
Shelbyville, KY **62** C2
Shelbyville, TN **64** B1
Sheldon, IA **48** A2
Sheldon, MO **50** C4
Sheldon, SC **65** D4
Sheldon, TX **97** E1
Sheldon Junction, VT **70** C5
Shell, WY **21** D5
Shelley, ID **22** E1
Shelter Cove, CA **12** A3
Shelter Is., NY **72** E5
Shelton, CT **113** B1
Shelton, WA **8** E4
Shenandoah, IA **48** B5
Shenandoah, PA **74** B2
Shenandoah Natl. Park, VA **61** E5
Sheperdsville, KY **62** C3
Shepherd, TX **54** C4
Sheppardsville, AL **66** B1
Sherard, MS **53** C4
Sherbrooke, PQ **70** D4
Sherburne, NY **72** B4
Sheridan, AR **53** A4
Sheridan, CO **93** B4
Sheridan, MT **20** E3
Sheridan, WY **21** E5
Sheridan Beach, WA **82** D1
Sheridan Lake, CO **36** E4
Sherman, ME **71** B3
Sherman, TX **52** A5
Sherwood, AR **53** A3
Sherwood, ND **30** E4
Sherwood, OR **83** A5
Shickshinny, PA **74** B1
Shidler, OK **52** A1
Shields, KS **37** B3
Shin Pond, ME **71** B2
Shiner, TX **56** A1
Shingleton, MI **47** E1
Shingletown, CA **12** D3
Shinnston, WV **61** C5
Ship Bottom, NJ **74** D3
Shippensburg, PA **74** A3
Shiprock, NM **27** B1
Shoal Lake, MB **31** A2
Shoals, IN **62** A2
Shoemakersville, PA **74** B2
Shooks, MN **44** B5
Shoreview, MN **100** C1
Shorewood, WI **101** E2
Shortwell, NC **119** E4
Shoshone, CA **17** D1
Shoshone, ID **22** B1
Shoshoni, WY **23** D2
Show Low, AZ **26** E4
Shreveport, LA **54** D1
Shrewbury, MO **104** D4
Shrewsbury, PA **74** B3
Shultz, OK **39** E1
Shuttletown, PA **107** C4
Sibley, IA **48** A2
Sicily Is., LA **55** B2
Sidney, BC **8** E2
Sidney, IA **48** B5
Sidney, MB **31** C3
Sidney, MT **32** C1
Sidney, NE **34** D5
Sidney, NY **72** B5
Sidney, OH **60** D4
Sierra Blanca, TX **40** A4
Sierra Mojada, COAH **42** C4
Sierra Vista, AZ **28** E3
Sierraville, CA **12** E5
Sifton, WA **83** E1
Signal Hill, CA **86** C5
Sigourney, IA **48** E4
Sigurd, UT **24** D2
Sikeston, MO **51** D5
Silas, AL **66** A2
Siler City, NC **63** E4
Silesia, MD **116** D5
Siloam Springs, AR **52** C1
Silsbee, TX **54** D4
Silva, MO **51** C5
Silver Bay, MN **46** E1
Silver City, MI **47** B1
Silver City, NM **29** B1
Silver Creek, NE **35** E5
Silver Creek, NY **59** C5
Silver Gate, MT **21** B4
Silver Hill, MD **116** D3
Silver Lake, IN **60** B4
Silver Lake, OR **11** A5
Silver Plume, CO **36** A2
Silver Spring, MD **116** C1
Silver Springs, FL **67** D4
Silver Springs, NV **13** A5
Silver Star, MT **20** E3
Silverdale, MN **44** C5
Silverpeak, NV **15** C3
Silverton, CO **25** D4
Silverton, OH **108** c2
Silverton, OR **10** E2
Silverton, TX **39** A4
Simcoe, ON **59** B5
Simi Valley, CA **16** E2
Simmesport, LA **55** B3
Simms, MT **19** A5
Simms, TX **52** D5
Simpleton, KS **37** B4
Simsbury, CT **72** E4
Sinclair, WY **23** E4
Singer, LA **54** E4
Sinking Spring, OH **62** E1
Sinton, TX **43** E3
Sioux City, IA **48** A3
Sioux Falls, SD **35** E1
Sirdar, BC **18** B2
Siren, WI **46** D3
Siskiyou, OR **12** D1
Sisseton, SD **33** E3
Sister Bay, WI **47** E3
Sisters, OR **10** E3
Sistersville, WV **61** B5
Sitka, AK **5** E5
Sitka, KS **37** B5
Six Corners, OR **83** A4
Six Forks, NC **119** B2
Six Lakes, MI **58** B5
Six Points, IN **105** A4
Skagway, AK **5** E4
Skaneateles, NY **72** A4
Skiatook, OK **52** B1
Skidmore, TX **43** E3
Skiff, AB **19** A3
Skokie, IL **102** C1
Skookumchuck, BC **18** C1
Skowhegan, ME **71** A4
Sky Lake, FL **120** D3
Skykomish, WA **9** B3
Slana, AK **5** D3
Slapout, OK **39** B1
Slaton, TX **40** E1
Slayton, MN **48** A1
Sleetmute, AK **5** B3
Slidell, LA **55** E4
Slip Up, KY **62** D2
Sloan, IA **48** A3
Slocomb, AL **66** D2
Smackover, AR **53** A5
Smethport, PA **61** D1
Smith, NV **15** A1
Smith Center, KS **37** C2
Smith Lake, NM **27** C2
Smith River, CA **12** B1
Smith Springs, TN **99** E4
Smith Valley, IN **105** C5
Smithers, BC **5** F5
Smithfield, NC **76** A4
Smithfield, UT **22** E3
Smithfield, VA **76** C2
Smiths Falls, ON **59** E1
Smithville, MO **50** C2
Smithville, OK **52** C4
Smithville, TN **64** C1
Smithville, TX **54** A5
Smithville, WV **61** B5
Smoot, WY **23** A2
Smyrna, DE **74** C4
Smyrna, GA **121** A1
Smyrna, PA **61** B4
Smyrna Mills, ME **71** B2
Snidercrest, OH **108** D1
Snow Hill, AL **66** C1
Snow Hill, NC **76** B4
Snow Shoe, PA **61** E2
Snowden, PA **107** D5
Snowflake, AZ **26** E3
Snowmass Village, CO **25** D2
Snowville, UT **22** D3
Snug Harbor, FL **122** D3
Snyder, CO **36** C1
Snyder, OK **39** C4
Snyder, TX **41** A2
Soap Lake, WA **9** C4
Society Hill, SC **65** E1
Socorro, NM **27** D4
Soda Springs, ID **22** E2
Soddy Daisy, TN **64** D1
Sodom, NY **72** C2
Solano, NM **38** B2
Solano Beach, CA **17** B4
Soldotna, AK **5** C4
Soledad, CA **14** C4
Solomons, MD **74** B5
Solon, ME **71** A4
Solon Springs, WI **46** E2
Solvang, CA **16** D2
Solvey, NY **72** A4
Somerdale, NJ **114** D4
Somers, NY **72** D5
Somerset, CO **25** D3
Somerset, KY **62** D4
Somerset, MD **116** B2
Somerset, MI **60** C2
Somerset, OH **61** A5
Somerset, PA **61** D4
Somerset, TX **96** A5
Somerset West, OR **83** A2
Somersworth, NH **73** A2
Somerville, MA **110** C3
Somerville, NJ **74** C2
Somerville, TN **53** D2
Somerville, TX **54** A5
Somes Bar, CA **12** B2
Sonnette, MT **32** A4
Sonoita, AZ **28** D2
Sonoma, CA **14** B1
Sonora, CA **14** E2
Sonora, TX **41** A5
Sonoyta, SON **28** B2
Sooke, BC **8** E2
Sopchoppy, FL **67** A3
Soperton, GA **65** C5
Sophia, WV **63** B2
Sorel, PQ **70** C4
Sorrento, LA **55** C4
Souk Centre, MN **46** B3
Souris, MB **31** B3
South Ardmore, PA **114** A3
South Arm, ME **70** E5
South Bay, FL **80** A2
South Beach, WA **82** A3
South Bend, IN **60** A3
South Bend, WA **8** D4
South Boston, VA **63** E3
South Braintree, MA **110** D5
South China, ME **71** B5
South Colby, WA **82** A4
South Cove, AZ **26** A1
South Elmonte, CA **87** A2
South Euclid, OH **106** E1
South Gate, CA **86** D3
South Hampton, NY **72** E5
South Haven, KS **37** E5
South Haven, MI **60** A2
South Hill, VA **76** A3
South Houston, TX **97** D4
South Jordan, UT **90** B5
South Lake Tahoe, CA **14** E1
South Lincoln, MA **110** A3
South Lynnfield, MA **110** D1
South Miami, FL **123** C5
South Milwaukee, WI **49** D1
South New Berlin, NY **72** B4
South Nyack, NY **112** A3
South Pasadena, FL **122** B4
South Pasadena, CA **86** D1
South Pittsburg, TN **64** C2
South Plains, TX **39** A4
South Saint Paul, MN **100** E4
South Salt Lake, UT **90** B3
South San Francisco, CA **85** B1
South Saugus, MA **110** D2
South Sioux City, NE **48** A3
South Slocan, BC **18** A2
South Wilton, CT **112** F1
Southaven, MS **53** D3
Southern Pines, NC **63** E5
Southey, SK **30** C1
Southfield, MI **103** A2
Southgate, KY **108** C4
Southgate, MD **115** D5
Southgate, MI **103** C5
Southglenn, CO **93** C5
Southport, CT **113** A4
Southport, FL **66** D3
Southport, IN **105** D5
Southport, LA **98** B4
Southport, NC **78** B1
Southside Place, TX **97** B3
Southville, KY **62** C3
Southwest Harbor, ME **71** C5
Southwick, MA **72** D4
Southworth, WA **82** A4
Spangler, PA **61** D3
Spanish Fork, UT **24** E1
Spanish Harbor, FL **80** A5
Spanish Lake, MO **104** E1
Sparkill, NY **112** A4
Sparks, GA **67** B2
Sparks, NV **13** A5
Sparrows Point, MD **115** E4
Sparta, GA **65** B4
Sparta, MI **60** A1
Sparta, TN **62** C5
Sparta, WI **47** A5
Spartanburg, SC **65** C1
Sparwood, BC **18** C2
Spavinaw, OK **52** C1
Spearfish, SD **32** C5
Spearman, TX **39** A2
Speculator, NY **72** B3
Speedway, IN **105** B3
Spencer, IA **48** B2
Spencer, IN **62** A1
Spencer, MA **72** E4
Spencer, NE **35** C2
Spencer, TN **64** C1
Spencer, WV **63** B1
Sperry, OK **52** B1
Sperryville, VA **61** E5
Spirit Lake, IA **48** B1
Spirit Lake, ID **18** A4
Spiro, OK **52** C3
Spofford, TX **43** B1
Spokane, WA **9** E4
Spooner, WI **46** E3
Spotted Horse, WY **32** A5
Sprague, WA **9** E5
Sprague, WV **63** C2
Sprague River, OR **12** E1
Sprakers, NY **72** C4
Spray, OR **11** B3
Spring City, TN **64** D1
Spring Green, WI **49** B1
Spring Hill, AL **66** D1
Spring Lake Park, MN **100** B1
Spring Mill, PA **114** A2
Spring Valley, CA **89** D3
Spring Valley, MN **48** E1
Spring Valley, TX **97** A2
Springdale, AR **52** D1
Springdale, CT **112** E2
Springdale, NJ **114** E3
Springdale, OH **108** B1
Springdale, PA **107** E1
Springdale, WA **9** E4
Springer, NM **38** B1
Springerville, AZ **27** A4
Springfield, CO **36** D5
Springfield, GA **65** D4
Springfield, ID **22** D1
Springfield, IL **51** C1
Springfield, KY **62** C3
Springfield, MA **72** E4
Springfield, ME **71** B3
Springfield, MN **46** B5
Springfield, MO **50** E5
Springfield, NB **71** C2
Springfield, OH **60** D5
Springfield, OR **10** D3
Springfield, PA **114** A4
Springfield, TN **62** B5
Springfield, VA **116** B5
Springfield, VT **72** D2
Springfield, WV **61** E4
Springhill, LA **54** E1
Springlake, KY **108** C5
Springlake, TX **38** D4
Springside, NJ **114** E1
Springtown, TX **41** E1
Springview, NE **35** B3
Springville, AL **64** C4
Springville, CA **15** A5
Springville, NY **59** D5
Springville, UT **24** E1
Spruce Pine, NC **63** B5
Spur, TX **39** A5
Spy Lake, NY **72** B3
Squantum, MA **110** D4
Square Butte, MT **21** B1
Squaw Valley, CA **15** A4
Stafford, KS **37** D4
Stafford, OR **83** B5
Stafford Springs, CT **72** E4
Stallings, NC **117** E4
Stamford, CT **74** D1
Stamford, NY **72** C4
Stamford, SD **35** A1
Stamps, AR **52** E5
Stanberry, MO **50** C1
Stand Off, AB **18** E2
Standing Rock, NM **27** C2
Standish, ME **73** A1
Standish, MI **58** C4
Standstone, MN **46** D3
Stanford, KY **62** D3
Stanford, MT **21** B1
Stanhope, PQ **70** D5
Stanley, ID **20** B4
Stanley, NB **71** C2
Stanley, ND **30** E5
Stanley, NM **27** E3
Stanton, CA **87** A5
Stanton, IA **48** B5
Stanton, MI **58** B5
Stanton, ND **33** A1
Stanton, TX **40** E2
Stanwich, CT **112** D2
Stanwick, NJ **114** E2
Staples, MN **46** B2
Stapleton, NE **35** B4
Star City, AR **53** B4
Star Lake, NY **72** B2
Starbuck, MB **31** D3
Starbuck, MN **46** A3
Starke, FL **67** D3
Starks, LA **54** E4
Starkville, MS **53** E5
Starkweather, ND **31** C5
State College, PA **61** E2
State Line, MS **66** A2
Stateline, CA **15** A1
Statenville, GA **67** B2
Statesboro, GA **65** C4
Statesville, NC **63** C5
Staunton, IL **51** C2
Staunton, VA **63** E1
Stavely, AB **18** E1
Steamboat, OR **10** D4
Steamboat Springs, CO **25** E1
Stearns, KY **62** D4
Steele, ND **33** B2
Steele Swamp, CA **12** E2
Steelville, MO **51** B4
Steinbach, MB **31** E3
Steinhatchee, FL **67** B4
Stephen, AR **52** E5
Stephens City, VA **61** E5
Stephenville, TX **41** D2
Stepney, CT **113** A2
Steptoe, WA **9** E5
Sterling, CO **36** D1
Sterling, IL **49** C3
Sterling, KS **37** D4
Sterling, ND **33** B2
Sterling City, TX **41** A3
Sterling Heights, MI **60** D1
Sterling Landing, AK **5** C3
Sterlington, LA **55** B1
Steubenville, OH **61** B3
Stevens Point, WI **47** B4
Stevenson, CT **113** A1
Stewart, BC **5** F5
Stewartville, MN **48** E1
Stickney, IL **102** C4
Stickney, SD **35** D1
Stickney Corner, ME **71** B5
Stigler, OK **52** C3
Stiles, TX **40** D3
Stiles, WI **47** D4
Stiles Junction, WI **47** D4
Stillwater, MN **46** D4
Stillwater, NV **13** B5
Stillwater, OK **39** E2
Stilwell, OK **52** C2
Stinnett, TX **38** E2
Stirling, AB **18** E2
Stockbridge, GA **121** E5
Stockdale, TX **43** E1
Stockton, AL **66** B3
Stockton, CA **14** D2
Stockton, GA **67** B2
Stockton, KS **37** C2
Stockton, MO **50** D4
Stockton, WI **49** B2
Stockton Springs, ME **71** B5
Stolle, IL **104** E4
Stone, ID **22** D3
Stone Harbor, NJ **74** D4
Stone Hill, MO **51** B4
Stone Lake, WI **46** E3
Stone Park, IL **102** B3
Stoneham, CO **36** C1
Stoneham, MA **110** C2
Stoner, CO **25** C4
Stonewall, GA **121** B5
Stonewall, MB **31** D2
Stonington, ME **71** B5
Stony Brook Station, MA **110** A3
Stony Creek, VA **76** B2
Stoops Ferry, PA **107** A2
Storm Lake, IA **48** B3
Stoughton, SK **30** D3
Stoughton, WI **49** C2
Stovepipe Wells Village, CA **15** C4
Stover, MO **50** E3
Stowe, PA **107** B3
Stowell, TX **54** D5
Strafford, MO **50** E5
Strasbourg, SK **30** B1
Strasburg, ND **33** B3
Strasburg, VA **61** E5
Stratford, CA **14** E4
Stratford, CT **113** B3
Stratford, NJ **114** E4
Stratford, OK **52** A4
Stratford, ON **59** A4
Stratford, TX **38** E2
Strathcona, MN **44** A4
Strathroy, ON **59** A5
Stratton, CO **36** D2
Stratton, ME **70** E4
Stratton, NE **37** A1
Strausstown, PA **74** B2
Strawberry Point, IA **49** A2
Strawn, TX **41** D2
Streator, IL **49** D4
Strevell, ID **22** C3
Stringtown, OK **52** B4
Stromsburg, NE **35** E5
Strong, AR **53** A5
Strong City, KS **50** A4
Strongsville, OH **61** A2
Stroud, OK **52** A2
Stroudsburg, PA **74** C1
Stuart, FL **80** B1
Stuart, NE **35** C3
Stuart, VA **63** D3
Studley, KS **37** B2
Sturbridge, MA **72** E4
Sturgeon, PA **107** A4
Sturgeon Bay, WI **47** E4
Sturgis, MI **60** B2
Sturgis, SD **32** C5
Stuttgart, AR **53** B3
Sublette, KS **37** A5
Success, MO **51** A4
Sudan, TX **38** D5
Suffern, NY **74** D1
Suffield, AB **19** B2
Suffolk, VA **76** C2
Sugar Creek, MO **92** D2
Sugar Land, TX **56** C1
Suitland, MD **116** D3
Sulligent, AL **64** A4
Sullivan, IL **51** D1
Sullivan, IN **62** A2
Sullivan, MO **51** B3
Sulphur, IN **62** B3
Sulphur, LA **54** E5
Sulphur, NV **13** B3
Sulphur, OK **52** A4
Sulphur Springs, TX **54** B1
Sumas, WA **9** A2
Sumatra, FL **66** E3
Sumatra, MT **21** E2
Summer Lake, OR **11** A5
Summerhaven, AZ **28** D1
Summerland, BC **9** C1
Summerland Key, FL **80** A5
Summerport Beach, FL **120** A3
Summerside, OH **108** D3
Summersville, WV **63** C1
Summerton, SC **65** E3
Summerville, GA **64** D2
Summerville, SC **65** E3
Summit, IL **102** C4
Summit, MS **55** D3
Summitville, CO **25** E5
Sumner, MD **116** B2
Sumter, SC **65** E2
Sun City, FL **122** E5
Sun Prairie, WI **49** C1
Sun Valley, ID **20** C5
Sunbeam, CO **23** C5
Sunbright, TN **62** D5
Sunbury, NC **76** C3
Sunbury, OH **60** E4
Sunbury, PA **74** A2
Suncook, NH **72** E2
Sundance WY **32** C5
Sunderland, MD **74** B5
Sunfish Lake, MN **100** D4
Sunflower, MS **53** C5
Sunland Gardens, FL **80** A1
Sunny Isles, FL **123** E2

Bold type indicates cities with 100,000 population or more.

Place Name / Page Number / Grid Number
Stantonburg **118** C5

Sunnydale, WA .. **82** C5
Sunnyside, CA **89** C4
Sunnyside, FL **66** D3
Sunnyside, OR **83** D4
Sunnyside, WA ... **11** C1
Sunnyvale, CA . **14** C2
Sunrise, WY **34** B3
Sunrise Trading Post, AZ **26** E2
Sunset, NM **40** A1
Sunset, UT **22** D4
Sunset Beach, HI .. **7** A2
Sunset Beach, WA **8** D3
Sunset Crater Natl. Mon., AZ **26** D2
Sunset Gardens, OR **83** A3
Sunset Hills, MO **104** C4
Superior, AZ **26** D5
Superior, MT **18** C5
Superior, NE **37** D1
Superior, WI **46** E2
Suplee, OR **11** B4
Suquamish, WA . **82** A1
Surf, CA **16** C1
Surf City, NC **78** B1
Surf City, NJ **74** D3
Surfside, FL **123** E3
Surfside Beach, SC **78** A2
Surprise, AZ **26** C4
Surrattsville, MD **116** E4
Surrency, GA **67** C1
Surry, VA **76** B2
Susanville, CA **12** E4
Susquehanna, MD **74** B3
Susquehanna, PA **72** B5
Sussex, NB **71** E2
Sussex, WI **101** A2
Sussex, WY **34** A1
Sussex Corner, NB **71** D2
Sutcliffe, NV **13** A4
Sutherland, NE ... **35** A5
Sutter Creek, CA . **14** D1
Sutton, NE **37** D1
Sutton, PQ **70** C5
Sutton, WV **63** C1
Suttons Bay, MI .. **58** A3
Suttons Corner, GA **66** F1
Suwannee, FL **67** C4
Swainsboro, GA . **65** C4
Swampscott, MA **110** E1
Swan Lake, MT .. **18** D4
Swan Quarter, NC **76** C4
Swan River, MN . **46** D1
Swan Valley, ID .. **22** E1
Swansboro, NC .. **76** C5
Swansea, SC **65** D3
Swanson Bay, BC . **5** F6
Swanton, VT **70** C5
Swarthmore, PA **114** A4
Swedeland, PA . **114** A2
Sweet Home, OR **10** D3
Sweet Springs, MO **50** D2
Sweet Springs, WV **63** D2
Sweetgrass, MT . **19** A3
Sweetwater, FL **123** D4
Sweetwater, TN . **64** F1
Sweetwater, TX . **41** B2
Sweetwater Station, WY **23** D3
Swenson, TX **41** B1
Swift Current, SK **19** E2
Swift Trail Junction, AZ **29** A1
Swiss, NC **63** B5
Swissvale, PA ... **107** D3
Sycamore, IL **49** D3
Sycamore Hills, MO **104** C2
Sylacauga, AL **64** C4
Sylva, NC **65** A1
Sylvania, GA **65** C4
Sylvania, OH **60** D2
Sylvester, GA **67** A1
Symmes Corner, MA **110** B2
Syracuse, KS **36** E4
Syracuse, NE **48** A5
Syracuse, NY ... **72** A4

T

T.B., MD **116** E5
Taber, AB **19** A2
Tachee, AZ **27** A1
Tacoma, WA **9** A4
Taft, CA **16** E1
Taft, FL **120** D4
Tahlequah, OK **52** C2
Tahoe City, CA **12** E5
Tahoka, TX **40** E1
Taholah, WA **8** D3
Takoma Park, MD **116** C2
Talala, OK **52** B1
Talbotton, GA **64** E5
Talihina, OK **52** C3
Talladega, AL **64** C4
Tallahassee, FL **67** A3
Tallassee, AL **64** D5
Tallmadge, OH **61** A3
Tallulah, LA **55** C1
Taloga, OK **39** C2
Tama, IA **48** E3
Tamaqua, PA **74** B2
Tampa, FL **69** D1
Taneytown, MD .. **74** A4
Tangelo Park, FL **120** C3
Tankersley, TX **41** A3
Taos, NM **38** A1
Tappahannock, VA **76** B1
Tarboro, NC **76** B4
Tarkio, MO **50** B1
Tarpon Springs, FL **69** C1
Tarryall, CO **36** A3
Tarrytown, FL **67** D5
Tarrytown, NY ... **112** A3
Tascosa, TX **38** E3
Tate Springs, TN **63** A5
Tatum, NM **40** C1
Taunton, MA **73** A4
Tavares, FL **67** F4
Tavernier, FL **80** B4
Tawas City, MI **58** C4
Tay Creek, NB **71** C2
Taylor, AZ **26** E4
Taylor, MI **103** B5
Taylor, MO **51** A1
Taylor, NE **35** C4
Taylor, TX **41** F4
Taylor Canyon, NV **13** E3
Taylor Mill, KY .. **108** B5
Taylor Station, OH **109** E3
Taylors Falls, MN **46** D4
Taylors Is., MD .. **74** B5
Taylorsville, MD . **74** A4
Taylorsville, NC .. **63** C5
Taylorville, IL **51** D1
Taymouth, NB **71** C2
Tazewell, TN **62** E4
Tazewell, VA **63** B3
Tchula, MS **53** D5
Teacup, TX **41** C5
Teague, TX **54** B3
Tealtown, OH **108** E3
Teanaway, WA **9** B4
Teaneck, NJ **111** B1
Teas Toh, AZ **26** E2
Tecate, BC **17** C5
Tecopa, CA **17** D1
Tecumseh, MI **60** C2
Tecumseh, NE **50** A1
Tecumseh, OK **52** A3
Ted's Place, CO .. **34** A5
Teec Nos Pos, AZ **25** B5
Tega Cay, SC **117** A5
Tehachapi, CA **17** A1
Tekamah, NE **48** A4
Tekoa, ID **18** A5
Tekonsha, MI **60** C2
Telegraph, TX **41** B5
Tell, GA **121** A5
Tell City, IN **62** B3
Telluride, CO **25** C4
Telma, WA **9** C3
Tempe, AZ **26** C5
Temple, NB **71** C2
Temple, TX **41** E4
Temple City, CA .. **07** A1
Ten Sleep, WY **23** E1
Tenafly, NJ **111** B1
Tenaha, TX **54** D2
Tenino, WA **8** E4
Tennyson, TX **41** B3
Tensed, ID **18** A5
Terese, AL **66** E1
Terlingua, TX **42** C1
Termo, CA **12** E3
Terrace, BC **5** F5
Terrace Park, OH **108** D3
Terre Haute, IN ... **62** A1
Terrell, TX **54** B1
Terrell Hills, TX ... **96** C3
Terrells, NC **118** A4
Terreon, NM **27** D2
Terreton, ID **20** E5
Terry, MT **32** B2
Tess Corners, WI **101** C4
Tetlin Junction, AK **5** D3
Teulon, MB **31** D2
Teutopolis, IL **51** E2
Texarkana, TX **52** D5
Texas, MD **115** B1
Texas City, TX **56** D1
Texas Creek, CO . **36** A4
Texhoma, TX **38** E1
Texline, TX **38** D1
Thatcher, AZ **29** A1
Thatcher, CO **36** B5
Thayer, MO **53** B1
Thayne, WY **23** A2
Thebes, IL **51** D4
Thedford, NE **35** A4
Theodore Roosevelt Natl. Park, ND .. **32** D1
Theresa, NY **72** A2
Thermopolis, WY **23** D1
Thetford Mines, PQ **70** D3
Thibodaux, LA **55** C5
Thief River Falls, MN **44** A5
Thistle, UT **24** E1
Thomas, OK **39** D2
Thomas, WV **61** D5
Thomaston, CT **72** D5
Thomaston, GA ... **64** E4
Thomaston, ME .. **71** B5
Thomaston Corner, NB **71** C2
Thomasville, AL .. **66** B1
Thomasville, GA . **67** A2
Thomasville, NC . **63** D4
Thompson, AL **66** D1
Thompson, MI **47** E2
Thompson, ND **33** E1
Thompson Falls, MT **18** B5
Thompson Springs, UT **25** B2
Thompsonville, CT **72** E4
Thompsonville, PA **107** B5
Thomson, GA **65** B3
Thoreau, NM **27** C3
Thornburg, PA ... **107** B3
Thornton, AR **53** A5
Thornton, CO **93** C1
Thornwood, NY **112** B3
Thorp, WI **47** A4
Thousand Oaks, CA **16** E2
Thousand Palms, CA **17** C3
Thousand Springs, NV **22** B3
Thrashers Corner, WA **82** E1
Three Creek, ID ... **22** A2
Three Forks, MT . **21** A3
Three Lakes, WI . **47** C3
Three Points [Robles Jct.], AZ **28** D2
Three Rivers, CA . **15** A4
Three Rivers, MI . **60** B2
Three Rivers, TX . **43** E2
Threeway, AZ **29** A1
Throckmorton, TX **41** C1
Thunder Bay, ON **45** B4
Thurman, CO **36** D2
Thurmont, MD **74** A4
Thurso, PQ **70** A5
Tiburon, CA **85** D2
Ticaboo, UT **24** E4
Tice, FL **69** E2
Ticonderoga, NY . **72** C2
Tidal Bore, NB **71** E1
Tidewater, OR **10** C2
Tie Siding, WY **34** A5
Tierra Amarilla, NM **27** E1
Tierra Verde, FL **122** C5
Tiffin, OH **60** E3
Tifton, GA **67** B1
Tigard, OR **83** B4
Tijuana, BC **17** D5
Tilden, NE **35** D4
Tilden, TX **43** D2
Tildenville, FL ... **120** A2
Tillamook, OR **10** D1
Tiller, OR **10** D5
Tillman, SC **65** D4
Tillsonburg, ON .. **59** B5
Tilly, AR **52** E2
Tilma, ID **18** A5
Timber Lake, SD . **33** A4
Timonium, MD .. **115** B1
Timpanogos Cave Natl. Mon., UT **22** E5
Timpas, CO **36** C4
Timpson, TX **54** D2
Tinaja, NM **27** C3
Tioga, ND **30** D5
Tioga, PA **61** E1
Tionesta, PA **61** C2
Tippett, MD **116** E5
Tipton, IN **60** B5
Tipton, KS **36** D2
Tipton, MO **50** E3
Tipton, OK **39** C4
Tiptonville, TN **53** D1
Tishomingo, MS . **52** A4
Titusville, FL **67** F4
Titusville, PA **61** C2
Tivoli, TX **56** A2
Tobasco, OH **108** D4
Tobe, CO **36** C5
Tobias, OR **83** A3
Toccoa, GA **65** A2
Toco Hills, GA ... **121** D2
Tofte, MN **45** A5
Togiak, AK **5** B4
Togo, MN **44** C5
Tok, AK **5** D3
Tokeland, WA **8** D4
Tolar, NM **38** C4
Tolchester Beach, MD **74** B4
Toledo, IA **48** E3
Toledo, OH **60** D2
Toledo, OR **10** C2
Tomah, WI **47** B5
Tomahawk, WI ... **47** B3
Tombstone, AZ ... **28** E2
Tompkins, SK **19** D2
Tompkinsville, KY **62** C5
Tom's Place, CA . **15** B3
Toms River, NJ ... **74** D2
Tonasket, WA **9** D2
Tonganoxie, KS .. **50** B2
Tonkawa, OK **39** E1
Tonopah, NV **15** C2
Tonquin, OR **83** A5
Tonsina, AK **5** D3
Tonto Natl. Mon., AZ **26** D5
Tooele, UT **22** D5
Toomsuba, MS ... **66** A1
Toonerville, CO ... **36** D4
Topawa, AZ **28** C2
Topaz, CA **15** A1
Topeka, KS **50** B3
Topock, AZ **17** E3
Toponas, CO **25** E1
Topsfield, ME **71** C3
Tornillo, TX **29** E3
Toronto, FL **120** B1
Toronto, OH **61** B3
Toronto, ON **59** C4
Torrance, CA **17** A3
Torrey, UT **24** E3
Torrington, CT **72** D4
Torrington, WY ... **34** C4
Tortilla Flat, AZ .. **28** D5
Toulon, IL **49** C4
Tourville, PQ **70** E1
Towanda, KS **37** E4
Tower, MN **44** D5
Tower Roosevelt, WY **21** B4
Town & Country, MO **104** B3
Towner, CO **36** E4
Towner, ND **31** B5
Townsend, VT ... **72** D3
Townsend, GA **67** D1
Townsend, MA ... **72** E3
Townsend, MT **21** A2
Towson, MD **115** C2
Toyah, TX **40** C3
Toyahvale, TX **40** B4
Tracey, CA **14** D2
Tracy, AZ **28** C1
Tracy, MN **46** A5
Tracy, NB **71** C2
Tracy, PQ **70** C4
Traer, IA **48** E3
Trafford, PA **107** F3
Trail, BC **18** A2
Trail, OR **10** D5
Trail City, SD **33** A4
Trainer, PA **114** A5
Travelers Rest, SC **65** B1
Traverse City, MI **58** A3
Treasure Is., FL . **122** B4
Treelon, SK **19** D4
Trogo, WI **40** E3
Tremont, PA **74** B2
Tremonton, UT **22** D3
Trenton, FL **67** C4
Trenton, GA **64** D2
Trenton, IL **51** C3
Trenton, MO **50** D1
Trenton, NE **37** A1
Trenton, NJ **74** C2
Trenton, ON **59** D3
Trenton, TN **53** E1
Tres Alamos, CHIH **29** B4
Tres Piedras, NM **27** E1
Treveskyn, PA ... **107** B5
Tribune, KS **36** E4
Tribune, SK **30** C3
Tring Junction, PQ **70** D3
Trinidad, CA **12** B2
Trinidad, CO **36** B5
Trinity, TX **54** C4
Trois Rivieres, PQ **70** C3
Trona, CA **17** B1
Trossachs, SK **30** C3
Trout Creek, MT . **18** B4
Trout Creek, UT .. **24** B1
Trout Lake, MI **58** A1
Trout Lake, WA ... **11** A1
Trout River, NY ... **72** B1
Trout Run, PA **74** A1
Troy, AL **66** D1
Troy, KS **50** B1
Troy, MI **103** B1
Troy, MO **51** B2
Troy, MT **18** B3
Troy, NC **63** E5
Troy, NH **72** E3
Troy, NY **72** C3
Troy, OH **60** D5
Troy, PA **74** A1
Troy, TN **53** D1
Truckee, CA **12** E5
Truckton, CO **36** C3
Trujillo, NM **38** B3
Trumann, AR **53** C2
Trumbull, CT **113** B2
Truscott, TX **39** B5
Truth or Consequences, NM **29** D1
Truxton, MD **116** A2
Truxton, NY **72** A4
Tryon, NE **35** A4
Tualatin, OR **83** A4
Tuba City, AZ **26** D1
Tubutama, SON .. **28** C3
Tuckahoe, NY ... **112** B5
Tucker, GA **121** E1
Tuckerman, AR .. **53** B2
Tuckerton, NJ **74** D3
Tucson, AZ **28** D1
Tucumcari, NM ... **38** C3
Tugaske, SK **30** A1
Tukwila, WA **82** C5
Tulare, CA **14** E5
Tularosa, NM **29** E1
Tulelake, CA **12** E1
Tulia, TX **38** E4
Tullahoma, TN **64** C1
Tullos, LA **55** A2
Tully, NY **72** A4
Tulsa, OK **52** B2
Tungsten, NT **5** F3
Tunica, LA **55** B3
Tunica, MS **53** C3
Tunitas, CA **84** C1
Tunkhannock, PA **74** B1
Tununak, AK **5** A3
Tuolumne Meadows, CA **15** A2
Tupelo, MS **53** E3
Tupper Lake, NY . **72** B2
Turin, IA **48** A3
Turin, NY **72** A3
Turkey, TX **39** A4
Turkey Creek, LA **55** A4
Turley, NM **27** C1
Turlock, CA **14** D2
Turner, ME **71** A5
Turner, MT **19** D4
Turners Corner, WA **82** E1
Turners Corners, NY **59** D5
Turnersville, NJ **114** D5
Turon, KS **37** D4
Turpin, OK **39** A1
Turtle Creek, PA **107** E3
Turtle Lake, ND .. **33** A1
Turtle Lake, WI ... **46** E3
Tusas, NM **27** E1
Tuscaloosa, AL .. **64** B5
Tuscarora, NV **13** E3
Tuscola, IL **51** E1
Tuscola, TX **41** B2
Tuscumbia, AL ... **64** A3
Tuscumbia, MO ... **50** E3
Tuskegee, AL **64** D5
Tustin, CA **88** C1
Tutwiler, MS **53** C4
Tuweep, AZ **24** B5
Tuxedo, TX **41** B1
Tuxford, SK **30** B2
Tuzigoot Natl. Mon., AZ **26** C3
Twenty Mile Stand, OH **108** D1
Twentynine Palms, CA **17** D3
Twin Bridges, MO **51** A5
Twin Bridges, MT **20** E3
Twin Butte, AB ... **18** D3
Twin Buttes, AZ . **28** D2
Twin City, GA **65** C4
Twin Falls, ID **22** B2
Twin Mountain, NH **72** E1
Twin Oaks, MO . **104** B4
Twin Oaks, NC ... **63** C4
Twin Sister, TX ... **41** D5
Twin Valley, MN . **46** A1
Twinsburg, OH ... **61** A2
Twisp, WA **9** C3
Two Harbors, MN **46** E1
Two Rivers, WI ... **47** D5
Tybee Is., GA **65** E5
Tygh Valley, OR .. **11** A2
Tyler, MN **46** A5
Tyler, TX **54** C2
Tylertown, MS **55** D3
Tynan, TX **43** F3
Tyndall, SD **35** D2
Tyner, KY **62** E3
Tyonek, AK **5** C4
Tyrone, PA **61** E2
Tyson Station, MO **104** A4
Tysons Corner, VA **116** A3

U

Ucluelet, BC **8** C1
Ucross, WY **21** E5
Udall, KS **37** E5
Ugashik, AK **5** B4
Uhrichsville, OH .. **61** B4
Ukiah, CA **12** B5
Ukiah, OR **11** C2
Ulmer, SC **65** D3
Ulysses, KS **37** A5
Umatilla, FL **67** E4
Umpire, AR **52** D4
Una, TN **99** D4
Unadilla, GA **65** A5
Unadilla, NY **72** B4
Unalakleet, AK **5** B3
Unalaska, AK **4** G5
Underwood, ND .. **33** A1
Unimak, AK **5** A5
Union, IN **60** D5
Union, MO **51** B3
Union, MS **55** E1
Union, OR **11** D3
Union, SC **65** C1
Union, WV **63** C2
Union City, CA **84** E4
Union City, GA .. **121** B5
Union City, NJ ... **111** B3
Union City, OH **60** C5
Union City, PA **61** C1
Union City, TN **51** D5
Union Creek, OR . **10** D5
Union Grove, WI . **49** D2
Union Hill, TN **99** B1
Union Springs, AL **66** D1
Uniontown, AL **66** B1
Uniontown, PA **61** C4
Unionville, MI **58** D5
Unionville, MO ... **48** D5
Unionville, NV **13** C4
Unity, ME **71** B5
Unity, OR **11** D4
Unity, PA **107** E2
Unity Lake, MO .. **92** E4
Unityville, PA **74** A1
Universal, PA **107** E2
Universal City, TX **96** E2
University City, MO **104** D2
University Heights, OH **106** D2
University Park, MD **116** D2
University Park, TX **95** C2
Upchurch, NC **118** E4
Upham, ND **31** A4
Upland, CA **87** E2
Upland, IN **60** B4
Upland, PA **114** A5
Upper Arlington, OH **109** B3
Upper Blackville, NB **71** D1
Upper Darby, PA **114** B3
Upper Lake, CA ... **12** B5
Upper St. Clair, PA **107** B5
Upper Sandusky, OH **60** E3
Upper Stepney, CT **113** A2
Upper Talley Cavey, PA **107** C1
Upthegrove Beach, FL **80** A1
Upton, KY **62** C4
Upton, ME **70** E5
Upton, WY **34** B1
Uravan, CO **25** D3
Urbana, IL **49** E5
Urbana, OH **60** D4
Urbancrest, OH . **109** B4
Uriah, AL **66** B2
Urich, MO **50** D3
Ursa, IL **51** A1
Ursine, NV **24** A3
Usta, SD **32** E4
Ute, CO **25** C4
Ute, IA **48** B3
Ute Park, NM **38** A1
Utica, KS **37** B3
Utica, MI **60** D1
Utica, MS **55** C2
Utica, MT **21** B1
Utica, NY **72** B3
Utica, OH **61** A4
Utuado, PR **6** A3
Uvalde, TX **43** B1

V

Vacaville, CA **14** C1
Vacherie, LA **55** D5
Vadnais Heights, MN **100** D2
Vado, NM **29** D2
Vaiden, MS **53** D5
Vail, AZ **28** D2
Vail, CO **25** E2
Val-Marie, SK **19** E3
Val Verda, UT **90** C1
Valdez, AK **5** D4
Valdosta, GA **67** B2
Vale, OR **11** E4
Valemont Heights, PA **107** E2
Valencia, NM **27** D3
Valentine, AZ **26** B2
Valentine, NE **35** A2
Valentine, TX **40** B4
Valhalla, NY **112** B3
Valie La Palmas, BC **17** B5
Valle, AZ **26** C2
Vallecillos, NL **43** B5
Vallecitos, NM **27** E1
Vallee-Junction, PQ **70** D3
Vallejo, CA **14** C1
Valley, WA **9** E4
Valley, WY **21** C5
Valley Center, KS **37** E4
Valley City, AL **64** D5
Valley City, ND **33** D2
Valley Club Acres, CO **93** F5
Valley Falls, KS .. **50** B2
Valley Falls, OR .. **13** A1
Valley Junction, OR **10** D2
Valley Mills, TX .. **41** E3
Valley Park, MO **104** B4
Valley Spring, TX **41** D4
Valley View, OH **106** D4
Valleyview, OH . **109** B3
Valmont, NM **29** E1
Valmy, NV **13** D4
Valparaiso, FL **66** C3
Valparaiso, IN **60** A3
Van Buren, AR **52** D2
Van Buren, IN **60** B4
Van Buren, ME **71** B1
Van Cleave, MS .. **66** A3
Van Etten, NY **72** A5
Van Horn, TX **40** A4
Van Tassel, WY .. **34** C3
Van Wert, OH **60** C4
Vananda, MT **21** E2
Vanceboro, ME ... **71** C3
Vanceboro, NC ... **76** C4
Vanceburg, KY ... **62** E1
Vancorum, CO **25** C4
Vancouver, BC ... **5** G7
Vancouver, WA ... **10** E1
Vandalia, MO **51** A2
Vandalia, OH **60** D5
Vandana, IL **51** D2
Vandergrift, PA ... **61** C3
Vanderhoof, BC **5** G5
Vanguard, SK **19** E2
Vankleek Hill, ON **70** A5
Varennes, PQ **70** B4
Variadero, NM **38** B3
Vashon, WA **82** A5
Vashon Center, WA **82** A5
Vashon Heights, WA **82** A4
Vassar, MI **58** D5
Vaughn, MT **19** A5
Vaughn, NM **38** A4
Vaughn, ON **59** B4
Vauxhall, AB **19** A2
Veedersburg, IN . **60** A5
Vega, TX **38** D3
Velva, ND **31** A5
Venango, NE **34** E5
Veneta, OR **10** D3
Venice, FL **69** D2
Venice, IL **104** E2
Venice, LA **55** E5
Venice, WA **82** A2
Venice Center, NY **72** A4
Ventana, AZ **28** C1
Ventura, CA **16** E2
Venus, TX **54** A2
Vera, TX **39** C5
Verdel, NE **35** C2
Verdigre, NE **35** D3
Vergennes, VT **72** C1
Vermillion, OH **60** E2
Vermillion, SD **35** E2
Vern, TN **64** A1
Vernal, UT **23** B5
Vernon, AL **64** A4
Vernon, CA **86** D2
Vernon, FL **66** D3
Vernon, TX **39** C5
Vernon, UT **24** D1
Vernon, WI **101** A5
Vero Beach, FL ... **80** A1
Verona, ND **33** D3
Verona, PA **107** D2
Verona, WI **49** C2
Veronia, OR **10** D1
Versailles, IN **62** C1
Versailles, KY **62** D2
Versailles, MO **50** E3
Versailles, OH **60** C4
Versailles, PA ... **107** E4
Vesta, MN **46** B5
Vetal, SD **35** A2
Vevay, IN **62** C2
Veyo, UT **24** B4
Vian, OK **52** C2
Vibank, SK **30** C2
Vichy, MO **51** A4
Vici, OK **39** C2
Vicksburg, MS **55** C1
Victor, ID **23** A1
Victoria, BC **5** G7
Victoria, TX **56** A2
Victoria, VA **76** A2
Victoria Beach, NS **71** E3
Victoriaville, PQ .. **70** D3
Victorville, CA **17** B2
Victory, NY **59** E4
Victory, OK **39** C4
Vida, MT **30** B5
Vida, OR **10** D3
Vidal, CA **17** E3
Vidalia, GA **65** C5
Vidalia, LA **55** B2
Vidor, TX **54** E5
Vienna, GA **65** A5
Vienna, IL **51** D4
Vienna, MO **51** A3
Vienna, VA **116** A3
Vieques, PR **6** C4
View Park, WA ... **82** A4
Villa Acuña, COAH **43** A1
Villa Frontera, COAH **43** A5
Villa Hidalgo, COAH **43** B3
Villa Hills, KY **108** A5
Villa Park, CA **88** D1
Villa Park, IL **102** A3
Villa Rica, GA **64** D3
Villa Unión, COAH **43** A3
Villaldama, NL **43** B5
Villanova, PA **114** A2
Ville Platte, LA ... **55** B4
Vincennes, IN **62** A2
Vincent, CA **17** A2
Vineland, CO **36** B4
Vineland, FL **120** B4
Vineland, NJ **74** C3
Vinings, GA **121** B1
Vinita, OK **52** C1
Vinita Park, MO **104** C2
Vinita Terrace, MO **104** C2
Vinson, OK **39** B4
Vinton, LA **54** E5
Viola, IL **49** B4
Viola, KS **37** E5
Violet, LA **98** E4
Virden, MB **31** A3
Virden, NM **29** A1
Virgin Is. Natl. Park, VI **6** D3
Virginia, IL **51** C1
Virginia, MN **46** D1
Virginia Beach, VA **76** C2
Virginia City, MT **20** E3
Virginia City, NV . **13** A5
Virginia Dale, CO **34** A5
Virginia Gardens, FL **123** C4
Virginia Hills, VA **116** C5
Viroqua, WI **49** A1
Visalia, CA **14** E4
Vista, NY **112** D1

Place Name · Page Number · Grid Number
Stantonburg **118** C5

Vivian, SD 35 B1
Voca, TX 41 C4
Volborg, MT 32 A3
Von Ormy, TX 96 A5
Votaw, TX 54 D4
Voyageurs Natl. Park, MN 44 D4
Vrooman, NY 72 C4
Vulcan, AB 18 E1
Vya, NV 13 A2

W

Waban, MA 110 B4
Wabash, IN 60 B4
Wabasha, MN 46 E5
Wabeno, WI 47 C3
Wachapreague, VA 76 C1
Waco, TN 64 B2
Waco, TX 54 A3
Waddington, NY 72 A1
Wade, MS 66 A3
Wadena, MN 46 B2
Wadesboro, NC 65 E1
Wadley, AL 64 D4
Wadley, GA 65 C4
Wadsworth, OH 61 A3
Wagarville, AL 66 A2
Waggaman, LA 98 A5
Wagner, SD 35 D2
Wagon Mound, NM 38 B2
Wagon Wheel Gap, CO 25 E4
Wagoner, OK 52 B2
Wagontire, OR 11 B5
Wahiawa, HI 7 A2
Wahoo, NE 48 A5
Wahpeton, ND 33 E3
Waianaé, HI 7 A2
Wailea, HI 7 C3
Wailuku, HI 7 C3
Waimea, HI 7 D4
Wainwright, AK 5 C1
Waite, ME 71 C3
Waitsburg, WA 11 D1
Waitsfield, VT 72 D1
Wake Crossroads, NC 119 D2
Wake Forest, NC 76 A4
WaKeeney, KS 37 B3
Wakefield, MA 110 C1
Wakefield, MI 47 B2
Wakefield, NE 35 E3
Wakefield, RI 73 A4
Wakefield, VA 76 B2
Wakulla, FL 67 A3
Walden, CO 23 E5
Walden, NY 72 C5
Waldenburg, AR 53 B2
Waldo, AR 52 E5
Waldo, FL 67 D3
Waldo, OH 60 E4
Waldorf, MD 74 B5
Waldport, OR 10 C2
Waldron, AR 52 D3
Wales, AK 5 A2
Walhalla, ND 31 D4
Walhalla, SC 65 A2
Walker, CA 15 A1
Walker, KS 37 C3
Walker, MI 60 A1
Walker, MN 46 B1
Walker, SD 33 A3
Walkers Mill, PA 107 B4
Walkerton, IN 60 A3
Wall, PA 107 E3
Wall, SD 34 E1
Wall, TX 41 B3
Walla Walla, WA 11 D1
Wallace, ID 18 B5
Wallace, NC 76 B5
Wallace, NE 35 A5
Wallhalla, SC 65 A2
Wallingford, PA 114 A4
Wallingford, VT 72 D2
Wallington, NJ 111 A2
Wallis, TX 56 B1
Wallowa, OR 11 E2
Wallula, WA 11 D1
Walnut, CA 87 C3
Walnut, MS 53 E2
Walnut Canyon Natl. Mon., AZ 26 D2
Walnut Cove, NC 63 D4
Walnut Grove, WA 83 D1
Walnut Ridge, AR 53 B1
Walnut Springs, TX 41 E2
Walsenburg, CO 36 B
Walsh, AB 19 C2
Walsh, CO 36 E5
Walsingham, FL 122 A3
Walterboro, SC 65 E4
Waltham, MA 110 A3
Waltman, WY 23 E2
Walton, NY 72 B5
Walton Hills, OH 106 E4
Wamego, KS 50 A2
Wamsutter, WY 23 D4
Wankers Corners, OR 83 B5
Wannaska, MN 44 A4
Wanship, UT 22 E5
Wapakoneta, OH 60 D4
Wapanucka, OK 52 A4
Wapella, SK 30 E2
Wapello, IA 49 A4
War, WV 63 B3
Wardner, BC 18 C2
Ware, IL 51 D4
Ware, MA 72 E4
Ware, TX 38 D2
Ware Shoals, SC 65 B2
Wareham, MA 73 B4
Warm Springs, NV 15 D2
Warm Springs, OR 11 A3
Warm Springs, VA 63 D1
Warner, AB 19 A3
Warner, OK 52 B2
Warner Robins, GA 65 A5
Warren, AR 53 A5
Warren, AZ 28 E3
Warren, MI 103 C1
Warren, MN 31 E5
Warren, MT 21 C4
Warren, NH 72 E1
Warren, OH 61 B2
Warren, PA 61 C1
Warrendale, PA 107 A1
Warrensburg, MO 50 D3
Warrensburg, NY 72 C2
Warrensville, OH 106 E2
Warrensville Heights, OH 106 E2
Warrenton, GA 65 B3
Warrenton, MO 51 B2
Warrenton, NC 76 A3
Warrenton, VA 74 A5
Warrington, FL 66 C3
Warrior, AL 64 B4
Warroad, MN 44 A4
Warsaw, MO 50 D3
Warsaw, IN 60 B3
Warsaw, NC 76 B5
Warsaw, NY 59 D5
Warsaw, VA 76 B1
Warson Woods, MO 104 C3
Wartburg, TN 62 D5
Warwick, ND 31 C5
Warwick, PQ 70 D4
Warwick, RI 73 A4
Wasa, BC 18 B2
Wasatch Natl. Forest, UT 90 E4
Wasco, CA 14 E5
Wasco, OR 11 B1
Waseca, MN 46 D5
Washburn, ME 71 B1
Washburn, WI 47 A2
Washington, AR 52 E5
Washington, DC 74 B4
Washington, GA 65 B3
Washington, IA 49 A4
Washington, IL 49 C5
Washington, IN 62 A2
Washington, KS 37 E2
Washington, LA 55 B4
Washington, MO 51 B3
Washington, NC 76 C4
Washington, NJ 74 D3
Washington, PA 61 C4
Washington, UT 24 B4
Washington Court House, OH 60 E5
George Washington Birthplace Natl. Mon., MD 74 B5
Washington Square, PA 114 A1
Washtucna, WA 9 D5
Waskish, MN 44 B5
Wasta, SD 34 E1
Watauga, TX 94 B2
Water Street, PA 61 E3
Waterbury, CT 72 D5
Waterbury, VT 72 D1
Waterford, NY 72 C3
Waterloo, IA 48 E2
Waterloo, IL 51 C3
Waterloo, IN 60 C3
Waterloo, MD 115 B5
Waterloo, NY 59 E4
Waterloo, OH 63 A1
Waterloo, ON 59 A4
Waterloo, PQ 70 C5
Waterman, WA 82 A3
Watersmeet, MI 47 B2
Waterton Lakes Natl. Park, AB 18 D3
Waterton Park, AB 18 D3
Watertown, MA 110 B3
Watertown, NY 72 A2
Watertown, SD 33 E5
Watertown, TN 62 C5
Watertown, WI 49 D1
Waterville, ME 71 A5
Waterville, MN 46 C5
Waterville, NY 72 B4
Waterville, WA 9 C4
Watervliet, MI 60 A2
Watford City, ND 32 D1
Wathena, KS 50 B1
Watkins, CO 36 B2
Watkins Glen, NY 59 E5
Watkinsville, GA 65 A3
Watonga, OK 39 D2
Watrous, NM 38 A2
Watseka, IL 49 E4
Watson, IL 51 D2
Watson Lake, YT 5 F4
Watsonville, CA 14 C3
Wattsburg, PA 61 C1
Wauchula, FL 69 E1
Wauconda, WA 9 D2
Waukegan, IL 49 E2
Waukesha, WI 49 D1
Waukon, IA 49 A1
Waupaca, WI 47 C5
Waupun, WI 49 C1
Waurika, OK 39 D4
Wausau, WI 47 B4
Wausaukee, WI 47 D3
Wautoma, WI 47 C5
Wauwatosa, WI 101 C3
Waveland, MA 110 E4
Waverly, GA 67 D1
Waverly, IA 48 E2
Waverly, MA 110 B3
Waverly, MO 50 D2
Waverly, NY 72 A5
Waverly, OH 62 E1
Waverly, TN 64 A1
Waverly, VA 76 B2
Wawbeek, NY 72 B2
Wawona, CA 14 E3
Wawota, SK 30 E3
Waxahachie, TX 54 A2
Wayan, ID 22 E2
Waycross, GA 67 C1
Wayland, MI 60 B1
Wayland, NY 59 E5
Wayne, MI 103 A5
Wayne, NE 35 E3
Wayne, WV 63 A2
Waynesboro, GA 65 C4
Waynesboro, MS 66 A2
Waynesboro, PA 74 A3
Waynesboro, TN 64 A2
Waynesboro, VA 63 E1
Waynesburg, OH 61 B3
Waynesburg, PA 61 C4
Waynesville, MO 51 A4
Waynesville, NC 65 A1
Waynesville, OH 60 D5
Waynoka, OK 39 C1
Weatherby Lake, MO 92 B1
Weatherford, OK 39 D3
Weatherford, TX 41 E1
Weaverville, CA 12 C3
Webb, TX 43 C3
Webster, MA 72 E4
Webster, ND 31 C5
Webster, NY 59 E4
Webster, SD 33 D4
Webster City, IA 48 C3
Webster Groves, MO 104 C4
Webster Springs, WV 63 C1
Wedgeport, NS 71 E5
Wedowee, AL 64 D4
Weed, CA 12 D2
Weedon-Centre, PQ 70 D4
Weedsport, NY 72 A4
Weehawken, NJ 111 B3
Weirton, WV 61 B3
Weiser, ID 11 E4
Weitchpec, CA 12 B2
Welby, CO 93 C1
Welch, TX 40 E1
Welch, WV 63 B3
Welcher, OK 50 C5
Weld, ME 71 A5
Weldon, NC 76 B3
Welland, ON 59 C5
Wellesley, MA 110 A4
Wellesley Farms, MA 110 A4
Wellesley Fells, MA 110 A4
Wellesley Hills, MA 110 A4
Wellfleet, NE 35 A5
Wellfleet, MA 73 B3
Wellington, KS 37 E5
Wellington, NV 15 A1
Wellington, OH 60 E3
Wellington, TX 39 B4
Wellington, UT 25 A2
Wellington, VA 116 C5
Wells, ME 73 A2
Wells, NV 22 A4
Wells, NY 72 C3
Wells River, VT 72 D1
Wellsboro, PA 61 E1
Wellsburg, WV 61 B4
Wellston, MO 104 D2
Wellston, OH 63 A1
Wellsville, NY 59 D5
Wellsville, OH 61 B3
Welsford, NB 71 C2
Welsh, LA 55 A5
Wenatchee, WA 9 B4
Wendell, ID 22 B2
Wenden, AZ 26 A4
Wendover, UT 22 B4
Wenona, IL 49 D4
Wentzville, MO 51 B2
Weott, CA 12 B3
Weskan, KS 36 E3
Weslaco, TX 43 E6
Wesley, ME 71 C3
Wessington, SD 33 C5
Wessington Springs, SD 35 C1
West, TN 99 A2
West Allis, WI 101 D3
West Bay, FL 66 D3
West Bend, WI 49 D1
West Berlin, NJ 114 E4
West Blakely, WA 82 A3
West Bountiful, UT 90 C1
West Branch, MI 58 C4
West Bridgewater, VT 72 D2
West Burlington, NJ 114 E1
West Chester, PA 74 C3
West Columbia, TX 56 C1
West Conshohocken, PA 114 A2
West Covina, CA 87 B2
West Dover, VT 72 D3
West Elizabeth, PA 107 D5
West End, LA 98 B3
West Fork, AR 52 D2
West Forks, ME 71 A4
West Frankfort, IL 51 D3
West Glacier, MT 18 D4
West Hamlin, WV 63 A2
West Haven, CT 72 E5
West Helena, AR 53 C3
West Hollywood, CA 86 B1
West Homestead, PA 107 D4
West Jefferson, OH 60 E5
West Jordan, UT 90 B4
West Lafayette, IN 60 A5
West Leyden, NY 72 A3
West Liberty, IA 49 A4
West Liberty, KY 62 E2
West Liberty, OH 60 D4
West Linn, OR 83 C5
West Manayunk, PA 114 B2
West Meade, TN 99 B4
West Memphis, AR 53 C2
West Miami, FL 123 C4
West Mifflin, PA 107 D4
West Milwaukee, WI 101 D3
West Monroe, LA 55 A1
West New Kensington, PA 107 E1
West New York, NJ 111 B3
West Newton, MA 110 B4
West Newton, PA 61 C3
West Ossipee, NH 72 E1
West Palm Beach, FL 80 B2
West Park, PA 107 B3
West Plains, MO 51 A5
West Point, CA 14 E1
West Point, GA 64 D5
West Point, KY 62 B3
West Point, MS 53 E4
West Point, NE 35 E4
West Point, NY 72 D5
West Point, VA 76 B1
West Poplar, SK 30 A4
West Port Madison, WA 82 B1
West Quincey, MA 110 D5
West Saint Paul, MN 100 D4
West Springfield, PA 61 B1
West Stewartstown, NH 70 E5
West Thumb, WY 21 A5
West Union, IA 48 E2
West Union, OH 62 E1
West Union, OR 83 A2
West Union, WV 61 B5
West Unity, OH 60 C3
West University Place, TX 97 B3
West Valley City, UT 90 B3
West View, PA 107 B2
West Wendover, NV 22 B4
West Wilmerding, PA 107 E3
West Woburn, MA 110 B2
West Yellowstone, WY 21 A4
Westbank, BC 9 D1
Westbay, FL 66 D3
Westboro, WI 47 A3
Westbourne, MB 31 C2
Westbridge, BC 9 D2
Westbrook Village, MA 110 B4
Westby, MT 30 C4
Westby, WI 49 A1
Westchester, IL 102 B4
Westchester Estates, FL 122 B4
Westcliffe, CO 36 A4
Westerly, RI 73 A4
Western Hills, OH 108 A4
Western Springs, IL 102 B4
Westernport, MD 61 D4
Westerville, OH 60 E4
Westfield, MA 72 E4
Westfield, NB 71 D3
Westfield, NY 61 C1
Westfield, PA 61 E1
Westgate Hills, PA 114 A3
Westhoff, TX 43 E1
Westhope, ND 31 A4
Westinghouse Village, PA 114 B4
Westland, MI 103 A5
Westminster, CA 88 A1
Westminster, CO 93 B1
Westminster, MD 74 A4
Westminster, SC 65 A2
Westmont, IL 102 A5
Westmont, NJ 114 D3
Westmoreland, CA 17 D5
Westmoreland, TN 62 B5
Weston, CT 72 D5
Weston, GA 66 E1
Weston, ID 22 E3
Weston, MA 110 A4
Weston, OR 11 D2
Weston, WV 61 C5
Westover HIlls, TX 94 A3
Westport, CA 12 B4
Westport, CT 72 D5
Westport, IN 62 C1
Westport, NS 71 E4
Westport, NY 72 C1
Westport, OR 8 D5
Westport, WA 8 D4
Westville, IL 49 E5
Westville, NJ 114 C4
Westville, OK 52 C2
Westwego, LA 98 B5
Westwood, KS 92 C3
Westwood, MA 110 B5
Westwood, MO 104 B3
Westwood Hills, KS 92 C3
Westworth, TX 94 A3
Wetmore, CO 36 B4
Wetumka, OK 52 A3
Wetumpka, AL 64 C5
Wetzels Corner, OR 83 E5
Wevertown, NY 72 C2
Wewahitchka, FL 66 E3
Wewela, SD 35 B2
Wewoka, OK 52 A3
Wexford, PA 107 B1
Weyburn, SK 30 C3
Weymouth, MA 110 E5
Weymouth, NS 71 E4
Weymouth Center, MA 110 E5
Weymouth Heights, MA 110 E5
Wharton, TX 56 B1
Wheat Ridge, CO 93 B2
Wheatland, CA 12 D5
Wheatland, NM 38 C3
Wheatland, WY 34 B3
Wheaton, IL 49 D3
Wheaton, MD 116 B1
Wheaton, MN 33 E3
Wheeler, KS 36 E2
Wheeler, TX 39 B3
Wheeling, IN 60 A4
Wheeling, WV 61 B4
Whispering Pines, FL 80 A1
Whitaker, PA 107 D3
Whitby, ON 59 C3
White Bear Lake, MN 100 E1
White Bird, ID 20 A2
White Butte, ND 32 E3
White Castle, LA 55 C4
White Center, WA 82 B4
White City, FL 66 E4
White Cloud, MI 58 A5
White Cross, NC 118 A3
White Deer, TX 39 A3
White Hall, IL 51 B1
White Lakes, NM 27 E3
White Marsh, MD 115 E2
White Oak, MD 116 C1
White Oak, PA 107 E4
White Pigeon, MI 60 B3
White Plains, NY 74 D1
White River, SD 35 A1
White River Junction, VT 72 D2
White Rock, BC 9 A1
White Rock, NM 27 E2
White Salmon, WA 11 A1
White Sands Natl. Mon., NM 29 E1
White Settlement, TX 41 E1
White Signal, NM 29 B1
White Springs, FL 67 C3
White Stone, VA 76 C1
White Sulpher Springs, MT 21 A2
White Sulphur Springs, WV 63 C2
White Swan, WA 9 B5
Whiteclay, NE 34 D2
Whiteface, TX 38 D5
Whitefield, OK 52 C3
Whitefish, MT 18 C4
Whitefish Bay, WI 101 D2
Whitefish Point, MI 58 A1
Whitehall, OH 109 D3
Whitehall, IN 60 E4
Whitehall, MI 58 A5
Whitehall, MT 20 E3
Whitehall, NY 72 C2
Whitehall, PA 107 C4
Whitehall, WI 47 A5
Whitehorse, YT 5 E4
Whitehorse Ranch, OR 13 C2
Whitemarsh, PA 114 B1
Whites City, NM 40 B2
Whites Creek, TN 99 B2
Whitesboro, TX 52 A5
Whitesburg, KY 63 A3
Whitetail, MT 30 B4
Whiteville, NC 78 A1
Whiteville, TN 53 E1
Whitewater, CO 25 C3
Whitewater, KS 37 E4
Whitewater, MT 19 E4
Whitewater, WI 49 D2
Whitewood, SK 30 E2
Whitingham, VT 72 D3
Whitley City, KY 62 D4
Whitman, NE 34 E4
Whitmire, SC 65 C2
Whitney, TX 41 E3
Whitney Point, NY 72 A5
Whitsett, TX 43 D2
Whittemore, MI 58 C4
Whittier, AK 5 C4
Whittier, CA 87 A3
Whitting, ME 71 D4
Wibaux, MT 32 C2
Wichita, KS 37 E5
Wichita Falls, TX 39 D5
Wickenburg, AZ 26 B4
Wickett, TX 40 D3
Wickles, AR 52 D4
Wickliffe, KY 51 D5
Wide Ruins, AZ 27 A2
Wiggins, CO 36 C1
Wiggins, MS 55 E3
Wikieup, AZ 26 A3
Wilbaux, MT 32 C2
Wilborn, MT 20 E1
Wilbur, WA 9 D4
Wilburton, OK 52 C3
Wild Horse, AB 19 B3
Wilder, KY 108 C4
Wilders Grove, NC 119 C4
Wildwood, FL 67 D4
Wildwood, NJ 74 D4
Wildwood, PA 107 C1
Wildwood, UT 22 E5
Wiley, CO 36 D4
Wilkes-Barre, PA 74 B1
Wilkins, PA 107 E3
Wilkinsburg, PA 107 D3
Willacoochee, GA 67 B1
Willard, NM 27 E4
Willcox, AZ 28 E2
Willernie, MN 100 E1
Willet, NY 72 A4
Williams, AZ 26 C2
Williams, CA 12 C5
Williams, MN 44 B4
Williams Station, PA 114 A1
Williamsburg, IA 48 E4
Williamsburg, KY 62 E4
Williamsburg, VA 76 B2
Williamson, NY 59 E4
Williamson, WV 63 A3
Williamsport, PA 74 A1
Williamston, NC 76 C4
Williamstown, KY 62 D2
Williamstown, MA 72 D3
Williamstown, NJ 74 C3
Williamstown, NY 72 A3
Williamstown, OH 60 D3
Williamstown, VT 72 D1
Willimantic, CT 72 E4
Willingboro, NJ 114 E1
Williston, FL 67 D4
Williston, ND 30 D5
Willits, CA 12 B4
Willliams Lake, BC 5 G6
Willmar, MN 46 B4
Willock, PA 107 C4
Willoughby, OH 61 A2
Willow Bunch, SK 30 B3
Willow Creek, CA 12 B2
Willow Creek, SK 19 C3
Willow Lake, SD 33 D5
Willow Springs, IL 102 B5
Willow Springs, MO 51 A5
Willowbrook, IL 102 A5
Willows, CA 12 C4
Wilmer, TX 95 D5
Wilmerding, PA 107 E3
Wilmington, IL 49 D4
Wilmington, MA 110 B1
Wilmington, NC 78 B1
Wilmington, OH 60 D5
Wilmington, VT 72 D3
Wilmot, OH 61 A3
Wilmurt, NY 72 B3
Wilson, AR 53 C2
Wilson, NC 76 B4
Wilson, PA 107 D5
Wilson Corner, OR 83 E5
Wilsons Mills, ME 70 E5
Wilsonville, NC 118 D5
Wilsonville, NE 37 B1
Wilsonville, OR 83 A5
Wilton, CT 112 E1
Wilton, ME 71 A5
Wilton, ND 33 A1
Winamac, IN 60 A4
Winchell, TX 41 C3
Winchendon, MA 72 E3
Winchester, IL 51 B1
Winchester, IN 60 C5
Winchester, KY 62 D2
Winchester, MA 110 B2
Winchester, MO 104 A4
Winchester, NH 72 E3
Winchester, TN 64 C2
Winchester, VA 61 E4
Winchester, WY 23 D1
Winchester Bay, OR 10 C3
Wind Cave Natl. Park, SD 34 D1
Windber, PA 61 D3
Windcrest, TX 96 D2
Winder, GA 65 A3
Windermere, FL 120 B4
Windham, MT 21 B1
Windom, MN 48 B1
Window Rock, AZ 27 B2
Windsor, MO 50 D3
Windsor, NC 76 C3
Windsor, NY 72 B5
Windsor, ON 60 D1
Windsor, PQ 70 D4
Windsor, VA 76 B2
Windsor, VT 72 D2
Windthorst, TX 39 D5
Winfield, AL 64 A4
Winfield, KS 37 E5
Winfred, SD 35 E1
Wing, AL 66 C2
Wingate, PA 61 E2
Winger, MN 46 A1
Winifred, MT 21 C1
Wink, TX 40 C3
Winkelman, AZ 26 D5
Winkler, MB 31 D4
Winn, ME 71 B3
Winnebago, MN 48 C1
Winnebago, NE 48 A3
Winnemucca, NV 13 C3
Winner, SD 35 B2
Winnett, MT 21 D1
Winnfield, LA 55 A2
Winnipeg, MB 31 E2
Winnsboro, LA 55 B2
Winnsboro, SC 65 D2
Winnsboro, TX 54 C1
Winona, AZ 26 D2
Winona, MN 46 E5
Winona, MO 51 B5
Winona, MS 53 D5
Winslow, AR 52 D2
Winslow, AZ 26 E3
Winslow, ME 71 A5
Winslow, NE 48 A4
Winslow, WA 82 A2
Winsted, CT 72 D4
Winston, MT 21 A2
Winston, OR 10 C4
Winston, VA 74 A5
Winston-Salem, NC 63 D4
Winter Garden, FL 67 E5
Winter Haven, FL 69 E1
Winter Park, FL 67 E5
Winterhaven, CA 17 E5
Winterport, ME 71 B4
Winters, TX 41 B3
Wintersburg, AZ 26 B5
Winterset, IA 48 C4
Winthrop, MA 110 D3
Winthrop, ME 71 A5
Winthrop, MN 46 C5
Winthrop, NY 72 B1
Winthrop, WA 9 C3
Winthrop Beach, MA 110 D3
Winthrop Highlands, MA 110 D3
Winton, NC 76 B3
Wisconsin Dells, WI 49 B1
Wisconsin Rapids, WI 47 B5
Wisdom, MT 20 D3
Wise River, MT 20 D3
Wishek, ND 33 B3
Wisner, NE 35 E4
Withamsville, OH 108 E4
Withrow, WA 9 C4
Wittenberg, WI 47 C4
Woburn, MA 110 B1
Woburn, PQ 70 E4
Woburn Highlands, MA 110 B2
Wofford Heights, CA 15 A5
Wolcott, CO 25 E2
Wolcott, IN 60 A4
Wolf Creek, MT 20 E1
Wolf Creek, OR 10 C5
Wolf Hole, AZ 24 B5
Wolf Point, MT 30 B5
Wollaston, MA 110 D5
Wolseley, SK 30 D2
Wolsey, SD 33 D5
Wolverine, MI 58 B3
Wood, SD 35 B2
Wood Dale, IL 102 A2
Wood Lake, NE 35 B3
Wood Mountain, SK 30 A3
Wood Ridge, NJ 111 A2
Wood Village, OR 83 E3
Woodbine, GA 67 D1
Woodbine, IA 48 B4
Woodbine, MD 115 D3
Woodbridge, CT 113 C1
Woodbrook, MD 115 C2
Woodbury, IN 105 E1

Woodbury - Zwolle

Woodbury, MI **60** B1
Woodbury, NJ .. **114** C4
Woodbury, TN **64** C1
Woodbury, VT **72** D1
Woodbury Heights, NJ
.... **114** C5
Woodcrest, NJ . **114** E4
Woodgate, NY **72** B3
Woodinville, WA **82** E1
Woodland, CA **14** C1
Woodland, ME **71** C3
Woodland, MN .. **46** D3
Woodland Beach, DE
.... **74** C3
Woodland Park, CO
.... **36** B3
Woodlands, MB .**31** D2
Woodlawn, KY .. **108** B4
Woodlawn, MD . **115** B3
Woodlawn, OH .. **108** B2
Woodmere, OH . **106** E2
Woodrow, CO **36** C1
Woodruff, UT **22** E4
Woodruff, WI **47** B3
Woods, KS **37** A5
Woods Cross, UT **90** C1
Woods Hole, MA **73** B4
Woodsfield, OH . **61** B4
Woodside, CA **84** D2
Woodson, TX **41** C1
Woodson Terrace, MO
.... **104** C2
Woodstock, Il. ... **49** D2
Woodstock, NB .. **71** B2
Woodstock, ON .. **59** A5
Woodstock, VA ... **61** E5
Woodstock, VT .. **72** D2
Woodstown, NJ . **74** C3
Woodsville, NH .. **72** D1
Woodville, MS ... **55** C3
Woodville, PA .. **107** B4
Woodville, TX **54** D4
Woodward, OK ... **39** C1
Woodward, PA ... **61** E2
Woody, CA **15** A5
Woodyard, MD . **116** E4
Woolwine, VA **63** D3
Woonsocket, RI ..**73** A4
Woonsocket, SD . **35** D1
Wooster, OH **61** A3
Worcester, MA 72 E3
Worden, MT **21** D3
Worland, WY **23** D1
Worthington, IN . **62** A1
Worthington, MN **48** B1
Worthington, OH
.... **109** C2
Wounded Knee, SD
.... **34** E2
Wrangell, AK **5** F5
Wrangell-St. Elias Natl.
Park and Preserve, AK
.... **5** D3
Wray, CO **36** E1
Wrens, GA **65** C4
Wrentham, AB .. **19** A2
Wrentham, MA .. **73** A4
Wright, KS **37** B4
Wrightsville, GA **65** B4
Wrightsville Beach, NC
.... **78** B1
Wupatki Natl. Mon., AZ
.... **26** D2
Wurtsboro, NY ... **72** C5
Wyalusing, PA .. **74** A1
Wyalusing, WI ... **49** A2
Wyandotte, MI **103** C5
Wyatt, NC **119** C2
Wycliffe, BC **18** B2
Wylliesburg, VA .**76** A3
Wymore, NE **50** A1

Wyndmere, ND ... **33** E3
Wynne, AR **53** C2
Wynnewood, PA
.... **114** A2
Wyoming, MI **60** B1
Wyoming, OH .. **108** B2
Wyomissing, PA **74** B2
Wytheville, VA ... **63** C3

Xenia, OH **60** D5

Y City, AR **52** D3
Yaak, MT **18** B3
Yabucoa, PR **6** C4
Yachats, OR **10** C2
Yadkinville, NC .. **63** D4
Yahk, BC **18** B3
Yakima, WA **9** B5
Yakutat, AK **5** D4
Yale, MI **36** E2
Yale, WA **10** E1
Yampa, CO **25** E1
Yanceyville, NC . **63** E4
Yankeetown, FL . **67** C4
Yankton, SD **35** E2
Yarmouth, NS ... **70** E4
Yarnell, AZ **26** B3
Yarrow Point, WA
.... **82** D3
Yates, NM **38** C2
Yates Center, KS **50** B4
Yava, AZ **26** B3
Yazoo City, MS .. **55** C1
Yeadon, PA **114** B4
Yeehaw Junction, FL
.... **80** A1
Yellow Grass, SK **30** C3
Yellow Pine, ID .. **20** B3
Yellowknife, NT ... **5** G3
Yellowstone National
Park, WY **21** A5
Yellville, AR **52** E1
Yelm, WA **8** E4
Yemassee, SC ... **65** D4
Yerington, NV ... **15** A1
Yermo, CA **17** C2
Yeso, NM **38** B4
Ymir, BC **18** A2
Yoakum, TX **56** A1
Yoder, CO **36** B3
Yoncalla, OR .... (no)
Yonkers, NY **74** D1
Yorba Linda, CA . **87** C5
York, AL **66** A1
York, ME **73** A7
York, MO **51** C4
York, NE **35** E5
York, ON **59** B4
York, PA **74** A3
York, SC **65** C1
York Center, IL . **102** A4
York Mills, NB ... **71** C2
Yorkton, SK **30** E1
Yorktown, TX **43** E2
Yorktown, VA **76** C2
Yorktown Heights, NY
.... **112** B1

Yosemite Natl. Park, CA
.... **15** A2
Yosemite Village, CA
.... **15** A2
Youbou, BC **8** D1
Young, AZ **26** E4
Youngs Cove, NB **71** C2
Youngstown, FL . **66** E3
Youngstown, NY **59** C4
Youngstown, OH
.... **61** B3
Ypsilanti, MI **60** D2
Yreka, CA **12** C1
Yuba City, CA ... **12** D5
Yucca, AZ **26** A2
Yucca Valley, CA **17** C3
Yulee, FL **67** D2
Yuma, AZ **17** E5
Yuma, CO **36** D1

Zahl, ND **30** C4
Zanesville, OH ... **61** A4
Zapata, TX **43** C5
Zaragosa, CHIH . **29** D3
Zaragosa, COAH . **43** A3
Zavalla, TX **54** D3
Zavalla, DGO **42** B5
Zebulon, NC **76** A4
Zeeland, MI **60** A1
Zelienople, PA ... **61** C3
Zeona, SD **32** D4
Zephyr, TX **41** D3
Zephyr Cove, NV **15** A1
Zephyrhills, FL ... **67** D5
Zerkel, MN **46** A1
Zero, MT **32** B2
Zion, IL **49** E2
Zion Natl. Park, UT
.... **24** C4
Zionsville, IN ... **105** B1
Zolfo Springs, FL **69** E1
Zumbrota, MN ... **46** D5
Zuni, NM **27** B3
Zwolle, LA **54** E3

Toll Free Numbers: Hotels

Comfort Inn/ Quality Inn
800/221-2222

Days Inn
800/325-2525

The Four Seasons
800/332-3442

Hilton
800/445-8667

Holiday Inn
800/465-4329

Hyatt
800/228-9000
800/233-1234

Marriott
800/228-9290

Sheraton
800/325-3535

Westin
800/228-3000

Toll Free Numbers: Car Rentals

Alamo
800/327-9633

American
800/527-0202

Avis
800/331-1212

Budget
800/527-0770

Dollar
800/421-6878

General
800/952-4896

Hertz
800/654-3131

National
800/227-7368

Payless
800/237-2804

Sears
800/527-0770

Thrifty
800/307-2277

Weather Information

Alabama
205/262-6800

Alaska
800/478-7675
907/586-7491

Arizona
602/957-8700
602/261-4000

Arkansas
501/834-0316

California
Northern:
415/364-7974
Southern:
213/575-7211

Colorado
303/757-9011

Connecticut
203/627-3440

Delaware
Kent County:
302/674-9262,
Sussex County:
302/855-9262,
Wilmington:
302/429-9000,

District of Columbia
202/936-1212

Florida
904/576-6318
305/661-5065

Georgia
404/762-6151

Hawaii
808/836-1021
808/836-2102

Idaho
208/342-6569

Illinois
312/976-1212

Indiana
317/248-4050

Iowa
515/285-6906

Kansas
913/267-6600

Kentucky
502/564-5358

Louisiana
504/388-5942

Maine
207/775-7781

Maryland
301/936-1212

Massachusetts
617/936-1234

Michigan
313/941-7192

Minnesota
612/725-6090
612/452-2323

Mississippi
601/936-2189

Missouri
314/882-6591

Montana
406/449-5204

Nebraska
402/447-6005

Nevada
702/793-1300
702/784-5402

New Hampshire
603/225-3161

New Jersey
609/646-6400

New Mexico
505/243-0702

New York
518/476-1122

North Carolina
919/860-1234

North Dakota
701/224-2898
800/472-2686

Ohio
614/469-1010
614/281-8211
614/841-2222
900/WEATHER

Oklahoma
405/425-2385

Oregon
503/236-7575

Pennsylvania
717/234-7379

Puerto Rico
809/253-4588

Rhode Island
401/737-5100

South Carolina
803/799-1010

South Dakota
605/773-3536

Tennessee
615/244-9393

Texas
512/463-8588

Utah
801/575-7669

Vermont
900/370-8728

Virgin Islands
809/774-1340

Virginia
804/222-7411

Washington
206/526-6087

West Virginia
304/348-3758
304/925-4906

Wisconsin
800/762-3947
La Crosse:
608/784-1930
Madison:
608/249-6645
Green Bay:
414/4942362
Milwaukee:
414/744-8000

Wyoming
307/635-9901

National Parks and Monuments

Use the following numbers for reservations and general information. Conditions and restrictions vary; many parks fill up quickly in peak season. Make sure you call for complete information before your trip.

Alabama

Russell Cave Natl. Mon.
205/495-2672

Alaska

Admiralty Island Natl. Mon.
907/788-3166

Denali Natl. Park & Preserve
907/683-2294

Gates of the Arctic
907/456-0281

Glacier Bay Natl. Park & Preserve
907/697-2230

Katmai Natl. Park & Preserve
907/246-3305

Kenai Fjords Natl. Park
907/224-3175

Kobuk Valley Natl. Park
907/442-3573

Lake Clark Natl. Park & Preserve
907/271-3751

Misty Fjords Natl. Mon.
907/225-2148

Nootak Natl. Preserve
907/442-3573

Wrangle-St. Elias Natl. Park & Preserve
907/822-5235

Arizona

Canyon de Chelly Natl. Mon.
602/674-5436

Casa Grande Ruins Natl. Mon.
602/723-3172

Chiricahua Natl. Mon.
602/824-3560

Grand Canyon Natl. Park
602/638-2401

Montezuma's Castle Natl. Mon.
602/567-3322

Navajo Natl. Mon.
602/ 672-2366

Petrified Forest Natl. Park
602/524-6228

Pipe Springs Natl. Mon.
602/643-7105

Rainbow Bridge Natl. Mon.
602/645-2471

Saguaro Natl. Mon. East
602/296-8576

Saguaro Natl. Mon. West
602/296-8576

Sunset Crater Natl. Mon.
602/527-7042

Tonto Natl. Mon.
602/467-2241

Tuzigoot Natl. Mon.
602/634-5564

Walnut Canyon Natl. Mon.
602/526-3367

Wupatki Natl. Mon.
602/527-7040

Arkansas

Hot Springs Natl. Park
501/321-4442

California

Cabrillo Natl. Mon.
619/557-5450

Channel Islands Natl. Park
805/644-8157

Death Valley Natl. Mon.
619/786-2331

Devils Hole Natl. Mon.
619/786-2331

Devils Postpile Natl. Mon.
619/934-2289

Joshua Tree Natl. Mon.
619/367-7511

Kings Canyon Natl. Park
209/335-2315

Lassen Volcanic Natl. Park
916/595-4444

Lava Beds Natl. Mon.
916/667-2282

Redwood Natl. Park
707/488-3461

Sequoia Natl. Park
209/565-3456

Yosemite Natl. Park
209/372-0264

Colorado

Black Canyon of the Gunnison Natl. Mon.
303/249-7036

Colorado Natl. Mon.
303/858-3617

Florissant Fossil Beds Natl. Mon.
719/748-3253

Great Sand Dunes Natl. Mon.
719/378-3212

Mesa Verde Natl. Park
303/529-4461

Rocky Mountain. Natl. Park
303/586-2371

Florida

Castillo de San Marcos Natl. Mon.
904/829-6506

Everglades Natl. Park
305/247-6211

Ft. Matanzas Natl. Mon.
904/471-0116

Georgia

Ft. Frederica Natl. Mon.
912/638-3639

Ft. Pulaski Natl. Mon.
912/786-5787

Hawaii

Haleakala Natl. Park
808/572-9306

Hawaii Volcanoes Natl. Park
808/967-7311

Idaho

Craters of the Moon Natl. Mon.
208/527-3257

Iowa

Effigy Mounds Natl. Mon.
319/873-3491

Maryland

Ft. McHenry Natl. Mon.
301/962-4290

George Washington Birthplace Natl. Mon.
804/224-1732

Michigan

Isle Royale Natl. Park
906/337-4993

Minnesota

Pipestone Natl. Mon.
507/825-5464

Voyageurs Natl. Park
218/283-9821

Montana

Custer Battlefield Natl. Mon. (Little Big Horn)
406/638-2621

Glacier Natl. Park
406/732-4424

Nebraska

Agate Fossil Beds Natl. Mon.
308/668-2211

Scotts Bluff Natl. Mon.
308/436-4340

New Mexico

Bandelier Natl. Mon.
505/672-3861

Capulin Mountain Natl. Mon.
505/278-2201

Carlsbad Caverns Natl. Park
505/785-2232

El Morro Natl. Mon.
505/783-4226

Ft. Union Natl. Mon.
505/425-8025

Gila Cliff Dwellings Natl. Mon.
505/536-9344

Salinas Natl. Mon. (Abo)
505/847-2400

Salinas Natl. Mon. (Gran Quivira)
505/847-2770

Salinas Natl. Mon. (Quarai)
505/847-2290

White Sands Natl. Mon.
505/479-6124

New York

Castle Clinton Natl. Mon.
212/344-7220

North Carolina

Great Smoky Mountains Natl. Park
704/488-3184

North Dakota

Theodore Roosevelt Natl. Park
701/623-4466
701/842-2333

Ohio

Mound City Group Natl. Mon.
614/774-1225

Oregon

Crater Lake Natl. Park
503/594-2211

John Day Fossil Beds Natl. Mon.
503/575-0721

South Carolina

Ft. Sumter/Ft. Moultrie Natl. Mon.
803/883-3123

South Dakota

Badlands Natl. Park
605/433-5361

Jewel Cave Natl. Mon.
605/673-2288

Mt. Rushmore Natl. Mon.
605/574-2523

Wind Caves Natl. Park
605/745-4600

Texas

Big Bend Natl. Park
915/477-2251

Guadalupe Mountains Natl. Park
915/828-3251

Utah

Arches Natl. Park
801/259-8161

Bryce Canyon Natl. Park
801/834-5322

Canyonlands Natl. Park
801/259-7165

Capitol Reef Natl. Park
801/425-3791

Dinosaur Natl. Mon.
303/374-2216

Zion Natl. Park
801/772-3256

Virgin Islands

Virgin Islands Natl. Park
809/775-6238

Virginia

Shenandoah Natl. Park
703/999-2229

Washington

Mt. Rainier Natl. Park
206/569-2211

Mt. St. Helens Natl. Volcanic Mon.
206/247-5473

North Cascades Natl. Park
206/856-5700

Olympic Natl. Park
206/452-4501

Wyoming

Devils Tower Natl. Mon.
307/467-5370

Fossil Butte Natl. Mon.
307/877-4455

Grand Teton Natl. Park
307/733-2880

Yellowstone Natl. Park
307/344-7381

Creative Director	**Richard Saul Wurman**

1991 Edition

Project Manager	Lynne Stiles
Assistant Project Manager	Scott Summers
Senior Researcher	Lisa Stage
Systems Director	Rajan Dev
Art Directors	Maria Giudice
	Michael Everitt
Assistant Art Director	Bonnie Scranton
Editorial Director	Maura Carey Damacion
Cartographic Design and Production	Tom Beatty
	Julie Bilski
	Cheryl Fitzgerald
	Kitti Homme
	Patricia Keelin
	Gary Mitchell Lang
	Laurie Miller
	Stuart Silberman
Production Assistance	Nathan Shedroff
	Jerry Stanton
	Ernest Abrams
Proofreading and Research	Caroline Scott *Senior*
	Karin Mullen
Cartography, H.M. Gousha	Cary A. Wilke
	Randall G. Sands
	Nancy G. Below
	Linda R. Lindner
	Francis S. Hohmann
	C. Arhelger
	Debra A. Cabaniss
	Michelle A. Mertz
Film Production	Sanjay & Janet Sakhuja
	Digital Pre-Press International
Printing	*Graphic Arts Center*

USATLAS is a joint venture between **ACCESS**Press, The *Understanding* Business, H. M. Gousha, and Prentice Hall Press, A Division of Simon & Schuster Inc., A Paramount Communications Co.

ACCESS Press
59 Wooster Street
New York, NY 10012

Jane Rosch *Director*

The Understanding Business
Rincon Center
101 Spear Street
Suite 203
San Francisco, CA 94105

Mark Johnson *Director*

H. M. Gousha/Prentice Hall Press
A Division of Simon & Schuster Inc.
A Paramount Communications Co.
15 Columbus Circle
New York, NY 10023

Katherine Cowles
  Vice President, Publishing
Al Cleveland
Mary Mulkern
Rosemarie Robotham
Brian Phair
Lisa Volpe

Since the publication of his first book in 1963, **Richard Saul Wurman** has distinguished his work with a singular passion: that for making information understandable. **US**ATLAS, his 47th book, remains faithful to the motivating principles found in his previous works. Each project has been based on the premise that you understand something only in relation to what you already understand. Applying this simple philosophy to cartography, he has produced one of his most influential works to date.

Receiving both bachelor's and master's degrees from the University of Pennsylvania, Wurman graduated in 1959 with highest honors. In the course of his studies, he established a close personal and professional relationship with architect Louis I. Kahn. A fellow of the American Institute of Architects, FAIA, Wurman is also a member of the Alliance Graphique Internationale and a Vice President of the American Institute of Graphic Arts. He has been the recipient of several grants from the National Endowment for the Arts, a Guggenheim fellowship, two Graham fellowships, and two Chandler fellowships.

The path of his career has been full of turns, twists, and diversions. He's held positions ranging from a partner in an architectural firm to professor then dean of an architectural school to deputy director of Philadelphia Housing and Community Development to corporate consultant. Along the way, he has applied his design expertise to the field of cartography, creating several revolutionary works which have culminated in the **US**ATLAS project. *CITIES: A Comparison of Form and Scale,* published in 1963, focused on the relative size and scale of 50 cities, allowing the reader to compare them accurately to one another. In 1967, Wurman developed city maps with standardized scale and legends, co-authoring them in a volume entitled *URBAN ATLAS: 20 American Cities.* One of his most notable mapmaking experiences was as a member of an archaeological expedition during the first year of exploration (1958) of the Mayan city of Tikal, in Guatemala, where he surveyed one-third of the city. In 1988 he wrote the paper *Mapping and Cartography in Metropolitan Areas* for the XVII Triennale in Milan.

Currently, Wurman is the owner of **ACCESS**®Press and of The **Understanding** Business. **ACCESS**® travel guides to London, Paris, Rome, Tokyo, and major U. S. cities answer tourists' questions, from the most common to the most obscure; the latest in the series is *"The Wall Street Journal Guide* to Understanding Money & Markets." Wurman restructured and redesigned the Pacific Bell Yellow Pages directories into a more coherently organized product, the **SMART** *Yellow Pages*®. *INFORMATION ANXIETY* (1989) is his breakthrough guide to handling the information glut.

Wurman, his wife, novelist Gloria Nagy, and their four children live in Manhattan and in Bridgehampton, New York.

Some technical notes...

USATLAS was designed and produced using Apple **Macintosh IIci**™ computers. Basic cartographic information supplied by **H.M. Gousha** was scanned at **300 dpi** with an **Agfa Focus II**™ flatbed scanner and was saved in **PICT** format. The PICT images were then used as templates in **Adobe Illustrator 88**™ **1.9.3.** Each map was redrawn using the vector-oriented drawing tools integral to Adobe Illustrator.

Research for margin notes was compiled using a flat-file data base program (**Record Holder Plus**™). Text was typed and laid out in Aldus' **PageMaker**™ **3.02** and **4.0** page-layout program. After layout and proofing, the PageMaker files were saved as encapsulated **Postscript**™ documents and were imported and positioned as graphic elements within the basic Adobe Illustrator map files.

The design staff at The **Understanding** Business maximized the potential of the software programs used in order to create the traps, spreads and other special image preparation requirements necessary for high speed commercial printing.

Map files were transferred to **Digital Pre-Press International**, where **Adobe Separator**™ was used to create electronically color separated files. **AGFA Compugraphic**™ image-setting equipment controlled by **RIP 3** image processors set the files at 2400 dpi resolution and produced negative film, "right reading emulsion down," 133 line screen, one negative per color.

USATLAS was printed by **Graphic Arts Center,** who also stripped the supplied individual page negatives into final composed flats, one piece film per color (six images per flat), ready for plate making. Five-color **Cromalins**® were made for color approvals. The book was printed with six matched colors, **Pantone Matching System**™ **299, 129, 5787, 185, 1565** and **process black,** on a **Harris M-200** web press, using **60# offset** stock. The book was bound using the **Otabind**™ method, which allows the pages to open flat.

RSW

Other travel titles available from
ACCESS®PRESS, Ltd:

USA

HAWAIIACCESS®
$12.95

SAN FRANCISCOACCESS®
$16.95

NYCACCESS®
$16.95

LAACCESS®
$16.95

DCACCESS®
$14.95

Europe

LONDONACCESS®
$16.95

PARISACCESS®
$16.95

ROMEACCESS®
$16.95

Organized by neighborhood, the way natives know a city and experience it.

Color-coded entries distinguish all restaurants, hotels, shops, architecture, and places of interest.

Generous use of maps with points of interest identified.

Easy to use and a pleasure to read.

Each city's flavor is conveyed by descriptions of its history, by lists of the personal favorites of people who know and love the city, by trivia and by lavish illustrations of important buildings and by places of interest.

Perfect preparation for a visit, enjoyment of a city or recollection of a trip.

Also available from
ACCESS®PRESS:

***The Wall Street Journal* Guide to Understanding Money & Markets**

A forthright, informative and entertaining ACCESS® Guide to the financial pages.

ACCESS® Travel Guides, as well as ACCESS® Guides on other subjects, are available through:

ACCESS® Press
Rincon Center
101 Spear Street
Suite 203
San Francisco, CA 94105

Each page in **US**ATLAS is approximately 10 1/4" wide. If you laid the 156 pages from one book edge to edge in a line, they would stretch about 133 feet.

Doing the same thing to 40 copies would take you just over a mile. Enough copies of **US**ATLAS were printed for this second edition that if you were to lay them all out the same way, in a line on the ground, the line would stretch clear across the country, from San Francisco to New York, and a few copies would be left over.

Please refer to the pages cited for complete questions.

pg. 4 Is Alaska the western-most or the easternmost of the 50 states? *Both—the Aleutian Islands straddle the 180° meridian.*

pg. 6 Who was the bride-killing pirate? *Bluebeard.*

pg. 7 What are the 12 letters of the Hawaiian alphabet? *a, e h, i, k, l, m, n, o, p, u, w.*

pg. 8 After whom is Astoria, OR named? *John Jacob Astor, 19th century plutocrat.*

pg. 9 Bigfoot has not been seen since 18 May 1980. What happened? *Mt. St. Helens erupted—the largest volcano eruption in US history.*

pg. 10 What record does Crater Lake hold? *The deepest lake in North America—1932 feet down.*

pg. 11 Hells Canyon National Recreation Area—the 8000 foot drop would leave you where? *In the deepest gorge on the continent.*

pg. 12 What's the worst that happened to the Donner Party? *Donner Party members resorted to cannibalism to survive.*

pg. 13 The McDermitt Mine is the Western Hemisphere's largest producer of what metal? *Mercury.*

pg. 14 What museum was built with planks from a single redwood tree? *Ripley's Believe It or Not Museum.*

pg. 15 Guess what the average temperature in July is in Death Valley? *110° F.*

pg. 16 Who lives at Rancho del Cielo? *Ronald and Nancy Reagan.*

pg. 17 What makes Boulder City unique in Nevada? *It's the only Nevada city in which gambling is illegal.*

pg. 18 Who were the first US citizens to see the Rocky Mountains and the Continental Divide? *Lewis and Clark.*

pg. 19 What weatherwise distinction does Great Falls, MT—and not Chicago—claim? *The windiest city in the US.*

pg. 20 What mineral made Montana's fame? *Copper.*

pg. 21 What two tribes fought General Custer at Little Big Horn? *The Cheyenne and the Sioux.*

pg. 22 How fast did the Blue Flame go to capture the speed record? *622 miles per hour.*

pg. 23 What's the Great Divide Basin? *Waters here flow to neither ocean; they flow to the middle of the basin.*

pg. 24 What's so special about the Bristlecone Pines on Wheeler Peak? *They are the oldest living things on earth—3000-4000 years old.*

pg. 25 Which four states can you touch at "Four Corners"? *Colorado, Arizona, Utah and New Mexico—the only four states that meet at one point.*

pg. 26 How long have people lived in Oraibi, AZ? *Since about 1100 AD.*

pg. 27 What is the official gem of Arizona? *Turquoise.*

pg. 28 What was the town motto of Tombstone? *"The Town Too Tough to Die."*

pg. 29 What did the first atomic bomb blast do to the desert sand? *Turned it to glass.*

pg. 30 Why shop in Montana? *There's no state sales tax.*

pg. 31 Where do the High Plains start? *The 98th meridian.*

pg. 32 What feature gives the Black Hills their name? *The dark coniferous trees that blanket them.*

pg. 33 Who was Lewis and Clark's Shoshone guide? *Sacagawea.*

pg. 34 Who are the presidents immortalized at Mt. Rushmore? *George Washington, Thomas Jefferson, Abraham Lincoln and Teddy Roosevelt.*

pg. 35 What holiday did Nebraskans initiate? *Arbor Day.*

pg. 36 Name the tune Katherine Lee Bates wrote as a result of her ascent of Pike's Peak. *America the Beautiful.*

pg. 37 What famous cowboy tune is the Kansas state song? *Home on the Range.*

pg. 38 What famous outlaw was killed in Fort Sumner, NM? *Billy the Kid.*

pg. 39 What unusual site will you see on the grounds of the State Capitol in Oklahoma City? *Oil derricks.*

pg. 40 What does a Texas rancher mean when he says his spread is the size of 5 "RIs"? *An "RI" is a "Rhode Island."*

pg. 41 Which six flags have flown over Texas? *Spain, France, Mexico, the Lone Star Republic, the Confederacy, the United States.*

pg. 42 Who was the famous Western justice of Langtry, and who was the actress he admired? *Judge Roy Bean and Lillie Langtry.*

pg. 43 Besides cattle, what other two herd animals are found in greatest number in Texas? *Sheep and goats.*

pg. 44 What's so special about Lake of the Woods, MN? *It's the northernmost point in the 48 states.*

pg. 45 What's Lake Superior's great claim to fame? *It's the world's largest freshwater lake.*

pg. 46 In what city in Minnesota can you see the Northern Lights about 40 nights of the year? *Duluth.*

pg. 47 What's Wisconsin's nickname? *"America's Dairyland."*

pg. 48 Who was the Duke from Winterset, IA? *John Wayne.*

pg. 49 Do you remember the price of the original McDonald's hamburgers? *A mere 15¢.*

pg. 50 Which aviatrix got her start in Atchison, KS? *Amelia Earhardt.*

pg. 51 What crime-fighting hero is celebrated in Metropolis, IL? *Superman.*

pg. 52 In what city will you find the largest population of Native Americans? *Tulsa.*

pg. 53 How many people would you guess stream through *Graceland* each year? *About 650,000.*

pg. 54 What legal system does Louisiana, alone of all the states, follow? *The Napoleonic Code.*

pg. 55 What exactly is Cajun? *"Cajun" is a corruption of "Arcadien"—and they were French Canadians who migrated down to Louisiana.*

pg. 56 What are the months commonly considered "hurricane season"? *August and September.*

pg. 58 What's significant about the Mackinac Bridge? *The world's longest suspension between anchorages.*

pg. 59 10 million people visit Niagara Falls each year. How many are on their honeymoon? *10 %—1 million lovebirds.*

pg. 60 What Michigan city was the site of the first auto plant? *Lansing, not Detroit.*

pg. 61 Chances are pretty good that the tires on your car have been in Ohio before. Why? *Akron, OH is the world's leading rubber producer.*

pg. 62 What infamous Indianan came to a bloody end on 22 July 1934? *John Dillinger.*

pg. 63 How many rooms are there in the world's largest private residence, Biltmore? *250.*

pg. 64 What local landmark near Lynchburg, TN has been operating since 1866? *The Jack Daniels Distillery.*

pg. 65 Which state is the largest east of the Mississippi? *Georgia.*

pg. 66 Montgomery, AL was the home of Jefferson Davis and a logical choice for what honor? *The first capital of the Confederacy—later moved to Richmond, VA.*

pg. 67 Jacksonville, FL holds a US record. What? *At 830 square miles, it's literally the largest city in the US.*

pg. 69 Thomas Edison "wintered" in which town? *Ft. Myers, FL.*

pg. 70 Montreal is Canada's largest and the world's second-largest what? *French-speaking city.*

pg. 71 Why stop driving when you hit West Quoddy Head, ME? *It's the easternmost point in the lower 48 states.*

pg. 72 Which of the New England states were not among the original 13 colonies? *Vermont and Maine.*

pg. 73 What sometime-New Englander said: "If you don't like the weather in New England, just wait a few minutes"? *Hartford, CT resident Mark Twain.*

pg. 74 Who wrote our national anthem? *Francis Scott Key.*

pg. 76 Can you recall the name of the ruling body of colonial Virginia? *The House of Burgesses.*

pg. 78 Do you know the nickname of South Carolina? *"The Palmetto State."*

pg. 80 The author of Cat on a Hot Tin Roof wrote in Key West. Who was he? *Tennessee Williams.*